Research Methods in Education

This completely rewritten and updated fifth edition of the long-running bestseller, *Research Methods in Education* covers the whole range of methods currently employed by educational researchers. It continues to be the standard text for students undertaking educational research whether at undergraduate or postgraduate level.

This new edition constitutes the largest reshaping of the text to date and includes new material on:

- qualitative, naturalistic and ethnographic research methods;
- curricular and evaluative research;
- critical theory and educational research;
- feminist perspectives on research;
- research and policy-making;
- planning educational research;
- critical action research;
- statistical analysis;
- sampling reliability and validity;
- event-history analysis;
- meta-analysis and multi-level modelling;
- nominal group technique and Delphi techniques;
- case study planning;
- qualitative data analysis;
- questionnaire design and construction;
- focus groups;
- testing;
- test construction and item response theory;
- recent developments in educational research including Internet usage, simulations, fuzzy logic, Geographical Information Systems, needs assessment and evidence-based education.

This user-friendly text provides both the theory that underpins research methodology and very practical guidelines for conducting educational research. It is essential reading for both the professional researcher and the consumer of research – the teacher, educational administrator, adviser, and all those concerned with educational research and practice.

Louis Cohen is Emeritus Professor of Education at Loughborough University. **Lawrence Manion** is former Principal Lecturer in Music at Didsbury School of Education, Manchester Metropolitan University. **Keith Morrison** is Professor of Education at the Inter-University Institute of Macau.

Research Methods in Education

Fifth edition

**Louis Cohen, Lawrence Manion
and Keith Morrison**

London and New York

First published 2000 by RoutledgeFalmer
11 New Fetter Lane, London EC4P 4EE

Simultaneously published in the USA and Canada by RoutledgeFalmer
29 West 35th Street, New York, NY 10001

Reprinted 2001

RoutledgeFalmer is an imprint of the Taylor & Francis Group

©2000 Louis Cohen, Lawrence Manion and Keith Morrison

Typeset in 10/12pt Goudy by J&L Composition Ltd, Filey, North Yorkshire
Printed and bound in Great Britain by TJ International Ltd, Padstow, Cornwall

British Library Cataloguing in Publication Data
A catalogue record for this book is available from the British Library

Library of Congress Cataloguing in Publication Data

Cohen, Louis
    Research methods in education / Louis Cohen, Lawrence Manion, and Keith
    Morrison.–5th ed.
        p. cm.
    Includes bibliographical references (p.) and index.
    ISBN 0-415-19541-1 (pbk.)
      1. Education–Research. 2. Education–Research–Great Britain. I. Manion, Lawrence.
    II. Morrison, Keith (Keith R. B.) III. Title.

LB 1028 .C572 2000
370'.7'2–dc21

ISBN 0–415–19541–1

'To understand is hard. Once one understands, action is easy.'
(Sun Yat Sen, 1866–1925)

Contents

Boxes

Acknowledgements

Our thanks are due to the following publishers and authors for permission to include materials in the text:

Academic Press Inc. London, for Bannister, D. and Mair, J. M. M. (1968) *The Evaluation of Personal Constructs*, **Box 19.2**; words from LeCompte, M., Millroy, W. L. and Preissle, J. (eds) (1992) *The Handbook of Qualitative Research in Education.*

Addison-Wesley Publishing Co., Wokingham, for words from Boyd-Barrett, D. and Scanlon, E., (1991) *Computers and Learning.*

Allyn & Bacon, Boston, Massachusetts, for words from Bogdan, R. G. and Biklen, S. K. (1992) *Qualitative Research for Education* (second edition).

Associated Book Publishers Ltd., London, for Fransella, F. (1975) *Need to Change?* **Box 19.3**.

Carfax Publishing Co., Abingdon, for McCormick, J. and Solman, R. (1992) Teachers' attributions of responsibility for occupational stress and satisfaction: an organisational perspective, *Educational Studies*, 18 (2), 201–22, **Box 20.5, Box 20.6, Box 20.7**; Halpin, D. *et al.* (1990) Teachers' perceptions of the effects of inservice education, *British Educational Research Journal*, 16 (2), 163–77, **Box 10.5**.

Cassell, London, for words from Tymms, P. (1996) Theories, models and simulations: school effectiveness at an impasse, in J. Gray, D. Reynolds, C. T. Fitz-Gibbon and D. Jesson (eds) *Merging Traditions: the Future of Research on School Effectiveness and School Improvement*, 121–35.

Centre for Applied Research in Education, Norwich, East Anglia, for words from MacDonald, B. (1987) *Research and Action in the Context of Policing*, paper commissioned by the Police Federation.

Corwin Press, Newbury Park, California, for words from Millman, J. and Darling-Hammond, L. (eds), (1991) *The New Handbook of Teacher Evaluation.*

Countryside Commission, Cheltenham, for Davidson, J. (1970) *Outdoor Recreation Surveys: the Design and Use of Questionnaires for Site Surveys*, **Box 8.1**.

Deakin University Press, Deakin, Australia, for words from Kemmis, S. and McTaggart, R. (1981) *The Action Research Planner*, and Kemmis, S. and McTaggart, R. (1992: 8 and 21–8) *The Action Research Planner* (third edition).

Elsevier Science Ltd, for words from Haig, B. D. (1997) Feminist research methodology, in J. P. Keeves (ed.) *Educational Research, Methodology, and Measurement: an International Handbook*, Oxford: Elsevier Science Ltd, 222–31.

Forgas, J. P. (1976) *Journal of Personal and Social Psychology*, 34 (2), 199–209, **Box 20.10**.

George Allen & Unwin, London, for Plummer, K. (1983) *Documents of Life: Introduction to the Problems and Literature of a Humanistic Method*, **Box 2.8**; Whyte, W. F. (1982) Interviewing in field research. In R. G. Burgess (ed.) *Field Research: a Sourcebook and Field Manual*, 111–22.

Harcourt Brace Jovanovich, Inc., New York, for Tuckman, B. W. (1972) *Conducting Educational Research*, **Box 16.5**, and **Box 15.2**.

Harper & Row Publishers, London, for Cohen, L. (1977) *Educational Research in Classrooms and Schools*, **Box 20.1, Box 20.2**, and **Box 20.3**.

Heinemann Educational Books Ltd, London, for Hoinville, G. and Jowell, R. (1978) *Survey Research Practice*, **Box 8.1**.

Hodder & Stoughton, Sevenoaks, for words from Frankfort-Nachmias, C. and Nachmias, D. (1992) *Research Methods in the Social Sciences.*

Jossey-Bass, San Francisco, for words from Reynolds, P. D. (1979) *Ethical Dilemmas and Social Science Research.*

Kogan Page, London, for words from Norris, N. (1990) *Understanding Educational Evaluation*.

Krejcie, R. V. and Morgan, D. W. (1970) Determining sample size for research activities, *Educational and Psychological Measurement* 30, 609, copyright Sage Publications Inc, reprinted by permission of Sage Publications Inc.

Kvale, S. (1996) *Interviews*, pp. 30, 88, 145, copyright Sage Publications Inc., reprinted by permission of Sage Publications Inc.

Lincoln, Y. S. and Guba, E. G. (1985) words from *Naturalistic Inquiry*, copyright Sage Publications Inc., reprinted by permission of Sage Publications Inc.

Methuen & Co, London, for words from Shipman, M. D. (1974) *Inside a Curriculum Project*.

Mies, M. (1993) for words from Towards a methodology for feminist research, in M. Hammersley (ed.) *Social Research: Philosophy, Politics and Practice*, reprinted by permission of Sage Publications Inc.

Multilingual Matters Ltd, Clevedon, for figures from Parsons, E., Chalkley, B. and Jones, A. (1996) The role of Geographic Information Systems in the study of parental choice and secondary school catchments, *Evaluation and Research in Education*, 10 (1), 23–34; for words from Stronach, I. and Morris, B. (1994) Polemical notes on educational evaluation in an age of 'policy hysteria', *Evaluation and Research in Education*, 8 (1 & 2), 5–19.

Open Books, London and Shepton Mallet, for Bennett, S. N. (1976), *Teaching Styles and Pupil Progress*, **Box 20.4**.

Open University Press, Milton Keynes, for words from Bell, J. (1987) *Doing Your Research Project*; Hopkins, D. (1985) *A Teacher's Guide to Classroom Research*; Pilliner, A. (1973) *Experiment in Educational Research*, E 341, Block 5; Rose, D.

and Sullivan, O. (1993) *Introducing Data Analysis for Social Scientists*.

Parsons, E., Chalkley, B. and Jones, A. (1996) The role of Geographic Information Systems in the study of parental choice and secondary school catchments, *Evaluation and Research in Education*, 10 (1), 23–34, published by Multilingual Matters Ltd, Clevedon, **Boxes 22.1** and **22.2**.

Patton, M.Q. (1980) *Qualitative Evaluation Methods*, p. 206, copyright Sage Publications Inc., reprinted by permission of Sage Publications Inc.

Peter Francis Publishers, Dereham, Norfolk, for material from Morrison, K. R. B. (1993) *Planning and Accomplishing School-Centred Evaluation*.

Prentice-Hall, Englewood Cliffs, New Jersey, for words from Denzin, N. K. (1989) *The Research Act* (third edition).

Routledge, London, for words from Hitchcock, G. and Hughes, D. (1989) *Research and the Teacher: a Qualitative Introduction to School-based Research*, **Box 7.2**; words from Hitchcock, G. and Hughes, D. (1995) *Research and the Teacher* (second edition); words from Carspecken, P. F. (1996) *Critical Ethnography in Educational Research*; Wragg, E. C. (1994) *An Introduction to Classroom Observation*.

Taylor & Francis, London, for words and figure from: Zuber-Skerritt, O. (ed.) (1996) *New Directions in Action Research*, published by Falmer, pp. 99 and 17; James, M. (1993) Evaluation for policy: rationality and political reality: the paradigm case of PRAISE, in R. G. Burgess (ed.) *Educational Research and Evaluation for Policy and Practice*, published by Falmer.

University of Chicago Press, Chicago, for words from Diener, E. and Crandall R. (1978) *Ethics in Social and Behavioral Research*.

Introduction

It is six years since the fourth edition of *Research Methods in Education* was published and we are indebted to RoutledgeFalmer for the opportunity to produce a fifth edition. The book continues to be received very favourably worldwide and we should like to thank reviewers for their constructive comments which have helped in the production of this fifth edition. In particular, this has led to the substantial increase in the coverage of qualitative approaches to educational research, which has resulted in a fairer balance to the book. This new edition constitutes the largest reshaping of the book to date, and includes a reorganization of the material into five parts that catch the range of issues in planning educational research: (a) the context of educational research; (b) planning educational research; (c) styles of educational research; (d) strategies for data collection and researching; (e) recent developments in educational research. Much of the material from the previous editions has been relocated within these five parts to make them more accessible to the reader, and the careful titling of chapters is designed to increase this accessibility. Within these main parts the book includes considerable additional material to give this edition greater balance and coverage, and to provide examples and greater practical guidance for those who are planning and conducting educational research. This edition includes, also, guidance on data analysis within both qualitative and quantitative approaches, and issues in reporting research. In particular the following are included:

Part One:

- additional material on interpretive, ethnographic, interactionist, phenomenological and qualitative perspectives;
- additional material on curricular and evaluative research;

- new material on critical perspectives on educational research, including ideology critique from Habermas and the Frankfurt School, and feminist perspectives;
- new material on research, politics and policy-making.

Part Two:

- an entirely new part that is designed to assist novice researchers to design and conduct educational research, from its earliest stages to its completion. It is envisaged that this part will be particularly useful for higher education students who are undertaking educational research as part of their course requirements.

Part Three:

- considerable new material on naturalistic, qualitative and ethnographic approaches, including critical ethnographies;
- additional material on action research, aligning it to the critical approaches set out in Part One;
- new material and chapters on sampling, reliability and validity, including qualitative approaches to educational research;
- additional explanations of frequently used concepts in quantitative educational research, for example statistical significance, correlations, regression, curvilinearity, and an indication of particular statistics to use for data analysis;
- new and additional material on event-history analysis, meta-analysis and multilevel modelling;
- an introduction to Nominal Group Technique and Delphi techniques;
- additional material on case study planning and implementation;
- additional material on data analysis for qualitative data, e.g. content analysis and coding,

analysis of field notes, cognitive mapping, patterning, critical events and incidents, analytic induction and constant comparison.

Part Four:

- new material and chapters on questionnaire design and construction, interviews, focus groups, telephone interviewing, observation, the laddering and pyramid designs of personal constructs, speech acts, and stories, including analysis of data derived from these instruments for data collection;
- a new chapter on testing, test construction, item response theory, item analysis, item difficulty and discriminability and computer adaptive testing;
- additional material on contingency tables and statistical significance.

Part Five:

- a new chapter on recent developments in educational research, including material on Internet usage, simulations, fuzzy logic, Geographical Information Systems, needs analysis/assessment and evidence-based education.

By careful cross-referencing and the provision of explanations and examples we have attempted to give both considerable coherence to the book and to provide researchers with clear and deliberately practical guidance on all stages of the research process, from planning to operationalization, ethics, methodology, sampling, reliability and validity, instrumentation and data collection, data analysis and reporting. We have attempted to show throughout how practices derive from, and are located within, the contexts of educational research that are set out in Part One. The guidance that we provide is couched in a view of educational research as an ethical activity, and care has been taken to ensure that ethical issues, in addition to the specific chapter on ethics, are discussed throughout the book. The significance of the ethical dimension of educational research is underlined by the relocation of the chapter on ethics to very early on in this edition.

We have deliberately reduced the more extended discussion of published examples in response to feedback on previous editions from reviewers, but we have included detailed backup reference to these and additional references to updated examples for the reader to follow up and consult at will.

We are joined by Keith Morrison for the authorship of this new edition. We welcome the additions and amendments that he has made, in the firm knowledge that these will guarantee the book's continuing success. Overall, this edition provides a balanced, structured and comprehensive introduction to educational research that sets out both its principles and practice for researchers in a user-friendly way, and which is guided by the principle of Occam's razor: all things being equal, the simplest explanation is frequently the best, or, as Einstein put it, one should make matters as simple as possible but no simpler! Balancing simplicity and the inescapable complexity of educational research is a high-wire act; we hope to have provided a useful introduction to this in the fifth edition of *Research Methods in Education*.

Louis Cohen, Ph.D., D. Litt., is Emeritus Professor of Education at Loughborough University.
Lawrence Manion, Ph.D., is former Principal Lecturer in Music in Didsbury School of Education, Manchester Metropolitan University.
Keith Morrison, Ph.D., is Professor of Education at the Inter-University Institute of Macau.

Part one

The context of educational research

This part locates the research enterprise in several contexts. It commences with positivist and scientific contexts of research and then proceeds to show the strengths and weaknesses of such traditions for educational research. As an alternative paradigm, the cluster of approaches that can loosely be termed interpretive, naturalistic, phenomenological, interactionist and ethnographic are brought together and their strengths and weaknesses for educational research are also examined. The rise of critical theory as a paradigm in which educational research is conducted has been meteoric and its implications for the research undertaking are addressed in several ways in this chapter, resonating with curriculum research and feminist research. Indeed critical theory links the conduct of educational research with politics and policy-making, and this is reflected in the discussions here of research and evaluation, arguing how much educational research has become evaluative in nature. That educational research serves a political agenda is seen in the later sections of this part, though the links between educational research and policy-making are typically far from straightforward. The intention in this section is to introduce the reader to different research traditions, and, rather than advocating slavish adherence to a single research paradigm, we suggest that 'fitness for purpose' must be the guiding principle: different research paradigms are suitable for different research purposes and questions. Different research traditions spawn different styles of research; researchers must make informed choices of research traditions, mindful of the political agendas that their research might serve.

▌ The nature of inquiry[1]

Introduction

This chapter explores the context of educational research. It sets out three significant lenses through which to examine the practice of research: (a) scientific and positivistic methodologies; (b) naturalistic and interpretive methodologies; (c) methodologies from critical theory. Our analysis takes as a starting point an important notion from Hitchcock and Hughes (1995: 21) who suggest that ontological assumptions give rise to epistemological assumptions; these, in turn, give rise to methodological considerations; and these, in turn, give rise to issues of instrumentation and data collection. This view moves us beyond regarding research methods as simply a technical exercise; it recognizes that research is concerned with understanding the world and that this is informed by how we view our world(s), what we take understanding to be, and what we see as the purposes of understanding. The chapter outlines the ontological, epistemological and methodological premises of the three lenses and examines their strengths and weaknesses. In so doing it recognizes that education, educational research, politics and decision-making are inextricably intertwined, a view which the lens of critical theory, for example, brings sharply into focus in its discussions of curriculum decision-making. Hence this introductory chapter draws attention to the politics of educational research and the implications that this has for undertaking research (e.g. the move towards applied and evaluative research and away from 'pure' research).

The search for truth

People have long been concerned to come to grips with their environment and to understand the nature of the phenomena it presents to their senses. The means by which they set out to achieve these ends may be classified into three broad categories: *experience, reasoning* and *research* (Mouly, 1978). Far from being independent and mutually exclusive, however, these categories must be seen as complementary and overlapping, features most readily in evidence where solutions to complex modern problems are sought.

In our endeavours to come to terms with the problems of day-to-day living, we are heavily dependent upon experience and authority and their value in this context should not be underestimated. Nor should their respective roles be overlooked in the specialist sphere of research where they provide richly fertile sources of hypotheses and questions about the world, though, of course, it must be remembered that as tools for uncovering ultimate truth they have decided limitations. The limitations of personal experience in the form of *common-sense knowing*, for instance, can quickly be exposed when compared with features of the scientific approach to problem-solving. Consider, for example, the striking differences in the way in which theories are used. Laypeople base them on haphazard events and use them in a loose and uncritical manner. When they are required to test them, they do so in a selective fashion, often choosing only that evidence that is consistent with their hunches and ignoring that which is counter to them. Scientists, by contrast, construct their theories carefully and systematically. Whatever hypotheses they formulate have to be tested empirically so that their explanations have a firm basis in fact. And there is the concept of *control* distinguishing the layperson's and the scientist's attitude to experience. Laypeople generally make no attempt to control any extraneous sources of influence when trying to explain an occurrence. Scientists, on the other hand, only too conscious of the multiplicity of causes for a given occurrence, resort to definite techniques and procedures to isolate and test the effect of one or more of the alleged causes. Finally, there is the difference of attitude to the relationships among phenomena. Laypeople's concerns with such relationships are loose, unsystematic and uncontrolled. The chance occurrence of two events in close proximity is sufficient reason to predicate a causal link between them. Scientists, however, display a much more serious professional concern with relationships and only as a result of rigorous experimentation will they postulate a relationship between two phenomena.

The second category by means of which people attempt to comprehend the world around them, namely, reasoning, consists of three types: *deductive reasoning, inductive reasoning*, and the *combined inductive–deductive* approach. Deductive reasoning is based on the syllogism which was Aristotle's great contribution to formal logic. In its simplest form the syllogism consists of a major premise based on an a priori or self-evident proposition, a minor premise providing a particular instance, and a conclusion. Thus:

> All planets orbit the sun;
> The earth is a planet;
> Therefore the earth orbits the sun.

The assumption underlying the syllogism is that through a sequence of formal steps of logic, from the general to the particular, a valid conclusion can be deduced from a valid premise. Its chief limitation is that it can handle only certain kinds of statement. The syllogism formed the basis of systematic reasoning from the time of its inception until the Renaissance. Thereafter its effectiveness was diminished because it was no longer related to observation and experience and

became merely a mental exercise. One of the consequences of this was that empirical evidence as the basis of proof was superseded by authority and the more authorities one could quote, the stronger one's position became. Naturally, with such abuse of its principal tool, science became sterile.

The history of reasoning was to undergo a dramatic change in the 1600s when Francis Bacon began to lay increasing stress on the observational basis of science. Being critical of the model of deductive reasoning on the grounds that its major premises were often preconceived notions which inevitably bias the conclusions, he proposed in its place the method of inductive reasoning by means of which the study of a number of individual cases would lead to a hypothesis and eventually to a generalization. Mouly (1978) explains it like this: 'His basic premise was that if one collected enough data without any preconceived notion about their significance and orientation – thus maintaining complete objectivity – inherent relationships pertaining to the general case would emerge to be seen by the alert observer.' Bacon's major contribution to science was thus that he was able to rescue it from the death-grip of the deductive method whose abuse had brought scientific progress to a standstill. He thus directed the attention of scientists to nature for solutions to people's problems, demanding empirical evidence for verification. Logic and authority in themselves were no longer regarded as conclusive means of proof and instead became sources of hypotheses about the world and its phenomena.

Bacon's inductive method was eventually followed by the inductive-deductive approach which combines Aristotelian deduction with Baconian induction. In Mouly's words, this consisted of:

> a back-and-forth movement in which the investigator first operates inductively from observations to hypotheses, and then deductively from these hypotheses to their implications, in order to check their validity from the standpoint of compatibility

with accepted knowledge. After revision, where necessary, these hypotheses are submitted to further test through the collection of data specifically designed to test their validity at the empirical level. This dual approach is the essence of the modern scientific method and marks the last stage of man's progress toward empirical science, a path that took him through folklore and mysticism, dogma and tradition, casual observation, and finally to systematic observation.

(Mouly, 1978)

Although both deduction and induction have their weaknesses, their contributions to the development of science are enormous and fall into three categories: (1) the suggestion of hypotheses; (2) the logical development of these hypotheses; and (3) the clarification and interpretation of scientific findings and their synthesis into a conceptual framework.

The third means by which we set out to discover truth is *research*. This has been defined by Kerlinger (1970) as the systematic, controlled, empirical and critical investigation of hypothetical propositions about the presumed relations among natural phenomena. Research has three characteristics in particular which distinguish it from the first means of problem-solving identified earlier, namely, experience. First, whereas experience deals with events occurring in a haphazard manner, research is systematic and controlled, basing its operations on the inductive–deductive model outlined above. Second, research is empirical. The scientist turns to experience for validation. As Kerlinger puts it, 'subjective belief . . . must be checked against objective reality. Scientists must always subject their notions to the court of empirical inquiry and test'. And, third, research is self-correcting. Not only does the scientific method have built-in mechanisms to protect scientists from error as far as is humanly possible, but also their procedures and results are open to public scrutiny by fellow professionals. As Mouly says, 'This self corrective function is the most important single aspect of science, guaranteeing that incorrect results will in time be found to be incorrect and

duly revised or discarded.' Research is a combination of both experience and reasoning and must be regarded as the most successful approach to the discovery of truth, particularly as far as the natural sciences are concerned (Borg, 1963).[2]

Educational research has at the same time absorbed two competing views of the social sciences – the established, traditional view and a more recent interpretive view. The former holds that the social sciences are essentially the same as the natural sciences and are therefore concerned with discovering natural and universal laws regulating and determining individual and social behaviour; the latter view, however, while sharing the rigour of the natural sciences and the same concern of traditional social science to describe and explain human behaviour, emphasizes how people differ from inanimate natural phenomena and, indeed, from each other. These contending views – and also their corresponding reflections in educational research – stem in the first instance from different conceptions of social reality and of individual and social behaviour. It will help our understanding of the issues to be developed subsequently if we examine these in a little more detail.

Two conceptions of social reality

The two views of social science that we have just identified represent strikingly different ways of looking at social reality and are constructed on correspondingly different ways of interpreting it. We can perhaps most profitably approach these two conceptions of the social world by examining the explicit and implicit assumptions underpinning them. Our analysis is based on the work of Burrell and Morgan (1979) who identified four sets of such assumptions.

First, there are assumptions of an ontological kind – assumptions which concern the very nature or essence of the social phenomena being investigated. Thus, the authors ask, is social reality external to individuals – imposing itself on their consciousness from without – or is it the product of individual consciousness? Is reality of an objective nature, or the result of individual cognition? Is it a given 'out there' in the world, or is it created by one's own mind? These questions spring directly from what is known in philosophy as the nominalist-realist debate. The former view holds that objects of thought are merely words and that there is no independently accessible thing constituting the meaning of a word. The realist position, however, contends that objects have an independent existence and are not dependent for it on the knower.

The second set of assumptions identified by Burrell and Morgan are of an epistemological kind. These concern the very bases of knowledge – its nature and forms, how it can be acquired, and how communicated to other human beings. The authors ask whether 'it is possible to identify and communicate the nature of knowledge as being hard, real and capable of being transmitted in tangible form, or whether knowledge is of a softer, more subjective, spiritual or even transcendental kind, based on experience and insight of a unique and essentially personal nature. The epistemological assumptions in these instances determine extreme positions on the issues of whether knowledge is something which can be acquired on the one hand, or is something which has to be personally experienced on the other' (Burrell and Morgan, 1979). How one aligns oneself in this particular debate profoundly affects how one will go about uncovering knowledge of social behaviour. The view that knowledge is hard, objective and tangible will demand of researchers an observer role, together with an allegiance to the methods of natural science; to see knowledge as personal, subjective and unique, however, imposes on researchers an involvement with their subjects and a rejection of the ways of the natural scientist. To subscribe to the former is to be positivist; to the latter, anti-positivist.

The third set of assumptions concern human nature and, in particular, the relationship between human beings and their environment. Since the human being is both its subject and object of study, the consequences for social science of assumptions of this kind are indeed far-reaching. Two images of human beings emerge from such assumptions – the one portrays them as responding mechanically to their environment; the other, as initiators of their own actions. Burrell and Morgan write lucidly on the distinction:

> Thus, we can identify perspectives in social science which entail a view of human beings responding in a mechanistic or even deterministic fashion to the situations encountered in their external world. This view tends to be one in which human beings and their experiences are regarded as products of the environment; one in which humans are conditioned by their external circumstances. This extreme perspective can be contrasted with one which attributes to human beings a much more creative role: with a perspective where 'free will' occupies the centre of the stage; where man [sic] is regarded as the creator of his environment, the controller as opposed to the controlled, the master rather than the marionette. In these two extreme views of the relationship between human beings and their environment, we are identifying a great philosophical debate between the advocates of *determinism* on the one hand and *voluntarism* on the other. Whilst there are social theories which adhere to each of these extremes, the assumptions of many social scientists are pitched somewhere in the range between.
>
> (Burrell and Morgan, 1979)

It would follow from what we have said so far that the three sets of assumptions identified above have direct implications for the methodological concerns of researchers, since the contrasting ontologies, epistemologies and models of human beings will in turn demand different research methods. Investigators adopting an objectivist (or positivist) approach to the social world and who treat it like the world of natural phenomena as being hard, real and external to the individual will choose from a range of traditional options – surveys, experiments, and the like. Others favouring the more subjectivist (or anti-positivist) approach and who view the social world as being of a much softer, personal and humanly created kind will select from a comparable range of recent and emerging techniques – accounts, participant observation and personal constructs, for example.

Where one subscribes to the view which treats the social world like the natural world – as if it were a hard, external and objective reality – then scientific investigation will be directed at analysing the relationships and regularities between selected factors in that world. It will be pre- dominantly quantitative. 'The concern', say Burrell and Morgan, 'is with the identification and definition of these elements and with the discovery of ways in which these relationships can be expressed. The methodological issues of importance are thus the concepts themselves, their measurement and the identification of underlying themes. This perspective expresses itself most forcefully in a search for universal laws which explain and govern the reality which is being observed' (Burrell and Morgan, 1979). An approach characterized by procedures and methods designed to discover general laws may be referred to as *nomothetic*.

However, if one favours the alternative view of social reality which stresses the importance of the subjective experience of individuals in the creation of the social world, then the search for understanding focuses upon different issues and approaches them in different ways. The principal concern is with an understanding of the way in which the individual creates, modifies and interprets the world in which he or she finds himself or herself. The approach now takes on a qualitative as well as quantitative aspect. As Burrell and Morgan observe,

> The emphasis in extreme cases tends to be placed upon the explanation and understanding of what is unique and particular to the individual rather than of what is general and universal. This approach questions whether there exists an external reality worthy of study. In methodological terms it is an approach which emphasizes the relativistic nature of the social world.
>
> (Burrell and Morgan, 1979)

Such a view is echoed by Kirk and Miller (1986: 14). In its emphasis on the particular and individual this approach to understanding individual behaviour may be termed *idiographic*.

In this review of Burrell and Morgan's analysis of the ontological, epistemological, human and methodological assumptions underlying two ways of conceiving social reality, we have laid the foundations for a more extended study of the two contrasting perspectives evident in the practices of researchers investigating human behaviour and, by adoption, educational problems. Box 1.1 summarizes these assumptions in graphic form along a subjective–objective dimension. It identifies the four sets of assumptions by

Box 1.1

The subjective–objective dimension

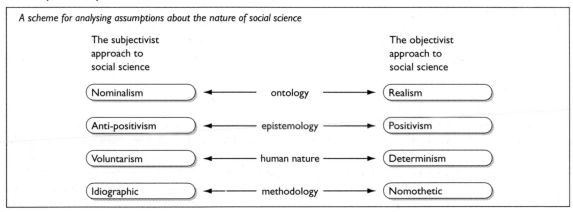

A scheme for analysing assumptions about the nature of social science

The subjectivist approach to social science		The objectivist approach to social science
Nominalism	← ontology →	Realism
Anti-positivism	← epistemology →	Positivism
Voluntarism	← human nature →	Determinism
Idiographic	← methodology →	Nomothetic

Source Burrell and Morgan, 1979

using terms we have adopted in the text and by which they are known in the literature of social philosophy.

Each of the two perspectives on the study of human behaviour outlined above has profound implications for research in classrooms and schools. The choice of problem, the formulation of questions to be answered, the characterization of pupils and teachers, methodological concerns, the kinds of data sought and their mode of treatment – all will be influenced or determined by the viewpoint held. Some idea of the considerable practical implications of the contrasting views can be gained by examining Box 1.2 which compares them with respect to a number of critical issues within a broadly societal and organizational framework. Implications of the two perspectives for research into classrooms and schools will unfold in the course of the text. Because of its significance to the epistemological basis of social science and its consequences for educational research, we devote much of the rest of this chapter to the positivist and anti-positivist debate.

Positivism

Although positivism has been a recurrent theme in the history of western thought from the Ancient Greeks to the present day, it is historically associated with the nineteenth-century French philosopher, Auguste Comte, who was the first thinker to use the word for a philosophical position (Beck, 1979). Here explanation proceeds by way of scientific description (Acton, 1975). In his study of the history of the philosophy and methodology of science, Oldroyd (1986) says:

> It was Comte who consciously 'invented' the new science of society and gave it the name to which we are accustomed. He thought that it would be possible to establish it on a 'positive' basis, just like the other sciences, which served as necessary preliminaries to it. For social phenomena were to be viewed in the light of physiological (or biological) laws and theories and investigated empirically, just

like physical phenomena. Likewise, biological phenomena were to be viewed in the light of chemical laws and theories; and so on down the line.

(Oldroyd, 1986)

Comte's position was to lead to a general doctrine of positivism which held that all genuine knowledge is based on sense experience and can only be advanced by means of observation and experiment. Following in the empiricist tradition, it limited inquiry and belief to what can be firmly established and in thus abandoning metaphysical and speculative attempts to gain knowledge by reason alone, the movement developed what has been described as a 'tough-minded orientation to facts and natural phenomena' (Beck, 1979).

Since Comte, the term positivism has been used in such different ways by philosophers and social scientists that it is difficult to assign it a precise and consistent meaning. Moreover, the term has also been applied to the doctrine of a school of philosophy known as 'logical positivism'.[3] The central belief of the logical positivists is that the meaning of a statement is, or is given by, the method of its verification. It follows from this that unverifiable statements are held to be meaningless, the utterances of traditional metaphysics and theology being included in this class.

However the term positivism is used by philosophers and social scientists, a residual meaning is always present and this derives from an acceptance of natural science as the paradigm of human knowledge (Duncan, 1968). This includes the following connected suppositions which have been identified by Giddens (1975). First, the methodological procedures of natural science may be directly applied to the social sciences. Positivism here implies a particular stance concerning the social scientist as an observer of social reality. Second, the end-product of investigations by social scientists can be formulated in terms parallel to those of natural science. This means that their analyses must be expressed in laws or law-like generalizations of the same kind that have been established in relation to natural

Box 1.2
Alternative bases for interpreting social reality

Dimensions of comparison	Conceptions of social reality	
	Objectivist	Subjectivist
Philosophical basis	Realism: the world exists and is knowable as it really is. Organizations are real entities with a life of their own.	Idealism: the world exists but different people construe it in very different ways. Organizations are invented social reality.
The role of social science	Discovering the universal laws of society and human conduct within it.	Discovering how different people interpret the world in which they live.
Basic units of social reality	The collectivity: society or organizations.	Individuals acting singly or together.
Methods of understanding	Identifying conditions or relationships which permit the collectivity to exist. Conceiving what these conditions and relationships are.	Interpretation of the subjective meanings which individuals place upon their action. Discovering the subjective rules for such action.
Theory	A rational edifice built by scientists to explain human behaviour.	Sets of meanings which people use to make sense of their world and behaviour within it.
Research	Experimental or quasi-experimental validation of theory.	The search for meaningful relationships and the discovery of their consequences for action.
Methodology	Abstraction of reality, especially through mathematical models and quantitative analysis.	The representation of reality for purposes of comparison. Analysis of language and meaning.
Society	Ordered. Governed by a uniform set of values and made possible only by those values.	Conflicted. Governed by the values of people with access to power.
Organizations	Goal oriented. Independent of people. Instruments of order in society serving both society and the individual.	Dependent upon people and their goals. Instruments of power which some people control and can use to attain ends which seem good to them.
Organizational pathologies	Organizations get out of kilter with social values and individual needs.	Given diverse human ends, there is always conflict among people acting to pursue them.
Prescription for change	Change the structure of the organization to meet social values and individual needs.	Find out what values are embodied in organizational action and whose they are. Change the people or change their values if you can.

Source Adapted from Barr Greenfield, 1975

phenomena. Positivism here involves a definite view of social scientists as analysts or interpreters of their subject matter. Positivism may be characterized by its claim that science provides us with the clearest possible ideal of knowledge.

Where positivism is less successful, however, is in its application to the study of human behaviour where the immense complexity of human nature and the elusive and intangible quality of social phenomena contrast strikingly with the order and regularity of the natural world. This point is nowhere more apparent than in the contexts of classroom and school where the problems of teaching, learning and human inter-action present the positivistic researcher with a mammoth challenge.

For further information on positivism within the history of the philosophy and methodology of science, see Oldroyd (1986). We now look more closely at some of its features.

The assumptions and nature of science

Since a number of the research methods we describe in this book draw heavily on the scientific method either implicitly or explicitly and can only be fully understood within the total framework of its principles and assumptions, we will here examine some of the characteristics of science a little more closely.

We begin with an examination of the tenets of scientific faith: the kinds of assumptions held by scientists, often implicitly, as they go about their daily work. First, there is the assumption of *determinism*. This means simply that events have causes, that events are determined by other circumstances; and science proceeds on the belief that these causal links can eventually be uncovered and understood, that the events are explicable in terms of their antecedents. Moreover, not only are events in the natural world determined by other circumstances, but there is regularity about the way they are determined: the universe does not behave capriciously. It is the ultimate aim of scientists to formulate laws to account for the happenings in the world around them, thus giving them a firm basis for prediction and control.

The second assumption is that of *empiricism*. We have already touched upon this viewpoint, which holds that certain kinds of reliable knowledge can only originate in experience. In practice, therefore, this means scientifically that the tenability of a theory or hypothesis depends on the nature of the empirical evidence for its support. Empirical here means that which is verifiable by observation; and evidence, data yielding proof or strong confirmation, in probability terms, of a theory or hypothesis in a research setting. The viewpoint has been summed up by Barratt who writes, 'The decision for empiricism as an act of scientific faith signifies that the best way to acquire reliable knowledge is the way of evidence obtained by direct experience' (Barratt, 1971).

Mouly (1978) has identified five steps in the process of empirical science:

1 *experience* – the starting point of scientific endeavour at the most elementary level;
2 *classification* – the formal systematization of otherwise incomprehensible masses of data;
3 *quantification* – a more sophisticated stage where precision of measurement allows more adequate analysis of phenomena by mathematical means;
4 *discovery of relationships* – the identification and classification of functional relationships among phenomena;
5 *approximation to the truth* – science proceeds by gradual approximation to the truth.

The third assumption underlying the work of the scientist is the principle of *parsimony*. The basic idea is that phenomena should be explained in the most economical way possible. The first historical statement of the principle was by William of Occam when he said that explanatory principles (entities) should not be needlessly multiplied. It may, of course, be interpreted in various ways: that it is preferable to account for a phenomenon by two concepts rather than three; that a simple theory is to be preferred to a complex one; or as Lloyd Morgan said as a guide to the study of animal behaviour: 'In no case may we interpret an action as the outcome of the exercise of a higher psychical faculty, if it can be interpreted as the outcome of the exercise of one which stands lower in the psychological scale.'

The final assumption, that of *generality*, played an important part in both the deductive and inductive methods of reasoning. Indeed, historically speaking, it was the problematic relationship between the concrete particular and the abstract general that was to result in two competing theories of knowledge – the rational and the empirical. Beginning with observations of the particular, scientists set out to generalize their findings to the world at large. This is so because they are concerned ultimately with explanation. Of course, the concept of generality presents much less of a problem to natural scientists working chiefly with inanimate matter than to human scientists who, of necessity having to deal with samples of larger human populations, have to exercise great caution when generalizing their findings to the particular parent populations.

Having identified the basic assumptions of science, we come now to the core question: What is science? Kerlinger (1970) points out that in the scientific world itself two broad views of science may be found: the static and the dynamic. The static view, which has particular appeal for laypeople, is that science is an activity that contributes systematized information to the world. The work of the scientist is to uncover new facts and add them to the existing corpus of knowledge. Science is thus seen as an accumulated body of findings, the emphasis being chiefly on the present state of knowledge and adding to it.[4] The dynamic view, by contrast, conceives science more as an activity, as something that scientists *do*. According to this conception it is important to have an accumulated body of knowledge, of course, but what really matter most are the discoveries that scientists make. The emphasis here, then, is more on the heuristic nature of science.

Contrasting views exist on the functions of science. We give a composite summary of these in Box 1.3. For the professional scientists however, science is seen as a way of comprehending the world; as a means of explanation and understanding, of prediction and control. For them the ultimate aim of science is theory. *Theory* has been defined by Kerlinger as 'a set of interrelated constructs [concepts], definitions, and propositions that presents a systematic view of phenomena by specifying relations among variables, with the purpose of explaining and predicting the phenomena' (Kerlinger, 1970). In a sense, theory gathers together all the isolated bits of empirical data into a coherent conceptual framework of wider applicability. Mouly expresses it

thus: 'If nothing else, a theory is a convenience – a necessity, really – organizing a whole slough of unassorted facts, laws, concepts, constructs, principles, into a meaningful and manageable form. It constitutes an attempt to make sense out of what we know concerning a given phenomenon' (Mouly, 1978). More than this, however, theory is itself a potential source of further information and discoveries. It is in this way a source of new hypotheses and hitherto unasked questions; it identifies critical areas for further investigation; it discloses gaps in our knowledge; and enables a researcher to postulate the existence of previously unknown phenomena.

Clearly there are several different types of theory, and each type of theory defines its own kinds of 'proof'. For example, Morrison (1995a) identifies *empirical theories*, '*grand*' *theories* and '*critical*' *theory*. Empirical theories and critical theories are discussed below. 'Grand theory' is a metanarrative, defining an area of study, being speculative, clarifying conceptual structures and frameworks, and creatively enlarging the way we consider behaviour and organizations (Layder, 1994). It uses fundamental ontological and epistemological postulates which serve to define a field of inquiry (Hughes, 1976). Here empirical material tends to be used by way of illustration

Box 1.3
The functions of science

1	Its problem-seeking, question-asking, hunch-encouraging, hypotheses-producing function.
2	Its testing, checking, certifying function; its trying out and testing of hypotheses; its repetition and checking of experiments; its piling up of facts.
3	Its organizing, theorizing, structuring, function; its search for larger and larger generalizations.
4	Its history-collecting, scholarly function.
5	Its technological side; instruments, methods, techniques.
6	Its administrative, executive, and organizational side.
7	Its publicizing and educational functions.
8	Its applications to human use.
9	Its appreciation, enjoyment, celebration, and glorification.

Source Maslow, 1954

rather than 'proof'. This is the stuff of some sociological theories, for example Marxism, consensus theory and functionalism. Whilst sociologists may be excited by the totalizing and all-encompassing nature of such theories, they have been subject to considerable undermining for half a century. For example, Merton (1949), Coser and Rosenberg (1969), Doll (1993) and Layder (1994) contend that whilst they might possess the attraction of large philosophical systems of considerable – Byzantine – architectonic splendour and logical consistency, nevertheless, they are scientifically sterile, irrelevant and out of touch with a postmodern world that is characterized by openness, fluidity, heterogeneity and fragmentation. This book does not endeavour to refer to this type of theory.

The status of theory varies quite considerably according to the discipline or area of knowledge in question. Some theories, as in the natural sciences, are characterized by a high degree of elegance and sophistication; others, like educational theory, are only at the early stages of formulation and are thus characterized by great unevenness. Popper (1968), Lakatos (1970),[5] Mouly (1978), Laudan (1990) and Rasmussen (1990) identify the following characteristics of an effective empirical theory:

- A theoretical system must permit deductions and generate laws that can be tested empirically; that is, it must provide the means for its confirmation or rejection. One can test the validity of a theory only through the validity of the propositions (hypotheses) that can be derived from it. If repeated attempts to disconfirm its various hypotheses fail, then greater confidence can be placed in its validity. This can go on indefinitely, until possibly some hypothesis proves untenable. This would constitute indirect evidence of the inadequacy of the theory and could lead to its rejection (or more commonly to its replacement by a more adequate theory that can incorporate the exception).
- Theory must be compatible with both observation and previously validated theories. It must be grounded in empirical data that have been verified and must rest on sound postulates and hypotheses. The better the theory, the more adequately it can explain the phenomena under consideration, and the more facts it can incorporate into a meaningful structure of ever-greater generalizability. There should be internal consistency between these facts. It should clarify the precise terms in which it seeks to explain, predict and generalize about empirical phenomena.
- Theories must be stated in simple terms; that theory is best that explains the most in the simplest way. This is the law of parsimony. A theory must explain the data adequately and yet must not be so comprehensive as to be unwieldy. On the other hand, it must not overlook variables simply because they are difficult to explain.
- A theory should have considerable explanatory and predictive potential.
- A theory should be able to respond to observed anomalies.
- A theory should spawn a research enterprise (echoing Siegel's (1987) comment that one of the characteristics of an effective theory is its fertility).
- A theory should demonstrate precision and universality, and set the grounds for its own falsification and verification, identifying the nature and operation of a 'severe test' (Popper, 1968). An effective empirical theory is tested in contexts which are different from those that gave rise to the theory, i.e. they should move beyond simply corroboration and induction and towards 'testing' (Laudan, 1990). It should identify the type of evidence which is required to confirm or refute the theory.
- A theory must be operationalizable precisely.
- A test of the theory must be replicable.

Sometimes the word *model* is used instead of, or interchangeably with, *theory*. Both may be seen as explanatory devices or schemes having a broadly conceptual framework, though models are often characterized by the use of analogies to give a more graphic or visual representation of a particular phenomenon. Providing they are accurate and do not misrepresent the facts, models can be of great help in achieving clarity and focusing on key issues in the nature of phenomena.

Hitchcock and Hughes (1995: 20–1) draw together the strands of the discussion so far when they describe a theory thus:

> Theory is seen as being concerned with the development of systematic construction of knowledge of the social world. In doing this theory employs the use of concepts, systems, models, structures, beliefs and ideas, hypotheses (theories) in order to make statements about particular types of actions, events or activities, so as to make analyses of their causes, consequences and process. That is, to explain events in ways which are consistent with a particular philosophical rationale or, for example, a particular sociological or psychological perspective. Theories therefore aim to both propose and analyze sets of relations existing between a number of variables when certain regularities and continuities can be demonstrated via empirical inquiry.
>
> (Hitchcock and Hughes, 1995: 20–1)

Scientific theories must, by their very nature, be provisional. A theory can never be complete in the sense that it encompasses all that can be known or understood about the given phenomenon. As Mouly says,

> Invariably, scientific theories are replaced by more sophisticated theories embodying more of the advanced state of the question so that science widens its horizons to include more and more of the facts as they accumulate. No doubt, many of the things about which there is agreement today will be found inadequate by future standards. But we must begin where we are.
>
> (Mouly, 1978)

We have already implied that the quality of a theory is determined by the state of development of the particular discipline. The early stages of a science must be dominated by empirical work, that is, the accumulation and classifi-cation of data. This is why, as we shall see, much of educational research is descriptive. Only as a discipline matures can an adequate body of theory be developed. Too premature a formulation of theory before the necessary empirical spadework has been done can lead to a slowing down of progress. Mouly optimistically suggests that some day a single theoretical system, unknown to us at the present time, will be used to explain the behaviour of molecules, animals and people.

In referring to theory and models, we have begun to touch upon the tools used by scientists in their work. We look now in more detail at two such tools which play a crucial role in science – the concept and the hypothesis.

The tools of science

Concepts express generalizations from particulars – anger, achievement, alienation, velocity, intelligence, democracy. Examining these examples more closely, we see that each is a word representing an idea: more accurately, a concept is the relationship between the word (or symbol) and an idea or conception. Whoever we are and whatever we do, we all make use of concepts. Naturally, some are shared and used by all groups of people within the same culture – child, love, justice, for example; others, however, have a restricted currency and are used only by certain groups, specialists, or members of professions – idioglossia, retroactive inhibition, anticipatory socialization.

Concepts enable us to impose some sort of meaning on the world; through them reality is given sense, order and coherence. They are the means by which we are able to come to terms with our experience. How we perceive the world, then, is highly dependent on the repertoire of concepts we can command. The more we have, the more sense data we can pick up and the surer will be our perceptual (and cognitive) grasp of whatever is 'out there'. If our perceptions of the world are determined by the concepts available to us, it follows that people with differing sets of concepts will tend to view the 'same' objective reality differently – a doctor diagnosing an illness will draw upon a vastly different range of concepts from, say, the restricted and simplistic notions of the layperson in that context; and a visitor to civilization from a distant primitive culture would be as confused by the frenetic bustle of urban life as would the mythical Martian.

So, you may ask, where is all this leading? Simply to this: that social scientists have likewise developed, or appropriated by giving precise meaning to, a set of concepts which enable them to shape their perceptions of the world in a particular way, to represent that slice of reality which is their special study. And collectively, these concepts form part of their wider meaning system which permits them to give accounts of that reality, accounts which are rooted and validated in the direct experience of everyday life. These points may be exemplified by the concept of social class. Hughes says that it offers 'a rule, a grid, even though vague at times, to use in talking about certain sorts of experience that have to do with economic position, life-style, life-chances, and so on. It serves to identify aspects of experience, and by relating the concept to other concepts we are able to construct theories about experience in a particular order or sphere' (Hughes, 1976: 34).

There are two important points to stress when considering scientific concepts. The first is that they do not exist independently of us: they are indeed our inventions enabling us to acquire some understanding at least of the apparent chaos of nature. The second is that they are limited in number and in this way contrast with the infinite number of phenomena they are required to explain.

A second tool of great importance to the scientist is the *hypothesis*. It is from this that much research proceeds, especially where cause-and-effect or concomitant relationships are being investigated. The hypothesis has been defined by Kerlinger (1970) as a conjectural statement of the relations between two or more variables. More simply, it has been termed 'an educated guess', though it is unlike an educated guess in that it is often the result of considerable study, reflective thinking and observation. Medawar (1972) writes incomparably of the hypothesis and its function in the following way:

> All advances of scientific understanding, at every level, begin with a speculative adventure, an imaginative preconception *of what might be true* – a preconception which always, and necessarily, goes a little way (sometimes a long way) beyond anything which we have logical or factual authority to believe in. It is the invention of a possible world, or of a tiny fraction of that world. The conjecture is then exposed to criticism to find out whether or not that imagined world is anything like the real one. Scientific reasoning is therefore at all levels an interaction between two episodes of thought – a dialogue between two voices, the one imaginative and the other critical; a dialogue, if you like, between the possible and the actual, between proposal and disposal, conjecture and criticism, between what might be true and what is in fact the case.
>
> (Medawar, 1972)

Kerlinger (1970) has identified two criteria for 'good' hypotheses. The first is that hypotheses are statements about the relations between variables; and second, that hypotheses carry clear implications for testing the stated relations. To these he adds two ancillary criteria: that hypotheses disclose compatibility with current knowledge; and that they are expressed as economically as possible. Thus if we conjecture that social class background determines academic achievement, we have a relationship between one variable, social class, and another, academic achievement. And since both can be measured, the primary criteria specified by Kerlinger can be met. Neither do they violate the ancillary criteria proposed by Kerlinger (see also Box 1.4).

He further identifies four reasons for the importance of hypotheses as tools of research. First, they organize the efforts of researchers. The relationship expressed in the hypothesis indicates what they should do. They enable them to understand the problem with greater clarity and provide them with a framework for collecting, analysing and interpreting their data. Sec-

Box 1.4
The hypothesis

> Once he has a hypothesis to work on, the scientist is in business; the hypothesis will guide him to make some observations rather than others and will suggest experiments that might not otherwise have been performed. Scientists soon pick up by experience the characteristics that make a good hypothesis; . . . almost all laws and hypotheses can be read in such a way as to *prohibit* the occurrence of certain phenomena . . . Clearly, a hypothesis so permissive as to accommodate *any* phenomenon tells us precisely nothing; the more phenomena it prohibits, the more informative it is.
>
>   Again, a good hypothesis must also have the character of *logical immediacy*, by which I mean that it must be rather specially an explanation of whatever it is that needs to be explained and not an explanation of a great many other phenomena besides . . . The great virtue of logical immediacy in a hypothesis is that it can be tested by comparatively direct and practicable means – that is, without the foundation of a new research institute or by making a journey into outer space. A large part of the *art of the soluble* is the art of devising hypotheses that can be tested by practicable experiments.

Source Medawar, 1981

ond, they are, in Kerlinger's words, the working instruments of theory. They can be deduced from theory or from other hypotheses. Third, they can be tested, empirically or experimentally, thus resulting in confirmation or rejection. And there is always the possibility that a hypothesis, once confirmed and established, may become a law. And fourth, hypotheses are powerful tools for the advancement of knowledge because, as Kerlinger explains, they enable us to get outside ourselves.

Hypotheses and concepts play a crucial part in the scientific method and it is to this that we now turn our attention.

The scientific method

If the most distinctive feature of science is its empirical nature, the next most important characteristic is its set of procedures which show not only how findings have been arrived at, but are sufficiently clear for fellow-scientists to repeat them, i.e. to check them out with the same or other materials and thereby test the results. As Cuff and Payne (1979) say: 'A scientific approach necessarily involves standards and procedures for demonstrating the "empirical warrant" of its findings, showing the match or fit between its statements and what is happening or has happened in the world' (Cuff and Payne, 1979: 4). These standards and procedures we will call for convenience 'the scientific method', though this can be somewhat misleading for the following reason: the combination of the definite article, adjective and singular noun conjures up in the minds of some people a single invariant approach to problem-solving, an approach frequently involving atoms or rats, and taking place within the confines of a laboratory peopled with stereotypical scientists wearing white coats and given to eccentric bouts of behaviour. Yet there is much more to it than this. The term in fact cloaks a number of methods which vary in their degree of sophistication depending on their function and the particular stage of development a science has reached. We refer you at this point to Box 1.5 which sets out the sequence of stages through which a science normally passes in its development or, perhaps more realistically, that are constantly present in its progress and on which scientists may draw depending on the kind of information they seek or the kind of problem confronting them. Of particular interest to us in our efforts to elucidate the term 'scientific method' are stages 2, 3 and 4. Stage 2 is a relatively uncomplicated point at which the researcher is content to observe and record facts and possibly arrive at some system of classification. Much research in the field of education, especially at classroom and school level, is conducted in this way, e.g. surveys and case studies. Stage 3 introduces a note of added sophistication as attempts are made to establish relationships between variables within a loose framework of inchoate theory. Stage 4 is the most sophisticated stage and often the one that many people equate exclusively with the scientific method. In order to arrive at causality, as distinct from mere measures of association, researchers here design experimental situations in which variables are manipulated to test their chosen hypotheses. Here is how one noted researcher describes the later stages:

First, there is a doubt, a barrier, an indeterminate situation crying out, so to speak, to be made determinate. The scientist experiences vague doubts, emotional disturbances, inchoate ideas. He struggles to formulate the problem, even if inadequately. He studies the literature, scans his own experience and the experience of others. Often he simply has to wait for an inventive leap of mind. Maybe it will occur; maybe not. With the problem formulated, with the basic question or questions properly asked, the rest is much easier. Then the hypothesis is constructed, after which its implications are deduced, mainly along experimental lines. In this process the original problem, and of course the original hypothesis, may be changed. It may be broadened or narrowed. It may even be abandoned.

Lastly, but not finally, the relation expressed by the hypothesis is tested by observation and experimentation. On the basis of the research evidence, the hypothesis is accepted or rejected. This information is then fed back to the original problem and it is kept or altered as dictated by the evidence. Dewey finally pointed out that one phase of the process may be expanded and be of great importance, another may be skimped, and there may be fewer or more steps involved. These things are not important. What is important is the overall fundamental idea of scientific research as a controlled rational process of reflective inquiry, the interdependent nature of the parts of the process, and the paramount importance of the problem and its statement.

(Kerlinger, 1970)

With stages 3 and 4 of Box 1.5 in mind, we may say that the scientific method begins consciously and deliberately by selecting from the total number of elements in a given situation. More recently Hitchcock and Hughes (1995: 23) suggest an eight-stage model of the scientific method that echoes Kerlinger. This is represented in Box 1.6. The elements the researchers fasten on to will naturally be suitable for scientific formulation; this means simply that they will possess quantitative aspects. Their principal working tool will be the hypothesis which, as we have seen, is a statement indicating a relationship (or its absence)

Box 1.5
Stages in the development of a science

1 Definition of the science and identification of the phenomena that are to be subsumed under it. 2 Observational stage at which the relevant factors, variables or items are identified and labelled; and at which categories and taxonomies are developed. 3 Correlational research in which variables and parameters are related to one another and information is systematically integrated as theories begin to develop. 4 The systematic and controlled manipulation of variables to see if experiments will produce expected results, thus moving from correlation to causality. 5 The firm establishment of a body of theory as the outcomes of the earlier stages are accumulated. Depending on the nature of the phenomena under scrutiny, laws may be formulated and systematized. 6 The use of the established body of theory in the resolution of problems or as a source of further hypotheses.

Box 1.6
An eight-stage model of the scientific method

Stage 1: Hypotheses, hunches and guesses Stage 2: Experiment designed; samples taken; variables isolated Stage 3: Correlations observed; patterns identified Stage 4: Hypotheses formed to explain regularities Stage 5: Explanations and predictions tested; falsifiability Stage 6: Laws developed or disconfirmation (hypothesis rejected) Stage 7: Generalizations made Stage 8: New theories

between two or more of the chosen elements and stated in such a way as to carry clear implications for testing. Researchers then choose the most appropriate method and put their hypotheses to the test.

Criticisms of positivism and the scientific method

In spite of the scientific enterprise's proven success – especially in the field of natural science – its ontological and epistemological bases have been the focus of sustained and sometimes vehement criticism from some quarters. Beginning in the second half of the nineteenth century, the revolt against positivism occurred on a broad front, attracting some of the best intellectuals in Europe – philosophers, scientists, social critics and creative artists. Essentially, it has been a reaction against the world picture projected by science which, it is contended, undermines life and mind. The precise target of the anti-positivists' attack has been science's mechanistic and reductionist view of nature which, by definition, excludes notions of choice, freedom, individuality, and moral responsibility.

One of the most sustained and consistent attacks in this respect came from the poet, William Blake, who perceived the universe not as a mechanism, but as a living organism:

> Blake would have us understand that mechanistic science and the philosophy of materialism eliminate the concept of life itself. All they can do is to define life in terms of biochemistry, biophysics, vibrations, wavelengths, and so on; they reduce 'life' to conceivable measurement, but such a conception of life does not embrace the most evident element of all: that life can only be known by a living being, by 'inner' experience. No matter how exact measurement may be, it can never give us an experience of life, for life cannot be weighed and measured on a physical scale.
>
> (Nesfield-Cookson, 1987)

Another challenge to the claims of positivism came from Søren Kierkegaard, the Danish philosopher, from whose work was to originate the movement that became known as Existentialism. Kierkegaard was concerned with individuals and their need to fulfil themselves to the highest level of development. This realization of a person's potential was for him the meaning of existence which he saw as 'concrete and individual, unique and irreducible, not amenable to conceptualization' (Beck, 1979). Characteristic features of the age in which we live – democracy's trust in the crowd mentality, the ascendancy of reason, scientific and technological progress – all militate against the achievement of this end and contribute to the dehumanization of the individual. In his desire to free people from their illusions, the illusion Kierkegaard was most concerned about was that of objectivity. By this he meant the imposition of rules of behaviour and thought, and the making of a person into an observer set on discovering general laws governing human behaviour. The capacity for subjectivity, he argued, should be regained. This he regarded as the ability to consider one's own relationship to whatever constitutes the focus of inquiry. The contrast he made between objectivity and subjectivity is brought out in the following passage:

> When the question of truth is raised in an objective manner, reflection is directed objectively to the truth as an object to which the knower is related. Reflection is not focused on the relationship, however, but upon the question of whether it is the truth to which the knower is related. If only the object to which he is related is the truth, the subject is accounted to be in the truth. When the question of truth is raised subjectively, reflection is directed subjectively to the nature of the individual's relationship; if only the mode of this relationship is in the truth, the individual is in the truth, even if he should happen to be thus related to what is not true.
>
> (Kierkegaard, 1974)

For Kierkegaard, 'subjectivity and concreteness of truth are together the light. Anyone who is committed to science, or to rule-governed morality, is benighted, and needs to be rescued from his state of darkness' (Warnock, 1970).

Also concerned with the dehumanizing effects of the social sciences is Ions (1977). While acknowledging that they can take much credit for throwing light in dark corners, he expresses serious concern at the way in which quantification and computation, assisted by statistical theory and method, are used. On this point, he writes:

> The argument begins when we quantify the process and interpret the human act. In this respect, behavioural science represents a form of collectivism which runs parallel to other developments this century. However high-minded the intention, the result is depersonalization, the effects of which can be felt at the level of the individual human being, not simply at the level of culture.
>
> (Ions, 1977)

His objection is not directed at quantification *per se*, but at quantification when it becomes an end in itself – 'a branch of mathematics rather than a humane study seeking to explore and elucidate the gritty circumstances of the human condition' (Ions, 1977). This echoes Horkheimer's (1972) powerful critique of positivism as the 'mathematication of nature'.

Another forceful critic of the objective consciousness has been Roszak. Writing of its alienating effect in contemporary life, he says:

> While the art and literature of our time tell us with ever more desperation that the disease from which our age is dying is that of alienation, the sciences, in their relentless pursuit of objectivity, raise alienation to its apotheosis as our *only* means of achieving a valid relationship to reality. Objective consciousness is alienated life promoted to its most honorific status as the scientific method. Under its auspices we subordinate nature to our command only by estranging ourselves from more and more of what we experience, until the reality about which objectivity tells us so much finally becomes a universe of congealed alienation.
>
> (Roszak, 1970)[6]

The justification for any intellectual activity lies in the effect it has on increasing our awareness and degree of consciousness. This increase, some claim, has been retarded in our time by the excessive influence the positivist paradigm has been allowed to exert on areas of our intellectual life. Holbrook, for example, affording consciousness a central position in human existence and deeply concerned with what happens to it, has written:

> [O]ur approaches today to the study of man [*sic*] have yielded little, and are essentially dead, because they cling to positivism – that is, to an approach which demands that nothing must be regarded as real which cannot be found by empirical science and rational methods, by 'objectivity'. Since the whole problem . . . belongs to 'psychic reality', to man's 'inner world', to his moral being, and to the subjective life, there can be no debate unless we are prepared to recognize the bankruptcy of positivism, and the failure of 'objectivity' to give an adequate account of existence, and are prepared to find new modes of inquiry.
>
> (Holbrook, 1977)

Other writers question the perspective adopted by positivist social science because it presents a misleading picture of the human being. Hampden-Turner (1970), for example, concludes that the social science view of human beings is biased in that it is conservative and ignores important qualities. This restricted image of humans, he contends, comes about because social scientists concentrate on the repetitive, predictable and invariant aspects of the person; on 'visible externalities' to the exclusion of the subjective world; and – at least as far as psychology is concerned – on the parts of the person in their endeavours to understand the whole. For a trenchant critique of science from the point of view of theology, see Philip Sherrard (1987), *The Eclipse of Man and Nature*.

Habermas (1972), in keeping with the Frankfurt School of critical theory (critical theory is discussed below), provides a corrosive critique of positivism, arguing that the scientific mentality has been elevated to an almost unassailable position – almost to the level of a religion (scientism) – as being the only epistemology of the west. In this view all knowledge becomes equated with scientific knowledge. This neglects hermeneutic, aesthetic, critical, moral, creative and other forms of knowledge. It reduces behaviour to technicism.

Positivism's concern for control and, thereby, its appeal to the passivity of behaviourism and for instrumental reason is a serious danger to the more open-ended, creative, humanitarian aspects of social behaviour. Habermas (1972, 1974) and Horkheimer (1972) are arguing that scientism silences an important debate about values, informed opinion, moral judgements and beliefs. Scientific explanation seems to be the only means of explaining behaviour, and, for them, this seriously diminishes the very characteristics that make humans human. It makes for a society without conscience. Positivism is unable to answer questions about many interesting or important areas of life (Habermas, 1972: 300). Indeed this is an echo of Wittgenstein's (1974) famous comment that when all possible scientific questions have been addressed they have left untouched the main problems of life.

Other criticisms are commonly levelled at positivistic social science from within its own ranks. One is that it fails to take account of our unique ability to interpret our experiences and represent them to ourselves. We can, and do construct theories about ourselves and our world; moreover, we act on these theories. In failing to recognize this, positivistic social science is said to ignore the profound differences between itself and the natural sciences. Social science, unlike natural science, 'stands in a subject–subject relation to its field of study, not a subject–object relation; it deals with a pre-interpreted world in which the meanings developed by active subjects enter the actual constitution or production of the world' (Giddens, 1976).

The difficulty in which positivism finds itself is that it regards human behaviour as passive, essentially determined and controlled, thereby ignoring intention, individualism and freedom. This approach suffers from the same difficulties that inhere in behaviourism, which has scarcely recovered from Chomsky's withering criticism in 1959 where he writes that a singular problem

of behaviourism is our inability to infer causes from behaviour, to identify the stimulus that has brought about the response – the weakness of Skinner's stimulus-response theory. This problem with positivism also rehearses the familiar problem in social theory, viz. the tension between agency and structure (Layder, 1994); humans exercise agency – individual choice and intention – not necessarily in circumstances of their own choosing, but nevertheless they do not behave simply, deterministically like puppets.

The findings of positivistic social science are often said to be so banal and trivial that they are of little consequence to those for whom they are intended, namely, teachers, social workers, counsellors, personnel managers, and the like. The more effort, it seems, that researchers put into their scientific experimentation in the laboratory by restricting, simplifying and controlling variables, the more likely they are to end up with a 'pruned, synthetic version of the whole, a constructed play of puppets in a restricted environment'.[7]

These are formidable criticisms; but what alternatives are proposed by the detractors of positivistic social science?

Alternatives to positivistic social science: naturalistic approaches

Although the opponents of positivism within social science itself subscribe to a variety of schools of thought each with its own subtly different epistemological viewpoint, they are united by their common rejection of the belief that human behaviour is governed by general, universal laws and characterized by underlying regularities. Moreover, they would agree that the social world can only be understood from the standpoint of the individuals who are part of the ongoing action being investigated; and that their model of a person is an autonomous one, not the plastic version favoured by positivist researchers. In rejecting the viewpoint of the detached, objective observer – a mandatory feature of traditional research – anti-positivists would argue that individuals' behaviour can only be understood by the researcher sharing their frame of reference: understanding of individuals' interpretations of the world around them has to come from the inside, not the outside. Social science is thus seen as a subjective rather than an objective undertaking, as a means of dealing with the direct experience of people in specific contexts. The following extract nicely captures the spirit in which the anti-positivist social scientist would work:

[T]he purpose of social science is to understand social reality as different people see it and to demonstrate how their views shape the action which they take within that reality. Since the social sciences cannot penetrate to what lies behind social reality, they must work directly with man's definitions of reality and with the rules he devises for coping with it. While the social sciences do not reveal ultimate truth, they do help us to make sense of our world. What the social sciences offer is explanation, clarification and demystification of the social forms which man has created around himself.

(Beck, 1979)

The anti-positivist movement has so influenced those constituent areas of social science of most concern to us, namely, psychology, social psychology and sociology, that in each case a movement reflecting its mood has developed collaterally with mainstream trends. Whether this development is seen in competitive or complementary terms depends to some extent on one's personal viewpoint. It cannot be denied, however, that in some quarters proponents of the contrasting viewpoints have been prepared to lock horns on some of the more contentious issues.

In the case of psychology, for instance, a school of humanistic psychology has emerged alongside the co-existing behaviouristic and psychoanalytic schools. Arising as a response to the challenge to combat the growing feelings of dehumanization which characterize much of the current social and cultural milieu, it sets out to study and understand the person as a *whole* (Buhler and Allen, 1972). Humanistic psycholo-

gists present a model of people that is positive, active and purposive, and at the same time stresses their own involvement with the life experience itself. They do not stand apart, introspective, hypothesizing. Their interest is directed at the intentional and creative aspects of the human being. The perspective adopted by humanistic psychologists is naturally reflected in their methodology. They are dedicated to studying the individual in preference to the group, and consequently prefer idiographic approaches to nomothetic ones. The implications of the movement's philosophy for the education of the human being have been drawn by Carl Rogers.[8]

Comparable developments within social psychology may be perceived in the 'science of persons' movement. Its proponents contend that because of our self-awareness and powers of language, we must be seen as systems of a different order of complexity from any other existing system whether natural, like an animal, or artificial, a computer, for instance. Because of this, no other system is capable of providing a sufficiently powerful model to advance our understanding of ourselves. It is argued, therefore, that we must use ourselves as a key to our understanding of others and conversely, our understanding of others as a way of finding out about ourselves. What is called for is an anthropomorphic model of people. Since anthropomorphism means, literally, the attribution of human form and personality, the implied criticism is that social psychology as traditionally conceived has singularly failed, so far, to model people as they really are. As one wry commentator has pleaded, 'For scientific purposes, treat people as if they were human beings' (Harré and Secord, 1972).

This approach would entail working from a model of humans that takes account of the following uniquely human attributes:

We are entities who are capable of monitoring our own performance. Further, because we are aware of this self-monitoring and have the power of speech, we are able to provide commentaries on those performances and to plan ahead of them as well. Such entities it is held, are much inclined to using rules, to devising plans, to developing strategies in getting things done the way they want them doing.

(Harré and Secord, 1972)

Social psychology's task is to understand people in the light of this anthropomorphic model. But what specifically would this involve? Proponents of this 'science of persons' approach place great store on the systematic and painstaking analysis of social episodes, i.e. behaviour in context. In Box 1.7 we give an example of such an episode taken from a classroom study. Note how the particular incident would appear on an interaction analysis coding sheet of a researcher employing a positivistic approach. Note, too, how this slice of classroom life can only be understood by knowledge of the specific organizational background and context in which it is embedded.

The approach to analysing social episodes in terms of the 'actors' themselves is known as the 'ethogenic method'.[9] Unlike positivistic social psychology which ignores or presumes its subjects' interpretations of situations, ethogenic social psychology concentrates upon the ways in which persons construe their social world. By probing their own accounts of their actions, it endeavours to come up with an understanding of what those persons were doing in the particular episode.

As an alternative to positivist approaches, naturalistic, qualitative, interpretive approaches of various hue possess particular distinguishing features:

- people are deliberate and creative in their actions, they act intentionally and make meanings in and through their activities (Blumer, 1969);
- people actively construct their social world – they are not the 'cultural dopes' or passive

Box 1.7
A classroom episode

Walker and Adelman describe an incident in the following manner:

In one lesson the teacher was listening to the boys read through short essays that they had written for homework on the subject of 'Prisons'. After one boy, Wilson, had finished reading out his rather obviously skimped piece of work the teacher sighed and said, rather crossly:
>   T: Wilson, we'll have to put you away if you don't change your ways, and do your homework. Is that all you've done?
>   P: Strawberries, strawberries. (Laughter)

Now at first glance this is meaningless. An observer coding with Flanders Interaction Analysis Categories (FIAC) would write down:

- '7' (teacher criticizes) followed by a,
- '4' (teacher asks question) followed by a,
- '9' (pupil irritation) and finally a,
- '10' (silence or confusion) to describe the laughter

Such a string of codings, however reliable and valid, would not help anyone to *understand* why such an interruption was funny. Human curiosity makes us want to know *why* everyone laughs – and so, I would argue, the social scientist needs to know too. Walker and Adelman asked subsequently why 'strawberries' was a stimulus to laughter and were told that the teacher frequently said the pupils' work was 'like strawberries – good as far as it goes, but it doesn't last nearly long enough'. Here a casual comment made in the past has become an integral part of the shared meaning system of the class. It can only be comprehended by seeing the relationship as developing over time.

Source Adapted from Delamont, 1976

dolls of positivism (Becker, 1970; Garfinkel, 1967);

- situations are fluid and changing rather than fixed and static; events and behaviour evolve over time and are richly affected by context – they are 'situated activities';
- events and individuals are unique and largely non-generalizable;
- a view that the social world should be studied in its natural state, without the intervention of, or manipulation by, the researcher (Hammersley and Atkinson, 1983);
- fidelity to the phenomena being studied is fundamental;
- people interpret events, contexts and situations, and act on the bases of those events (echoing Thomas's (1928) famous dictum that if people define their situations as real then they are real in their consequences – if I believe there is a mouse under the table, I will act as though there is a mouse under the table, whether there is or not (Morrison, 1998));
- there are multiple interpretations of, and perspectives on, single events and situations;
- reality is multi-layered and complex;
- many events are not reducible to simplistic interpretation, hence 'thick descriptions' (Geertz, 1973) are essential rather than reductionism;
- we need to examine situations through the eyes of participants rather than the researcher.

The anti-positivist movement in sociology is represented by three schools of thought – phenomenology, ethnomethodology and symbolic interactionism. A common thread running through the three schools is a concern with phenomena, that is, the things we directly apprehend through our senses as we go about our daily lives, together with a consequent emphasis on qualitative as opposed to quantitative methodology. The differences between them and the significant roles each phenomenon plays in research in classrooms and schools are such as to warrant a more extended consideration of them in the discussion below (p. 23).

A question of terminology: the normative and interpretive paradigms

We so far have introduced and used a variety of terms to describe the numerous branches and schools of thought embraced by the positivist and anti-positivist viewpoints. We clarify at this point two generic terms conventionally used to describe these two perspectives and the categories subsumed under each, particularly as they refer to social psychology and sociology. The terms in question are 'normative' and 'interpretive'. The normative paradigm (or model) contains two major orienting ideas (Douglas, 1973): first, that human behaviour is essentially rule-governed; and second, that it should be investigated by the methods of natural science. The interpretive paradigm, in contrast to its normative counterpart, is characterized by a concern for the individual. Whereas normative studies are positivist, all theories constructed within the context of the interpretive paradigm tend to be anti-positivist.[10] As we have seen, the central endeavour in the context of the interpretive paradigm is to understand the subjective world of human experience. To retain the integrity of the phenomena being investigated, efforts are made to get inside the person and to understand from within. The imposition of external form and structure is resisted, since this reflects the viewpoint of the observer as opposed to that of the actor directly involved.

Two further differences between the two paradigms may be identified at this stage: the first concerns the concepts of 'behaviour' and 'action'; the second, the different conceptions of 'theory'. A key concept within the normative paradigm, behaviour refers to responses either to external environmental stimuli (another person, or the demands of society, for instance) or to internal stimuli (hunger, or the need to achieve, for example). In either case, the cause of the behaviour lies in the past. Interpretive approaches, on the other hand, focus on action.

This may be thought of as behaviour-with-meaning; it is intentional behaviour and as such, future oriented. Actions are only meaningful to us in so far as we are able to ascertain the intentions of actors to share their experiences. A large number of our everyday interactions with one another rely on such shared experiences.

As regards theory, normative researchers try to devise general theories of human behaviour and to validate them through the use of increasingly complex research methodologies which, some believe, push them further and further from the experience and understanding of the everyday world and into a world of abstraction. For them, the basic reality is the collectivity; it is external to the actor and manifest in society, its institutions and its organizations. The role of theory is to say how reality hangs together in these forms or how it might be changed so as to be more effective. The researcher's ultimate aim is to establish a comprehensive 'rational edifice', a universal theory, to account for human and social behaviour.

But what of the interpretive researchers? They begin with individuals and set out to understand their interpretations of the world around them. Theory is emergent and must arise from particular situations; it should be 'grounded' on data generated by the research act (Glaser and Strauss, 1967). Theory should not precede research but follow it.

Investigators work directly with experience and understanding to build their theory on them. The data thus yielded will be glossed with the meanings and purposes of those people who are their source. Further, the theory so generated must make sense to those to whom it applies. The aim of scientific investigation for the interpretive researcher is to understand how this glossing of reality goes on at one time and in one place and compare it with what goes on in different times and places. Thus theory becomes sets of meanings which yield insight and understanding of people's behaviour. These theories are likely to be as diverse as the sets of human meanings and understandings that they are to explain. From an interpretive perspective the hope of a universal theory which characterizes the normative outlook gives way to multifaceted images of human behaviour as varied as the situations and contexts supporting them.

Phenomenology, ethnomethodology and symbolic interactionism

There are many variants of qualitative, naturalistic approaches (Jacob, 1987; Hitchcock and Hughes, 1995). Here we focus on three significant 'traditions' in this style of research – phenomenology, ethnomethodology and symbolic interactionism. In its broadest meaning, phenomenology is a theoretical point of view that advocates the study of direct experience taken at face value; and one which sees behaviour as determined by the phenomena of experience rather than by external, objective and physically described reality (English and English, 1958). Although phenomenologists differ among themselves on particular issues, there is fairly general agreement on the following points identified by Curtis (1978) which can be taken as distinguishing features of their philosophical viewpoint:

- a belief in the importance, and in a sense the primacy, of subjective consciousness;
- an understanding of consciousness as active, as meaning bestowing; and
- a claim that there are certain essential structures to consciousness of which we gain direct knowledge by a certain kind of reflection. Exactly what these structures are is a point about which phenomenologists have differed.

Various strands of development may be traced in the phenomenological movement: we shall briefly examine two of them – the transcendental phenomenology of Husserl; and existential phenomenology, of which Schutz is perhaps the most characteristic representative.

Husserl, regarded by many as the founder of phenomenology, was concerned with investigating the source of the foundation of science and with questioning the commonsense, 'taken-for-granted' assumptions of everyday life (see

Burrell and Morgan, 1979). To do this, he set about opening up a new direction in the analysis of consciousness. His catch-phrase was 'back to the things!' which for him meant finding out how things appear directly to us rather than through the media of cultural and symbolic structures. In other words, we are asked to look beyond the details of everyday life to the essences underlying them. To do this, Husserl exhorts us to 'put the world in brackets' or free ourselves from our usual ways of perceiving the world. What is left over from this reduction is our consciousness of which there are three elements – the 'I' who thinks, the mental acts of this thinking subject, and the intentional objects of these mental acts. The aim, then, of this method of *epoché*, as Husserl called it, is the dismembering of the constitution of objects in such a way as to free us from all preconceptions about the world (see Warnock, 1970).

Schutz was concerned with relating Husserl's ideas to the issues of sociology and to the scientific study of social behaviour. Of central concern to him was the problem of understanding the meaning structure of the world of everyday life. The origins of meaning he thus sought in the 'stream of consciousness' – basically an unbroken stream of lived experiences which have no meaning in themselves. One can only impute meaning to them retrospectively, by the process of turning back on oneself and looking at what has been going on. In other words, meaning can be accounted for in this way by the concept of reflexivity. For Schutz, the attribution of meaning reflexively is dependent on the people identifying the purpose or goal they seek (see Burrell and Morgan, 1979).

According to Schutz, the way we understand the behaviour of others is dependent on a process of typification by means of which the observer makes use of concepts resembling 'ideal types' to make sense of what people do. These concepts are derived from our experience of everyday life and it is through them, claims Schutz, that we classify and organize our everyday world. As Burrell and Morgan observe, 'The typifications are learned through our biographi-

cal situation. They are handed to us according to our social context. Knowledge of everyday life is thus socially ordered. The notion of typification is thus . . . an inherent feature of our everyday world' (Burrell and Morgan, 1979).

The fund of everyday knowledge by means of which we are able to typify other people's behaviour and come to terms with social reality varies from situation to situation. We thus live in a world of multiple realities:

> The social actor shifts between these provinces of meaning in the course of his everyday life. As he shifts from the world of work to that of home and leisure or to the world of religious experience, different ground rules are brought into play. While it is within the normal competence of the acting individual to shift from one sphere to another, to do so calls for a 'leap of consciousness' to overcome the differences between the different worlds.
>
> (Burrell and Morgan, 1979)

Like phenomenology, ethnomethodology is concerned with the world of everyday life. In the words of its proponent, Harold Garfinkel, it sets out 'to treat practical activities, practical circumstances, and practical sociological reasonings as topics of empirical study, and by paying to the most commonplace activities of daily life the attention usually accorded extraordinary events, seeks to learn about them as phenomena in their own right' (Garfinkel, 1967). He maintains that students of the social world must doubt the reality of that world; and that in failing to view human behaviour more sceptically, sociologists have created an ordered social reality that bears little relationship to the real thing. He thereby challenges the basic sociological concept of order.

Ethnomethodology, then, is concerned with how people make sense of their everyday world. More especially, it is directed at the mechanisms by which participants achieve and sustain interaction in a social encounter – the assumptions they make, the conventions they utilize, and the practices they adopt. Ethnomethodology thus seeks to understand social accomplishments in their own terms; it is concerned to understand them from within (see Burrell and Morgan, 1979).

In identifying the 'taken-for-granted' assumptions characterizing any social situation and the ways in which the people involved make their activities rationally accountable, ethnomethodologists use notions like 'indexicality' and 'reflexivity'. Indexicality refers to the ways in which actions and statements are related to the social contexts producing them; and to the way their meanings are shared by the participants but not necessarily stated explicitly. Indexical expressions are thus the designations imputed to a particular social occasion by the participants in order to locate the event in the sphere of reality. Reflexivity, on the other hand, refers to the way in which all accounts of social settings – descriptions, analyses, criticisms, etc. – and the social settings occasioning them are mutually interdependent.

It is convenient to distinguish between two types of ethnomethodologists: linguistic and situational. The linguistic ethnomethodologists focus upon the use of language and the ways in which conversations in everyday life are structured. Their analyses make much use of the unstated 'taken-for-granted' meanings, the use of indexical expressions and the way in which conversations convey much more than is actually said. The situational ethnomethodologists cast their view over a wider range of social activity and seek to understand the ways in which people negotiate the social contexts in which they find themselves. They are concerned to understand how people make sense of and order their environment. As part of their empirical method, ethnomethodologists may consciously and deliberately disrupt or question the ordered 'taken-for-granted' elements in everyday situations in order to reveal the underlying processes at work.

The substance of ethnomethodology thus largely comprises a set of specific techniques and approaches to be used in the study of what Garfinkel has described as the 'awesome indexicality' of everyday life. It is geared to empirical study, and the stress which its practitioners place upon the uniqueness of the situation encountered, projects its essentially relativist standpoint. A commitment to the development of methodology and field-work has occupied first place in the interests of its adherents, so that related issues of ontology, epistemology and the nature of human beings have received less attention than perhaps they deserve.

Essentially, the notion of symbolic interactionism derives from the work of G. H. Mead (1934). Although subsequently to be associated with such noted researchers as Blumer, Hughes, Becker and Goffman, the term does not represent a unified perspective in that it does not embrace a common set of assumptions and concepts accepted by all who subscribe to the approach. For our purposes, however, it is possible to identify three basic postulates. These have been set out by Woods (1979) as follows. First, human beings act towards things on the basis of the meanings they have for them. Humans inhabit two different worlds: the 'natural' world wherein they are organisms of drives and instincts and where the external world exists independently of them, and the social world where the existence of symbols, like language, enables them to give meaning to objects. This attribution of meanings, this interpreting, is what makes them distinctively human and social. Interactionists therefore focus on the world of subjective meanings and the symbols by which they are produced and represented. This means not making any prior assumptions about what is going on in an institution, and taking seriously, indeed giving priority to, inmates' own accounts. Thus, if pupils appear preoccupied for too much of the time – 'being bored', 'mucking about', 'having a laugh', etc. the interactionist is keen to explore the properties and dimensions of these processes. Second, this attribution of meaning to objects through symbols is a continuous process. Action is not simply a consequence of psychological attributes such as drives, attitudes, or personalities, or determined by external social facts such as social structure or roles, but results from a continuous process of meaning attribution which is always emerging in a state of flux and subject to change. The individual constructs, modifies, pieces together, weighs up the pros and cons and bargains. Third, this process takes place in a social context. Individuals align their actions to those of others. They do this by 'taking the role of the other', by making indications to 'themselves' about the likely responses of 'others'. They construct how others wish or might act in certain circumstances, and how they themselves might act. They might try to 'manage' the impressions others have of them, put on a 'performance', try to influence others' 'definition of the situation'.

Instead of focusing on the individual, then, and his or her personality characteristics, or on how the social structure or social situation causes individual behaviour, symbolic interactionists direct their attention at the nature of interaction, the dynamic activities taking place between people. In focusing on the interaction itself as a unit of study, the symbolic interactionist creates a more active image of the human being and rejects the image of the passive, determined organism. Individuals interact; societies are made up of interacting individuals. People are constantly undergoing change in interaction and society is changing through interaction. Interaction implies human beings acting in relation to each other, taking each other into account, acting, perceiving, interpreting, acting again. Hence, a more dynamic and active human being emerges rather than an actor merely responding to others. Woods (1983: 15–16) summarizes key emphases of symbolic interaction thus:

- individuals as constructors of their own actions;
- the various components of the self and how they interact; the indications made to self, meanings attributed, interpretive mechanisms, definitions of the situation; in short, the world of subjective meanings, and the symbols by which they are produced and represented;
- the process of negotiation, by which meanings are continually being constructed;

- the social context in which they occur and whence they derive;
- by taking the 'role of the other' – a dynamic concept involving the construction of how others wish to or might act in a certain circumstance, and how individuals themselves might act – individuals align their actions to those of others.

A characteristic common to the phenomenological, ethnomethodological and symbolic interactionist perspectives – and one which makes them singularly attractive to the would-be educational researcher – is the way they fit naturally to the kind of concentrated action found in classrooms and schools. Yet another shared characteristic is the manner in which they are able to preserve the integrity of the situation where they are employed. This is to say that the influence of the researcher in structuring, analysing and interpreting the situation is present to a much smaller degree than would be the case with a more traditionally oriented research approach.

Criticisms of the naturalistic and interpretive approaches

Critics have wasted little time in pointing out what they regard as weaknesses in these newer qualitative perspectives. They argue that while it is undeniable that our understanding of the actions of our fellow-beings necessarily requires knowledge of their intentions, this, surely, cannot be said to comprise *the* purpose of a social science. As Rex has observed:

Whilst patterns of social reactions and institutions may be the product of the actors' definitions of the situations there is also the possibility that those actors might be falsely conscious and that sociologists have an obligation to seek an objective perspective which is not necessarily that of any of the participating actors at all . . . We need not be confined purely and simply to that . . . social reality which is made available to us by participant actors themselves.

(Rex, 1974)

Giddens similarly argues against the likely relativism of this paradigm:

> No specific person can possess detailed knowledge of anything more than the particular sector of society in which he participates, so that there still remains the task of making into an explicit and comprehensive body of knowledge that which is only known in a partial way by lay actors themselves.

(Giddens, 1976)

While these more recent perspectives have presented models of people that are more in keeping with common experience, their methodologies are by no means above reproof. Some argue that advocates of an anti-positivist stance have gone too far in abandoning scientific procedures of verification and in giving up hope of discovering useful generalizations about behaviour (see Mead, 1934). Are there not dangers, it is suggested, in rejecting the approach of physics in favour of methods more akin to literature, biography and journalism? Some specific criticisms of the methodologies used are well directed:

> If the carefully controlled interviews used in social surveys are inaccurate, how about the uncontrolled interviews favoured by the (newer perspectives)? If sophisticated ethological studies of behaviour are not good enough, are participant observation studies any better?

(Argyle, 1978)

> And what of the insistence of the interpretive methodologies on the use of verbal accounts to get at the meaning of events, rules and intentions? Are there not dangers? Subjective reports are sometimes incomplete and they are sometimes misleading.

(Bernstein, 1974)

Bernstein's criticism is directed at the overriding concern of phenomenologists and ethnomethodologists with the meanings of situations and the ways in which these meanings are negotiated by the actors involved. What is overlooked about such negotiated meanings, observes Bernstein, is that they 'presuppose a structure of meanings (and their history) wider than the area of negotiation. Situated activities presuppose a situation; they presuppose relationships between situations; they presuppose sets of situations' (Bernstein, 1974).

Bernstein's point is that the very process whereby one interprets and defines a situation is itself a product of the circumstances in which one is placed. One important factor in such circumstances that must be considered is the power of others to impose their own definitions of situations upon participants. Doctors' consulting rooms and headteachers' studies are locations in which inequalities in power are regularly imposed upon unequal participants. The ability of certain individuals, groups, classes and authorities to persuade others to accept their definitions of situations demonstrates that while – as ethnomethodologists insist – social structure is a consequence of the ways in which we perceive social relations, it is clearly more than this. Conceiving of social structure as external to ourselves helps us take its self-evident effects upon our daily lives into our understanding of the social behaviour going on about us. Here is rehearsed the tension between agency and structure of social theorists (Layder, 1994); the danger of interactionist and interpretive approaches is their relative neglect of the power of external – structural – forces to shape behaviour and events. There is a risk in interpretive approaches that they become hermetically sealed from the world outside the participants' theatre of activity – they put artificial boundaries around subjects' behaviour. Just as positivistic theories can be criticized for their macro-sociological persuasion, so interpretive and qualitative can be criticized for their narrowly micro-sociological persuasion.

Critical theory and critical educational research

Positivist and interpretive paradigms are essentially concerned with understanding phenomena through two different lenses. Positivism strives for objectivity, measurability, predictability, controllability, patterning, the construction of laws and rules of behaviour, and the ascription of causality; the interpretive paradigms strive to understand and interpret the world in terms of its actors. In the former, observed phenomena are important; in the latter, meanings and interpretations are paramount. Habermas (1984: 109–10) describes this latter as a 'double hermeneutic', where people strive to interpret and operate in an already interpreted world. By way of contrast, an emerging approach to educational research is the paradigm of *critical educational research*. This regards the two previous paradigms as presenting incomplete accounts of social behaviour by their neglect of the political and ideological contexts of much educational research. Positivistic and interpretive paradigms are seen as preoccupied with technical and hermeneutic knowledge respectively (Gage, 1989). The paradigm of critical educational research is heavily influenced by the early work of Habermas and, to a lesser extent, his predecessors in the Frankfurt School, most notably Adorno, Marcuse, Horkheimer and Fromm. Here the expressed intention is deliberately political – the emancipation of individuals and groups in an egalitarian society.

Critical theory is explicitly prescriptive and normative, entailing a view of what behaviour in a social democracy *should* entail (Fay, 1987; Morrison, 1995a). Its intention is not merely to give an account of society and behaviour but to realize a society that is based on equality and democracy for all its members. Its purpose is not merely to understand situations and phenomena but to change them. In particular it seeks to emancipate the disempowered, to redress inequality and to promote individual freedoms within a democratic society.

In this enterprise critical theory identifies the 'false' or 'fragmented' consciousness (Eagleton, 1991) that has brought an individual or social group to relative powerlessness or, indeed, power, and it questions the legitimacy of this. It holds up to the lights of legitimacy and equality issues of repression, voice, ideology, power, participation, representation, inclusion, and interests. It argues that much behaviour (including research behaviour) is the outcome of particular illegitimate, dominatory and repressive factors, illegitimate in the sense that they do not operate in the general interest – one person's or group's freedom and power is bought at the price of another's freedom and power. Hence critical theory seeks to uncover the *interests* at work in particular situations and to interrogate the legitimacy of those interests – identifying the extent to which they are legitimate in their service of equality and democracy. Its intention is *transformative*: to transform society and individuals to social democracy. In this respect the purpose of critical educational research is intensely practical – to bring about a more just, egalitarian society in which individual and collective freedoms are practised, and to eradicate the exercise and effects of illegitimate power. The pedigree of critical theory in Marxism, thus, is not difficult to discern. For critical theorists, researchers can no longer claim neutrality and ideological or political innocence.

Critical theory and critical educational research, then, have their substantive agenda – for example examining and interrogating: the relationships between school and society – how schools perpetuate or reduce inequality; the social construction of knowledge and curricula, who defines worthwhile knowledge, what ideological interests this serves, and how this reproduces inequality in society; how power is produced and reproduced through education; whose interests are served by education and how legitimate these are (e.g. the rich, white, middle-class males rather than poor, non-white, females).

The significance of critical theory for research is immense, for it suggests that much social research is comparatively trivial in that it accepts rather than questions given agendas for research. That this is compounded by the nature of funding for research underlines the political dimension of research sponsorship (discussed later) (Norris, 1990). Critical theorists would argue that the positivist and interpretive paradigms are essentially technicist, seeking to understand and render more efficient an existing situation, rather than to question or transform it.

Habermas (1972) offers a useful tripartite conceptualization of interests that catches the three paradigms of research in this chapter. He suggests that knowledge – and hence research knowledge – serves different interests. Interests, he argues, are socially constructed, and are 'knowledge-constitutive', because they shape and determine what counts as the objects and types of knowledge. Interests have an ideological function (Morrison, 1995a), for example a 'technical interest' (discussed below) can have the effect of keeping the empowered in their empowered position and the disempowered in their powerlessness – i.e. reinforcing and perpetuating the *status quo*. An 'emancipatory interest' (discussed below) threatens the status quo. In this view knowledge – and research knowledge – is not neutral (see also Mannheim, 1936). What counts as worthwhile knowledge is determined by the social and positional power of the advocates of that knowledge. The link here between objects of study and communities of scholars echoes Kuhn's (1962) notions of paradigms and paradigm shifts, where the field of knowledge or paradigm is seen to be only as good as the evidence and the respect in which it is held by 'authorities'. Knowledge and definitions of knowledge reflect the interests of the community of scholars who operate in particular paradigms. Habermas (1972) constructs the definition of worthwhile knowledge and modes of understanding around three cognitive interests:

1   prediction and control;
2   understanding and interpretation;
3   emancipation and freedom.

He names these the '*technical*', '*practical*' and '*emancipatory*' interests respectively. The technical interest characterizes the scientific, positivist method outlined earlier, with its emphasis on laws, rules, prediction and control of behaviour, with passive research objects – instrumental knowledge. The 'practical' interest, an attenua-

tion of the positivism of the scientific method, is exemplified in the hermeneutic, interpretive methodologies outlined in the qualitative approaches earlier (e.g. symbolic interactionism). Here research methodologies seek to clarify, understand and interpret the communications of 'speaking and acting subjects' (Habermas, 1974: 8). Hermeneutics focuses on interaction and language; it seeks to understand situations through the eyes of the participants, echoing the *verstehen* approaches of Weber and premised on the view that reality is socially constructed (Berger and Luckmann, 1967). Indeed Habermas (1988: 12) suggests that sociology must understand social facts in their cultural significance and as socially determined. Hermeneutics involves recapturing the *meanings* of interacting others, recovering and reconstructing the *intentions* of the other actors in a situation. Such an enterprise involves the analysis of *meaning in a social context* (Held, 1980). Gadamer (1975: 273) argues that the hermeneutic sciences (e.g. qualitative approaches) involve the *fusion of horizons* between participants. Meanings rather than phenomena take on significance in this paradigm.

The emancipatory interest subsumes the previous two paradigms; it requires them but goes beyond them (Habermas, 1972: 211). It is concerned with *praxis* – action that is informed by reflection with the aim to emancipate (Kincheloe, 1991: 177). The twin intentions of this interest are to expose the operation of power and to bring about social justice as domination and repression act to prevent the full existential realization of individual and social freedoms (Habermas, 1979: 14). The task of this knowledge-constitutive interest, indeed of critical theory itself, is to restore to consciousness those suppressed, repressed and submerged determinants of unfree behaviour with a view to their dissolution (Habermas, 1984: 194–5).

What we have in effect, then, in Habermas's early work is an attempt to conceptualize three research styles: the scientific, positivist style; the interpretive style; and the emancipatory, ideology critical style. Not only does critical theory have its own research agenda, but it also has its own research methodologies, in particular ideology critique and action research. With regard to ideology critique, a particular reading of ideology is being adopted here, as the *suppression of generalizable interests* (Habermas, 1976: 113), where systems, groups and individuals operate in rationally indefensible ways because their power to act relies on the disempowering of other groups, i.e. that their principles of behaviour are not universalizable. Ideology – the values and practices emanating from particular dominant groups – is the means by which powerful groups promote and legitimate their particular – sectoral – interests at the expense of disempowered groups. Ideology critique exposes the operation of ideology in many spheres of education, the working out of vested interests under the mantle of the general good. The task of ideology critique is to uncover the vested interests at work which may be occurring consciously or subliminally, revealing to participants how they may be acting to perpetuate a system which keeps them either empowered or disempowered (Geuss, 1981), i.e. which suppresses a generalizable interest. Explanations for situations might be other than those 'natural', taken for granted, explanations that the participants might offer or accept. Situations are not natural but problematic (Carr and Kemmis, 1986). They are the outcomes or processes wherein interests and powers are protected and suppressed, and one task of ideology critique is to expose this (Grundy, 1987). The interests at work are uncovered by ideology critique, which, itself, is premised on reflective practice (Morrison, 1995a, 1995b, 1996a).

Habermas (1972: 230) suggests that ideology critique through reflective practice can be addressed in four stages:

Stage 1 A description and interpretation of the existing situation – a hermeneutic exercise that identifies and attempts to make sense of the current situation (echoing the *verstehen* approaches of the interpretive paradigm).

Stage 2 A penetration of the reasons that brought the existing situation to the form that it takes – the causes and purposes of a situation and an evaluation of their legitimacy, involving an analysis of interests and ideologies at work in a situation, their power and legitimacy (both in micro- and macro-sociological terms). In Habermas's early work (1972) he likens this to psychoanalysis as a means for bringing into consciousness of 'patients' those repressed, distorted and oppressive conditions, experiences and factors that have prevented them from a full, complete and accurate understanding of their conditions, situations and behaviour, and that, on such exposure and examination, will be liberatory and emancipatory. Critique here serves to reveal to individuals and groups how their views and practices might be ideological distortions that, in their effects, are perpetuating a social order or situation that works against their democratic freedoms, interests and empowerment (see also Carr and Kemmis, 1986: 138–9).

Stage 3 An agenda for altering the situation – in order for moves to an egalitarian society to be furthered.

Stage 4 An evaluation of the achievement of the situation in practice.

In the world of education Habermas's stages are paralleled by Smyth (1989) who, too, denotes a four-stage process: *description* (what am I doing?); *information* (what does it mean?); *confrontation* (how did I come to be like this?); and *reconstruction* (how might I do things differently?). It can be seen that ideology critique here has both a reflective, theoretical and a practical side to it; without reflection it is hollow and without practice it is empty.

As ideology is not mere theory but impacts directly on practice (Eagleton, 1991) there is a strongly practical methodology implied by critical theory, which articulates with action research (Callewaert, 1999). Action research (discussed in Chapter 13) as its name suggests, is about research that impacts on, and focuses on, practice. In its espousal of practitioner research, for example teachers in schools, participant observers and curriculum developers, action research recognizes the significance of *contexts* for practice – locational, ideological, historical, managerial, social. Furthermore it accords power to those who are operating in those contexts, for they are both the engines of research and of practice. In that sense the claim is made that action research is strongly empowering and emancipatory in that it gives practitioners a 'voice' (Carr and Kemmis, 1986; Grundy, 1987), participation in decision-making, and control over their environment and professional lives. Whether the strength of the claims for empowerment are as strong as their proponents would hold is another matter, for action research might be relatively powerless in the face of mandated changes in education. Here action research might be more concerned with the intervening in existing practice to ensure that mandated change is addressed efficiently and effectively.

Morrison (1995a) suggests that critical theory, because it has a practical intent to transform and empower, can – and should – be examined and perhaps tested empirically. For example, critical theory claims to be empowering; that is a testable proposition. Indeed, in a departure from some of his earlier writing, in some of his later work Habermas (1990) acknowledges this; he argues for the need to find 'counter examples' (p. 6), to 'critical testing' (p. 7) and empirical verification (p. 117). He acknowledges that his views have only 'hypothetical status' (p. 32) that need to be checked against specific cases (p. 9). One could suggest, for instance, that the effectiveness of his critical theory can be examined by charting the extent to which equality, freedom, democracy, emancipation, empowerment have been realized by dint of his theory, the extent to which transformative practices have been addressed or occurred as a result of his theory, the extent to which subscribers to his theory have been able to assert their agency, the extent to which his theories have broken down the barriers of instrumental rationality. The operationalization and testing (or empirical investigation) of his theories clearly is a major undertaking, and one which Habermas has not done. In this respect critical theory, a theory that strives to improve practical living, runs the risk of becoming merely contemplative.

Criticisms of approaches from critical theory

There are several criticisms that have been voiced against critical approaches. Morrison (1995a) suggests that there is an artificial separation between Habermas's three interests – they are drawn far more sharply (Hesse, 1982; Bernstein, 1976; 1983: 33). For example, one has to bring hermeneutic knowledge to bear on positivist science and *vice versa* in order to make meaning of each other and in order to judge their own status. Further, the link between ideology critique and emancipation is neither clear nor proven, nor a logical necessity (Morrison, 1995a: 67) – whether a person or society can become emancipated simply by the exercise of ideology critique or action research is an empirical rather than a logical matter (Morrison, 1995a; Wardekker and Miedama, 1997). Indeed one can become emancipated by means other than ideology critique; emancipated societies do not necessarily demonstrate or require an awareness of ideology critique. Moreover, it could be argued that the rationalistic appeal of ideology critique actually obstructs action designed to bring about emancipation. Roderick (1986: 65), for example, questions whether the espousal of ideology critique is itself as ideological as the approaches that it proscribes. Habermas, in his allegiance to the view of the social construction of knowledge through 'interests', is inviting the charge of relativism.

Whilst the claim to there being three forms of knowledge has the epistemological attraction of simplicity, one has to question this very simplicity (e.g. Keat, 1981: 67); there are a multitude of interests and ways of understanding the world and it is simply artificial to reduce these to three. Indeed it is unclear whether Habermas, in his three knowledge-constitutive interests, is dealing with a conceptual model, a political analysis, a set of generalities, a set of transhistorical principles, a set of temporally specific observations, or a set of loosely defined slogans (Morrison, 1995a: 71) that survive only by dint of their ambiguity (Kolakowsi, 1978). Lakomski (1999) questions the acceptability of the consensus theory of truth on which Habermas's work is premised (pp. 179–82); she argues that Habermas's work is silent on social change, and is little more than speculation, a view echoed by Fendler's (1999) criticism of critical theory as inadequately problematizing subjectivity and ahistoricity.

More fundamental to a critique of this approach is the view that critical theory has a deliberate political agenda, and that the task of the researcher is not to be an ideologue or to have an agenda, but to be dispassionate, disinterested and objective (Morrison, 1995a). Of course, critical theorists would argue that the call for researchers to be ideologically neutral is itself ideologically saturated with *laissez-faire* values which allow the *status quo* to be reproduced, i.e. that the call for researchers to be neutral and disinterested is just as value laden as is the call for them to intrude their own perspectives. The rights of the researcher to move beyond disinterestedness are clearly contentious, though the safeguard here is that the researcher's is only one voice in the community of scholars (Kemmis, 1982). Critical theorists as researchers have been hoisted by their own petard, for if they are to become more than merely negative Jeremiahs and skeptics, berating a particular social order that is dominated by scientism and instrumental rationality (Eagleton, 1991; Wardekker and Miedama, 1997), then they have to generate a positive agenda, but in so doing they are violating the traditional objectivity of researchers. Because their focus is on an ideological agenda, they themselves cannot avoid acting ideologically (Morrison, 1995a).

Claims have been made for the power of action research to empower participants as researchers (e.g. Carr and Kemmis, 1986; Grundy, 1987). This might be over-optimistic in a world in which power is often through statute; the reality of political power seldom extends to teachers. That teachers might be able to exercise some power in schools but that this has little effect on the workings of society at large was caught in Bernstein's famous comment (1970) that 'education cannot compensate for society'. Giving action researchers a small degree of power (to research their own situations) has little effect on the *real* locus of power and decision-making, which often lies outside the control of action researchers. Is action research genuinely and full-bloodedly empowering and emancipatory? Where is the evidence?

Critical theory and curriculum research

In terms of a book on research methods, the tenets of critical theory suggest their own substantive fields of inquiry and their own methods (e.g. ideology critique and action research). Beyond that the contribution to this text on empirical research methods is perhaps limited by the fact that the agenda of critical theory is highly particularistic, prescriptive and, as has been seen, problematical. Though it is an influential paradigm, it is influential in certain fields rather than in others. For example, its impact on curriculum research has been far-reaching.

It has been argued for many years that the most satisfactory account of the curriculum is given by a modernist, positivist reading of the development of education and society. This has its curricular expression in Tyler's (1949) famous and influential rationale for the curriculum in terms of four questions:

1   What educational purposes should the school seek to attain?
2   What educational experiences can be provided that are likely to attain these purposes?
3   How can these educational experiences be effectively organized?
4   How can we determine whether these purposes are being attained?

Underlying this rationale is a view that the curriculum is controlled (and controllable), ordered, pre-determined, uniform, predictable and largely behaviourist in outcome – all elements of the positivist mentality that critical theory eschews. Tyler's rationale resonates sympathetically with a modernist, scientific, managerialist mentality of society and education that regards ideology and power as unproblematic, indeed it claims the putative political neutrality and objectivity of positivism (Doll, 1993); it ignores the advances in psychology and psychopedagogy made by constructivism.

However, this view has been criticized for precisely these sympathies. Doll (1993) argues that it represents a *closed* system of planning and practice that sits uncomfortably with the notion of education as an *opening* process and with the view of postmodern society as open and diverse, multidimensional, fluid and with power less monolithic and more problematical. This view takes seriously the impact of chaos and complexity theory and derives from them some important features for contemporary curricula. These are incorporated into a view of curricula as being *rich*, *relational*, *recursive* and *rigorous* (Doll, 1993) with an emphasis on *emergence*, *process epistemology* and *constructivist psychology*.

Not all knowledge can be included in the curriculum; the curriculum is a selection of what is deemed to be worthwhile knowledge. The justification for that selection reveals the ideologies and power in decision-making in society and through the curriculum. Curriculum is an ideological selection from a range of possible knowledge. This resonates with a principle from Habermas (1972) that knowledge and its selection are neither neutral nor innocent.

Ideologies can be treated unpejoratively as sets of beliefs or, more sharply, as sets of beliefs emanating from powerful groups in society, designed to protect the interests of the dominant. If curricula are value-based then why is it that some values hold more sway than others? The link between values and power is strong. This theme asks not only *what* knowledge is important but *whose* knowledge is important in curricula, *what and whose interests* such knowledge serves, and *how* the curriculum and pedagogy serve (or do not serve) differing interests. Knowledge is not neutral (as was the tacit view in modernist curricula). The curriculum is ideologically contestable terrain.

The study of the sociology of knowledge indi-

cates how the powerful might retain their power through curricula and how knowledge and power are legitimated in curricula. The study of the sociology of knowledge suggests that the curriculum should be both subject to ideology critique and itself promote ideology critique in students. A research agenda for critical theorists, then is how the curriculum perpetuates the societal *status quo* and how can it (and should it) promote equality in society.

The notion of ideology critique engages the early writings of Habermas (1972), in particular his theory of three knowledge-constitutive interests. His *technical interest* (in control and predictability) resonates with Tyler's model of the curriculum and reveals itself in technicist, instrumentalist and scientist views of curricula that are to be 'delivered' to passive recipients – the curriculum is simply another commodity in a consumer society in which differential cultural capital is inevitable. Habermas's 'hermeneutic' *interest* (in understanding others' perspectives and views) resonates with a *process* view of the curriculum. His *emancipatory interest* (in promoting social emancipation, equality, democracy, freedoms and individual and collective empowerment) requires an exposure of the ideological interests at work in curricula in order that teachers and students can take control of their own lives for the collective, egalitarian good. Habermas's emancipatory interest denotes an inescapably political reading of the curriculum and the purposes of education – the movement away from authoritarianism and elitism and towards social democracy.

Habermas's work underpins and informs much contemporary and recent curriculum theory (e.g. Grundy, 1987; Apple, 1990; UNESCO, 1996) and is a useful heuristic device for understanding the motives behind the heavy prescription of curriculum content in, for example, the UK, New Zealand, the USA and France. For instance, one can argue that the National Curriculum of England and Wales is heavy on the technical and hermeneutic interests but very light on the emancipatory interest (Morrison, 1995a), and that this (either deliberately or in its effects) supports – if not contributes to – the reproduction of social inequality. As Bernstein (1971) argues: 'how a society selects, classifies, distributes, transmits and evaluates the educational knowledge it considers to be public, reflects both the distribution of power and the principles of social control' (p. 47).

Further, one can argue that the move towards modular and competence-based curricula reflects the commodification, measurability and trivialization of curricula, the technicist control of curricula, a move toward the behaviourism of positivism and a move away from the transformatory nature of education, a silencing of critique, and the imposition of a narrow ideology of instrumental utility on the curriculum.

Several writers on contemporary curriculum theory (e.g. McLaren, 1995; Leistna, Woodrum and Sherblom, 1996) argue that power is a central, defining concept in matters of the curriculum. Here considerable importance is accorded to the political agenda of the curriculum, and the empowerment of individuals and societies is an inescapable consideration in the curriculum. One means of developing student and societal empowerment finds its expression in Habermas's (1972) emancipatory interest and critical pedagogy.

In the field of critical pedagogy the argument is advanced that educators must work with, and on, the lived experience that students bring to the pedagogical encounter rather than imposing a dominatory curriculum that reproduces social inequality. In this enterprise teachers are to transform the experience of domination in students and empower them to become 'emancipated' in a full democracy. Students' everyday experiences of oppression, of being 'silenced', of having their cultures and 'voices' excluded from curricula and decision-making are to be interrogated for the ideological messages that are contained in such acts. Raising awareness of such inequalities is an important step to overcoming them. Teachers and students together move forward in the progress towards 'individual autonomy within a just society' (Mass-

chelein, 1991: 97). In place of centrally prescribed and culturally biased curricula that students simply receive, critical pedagogy regards the curriculum as a form of cultural politics in which *participants in* (rather than *recipients of*) curricula question the cultural and dominatory messages contained in curricula and replace them with a 'language of possibility' and empowering, often community-related curricula. In this way curricula serve the 'socially critical' rather than the culturally and ideologically passive school.

One can discern a utopian and generalized tenor in some of this work, and applying critical theory to education can be criticized for its limited comments on practice. Indeed Miedama and Wardekker (1999: 68) go so far as to suggest that critical pedagogy has had its day, and that it was a stillborn child and that critical theory is a philosophy of science without a science (p. 75)! Nevertheless it is an important field for it recognizes and makes much of the fact that curricula and pedagogy are problematical and political.

A summary of the three paradigms[11]

Box 1.8 summarizes some of the broad differences between the three approaches that we have made so far.

Feminist research

It is perhaps no mere coincidence that feminist research should surface as a serious issue at the same time as ideology-critical paradigms for research; they are closely connected. Usher (1996), although criticizing Habermas (p. 124) for his faith in family life as a haven from a heartless, exploitative world, nevertheless sets out several principles of feminist research that resonate with the ideology critique of the Frankfurt School:

1   The acknowledgement of the pervasive influence of gender as a category of analysis and organization.

Box 1.8
Differing approaches to the study of behaviour

Normative	*Interpretive*	*Critical*
Society and the social system	The individual	Societies, groups and individuals
Medium/large-scale research	Small-scale research	Small-scale research
Impersonal, anonymous forces regulating behaviour	Human actions continuously recreating social life	Political, ideological factors, power and interests shaping behaviour
Model of natural sciences	Non-statistical	Ideology critique and action research
'Objectivity'	'Subjectivity'	Collectivity
Research conducted 'from the outside'	Personal involvement of the researcher	Participant researchers, researchers and facilitators
Generalizing from the specific	Interpreting the specific	Critiquing the specific
Explaining behaviour/seeking causes	Understanding actions/meanings rather than causes	Understanding, interrogating, critiquing, transforming actions and interests
Assuming the taken-for-granted	Investigating the taken-for-granted	Interrogating and critiquing the taken-for-granted
Macro-concepts: society, institutions, norms, positions, roles, expectations	Micro-concepts: individual perspective, personal constructs, negotiated meanings, definitions of situations	Macro- and micro-concepts: political and ideological interests, operations of power
Structuralists	Phenomenologists, symbolic interactionists, ethnomethodologists	Critical theorists, action researchers, practitioner researchers
Technical interest	Practical interest	Emancipatory interest

2   The deconstruction of traditional commitments to truth, objectivity and neutrality.

3   The adoption of an approach to knowledge creation which recognizes that all theories are perspectival.

4   The utilization of a multiplicity of research methods.

5   The inter-disciplinary nature of feminist research.

6   Involvement of the researcher and the people being researched.

7   The deconstruction of the theory/practice relationship.

Her suggestions build on earlier recognition of the significance of addressing the 'power issue' in research ('whose research', 'research for whom', 'research in whose interests') and the need to address the emancipatory element of educational research – that research should be empowering to all participants. The paradigm of critical theory questioned the putative objective, neutral, value-free, positivist, 'scientific' paradigm for the splitting of theory and practice and for its reproduction of asymmetries of power

(reproducing power differentials in the research community and for treating participants/respondents instrumentally – as objects).

Feminist research, too, challenges the legitimacy of research that does not empower oppressed and otherwise invisible groups – women. Positivist research served a given set of power relations, typically empowering the white, male-dominated research community at the expense of other groups whose voices were silenced. It had this latent, if not manifest or deliberate (Merton, 1967) function or outcome; it had this substantive effect (or maybe even agenda). Feminist research seeks to demolish and replace this with a different substantive agenda – of empowerment, voice, emancipation, equality and representation for oppressed groups. In doing so, it recognizes the necessity for foregrounding issues of power, silencing and voicing, ideology critique and a questioning of the legitimacy of research that does not emancipate hitherto disempowered groups.

The issue of empowerment resonates with the work of Freire (1970) on 'conscientization', wherein oppressed groups – in his case the illiterate poor – are taught to read and write by focusing on their lived experiences, e.g. of power, poverty, oppression, such that a political agenda is raised in their learning. In feminist research, women's consciousness of oppression, exploitation and disempowerment becomes a focus for research – the paradigm of ideology critique.

Far from treating educational research as objective and value-free, feminists argue that this is merely a smokescreen that serves the existing, disempowering *status quo*, and that the subject and value-laden nature of research must be surfaced, exposed and engaged (Haig, 1999: 223). This entails taking seriously issues of reflexivity, the effects of the research on the researched and the researchers, the breakdown of the positivist paradigm, and the raising of consciousness of the purposes and effects of the research. Indeed Ribbens and Edwards (1997) suggest that it is important to ask how researchers can produce work with reference to theoretical perspectives and formal traditions and requirements of public, academic knowledge whilst still remaining faithful to the experiences and accounts of research participants. Denzin (1989), Mies (1993) and Haig (1999) argue for several principles in feminist research:

- The asymmetry of gender relations and representation must be studied reflexively as constituting a fundamental aspect of social life (which includes educational research).
- Women's issues, their history, biography and biology, feature as a substantive agenda/focus in research – moving beyond mere perspectival/methodological issues to setting a research agenda.
- The raising of consciousness of oppression, exploitation, empowerment, equality, voice and representation is a methodological tool.
- The acceptability and notion of objectivity and objective research must be challenged.
- The substantive, value-laden dimensions and purposes of feminist research must be paramount.
- Research must empower women.

- Research need not only be undertaken by academic experts.
- Collective research is necessary – women need to collectivize their own individual histories if they are to appropriate these histories for emancipation.
- There is a commitment to revealing core processes and recurring features of women's oppression.
- An insistence on the inseparability of theory and practice.
- An insistence on the connections between the private and the public, between the domestic and the political.
- A concern with the construction and reproduction of gender and sexual difference.
- A rejection of narrow disciplinary boundaries.
- A rejection of the artificial subject/researcher dualism.
- A rejection of positivism and objectivity as male mythology.
- The increased use of qualitative, introspective biographical research techniques.
- A recognition of the gendered nature of social research and the development of anti-sexist research strategies.
- A review of the research process as consciousness and awareness raising and as fundamentally participatory.
- The primacy of women's personal subjective experience.
- The rejection of hierarchies in social research.
- The vertical, hierarchical relationships of researchers/research community and research objects, in which the research itself can become an instrument of domination and the reproduction and legitimation of power elites has to be replaced by research that promotes the interests of dominated, oppressed, exploited groups.
- The recognition of equal status and reciprocal relationships between subjects and researchers.
- There is a need to change the *status quo*, not merely to understand or interpret it.

- The research must be a process of conscientiza-tion, not research solely by experts for experts, but to empower oppressed participants.

Gender shapes research agendas, the choice of topics and foci, the choice of data collection techniques and the relationships between researchers and researched. Several methodolog-ical principles flow from a 'rationale' for femi-nist research (Denzin, 1989; Mies, 1993; Haig, 1997, 1999):

- The replacement of quantitative, positivist, objective research with qualitative, interpre-tive, ethnographic reflexive research.
- Collaborative, collectivist research under-taken by collectives – often of women – com-bining researchers and researched in order to break subject/object and hierarchical, non-reciprocal relationships.
- The appeal to alleged value-free, neutral, indifferent and impartial research has to be replaced by conscious, deliberate partiality – through researchers identifying with partici-pants.
- The use of ideology-critical approaches and paradigms for research.
- The spectator theory or contemplative theory of knowledge in which researchers research from ivory towers has to be replaced by a participatory approach – per-haps action research – in which all partici-pants (including researchers) engage in the struggle for women's emancipation – a liber-atory methodology.
- The need to change the *status quo* is the starting point for social research – if we want to know something we change it. (Mies (1993) cites the Chinese saying that if you want to know a pear then you must chew it!).
- The extended use of triangulation and multi-ple methods (including visual techniques such as video, photograph and film).
- The use of linguistic techniques such as con-versational analysis.
- The use of textual analysis such as decon-struction of documents and texts about women.

- The use of meta-analysis to synthesize find-ings from individual studies (see Chapter 12).
- A move away from numerical surveys and a critical evaluation of them, including a cri-tique of question wording.

The drive towards collective, egalitarian and emancipatory qualitative research is seen as nec-essary if women are to avoid colluding in their own oppression by undertaking positivist, unin-volved, objective research. Mies (ibid.: 67) argues that for women to undertake this latter form of research puts them into a schizophrenic position of having to adopt methods which con-tribute to their own subjugation and repression by ignoring their experience (however vicarious) of oppression and by forcing them to abide by the 'rules of the game' of the competitive, male-dominated academic world. In this view, argue Roman and Apple (1990: 59) it is not enough for women simply to embrace ethnographic forms of research, as this does not necessarily chal-lenge the existing and constituting forces of oppression or asymmetries of power. Ethno-graphic research, they argue, has to be accompa-nied by ideology critique, indeed they argue that the transformative, empowering, emancipatory potential of a piece of research is a critical stan-dard for evaluating that piece of research.

However, these views of feminist research and methodology are not unchallenged by other fem-inist researchers. For example Jayaratne (1993: 109) argues for 'fitness for purpose', suggesting that exclusive focus on qualitative methodolo-gies might not be appropriate either for the research purposes or, indeed, for advancing the feminist agenda. She refutes the argument that quantitative methods are unsuitable for femi-nists because they neglect the emotions of the people under study. Indeed she argues for beat-ing quantitative research on its own grounds (p. 121), suggesting the need for feminist quantita-tive data and methodologies in order to counter sexist quantitative data in the social sciences. She suggests that feminist researchers can accom-plish this without 'selling out' to the positivist, male-dominated academic research community.

An example of a feminist approach to research is the Girls Into Science and Technology (GIST) action research project. This took place over three years and involved 2,000 students and their teachers in ten co-educational, comprehensive schools in the Greater Manchester area of the UK, eight schools serving as the bases of the 'action', the remaining two acting as 'controls'. Several publications have documented the methodologies and findings of the GIST study (Whyte, 1986; Kelly, 1986, 1989a, 1989b; Kelly and Smail, 1986), described by its co-director as 'simultaneous-integrated action research' (Kelly, 1987) (i.e. integrating action and research).

Research and evaluation

The preceding discussion has suggested that research and politics are inextricably bound together. This can be taken further, as researchers in education will be advised to pay serious consideration to the politics of their research enterprise and the ways in which politics can steer research. For example one can detect a trend in educational research towards more evaluative research, where, for instance, a researcher's task is to evaluate the effectiveness (often of the implementation) of given policies and projects. This is particularly true in the case of 'categorically funded' and commissioned research – research which is funded by policy-makers (e.g. governments, fund-awarding bodies) under any number of different headings that those policy-makers devise (Burgess, 1993). On the one hand this is laudable, for it targets research directly towards policy; on the other hand it is dangerous in that it enables others to set the research agenda. Research ceases to become open-ended, pure research, and, instead, becomes the evaluation of *given* initiatives. Less politically charged, much research is evaluative, and indeed there are many similarities between research and evaluation. The two overlap but possess important differences. The problem of trying to identify differences between evaluation and research is compounded because not only

do they share several of the same methodological characteristics but one branch of research is called *evaluative research* or *applied research*. This is often kept separate from 'blue skies' research in that the latter is open-ended, exploratory, contributes something original to the substantive field and extends the frontiers of knowledge and theory whereas in the former the theory is *given* rather than *interrogated* or *tested*.

One can detect many similarities between the two in that they both use methodologies and methods of social science research generally, covering, for example:

- the need to clarify the *purposes* of the investigation;
- the need to *operationalize* purposes and areas of investigation;
- the need to address principles of *research design* that include:

  (a) formulating operational questions;
  (b) deciding appropriate methodologies;
  (c) deciding which instruments to use for data collection;
  (d) deciding on the sample for the investigation;
  (e) addressing reliability and validity in the investigation and instrumentation;
  (f) addressing ethical issues in conducting the investigation;
  (g) deciding on data analysis techniques;
  (h) deciding on reporting and interpreting results.

Indeed Norris (1990) argues that evaluation applies research methods to shed light on a problem of action (Norris, 1990: 97); he suggests that evaluation can be viewed as an extension of research, because it shares its methodologies and methods, and because evaluators and researchers possess similar skills in conducting investigations. In many senses the eight features outlined above embrace many elements of the *scientific method*, which Smith and Glass (1987) set out thus:

Step 1 A *theory* about the phenomenon exists.
Step 2 A *research problem* within the theory is detected and a *research question* is devised.

Step 3   A *research hypothesis* is deduced (often about the relationship between constructs).

Step 4   A *research design* is developed, *operationalizing* the research question and stating the *null hypothesis*.

Step 5   The research is conducted.

Step 6   The null hypothesis is tested based on the data gathered.

Step 7   The original theory is revised or supported based on the results of the hypothesis testing.

Indeed, if steps 1 and 7 were removed then there would be nothing to distinguish between research and evaluation. Both researchers and evaluators pose questions and hypotheses, select samples, manipulate and measure variables, compute statistics and data, and state conclusions. Nevertheless several commentators suggest that there are important differences between evaluation and research that are not always obvious simply by looking at publications. Publications do not always make clear the background events that gave rise to the investigation, nor do they always make clear the uses of the material that they report, nor do they always make clear what the dissemination rights (Sanday, 1993) are and who holds them.

Several commentators set out some of the differences between evaluation and research. For example Smith and Glass (1987) offer eight main differences:

1   *The intents and purposes of the investigation* The researcher wants to advance the frontiers of knowledge of phenomena, to contribute to theory and to be able to make generalizations; the evaluator is less interested in contributing to theory or general body of knowledge. Evaluation is more parochial than universal (pp. 33–4).

2   *The scope of the investigation* Evaluation studies tend to be more comprehensive than research in the number and variety of aspects of a programme that are being studied (p. 34).

3   *Values in the investigation* Research aspires to value neutrality, evaluations must represent multiple sets of values and include data on these values.

4   *The origins of the study* Research has its origins and motivation in the researcher's curiosity and desire to know (p. 34). The researcher is answerable to colleagues and scientists (i.e. the research community) whereas the evaluator is answerable to the 'client'. The researcher is autonomous whereas the evaluator is answerable to clients and stakeholders. The researcher is motivated by a search for knowledge, the evaluator is motivated by the need to solve problems, allocate resources and make decisions. Research studies are public, evaluations are for a restricted audience.

5   *The uses of the study*   The research is used to further knowledge, evaluations are used to inform decisions.

6   *The timeliness of the study*   Evaluations must be timely, research need not be. Evaluators' time scales are given, researchers' time scales need not be given.

7   *Criteria for judging the study*   Evaluations are judged by the criteria of utility and credibility, research is judged methodologically and by the contribution that it makes to the field (i.e. internal and external validity).

8   *The agendas of the study*   An evaluator's agenda is given, a researcher's agenda is her own.

Norris (1990) reports an earlier piece of work by Glass and Worthen in which they identified important differences between evaluation and research:

- *The motivation of the enquirer*   Research is pursued largely to satisfy curiosity, evaluation is undertaken to contribute to the solution of a problem.

- *The objectives of the search*   Research and evaluation seek different ends. Research seeks conclusions, evaluation leads to decisions.

- *Laws versus description*   Research is the quest for laws (nomothetic), evaluation merely seeks to describe a particular thing (idiographic).

- *The role of explanation* Proper and useful evaluation can be conducted without producing an explanation of why the product or project is good or bad or of how it operates to produce its effects.
- *The autonomy of the inquiry* Evaluation is undertaken at the behest of a client, while researchers set their own problems.
- *Properties of the phenomena that are assessed* Evaluation seeks to assess social utility directly, research may yield evidence of social utility but often only indirectly.
- *Universality of the phenomena studied* Researchers work with constructs having a currency and scope of application that make the objects of evaluation seem parochial by comparison.
- *Salience of the value question* In evaluation value questions are central and usually determine what information is sought.
- *Investigative techniques* While there may be legitimate differences between research and evaluation methods, there are far more similarities than differences with regard to techniques and procedures for judging validity.
- *Criteria for assessing the activity* The two most important criteria for judging the adequacy of research are internal and external validity, for evaluation they are utility and credibility.
- *Disciplinary base* The researcher can afford to pursue inquiry within one discipline and the evaluator cannot.

A clue to some of the differences between evaluation and research can be seen in the definition of evaluation. Most definitions of evaluation include reference to several key features: (1) answering specific, given questions; (2) gathering information; (3) making judgements; (4) taking decisions; (5) addressing the politics of a situation (Morrison, 1993: 2). Morrison provides one definition of evaluation as: *the provision of information about specified issues upon which judgements are based and from which decisions for action*

are taken (ibid., p. 2). This view echoes MacDonald (1987) in his comments that the evaluator:

> is faced with competing interest groups, with divergent definitions of the situation and conflicting informational needs ... He has to decide which decision-makers he will serve, what information will be of most use, when it is needed and how it can be obtained. I am suggesting that the resolution of these issues commits the evaluator to a political stance, an attitude to the government of education. No such commitment is required of the researcher. He stands outside the political process, and values his detachment from it. For him the production of new knowledge and its social use are separated. The evaluator is embroiled in the action, built into a political process which concerns the distribution of power, i.e. the allocation of resources and the determination of goals, roles and tasks ... When evaluation data influences power relationships the evaluator is compelled to weight carefully the consequences of his task specification ... The researcher is free to select his questions, and to seek answers to them. The evaluator, on the other hand, must never fall into the error of answering questions which no one but he is asking.
>
> (MacDonald, 1987: 42)

MacDonald argues that evaluation is an inherently political enterprise. His much-used threefold typification of evaluations as autocratic, bureaucratic and democratic is premised on a political reading of evaluation (a view echoed by Chelinsky and Mulhauser, 1993, who refer to 'the inescapability of politics' (p. 54) in the world of evaluation). MacDonald (1987), noting that 'educational research is becoming more evaluative in character' (p. 101), argues for research to be kept out of politics and for evaluation to square up to the political issues at stake:

> The danger therefore of conceptualizing evaluation as a branch of research is that evaluators become trapped in the restrictive tentacles of research respectability. Purity may be substituted for utility, trivial proofs for clumsy attempts to grasp complex significance. How much more productive it would be to define research as a branch of evaluation, a

branch whose task it is to solve the technological problems encountered by the evaluator.

(MacDonald, 1987: 43)

However, these typifications are very much 'ideal types'; the truth of the matter is far more blurred than these distinctions suggest. Two principal causes of this blurring lie in the *funding* and the *politics* of both evaluation and research. For example, the view of research as uncontaminated by everyday life is naive and simplistic; Norris (1990) argues that such an antiseptic view of research

ignores the social context of educational inquiry, the hierarchies of research communities, the reward structure of universities, the role of central government in supporting certain projects and not others, and the long-established relationships between social research and reform. It is, in short, an asocial and ahistorical account.

(Norris, 1990: 99)

The quotation from Norris (in particular the first three phrases) has a pedigree that reaches back to Kuhn (1962). After that his analysis becomes much more contemporaneous. Norris is making an important comment on the politics of research funding and research utilization. Since the early 1980s one can detect a massive rise in 'categorical' funding of projects, i.e. defined, *given* projects (often by government or research sponsors) for which bids have to be placed. This may seem unsurprising if one is discussing research grants by the Department for Education and Employment in the UK, which are deliberately policy-oriented, though one can also detect in projects that have been granted by non-governmental organizations (e.g. the Economic and Social Research Council in the UK) a move towards sponsoring policy-oriented projects rather than the 'blue-skies' research mentioned earlier. Indeed Burgess (1993) argues that 'researchers are little more than contract workers . . . research in education must become policy relevant . . . research must come closer to the requirement of practitioners' (Burgess, 1993: 1). This view is reinforced by several articles in

the collection edited by Anderson and Biddle (1991) which show that research and politics go together uncomfortably because researchers have different agendas and longer time scales than politicians and try to address the complexity of situations, whereas politicians, anxious for short-term survival want telescoped time scales, simple remedies and research that will be consonant with their political agendas. Indeed James (1993) argues that

the power of research-based evaluation to provide evidence on which rational decisions can be expected to be made is quite limited. Policy-makers will always find reasons to ignore, or be highly selective of, evaluation findings if the information does not support the particular political agenda operating at the time when decisions have to be made.

(James, 1993: 135)

The politicization of research has resulted in funding bodies awarding research grants for categorical research that specify time scales and the terms of reference. Burgess's view also points to the constraints under which research is undertaken; if it is not concerned with policy issues then research tends not to be funded. One could support Burgess's view that research must have some impact on policy-making.

Not only is *research* becoming a political issue, but this extends to the use being made of *evaluation* studies. It was argued above that evaluations are designed to provide useful data to inform decision-making. However, as evaluation has become more politicized so its uses (or non-uses) have become more politicized. Indeed Norris (1990) shows how politics frequently overrides evaluation or research evidence. He writes:

When the national extension of the TVEI was announced, neither the Leeds nor NFER team had reported and it had appeared that the decision to extend the initiative had been taken irrespective of any evaluation findings.

(Norris, 1990: 135)

This echoes James (1993) where she writes:

The classic definition of the role of evaluation as providing information for decision-makers . . . is a fiction if this is taken to mean that policy-makers who commission evaluations are expected to make rational decisions based on the best (valid and reliable) information available to them.

(James, 1993: 119)

Where evaluations are commissioned and have heavily political implications, Stronach and Morris (1994) argue that the response to this is that evaluations become more 'conformative'. 'Conformative evaluations', they argue, have several characteristics:

- Short-term, taking project goals as given, and supporting their realization.
- Ignoring the evaluation of longer-term learning outcomes, or anticipated economic/social consequences of the programme.
- Giving undue weight to the perceptions of programme participants who are responsible for the successful development and implementation of the programme; as a result, tending to 'over-report' change.
- Neglecting and 'under-reporting' the views of classroom practitioners, and programme critics.
- Adopting an atheoretical approach, and generally regarding the aggregation of opinion as the determination of overall significance.
- Involving a tight contractual relationship with the programme sponsors that either disbars public reporting, or encourages self-censorship in order to protect future funding prospects.
- Undertaking various forms of implicit advocacy for the programme in its reporting style.
- Creating and reinforcing a professional schizophrenia in the research and evaluation community, whereby individuals come to hold divergent public and private opinions, or offer criticisms in general rather than in particular, or quietly develop 'academic' critiques which are at variance with their contractual evaluation activities, alternating between 'critical' and 'conformative' selves.

The argument so far has been confined to large-scale projects that are influenced by and may or may not influence political decision-making. However the argument need not remain there. Morrison (1993) for example indicates how evaluations might influence the 'micro-politics of the school'. Hoyle (1986) asks whether evaluation data are used to bring resources into, or take resources out of, a department or faculty. The issue does not relate only to evaluations, for school-based research, far from the emancipatory claims for it made by action researchers (e.g. Carr and Kemmis, 1986; Grundy, 1987), is often concerned more with finding out the most successful ways of organization, planning, teaching and assessment of a *given agenda* rather *than setting agendas* and following one's own research agendas. This is *problem-solving* rather than *problem-setting*. That evaluation and research are being drawn together by politics at both a macro and micro level is evidence of a growing interventionism by politics into education, thus reinforcing the hegemony of the government in power. Several points have been made here:

- there is considerable overlap between evaluation and research;
- there are some *conceptual* differences between evaluation and research, though, in practice, there is considerable blurring of the edges of the differences between the two;
- the funding and control of research and research agendas reflect the persuasions of political decision-makers;
- evaluative research has increased in response to categorical funding of research projects;
- the attention being given to, and utilization of, evaluation varies according to the consonance between the findings and their political attractiveness to political decision-makers.

In this sense the views expressed earlier by Mac-Donald are now little more than an historical relic; there is very considerable blurring of the edges between evaluation and research because of the political intrusion into, and use of, these two types of study. One response to this can be seen in Burgess's (1993) view that a researcher needs to be able to meet the sponsor's requirements for evaluation whilst also generating research data (engaging the issues of the need to negotiate ownership of the data and intellectual property rights).

Research, politics and policy-making

The preceding discussion has suggested that there is an inescapable political dimension to educational research, both in the macro- and micro-political senses. In the macro-political sense this manifests itself in funding arrangements, where awards are made provided that the research is 'policy-related' (Burgess, 1993) – guiding policy decisions, improving quality in areas of concern identified by policy-makers, facilitating the implementation of policy decisions, evaluating the effects of the implementation of policy. Burgess notes a shift here from a situation where the researcher specifies the topic of research and towards the sponsor specifying the focus of research. The issue of sponsoring research reaches beyond simply commissioning research towards the dissemination (or not) of research – who will receive or have access to the findings and how the findings will be used and reported. This, in turn, raises the fundamental issue of who owns and controls data, and who controls the release of research findings. Unfavourable reports might be withheld for a time, suppressed or selectively released! Research can be brought into the service of wider educational purposes – the politics of a local education authority, or indeed the politics of government agencies.

On a micro-scale Morrison (1993) suggests that research and evaluation are not politically innocent because they involve people. Research is brought into funding decisions in institutions – for example to provide money or to withhold money, to promote policies or to curtail them, to promote people or to reduce their status (Usher and Scott, 1996: 177). Micro-politics, Usher and Scott argue, influence the commissioning of research, the kind of field-work and

field relations that are possible, funding issues, and the control of dissemination. Morrison suggests that this is particularly the case in evaluative research, where an evaluation might influence prestige, status, promotion, credibility, or funding. For example, in a school a negative evaluation of one area of the curriculum might attract more funding into that department, or it might have the effect of closing down the department and the loss of staff.

Though research and politics intertwine, the relationships between educational research, politics and policy-making are complex because research designs strive to address a complex social reality (Anderson and Biddle, 1991); a piece of research does not feed simplistically or directly into a specific piece of policy-making. Rather, research generates a range of different types of knowledge – concepts, propositions, explanations, theories, strategies, evidence, methodologies (Caplan, 1991). These feed subtly and often indirectly into the decision-making process, providing, for example, direct inputs, general guidance, a scientific gloss, orienting perspectives, generalizations and new insights. Basic and applied research have significant parts to play in this process.

The degree of influence exerted by research depends on careful dissemination; too little and its message is ignored, too much and data overload confounds decision-makers and makes them cynical – the syndrome of the boy who cried wolf (Knott and Wildavsky, 1991). Hence researchers must give more care to utilization by policy-makers (Weiss, 1991a), reduce jargon, provide summaries, and improve links between the two cultures of researchers and policy-makers (Cook, 1991) and, further, to the educational community. Researchers must cultivate ways of influencing policy, particularly when policy-makers can simply ignore research findings, commission their own research (Cohen and Garet, 1991) or underfund research into social problems (Coleman, 1991; Thomas, 1991). Researchers must recognize their links with the power groups who decide policy. Research utilization takes many forms depending on its location in the process of policy-making, e.g. in research and development, problem solving, interactive and tactical models (Weiss, 1991b). Researchers will have to judge the most appropriate forms of utilization of their research (Alkin, Daillak and White, 1991).

The impact of research on policy-making depends on its degree of consonance with the political agendas of governments (Thomas, 1991) and policy-makers anxious for their own political survival (Cook, 1991) and the promotion of their social programmes. Research is used if it is politically acceptable. That the impact of research on policy is intensely and inescapably political is a truism (Selleck, 1991; Kamin, 1991; Horowitz and Katz, 1991; Wineburg, 1991). Research too easily becomes simply an 'affirmatory text' which 'exonerates the system' (Wineburg, 1991) and is used by those who seek to hear in it only echoes of their own voices and wishes (Kogan and Atkin, 1991).

There is a significant tension between researchers and policy-makers. The two parties have different, and often conflicting, interests, agendas, audiences, time scales, terminology, and concern for topicality (Levin, 1991). These have huge implications for research styles. Policy-makers anxious for the quick fix of superficial facts, short-term solutions and simple remedies for complex and generalized social problems (Cartwright, 1991; Cook, 1991) – the Simple Impact model (Biddle and Anderson, 1991; Weiss, 1991a, 1991b) – find positivist methodologies attractive, often debasing the data through illegitimate summary. Moreover policy-makers find much research uncertain in its effects (Kerlinger, 1991; Cohen and Garet, 1991), dealing in a *Weltanschauung* rather than specifics, and being too complex in its designs and of limited applicability (Finn, 1991). This, reply the researchers, misrepresents the nature of their work (Shavelson and Berliner, 1991) and belies the complex reality which they are trying to investigate (Blalock, 1991). Capturing social complexity and serving political utility can run counter to each other.

The issue of the connection between research

and politics – power and decision-making – is complex. On another dimension, the notion that research is inherently a political act because it is part of the political processes of society has not been lost on researchers. Usher and Scott (1996: 176) argue that positivist research has allowed a traditional conception of society to be preserved relatively unchallenged – the white, male, middle-class researcher – to the relative exclusion of 'others' as legitimate knowers. That this reaches into epistemological debate is evidenced in the issues of who defines the 'traditions of knowledge' and the disciplines of knowledge; the social construction of knowledge has to take into account the differential power of groups to define what is worthwhile research knowledge, what constitutes acceptable focuses and methodologies of research and how the findings will be used.

Methods and methodology

We return to our principal concern, methods and methodology in educational research. By methods, we mean that range of approaches used in educational research to gather data which are to be used as a basis for inference and interpretation, for explanation and prediction. Traditionally, the word refers to those techniques associated with the positivistic model – eliciting responses to predetermined questions, recording measurements, describing phenomena and performing experiments. For our purposes, we will extend the meaning to include not only the methods of normative research but also those associated with interpretive paradigms – participant observation, role-playing, non-directive interviewing, episodes and accounts. Although methods may also be taken to include the more specific features of the scientific enterprise such as forming concepts and hypotheses, building models and theories, and sampling procedures, we will limit ourselves principally to the more general techniques which researchers use.

If methods refer to techniques and procedures used in the process of data-gathering, the aim of methodology then is, in Kaplan's words:

to describe and analyze these methods, throwing light on their limitations and resources, clarifying their presuppositions and consequences, relating their potentialities to the twilight zone at the frontiers of knowledge. It is to venture generalizations from the success of particular techniques, suggesting new applications, and to unfold the specific bearings of logical and metaphysical principles on concrete problems, suggesting new formulations.

(Kaplan, 1973)

In summary, he suggests, the aim of methodology is to help us to understand, in the broadest possible terms, not the products of scientific inquiry but the process itself.

We, for our part, will attempt to present normative and interpretive perspectives in a complementary light and will try to lessen the tension that is sometimes generated between them. Merton and Kendall[12] express the same sentiment when they say, 'Social scientists have come to abandon the spurious choice between qualitative and quantitative data: they are concerned rather with that combination of both which makes use of the most valuable features of each. The problem becomes one of determining *at which points* they should adopt the one, and at which the other, approach' (Merton and Kendall, 1946).

Our earlier remarks on the nature of research may best be summarized by quoting Mouly's definitive statement on the subject. He writes, 'Research is best conceived as the process of arriving at dependable solutions to problems through the planned and systematic collection, analysis, and interpretation of data. It is a most important tool for advancing knowledge, for promoting progress, and for enabling man [*sic*] to relate more effectively to his environment, to accomplish his purposes, and to resolve his conflicts' (Mouly, 1978).

The term *research* itself may take on a range of meanings and thereby be legitimately applied to a variety of contexts from, say, an investigation into the techniques of Dutch painters of the seventeenth century to the problem of finding more efficient means of improving traffic flow in major city centres. For our purposes, however, we will restrict its usages to those activities and undertakings aimed at developing a science of behaviour, the word *science* itself implying both normative and interpretive perspectives. Accordingly, when we speak of social research, we have in mind the systematic and scholarly application of the principles of a science of behaviour to the problems of people within their social contexts and when we use the term educational research, we likewise have in mind the application of these same principles to the problems of teaching and learning within the formal educational framework and to the clarification of issues having direct or indirect bearing on these concepts.

The particular value of scientific research in education is that it will enable educators to develop the kind of sound knowledge base that characterizes other professions and disciplines; and one that will ensure education a maturity and sense of progression it at present lacks.

Part two

Planning educational research

The planning of educational research is not an arbitrary matter, the research itself being an inescapably ethical enterprise. The research community and those using the findings of research have a right to expect that research be conducted rigorously, scrupulously and in an ethically defensible manner. All this necessitates careful planning, with thought being given particularly to the consequences of the research. It is no accident, therefore, that we place the chapter on ethical issues at an early point in the book, for such matters must be a touchstone of acceptable practice. In addition, the parameters of the research need to be considered and made explicit by researchers at this initial stage; subsequent chapters in this part indicate how this might be achieved. A new chapter on planning educational research is intended to give novice researchers an overview of, and introduction to, planning issues, the intention being deliberately practical, for educational research has to work!

In planning research and identifying its parameters, we need to consider the issues of sampling, reliability, and validity *at the very outset*. We regard these factors as so important that in this edition we have included new chapters to address them. All are complex in nature, for there is no singular or exclusive version of reliability, validity, or what constitutes an acceptable sample. However, we believe that it is essential for planners to embark on research 'with their eyes open' so that they can consider what avenues of approach are open to them. What follows in this part of the book sets out to do just this: to make clear the range of possibilities and interpretations in these respects so that the eventual selection of sampling procedures and versions of reliability and validity will be made on the basis of *fitness for purpose* rather than caprice. The intention is that by the end of this part of the book researchers, however inexperienced, will be able to make informed decisions about the parameters and conduct of the research.

2 The ethics of educational and social research

Introduction

Developments in the field of social science in recent years have been accompanied by a growing awareness of the attendant moral issues implicit in the work of social researchers and of their need to meet their obligations with respect to those involved in, or affected by, their investigations. This awareness, focusing chiefly, but by no means exclusively, on the subject matter and methods of research in so far as they affect the participants, is reflected in the growth of relevant literature and in the appearance of regulatory codes of research practice formulated by various agencies and professional bodies.[1] Ethical concerns encountered in educational research in particular can be extremely complex and subtle and can frequently place researchers in moral predicaments which may appear quite unresolvable. One such dilemma is that which requires researchers to strike a balance between the demands placed on them as professional scientists in pursuit of truth, and their subjects' rights and values potentially threatened by the research. This is known as the 'costs/benefits ratio', the essence of which is outlined by Frankfort-Nachmias and Nachmias (1992) in Box 2.1, and is a concept we return to later in the chapter when we consider how ethical dilemmas arise from various sources of tension. It is a particularly thorny dilemma because, as Aronson *et al.* (1990) note, it cannot be shrugged off either by making pious statements about the inviolability of human dignity or by pledging glib allegiance to the cause of science. Most standard textbooks on ethics in social research would, in this case, advise researchers to proceed ethically without threatening the validity of the research endeavour in so far as it is possible to do so. Conventional wisdom of this kind is admirable in its way, but the problems for researchers can multiply surprisingly when the principle comes to be applied: when they move from the general to the particular, from the abstract to the concrete. Each research undertaking is different and investigators may find that on one occasion their work proceeds smoothly without the Hydra-headed creature of ethical concern breaking surface. At another time, they may come to realize that, suddenly and without prior indication, they are in the middle of an ethical minefield, and that the residual problems of a technical and administrative nature that one expects as a matter of course when pursuing educational research are compounded by unforeseen moral questions.

Ethical issues may stem from the kinds of problems investigated by social scientists and the methods they use to obtain valid and reliable data. In theory at least, this means that each stage in the research sequence may be a potential source of ethical problems. Thus, they may arise from the nature of the research project itself (ethnic differences in intelligence, for example); the context for the research (a remand home); the procedures to be adopted (producing high levels of anxiety); methods of data collection (covert observation); the nature of the participants (emotionally disturbed adolescents); the type of data collected (highly personal information of a sensitive kind); and what is to be done with the data (publishing in a manner that causes the participants embarrassment).

Our initial observations would seem to indicate

Box 2.1
The costs/benefits ratio

The *costs/benefits ratio* is a fundamental concept expressing the primary ethical dilemma in social research. In planning their proposed research, social scientists have to consider the likely social benefits of their endeavours against the personal costs to the individuals taking part. Possible benefits accruing from the research may take the form of crucial findings leading to significant advances in theoretical and applied knowledge. Failure to do the research may cost society the advantages of the research findings and ultimately the opportunity to improve the human condition. The costs to participants may include affronts to dignity, embarrassment, loss of trust in social relations, loss of autonomy and self-determination, and lowered self-esteem. On the other hand, the benefits to participants could take the form of satisfaction in having made a contribution to science and a greater personal understanding of the research area under scrutiny. The process of balancing benefits against possible costs is chiefly a subjective one and not at all easy. There are few or no absolutes and researchers have to make decisions about research content and procedures in accordance with professional and personal values. This *costs/benefits ratio* is the basic dilemma residual in a great deal of social research.

Source Adapted from Frankfort-Nachmias and Nachmias, 1992

that the subject of ethics in social research is potentially a wide-ranging and challenging one. It is fitting, therefore, if in this chapter we present a conspectus of the main issues that may confront workers in the field. Although what follows offers advice and guidance in liberal amounts drawn from the work of seasoned researchers and from a range of empirical studies, we do not intend to be unduly prescriptive or proscriptive. As we suggested in our opening comments, each research undertaking is an event *sui generis*, and the conduct of researchers cannot be, indeed should not be, forced into a procrustean system of ethics. When it comes to the resolution of a specific moral problem, each situation frequently offers a spectrum of possibilities. In what follows, we have indulged in a certain amount of repetition without, we hope, being repetitious. This has advantages since some of the ideas discussed are multi-faceted

and their reappearance in different contexts may assist greater understanding.

From what we have said so far, we hope that we will be seen as informants rather than arbiters, and that our counsels will be perceived as markers and signposts in what for many readers will be a largely unexplored *terra incognita*. It is in this spirit that we review seriatim the problems of access to the research setting; the nature of ethics in social research generally; sources of tension in the ethical debate; problems and dilemmas confronting the researcher, including matters of privacy, anonymity, confidentiality, betrayal and deception; ethical problems endemic in particular research methods; ethics and teacher evaluation; regulations affecting research; and a final word on personal codes of practice. Before this, however, we examine another fundamental concept which, along with the *costs/benefits ratio*, contributes to the bedrock of ethical procedure – that of *informed consent*.

Informed consent

Much social research necessitates obtaining the consent and co-operation of subjects who are to assist in investigations and of significant others in the institutions or organizations providing the research facilities. In some cultures, informed consent is absolutely essential whenever participants are exposed to substantial risks or asked to forfeit personal rights. Writing of the situation in the USA, for instance, Frankfort-Nachmias and Nachmias say:

> When research participants are to be exposed to pain, physical or emotional injury, invasions of privacy, or physical or psychological stress, or when they are asked to surrender their autonomy temporarily (as, for example, in drug research), informed consent must be fully guaranteed. Participants should know that their involvement is voluntary at all times, and they should receive a thorough explanation beforehand of the benefits, rights, risks, and dangers involved as a consequence of their participation in the research project.
>
> (Frankfort-Nachmias and Nachmias, 1992)

The principle of informed consent arises from the subject's right to freedom and self-determination. Being free is a condition of living in a democracy and when restrictions and limitations are placed on that freedom they must be justified and consented to, even in research proceedings. Consent thus protects and respects the right of self-determination and places some of the responsibility on the participant should anything go wrong in the research. Another aspect of the right to self-determination is that the subject has the right to refuse to take part, or to withdraw once the research has begun (see Frankfort-Nachmias and Nachmias, 1992). Thus informed consent implies informed refusal.

Informed consent has been defined by Diener and Crandall as 'the procedures in which individuals choose whether to participate in an investigation after being informed of facts that would be likely to influence their decisions' (Diener and Crandall, 1978). This definition involves four elements: competence, voluntarism, full information and comprehension. 'Competence' implies that responsible, mature individuals will make correct decisions if they are given the relevant information. It is incumbent on researchers to ensure they do not engage individuals incapable of making such decisions either because of immaturity or some form of psychological impairment. 'Voluntarism' entails applying the principle of informed consent and thus ensuring that participants freely choose to take part (or not) in the research and guarantees that exposure to risks is undertaken knowingly and voluntarily. This element can be problematical, especially in the field of medical research when unknowing patients are used as guinea-pigs. 'Full information' implies that consent is fully informed, though in practice it is often impossible for researchers to inform subjects on everything, e.g. on the statistical treatment of data; and, as we shall see below, on those occasions when the researchers themselves do not know everything about the investigation. In such circumstances, the strategy of reasonably informed consent has to be applied. Box 2.2 illustrates a set of guidelines used in the USA

that are based on the idea of *reasonably informed consent.*[2] 'Comprehension' refers to the fact that participants fully understand the nature of the research project, even when procedures are complicated and entail risks. Suggestions have been made to ensure that subjects fully comprehend the situation they are putting themselves into, e.g. by using highly educated subjects, by engaging a consultant to explain difficulties or by building into the research scheme a time lag between the request for participation and decision time. If these four elements are present, researchers can be assured that subjects' rights will have been given appropriate consideration. As Frankfort-Nachmias and Nachmias note, however:

> The principle of informed consent should not . . . be made an absolute requirement of all social science research. Although usually desirable, it is not absolutely necessary to studies where no danger or risk is involved. The more serious the risk to research participants, the greater becomes the obligation to obtain informed consent.
>
> (Frankfort-Nachmias and Nachmias, 1992)

It must also be remembered that there are some research methods where it is impossible to seek informed consent. Covert observation, for

Box 2.2
Guidelines for reasonably informed consent

1 A fair explanation of the procedures to be followed and their purposes.
2 A description of the attendant discomforts and risks reasonably to be expected.
3 A description of the benefits reasonably to be expected.
4 A disclosure of appropriate alternative procedures that might be advantageous to the participants.
5 An offer to answer any inquiries concerning the procedures.
6 An instruction that the person is free to withdraw consent and to discontinue participation in the project at any time without prejudice to the participant.

Source United States Department of Health, Education and Welfare, *Institutional Guide to DHEW Policy,* 1971

example, as used in Patrick's study of a Glasgow gang (Chapter 9), or experimental techniques involving deception, as in Milgram's Obedience-to-authority experiments (Chapter 21), would, by their very nature, rule out the option. And, of course, there may be occasions when problems arise even though consent has been obtained. Burgess (1989a), for example, cites his own research in which teachers had been informed that research was taking place but in which it was not possible to specify exactly what data would be collected or how they would be used. It could be said, in this particular case, that individuals were not fully informed, that consent had not been obtained, and that privacy had been violated. As a general rule, however, informed consent is an important principle to abide by and the fact that moral philosophers have joined in the debate engendered by the concept is testimony to the seriousness with which it is viewed (Soble, 1978). It is this principle that will form the basis, so to speak, of an implicit contractual relationship between the researcher and the researched and will serve as a foundation on which subsequent ethical considerations can be structured.

From our remarks and citations so far on this subject of informed consent, we may appear to be assuming relationships between peers – researcher and teachers, for example, or research professor and post-graduate students; and this assumption would seem to underpin many of the discussions of an ethical nature in the research literature generally. Readers will be aware, however, that much educational research involves children who cannot be regarded as being on equal terms with the researcher, and it is important to keep this in mind at all stages in the research process including the point where informed consent is sought. In this connection we refer to the important work of Fine and Sandstrom (1988), whose ethnographic and participant observational studies of children and young people focus, among other issues, on this asymmetry with respect to the problems of obtaining informed consent from their young subjects and explaining the research in a com-

prehensible fashion. As a guiding principle they advise that while it is desirable to lessen the power differential between children and adult researchers, the difference will remain and its elimination may be ethically inadvisable.

It may be of some help to readers if we refer briefly to other aspects of the problem of informed consent (or refusal) in relation to young, or very young, children. Seeking informed consent with regard to minors involves two stages. First, researchers consult and seek permission from those adults responsible for the prospective subjects; and, second, they approach the young people themselves. The adults in question will be, for example, parents, teachers, tutors, or psychiatrists, youth leaders, or team coaches, depending on the research context. The point of the research will be explained, questions invited and permission to proceed to the next stage sought. Objections, for whatever reason, will be duly respected. Obtaining approval from relevant adults may be more difficult than in the case of the children, but at a time of increasing sensitivity to children's welfare it is vital that researchers secure such approval. It may be useful if, in seeking the consent of children, researchers bear in mind the provisory comments below.

While seeking children's permission and co-operation is an automatic part of quantitative research (a child cannot unknowingly complete a simple questionnaire), the importance of informed consent in qualitative research is not always recognized. Speaking of participant observation, for example, Fine and Sandstrom say that researchers must provide a credible and meaningful explanation of their research intentions, especially in situations where they have little authority, and that children must be given a real and legitimate opportunity to say that they do not want to take part. The authors advise that where subjects do refuse, they should not be questioned, their actions should not be recorded, and they should not be included in any book or article (even under a pseudonym). Where they form part of a group, they may be included as part of a collectivity. Fine and

Sandstrom consider that such rejections are sometimes a result of mistrust of the researcher. They suggest that at a later date, when the researcher has been able to establish greater rapport with the group, those who refused initially may be approached again, perhaps in private.

Two particular groups of children require special mention: very young children, and those not capable of making a decision. Researchers intending to work with pre-school or nursery children may dismiss the idea of seeking informed consent from their would-be subjects because of their age, but Fine and Sandstrom would recommend otherwise. Even though such children would not understand what research was, the authors advise that the children be given some explanation. For example, one to the effect that an adult will be watching and playing with them might be sufficient to provide a measure of informed consent consistent with the children's understanding. As Fine and Sandstrom comment:

> Our feeling is that children should be told as much as possible, even if some of them cannot understand the full explanation. Their age should not diminish their rights, although their level of understanding must be taken into account in the explanations that are shared with them.
>
> (Fine and Sandstrom, 1988)

The second group consists of those children who are to be used in a research project and who may not meet Diener and Crandall's (1978) criterion of 'competence' (a group of psychologically impaired children, for example – the issue of 'advocacy' applies here). In such circumstances there may be LEA guidelines to follow. In the absence of these, the requirements of informed consent would be met by obtaining the permission of headteachers who will be acting *in loco parentis* or who have had delegated to them the responsibility for providing informed consent by the parents.

Two final cautions: first, where an extreme form of research is planned, parents would have to be fully informed in advance and their consent obtained; and second, whatever the nature of the research and whoever is involved, should a child show signs of discomfort or stress, the research should be terminated immediately. For further discussion on the care that needs to be exercised in working with children we refer readers to Greig and Taylor (1998), Holmes (1998) and Graue and Walsh (1998).

Access and acceptance

The relevance of the principle of informed consent becomes apparent at the initial stage of the research project – that of access to the institution or organization where the research is to be conducted, and acceptance by those whose permission one needs before embarking on the task. We highlight this stage of access and acceptance in particular at this point because it offers the best opportunity for researchers to present their credentials as serious investigators and establish their own ethical position with respect to their proposed research.

Investigators cannot expect access to a nursery, school, college, or factory as a matter of right. They have to demonstrate that they are worthy, as researchers and human beings, of being accorded the facilities needed to carry out their investigations. The advice of Bell (1987) is particularly apposite in this connection:

> Permission to carry out an investigation must always be sought at an early stage. As soon as you have an agreed project outline and have read enough to convince yourself that the topic is feasible, it is advisable to make a formal, written approach to the individuals and organization concerned, outlining your plans. Be honest. If you are carrying out an investigation in connection with a diploma or degree course, say that is what you are doing. If you feel the study will probably yield useful and/or interesting information, make a particular point of that fact – but be careful not to claim more than the investigation merits.
>
> (Bell, 1987: 42)

The first stage thus involves the gaining of official permission to undertake one's research in the target community. This will mean contacting, in person or in writing, an LEA official and/or the chairperson of the governors, if one is to work in a school, along with the headteacher or principal. At a later point, significant figures who will be responsible for, or assist in, the organization and administration of the research will also need to be contacted – the deputy head or senior teacher, for instance, and most certainly the classteacher if children are to be used in the research. Since the researcher's potential for intrusion and perhaps disruption is considerable, amicable relations with the classteacher in particular should be fostered as expeditiously as possible. If the investigation involves teachers as participants, propositions may have to be put to a full staff meeting and conditions negotiated. Where the research is to take place in another kind of institution – a youth club or detention centre, for example – the principle of approach will be similar, although the organizational structure will be different.

Achieving goodwill and co-operation is especially important where the proposed research extends over a period of time: days, perhaps, in the case of an ethnographic study; months (or perhaps years!) where longitudinal research is involved. Access does not present quite such a problem when, for example, a one-off survey requires respondents to give up half-an-hour of their time; or when a researcher is normally a member of the organization where the research is taking place (an insider), though in the case of the latter, it is generally unwise to take co-operation for granted. Where research procedures are extensive and complicated, however, or where the design is developmental or longitudinal, or where researchers are not normally based in the target community, the problems of access are more involved and require greater preparation. Box 2.3 gives a flavour of the kinds of accessibility problems that can be experienced (Foster, 1989).

Having identified the official and significant figures whose permission must be sought, and before actually meeting them, researchers will need to clarify in their own minds the precise nature and scope of their research. In this respect researchers could, for instance, identify

Box 2.3
Close encounters of a researcher kind

My first entry into a staffroom at the college was the occasion of some shuffling and shifting of books and chairs so that I could be given a comfortable seat whilst the tutor talked to me from a standing position. As time progressed my presence was almost taken for granted and later, when events threatened the security of the tutors, I was ignored. No one inquired as to whether they could assist me and my own inquiries were met with cursory answers and confused looks, followed by the immediate disappearance of the individuals concerned, bearing a pile of papers. I learned not to make too many inquiries. Unfortunately, when individuals feel insecure, when their world is threatened with change that is beyond their control, they are likely to respond in an unpredictable manner to persons within their midst whose role is unclear, and the role of the researcher is rarely understood by those not engaged in research.

Source Foster, 1989

the aims of the research; its practical applications, if any; the design, methods and procedures to be used; the nature and size of samples or groups; what tests are to be administered and how; what activities are to be observed; what subjects are to be interviewed; observational needs; the time involved; the degree of disruption envisaged; arrangements to guarantee confidentiality with respect to data (if this is necessary); the role of feedback and how findings can best be disseminated; the overall timetable within which the research is to be encompassed; and finally, whether assistance will be required in the organization and administration of the research. By such planning and foresight, both researchers and institutions will have a good idea of the demands likely to be made on both subjects (be they children or teachers) and organizations. It is also a good opportunity to anticipate and resolve likely problems, especially those of a practical kind. A long, complicated questionnaire, for example, may place undue demands on the comprehension skills and attention spans of a particular class of 13-year-olds; or a relatively inexperienced teacher could feel threatened by sustained research scrutiny. Once this kind of information has been sorted out and clarified, researchers will be in a strong position to discuss their proposed plans in an informed, open and frank manner (though not necessarily too open, as we shall see) and will thereby more readily gain permission, acceptance, and support. It must be remembered that hosts will have perceptions of researchers and their intentions and that these need to be positive. Researchers can best influence such perceptions by presenting themselves as competent, trustworthy, and accommodating.

Once this preliminary information has been collected, researchers are duly prepared for the next stage: making actual contact in person, perhaps after an introductory letter, with appropriate people in the organization with a view to negotiating access. If the research is college-based, they will have the support of their college and course supervisors. Festinger and Katz (1966) consider that there is real economy in going to the very top of the organization or system in question to obtain assent and co-operation. This is particularly so where the structure is clearly hierarchical and where lower levels are always dependent on their superiors. They consider that it is likely that the nature of the research will be referred to the top of the organization sooner or later, and that there is a much better chance for a favourable decision if leaders are consulted at the outset. It may also be the case that heads will be more open-minded than those lower down, who because of their insecurity, may be less co-operative. The authors also warn against using the easiest entrances into the organization when seeking permission. Researchers may perhaps seek to come in as allies of individuals or groups who have a special interest to exploit and who see research as a means to their ends. As Festinger and Katz put it, 'The researcher's aim should be to enter the situation in the common interests of all parties, and his findings should be equally available to all groups and individuals' (Festinger and Katz, 1966). Investigators should thus seek as broad a basis for their support as possible. Other potential problems may be circumvented by making use of accepted channels of communication in the institution or organization. In a school, for example, this may take the form of a staff forum. As Festinger and Katz say in this regard, 'If the information is limited to a single channel, the study may become identified with the interests associated with that channel' (Festinger and Katz, 1966).

Following contact, there will be a negotiation process. At this point researchers will give as much information about the aims, nature and procedures of the research as is appropriate. This is very important: information that may prejudice the results of the investigation should be withheld. Aronson and Carlsmith (1969), for instance, note that one cannot imagine researchers who are studying the effects of group pressure on conformity announcing their intentions in advance. On the other hand, researchers may find themselves on dangerous ground if they go to the extreme of maintaining a 'conspiracy of silence', because, as Festinger and Katz note, such a stance is hard to keep up if the research is extensive and lasts over several days or weeks. As they say in this respect, 'An attempt to preserve secrecy merely increases the spread and wildness of the rumours' (Festinger and Katz, 1966). If researchers do not want their potential hosts and/or subjects to know too much about specific hypotheses and objectives, then a simple way out is to present an explicit statement at a fairly general level with one or two examples of items that are not crucial to the study as a whole. As most research entails some risks, especially where field studies are concerned, and as the presence of an observer scrutinizing various aspects of community or school life may not be relished by all in the group, investigators must at all times manifest a sensitive appreciation of their hosts' and subjects' position and reassure anyone who feels threatened by the work. Such reassurance could take the form of a statement of conditions and guarantees given by researchers at this negotiation stage. By way of illustration, Box 2.4 contains conditions laid down by an Open University student for a school-based research project.

Box 2.4
Conditions and guarantees proffered for a school-based research project

---

1   All participants will be offered the opportunity to remain anonymous.
2   All information will be treated with the strictest confidentiality.
3   Interviewees will have the opportunity to verify statements when the research is in draft form.
4   Participants will receive a copy of the final report.
5   The research is to be assessed by the Open University for examination purposes only, but should the question of publication arise at a later date, permission will be sought from the participants.
6   The research will attempt to explore educational management in practice. It is hoped the final report may be of benefit to the school and to those who take part.

Source Bell, 1991

We conclude this section by reminding beginning researchers in particular that there will be times when ethical considerations will pervade much of their work and that these will be no more so than at the stage of access and acceptance, where appropriateness of topic, design, methods, guarantees of confidentiality, analysis and dissemination of findings must be negotiated with relative openness, sensitivity, honesty, accuracy and scientific impartiality. As we have indicated earlier, there can be no rigid rules in this context. It will be a case of formulating and abiding by one's own situational ethics. These will determine what is acceptable and what is not acceptable. As Hitchcock and Hughes (1989) say in this regard:

> Individual circumstances must be the final arbiter. As far as possible it is better if the teacher can discuss the research with all parties involved. On other occasions it may be better for the teacher to develop a pilot study and uncover some of the problems in advance of the research proper. If it appears that the research is going to come into conflict with aspects of school policy, management styles, or individual personalities, it is better to confront the issues head on, consult relevant parties,

and make rearrangements in the research design where possible or necessary.

> (Hitchcock and Hughes, 1989: 198)

Where a pilot study is not feasible it may be possible to arrange one or two scouting forays to assess possible problems and risks. By way of summary, we refer the reader to Box 2.5.

Ethics of social research

Social scientists generally have a responsibility not only to their profession in its search for knowledge and quest for truth, but also for the subjects they depend on for their work. Whatever the specific nature of their work, social researchers must take into account the effects of the research on participants, and act in such a way as to preserve their dignity as human beings. Such is ethical behaviour. Indeed, ethics has been defined as:

> a matter of principled sensitivity to the rights of others. Being ethical limits the choices we can make in the pursuit of truth. Ethics say that while truth is good, respect for human dignity is better, even if, in the extreme case, the respect of human nature leaves one ignorant of human nature.

> (Cavan, 1977: 810)

Kimmel (1988) has pointed out that when attempting to describe ethical issues, it is important we remember to recognize that the distinction between ethical and unethical behaviour is not dichotomous, even though the normative code of prescribed ('ought') and proscribed ('ought not') behaviours, as represented by the ethical standards of a profession, seem to imply that it is. Judgements about whether behaviour conflicts with professional values lie on a continuum that ranges from the clearly ethical to the clearly unethical. The point to be borne in mind is that ethical principles are not absolute, generally speaking, though some maintain that they are as we shall see shortly, but must be interpreted in the light of the research context and of other values at stake.

It is perhaps worthwhile at this point to

Box 2.5
Negotiating access checklist

1 **Clear official channels by formally requesting permission to carry out your investigation as soon as you have an agreed project outline.**
Some LEAs insist that requests to carry out research are channelled through the LEA office. Check what is required in your area.

2 **Speak to the people who will be asked to co-operate.**
Getting the LEA or head's permission is one thing, but you need to have the support of the people who will be asked to give interviews or complete questionnaires.

3 **Submit the project outline to the head, if you are carrying out a study in your or another educational institution.**
List people you would like to interview or to whom you wish to send questionnaires and state conditions under which the study will be conducted.

4 **Decide what you mean by anonymity and confidentiality.**
Remember that if you are writing about 'the head of English' and there is only one head of English in the school, the person concerned is immediately recognizable.

5 **Decide whether participants will receive a copy of the report and/or see drafts or interview transcripts.**
There are cost and time implications. Think carefully before you make promises.

6 **Inform participants what is to be done with the information they provide.**
Your eyes and those of the examiner only? Shown to the head, the LEA etc.?

7 **Prepare an outline of intentions and conditions under which the study will be carried out to hand to the participants.**
Even if you explain the purpose of the study the conditions and the guarantees, participants may forget.

8 **Be honest about the purpose of the study and about the conditions of the research.**
If you say an interview will last ten minutes, you will break faith if it lasts an hour. If you are conducting the investigation as part of a degree or diploma course, say so.

9 **Remember that people who agree to help are doing you a favour.**
Make sure you return papers and books in good order and on time. Letters of thanks should be sent, no matter how busy you are.

10 **Never assume 'it will be all right'. Negotiating access is an important stage in your investigation.**
If you are an inside researcher, you will have to live with your mistakes, so take care.

Source Adapted from Bell, 1991

pause and remind ourselves that a considerable amount of research does not cause pain or indignity to the participants, that self-esteem is not necessarily undermined nor confidences betrayed, and that the social scientist may only infrequently be confronted with an unresolvable ethical dilemma. Where research is ethically sensitive, however, many factors may need to be taken into account and these may vary from situation to situation. By way of example, we identify a selection of such variables, the prior consideration of which will perhaps reduce the number of problems subsequently faced by the researcher. Thus, the age of those being researched; whether the

subject matter of the research is a sensitive area; whether the aims of the research are in any way subversive (vis-à-vis subjects, teachers, or institution); the extent to which the researcher and researched can participate and collaborate in planning the research; how the data are to be processed, interpreted, and used (and Laing (1967: 53) offers an interesting, cautionary view of data where he writes that they are 'not so much given as *taken* out of a constantly elusive matrix of happenings. We should speak of *capta* rather than data'); the dissemination of results; and guarantees of confidentiality are just some of the parameters that can form the basis of, to use Aronson and Carlsmith's phrase, 'a specification of democratic ethics'. Readers will no doubt be in a position to develop their own schema from the ideas and concepts expressed in this chapter as well as from their own widening experience as researchers.

Sources of tension

We noted earlier that the question of ethics in research is a highly complex subject. This complexity stems from numerous sources of tension. We consider two of the most important. The first, as expressed by Aronson and Carlsmith (1969), is the tension that exists between two sets of related values held by society: a belief in the value of free scientific inquiry in pursuit of truth and knowledge; and a belief in the dignity of individuals and their right to those considerations that follow from it. It is this polarity that we referred to earlier as the costs/benefits ratio and by which 'greater consideration must be given to the risks to physical, psychological, humane, proprietary and cultural values than to the potential contribution of research to knowledge' (Social Sciences and Humanities Research Council of Canada, 1981), i.e. the issue of 'non-maleficence' (where no harm befalls the subjects). When researchers are confronted with this dilemma (and it is likely to occur much less in education than in social psychology or medicine), it is generally considered that they resolve it in a manner that avoids the extremes of, on the one hand, giving up the idea of research and, on the other, ignoring the rights of the subjects. At all times, the welfare of subjects should be kept in mind (though this has not always been the case, as we shall see), even if it involves compromising the impact of the research. Researchers should never lose sight of the obligations they owe to those who are helping, and should constantly be on the alert for alternative techniques should the ones they are employing at the time prove controversial (see the penultimate paragraph in this chapter on personal codes of ethical practice). Indeed, this polarity between the research and the researched

is reflected in the principles of the American Psychological Association who, as Zechmeister and Shaughnessy (1992) show, attempt to strike a balance between the rights of investigators to seek an understanding of human behaviour, and the rights and welfare of individuals who participate in the research. In the final reckoning, the decision to go ahead with a research project rests on a subjective evaluation of the costs both to the individual and society.

The second source of tension in this context is that generated by the competing absolutist and relativist positions. The absolutist view holds that clear, set principles should guide the researchers in their work and that these should determine what ought and what ought not to be done (see Box 2.6). To have taken a wholly absolutist stance, for example, in the case of the Stanford Prison Experiment (see Chapter 21) where the researchers studied interpersonal dynamics in a simulated prison, would have meant that the experiment should not have taken place at all or that it should have been terminated well before the sixth day. Zimbardo has stated the ethical position:

Box 2.6
Absolute ethical principles in social research

> Ethics embody individual and communal codes of conduct based upon adherence to a set of principles which may be explicit and codified or implicit and which may be abstract and impersonal or concrete and personal. For the sake of brevity, we may say that ethics can be dichotomized as 'absolute' and 'relative'. When behaviour is guided by absolute ethical standards, a higher-order moral principle can be postulated which is *invariant* with regard to the conditions of its applicability – across time, situations, persons and expediency. Such principled ethics allow no degree of freedom for ends to justify means or for any positive consequences to qualify instances where the principle is suspended or applied in an altered, watered-down form. In the extreme, there are no extenuating circumstances to be considered or weighed as justifying an abrogation of the ethical standard.

Source Zimbardo, 1984

To search for those conditions which justify experiments that induce human suffering is not an appropriate enterprise to anyone who believes in the absolute ethical principle that human life is sacred and must not in any way be knowingly demeaned physically or mentally by experimental interventions. From such a position it is even reasonable to maintain that *no* research should be conducted in psychology or medicine which violates the biological or psychological integrity of any human being regardless of the benefits that might, or even would definitely, accrue to the society at large.

(Zimbardo, 1984)

By this absolute principle, the Stanford Prison Experiment must be regarded as unethical because the participants suffered considerably.

Those who hold a relativist position, by contrast to this, would argue that there can be no absolute guidelines and that the ethical considerations will arise from the very nature of the particular research being pursued at the time: situation determines behaviour. There are some contexts, however, where neither the absolutist nor the relativist position is clear cut. Writing of the application of the principle of informed consent with respect to life history studies, Plummer says:

Both sides have a weakness. If, for instance, as the absolutists usually insist, there should be informed consent, it may leave relatively privileged groups under-researched (since they will say 'no') and underprivileged groups over-researched (they have nothing to lose and say 'yes' in hope). If the individual conscience is the guide, as the relativists insist, the door is wide open for the unscrupulous – even immoral – researcher.

(Plummer, 1983)

He suggests that broad guidelines laid down by professional bodies which offer the researcher room for personal ethical choice are a way out of the problem. Raffe *et al.* (1989) have identified other sources of tension which arose in their own research: that between different ethical principles, for instance, and between groups and other individuals or groups. Before we consider the problems set by ethical dilemmas, we touch upon one or two other trip-wires disclosed by empirical research.

Voices of experience

Whatever the ethical stance one assumes and no matter what forethought one brings to bear on one's work, there will always be unknown, unforeseen problems and difficulties lying in wait (Kimmel, 1988). It may therefore be of assistance to readers if we dip into the literature and identify some of these. Baumrind (1964), for example, warns of the possible failure on the researchers' part to perceive a positive indebtedness to their subjects for their services, perhaps, she suggests, because the detachment which investigators bring to their task prevents appreciation of subjects as individuals. This kind of omission can be averted if the experimenters are prepared to spend a few minutes with subjects afterwards in order to thank them for their participation, answer their questions, reassure them that they did well, and generally talk to them for a time. If the research involves subjects in a failure experience, isolation, or loss of self-esteem, for example, researchers must ensure that the subjects do not leave the situation more humiliated, insecure, and alienated than when they arrived. From the subject's point of view, procedures which involve loss of dignity, injury to self-esteem, or affect trust in rational authority are probably most harmful in the long run and may require the most carefully organized ways of recompensing the subject in some way if the researcher chooses to carry on with such methods. With particularly sensitive areas, participants need to be fully informed of the dangers of serious after-effects. There is reason to believe that at least some of the obedient subjects in Milgram's (1963) experiments (see Chapter 21) came away from the experience with a lower self-esteem, having to live with the realization that they were willing to yield to destructive authority to the point of inflicting extreme pain on a fellow human being (Kelman, 1967). It follows that researchers need to reflect attitudes of compassion, respect, gratitude and common sense without being too effusive. Subjects clearly have a right to expect that the researchers with whom they are interacting have some concern for the welfare of participants. Further, the subject's sensibilities need also to be taken into account when the researcher comes to write up the research. There have been notorious instances in the research literature when even experienced researchers have shown scant regard for subjects' feelings at the report stage. A related and not insignificant issue concerns the formal recognition of those who have assisted in the investigation, if such be the case. This means that whatever form the written account takes, be it a report, article, chapter, or course thesis, and no matter the readership for which it is intended, its authors must acknowledge and thank all who helped in the research, even to the extent of identifying by name those whose contribution was significant. This can be done in a foreword, introduction or footnote. All this is really a question of common-sensical ethics, an approach that will go a long way in enabling researchers to overcome many of the challenges that beset them.

Ethical problems in educational research can often result from thoughtlessness, oversight, or taking matters for granted. For example, a researcher may be completely oblivious to attendant moral issues and perceive his or her work in an ethical void (not to be compared with the situation where a researcher knowingly treats moral issues as if they do not matter, with, as it were, 'metaethical disdain'). Again, researchers engaged in sponsored research may feel they do not have to deal with ethical issues, believing their sponsors to have them in hand.

Likewise, each researcher in a collaborative venture may take it for granted, wrongly, that colleagues have the relevant ethical questions in mind; consequently, appropriate precautions go by default. A student whose research is part of a course requirement and who is motivated wholly by self-interest, or the academic researchers with professional advancement in mind, may overlook the 'oughts' and 'ought nots'. There is nothing wrong with either motivation providing that eth-

ical issues are borne in mind. Finally, researchers should beware of adopting *modi operandi* in which correct ethical procedure unwittingly becomes a victim of convenience.

Ethical dilemmas

At the beginning of this chapter, we spoke of the costs/benefits ratio. This has been explained by Frankfort-Nachmias and Nachmias as a conflict between two rights which they express as:

> the right to research and acquire knowledge and the right of individual research participants to self-determination, privacy and dignity. A decision not to conduct a planned research project because it interferes with the participants' welfare is a limit on the first of these rights. A decision to conduct research despite an ethically questionable practice … is a limit on the second right.
>
> (Frankfort-Nachmias and Nachmias, 1992)

This constitutes the fundamental ethical dilemma of the social scientist for whom there are no absolute right or wrong answers. Which proposition is favoured, or how a balance between the two is struck will depend very much on the background, experience, and personal values of the individual researcher. With this issue in mind, we now examine other dilemmas that may confront investigators once they have come to some accommodation with this fundamental dilemma and decided to proceed with their research.

Privacy

For the most part, individual 'right to privacy' is usually contrasted with public 'right to know' (Pring, 1984) and this has been defined in the *Ethical Guidelines for the Institutional Review Committee for Research with Human Subjects* as that which:

> extends to all information relating to a person's physical and mental condition, personal circumstances and social relationships which is not already in the public domain. It gives to the individual or

collectivity the freedom to decide for themselves when and where, in what circumstances and to what extent their personal attitudes, opinions, habits, eccentricities, doubts and fears are to be communicated to or withheld from others.

(Social Sciences and Humanities Research Council of Canada, 1981)

In the context of research, therefore, 'right to privacy' may easily be violated during the course of an investigation or denied after it has been completed. At either point the participant is vulnerable.

Privacy has been considered from three different perspectives by Diener and Crandall (1978). These are: the sensitivity of the information being given, the setting being observed, and dissemination of information. Sensitivity of information refers to how personal or potentially threatening the information is that is being collected by the researcher. Certain kinds of information are more personal than others and may be more threatening. According to a report by the American Psychological Association for example, 'Religious preferences, sexual practices, income, racial prejudices, and other personal attributes such as intelligence, honesty, and courage are more sensitive items than "name, rank, and serial number"' (American Psychological Association, 1973). Thus, the greater the sensitivity of the information, the more safeguards are called for to protect the privacy of the research participant. The setting being observed may vary from very private to completely public. The home, for example, is considered one of the most private settings, and intrusions into people's homes without their consent are forbidden by law. Dissemination of information concerns the ability to match personal information with the identity of the research participants. Indeed, personal data are defined at law as those data which uniquely identify the individual providing them. When such information is publicized with names through the media, for example, privacy is seriously violated. The more people there are who can learn about the information, the more concern there must be about privacy (see Diener and Crandall, 1978).

As is the case with most rights, privacy can be voluntarily relinquished. Research participants may choose to give up their right to privacy by either allowing a researcher access to sensitive topics or settings or by agreeing that the research report may identify them by name. The latter case at least would be an occasion where informed consent would need to be sought.

Generally speaking, if researchers intend to probe into the private aspects or affairs of individuals, their intentions should be made clear and explicit and informed consent should be sought from those who are to be observed or scrutinized in private contexts. Other methods to protect participants are anonymity and confidentiality and our examination of these follows.

Anonymity

As Frankfort-Nachmias and Nachmias say, 'The obligation to protect the anonymity of research participants and to keep research data confidential is all-inclusive. It should be fulfilled at all costs unless arrangements to the contrary are made with the participants in advance' (Frankfort-Nachmias and Nachmias, 1992).

The essence of anonymity is that information provided by participants should in no way reveal their identity. The obverse of this is, as we saw earlier, personal data that uniquely identify their supplier. A participant or subject is therefore considered anonymous when the researcher or another person cannot identify the participant or subject from the information provided. Where this situation holds, a participant's privacy is guaranteed, no matter how personal or sensitive the information is. Thus a respondent completing a questionnaire that bears absolutely no identifying marks – names, addresses, occupational details, or coding symbols – is ensured complete and total anonymity. A subject agreeing to a face-to-face interview, on the other hand, can in no way expect anonymity. At most, the interviewer can promise confidentiality. Non-traceability is an important matter, and this extends to aggregating data in some cases, so that an individual's response is not identifiable.

The principal means of ensuring anonymity then, is not using the names of the participants or any other personal means of identification. Further ways of achieving anonymity have been listed by Frankfort-Nachmias and Nachmias as follows:

> participants may be asked to use an alias of their own creation or to transfer well-remembered personal data (birthdays or National Insurance number, for instance). Anonymity may be enhanced if names and other identifiers are linked to the information by a code number. Once the data have been prepared for analysis, anonymity can be maintained by separating identifying information from the research data. Further safeguards include the prevention of duplication of records and passwords to control access to data.
>
> (Frankfort-Nachmias and Nachmias, 1992)[3]

These directives may work satisfactorily in most situations, but as Raffe and his colleagues (1989) have shown, there is sometimes the difficulty of maintaining an assurance of anonymity when, for example, categorization of data may uniquely identify an individual or institution or when there is access to incoming returns by support staff. Plummer (1983), likewise, refers to life studies in which names have been changed, places shifted, and fictional events added to prevent acquaintances of subjects discovering their identity. Although one can go a long way down this path, there is no absolute guarantee of total anonymity as far as life studies are concerned. Fortunately, in experimental social psychological research the experimenter is interested in 'human' behaviour rather than in the behaviour of specific individuals, as Aronson and Carlsmith (1969) note. Consequently the researcher has absolutely no interest in linking the person as a unique, named individual to actual behaviour, and the research data can be transferred to coded, unnamed data sheets. As they comment, 'the very impersonality of the process is a great advantage ethically because it eliminates some of the negative consequences of the invasion of privacy' (Aronson and Carlsmith, 1969: 33).

Confidentiality

The second way of protecting a participant's right to privacy is through the promise of confidentiality. This means that although researchers know who has provided the information or are able to identify participants from the information given, they will in no way make the connection known publicly; the boundaries surrounding the shared secret will be protected. The essence of the matter is the extent to which investigators keep faith with those who have helped them. It is generally at the access stage or at the point where researchers collect their data that they make their position clear to the hosts and/or subjects. They will thus be quite explicit in explaining to subjects what the meaning and limits of confidentiality are in relation to the particular research project. On the whole, the more sensitive, intimate, or discrediting the information, the greater is the obligation on the researcher's part to make sure that guarantees of confidentiality are carried out in spirit and letter. Promises must be taken seriously.

In his account of confidentiality and the right to privacy, Kimmel (1988) notes that one general finding that emerges from the empirical literature is that some potential respondents in research on sensitive topics will refuse to co-operate when an assurance of confidentiality is weak, vague, not understood, or thought likely to be breached. He concludes that the usefulness of data in sensitive research areas may be seriously affected by the researcher's inability to provide a credible promise of confidentiality. Assurances do not appear to affect co-operation rates in innocuous studies perhaps because, as Kimmel suggests, there is expectation on the part of most potential respondents that confidentiality will be protected.

A number of techniques have been developed to allow public access to data and information without confidentiality being betrayed. These have been listed by Frankfort-Nachmias and Nachmias (1992) as follows:

1   Deletion of identifiers (for example, deleting the names, addresses, or other means of identification from the data released on individuals).

2   Crude report categories (for example, releasing the year of birth rather than the specific date, profession but not the speciality within that profession, general information rather than specific).

3   Microaggregation (that is, the construction of 'average persons' from data on individuals and the release of these data, rather than data on individuals).

4   Error inoculation (deliberately introducing errors into individual records while leaving the aggregate data unchanged). Such techniques ensure that the notion of non-traceability is upheld.

Betrayal

The term 'betrayal' is usually applied to those occasions where data disclosed in confidence are revealed publicly in such a way as to cause embarrassment, anxiety, or perhaps suffering to the subject or participant disclosing the information. It is a breach of trust, in contrast to confidentiality, and is often a consequence of selfish motives of either a personal or professional nature. Plummer comments, 'in sociology, there is something slightly awry when a sociologist can enter a group and a person's life for a lengthy period, learn their most closely guarded secrets, and then expose all in a critical light to the public' (Plummer, 1983). One of the research methods we deal with in this book that is perhaps most vulnerable to betrayal is action research. As Kelly (1989a) notes, this can produce several ethical problems. She says that if we treat teachers as collaborators in our day-to-day interactions, it may seem like betrayal of trust if these interactions are recorded and used as evidence. This is particularly the case where the evidence is negative. One way out, Kelly suggests, could be

to submit reports and evaluations of teachers' reactions to the teachers involved for comment; to get them to assess their own changing attitudes. She warns, however, that this might work well with teachers who have become converts, but is more problematic where teachers remain indifferent or hostile to the aims of the research project. How does one write an honest but critical report of teachers' attitudes, she asks, if one hopes to continue to work with those involved? As she concludes, 'Our position lies uncomfortably between that of the internal evaluator whose main loyalty is to colleagues and the school, and the external researcher for whom informal comments and small incidents may provide the most revealing data' (Kelly, 1989a).

Deception

The use of deception in social psychological and sociological research has attracted a certain amount of adverse publicity. In social psychological research, the term is applied to that kind of experimental situation where the researcher knowingly conceals the true purpose and conditions of the research, or else positively misinforms the subjects, or exposes them to unduly painful, stressful or embarrassing experiences, without the subjects having knowledge of what is going on. The deception lies in not telling the whole truth. Advocates of the method feel that if a deception experiment is the only way to discover something of real importance, the truth so discovered is worth the lies told in the process, so long as no harm comes to the subject (see Aronson et al., 1990). Objections to the technique, on the other hand, are listed in Chapter 21, where the approach is contrasted with role playing. The problem from the researcher's point of view is: 'What is the proper balance between the interests of science and the thoughtful, humane treatment of people who, innocently, provide the data?' In other words, the problem again hinges on the costs/benefits ratio.

The pervasiveness of the problem of deception becomes even more apparent when we remember that it is even built into many of our measurement devices, since it is important to keep the respondent ignorant of the personality and attitude dimensions that we wish to investigate.

There are many problems that cannot be investigated without deception and although there is some evidence that most subjects accept without resentment the fact of having been duped once they understand the necessity for it (see, for instance, Festinger and Katz, 1966), it is important to keep in the forefront of one's mind the question of whether the amount and type of deception is justified by the significance of the study and the unavailability of alternative procedures.

Ethical considerations loom particularly large when second-order deception is involved; that is, letting persons believe they are acting as researchers or researchers' accomplices when they are in fact serving as the subjects (i.e., as unknowing participants). Such procedures can undermine the relationship between the researcher and subject even more than simply misinforming them. The use of deception resulting in particularly harmful consequences would be another occasion where ethical considerations would need to be given priority. An example here would be the study by Campbell, Sanderson and Laverty (1964) which created extremely stressful conditions by using drugs to induce temporary interruption of breathing (see Box 2.7).

Kelman (1967) has suggested three ways of dealing with the problem of deception. First, it is important that we increase our active awareness that it exists as a problem. It is crucial that we always ask ourselves the question whether deception is necessary and justified. We must be wary of the tendency to dismiss the question as irrelevant and to accept deception as a matter of course. Active awareness is thus in itself part of the solution, for it makes the use of deception a focus for discussion, deliberation, investigation, and choice.

The second way of approaching the problem concerns counteracting and minimizing the negative effects of deception. For example, subjects must be selected in a way that will exclude indi-

Box 2.7
An extreme case of deception

In an experiment designed to study the establishment of a conditioned response in a situation that is traumatic but not painful, Campbell, Sanderson and Laverty induced – through the use of a drug – a temporary interruption of respiration in their subjects. The subjects' reports confirmed that this was a 'horrific' experience for them. All the subjects thought they were dying. The subjects, male alcoholic patients who had volunteered for the experiment when they were told that it was connected with a possible therapy for alcoholism, were not warned in advance about the effect of the drug, since this information would have reduced the traumatic impact of the experience.

Source Adapted from Kelman, 1967

viduals who are especially vulnerable; any potentially harmful manipulation must be kept to a moderate level of intensity; researchers must be sensitive to danger signals in the reactions of subjects and be prepared to deal with crises when they arise; and at the conclusion of the research, they must take time not only to reassure subjects, but also help them work through their feelings about the experience to whatever degree may be required. The principle that subjects ought not to leave the research situation with greater anxiety or lower levels of self-esteem than they came with is a good one to follow (the issue of non-maleficence again). Desirably, subjects should be enriched by the experience and should leave it with the feeling that they have learned something.

The primary way of counteracting negative effects of research employing deception is to ensure that adequate feedback is provided at the end of the research or research session. Feedback must be kept inviolable and in no circumstances should subjects be given false feedback or be misled into thinking they are receiving feedback when the researcher is in fact introducing another experimental manipulation.

Even here, however, there are dangers. As Aronson and Carlsmith say:

debriefing a subject is not simply a matter of exposing him to the truth. There is nothing magically curative about the truth; indeed . . . if harshly presented, the truth can be more harmful than no explanation at all. There are vast differences in how this is accomplished, and it is precisely these differences that are of crucial importance in determining whether or not a subject is uncomfortable when he leaves the experimental room.

(Aronson and Carlsmith, 1969: 31)

They consider that the one essential aspect of the debriefing process is that researchers communicate their own sincerity as scientists seeking the truth and their own discomfort about the fact that they found it necessary to resort to deception in order to uncover the truth. As they say, 'No amount of postexperimental gentleness is as effective in relieving a subject's discomfort as an honest accounting of the experimenter's *own* discomfort in the situation' (Aronson and Carlsmith, 1969: 31–2).

The third way of dealing with the problem of deception is to ensure that new procedures and novel techniques are developed. It is a question of tapping one's own creativity in the quest for alternative methods. It has been suggested that role-playing, or 'as-if' experiments, could prove a worthwhile avenue to explore – the 'role-playing versus deception' debate we raise in Chapter 21. By this method, as we shall see, the subject is asked to behave as if he/she were a particular person in a particular situation. Whatever form they take, however, new approaches will involve a radically different set of assumptions about the role of the subject in this type of research. They require us to use subjects' motivations rather than bypassing them. They may even call for increasing the sophistication of potential subjects, rather than maintaining their naivety.

Plummer (1983) informs us that even in an unlikely area like life history, deceptions of a lesser nature occur. Thus, for example, the general description given of research may leave out some key issues; indeed, to tell the subject what it is you are looking for may bias the outcome quite substantially. Further, different accounts of

the research may have to be presented to different groups. He quotes an instance from his own research, a study of sexual minorities, which required various levels of release – for the subjects, for colleagues, for general inquiries, and for outside friends. None of these accounts actually lied, they merely emphasized a different aspect of the research.

In the social sciences, the dilemma of deception, as we have seen, has played an important part in experimental social psychology where subjects are not told the true nature of the experiment. Another area where it has been increasingly used in recent years is that of sociology, where researchers conceal their identities and 'con' their way into alien groups – the overt/covert debate (Mitchell, 1993). Covert, or secret participation, then, refers to that kind of research where researchers spend an extended period of time in particular research settings, concealing the fact that they are researchers and pretending to play some other role. Bulmer (1982) notes that such methods have produced an extremely lively on-going debate and that there are no simple and universally agreed answers to the ethical issues the method produces. Erikson (1967), for example, makes a number of points against covert research; among them, that sociologists have responsibilities to their subjects in general and that secret research can injure other people in ways that cannot be anticipated or compensated for afterwards; and that sociologists have responsibilities towards fellow-sociologists. Douglas (1976), by contrast, argues that covert observation is a necessary, useful and revealing method. And Bulmer (1982) concludes that the most compelling argument in favour of covert observation is that it has produced good social science which would not have been possible without the method. It would be churlish, he adds, not to recognize that the use of covert methods has advanced our understanding of society.

The final word on the subject of deception in general goes to Kimmel (1988) who claims that few researchers feel that they can do without deception entirely, since the adoption of an overtly conservative approach could deem the study of important research hardly worth the effort. A study of racial prejudice, for example, accurately labelled as such would certainly affect the behaviour of the subjects taking part. Deception studies, he considers, differ so greatly that even the harshest critics would be hard pressed to state unequivocally that all deception has potentially harmful effects on participants or is otherwise wrong. We turn now to research methods used in educational settings and to some ethical issues associated with them.

Ethics and research methods in education

Ethical problems arising from research methods used in educational contexts occur *passim* in Burgess's (1989a) edited collection of papers, *The Ethics of Educational Research*, and the book is recommended to readers for their perusal. Burgess himself considers ethical issues emerging from ethnographic research (1989b). Similar themes characterize Riddell's paper in which she examines feminist research in two rural comprehensive schools. Her work illustrates how feminist investigations raise questions about honesty, power relations, the responsibility of the researcher to the researched, and collaboration. Corresponding topics are broached for action researchers by Kelly (1989b), who was co-director of the 'Girls into Science and Technology' project, a study focusing on girls' under-involvement in science and technology. A range of questions are considered – researcher power and values, the problem of informed consent, and the manner in which research data are presented to the participants in the project with respect to empirical research are considered in the second part of the book.

Reflection on the articles in Burgess (1989a) will show that the issues thrown up by the complexities of research methods in educational institutions and their ethical consequences are probably among the least anticipated, particularly among the more inexperienced researchers.

The latter need to be aware of those kinds of research which, by their nature, lead from one problem to another. Serial problems of this sort may arise in survey methods or ethnographic studies, for example, or in action research or the evaluation of developments. Indeed, the researcher will frequently find that methodological and ethical issues are inextricably interwoven in much of the research we have designated as qualitative or interpretive. As Hitchcock and Hughes note:

> Doing participant observation or interviewing one's peers raises ethical problems that are directly related to the nature of the research technique employed. The degree of openness or closure of the nature of the research and its aims is one that directly faces the teacher researcher.
> (Hitchcock and Hughes, 1989: 199)

They go on to pose the kinds of question that may arise in such a situation. 'Where for the researcher does formal observation end and informal observation begin?' 'Is it justifiable to be open with some teachers and closed with others?' 'How much can the researcher tell the pupils about a particular piece of research?' 'When is a casual conversation part of the research data and when is it not?' 'Is gossip legitimate data and can the researcher ethically use material that has been passed on in confidence?' As Hitchcock and Hughes conclude, the list of questions is endless yet they can be related to the nature of both the research technique involved and the social organization of the setting being investigated. The key to the successful resolution of such questions lies in establishing good relations. This will involve the development of a sense of rapport between researchers and their subjects that will lead to feelings of trust and confidence. Mention must be made once again in this particular context of the work of Fine and Sandstrom (1988) who discuss in some detail the ethical and practical aspects of doing field-work with children. In particular they show how the ethical implications of participant observation research differ with the age of the children. Another feature of qualitative methods in this connection has been identified by Finch who observes that:

> there can be acute ethical and political dilemmas about how the material produced is *used*, both by the researcher her/himself, and by other people. Such questions are not absent in quantitative research, but greater distancing of the researcher from the research subjects may make them less personally agonizing. Further, in ethnographic work or depth interviewing, the researcher is very much in a position of trust in being accorded privileged access to information which is usually private or invisible. Working out how to ensure that such trust is not betrayed is no simple matter . . . Where qualitative research is targeted upon social policy issues, there is the special dilemma that findings could be used to worsen the situation of the target population in some way.
>
> (Finch, 1985)

Kelly's (1989a) paper would seem to suggest, as we have noted elsewhere in this chapter, that the area in qualitative research where one's ethical antennae need to be especially sensitive is that of action research, and it is here that researchers, be they teachers or outsiders, must show particular awareness of the traps that lie in wait. These difficulties have been nowhere better summed up than in Hopkins when he says:

> [The researchers'] actions are deeply embedded in an existing social organization and the failure to work within the general procedures of that organization may not only jeopardize the process of improvement but existing valuable work. Principles of procedures for action research accordingly go beyond the usual concerns for confidentiality and respect for persons who are the subjects of enquiry and define in addition, appropriate ways of working with other participants in the social organization.
>
> (Hopkins, 1985: 135)

Box 2.8 presents a set of principles specially formulated for action researchers by Kemmis and McTaggart (1981) and quoted by Hopkins (1985).

We conclude by reminding readers who may

become involved in action research that the problem of access is not resolved once one has been given permission to use the school or organization. The advice given by Hammersley and Atkinson with respect to ethnographic research is equally applicable to action research. As they say:

> [having] gained entry to a setting . . . by no means guarantees access to all the data available within it. Not all parts of the setting will be equally open to observation, not everyone may be willing to talk, and even the most willing informant will not be prepared, or perhaps even able, to divulge all the information available to him or her. If the data required to develop and test the theory are to be acquired, negotiation of access is therefore likely to be a recurrent preoccupation for the ethnographer.
>
> (Hammersley and Atkinson, 1983: 76)

As the authors observe, different kinds of data will demand different roles, and these in turn result in varying ethical principles being applied to the various negotiating stances.

Ethics and teacher evaluation

After our brief excursus on the problems of ethics in relation to action research, an approach to classroom activities frequently concerned with the improvement of teacher performance and efficiency, it would seem logical to acknowledge the role and importance of ethics in teacher evaluation. The appraisal of teacher and headteacher performance is one that is going to play an increasingly important part as accountability, teacher needs, and management efficiency assume greater significance, as governments introduce pedagogic and curricular changes, and as market forces exert pressure on the educational system generally. By thus throwing teacher appraisal into greater relief, it becomes very important that training appraisal programmes are planned and designed in such a way as to give due recognition to the ethical implications at both school and LEA levels. With this in mind, we briefly review some basic principles

Box 2.8
Ethical principles for the guidance of action researchers

Observe protocol: Take care to ensure that the relevant persons, committees, and authorities have been consulted, informed and that the necessary permission and approval have been obtained.

Involve participants: Encourage others who have a stake in the improvement you envisage to shape and form the work.

Negotiate with those affected: Not everyone will want to be directly involved; your work should take account of the responsibilities and wishes of others.

Report progress: Keep the work visible and remain open to suggestions so that unforeseen and unseen ramifications can be taken account of; colleagues must have the opportunity to lodge a protest to you.

Obtain explicit authorizations: This applies where you wish to observe your professional colleagues; and where you wish to examine documentation.

Negotiate descriptions of people's work: Always allow those described to challenge your accounts on the grounds of fairness, relevance and accuracy.

Negotiate accounts of others' points of view (e.g. in accounts of communication): Always allow those involved in interviews, meetings and written exchanges to require amendments which enhance fairness, relevance and accuracy.

Obtain explicit authorization before using quotations: Verbatim transcripts, attributed observations, excerpts of audio and video recordings, judgements, conclusions or recommendations in reports (written or to meetings).

Negotiate reports for various levels of release: Remember that different audiences require different kinds of reports; what is appropriate for an informal verbal report to a faculty meeting may not be appropriate for a staff meeting, a report to council, a journal article, a newspaper, a newsletter to parents; be conservative if you cannot control distribution.

Accept responsibility for maintaining confidentiality.

Retain the right to report your work: Provided that those involved are satisfied with the fairness, accuracy and relevance of accounts which pertain to them, and that the accounts do not unnecessarily expose or embarrass those involved, then accounts should not be subject to veto or be sheltered by prohibitions of confidentiality.

Make your principles of procedure binding and known: All of the people involved in your action research project must agree to the principles before the work begins; others must be aware of their rights in the process.

Source Adapted from Kemmis and McTaggart (1981) and quoted in Hopkins (1985)

and concepts formulated in the USA that may sensitize all those involved in appraisal procedures to the concomitant ethical factors.

Strike (1990), in his paper on the ethics of educational evaluation, offers two broad principles which may form the basis of further considerations in the field of evaluation. These are the principle of benefit maximization and the principle of equal respect. The former, the principle of benefit maximization, holds that the best decision is the one that results in the greatest benefit for most people. It is pragmatic in the sense that it judges the rightness of our actions by their consequences or, as Strike says, the best action is the one with the best results. In British philosophical circles it is known as utilitarianism and requires us to identify the particular benefits we wish to maximize, to identify a suitable population for maximization, specify what is to count as maximization, and fully understand the consequences of our actions. The second principle, that of equal respect, demands that we respect the equal worth of all people. This requires us to treat people as ends rather than means; to regard them as free and rational; and to accept that they are entitled to the same basic rights as others.

Strike then goes on to list the following ethical principles which he regards as particularly important to teacher evaluation and which may be seen in the light of the two broad principles outlined above:

1   *Due process* Evaluative procedures must ensure that judgements are reasonable: that known and accepted standards are consistently applied from case to case, that evidence is reasonable and that there are systematic and reasonable procedures for collecting and testing evidence.

2   *Privacy* This involves a right to control information about oneself, and protects people from unwarranted interference in their affairs. In evaluation, it requires that procedures are not overtly intrusive and that such evaluation pertains only to those aspects of a teacher's activity that are job related. It also protects the confidentiality of evaluation information.

3   *Equality* In the context of evaluation, this can best be understood as a prohibition against making decisions on irrelevant grounds, such as race, religion, gender, ethnicity or sexual orientation.

4   *Public perspicuity* This principle requires openness to the public concerning evaluative procedures, their purposes and their results.

5   *Humaneness* This principle requires that consideration is shown to the feelings and sensitivities of those in evaluative contexts.

6   *Client benefit* This principle requires that evaluative decisions are made in a way that respects the interests of students, parents and the public, in preference to those of educational institutions and their staff. This extends to treating participants as subjects rather than as 'research fodder'.

7   *Academic freedom* This requires that an atmosphere of intellectual openness is maintained in the classroom for both teachers and students. Evaluation should not be conducted in a way that chills this environment.

8   *Respect for autonomy* Teachers are entitled to reasonable discretion in, and to exercise reasonable judgement about, their work. Evaluations should not be conducted so as to unreasonably restrict discretion and judgement.

Strike has developed these principles in a more extended and systematic form in his article. Finally, we note the three principles that Strike applies to the task of conflict resolution, to resolving the differences between teachers and the institutions in which they work as a result of the evaluation process. He recommends that where a conflict has to be resolved, remediation is to be preferred, where possible, to disciplinary action or termination; mediation is to be preferred, where possible, to more litigious forms and solutions; and that informal attempts to settle disputes should precede formal ones.

We have seen throughout this chapter and in this particular section how the codification and regulation of ethical principles is proceeding apace in the USA; and that this is occurring at both a formal and informal level. In this next, penultimate, section we look a little closer at these matters and their implications for the UK.

Research and regulation

A glance at any current American textbook in the social sciences will reveal the extent to which professional researchers in the USA are governed by laws and regulations (Zechmeister and Shaughnessy, 1992). These exist at several levels: federal and state legal statutes, ethics review committees to oversee research in universities and other institutions (these can constitute a major hurdle for those planning to undertake research), ethical codes of the professional bodies and associations as well as the personal ethics of individual researchers are all important regulatory mechanisms. All investigators, from undergraduates pursuing a course-based research project to professional researchers striving at the frontiers of knowledge, must take cognizance of the ethical codes and regulations governing their practice. Indeed, we have sampled some of the ethical research requirements of American investigators in this chapter. Failure to meet these responsibilities on the part of researchers is perceived as undermining the whole scientific process and may lead to legal and financial penalties for individuals and institutions.

If Britain has not yet gone as far as the USA down this path of regulation and litigation, it may only be a question of time. Even in the UK, however, professional societies have formulated working codes of practice which express the consensus of values within a particular group and which help individual researchers in indicating what is desirable and what is to be avoided. Of course, this does not solve all the problems, for there are few absolutes and in consequence ethical principles may be open to a wide range of interpretations. In addition, more informal codes of ethical principles have emerged as a result of individual initiative. The establishment of comprehensive regulatory mechanisms is thus well in hand in the UK, but it is perhaps in the field of information and data – how they are stored and the uses to which they are put, for example – that educational researchers are likely to find growing interest. This category would include, for instance, statistical data, data used as the basis for evaluation, curricular records, written records, transcripts, data sheets, personal documents, research data, computer files, and audio and video recordings.

As information technology establishes itself in a centre-stage position and as society becomes increasingly dependent on information economically and functionally, so we realize just how important the concept of information is to us. It is important not only for what it is, but for what it can do. Numerous writers have pointed out the connection between information and power. Harris, Pearce and Johnstone (1992), for instance, say:

> Information and power have a very close relationship . . . Power over individuals . . . relies on the control of personal information. Power of professionalism involves both submission of the client to the professional's better judgment and a network of professional and inter-professional relationships, and probably rivalries, buttressed by exclusive sharing of information. It is well to recognize that decisions about information-holding or access are, to an extent, always decisions about power.
>
> (Harris, Pearce and Johnstone, 1992)

When we reflect on the extent to which two key concepts in the world of contemporary education, namely 'evaluation' (or appraisal) and 'accountability', depend wholly on information in one form or another, that it is their very life blood, we realize just how powerful it is. Its misuse, therefore, or disclosure at the wrong time or to the wrong client or organ, can result in the most unfortunate consequences for an individual, group, or institution. And matters are greatly exacerbated if it is the wrong information, or incomplete, or deliberately misleading.

In an increasingly information-rich world, it is essential that safeguards be established to protect it from misuse or abuse. The Data Protection Act (1984) was designed to achieve such an end. This covered the principles of data protection, the responsibilities of data users, and the rights of data subjects, and its broad aims are embodied in eight principles. However, data held for 'historical and research' purposes are exempted from the principle which gives individuals the right of access to personal data about themselves, provided the data are not made available in a form which identifies individuals. Research data also have partial exemption from two further principles, with the effect that such data may be held indefinitely and the use of the data for research purposes need not be disclosed at the time of data collection.

Of the two most important principles which do concern research data, one states that personal data (i.e., data that uniquely identifies the person supplying it) shall be held only for specified and lawful purposes. The second principle states that appropriate security measures shall be taken against unauthorized access to, or alteration, disclosure, or destruction of personal data and against accidental loss or destruction of personal data. For a study of the effects of the Data Protection Act on the work of the Centre for Educational Sociology, see Raffe, Bundell and Bibby (1989).

Conclusion

This book is concerned with the methods used in educational research and in this chapter we have attempted to acquaint readers with some of the ethical difficulties they are likely to experience in the conduct of such research. To this end, we have drawn on key concepts and ideas from deliberations and investigations in the educational, psychological, social psychological, and sociological domains in order to elucidate some of the more important dilemmas and issues that are an inevitable part of social research. In doing this we are well aware that it is not possible to identify all potential ethical questions or adjudicate on what is correct researcher behaviour.[4] On the other hand, perhaps some of the things we have said will seem irrelevant to readers who are unlikely to be called upon to submit subjects to painful electric shocks, provoke aggression, embarrass them, have them tell lies, or eat grasshoppers, as Aronson and Carlsmith (1969) put it. Nevertheless, it is hoped that these few pages will have induced in readers a certain disposition that will enable them to approach their own more temperate projects with a greater awareness and fuller understanding of the ethical dilemmas and moral issues lurking in the interstices of the research process. However inexperienced in these matters researchers are, they will bring to the world of social research a sense of rightness[5] on which they can construct a set of rational principles appropriate to their own circumstances and based on personal, professional, and societal values (we stress the word 'rational' since reason is a prime ingredient of ethical thinking and it is the combination of reason and a sense of rightness that researchers must keep faith with if they are to bring a rich ethical quality to their work).[6]

Although no code of practice can anticipate or resolve all problems, there is a six-fold advantage in fashioning a personal code of ethical practice.[7] First, such a code establishes one as a member of the wider scientific community having a shared interest in its values and concerns. Second, a code of ethical practice makes researchers aware of their obligations to their subjects and also to those problem areas where there is a general consensus about what is acceptable and what is not. In this sense it has a

Box 2.9
An ethical code: an illustration

1	It is important for the researcher to reveal fully his or her identity and background.
2	The purpose and procedures of the research should be fully explained to the subjects at the outset.
3	The research and its ethical consequences should be seen from the subjects' and institution's point of view.
4	Ascertain whether the research benefits the subjects in any way (beneficence).
5	Where necessary, ensure the research does not harm the subjects in any way (non-maleficence).
6	Possible controversial findings need to be anticipated and where they ensue, handled with great sensitivity.
7	The research should be as objective as possible. This will require careful thought being given to the design, conduct and reporting of research.
8	Informed consent should be sought from all participants. All agreements reached at this stage should be honoured.
9	Sometimes it is desirable to obtain informed consent in writing.
10	Subjects should have the option to refuse to take part and know this; and the right to terminate their involvement at any time and know this also.
11	Arrangements should be made during initial contacts to provide feedback for those requesting it. It may take the form of a written résumé of findings.
12	The dignity, privacy and interests of the participants should be respected. Subsequent privacy of the subjects after the research is completed should be guaranteed (non-traceability).
13	Deceit should only be used when absolutely necessary.
14	When ethical dilemmas arise, the researcher may need to consult other researchers or teachers.

Source Adapted from Reynolds, 1979

clarificatory value. Third, when one's professional behaviour is guided by a principled code of ethics, then it is possible to consider that there may be alternative ways of doing the same thing, ways that are more ethical or less unethical should one be confronted by a moral challenge. Fourth, a balanced code can be an important organizing factor in researchers' perceptions of the research situation, and as such may assist them in their need to anticipate and prepare. Fifth, a code of practice validated by their own sense of rightness will help researchers to develop an intuitive sensitivity that will be particularly helpful to them in dealing with the unknown and the unexpected, especially where the more fluidic methods such as ethnography and participant observation are concerned. And sixth, a code of practice will bring discipline to researchers' awareness. Indeed, it should be their aim to strike a balance between discipline and awareness. Discipline without awareness may result in largely mechanical behaviour; whereas awareness without discipline can produce inappropriate responses. Box 2.9 gives a short ethical code, by way of example. It must be stressed, however, that bespoke items, i.e. ones designed to meet the needs of a specific project, are preferable to standard ones. The items in Box 2.9 are illustrative, and in no way exhaustive. Finally, we live in a relative universe and it has been said that relativity seeks adjustment; that adjustment is art; and that the art of life lies in a constant readjustment to one's surroundings (Okakura, 1991). What better precept for the art of the ethical researcher?

Research design issues: planning research

Introduction

There is no single blueprint for planning research. Research design is governed by the notion of 'fitness for purpose'. The purposes of the research determine the methodology and design of the research. For example, if the purpose of the research is to map the field, or to make generalizable comments then a survey approach might be desirable, using some form of stratified sample; if the effects of a specific intervention are to be evaluated then maybe an experimental or action research model is appropriate; if an in-depth study of a particular situation or group is important then an ethnographic model might be more appropriate.

That said, it is possible, nevertheless, to identify a set of issues that researchers need to address, regardless of the specifics of their research. It is this set of issues that this chapter addresses. It acts as a bridge between the theoretical discussions of the opening chapter and the subsequent chapters that cover: (a) specific styles of research (Part Three); (b) specific issues in planning a research design, e.g. sampling, validity, reliability, ethics (Part Two); (c) planning data collection (instrumentation, Part Four); (d) data analysis. The intention here is to provide a set of issues that need to be addressed in practice so that an area of research interest can become practicable, feasible and capable of being undertaken. This chapter indicates how research might be operationalized, i.e. how a general set of research aims and purposes can be translated into a practical, researchable topic.

To change the 'rules of the game' in midstream once the research has commenced is a sure recipe for problems. The terms of the research and the mechanism of its operation must be ironed out in advance if it is to be credible, legitimate and practicable. Once they have been decided upon the researcher is in a very positive position to undertake the research. The setting up of the research is a balancing act, for it requires the harmonizing of *planned possibilities* with *workable, coherent practice*, i.e. the resolution of the difference between idealism and reality, between what could be done and what will actually work, for at the end of the day research has to work. In planning research there are two phases – a divergent phase and a convergent phase. The divergent phase will open up a range of possible options facing the researcher, whilst the convergent phase will sift through these possibilities, see which ones are desirable, which ones are compatible with each other, which ones will actually work in the situation, and move towards an action plan that can realistically operate. This can be approached through the establishment of a framework of planning issues.

A framework for planning research

Though, clearly, the set of issues that constitute a framework for planning research will need to be interpreted differently for different styles of research, nevertheless, it is useful to indicate what those issues might be. These include:

1   the general aims and purposes of the research;
2   how to operationalize research aims and purposes;

3 generating research questions;
4 identifying and setting in order the priorities for and constraints on the research;
5 approaching the research design;
6 focusing the research;
7 research methodology;
8 ethical issues;
9 audiences of the research;
10 instrumentation;
11 sampling;
12 time frames;
13 resources required;
14 validity and reliability;
15 data analysis;
16 verifying and validating the data;
17 reporting and writing up the research.

These can be arranged into four main areas (Morrison, 1993):

(i) orienting decisions;
(ii) research design and methodology;
(iii) data analysis;
(iv) presenting and reporting the results.

Orienting decisions are those decisions which will set the boundaries or the parameters of constraints on the research. For example, let us say that the overriding feature of the research is that it has to be completed within six months; this will exert an effect on the enterprise. On the one hand it will 'focus the mind', really requiring priorities to be settled and data to be provided in a relatively short time. On the other hand this may reduce the variety of possibilities available to the researcher. Hence questions of time scale will affect:

- the research questions which might be answered feasibly and fairly (for example, some research questions might require a long data collection period);
- the number of data collection instruments used (for example, there might be only enough time for a few instruments to be used);
- the sources (people) to whom the researcher might go (for example, there might only be enough time to interview a handful of people);

- the number of foci which can be covered in the time (for example, for some foci it will take a long time to gather relevant data);
- the size and nature of the reporting (there might only be time to produce one interim report).

By clarifying the time scale a valuable note of realism is injected into the research, which enables questions of practicability to be answered.

Let us take another example. Suppose the overriding feature of the research is that the costs in terms of time, people and materials for carrying it out are to be negligible. This, too, will exert an effect on the research. On the one hand it will inject a sense of realism into proposals, identifying what is and what is not manageable. On the other it will reduce, again, the variety of possibilities which are available to the researcher. Questions of cost will affect:

- the research questions which might be feasibly and fairly answered (for example, some research questions might require: (a) interviewing which is costly in time both to administer and transcribe; (b) expensive commercially produced data collection instruments, e.g. tests, and costly computer services, which may include purchasing software for example);
- the number of data collection instruments used (for example, some data collection instruments, e.g. postal questionnaires, are costly for reprographics and postage);
- the people, to whom the researcher might go (for example, if teachers are to be released from teaching in order to interviewed then cover for their teaching may need to be found);
- the number of foci which can be covered in the time (for example, in uncovering relevant data, some foci might be costly in researcher's time);
- the size and nature of the reporting (for example, the number of written reports produced, the costs of convening meetings).

Certain time scales permit certain types of research, e.g. a short time scale permits answers to short-term issues, whilst long-term or large questions might require a long-term data collection period to cover a range of foci. Costs in terms of time, resources and people might affect the choice of data collection instruments. Time and cost will require the researcher to determine, for example, what will be the minimum representative sample of teachers or students in a school, for interviews are time-consuming and questionnaires are expensive to produce. These are only two examples of the real constraints on the research which must be addressed. Planning the research early on will enable the researcher to identify the boundaries within which the research must operate and what the constraints are on it.

With these preliminary comments, let us turn to the four main areas of the framework for planning research.

Orienting decisions

Decisions in this field are strategic; they set the general nature of the research, and the questions that researchers may need to consider are:

Who wants the research?
Who will receive the research/who is it for?
Who are the possible/likely audiences of the research?
What powers do the recipients of the research have?
What are the general aims and purposes of the research?
What are the main priorities for and constraints on the research?
What are the time scales and time frames of the research?
Who will own the research?
At what point will the ownership of the research pass from the participants to the researcher and from the researcher to the recipients of the research?
Who owns the data?

What ethical issues are to be faced in undertaking the research?
What resources (e.g. physical, material, temporal, human, administrative) are required for the research?

It can be seen that decisions here establish some key parameters of the research, including some political decisions (for example, on ownership and on the power of the recipients to take action on the basis of the research). At this stage the overall feasibility of the research will be addressed.

Research design and methodology

If the preceding orienting decisions are strategic then decisions in this field are tactical; they establish the practicalities of the research, assuming that, generally, it is feasible (i.e. that the orienting decisions have been taken). Decisions here include addressing such questions as:

What are the specific purposes of the research?
How are the general research purposes and aims operationalized into specific research questions?
What are the specific research questions?
What needs to be the focus of the research in order to answer the research questions?
What is the main methodology of the research (e.g. a quantitative survey, qualitative research, an ethnographic study, an experiment, a case study, a piece of action research etc.)?
How will validity and reliability be addressed?
What kinds of data are required?
From whom will data be acquired (i.e. sampling)?
Where else will data be available (e.g. documentary sources)?
How will the data be gathered (i.e. instrumentation)?
Who will undertake the research?

The process of *operationalization* is critical for effective research. What is required here is translating a very general research aim or purpose into specific, concrete questions to which specific, concrete answers can be given. The process moves from the general to the particular, from the abstract to the concrete. Thus the researcher breaks down each general research purpose or general aim into more specific research purposes and constituent elements, continuing the process until specific, concrete questions have been reached to which specific answers can be provided. An example of this is provided below.

Let us imagine that the overall research aim is to ascertain the continuity between primary and secondary education (Morrison, 1993: 31–3). This is very general, and needs to be translated into more specific terms. Hence the researcher might deconstruct the term 'continuity' into several components, for example experiences, syllabus content, teaching and learning styles, skills, concepts, organizational arrangements, aims and objectives, ethos, assessment. Given the vast scope of this, the decision is taken to focus on continuity of pedagogy. This is then broken down into its component areas:

the level of continuity of pedagogy;
the nature of continuity of pedagogy;
the degree of success of continuity of pedagogy;
the responsibility for continuity;
record keeping and documentation of continuity;
resources available to support continuity.

The researcher might take this further into investigating: the *nature* of the continuity (i.e. the provision of information about continuity); the *degree* of continuity (i.e. a measure against a given criterion); the *level of success of the continuity* (i.e. a judgement). An operationalized set of research questions, then, might be:

- How much continuity of pedagogy is occurring across the transition stages in each curriculum area? What kind of evidence is required to answer this question? On what criteria will the level of continuity be decided?

- What pedagogical styles operate in each curriculum area? What are the most frequent and most preferred? What is the balance of pedagogical styles? How is pedagogy influenced by resources? To what extent is continuity planned and recorded? On what criteria will the nature of continuity be decided? What kind of evidence is required to answer this question?

- On what aspects of pedagogy does planning take place? By what criteria will the level of success of continuity be judged? Over how many students/teachers/curriculum areas will the incidence of continuity have to occur for it to be judged successful? What kind of evidence is required to answer this question?

- Is continuity occurring by accident or design? How will the extent of planned and unplanned continuity be gauged? What kind of evidence is required to answer this question?

- Who has responsibility for continuity at the transition points? What is being undertaken by these people?

- How are records kept on continuity in the schools? Who keeps these records? What is recorded? How frequently are the records updated and reviewed? What kind of evidence is required to answer this question?

- What resources are there to support continuity at the point of transition? How adequate are these resources? What kind of evidence is required to answer this question?

It can be seen that these questions, several in number, have moved the research from simply an expression of interest (or a general aim) into a series of issues that lend themselves to being investigated in concrete terms. This is precisely what we mean by *the process of operationalization*. It is now possible not only to formulate the specific questions to be posed, but also to select appropriate instruments that will gather the data to answer them (e.g. semi-structured interviews, rating scales on questionnaires, or documentary analysis). By this process of operationalization we thus make a general purpose amenable to investigation, e.g. by measurement (Rose and Sullivan, 1993: 6) or some other means.

In planning research it is important to clarify a distinction that needs to be made between methodology and methods, approaches and instruments, styles of research and ways of collecting data. Several of the later chapters of this book are devoted to specific instruments for collecting data, e.g.:

- interviews;
- questionnaires;
- observation;
- tests;
- accounts;
- biographies and case studies;
- role playing;
- simulations;
- personal constructs.

The decision on which instrument to use frequently follows from an important earlier decision on which kind of research to undertake, for example:

- a survey;
- an experiment;
- an in-depth ethnography;
- action research;
- case study research;
- testing and assessment.

Subsequent chapters of this book examine each of these research styles, their principles, rationales and purposes, and the instrumentation and data types that seem suitable for them. For conceptual clarity it is possible to set out some key features of these models (Box 3.1).[1] It is intended that, when decisions have been reached on the stage of research design and methodology, a clear plan of action will have been prepared. To this end, considering models of research might be useful (Morrison, 1993).

Data analysis

The prepared researcher will need to consider the mode of data analysis to be employed. In some cases this is very important as it has a specific bearing on the form of the instrumentation. For example, a researcher will need to plan the layout and structure of a questionnaire survey very carefully in order to assist data entry for computer reading and analysis; an inappropriate layout may obstruct data entry and subsequent analysis by computer. The planning of data analysis will need to consider:

> What needs to be done with the data when they have been collected – how will they be processed and analysed?
>
> How will the results of the analysis be verified, cross-checked and validated?

Decisions will need to be taken with regard to the statistical tests that will be used in data analysis as this will affect the layout of research items (for example in a questionnaire), and the computer packages that are available for processing quantitative and qualitative data, e.g. SPSS and NUD.IST respectively.

For statistical processing the researcher will need to ascertain the level of data being processed – nominal, ordinal, interval or ratio (discussed in Chapter 10). Nominal and ordinal scales yield non-parametric data, i.e. data from populations, where few or no assumptions are made about the distribution of the population or the characteristics of that population; the parameters of the population are unknown. Interval and ratio scales yield parametric data, on the basis of which assumptions are made about the characteristics and distribution of the wider population, i.e. the parameters of the population are known, and usually assume a normal, Gaussian curve of distribution, as in reading scores, for example. Non-parametric data are often derived from questionnaires and surveys (though these can also yield parametric data, see 'survey' in Box 3.1), whilst parametric data tend to be derived from experiments and tests.

The choice of which statistics to employ is not arbitrary, and Box 3.2 sets out the commonly used statistics for data types (Siegel, 1956; Cohen and Holliday, 1996; Hopkins, Hopkins and Glass, 1996). For qualitative data analysis the researchers have at their disposal a range of techniques, for example (Hammersley, 1979):

- coding of field notes (Miles and Huberman, 1984);
- content analysis of field notes or qualitative data (see chapter 6);

Box 3.1
Elements of research styles

Model	Purposes	Foci	Key terms	Characteristics
Survey	Gathering large scale data in order to make generalizations Generating statistically manipulable data Gathering context-free data	Opinions Scores Outcomes Conditions Ratings	Measuring Testing Representativeness Generalizability	Describes and explains Represents wide population Gathers numerical data Much use of questionnaires and assessment/test data
Experiment	Comparing under controlled conditions Making generalizations about efficacy Objective measurement of treatment Establishing causality	Initial states, intervention and outcomes Randomized controlled trials	Pretest and post-test Identification, isolation and control of key variables Generalizations Comparing Causality	Control and experimental groups Treats situations like a laboratory Causes due to experimental intervention Does not judge worth Simplistic
Ethnography	Portrayal of events in subjects' terms Subjective and reporting of multiple perspectives Description, understanding and explanation of a specific situation	Perceptions and views of participants Issues as they emerge over time	Subjectivity Honesty, authenticity Non-generalizable Multiple perspectives Exploration and rich reporting of a specific context Emergent issues	Context-specific Formative and emergent Responsive to emerging features Allows room for judgements and multiple perspectives Wide data base gathered over a long period of time Time consuming to process data

continued

Chapter 3

Box 3.1
continued

Model	Purposes	Foci	Key terms	Characteristics
Action research	To plan, implement, review and evaluate an intervention designed to improve practice/solve local problem	Everyday practices Outcomes of interventions	Action Improvement Reflection Monitoring Evaluation Intervention Problem-solving Empowering Planning Reviewing	Context-specific Participants as researchers Reflection on practice
	To empower participants through research involvement and ideology critique	Participant empowerment		Interventionist – leading to solution of 'real' problems and meeting 'real' needs
	To develop reflective practice			Empowering for participants
	To promote equality democracy	Reflective practice		Collaborative
	To link practice and research	Social democracy and equality		Promoting praxis and equality
	To promote collaborative research	Decision-making		Stakeholder research
Case study	To portray, analyse and interpret the uniqueness of real individuals and situations through accessible accounts	Individuals and local situations Unique instances A single case	Individuality, uniqueness In-depth analysis and portrayal Interpretive and inferential analysis	In-depth, detailed data from wide data source Participant and non-participant observation Non-interventionist
	To catch the complexity and situatedness of behaviour	Bounded phenomena and systems: • individual • group • roles • organizations • community	Subjective Descriptive Analytical Understanding specific situations	Empathic Holistic treatment of phenomena
	To contribute to action and intervention			What can be learned from the particular case
	To present and represent reality – to give a sense of 'being there'		Sincerity Complexity Particularity	

continued

Box 3.1
continued

Model	Purposes	Foci	Key terms	Characteristics
Testing and assessment	To measure achievement and potential	Academic and non-academic, cognitive, affective and psychomotor domains – low order to high order	Reliability Validity Criterion-referencing Norm-referencing Domain-referencing Item-response Formative	Materials designed to provide scores that can be aggregated
	To diagnose strengths and weaknesses			Enables individuals and groups to be compared
	To assess performance and abilities	Performance, achievement, potential, abilities	Summative Diagnostic Standardization Moderation	In-depth diagnosis
		Personality characteristics		Measures performance

Box 3.2
Statistics available for different types of data

Data type	Legitimate statistics	Points to observe/questions/examples
Nominal	1 Mode (the score achieved by the greatest number of people)	Is there a clear 'front runner' that receives the highest score with low scoring on other categories, or is the modal score only narrowly leading the other categories? Are there two scores which are vying for the highest score – a bi-modal score?
	2 Frequencies	Which are the highest/lowest frequencies? Is the distribution even across categories?
	3 Chi-square (χ^2) (a statistic that charts the difference between statistically expected and actual scores)	Are differences between scores caused by chance/accident or are they statistically significant, i.e. not simply caused by chance?
Ordinal	1 Mode	Which score on a rating scale is the most frequent?
	2 Median (the score gained by the middle person in a ranked group of people or, if there is an even number of cases, the score which is midway between the highest score obtained in the lower half of the cases and the lowest score obtained in the higher half of the cases)	What is the score of the middle person in a list of scores?
	3 Frequencies	Do responses tend to cluster around one or two categories of a rating scale? Are the responses skewed towards one end of a rating scale (e.g. 'strongly agree')? Do the responses pattern themselves consistently across the sample? Are the frequencies generally high or generally low (i.e. whether respondents tend to feel strongly about an issue)? Is there a clustering of responses around the central categories of a rating scale (the central tendency, respondents not wishing to appear to be too extreme)?

continued

Box 3.2
continued

Data type	Legitimate statistics	Points to observe/questions/examples
	4 Chi-square (χ^2)	Are the frequencies of one set of nominal variables (e.g. sex) significantly related to a set of ordinal variables?
	5 Spearman rank order correlation (a statistic to measure the degree of association between two ordinal variables)	Do the results from one rating scale correlate with the results from another rating scale? Do the rank order positions for one variable correlate with the rank order positions for another variable?
	6 Mann–Whitney U-test (a statistic to measure any significant difference between two independent samples)	Is there a significant difference in the results of a rating scale for two independent samples (e.g. males and females)?
	7 Kruskal–Wallis analysis of variance (a statistic to measure any significant differences between three or more independent samples)	Is there a significant difference between three or more nominal variables (e.g. membership of political parties) and the results of a rating scale?
Interval and ratio	1 Mode	
	2 Mean	What is the average score for this group?
	3 Frequencies	
	4 Median	
	5 Chi-square (χ^2)	
	6 Standard deviation (a measure of the dispersal of scores)	Are the scores on a parametric test evenly distributed? Do scores cluster closely around the mean? Are scores widely spread around the mean? Are scores dispersed evenly? Are one or two extreme scores ('outliers') exerting a disproportionate influence on what are otherwise closely clustered scores?
	7 z-scores (a statistic to convert scores from different scales, i.e. with different means and standard deviations, to a common scale, i.e. with the same mean and standard deviation, enabling different scores to be compared fairly)	How do the scores obtained by students on a test which was marked out of 20 compare to the scores by the same students on a test which was marked out of 50?
	8 Pearson product moment correlation (a statistic to measure the degree of association between two interval or ratio variables)	Is there a correlation between one set of interval data (e.g. test scores for one examination) and another set of interval data (e.g. test scores on another examination)?
	9 t-tests (a statistic to measure the difference between the means of one sample on two separate occasions or between two samples on one occasion)	Are the control and experimental groups matched in their mean scores on a parametric test? Is there a significant difference between the pretest and post-test scores of a sample group?
	10 Analysis of variance (a statistic to ascertain whether two or more means differ significantly)	Are the differences in the means between test results of three groups statistically significant?

- cognitive mapping (Jones, 1987; Morrison, 1993);
- seeking patterning of responses;
- looking for causal pathways and connections (Miles and Huberman, 1984);
- presenting cross-site analysis (ibid.);
- case studies;
- personal constructs;
- narrative accounts;
- action research analysis;
- analytic induction (Denzin, 1970);
- constant comparison (Glaser and Strauss, 1967);
- grounded theory (Glaser and Strauss, 1967);
- discourse analysis (Stillar, 1998);
- biographies and life histories (Atkinson, 1998).

The criteria for deciding which forms of data analysis to undertake are governed both by fitness for purpose and legitimacy – the form of data analysis must be appropriate for the kinds of data gathered. For example, it would be inappropriate to use certain statistics with certain kinds of numerical data (e.g. using means on nominal data), or to use causal pathways on unrelated cross-site analysis.

Presenting and reporting the results

As with the stage of planning data analysis, the prepared researcher will need to consider the form of the reporting of the research and its results, giving due attention to the needs of different audiences (for example, an academic audience may require different contents from a wider professional audience and, *a fortiori*, from a lay audience). Decisions here will need to consider:

How to write up and report the research?
When to write up and report the research (e.g. ongoing or summative)?
How to present the results in tabular and/or written-out form?
How to present the results in non-verbal forms?
To whom to report (the necessary and possible audiences of the research)?
How frequently to report?

A planning matrix for research

In planning a piece of research the range of questions to be addressed can be set into a matrix. Box 3.3 provides such a matrix, in the left hand column of which are the questions which figure in the four main areas set out so far:
(i)   orienting decisions;
(ii) research design and methodology;
(iii) data analysis;
(iv) presenting and reporting the results.

Questions 1–10 are the orienting decisions, questions 11–22 concern the research design and methodology, questions 23–4 cover data analysis, and questions 25–30 deal with presenting and reporting the results. Within each of the 30 questions there are several sub-questions which research planners may need to address. For example, within question 5 ('What are the purposes of the research?') the researcher would have to differentiate major and minor purposes, explicit and maybe implicit purposes, whose purposes are being served by the research, and whose interests are being served by the research. An example of these sub-issues and problems is contained in the second column.

At this point the planner is still at the divergent phase of the research planning, dealing with *planned possibilities* (Morrison, 1993: 19), opening up the research to all facets and interpretations. In the column headed 'decisions' the research planner is moving towards a convergent phase, where planned possibilities become visible within the terms of constraints available to the researcher. To do this the researcher has to move down the column marked 'decisions' to see how well the decision which is taken in regard to one issue/question fits in with the decisions in regard to other issues/questions. For one decision to fit with another, four factors must be present:

1   All of the cells in the 'decisions' column must be coherent – they must not contradict each other.
2   All of the cells in the 'decisions' column must be mutually supporting.

Chapter 3

Box 3.3

A matrix for planning research

Orienting decisions

Question	Sub-issues and problems	Decisions
1 Who wants the research?	Is the research going to be useful? Who might wish to use the research? Are the data going to be public? What if different people want different things from the research? Can people refuse to participate?	Find out the controls over the research which can be exercised by respondents. What are the scope and audiences of the research? Determine the reporting mechanisms.
2 Who will receive the research?	Will participants be able to veto the release of parts of the research to specified audiences? Will participants be able to give the research to whomsoever they wish? Will participants be told to whom the research will go?	Determine the proposed internal and external audiences of the research. Determine the controls over the research which can be exercised by the participants. Determine the rights of the participants and the researcher to control the release of the research.
3 What powers do the recipients of the research have?	What use will be made of the research? How might the research be used for or against the participants? What might happen if the data fall into the 'wrong' hands? Will participants know in advance what use will and will not be made of the research?	Determine the rights of recipients to do what they wish with the research. Determine the respondents' rights to protection as a result of the research.
4 What are the time scales of the research?	Is there enough time to do all the research? How to decide what to be done within the time scale?	Determine the time scales and timing of the research.
5 What are the purposes of the research?	What are the formal and hidden agendas here? Whose purposes are being served by the research? Who decides the purposes of the research? How will different purposes be served in the research?	Determine all the possible uses of the research. Determine the powers of the respondents to control the uses made of the research. Decide on the form of reporting and the intended and possible audiences of the research.
6 What are the research questions?	Who decides what the questions will be? Do participants have rights to refuse to answer or take part? Can participants add their own questions?	Determine the participants' rights and powers to participate in the planning, form and conduct of the research. Decide the balance of all interests in the research.
7 What must be the focus in order to answer the research questions?	Is sufficient time available to focus on all the necessary aspects of the research? How will the priority foci be decided? Who decides the foci?	Determine all the aspects of the research, prioritize them, and agree on the minimum necessary areas of the research. Determine decision-making powers on the research.

continued

Box 3.3
continued

Question	Sub-issues and problems	Decisions
8 What costs are there – human, material, physical, administrative, temporal?	What support is available for the researcher? What materials are necessary?	Cost out the research.
9 Who owns the research?	Who controls the release of the report? What protection can be given to participants? Will participants be identified and identifiable/traceable? Who has the ultimate decision on what data are included?	Determine who controls the release of the report. Decide the rights and powers of the researcher. Decide the rights of veto. Decide how to protect those who may be identified/identifiable in the research.
10 At what point does the ownership pass from the respondent to the researcher and from the researcher to the recipients?	Who decides the ownership of the research? Can participants refuse to answer certain parts if they wish, or, if they have the option not to take part, must they opt out of everything? Can the researcher edit out certain responses?	Determine the ownership of the research at all stages of its progress. Decide the options available to the participants. Decide the rights of different parties in the research, e.g. respondents, researcher, recipients.

Research design and methodology

Question	Sub-issues and problems	Decisions
11 What are the specific purposes of the research?	How do these purposes derive from the overall aims of the research? Will some areas of the broad aims be covered, or will the specific research purposes have to be selective? What priorities are there?	Decide the specific research purposes and write them as concrete questions.
12 How are the general research purposes and aims operationalized into specific research questions?	Do the specific research questions together cover all the research purposes? Are the research questions sufficiently concrete as to suggest the kinds of answers and data required and the appropriate instrumentation and sampling? How to balance adequate coverage of research purposes with the risk of producing an unwieldy list of sub-questions?	Ensure that each main research purpose is translated into specific, concrete questions that, together, address the scope of the original research questions. Ensure that the questions are sufficiently specific as to suggest the most appropriate data types, kinds of answers required, sampling, and instrumentation. Decide how to ensure that any selectivity still represents the main fields of the research questions.
13 What are the specific research questions?	Do the specific research questions demonstrate construct and content validity?	Ensure that the coverage and operationalization of the specific questions addresses content and construct validity respectively.

continued

Box 3.3
continued

Question	Sub-issues and problems	Decisions
14 What needs to be the focus of the research in order to answer the research questions?	How may foci are necessary? Are the foci clearly identifiable and operationalizable?	Decide the number of foci of the research questions. Ensure that the foci are clear and can be operationalized.
15 What is the main methodology of the research?	How many methodologies are necessary? Are several methodologies compatible with each other? Will a single focus/research question require more than one methodology (e.g. for triangulation and concurrent validity)?	Decide the number, type and purposes of the methodologies to be used. Decide whether one or more methodologies is necessary to gain answers to specific research questions. Ensure that the most appropriate form of methodology is employed.
16 How will validity and reliability be addressed?	Will there be the opportunity for cross-checking? Will the depth and breadth required for content validity be feasible within the constraints of the research (e.g. time constraints, instrumentation)? In what senses are the research questions valid (e.g. construct validity)? Are the questions fair? How does the researcher know if people are telling the truth? What kinds of validity and reliability are to be addressed? How will the researcher take back the research to respondents for them to check that the interpretations are fair and acceptable? How will data be gathered consistently over time? How to ensure that each respondent is given the same opportunity to respond?	Determine the process of respondent validation of the data. Decide a necessary minimum of topics to be covered. Subject the plans to scrutiny by critical friends ('jury' validity). Pilot the research. Build in cross-checks on data. Address the appropriate forms of reliability and validity. Decide the questions to be asked and the methods used to ask them. Determine the balance of open and closed questions.
17 How will reflexivity be addressed?	How will reflexivity be recognized? Is reflexivity a problem? How can reflexivity be included in the research?	Determine the need to address reflexivity and to make this public. Determine how to address reflexivity in the research.
18 What kinds of data are required?	Does the research need words, numbers or both? Does the research need opinions, facts or both? Does the research seek to compare responses and results or simply to illuminate an issue?	Determine the most appropriate types of data for the foci and research questions. Balance objective and subjective data. Determine the purposes of collecting different types of data and the ways in which they can be processed.

continued

Box 3.3
continued

Question	Sub-issues and problems	Decisions
19 From whom will data be acquired (i.e. sampling)?	Will there be adequate time to go to all the relevant parties? What kind of sample is required (e.g. probability/non-probability/random/stratified etc.)? How to achieve a representative sample (if required)?	Determine the minimum and maximum sample. Decide on the criteria for sampling. Decide the kind of sample required. Decide the degree of representativeness of the sample. Decide how to follow up and not to follow up on the data gathered.
20 Where else will data be available?	What documents and other written sources of data can be used? How to access and use confidential material? What will be the positive or negative effects on individuals of using certain documents?	Determine the necessary/desirable/possible documentary sources. Decide access and publication rights and protection of sensitive data.
21 How will the data be gathered (i.e. instrumentation)?	What methods of data gathering are available and appropriate to yield data to answer the research questions? What methods of data gathering will be used? How to construct interview schedules/questionnaires/tests/observation schedules? What will be the effects of observing participants? How many methods should be used (e.g. to ensure reliability and validity)? Is it necessary or desirable to use more than one method of data collection on the same issue? Will many methods yield more reliable data? Will some methods be unsuitable for some people or for some issues?	Determine the most appropriate data collection instruments to gather data to answer the research questions. Pilot the instruments and refine them subsequently. Decide the strengths and weaknesses of different data collection instruments in the short and long term. Decide which methods are most suitable for which issues. Decide which issues will require more than one data collection instrument. Decide whether the same data collection methods will be used with all the participants.
22 Who will undertake the research?	Can different people plan and carry out different parts of the research?	Decide who will carry out the data collection, processing and reporting.
Data analysis *Question* 23 How will the data be analysed?	*Sub-issues and problems* Are the data to be processed numerically or verbally? What computer packages are available to assist data processing and analysis? What statistical tests will be needed? How to perform a content analysis of word data? How to summarize and present word data? How to process all the different responses to open-ended questions? Will the data be presented person by person, issue by issue, aggregated to groups, or a combination of these? Does the research seek to make generalizations? Who will process the data?	*Decisions* Clarify the legitimate and illegitimate methods of data processing and analysis of quantitative and qualitative data. Decide which methods of data processing and analysis are most appropriate for which types of data and for which research questions. Check that the data processing and analysis will serve the research purposes. Determine the data protection issues if data are to be processed by 'outsiders' or particular 'insiders'.

continued

Box 3.3
continued

Question	Sub-issues and problems	Decisions
24 How to verify and validate the data and their interpretation?	What opportunities will there be for respondents to check the researcher's interpretation? At what stages of the research is validation necessary? What will happen if respondents disagree with the researcher's interpretation?	Determine the process of respondent validation during the research. Decide the reporting of multiple perspectives and interpretations. Decide respondents' rights to have their views expressed or to veto reporting.

Presenting and reporting the results

Question	Sub-issues and problems	Decisions
25 How to write up and report the research?	Who will write the report and for whom? How detailed must the report be? What must the report contain? What channels of dissemination of the research are to be used?	Ensure that the most appropriate form of reporting is used for the audiences. Keep the report as short, clear and complete as possible. Provide summaries if possible/fair. Ensure that the report enables fair critique and evaluation to be undertaken.
26 When to write up and report the research (e.g. ongoing or summative)?	How many times are appropriate for reporting? For whom are interim reports compiled? Which reports are public?	Decide the most appropriate timing, purposes and audiences of the reporting. Decide the status of the reporting (e.g. formal, informal, public, private).
27 How to present the results in tabular and/or written-out form?	How to ensure that everyone will understand the language or the statistics? How to respect the confidentiality of the participants? How to report multiple perspectives?	Decide the most appropriate form of reporting. Decide whether to provide a glossary of terms. Decide the format(s) of the reports. Decide the number and timing of the reports. Decide the protection of the individual's rights, balancing this with the public's rights to know.
28 How to present the results in non-verbal forms?	Will different parties require different reports? How to respect the confidentiality of the participants? How to report multiple perspectives?	Decide the most appropriate form of reporting. Decide the number and timing of the reports. Ensure that a written record is kept of oral reports. Decide the protection of the individual's rights, balancing this with the public's rights to know.
29 To whom to report (the necessary and possible audiences of the research)?	Do all participants receive a report? What will be the effects of not reporting to stakeholders?	Identify the stakeholders. Determine the least and most material to be made available to the stakeholders.
30 How frequently to report?	Is it necessary to provide interim reports? If interim reports are provided, how might this affect the future reports or the course of the research?	Decide on the timing and frequency of the reporting. Determine the formative and summative nature of the reports.

3   All of the cells in the 'decisions' column must be practicable when taken separately.
4   All of the cells in the 'decisions' column must be practicable when taken together.

Not all of the planned possibilities might be practicable when these four criteria are applied. It would be of very little use if the methods of data collection listed in the 'decisions' column of question 21 ('How will the data be gathered?') offered little opportunity to fulfil the needs of acquiring information to answer question 7 ('What must be the focus in order to answer the research questions?'), or if the methods of data collection were impracticable within the time scales available in question 4.

In the matrix of Box 3.3 the cells have been completed in a deliberately content-free way, i.e. the matrix as presented here does not deal with the specific, actual points which might emerge in a particular research proposal. If the matrix were to be used for planning an actual piece of research, then, instead of couching the wording of each cell in generalized terms, it would be more useful if *specific, concrete* responses were given which addressed particular issues and concerns in the research proposal in question.

Many of these questions concern rights, responsibilities and the political uses (and abuses) of the research. This underlines the view that research is an inherently political and moral activity; it is not politically or morally neutral. The researcher has to be concerned with the uses as well as the conduct of the research.

Managing the planning of research

The preceding discussion has revealed the complexity of planning a piece of research, yet it should not be assumed that research will always go according to plan! For example, the mortality of the sample might be a feature (participants leaving during the research), or a poor response rate to questionnaires might be encountered, rendering subsequent analysis, reporting and generalization problematic; administrative support might not be forthcoming, or there might be serious slippage in the timing. This is not to say that a plan for the research should not be made; rather it is to suggest that it is dangerous to put absolute faith in it!

To manage the complexity in planning outlined above a simple four-stage model can be proposed:

Stage 1   Identify the purposes of the research.
Stage 2   Identify and give priority to the constraints under which the research will take place.
Stage 3   Plan the possibilities for the research within these constraints.
Stage 4   Decide the research design.

Each stage contains several operations. Box 3.4 clarifies this four stage model, drawing out the various operations contained in each stage. It may be useful for research planners to consider which instruments will be used at which stage of the research and with which sectors of the sample population. Box 3.5 sets out a matrix of these for planning (see also Morrison, 1993: 109), for example, of a small-scale piece of research.

A matrix approach such as this enables research planners to see at a glance their coverage of the sample and of the instruments used at particular points in time, making omissions clear, and promoting such questions as:

Why are certain instruments used at certain times and not at others?
Why are certain instruments used with certain people and not with others?
Why do certain times in the research use more instruments than other times?
Why is there such a heavy concentration of instruments at the end of the study?
Why are certain groups involved in more instruments than other groups?
Why are some groups apparently neglected (e.g. parents), e.g. is there a political dimension to the research?
Why are questionnaires the main kinds of instrument to be used?

Box 3.4
A planning sequence for research

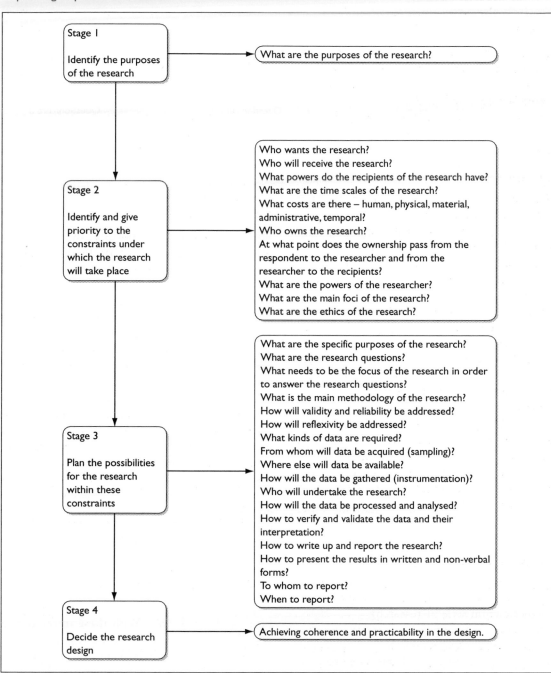

Stage 1

Identify the purposes of the research

What are the purposes of the research?

Stage 2

Identify and give priority to the constraints under which the research will take place

Who wants the research?
Who will receive the research?
What powers do the recipients of the research have?
What are the time scales of the research?
What costs are there – human, physical, material, administrative, temporal?
Who owns the research?
At what point does the ownership pass from the respondent to the researcher and from the researcher to the recipients?
What are the powers of the researcher?
What are the main foci of the research?
What are the ethics of the research?

Stage 3

Plan the possibilities for the research within these constraints

What are the specific purposes of the research?
What are the research questions?
What needs to be the focus of the research in order to answer the research questions?
What is the main methodology of the research?
How will validity and reliability be addressed?
How will reflexivity be addressed?
What kinds of data are required?
From whom will data be acquired (sampling)?
Where else will data be available?
How will the data be gathered (instrumentation)?
Who will undertake the research?
How will the data be processed and analysed?
How to verify and validate the data and their interpretation?
How to write up and report the research?
How to present the results in written and non-verbal forms?
To whom to report?
When to report?

Stage 4

Decide the research design

Achieving coherence and practicability in the design.

Box 3.5
A planning matrix for research

Time sample	Stage 1 (start)	Stage 2 (3 months)	Stage 3 (6 months)	Stage 4 (9 months)	Stage 5 (12 months)
Principal/ headteacher	Documents Interview Questionnaire 1	Interview	Documents Questionnaire 2	Interview	Documents Interview Questionnaire 3
Teacher group 1	Questionnaire 1		Questionnaire 2		Questionnaire 3
Teacher group 2	Questionnaire 1		Questionnaire 2		Questionnaire 3
Teacher group 3	Questionnaire 1		Questionnaire 2		Questionnaire 3
Students			Questionnaire 2		Interview
Parents	Questionnaire 1		Questionnaire 2		Questionnaire 3
University teacher educators	Interview Documents				Interview Documents

Why are some instruments (e.g. observation, testing) not used at all?

What makes the five stages separate?

Are documents only held by certain parties (and, if so, might one suspect an 'institutional line' to be revealed in them)?

Are some parties more difficult to contact than others (e.g. University teacher educators)?

Are some parties more important to the research than others (e.g. the principals)?

Why are some parties excluded from the sample (e.g. school governors, policy-makers, teachers' associations and unions)?

What is the difference between the three groups of teachers?

Matrix planning is useful for exposing key features of the planning of research. Further matrices might be constructed to indicate other features of the research, for example:

- the timing of the identification of the sample;
- the timing of the release of interim reports;
- the timing of the release of the final report;
- the timing of pretests and post-tests (in an experimental style of research);
- the timing of intensive necessary resource support (e.g. reprographics);
- the timing of meetings of interested parties.

These examples cover timings only; other matrices might be developed to cover other combinations, for example: reporting by audiences; research team meetings by reporting; instrumentation by participants etc. They are useful summary devices.

Conclusion

This chapter has suggested how a research plan can be formulated and operationalized, moving from general areas of interest, questions and purposes to very specific research questions which can be answered using appropriate sampling procedures, methodologies and instruments, and with the gathering of relevant data. The message from this chapter is that, while research may not always unfold according to plan, it is important to have thought out the several stages and elements of research so that coherence and practicability have been addressed within an ethically defensible context. Such planning can be usefully informed by models of research, and, indeed, these are addressed in several chapters of the book. The planning of research begins with the identification of purposes and constraints. With these in mind, the researcher can now decide on a research design and strategy that will provide him or her with answers to specific research questions. These in turn will serve more general research purposes and aims. Both the novice and experienced researcher alike have to confront the necessity of having a clear plan of action if the research is to have momentum and purpose. The notion of 'fitness for purpose' reigns here; the research plan must suit the purposes of the research. If the reader is left feeling, at the end of this chapter, that the task of research is complex, then that is an important message, for rigour and thoughtful, thorough planning are necessary if the research is to be worthwhile and effective.

Chapter 3

4 Sampling

Introduction

The quality of a piece of research not only stands or falls by the appropriateness of methodology and instrumentation but also by the suitability of the sampling strategy that has been adopted (see also Morrison, 1993: 112–17). Questions of sampling arise directly out of the issue of defining the population on which the research will focus. Researchers must take sampling decisions early in the overall planning of a piece of research. Factors such as expense, time and accessibility frequently prevent researchers from gaining information from the whole population. Therefore they often need to be able to obtain data from a smaller group or subset of the total population in such a way that the knowledge gained is representative of the total population (however defined) under study. This smaller group or subset is the sample. Experienced researchers start with the total population and work down to the sample. By contrast, less experienced researchers often work from the bottom up; that is, they determine the minimum number of respondents needed to conduct the research (Bailey, 1978). However, unless they identify the total population in advance, it is virtually impossible for them to assess how representative the sample is that they have drawn.

Suppose that a class teacher has been released from her teaching commitments for one month in order to conduct some research into the abilities of 13-year-old students to undertake a set of science experiments and that the research is to draw on three secondary schools which contain 300 such students each, a total of 900 students, and that the method that the teacher has been asked to use for data collection is a semi-structured interview. Because of the time available to the teacher it would be impossible for her to interview all 900 students (the total population being all the cases). Therefore she has to be selective and to interview fewer than all 900 students. How will she decide that selection; how will she select which students to interview?

If she were to interview 200 of the students, would that be too many? If she were to interview just twenty of the students would that be too few? If she were to interview just the males or just the females, would that give her a fair picture? If she were to interview just those students whom the science teachers had decided were 'good at science', would that yield a true picture of the total population of 900 students? Perhaps it would be better for her to interview those students who were experiencing difficulty in science and who did not enjoy science, as well as those who were 'good at science'. So she turns up on the days of the interviews only to find that those students who do not enjoy science have decided to absent themselves from the science lesson. How can she reach those students?

Decisions and problems such as these face researchers in deciding the sampling strategy to be used. Judgements have to be made about four key factors in sampling:

1 the sample size;
2 the representativeness and parameters of the sample;
3 access to the sample;
4 the sampling strategy to be used.

The decisions here will determine the sampling strategy to be used.

The sample size

A question that often plagues novice researchers is just how large their samples for the research should be. There is no clear-cut answer, for the correct sample size depends on the purpose of the study and the nature of the population under scrutiny. However it is possible to give some advice on this matter. Thus, a sample size of thirty is held by many to be the minimum number of cases if researchers plan to use some form of statistical analysis on their data. Of more import to researchers is the need to think out in advance of any data collection the sorts of relationships that they wish to explore within subgroups of their eventual sample. The number of variables researchers set out to control in their analysis and the types of statistical tests that they wish to make must inform their decisions about sample size prior to the actual research undertaking.

As well as the requirement of a minimum number of cases in order to examine relationships between subgroups, researchers must obtain the minimum sample size that will accurately represent the population being targeted. With respect to size, will a large one guarantee representativeness? Surely not! In the example above the researcher could have interviewed a total sample of 450 females and still not have represented the male population. Will a small size guarantee representativeness? Again, surely not! The latter falls into the trap of saying that 50 per cent of those who expressed an opinion said that they enjoyed science, when the 50 per cent was only one student, a researcher having interviewed only two students in all. Furthermore, too large a sample might become unwieldy and too small a sample might be unrepresentative (e.g. in the first example, the researcher might have wished to interview 450 students but this would have been unworkable in practice or the researcher might have interviewed only ten students, which would have been unrepresentative of the total population of 900 students).

Where simple random sampling is used, the sample size needed to reflect the population value of a particular variable depends both on the size of the population and the amount of heterogeneity in the population (Bailey, 1978). Generally, for populations of equal heterogeneity, the larger the population, the larger the sample that must be drawn. For populations of equal size, the greater the heterogeneity on a particular variable, the larger the sample that is needed. To the extent that a sample fails to represent accurately the population involved, there is sampling error, discussed below.

Sample size is also determined to some extent by the style of the research. For example, a survey style usually requires a large sample, particularly if inferential statistics are to be calculated. In an ethnographic or qualitative style of research it is more likely that the sample size will be small. Sample size might also be constrained by cost – in terms of time, money, stress, administrative support, the number of researchers, and resources. Borg and Gall (1979: 194–5) suggest that correlational research requires a sample size of no fewer than thirty cases, that causal-comparative and experimental methodologies require a sample size of no fewer than fifteen cases, and that survey research should have no fewer than 100 cases in each major subgroup and twenty to fifty in each minor subgroup.

They advise (ibid.: 186) that sample size has to begin with an estimation of the smallest number of cases in the smallest subgroup of the sample, and 'work up' from that, rather than *vice versa*. So, for example, if 5 per cent of the sample must be teenage boys, and this sub-sample must be thirty cases (e.g. for correlational research), then the total sample will be $30 \div 0.05 = 600$; if 15 per cent of the sample must be teenage girls and the sub-sample must be forty-five cases, then the total sample must be $45 \div 0.15 = 300$ cases.

The size of a probability (random) sample can be determined in two ways, either by the researcher exercising prudence and ensuring that the sample represents the wider features of the population with the minimum number of cases or by using a table which, from a mathematical formula, indicates the appropriate size of a random sample for a given number of the wider population (Morrison, 1993: 117). One such example is provided by Krejcie and Morgan (1970) in Box 4.1. This suggests that if the researcher were devising a sample from a wider population of thirty or fewer (e.g. a class of students or a group of young children in a class) then she/he would be well advised to include the whole of the wider population as the sample.

The key point to note about the sample size in Box 4.1 is that the smaller the number of cases there are in the wider, whole population, the larger the proportion of that population must

Box 4.1
Determining the size of a random sample

N	S	N	S	N	S
10	10	220	140	1,200	291
15	14	230	144	1,300	297
20	19	240	148	1,400	302
25	24	250	152	1,500	306
30	28	260	155	1,600	310
35	32	270	159	1,700	313
40	36	280	162	1,800	317
45	40	290	165	1,900	320
50	44	300	169	2,000	322
55	48	320	175	2,200	327
60	52	340	181	2,400	331
65	56	360	186	2,600	335
70	59	380	191	2,800	338
75	63	400	196	3,000	341
80	66	420	201	3,500	346
85	70	440	205	4,000	351
90	73	460	210	4,500	354
95	76	480	214	5,000	357
100	80	500	217	6,000	361
110	86	550	226	7,000	364
120	92	600	234	8,000	367
130	97	650	242	9,000	368
140	103	700	248	10,000	370
150	108	750	254	15,000	375
160	113	800	260	20,000	377
170	118	850	265	30,000	379
180	123	900	269	40,000	380
190	127	950	274	50,000	381
200	132	1,000	278	75,000	382
210	136	1,100	285	1,000,000	384

Notes
N = population size
S = sample size
Source Krejcie and Morgan, 1970[1]

be which appears in the sample; the converse of this is true: the larger the number of cases there are in the wider, whole population, the smaller the proportion of that population can be which appears in the sample. Krejcie and Morgan (1970) note that 'as the population increases the sample size increases at a diminishing rate and remains constant at slightly more than 380 cases' (ibid.: 610). Hence, for example, a piece of research involving all the children in a small primary or elementary school (up to 100 students in all) might require between 80 per cent and 100 per cent of the school to be included in the sample, whilst a large secondary school of 1,200 students might require a sample of 25 per cent of the school in order to achieve randomness. As a rough guide in a random sample, the larger the sample, the greater is its chance of being representative.

This approach to determining sample size for a probability sample is in relation to the confidence level and sampling error. For example, with confidence levels of 95 per cent and 99 per cent and sampling errors of 5 per cent and 1 per cent respectively, the following can be set as sample sizes (Box 4.2). As with the table from Krejcie and Morgan earlier, we can see that the size of the sample reduces at an increasing rate as the population size increases; generally (but, clearly, not always) the larger the population, the smaller the proportion of the probability sample can be.

Borg and Gall (1979: 195) suggest that, as a general rule, sample sizes should be large where:

- there are many variables;
- only small differences or small relationships are expected or predicted;
- the sample will be broken down into sub-groups;
- the sample is heterogeneous in terms of the variables under study;
- reliable measures of the dependent variable are unavailable.

Oppenheim (1992: 44) adds to this the view that the nature of the scales to be used also exerts an influence on the sample size. For nominal data the sample sizes may well have to be larger than

Box 4.2
Sample size, confidence levels and sampling error

Size of total population (N)	Sampling error of 5% with a confidence level of 95% Size of sample population (S)	Sampling error of 1% with a confidence level of 99% Size of sample population (S)
50	44	50
100	79	99
200	132	196
500	217	476
1,000	278	907
2,000	322	1,661
5,000	357	3,311
10,000	370	4,950
20,000	377	6,578
50,000	381	8,195
100,000	383	8,926
1,000,000	384	9,706

for interval and ratio data (i.e. a variant of the issue of the number of subgroups to be addressed, the greater the number of subgroups or possible categories, the larger the sample will have to be).

Borg and Gall (ibid.) set out a formula-driven approach to determining sample size (see also Moser and Kalton, 1977; Ross and Rust, 1997: 427–38), and they also suggest using correlational tables for correlational studies – available in most texts on statistics – 'in reverse' as it were, to determine sample size (p. 201), i.e. looking at the significance levels of correlation co-efficients and then reading off the sample sizes usually required to demonstrate that level of significance. For example, a correlational significance level of 0.01 would require a sample size of 10 if the estimated co-efficient of correlation is 0.65, or a sample size of 20 if the estimated correlation co-efficient is 0.45, and a sample size of 100 if the estimated correlation co-efficient is 0.20. Again, an inverse proportion can be seen – the larger the sample size, the smaller the estimated correlation co-efficient can be to be deemed significant.

With both qualitative and quantitative data, the essential requirement is that the sample is representative of the population from which it is drawn. In a dissertation concerned with a life history (i.e. n = 1), the sample is the population!

Qualitative data

In a qualitative study of thirty highly able girls of similar socio-economic background following an A-level Biology course, a sample of five or six may suffice the researcher who is prepared to obtain additional corroborative data by way of validation.

Where there is heterogeneity in the population, then a larger sample must be selected on some basis that respects that heterogeneity. Thus, from a staff of sixty secondary school teachers differentiated by gender, age, subject specialism, management or classroom responsibility, etc., it would be insufficient to construct a sample consisting of ten female classroom teachers of Arts and Humanities subjects.

Quantitative data

For quantitative data, a precise sample number can be calculated according to the *level of accuracy* and the *level of probability* that the researcher requires in her work. She can then report in her study the rationale and the basis of her research decision (Blalock, 1979).

By way of example, suppose a teacher/researcher wishes to sample opinions among 1,000 secondary school students. She intends to use a 10-point scale ranging from 1 = totally unsatisfactory to 10 = absolutely fabulous. She already has data from her own class of thirty students and suspects that the responses of other students will be broadly similar. Her own students rated the activity (an extra-curricular event) as follows: mean score = 7.27; standard deviation = 1.98. In other words, her students were pretty much 'bunched' about a warm, positive appraisal on the 10-point scale. How many of the 1,000 students does she need to sample in order to gain an accurate (i.e. reliable) assessment of what the whole school (n = 1,000) thinks of the extra-curricular event?

> It all depends on what degree of accuracy and what level of probability she is willing to accept.

A simple calculation from a formula by Blalock (1979: 215–18) shows that:

- if she is happy to be within + or – 0.5 of a scale point and accurate 19 times out of 20, then she requires a sample of 60 out of the 1,000;
- if she is happy to be within + or – 0.5 of a scale point and accurate 99 times out of 100, then she requires a sample of 104 out of the 1,000;
- if she is happy to be within + or – 0.5 of a scale point and accurate 999 times out of 1,000, then she requires a sample of 170 out of the 1,000;
- if she is a perfectionist and wishes to be within + or – 0.25 of a scale point and accurate 999 times out of 1,000, then she requires a sample of 679 out of the 1,000.

Determining the size of the sample will also have to take account of attrition and respondent mortality, i.e. that some participants will leave the research or fail to return questionnaires. Hence it is advisable to overestimate rather than to underestimate the size of the sample required.

It is clear that sample size is a matter of judgement as well as mathematical precision; even formula-driven approaches make it clear that there are elements of prediction, standard error and human judgement involved in determining sample size.

Sampling error

If many samples are taken from the same population, it is unlikely that they will all have characteristics identical with each other or with the population; their means will be different. In brief, there will be sampling error (see Cohen and Holliday, 1979; 1996). Sampling error is often taken to be the difference between the sample mean and the population mean. Sampling error is not necessarily the result of mistakes made in sampling procedures. Rather, variations may occur due to the chance selection of different individuals. For example, if we take a large number of samples from the population and measure the mean value of each sample, then the sample means will not be identical. Some will be relatively high, some relatively low, and many will cluster around an average or mean value of the samples. We show this diagrammatically in Box 4.3.

Why should this occur? We can explain the phenomenon by reference to the Central Limit Theorem which is derived from the laws of probability. This states that if random large samples of equal size are repeatedly drawn from any population, then the mean of those samples will

Box 4.3

Distribution of sample means showing the spread of a selection of sample means around the population mean

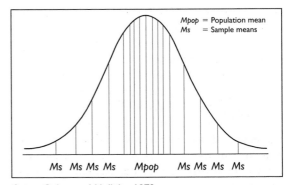

Source Cohen and Holliday, 1979

be approximately normally distributed. The distribution of sample means approaches the normal distribution as the size of the sample increases, regardless of the shape – normal or otherwise – of the parent population (Hopkins, Hopkins and Glass, 1996: 159, 388). Moreover, the average or mean of the sample means will be approximately the same as the population mean. The authors demonstrate this (pp. 159–62) by reporting the use of computer simulation to examine the sampling distribution of means when computed 10,000 times (a method that we discuss in the final chapter of this book). Rose and Sullivan (1993: 144) remind us that 95 per cent of all sample means fall between plus or minus 1.96 standard errors of the sample and population means, i.e. that we have a 95 per cent chance of having a single sample mean within these limits, that the sample mean will fall within the limits of the population mean.

By drawing a large number of samples of equal size from a population, we create a sampling distribution. We can calculate the error involved in such sampling. The standard deviation of the theoretical distribution of sample means is a measure of sampling error and is called the standard error of the mean (SE_M). Thus,

$$SE = \frac{SD_S}{\sqrt{N}}$$

where

SD_S = the standard deviation of the sample and
N = the number in the sample.

Strictly speaking, the formula for the standard error of the mean is:

$$SE = \frac{SD_{pop}}{\sqrt{N}}$$

where SD_{pop} = the standard deviation of the population.

However, as we are usually unable to ascertain the SD of the total population, the standard deviation of the sample is used instead. The standard error of the mean provides the best estimate of the sampling error. Clearly, the sampling error depends on the variability (i.e. the heterogeneity) in the population as measured by SD_{pop} as well as the sample size (N) (Rose and Sullivan, 1993: 143). The smaller the SD_{pop} the smaller the sampling error; the larger the N, the smaller the sampling error. Where the SD_{pop} is very large, then N needs to be very large to counteract it. Where SD_{pop} is very small, then N, too, can be small and still give a reasonably small sampling error. As the sample size increases the sampling error decreases. Hopkins, Hopkins and Glass (1996: 159) suggest that, unless there are some very unusual distributions, samples of twenty-five or greater usually yield a normal sampling distribution of the mean. For further analysis of steps that can be taken to cope with the estimation of sampling in surveys we refer the reader to Ross and Wilson (1997).

The standard error of proportions

We said earlier that one answer to 'How big a sample must I obtain?' is 'How accurate do I want my results to be?' This is well illustrated in the following example:

> A school principal finds that the 25 students she talks to at random are reasonably in favour of a proposed change in the lunch break hours, 66 per cent being in favour and 34 per cent being against. How can she be sure that these proportions are truly representative of the whole school of 1,000 students?

A simple calculation of the standard error of proportions provides the principal with her answer.

$$SE = \sqrt{\frac{P \times Q}{N}}$$

where

P = the percentage in favour
Q = 100 per cent – P
N = the sample size

The formula assumes that each sample is drawn on a simple random basis. A small correction factor called the finite population correction (fpc) is generally applied as follows:

$$SE \text{ of proportions} = \sqrt{\frac{(1-f)P \times Q}{N}}$$ where f is the proportion included in the sample.

Where, for example, a sample is 100 out of 1,000, f is 0.1.

$$SE \text{ of proportions} = \sqrt{\frac{(1-0.1)(66 \times 34)}{100}} = 4.49$$

In our example above, of the school principal's interest in lunch break hours, with a sample of 25, the SE = 9.4. In other words, the favourable vote can vary between 56.6 per cent and 75.4 per cent; likewise, the unfavourable vote can vary between 43.4 per cent and 24.6 per cent. Clearly, a voting possibility ranging from 56.6 per cent in favour to 43.4 per cent against is less decisive than 66 per cent as opposed to 34 per cent. Should the school principal enlarge her sample to include 100 students, then the SE becomes 4.5 and the variation in the range is reduced to 61.5 per cent–70.5 per cent in favour and 38.5 per cent–29.5 per cent against. Sampling the whole school's opinion (n = 1,000) reduces the SE to 1.5 and the ranges to 64.5 per cent–67.5 per cent in favour and 35.5 per cent–32.5 per cent against. It is easy to see why political opinion surveys are often based upon sample sizes of 1,000 to 1,500 (Gardner, 1978).

The representativeness of the sample

The researcher will need to consider the extent to which it is important that the sample in fact represents the whole population in question (in the example above, the 1,000 students), if it is to be a valid sample. The researcher will need to be clear what it is that is being represented, i.e. to set the parameter characteristics of the wider population – the sampling frame – clearly and correctly. There is a popular example of how poor sampling may be unrepresentative and unhelpful for a researcher. A national newspaper reports that one person in every two suffers from backache; this headline stirs alarm in every doctor's surgery throughout the land. However, the newspaper fails to make clear the parameters of the study which gave rise to the headline. It turns out that the research took place (a) in a damp part of the country where the incidence of backache might be expected to be higher than elsewhere, (b) in a part of the country which contained a disproportionate number of elderly people, again who might be expected to have more backaches than a younger population, (c) in an area of heavy industry where the working population might be expected to have more backache than in an area of lighter industry or service industries, (d) by using two doctors' records only, overlooking the fact that many backache sufferers did not go to those doctors' surgeries because the two doctors concerned were known to regard backache sufferers with suspicion – as shirkers from work.

These four variables – climate, age group, occupation and reported incidence – were seen to exert a disproportionate effect on the study, i.e. if the study were to have been carried out in an area where the climate, age group, occupation and reporting were to have been different, then the results might have been different. The newspaper report sensationally generalized beyond the parameters of the data, thereby overlooking the limited representativeness of the study.

The access to the sample

Researchers will need to ensure not only that access is permitted, but is, in fact, practicable. For example, if a researcher were to conduct research into truancy and unauthorized absence from school, and she decided to interview a sample of truants, the research might never commence as the truants, by definition, would not be present! Similarly access to sensitive areas might not only be difficult but problematical both legally and administratively, for example, access to child abuse victims, child abusers, disaffected students, drug addicts, school refusers, bullies and victims of bullying. In some sensitive areas access to a sample might be denied by the potential sample participants themselves, for example an AIDS counsellor might be so seriously distressed by her work that she simply cannot face discussing with a researcher its traumatic subject matter; it is distressing enough to do the job without living through it again with a researcher. Access might also be denied by the potential sample participants themselves for very practical reasons, for example a doctor or a teacher simply might not have the time to spend with the researcher. Further, access might be denied by people who have something to protect, for example, a person who has made an important discovery or a new invention and who does not wish to disclose the secret of her success; the trade in intellectual property has rendered this a live issue for many researchers. There are very many reasons which might prevent access to the sample, and researchers cannot afford to neglect this potential source of difficulty in planning research.

Not only might access be problematic, but its corollary – release of information – might also be problematic. For example, a researcher might gain access to a wealth of sensitive information and appropriate people, but there might be a restriction on the release of the data collection: in the field of education in the UK, reports have been known to be suppressed, delayed or 'doctored'. It is not always enough to be able to 'get to' the sample, the problem might be to 'get the information out' to the wider public, particularly if it could be critical of powerful people.

The sampling strategy to be used

There are two main methods of sampling (Cohen and Holliday, 1979, 1982, 1996; Schofield, 1996). The researcher must decide whether to opt for a probability (also known as a random sample) or a non-probability sample (also known as a purposive sample). The difference between them is this: in a probability sample the chances of members of the wider population being selected for the sample are known, whereas in a non-probability sample the chances of members of the wider popula-

tion being selected for the sample are unknown. In the former (probability sample) every member of the wider population has an equal chance of being included in the sample; inclusion or exclusion from the sample is a matter of chance and nothing else. In the latter (non-probability sample) some members of the wider population definitely will be excluded and others definitely included (i.e. every member of the wider population does not have an equal chance of being included in the sample). In this latter type the researcher has deliberately – purposely – selected a particular section of the wider population to include in or exclude from the sample.

Probability samples

A probability sample, because it draws randomly from the wider population, will be useful if the researcher wishes to be able to make generalizations, because it seeks representativeness of the wider population. This is a form of sampling that is popular in randomized controlled trials. On the other hand, a non-probability sample deliberately avoids representing the wider population; it seeks only to represent a particular group, a particular named section of the wider population, e.g. a class of students, a group of students who are taking a particular examination, a group of teachers.

A probability sample will have less risk of bias than a non-probability sample, whereas, by contrast, a non-probability sample, being unrepresentative of the whole population, may demonstrate skewness or bias. This is not to say that the former is bias-free; there is still likely to be sampling error in a probability sample (discussed below), a feature that has to be acknowledged, for example opinion polls usually declare their error factors, e.g. ± 3 per cent.

There are several types of probability samples: simple random samples; systematic samples; stratified samples; cluster samples; stage samples, and multi-phase samples. They all have a measure of randomness built into them and therefore have a degree of generalizability.

Simple random sampling

In simple random sampling, each member of the population under study has an equal chance of being selected and the probability of a member of the population being selected is unaffected by the selection of other members of the population, i.e. each selection is entirely independent of the next. The method involves selecting at random from a list of the population (a sampling frame) the required number of subjects for the sample. This can be done by drawing names out of a hat until the required number is reached, or by using a table of random numbers set out in matrix form (these are reproduced in many books on quantitative research methods and statistics), and allocating these random numbers to participants or cases (e.g. Hopkins, Hopkins and Glass, 1996: 148–9). Because of probability and chance, the sample should contain subjects with characteristics similar to the population as a whole; some old, some young, some tall, some short, some fit, some unfit, some rich, some poor etc. One problem associated with this particular sampling method is that a complete list of the population is needed and this is not always readily available.

Systematic sampling

This method is a modified form of simple random sampling. It involves selecting subjects from a population list in a systematic rather than a random fashion. For example, if from a population of, say, 2,000, a sample of 100 is required, then every twentieth person can be selected. The starting point for the selection is chosen at random.

One can decide how frequently to make systematic sampling by a simple statistic – the total number of the wider population being represented divided by the sample size required:

$$f = \frac{N}{sn}$$

where

f = the frequency interval

N = the total number of the wider population
sn = the required number in the sample.

Let us say that the researcher is working with a school of 1,400 students; by looking at the table of sample size (Box 4.1) required for a random sample of these 1,400 students we see that 302 students are required to be in the sample. Hence the frequency interval (f) is:

$$\frac{1400}{302} = 4.635 \text{ (which rounds up to 5.0)}$$

Hence the researcher would pick out every fifth name on the list of cases.

Such a process, of course, assumes that the names on the list themselves have been listed in a random order. A list of females and males might list all the females first, before listing all the males; if there were 200 females on the list, the researcher might have reached the desired sample size before reaching that stage of the list which contained males, thereby distorting (skewing) the sample. Another example might be where the researcher decides to select every thirtieth person identified from a list of school students, but it happens that:

1   the school has approximately thirty students in each class;
2   each class is listed from high ability to low ability students;
3   the school listing identifies the students by class.

In this case, although the sample is drawn from each class, it is not fairly representing the whole school population since it is drawing almost exclusively on the lower ability students. This is the issue of periodicity (Calder, 1979). Not only is there the question of the order in which names are listed in systematic sampling, but there is also the issue that this process may violate one of the fundamental premises of probability sampling, namely that every person has an equal chance of being included in the sample. In the example above where every fifth name is selected, this guarantees that names 1–4, 6–9 etc. will not be selected, i.e. that everybody does not have an equal chance to be chosen. The ways to minimize this problem are to ensure that the initial listing is selected randomly and that the starting point for systematic sampling is similarly selected randomly.

Stratified sampling

Stratified sampling involves dividing the population into homogenous groups, each group containing subjects with similar characteristics. For example, group A might contain males and group B, females. In order to obtain a sample representative of the whole population in terms of sex, a random selection of subjects from group A and group B must be taken. If needed, the exact proportion of males to females in the whole population can be reflected in the sample. The researcher will have to identify those characteristics of the wider population which must be included in the sample, i.e. to identify the parameters of the wider population. This is the essence of establishing the sampling frame.

To organize a stratified random sample is a simple two-stage process. First, identify those characteristics which appear in the wider population which must also appear in the sample, i.e. divide the wider population into homogeneous and, if possible, discrete groups (strata), for example males and females. Second, randomly sample within these groups, the size of each group being determined either by the judgement of the researcher or by reference to Boxes 4.1 or 4.2.

The decision on which characteristics to include should strive for simplicity as far as possible, as the more factors there are, not only the more complicated the sampling becomes, but often the larger the sample will have to be to include representatives of all strata of the wider population.

A stratified random sample is, therefore, a useful blend of randomization and categorization, thereby enabling both a quantitative and qualitative piece of research to be undertaken. A quantitative piece of research will be able to use analytical and inferential statistics, whilst a qualitative piece of research will be able to target those groups in institutions or clusters of participants who will be able to be approached to participate in the research.

Cluster sampling

When the population is large and widely dispersed, gathering a simple random sample poses administrative problems. Suppose we want to survey students' fitness levels in a particularly large community. It would be completely impractical to select students and spend an inordinate amount of time travelling about in order to test them. By cluster sampling, the researcher can select a specific number of schools and test all the students in those selected schools, i.e. a geographically close cluster is sampled.

Cluster samples are widely used in small scale research. In a cluster sample the parameters of the wider population are often drawn very sharply; a researcher, therefore, would have to comment on the generalizability of the findings. The researcher may also need to stratify within this cluster sample if useful data, i.e. those which are focused and which demonstrate discriminability, are to be acquired.

Stage sampling

Stage sampling is an extension of cluster sampling. It involves selecting the sample in stages, that is, taking samples from samples. Using the large community example in cluster sampling, one type of stage sampling might be to select a number of schools at random, and from within each of these schools, select a number of classes at random, and from within those classes select a number of students.

Morrison (1993: 121–2) provides an example of how to address stage sampling in practice. Let us say that a researcher wants to administer a questionnaire to all 16-year-olds in each of eleven secondary schools in one region. By contacting the eleven schools she finds that there are 2,000 16-year-olds on roll. Because of questions of confidentiality she is unable to find out the names of all the students so it is impossible to draw their names out of a hat to achieve randomness (and even if she had the names, it would be a mind-numbing activity to write out 2,000 names to draw out of a hat!). From looking at Box 4.1 she finds that, for a random sample of the 2,000 students, the sample size is 322 students. How can she proceed?

The first stage is to list the eleven schools on a piece of paper and then to put the names of the eleven schools onto a small card and place each card in a hat. She draws out the first name of the school, puts a tally mark by the appropriate school on her list and returns the card to the hat. The process is repeated 321 times, bringing the total to 322. The final totals might appear thus:

School	1	2	3	4	5	6	7	8	9	10	11	Total
Required no. of students	22	31	32	24	29	20	35	28	32	38	31	322

For the second stage she then approaches each of the eleven schools and asks them to select randomly the required number of students for each school. Randomness has been maintained in two stages and a large number (2,000) has been rendered manageable. The process at work here is to go from the general to the specific, the wide to the focused, the large to the small.

Multi-phase sampling

In stage sampling there is a single unifying purpose throughout the sampling. In the previous example the purpose was to reach a particular group of students from a particular region. In a multi-phase sample the purposes change at each phase, for example, at phase one the selection of the sample might be based on the criterion of geography (e.g. students living in a particular region); phase two might be based on an economic criterion (e.g. schools whose budgets are administered in markedly different ways); phase three might be based on a political criterion (e.g. schools whose students are drawn from areas with a tradition of support for a particular political party), and so on. What is evident here is

that the sample population will change at each phase of the research.

Non-probability samples

The selectivity which is built into a non-probability sample derives from the researcher targeting a particular group, in the full knowledge that it does not represent the wider population; it simply represents itself. This is frequently the case in small scale research, for example, as with one or two schools, two or three groups of students, or a particular group of teachers, where no attempt to generalize is desired; this is frequently the case for some ethnographic research, action research or case study research.

Small scale research often uses non-probability samples because, despite the disadvantages that arise from their non-representativeness, they are far less complicated to set up, are considerably less expensive, and can prove perfectly adequate where researchers do not intend to generalize their findings beyond the sample in question, or where they are simply piloting a questionnaire as a prelude to the main study.

Just as there are several types of probability sample, so there are several types of non-probability sample: convenience sampling, quota sampling, dimensional sampling, purposive sampling and snowball sampling. Each type of sample seeks only to represent itself or instances of itself in a similar population, rather than attempting to represent the whole, undifferentiated population.

Convenience sampling

Convenience sampling – or as it is sometimes called, accidental or opportunity sampling – involves choosing the nearest individuals to serve as respondents and continuing that process until the required sample size has been obtained. Captive audiences such as students or student teachers often serve as respondents based on convenience sampling. The researcher simply chooses the sample from those to whom she has easy access. As it does not represent any group apart from itself, it does not seek to generalize about the wider population; for a convenience sample that is an irrelevance. The researcher, of course, must take pains to report this point – that the parameters of generalizability in this type of sample are negligible. A convenience sample may be the sampling strategy selected for a case study or a series of case studies.

Quota sampling

Quota sampling has been described as the non-probability equivalent of stratified sampling (Bailey, 1978). Like a stratified sample, a quota sample strives to represent significant characteristics (strata) of the wider population; unlike stratified sampling it sets out to represent these in the proportions in which they can be found in the wider population. For example, suppose that the wider population (however defined) were composed of 55 per cent females and 45 per cent males, then the sample would have to contain 55 per cent females and 45 per cent males; if the population of a school contained 80 per cent of students up to and including the age of 16, and 20 per cent of students aged 17 and over, then the sample would have to contain 80 per cent of students up to the age of 16 and 20 per cent of students aged 17 and above. A quota sample, then, seeks to give proportional weighting to selected factors (strata) which reflects their weighting in which they can be found in the wider population. The researcher wishing to devise a quota sample can proceed in three stages:

Stage 1 Identify those characteristics (factors) which appear in the wider population which must also appear in the sample, i.e. divide the wider population into homogeneous and, if possible, discrete groups (strata), for example, males and females, Asian, Chinese and Afro-Caribbean.
Stage 2 Identify the proportions in which the selected characteristics appear in the wider population, expressed as a percentage.
Stage 3 Ensure that the percentaged proportions of the characteristics selected from the wider population appear in the sample.

Ensuring correct proportions in the sample may be difficult to achieve where the proportions in the wider community are unknown; sometimes a pilot survey might be necessary in order to establish those proportions (and even then sampling error or a poor response rate might render the pilot data problematical).

It is straightforward to determine the minimum number required in a quota sample. Let us say that that the total number of students in a school is 1,700, made up thus:

Performing arts	300 students
Natural sciences	300 students
Humanities	600 students
Business and social sciences	500 students

The proportions being 3:3:6:5, a minimum of 17 students might be required (3 + 3 + 6 + 5) for the sample. Of course this would be a minimum only, and it might be desirable to go higher than this. The price of having too many characteristics (strata) in quota sampling is that the minimum number in the sample very rapidly could become very large, hence in quota sampling it is advisable to keep the numbers of strata to a minimum. The larger the number of strata the larger the number in the sample will become, usually at a geometric rather than an arithmetic rate of progression.

Purposive sampling

In purposive sampling, researchers handpick the cases to be included in the sample on the basis of their judgement of their typicality. In this way, they build up a sample that is satisfactory to their specific needs. As its name suggests, the sample has been chosen for a specific purpose, for example: (a) a group of principals and senior managers of secondary schools is chosen as the research is studying the incidence of stress amongst senior managers; (b) a group of disaffected students has been chosen because they might indicate most distinctly the factors which contribute to students' disaffection (they are 'critical cases' akin to 'critical events' discussed in Chapter 17); (c) one class of students has been selected to be tracked throughout a week in order to report on the curricular and pedagogic diet which is offered to them so that other teachers in the school might compare their own teaching to that reported. Whilst it may satisfy the researcher's needs to take this type of sample, it does not pretend to represent the wider population; it is deliberately and unashamedly selective and biased.

Dimensional sampling

One way of reducing the problem of sample size in quota sampling is to opt for dimensional sampling. Dimensional sampling is a further refinement of quota sampling. It involves identifying various factors of interest in a population and obtaining at least one respondent of every combination of those factors. Thus, in a study of race relations, for example, researchers may wish to distinguish first, second and third generation immigrants. Their sampling plan might take the form of a multi-dimensional table with 'ethnic group' across the top and 'generation' down the side. A second example might be of a researcher who may be interested in studying disaffected students, girls and secondary aged students and who may find a single disaffected secondary female student, i.e. a respondent who is the bearer of all of the sought characteristics.

Snowball sampling

In snowball sampling researchers identify a small number of individuals who have the characteristics in which they are interested. These people are then used as informants to identify, or put the researchers in touch with, others who qualify for inclusion and these, in turn, identify yet others – hence the term snowball sampling. This method is useful for sampling a population where access is difficult, maybe because it is a sensitive topic (e.g. teenage solvent abusers) or where communication networks are undeveloped (e.g. where a researcher wishes to interview stand-in 'supply' teachers – teachers who are brought in on an *ad hoc* basis to cover for absent regular members of a school's teaching staff – but finds it difficult to acquire a list of these stand-in teachers, or where a researcher wishes to contact curriculum co-ordinators who have attended a range of in-service courses and built up an informal network of inter-school communication). The task for the researcher is to establish who are the critical or key informants with whom initial contact must be made.

Conclusion

The message from this chapter is the same as for many of the others – that every element of the research should not be arbitrary but planned and deliberate, and that, as before, the criterion of planning must be fitness for purpose. The selection of a sampling strategy must be governed by the criterion of suitability. The choice of which strategy to adopt must be mindful of the purposes of the research, the time scales and constraints on the research, the methods of data collection, and the methodology of the research. The sampling chosen must be appropriate for all of these factors if validity is to be served.

5 Validity and reliability

The concepts of validity and reliability are multi-faceted; there are many different types of validity and different types of reliability. Hence there will be several ways in which they can be addressed. It is unwise to think that threats to validity and reliability can ever be erased completely; rather, the effects of these threats can be attenuated by attention to validity and reliability throughout a piece of research.

This chapter discusses validity and reliability in quantitative and qualitative, naturalistic research. It suggests that both of these terms can be applied to these two types of research, though how validity and reliability are addressed in these two approaches varies. Finally validity and reliability using different instruments for data collection are addressed. It is suggested that reliability is a necessary but insufficient condition for validity in research; reliability is a necessary precondition of validity. Brock-Utne (1996: 612) contends that the widely held view that reliability is the sole preserve of quantitative research has to be exploded, and this chapter demonstrates the significance of her view.

Defining validity

Validity is an important key to effective research. If a piece of research is invalid then it is worthless. Validity is thus a requirement for both quantitative and qualitative/naturalistic research.

Whilst earlier versions of validity were based on the view that it was essentially a demonstration that a particular instrument in fact measures what it purports to measure, more recently valid-ity has taken many forms. For example, in qualitative data validity might be addressed through the honesty, depth, richness and scope of the data achieved, the participants approached, the extent of triangulation and the disinterestedness or objectivity of the researcher. In quantitative data validity might be improved through careful sampling, appropriate instrumentation and appropriate statistical treatments of the data. It is impossible for research to be 100 per cent valid; that is the optimism of perfection. Quantitative research possesses a measure of standard error which is inbuilt and which has to be acknowledged. In qualitative data the subjectivity of respondents, their opinions, attitudes and perspectives together contribute to a degree of bias. Validity, then, should be seen as a matter of degree rather than as an absolute state (Gronlund, 1981). Hence at best we strive to minimize invalidity and maximize validity.

There are several different kinds of validity, for example:

- content validity;
- criterion-related validity;
- construct validity;
- internal validity;
- external validity;
- concurrent validity;
- face validity;
- jury validity;
- predictive validity;
- consequential validity;
- systemic validity;
- catalytic validity;
- ecological validity;

- cultural validity;
- descriptive validity;
- interpretive validity;
- theoretical validity;
- evaluative validity.

It is not our intention in this chapter to discuss all of these terms in depth. Rather, the main types of validity will be addressed. The argument will be made that, whilst some of these terms are more comfortably the preserve of quantitative methodologies, this is not exclusively the case. Indeed, validity is the touchstone of all types of educational research. That said, it is important that validity in different research traditions is faithful to those traditions; it would be absurd to declare a piece of research invalid if it were not striving to meet certain kinds of validity, e.g. generalizability, replicability, controllability. Hence the researcher will need to locate her discussions of validity within the research paradigm that is being used. This is not to suggest, however, that research should be paradigm-bound, that is a recipe for stagnation and conservatism. Nevertheless, validity must be faithful to its premises and positivist research has to be faithful to positivist principles, e.g.:

- controllability;
- replicability;
- predictability;
- the derivation of laws and universal statements of behaviour;
- context-freedom;
- fragmentation and atomization of research;
- randomization of samples;
- observability.

By way of contrast, naturalistic research has several principles (Lincoln and Guba, 1985; Bogdan and Biklen, 1992):

- the natural setting is the principal source of data;
- context-boundedness and 'thick description';
- data are socially situated, and socially and culturally saturated;
- the researcher is part of the researched world;

- as we live in an already interpreted world, a doubly hermeneutic exercise (Giddens, 1979) is necessary to understand others' understandings of the world; the paradox here is that the most sufficiently complex instrument to understand human life is another human (Lave and Kvale, 1995; 220), but that this risks human error in all its forms;
- holism in the research;
- the researcher – rather than a research tool – is the key instrument of research;
- the data are descriptive;
- there is a concern for processes rather than simply with outcomes;
- data are analysed inductively rather than using a priori categories;
- data are presented in terms of the respondents rather than researchers;
- seeing and reporting the situation through the eyes of participants – from the native's point of view (Geertz, 1974);
- respondent validation is important;
- catching meaning and intention are essential.

Indeed Maxwell (1992) argues that qualitative researchers need to be cautious not to be working within the agenda of the positivists in arguing for the need for research to demonstrate concurrent, predictive, convergent, criterion-related, internal and external validity. The discussion below indicates that this need not be so. He argues, with Guba and Lincoln (1989), for the need to replace positivist notions of validity in qualitative research with the notion of authenticity. Maxwell, echoing Mishler (1990), suggests that 'understanding' is a more suitable term than 'validity' in qualitative research. We, as researchers, are part of the world that we are researching, and we cannot be completely objective about that, hence other people's perspectives are equally as valid as our own, and the task of research is to uncover these. Validity, then, attaches to accounts, not to data or methods (Hammersley and Atkinson, 1983); it is the meaning that subjects give to data and inferences drawn from the data that are important. 'Fidelity' (Blumenfeld-Jones, 1995) requires the researcher to be as honest as possible to the self-reporting of the researched.

The claim is made (Agar, 1993) that, in qualitative data collection, the intensive personal involvement and in-depth responses of individuals secure a sufficient level of validity and reliability. This claim is contested by Hammersley (1992: 144) and Silverman (1993: 153), who argue that these are insufficient grounds for validity and reliability, and that the individuals concerned have no privileged position on interpretation. (Of course, neither are actors 'cultural dopes' who need a sociologist or researcher to tell them what is 'really' happening!) Silverman argues that, whilst immediacy and authenticity make for interesting journalism, ethnography must have more rigorous notions of validity and reliability. This involves moving beyond selecting data simply to fit a preconceived or ideal conception of the phenomenon or because they are spectacularly interesting (Fielding and Fielding, 1986). Data selected must be representative of the sample, the whole data set, the field, i.e. they must address content, construct and concurrent validity.

Hammersley (1992: 50–1) suggests that validity in qualitative research replaces certainty with confidence in our results, and that, as reality is independent of the claims made for it by researchers, our accounts will only be representations of that reality rather than reproductions of it.

Maxwell (1992) argues for five kinds of validity in qualitative methods that explore his notion of 'understanding':

- *descriptive validity* (the factual accuracy of the account, that it is not made up, selective, or distorted); in this respect validity subsumes reliability; it is akin to Blumenfeld-Jones's (1995) notion of 'truth' in research – what actually happened (objectively factual);
- *interpretive validity* (the ability of the research to catch the meaning, interpretations, terms, intentions that situations and events, i.e. data, have for the participants/subjects themselves, in their terms); it is akin to Blumenfeld-

Jones's (1995) notion of 'fidelity' – what it means to the researched person or group (subjectively meaningful); interpretive validity has no clear counterpart in experimental/positivist methodologies;
- *theoretical validity* (the theoretical constructions that the researcher brings to the research (including those of the researched)); theory here is regarded as explanation. Theoretical validity is the extent to which the research explains phenomena; in this respect is it akin to construct validity (discussed below); in theoretical validity the constructs are those of all the participants;
- *generalizability* (the view that the theory generated may be useful in understanding other similar situations); generalizing here refers to generalizing *within* specific groups or communities, situations or circumstances validly) and, beyond, to specific *outsider* communities, situations or circumstance (external validity); internal validity has greater significance here than external validity;
- *evaluative validity* (the application of an evaluative framework, judgemental of that which is being researched, rather than a descriptive, explanatory or interpretive one). Clearly this resonates with critical-theoretical perspectives, in that the researchers' own evaluative agenda might intrude.

Both qualitative and quantitative methods can address internal and external validity.

Internal validity

Internal validity seeks to demonstrate that the explanation of a particular event, issue or set of data which a piece of research provides can actually be sustained by the data. In some degree this concerns accuracy, which can be applied to quantitative and qualitative research. The findings must accurately describe the phenomena being researched.

This chapter sets out the conventional notions of validity as derived from quantitative methodologies. However, in ethnographic research internal validity can be addressed in several ways (LeCompte and Preissle, 1993: 338):

- using low-inference descriptors;
- using multiple researchers;
- using participant researchers;
- using peer examination of data;
- using mechanical means to record, store and retrieve data.

In ethnographic, qualitative research there are several overriding kinds of internal validity (LeCompte and Preissle, 1993: 323–4):

- confidence in the data;
- the authenticity of the data (the ability of the research to report a situation through the eyes of the participants);
- the cogency of the data;
- the soundness of the research design;
- the credibility of the data;
- the auditability of the data;
- the dependability of the data;
- the confirmability of the data.

The writers provide greater detail on the issue of authenticity, arguing for the following:

- *fairness* (that there should be a complete and balanced representation of the multiple realities in and constructions of a situation);
- *ontological authenticity* (the research should provide a fresh and more sophisticated understanding of a situation, e.g. making the familiar strange, a significant feature in reducing 'cultural blindness' in a researcher, a problem which might be encountered in moving from being a participant to being an observer (Brock-Utne, 1996: 610));
- *educative authenticity* (the research should generate a new appreciation of these understandings);
- *catalytic authenticity* (the research gives rise to specific courses of action);
- *tactical authenticity* (the research should benefit all those involved – the ethical issue of 'beneficence').

Hammersley (1992: 71) suggests that internal validity for qualitative data requires attention to:

- plausibility and credibility;
- the kinds and amounts of evidence required (such that the greater the claim that is being made, the more convincing the evidence has to be for that claim);
- clarity on the kinds of claim made from the research (e.g. definitional, descriptive, explanatory, theory generative).

Lincoln and Guba (1985: 219, 301) suggest that credibility in naturalistic inquiry can be addressed by:

- prolonged engagement in the field;
- persistent observation (in order to establish the relevance of the characteristics for the focus);
- triangulation (of methods, sources, investigators and theories);
- peer debriefing (exposing oneself to a disinterested peer in a manner akin to cross-examination, in order to test honesty, working hypotheses and to identify the next steps in the research);
- negative case analysis (in order to establish a theory that fits every case, revising hypotheses retrospectively);
- member checking (respondent validation) to assess intentionality, to correct factual errors, to offer respondents the opportunity to add further information or to put information on record; to provide summaries and to check the adequacy of the analysis).

Whereas in positivist research history and maturation are viewed as threats to the validity of the research, ethnographic research simply assumes that this will happen; ethnographic research allows for change over time – it builds it in. Internal validity in ethnographic research is also addressed by the reduction of observer effects by having the observers sample both widely and stay in the situation long enough for their presence to be taken for granted. Further, by tracking and storing information, it is possible for the ethnographer to eliminate rival explanations of events and situations.

External validity

External validity refers to the degree to which the results can be generalized to the wider population, cases or situations. The issue of generalization is problematical. For positivist researchers generalizability is a *sine qua non*, whilst this is attenuated in naturalistic research. For one school of thought, generalizability through stripping out contextual variables is fundamental, whilst, for another, generalizations that say little about the context have little that is useful to say about human behaviour (Schofield, 1993: 200). For positivists variables have to be isolated and controlled, and samples randomized, whilst for ethnographers human behaviour is infinitely complex, irreducible, socially situated and unique.

Generalizability in naturalistic research is interpreted as comparability and transferability (Lincoln and Guba, 1985; Eisenhart and Howe, 1992: 647). These writers suggest that it is possible to assess the typicality of a situation – the participants and settings, to identify possible comparison groups, and to indicate how data might translate into different settings and cultures (see also LeCompte and Preissle, 1993: 348). Schofield (1992: 200) suggests that it is important in qualitative research to provide a clear, detailed and in-depth description so that others can decide the extent to which findings from one piece of research are generalizable to another situation, i.e. to address the twin issues of *comparability* and *translatability*. Indeed, qualitative research can be generalizable, the paper argues (p. 209), by studying the typical (for its applicability to other situations – the issue of *transferability* (LeCompte and Preissle, 1993: 324)) and by performing multi-site studies (e.g. Miles and Huberman, 1984), though it could be argued that this is injecting (or infecting!) a degree of positivism into non-positivist research. Lincoln and Guba (1985: 316) caution the naturalistic researcher against this; they argue that it is not the researcher's task to provide an index of transferability; rather, they suggest, researchers should provide sufficiently rich data for the readers and users of research to determine whether transferability is possible. In this respect transferability requires thick description.

Bogdan and Biklen (1992: 45) argue that generalizability, construed differently from its usage in positivist methodologies, can be addressed in qualitative research. Positivist researchers, they argue, are more concerned to derive universal statements of general social processes rather than to provide accounts of the degree of commonality between various social settings (e.g. schools and classrooms). Bogdan and Biklen are more interested not with the issue of whether their findings are generalizable in the widest sense but with the question of the settings, people and situations to which they might be generalizable.

In naturalistic research threats to external validity include (Lincoln and Guba, 1985: 189, 300):

- selection effects (where constructs selected in fact are only relevant to a certain group);
- setting effects (where the results are largely a function of their context);
- history effects (where the situations have been arrived at by unique circumstances and, therefore, are not comparable);
- construct effects (where the constructs being used are peculiar to a certain group).

Content validity

To demonstrate this form of validity the instrument must show that it fairly and comprehensively covers the domain or items that it purports to cover. It is unlikely that each issue will be able to be addressed in its entirety simply because of the time available or respondents' motivation to complete, for example, a long questionnaire. If this is the case, then the researcher must ensure that the elements of the main issue to be covered in the research are both a fair representation of the wider issue under investigation (and its weighting) and that the elements chosen for the research sample are themselves addressed in depth and breadth. Careful sampling of items is required to ensure their representativeness. For example, if the researcher wished to see how well a group of students could spell 1,000 words in French but decided only to have a sample of fifty words for the spelling test, then that test would have to ensure that it represented the range of spellings in the 1,000 words – maybe by ensuring that the spelling rules had all been included or that possible spelling errors had been covered in the test in the proportions in which they occurred in the 1,000 words.

Construct validity

A construct is an abstract; this separates it from the previous types of validity which dealt in actualities – defined content. In this type of validity agreement is sought on the 'operational-ized' forms of a construct, clarifying what we mean when we use this construct. Hence in this form of validity the articulation of the construct is important; is my understanding of this construct similar to that which is generally accepted to be the construct? For example, let us say that I wished to assess a child's intelligence (assuming, for the sake of this example, that it is a unitary quality). I could say that I construed intelligence to be demonstrated in the ability to sharpen a pencil. How acceptable a construction of intelligence is this? Is not intelligence something else (e.g. that which is demonstrated by a high result in an intelligence test)?

To establish construct validity I would need to be assured that *my construction* of a particular issue agreed with other constructions of the same underlying issue, e.g. intelligence, creativity, anxiety, motivation. This can be achieved through correlations with other measures of the issue or by rooting my construction in a wide literature search which teases out the meaning of a particular construct (i.e. a theory of what that construct is) and its constituent elements. Demonstrating construct validity means not only confirming the construction with that given in relevant literature, but looking for counter examples which might falsify my construction. When I have balanced confirming and refuting evidence I am in a position to demonstrate construct validity. I am then in a position to stipulate what I take this construct to be. In the case of conflicting interpretations of a construct, I might have to acknowledge that conflict and then stipulate the interpretation that I shall use.

In qualitative/ethnographic research construct validity must demonstrate that the categories that the researchers are using are meaningful *to the participants themselves* (Eisenhart and Howe, 1992: 648), i.e. that they reflect the way in which the participants actually experience and construe the situations in the research; that they see the situation through the actors' eyes.

Campbell and Fiske (1959) and Brock-Utne (1996) suggest that *convergent validity* implies that different methods for researching the same construct should give a relatively high inter-correlation, whilst *discriminant validity* suggests that using similar methods for researching different constructs should yield relatively low inter-correlations.

Ecological validity

In quantitative, positivist research variables are frequently isolated, controlled and manipulated in contrived settings. For qualitative, naturalistic research a fundamental premise is that the researcher deliberately does not try to manipulate variables or conditions, that the situations in the research occur naturally. The intention here is to give accurate portrayals of the realities of social situations in their own terms, in their natural or conventional settings. In education, ecological validity is particularly important and useful in charting how policies are actually happening 'at the chalk face' (Brock-Utne, 1996: 617). For ecological validity to be demonstrated it is important to include and address in the research as many characteristics in, and factors of, a given situation as possible. The difficulty for this is that the more characteristics are included and described, the more difficult it is to abide by central ethical tenets of much research – non-traceability, anonymity and non-identifiability.

A related type of validity is the emerging notion of cultural validity (Morgan, 1999). This is particularly an issue in cross-cultural, inter-cultural and comparative kinds of research, where the intention is to shape research so that it is appropriate to the culture of the researched. Cultural validity, Morgan (1999) suggests, applies at all stages of the research, and affects its planning, implementation and dissemination. It involves a degree of sensitivity to the participants, cultures and circumstances being studied.

Catalytic validity

Catalytic validity embraces the paradigm of critical theory discussed in Chapter 1. Put neutrally, catalytic validity simply strives to ensure that research leads to action. However, the story does not end there, for discussions of catalytic validity are substantive; like critical theory, catalytic validity suggests an agenda. Lather (1986, 1991), Kincheloe and McLaren (1994) suggest that the agenda for catalytic validity is to help participants to understand their worlds in order to transform them. The agenda is explicitly political, for catalytic validity suggests the need to expose whose definitions of the situation are operating in the situation. Lincoln and Guba (1986) suggest that the criterion of 'fairness' should be applied to research, meaning that it should (a) augment and improve the participants' experience of the world, and (b) that it should improve the empowerment of the participants. In this respect the research might focus on what *might* be (the leading edge of innovations and future trends) and what *could* be (the ideal, possible futures) (Schofield, 1992: 209).

Catalytic validity – a major feature in feminist research which, Usher (1996) suggests, needs to permeate all research – requires solidarity in the participants, an ability of the research to promote emancipation, autonomy and freedom within a just, egalitarian and democratic society (Masschelein, 1991), to reveal the distortions, ideological deformations and limitations that reside in research, communication and social structures (see also LeCompte and Preissle, 1993). Validity, it is argued (Mishler, 1990; Scheurich, 1996), is no longer an ahistorical given, but contestable, suggesting that the definitions of valid research reside in the academic communities of the powerful. Lather (1986) calls for research to be emancipatory and to empower those who are being researched, suggesting that catalytic validity, akin to Freire's notion of 'conscientization', should empower participants to understand and transform their oppressed situation.

Validity, it is proposed (Scheurich, 1996), is but a mask that in fact polices and sets boundaries to what is considered to be acceptable research by powerful research communities; discourses of validity, in fact, are discourses of power to define worthwhile knowledge. Valid research, if it is to meet the demands of catalytic validity, must demonstrate its ability to empower the researched as well as the researchers.

How defensible it is to suggest that researchers should have such ideological intents is, perhaps, a moot point, though not to address this area is to perpetuate inequality by omission and neglect. Catalytic validity reasserts the centrality of ethics in the research process, for it requires the researcher to interrogate her allegiances, responsibilities and self-interestedness (Burgess, 1989a).

Criterion-related validity

This form of validity endeavours to relate the results of one particular instrument to another external criterion. Within this type of validity there are two principal forms: predictive validity and concurrent validity.

Predictive validity is achieved if the data acquired at the first round of research correlate highly with data acquired at a future date. For example, if the results of examinations taken by 16-year-olds correlate highly with the examination results gained by the same students when aged 18, then we might wish to say that the first examination demonstrated strong predictive validity.

A variation on this theme is encountered in the notion of concurrent validity. To demonstrate this form of validity the data gathered from using one instrument must correlate highly with data gathered from using another instrument. For example, suppose I wished to research a student's problem-solving ability. I might observe the student working on a problem, or I might talk to the student about how she is tackling the problem, or I might ask the student to write down how she tackled the problem. Here I have three different data-collecting instruments – observation, interview and documentation respectively. If the results all agreed – concurred – that, according to given criteria for problem-solving ability, the student demonstrated a good ability to solve a problem, then I would be able to say with greater confidence (validity) that the student was good at problem-solving than if I had arrived at that judgement simply from using one instrument.

Concurrent validity is very similar to its partner – predictive validity – in its core concept (i.e. agreement with a second measure); what differentiates concurrent and predictive validity is the absence of a time element in the former; concurrence can be demonstrated simultaneously with another instrument.

An important partner to concurrent validity, which is also a bridge into later discussions of reliability, is triangulation.

Triangulation

Triangulation may be defined as the use of two or more methods of data collection in the study of some aspect of human behaviour. It is a technique of research to which many subscribe in principle, but which only a minority use in practice. In its original and literal sense, triangulation is a technique of physical measurement: maritime navigators, military strategists and surveyors, for example, use (or used to use) several locational markers in their endeavours to pinpoint a single spot or objective. By analogy, triangular techniques in the social sciences attempt to map out, or explain more fully, the richness and complexity of human behaviour by studying it from more than one standpoint and, in so doing, by making use of both quantitative and qualitative data. Triangulation is a powerful way of demonstrating concurrent validity, particularly in qualitative research (Campbell and Fiske, 1959).

The advantages of the multimethod approach in social research are manifold and we examine two of them. First, whereas the single observation in fields such as medicine, chemistry and physics normally yields sufficient and unambiguous information on selected phenomena, it provides only a limited view of the complexity of human behaviour and of situations in which human beings interact. It has been observed that as research methods act as filters through which the environment is selectively experienced, they are never atheoretical or neutral in representing the world of experience (Smith, 1975). Exclusive reliance on one method, therefore, may bias or distort the researcher's picture of the particular slice of reality she is investigating. She needs to be confident that the data generated are not simply artefacts of one specific method of collection (Lin, 1976). And this confidence can only be achieved as far as normative research is concerned when different methods of data collection yield substantially the same results. (Where triangulation is used in interpretive research to investigate different actors' viewpoints, the same method, e.g. accounts, will naturally produce different sets of data.) Further, the more the methods contrast with each other, the greater the researcher's confidence. If, for example, the outcomes of a questionnaire survey correspond to those of an observational study of the same phenomena, the more the researcher will be confident about the findings. Or, more extreme, where the results of a rigorous experimental investigation are replicated in, say, a role-playing exercise, the researcher will experience even greater assurance. If findings are artefacts of method, then the use of contrasting methods considerably reduces the chances that any consistent findings are attributable to similarities of method (Lin, 1976).

We come now to a second advantage: some theorists have been sharply critical of the limited use to which existing methods of inquiry in the social sciences have been put (Smith, 1975). The use of triangular techniques, it is argued, will help to overcome the problem of 'method-boundedness', as it has been termed. One of the earliest scientists to predict such a condition was Boring, who wrote:

> as long as a new construct has only the single operational definition that it received at birth, it is just a construct. When it gets two alternative operational definitions, it is beginning to be validated. When the defining operations, because of proven correlations, are many, then it becomes reified.
>
> (Boring, 1953)

In its use of multiple methods, triangulation may utilize either normative or interpretive techniques; or it may draw on methods from both these approaches and use them in combination.

Types of triangulation and their characteristics

We have just seen how triangulation is characterized by a multi-method approach to a problem in contrast to a single-method approach. Denzin (1970) has, however, extended this view of triangulation to take in several other types as well as the multi-method kind which he terms 'methodological triangulation', including:

- *time triangulation* (expanded by Kirk and Miller (1986) to include *diachronic reliability* – stability over time – and *synchronic reliability* – similarity of data gathered at the same time);
- *space triangulation*;
- *combined levels of triangulation* (e.g. individual, group, organization, societal);
- *theoretical triangulation* (drawing on alternative theories);
- *investigator triangulation* (more than one observer);

- *methodological triangulation* (using the same method on different occasions or different methods on the same object of study).

The vast majority of studies in the social sciences are conducted at one point only in time, thereby ignoring the effects of social change and process. Time triangulation goes some way to rectifying these omissions by making use of cross-sectional and longitudinal approaches. Cross-sectional studies collect data concerned with time-related processes from different groups at one point in time; longitudinal studies collect data from the same group at different points in the time sequence. The use of panel studies and trend studies may also be mentioned in this connection. The former compare the same measurements for the same individuals in a sample at several different points in time; and the latter examine selected processes continually over time. The weaknesses of each of these methods can be strengthened by using a combined approach to a given problem.

Space triangulation attempts to overcome the limitations of studies conducted within one culture or subculture. As one writer says, 'Not only are the behavioural sciences culture-bound, they are sub-culture-bound. Yet many such scholarly works are written as if basic principles have been discovered which would hold true as tendencies in any society, anywhere, anytime' (Smith, 1975). Cross-cultural studies may involve the testing of theories among different people, as in Piagetian and Freudian psychology; or they may measure differences between populations by using several different measuring instruments. Levine describes how he used this strategy of convergent validation in his comparative studies:

> I have studied differences of achievement motivation among three Nigerian ethnic groups by the analysis of dream reports, written expressions of values, and public opinion survey data. The convergence of findings from the diverse set of data (and samples) strengthens my conviction . . . that the differences among the groups are not artifacts produced by measuring instruments.
>
> (Levine, 1966)

Social scientists are concerned in their research with the individual, the group and society. These reflect the three levels of analysis adopted by researchers in their work. Those who are critical of much present-day research argue that some of it uses the wrong level of analysis, individual when it should be societal, for instance, or limits itself to one level only when a more meaningful picture would emerge by using more than one level. Smith extends this analysis and identifies seven possible levels: the aggregative or individual level, and six levels that are more global in that 'they characterize the collective as a whole, and do not derive from an accumulation of individual characteristics' (Smith, 1975). The six include:

- group analysis (the interaction patterns of individuals and groups);
- organizational units of analysis (units which have qualities not possessed by the individuals making them up);
- institutional analysis (relationships within and across the legal, political, economic and familial institutions of society);
- ecological analysis (concerned with spatial explanation);
- cultural analysis (concerned with the norms, values, practices, traditions and ideologies of a culture); and
- societal analysis (concerned with gross factors such as urbanization, industrialization, education, wealth, etc.)

Where possible, studies combining several levels of analysis are to be preferred.

Researchers are sometimes taken to task for their rigid adherence to one particular theory or theoretical orientation to the exclusion of competing theories. Thus, advocates of Piaget's developmental theory of cognition rarely take into consideration Freud's psychoanalytic theory of development in their work; and Gestaltists work without reference to S–R theorists. Few published works, as Smith (1975) points out, even go as far as to discuss alternative theories after a study in the light of methods used, much less consider alternatives prior to the research. As he recommends:

The investigator should be more active in designing his research so that competing theories can be tested. Research which tests competing theories will normally call for a wider range of research techniques than has historically been the case; this virtually assures more confidence in the data analysis since it is more oriented towards the testing of rival hypotheses.

(Smith, 1975)

Investigator triangulation refers to the use of more than one observer (or participant) in a research setting (Silverman, 1993: 99). Observers and participants working on their own each have their own observational styles and this is reflected in the resulting data. The careful use of two or more observers or participants independently, therefore, can lead to more valid and reliable data. Smith comments:

Perhaps the greatest use of investigator triangulation centres around validity rather than reliability checks. More to the point, investigators with differing perspectives or paradigmatic biases may be used to check out the extent of divergence in the data each collects. Under such conditions if data divergence is minimal then one may feel more confident in the data's validity. On the other hand, if their data are significantly different, then one has an idea as to possible sources of biased measurement which should be further investigated.

(Smith, 1975)

In this respect the notion of triangulation bridges issues of reliability and validity. We have already considered methodological triangulation earlier. Denzin identifies two categories in his typology: 'within methods' triangulation and 'between methods' triangulation. Triangulation within methods concerns the replication of a study as a check on reliability and theory confirmation (see Smith, 1975). Triangulation between methods, as we have seen, involves the use of more than one method in the pursuit of a given objective. As a check on validity, the between methods approach embraces the notion of convergence between independent measures of the same objective as has been defined by Campbell and Fiske (1959).

Of the six categories of triangulation in Denzin's typology, four are frequently used in education. These are: time triangulation with its longitudinal and cross-sectional studies; space triangulation as on the occasions when a number of schools in an area or across the country are investigated in some way; investigator triangulation as when two observers independently rate the same classroom phenomena; and methodological triangulation. Of these four, methodological triangulation is the one used most frequently and the one that possibly has the most to offer.

Triangular techniques are suitable when a more holistic view of educational outcomes is sought. An example of this can be found in Mortimore et al.'s (1988) search for school effectiveness.

Triangulation has special relevance where a complex phenomenon requires elucidation. Multiple methods are suitable where a controversial aspect of education needs to be evaluated more fully. Triangulation is useful when an established approach yields a limited and frequently distorted picture. Finally, triangulation can be a useful technique where a researcher is engaged in case study, a particular example of complex phenomena (Adelman et al., 1980). For an example of the use of triangular techniques in educational research we refer the reader to Blease and Cohen's (1990) account of investigator triangulation and methodological triangulation.

Triangulation is not without its critics. For example, Silverman (1985) suggests that the very notion of triangulation is positivistic, and that this is exposed most clearly in data triangulation, as it is presumed that a multiple data source (concurrent validity) is superior to a single data source or instrument. The assumption that a single unit can always be measured more than once violates the interactionist principles of emergence, fluidity, uniqueness and specificity (Denzin, 1997: 320). Further, Patton (1980) suggests that even having multiple data sources, particularly of qualitative data, does not ensure consistency or replication. Fielding and Fielding (1986) hold that methodological triangulation does not necessarily increase validity, reduce bias or bring objectivity to research.

With regard to investigator triangulation Lincoln and Guba (1985: 307) contend that it is erroneous to assume that one investigator will corroborate another, nor is this defensible, particularly in qualitative, reflexive inquiry. They extend their concern to include theory and methodological triangulation, arguing that the search for theory and methodological triangulation is epistemologically incoherent and empirically empty (see also Patton, 1980). No two theories, it is argued, will ever yield a sufficiently complete explanation of the phenomenon being researched.

These criticisms are trenchant, but they have been answered equally trenchantly by Denzin (1997).

Ensuring validity

It is very easy to slip into invalidity; it is both insidious and pernicious as it can enter at every stage of a piece of research. The attempt to build out invalidity is essential if the researcher is to be able to have confidence in the elements of the research plan, data acquisition, data processing analysis, interpretation and its ensuing judgement.

At the design stage threats to validity can be minimized by:

- choosing an appropriate time scale;
- ensuring that there are adequate resources for the required research to be undertaken;
- selecting an appropriate methodology for answering the research questions;
- selecting appropriate instrumentation for gathering the type of data required;
- using an appropriate sample (e.g. one which is representative, not too small or too large);
- demonstrating internal, external, content, concurrent and construct validity; 'operationalizing,' the constructs fairly;
- ensuring reliability in terms of stability (consistency, equivalence, split-half analysis of test material);

- selecting appropriate foci to answer the research questions;
- devising and using appropriate instruments (for example, to catch accurate, representative, relevant and comprehensive data (King, Morris and Fitz-Gibbon, 1987)); ensuring that readability levels are appropriate; avoiding any ambiguity of instructions, terms and questions; using instruments that will catch the complexity of issues; avoiding leading questions; ensuring that the level of test is appropriate – e.g. neither too easy nor too difficult; avoiding test items with little discriminability; avoiding making the instruments too short or too long; avoiding too many or too few items for each issue;
- avoiding a biased choice of researcher or research team (e.g. insiders or outsiders as researchers).

There are several areas where invalidity or bias might creep into the research at the stage of data gathering; these can be minimized by:

- reducing the Hawthorne effect;
- minimizing reactivity effects (respondents behaving differently when subjected to scrutiny or being placed in new situations, for example, the interview situation – we distort people's lives in the way we go about studying them (Lave and Kvale, 1995: 226));
- trying to avoid dropout rates amongst respondents;
- taking steps to avoid non-return of questionnaires;
- avoiding having too long or too short an interval between pretests and post-tests;
- ensuring inter-rater reliability;
- matching control and experimental groups fairly;
- ensuring standardized procedures for gathering data or for administering tests;
- building on the motivations of the respondents;
- tailoring the instruments to the concentration span of the respondents and addressing other situational factors (e.g. health, environment, noise, distraction, threat);

- addressing factors concerning the researcher (particularly in an interview situation); for example, the attitude, gender, race, age, personality, dress, comments, replies, questioning technique, behaviour, style and non-verbal communication of the researcher.

At the stage of data analysis there are several areas where invalidity lurks; these might be minimized by:

- using respondent validation;
- avoiding subjective interpretation of data (e.g. being too generous or too ungenerous in the award of marks), i.e. lack of standardization and moderation of results;
- reducing the halo effect, where the researcher's knowledge of the person or knowledge of other data about the person or situation exerts an influence on subsequent judgements;
- using appropriate statistical treatments for the level of data (e.g. avoiding applying techniques from interval scaling to ordinal data or using incorrect statistics for the type, size, complexity, sensitivity of data);
- recognizing spurious correlations and extraneous factors which may be affecting the data (i.e. tunnel vision);
- avoiding poor coding of qualitative data;
- avoiding making inferences and generalizations beyond the capability of the data to support such statements;
- avoiding the equating of correlations and causes;
- avoiding selective use of data;
- avoiding unfair aggregation of data (particularly of frequency tables);
- avoiding unfair telescoping of data (degrading the data);
- avoiding Type I and/or Type II errors.

A Type I error is committed where the researcher rejects the null hypothesis when it is in fact true (akin to convicting an innocent person (Mitchell and Jolley, 1988: 121)); this can be addressed by setting a more rigorous level of significance (e.g. $\rho < 0.01$ rather than $\rho < 0.05$). A

Type II error is committed where the null hypothesis is accepted when it is in fact not true (akin to finding a guilty person innocent (Mitchell and Jolley, ibid.)). Boruch (1997: 211) suggests that a Type II error may occur if: (a) the measurement of a response to the intervention is insufficiently valid; (b) the measurement of the intervention is insufficiently relevant; (c) the statistical power of the experiment is too low; (d) the wrong population was selected for the intervention.

A Type II error can be addressed by reducing the level of significance (e.g. $\rho < 0.20$ or $\rho < 0.30$ rather than $\rho < 0.05$). Of course, the more one reduces the chance of a Type I error the more chance there is of committing a Type II error, and *vice versa*. In qualitative data a Type I error is committed when a statement is believed when it is, in fact, not true, and a Type II error is committed when a statement is rejected when it is in fact true.

At the stage of data reporting invalidity can show itself in several ways; the researcher must take steps to minimize this by, for example:

- avoiding using data very selectively and unrepresentatively (for example, accentuating the positive and neglecting or ignoring the negative);
- indicating the context and parameters of the research in the data collection and treatment, the degree of confidence which can be placed in the results, the degree of context-freedom or context-boundedness of the data (i.e. the level to which the results can be generalized);
- presenting the data without misrepresenting their message;
- making claims which are sustainable by the data;
- avoiding inaccurate or wrong reporting of data (i.e. technical errors or orthographic errors);
- ensuring that the research questions are answered; releasing research results neither too soon nor too late.

Having identified the realms in which invalidity lurks, the researcher can take steps to ensure that, as far as possible, invalidity has been minimized in all areas of the research.[1]

Defining reliability

Reliability in quantitative research

Reliability is essentially a synonym for consistency and replicability over time, over instruments and over groups of respondents. It is concerned with precision and accuracy; some features, e.g. height, can be measured precisely, whilst others, e.g. musical ability, cannot. For research to be reliable it must demonstrate that if it were to be carried out on a similar group of respondents in a similar context (however defined), then similar results would be found. There are three principal types of reliability: stability, equivalence and internal consistency.

Reliability as stability

In this form reliability is a measure of consistency over time and over similar samples. A reliable instrument for a piece of research will yield similar data from similar respondents over time. A leaking tap which each day leaks one litre is leaking reliably whereas a tap which leaks one litre some days and two litres on others is not. In the experimental and survey models of research this would mean that if a test and then a re-test were undertaken within an appropriate time span, then similar results would be obtained. The researcher has to decide what an appropriate length of time is; too short a time and respondents may remember what they said or did in the first test situation, too long a time and there may be extraneous effects operating to distort the data (for example, maturation in students, outside influences on the students). A researcher seeking to demonstrate this type of reliability will have to choose an appropriate time scale between the test and re-test. Correlation coefficients can be calculated for the reliability of pre- and post-tests, using formulae which are readily available in books on statistics and test construction.

In addition to stability over time, reliability as stability can also be stability over a similar sample. For example, we would assume that if we were to administer a test or a questionnaire simultaneously to two groups of students who were very closely matched on significant characteristics (e.g. age, gender, ability etc. – whatever characteristics are deemed to have a significant bearing, on the responses), then similar results (on a test) or responses (to a questionnaire) would be obtained. The correlation co-efficient on this method can be calculated either for the whole test (e.g. by using the Pearson statistic) or for sections of the questionnaire (e.g. by using the Spearman or Pearson statistic as appropriate). The statistical significance of the correlation co-efficient can be found and should be 0.05 or higher if reliability is to be guaranteed. This form of reliability over a sample is particularly useful in piloting tests and questionnaires.

Reliability as equivalence

Within this type of reliability there are two main sorts of reliability. Reliability may be achieved, firstly, through using equivalent forms (also known as alternative forms) of a test or data-gathering instrument. If an equivalent form of the test or instrument is devised and yields similar results, then the instrument can be said to demonstrate this form of reliability. For example, the pretest and post-test in the experimental model of evaluation are predicated on this type of reliability, being alternate forms of instrument to measure the same issues. This type of reliability might also be demonstrated if the equivalent forms of a test or other instrument yield consistent results if applied simultaneously to matched samples (e.g., a control and experimental group or two random stratified samples in a survey). Here reliability can be measured through a t-test, through the demonstration of a high correlation co-efficient and through the demonstration of similar means and standard deviations between two groups.

Secondly, reliability as equivalence may be achieved through inter-rater reliability. If more than one researcher is taking part in a piece of research then, human judgement being fallible, agreement between all researchers must be achieved through ensuring that each researcher enters data in the same way. This would be particularly pertinent to a team of researchers gathering structured observational or semi-structured interview data where each member of the team would have to agree on which data would be entered in which categories. For observational data reliability is addressed in the training sessions for researchers where they work on video material to ensure parity in how they enter the data.

Reliability as internal consistency

Whereas the test/re-test method and the equivalent forms method of demonstrating reliability require the tests or instruments to be done twice, demonstrating internal consistency demands that the instrument or tests be run once only through the split-half method.

Let us imagine that a test is to be administered to a group of students. Here the test items are divided into two halves, ensuring that each half is matched in terms of item difficulty and content. Each half is marked separately. If the test is to demonstrate split-half reliability, then the marks obtained on each half should be correlated highly with the other. Any student's marks on the one half should match his or her marks on the other half. This can be calculated using, the Spearman–Brown formula:

$$\text{Reliability} = \frac{2r}{1 + r}$$

where r = the actual correlation between the halves of the instrument.

This calculation requires a correlation co-efficient to be calculated, e.g. a Spearman rank order correlation or a Pearson product moment correlation.

Let us say that using the Spearman–Brown formula the correlation co-efficient is 0.85; in this case the formula for reliability is set out thus:

$$\text{Reliability} = \frac{2\,(0.85)}{1 + 0.85} = \frac{1.70}{1.85} = 0.919$$

Given that the maximum value of the co-efficient is 1.00 we can see that the reliability of this instrument, calculated for the split-half form of reliability, is very high indeed.

This type of reliability assumes that the test administered can be split into two matched halves; many tests have a gradient of difficulty or different items of content in each half. If this is the case and, for example, the test contains twenty items, then the researcher, instead of splitting the test into two by assigning items one to ten to one half and items eleven to twenty to the second half may assign all the even numbered items to one group and all the odd numbered items to another. This would move towards the two halves being matched in terms of content and cumulative degrees of difficulty.

Reliability, thus construed, makes several assumptions, for example: that instrumentation, data and findings should be controllable, predictable, consistent and replicable. This presupposes a particular style of research, typically within the positivist paradigm.

Reliability in qualitative research

LeCompte and Preissle (1993: 332) suggest that the canons of reliability for quantitative research may be simply unworkable for qualitative research. Quantitative research assumes the possibility of replication; if the same methods are used with the same sample then the results should be the same. Typically, quantitative methods require a degree of control and manipulation of phenomena. This distorts the natural occurrence of phenomena (see earlier: ecological validity). Indeed the premises of naturalistic studies include the uniqueness and idiosyncrasy of situations, such that the study cannot be replicated – that is their strength rather than their weakness.

On the other hand, this is not to say that qualitative research need not strive for replication in generating, refining, comparing and validating constructs. Indeed LeCompte and Preissle (ibid.: 334) argue that such replication might include repeating:

- the status position of the researcher;
- the choice of informant/respondents;
- the social situations and conditions;
- the analytic constructs and premises that are used;
- the methods of data collection and analysis.

Further, Denzin and Lincoln (1994) suggest that reliability as replicability in qualitative research can be addressed in several ways:

- *stability of observations* (whether the researcher would have made the same observations and interpretation of these if they had been observed at a different time or in a different place);
- *parallel forms* (whether the researcher would have made the same observations and interpretations of what had been seen if she had paid attention to other phenomena during the observation);
- *inter-rater reliability* (whether another observer with the same theoretical framework and observing the same phenomena would have interpreted them in the same way).

Clearly this is a contentious issue, for it is seeking to apply to qualitative research the canons of reliability of quantitative research. Purists might argue against the legitimacy, relevance or need for this in qualitative studies.

In qualitative research reliability can be regarded as a fit between what researchers record as data and what actually occurs in the natural setting that is being researched, i.e. a degree of accuracy and comprehensiveness of coverage (Bogdan and Biklen, 1992: 48). This is not to strive for uniformity; two researchers who are studying a single setting may come up with very different findings but both sets of findings might be reliable. Indeed Kvale (1996: 181) suggests that, in interviewing, there might be as many different interpretations of the qualitative data as there are researchers. A clear example of this is the study of the Nissan automobile factory in the UK, where Wickens (1987) found a 'virtuous circle' of work organization practices that demonstrated flexibility, teamwork and quality consciousness, whereas the same practices were investigated by Garrahan and Stewart (1992) who found a 'vicious circle' of exploitation, surveillance and control respectively. Both versions of the same reality co-exist because reality is multi-layered. What is being argued for here is the notion of reliability through an eclectic use of instruments, researchers, perspectives and interpretations (echoing the comments earlier about triangulation) (see also Eisenhart and Howe, 1992).

Brock-Utne (1996) argues that qualitative research, being holistic, strives to record the multiple interpretations of, intention in and meanings given to situations and events. Here the notion of reliability is construed as *dependability* (Guba and Lincoln, 1985: 108–9), recalling the earlier discussion on internal validity. For them, dependability involves member checks (respondent validation), debriefing by peers, triangulation, prolonged engagement in the field, persistent observations in the field, reflexive journals, and independent audits (identifying acceptable processes of conducting the inquiry so that the results are consistent with the data). Audit trails enable the research to address the issue of confirmability of results. These, argue the authors (ibid.: 289), are a safeguard against the charge levelled against qualitative researchers, *viz.* that they respond only to the 'loudest bangs or the brightest lights'.

Dependability raises the important issue of *respondent validation* (see also McCormick and James, 1988). Whilst dependability might suggest that researchers need to go back to respondents to check that their findings are dependable, researchers also need to be cautious in placing exclusive store on respondents, for, as Hammersley and Atkinson (1983) suggest, they are not in a privileged position to be sole commentators on their actions.

Bloor (1978) suggests three means by which respondent validation can be addressed:

- researchers attempt to predict what the participants' classifications of situations will be;
- researchers prepare hypothetical cases and then predict respondents' likely responses to them;
- researchers take back their research report to the respondents and record their reactions to that report.

The argument rehearses the paradigm wars discussed in the opening chapter: quantitative measures are criticized for combining sophistication and refinement of process with crudity of concept (Ruddock, 1981) and for failing to distinguish between educational and statistical significance (Eisner, 1985); qualitative methodologies, whilst possessing immediacy, flexibility, authenticity, richness and candour, are criticized for being impressionistic, biased, commonplace, insignificant, ungeneralizable, idiosyncratic, subjective and short-sighted (Ruddock, 1981). This is an arid debate; rather, the issue is one of fitness for purpose. For our purposes here we need to note that criteria of reliability in quantitative methodologies differ from those in qualitative methodologies. In qualitative methodologies reliability includes fidelity to real life, context- and situation-specificity, authenticity, comprehensiveness, detail, honesty, depth of response and meaningfulness to the respondents.

Validity and reliability in interviews

Studies reported by Cannell and Kahn (1968), in which the interview was used, seemed to indicate that validity was a persistent problem. In one such study, subjects interviewed on the existence and state of their bank accounts often presented a misleading picture: fewer accounts were reported than actually existed and the amounts declared frequently differed from bank records, often in the direction of understating assets. The cause of invalidity, they argue, is bias which they define as 'a systematic or persistent tendency to make errors in the same direction, that is, to overstate or understate the "true value" of an attribute'. (Lansing, Ginsberg and Braaten, 1961).

The problem, it seems, is not limited to a narrow range of data but is widespread. One way of validating interview measures is to compare the interview measure with another measure that has already been shown to be valid. This kind of comparison is known as 'convergent validity'. If the two measures agree, it can be assumed that the validity of the interview is comparable with the proven validity of the other measure.

Perhaps the most practical way of achieving greater validity is to minimize the amount of bias as much as possible. The sources of bias are the characteristics of the interviewer, the characteristics of the respondent, and the substantive content of the questions. More particularly, these will include:

- the attitudes, opinions, and expectations of the interviewer;
- a tendency for the interviewer to see the respondent in her own image;
- a tendency for the interviewer to seek answers that support her preconceived notions;
- misperceptions on the part of the interviewer of what the respondent is saying;
- misunderstandings on the part of the respondent of what is being asked.

Studies have also shown that race, religion, gender, sexual orientation, status, social class and age in certain contexts can be potent sources of bias, i.e. interviewer effects (Lee, 1993; Scheurich, 1995). Interviewers and interviewees alike bring their own, often unconscious experiential and biographical baggage with them into the interview situation. Indeed Hitchcock and Hughes (1989) argue that because interviews are interpersonal, humans interacting with humans, it is inevitable that the researcher will have some influence on the interviewee and, thereby, on the data. Fielding and Fielding (1986: 12) make the telling comment that even the most sophisticated surveys only manipulate data that at some time had to be gained by asking people! Interviewer neutrality is a chimera (Denscombe, 1995).

Lee (1993) indicates the problems of conducting interviews perhaps at their sharpest, where the researcher is researching sensitive subjects, i.e. research that might pose a significant threat to those involved (be they interviewers or interviewees). Here the interview might be seen as an intrusion into private worlds, or the interviewer might be regarded as someone who can impose sanctions on the interviewee, or as someone who can exploit the powerless; the interviewee is in the searchlight that is being held by the interviewer (see also Scheurich, 1995). The issues also embrace *transference* and *countertransference*, which have their basis in psychoanalysis. In transference the interviewees project onto the interviewer their feelings, fears, desires, needs and attitudes that derive from their own experiences (Scheurich, 1995). In countertransference the process is reversed.

One way of controlling for reliability is to have a highly structured interview, with the same format and sequence of words and questions for each respondent (Silverman, 1993), though Scheurich (1995: 241–9) suggests that this is to misread the infinite complexity and open-endedness of social interaction: controlling the wording is no guarantee of controlling the interview. Oppenheim (1992: 147) argues that wording is a particularly important factor in attitudinal questions rather than factual questions. He suggests that changes in wording, context and emphasis undermine reliability, because it ceases to be the same question for each respondent. Indeed he argues that error and bias can stem from alterations to wording, procedure, sequence, recording, rapport, and that training for interviewers is essential to minimize this. Silverman (1993) suggests that it is important for each interviewee to understand the question in the same way. He suggests that the reliability of interviews can be enhanced by: careful piloting of interview schedules; training of interviewers; inter-rater reliability in the coding of responses; and the extended use of closed questions.

On the other hand Silverman (1993) argues for the importance of open-ended interviews, as this enables respondents to demonstrate their unique way of looking at the world – their definition of the situation. It recognizes that what is a suitable sequence of questions for one respondent might be less suitable for another, and open-ended questions enable important but unanticipated issues to be raised.

Oppenheim (1992: 96–7) suggests several causes of bias in interviewing:

- biased sampling (sometimes created by the researcher not adhering to sampling instructions);
- poor rapport between interviewer and interviewee;
- changes to question wording (e.g. in attitudinal and factual questions);
- poor prompting and biased probing;
- poor use and management of support materials (e.g. show cards);
- alterations to the sequence of questions;
- inconsistent coding of responses;
- selective or interpreted recording of data/ transcripts;
- poor handling of difficult interviews.

There is also the issue of *leading questions*. A leading question is one which makes assumptions about interviewees or 'puts words into their mouths', i.e. where the question influences the answer perhaps illegitimately. For example (Morrison, 1993: 66–7) the question 'when did you stop complaining to the headteacher?' assumes that the interviewee had been a frequent complainer, and the question 'how satisfied are you with the new Mathematics scheme?' assumes a degree of satisfaction with the scheme. The leading questions here might be rendered less leading by rephrasing, for example: 'how frequently do you have conversations with the headteacher?' and 'what is your opinion of the new Mathematics scheme?' respectively.

In discussing the issue of leading questions we are not necessarily suggesting that there is not a place for them. Indeed Kvale (1996: 158) makes a powerful case *for* leading questions, arguing that they may be necessary in order to obtain information that the interviewer suspects the interviewee might be withholding. Here it might be important to put the 'burden of denial' onto the

interviewee (e.g. 'when did you last stop beating your wife?'). Leading questions, frequently used in police interviews, may be used for reliability checks with what the interviewee has already said, or may be deliberately used to elicit particular non-verbal behaviours that give an indication of the sensitivity of the interviewee's remarks.

Hence reducing bias becomes more than simply: careful formulation of questions so that the meaning is crystal clear; thorough training procedures so that an interviewer is more aware of the possible problems; probability sampling of respondents; and sometimes matching interviewer characteristics with those of the sample being interviewed. Oppenheim (1992: 148) argues, for example, that interviewers seeking attitudinal responses have to ensure that people with known characteristics are included in the sample – the criterion group. We need to recognize that the interview is a shared, negotiated and dynamic social moment.

The notion of power is significant in the interview situation, for the interview is not simply a data collection situation but a social and frequently a political situation. Power can reside with interviewer and interviewee alike, though Scheurich (1995: 246) argues that, typically, more power resides with the interviewer: the interviewer generates the questions and the interviewee answers them; the interviewee is under scrutiny whilst the interviewer is not. This view is supported by Kvale (1996: 126), who suggests that there are definite asymmetries of power as the interviewer tends to define the situation, the topics, and the course of the interview.

Cassell (in Lee, 1993) suggests that elites and powerful people might feel demeaned or insulted when being interviewed by those with a lower status or less power. Further, those with power, resources and expertise might be anxious to maintain their reputation, and so will be more guarded in what they say, wrapping this up in well-chosen, articulate phrases. Lee (1993) comments on the asymmetries of power in several interview situations, with one party having more power and control over the interview than the other. Interviewers need to be aware of the potentially distorting effects of power, a significant feature of critical theory, as discussed in the opening chapter.

Neal (1995) draws attention to the feelings of powerlessness and anxieties about physical presentation and status on the part of interviewers when interviewing powerful people. This is particularly so for frequently lone, low status research students interviewing powerful people; a low status female research student might find that an interview with a male in a position of power (e.g. a university vice-chancellor, a dean or a senior manager) might turn out to be very different from an interview with the same person if conducted by a male university professor where it is perceived by the interviewee to be more of a dialogue between equals (see also Gewirtz and Ozga, 1993, 1994). Ball (1994b) comments that, when powerful people are being interviewed, interviews must be seen as an extension of the 'play of power' – with its game-like connotations. He suggests that powerful people control the agenda and course of the interview, and are usually very adept at this because they have both a personal and professional investment in being interviewed (see also Batteson and Ball, 1995; Phillips, 1998).

The effect of power can be felt even before the interview commences, notes Neal (1995), where she instances being kept waiting, and subsequently being interrupted, being patronized, and being interviewed by the interviewee (see also Walford, 1994). Indeed Scheurich (1995) suggests that many powerful interviewees will rephrase or not answer the question. Connell, Ashenden, Kessler and Dowsett (in Limerick, Burgess-Limerick and Grace (1996)) argue that a working-class female talking with a multinational director will be very different from a middle-class professor talking to the same person. Limerick, Burgess-Limerick and Grace (1996) comment on occasions where interviewers have felt themselves to be passive, vulnerable, helpless and indeed manipulated. One way of overcoming this is to have two interviewers conducting each interview (Walford, 1994: 227). On

the other hand, Hitchcock and Hughes (1989) observe that if the researchers are known to the interviewees and they are peers, however powerful, then a degree of reciprocity might be taking place, with interviewees giving answers that they think the researchers might want to hear.

The issue of power has not been lost on feminist research; that is, research that emphasizes subjectivity, equality, reciprocity, collaboration, non-hierarchical relations and emancipatory potential (catalytic validity) (Neal, 1995), echoing the comments about research that is influenced by the paradigm of critical theory. Here feminist research addresses a dilemma of interviews that are constructed in the dominant, male paradigm of pitching questions that demand answers from a passive respondent. Limerick, Burgess-Limerick and Grace (1996) suggest that, in fact, it is wiser to regard the interview as a gift, as interviewees have the power to withhold information, to choose the location of the interview, to choose how seriously to attend to the interview, how long it will last, when it will take place, what will be discussed – and in what and whose terms – what knowledge is important, even how the data will be analysed and used. Echoing Foucault, they argue that power is fluid and is discursively constructed through the interview rather than being the province of either party.

Miller and Cannell (1997) identify some particular problems in conducting telephone interviews, where the reduction of the interview situation to just auditory sensory cues can be particularly problematical. There are sampling problems, as not everyone will have a telephone. Further, there are practical issues, for example, the interviewee can only retain a certain amount of information in her/his short term memory, so bombarding the interviewee with too many choices (the non-written form of 'show cards' of possible responses) becomes unworkable. Hence the reliability of responses is subject to the memory capabilities of the interviewee – how many scale points and descriptors, for example, can an interviewee retain in her head about a single item? Further, the absence of non-verbal cues is significant, e.g. facial expression, gestures, posture, the significance of silences and pauses (Robinson, 1982), as interviewees may be unclear about the meaning behind words and statements. This problem is compounded if the interviewer is unknown to the interviewee.

Miller and Cannell present important research evidence to support the significance of the non-verbal mediation of verbal dialogue. As was discussed earlier, the interview is a social situation; in telephone interviews the absence of essential social elements could undermine the salient conduct of the interview, and hence its reliability and validity. Non-verbal paralinguistic cues affect the conduct, pacing, and relationships in the interview and the support, threat, confidence felt by the interviewees. Telephone interviews can easily slide into becoming mechanical and cold.

Further, telephone interviewing is becoming increasingly used by general medical practitioners (the practice of 'triaging'). Here the problem of loss of non-verbal cues is compounded by the asymmetries of power that often exist between doctor and patient. This contains a useful lesson for telephone interviews in educational research – the issue of power is itself a cogent mediating influence between researcher and researched; the interviewer will need to take immediate steps to address these issues (e.g. by putting interviewees at their ease).

On the other hand, Nias (1991) and Miller and Cannell (1997) suggest that the very factor that interviews are not face-to-face may strengthen their reliability, as the interviewee might disclose information that may not be so readily forthcoming in a face-to-face, more intimate situation. Hence, telephone interviews have their strengths and weaknesses, and their use should be governed by the criterion of fitness-for-purpose. They tend to be shorter, more focused and useful for contacting busy people (Harvey, 1988; Miller, 1995).

In his critique of the interview as a research tool, Kitwood draws attention to the conflict it generates between the traditional concepts of validity and reliability. Where increased reliability of the interview is brought about by greater control of its elements, this is achieved, he argues, at the cost of reduced validity. He explains:

> In proportion to the extent to which 'reliability' is enhanced by rationalization, 'validity' would decrease. For the main purpose of using an interview in research is that it is believed that in an interpersonal encounter people are more likely to disclose aspects of themselves, their thoughts, their feelings and values, than they would in a less human situation. At least for some purposes, it is necessary to generate a kind of conversation in which the 'respondent' feels at ease. In other words, the distinctively human element in the interview is necessary to its 'validity'.
>
> (Kitwood, 1977)

Kitwood suggests that a solution to the problem of validity and reliability might lie in the direction of a 'judicious compromise'.

A cluster of problems surround the person being interviewed. Tuckman (1972), for example, has observed that when formulating her questions an interviewer has to consider the extent to which a question might influence the respondent to show herself in a good light; or the extent to which a question might influence the respondent to be unduly helpful by attempting to anticipate what the interviewer wants to hear; or the extent to which a question might be asking for information about a respondent that she is not certain or likely to know herself. Further, interviewing procedures are based on the assumption that the person interviewed has insight into the cause of her behaviour. It has now come to be realized that insight of this kind is rarely achieved and that when it is, it is after long and difficult effort, usually in the context of repeated clinical interviews.

In educational circles interviewing might be a particular problem in working with children. Simons (1982) and McCormick and James (1988) comment on particular problems involved in interviewing children, for example:

- establishing trust;
- overcoming reticence;

- maintaining informality;
- avoiding assuming that children 'know the answers';
- overcoming the problems of inarticulate children;
- pitching the question at the right level;
- choice of vocabulary;
- non-verbal cues;
- moving beyond the institutional response or receiving what children think the interviewer wants to hear;
- avoiding the interviewer being seen an authority spy or plant;
- keeping to the point;
- breaking silences on taboo areas and those which are reinforced by peer-group pressure;
- children being seen as of lesser importance than adults (maybe in the sequence in which interviews are conducted, e.g. the head-teacher, then the teaching staff, then the children).

These are not new matters. The studies by Labov in the 1970s showed how students reacted very strongly to contextual matters in an interview situation (Labov, 1969). The language of children varied according to the ethnicity of the interviewer, the friendliness of the surroundings, the opportunity for the children to be interviewed with friends, the ease with which the scene was set for the interview, the demeanour of the adult (e.g. whether the adult was standing or sitting), the nature of the topics covered. The differences were significant, varying from monosyllabic responses by children in unfamiliar and uncongenial surroundings to extended responses in the more congenial and less threatening surroundings – more sympathetic to the children's everyday world. The language, argot and jargon (Edwards, 1976), social and cultural factors of the interviewer and interviewee all exert a powerful influence on the interview situation.

The issue is also raised here (Lee, 1993) of whether there should be a single interview that maintains the detachment of the researcher (perhaps particularly useful in addressing sensitive topics), or whether there should be repeated

interviews to gain depth and to show fidelity to the collaborative nature of research (a feature, as was noted above, which is significant for feminist research (Oakley, 1981)).

Kvale (1996: 148–9) sets out a range of qualifications for an effective interviewer, that she should be:

- *knowledgeable* (of the subject matter so that an informed conversation can be held);
- *structuring* (making clear the purpose, conduct, completion of the interview);
- *clear* (in choice of language, in presentation of subject matter);
- *gentle* (enabling subjects to say what they want to say in its entirety and in their own time and way);
- *sensitive* (employing empathic, active listening, taking account of non-verbal communication and how something is said);
- *open* (sensitive to which aspects of the interview are significant for the interviewee);
- *steering* (keeping to the point);
- *critical* (questioning to check the reliability, consistency and validity of what is being said);
- *remembering* (recalling earlier statements and relating to them during the interview);
- *interpreting* (clarifying, confirming and disconfirming the interviewee's statements with the interviewee).

Walford (1994: 225) adds to this the need for the interviewer to have done her homework when interviewing powerful people, as such people could well interrogate the interviewer – they will assume up-to-dateness, competence and knowledge in the interviewer. Powerful interviewees are usually busy people and will expect the interviewer to have read the material that is in the public domain.

The issues of reliability do not reside solely in the preparations for and conduct of the interview; they extend to the ways in which interviews are analysed. For example, Lee (1993) and Kvale (1996: 163) comment on the issue of 'transcriber selectivity'. Here transcripts of interviews, however detailed and full they might be, remain selective, since they are interpretations of social situations. They become decontextualized, abstracted, even if they record silences, intonation, non-verbal behaviour etc. The issue, then, is how useful they are to researchers overall rather than whether they are completely reliable.

One of the problems that has to be considered when open-ended questions are used in the interview is that of developing a satisfactory method of recording replies. One way is to summarize responses in the course of the interview. This has the disadvantage of breaking the continuity of the interview and may result in bias because the interviewer may unconsciously emphasize responses that agree with her expectations and fail to note those that do not. It is sometimes possible to summarize an individual's responses at the end of the interview. Although this preserves the continuity of the interview, it is likely to induce greater bias because the delay may lead to the interviewer forgetting some of the details. It is these forgotten details that are most likely to be the ones that disagree with her own expectations.

Validity and reliability in experiments

As we have seen, the fundamental purpose of experimental design is to impose control over conditions that would otherwise cloud the true effects of the independent variables upon the dependent variables.

Clouding conditions that threaten to jeopardize the validity of experiments have been identified by Campbell and Stanley (1963), Bracht and Glass (1968) and Lewis-Beck (1993), conditions incidentally that are of greater consequence to the validity of quasi-experiments (more typical in educational research) than to true experiments in which random assignment to treatments occurs and where both treatment and measurement can be more adequately controlled by the researcher. The following summaries adapted from Campbell and Stanley, Bracht and Glass, and Lewis-Beck distinguish between 'internal validity' and 'external validity'. Internal validity is concerned with the question, do the experimental treatments, in fact, make a difference in the specific experiments under scrutiny? External validity, on the other hand, asks the question, given these demonstrable effects, to what populations or settings can they be generalized?

Threats to internal validity

- *History* Frequently in educational research, events other than the experimental treatments occur during the time between pretest and post-test observations. Such events produce effects that can mistakenly be attributed to differences in treatment.
- *Maturation* Between any two observations subjects change in a variety of ways. Such changes can produce differences that are independent of the experimental treatments. The problem of maturation is more acute in protracted educational studies than in brief laboratory experiments.
- *Statistical regression* Like maturation effects, regression effects increase systematically with the time interval between pretests and post-tests. Statistical regression occurs in educational (and other) research due to the unreliability of measuring instruments and to extraneous factors unique to each experimental group. Regression means, simply, that subjects scoring highest on a pretest are likely to score relatively lower on a post-test; conversely, those scoring lowest on a pretest are likely to score relatively higher on a post-test. In short, in pretest-post-test situations, there is regression to the mean. Regression effects can lead the educational researcher mistakenly to attribute post-test gains and losses to low scoring and high scoring respectively.
- *Testing* Pretests at the beginning of experiments can produce effects other than those due to the experimental treatments. Such effects can include sensitizing subjects to the true purposes of the experiment and practice effects which produce higher scores on post-test measures.
- *Instrumentation* Unreliable tests or instru-

ments can introduce serious errors into experiments. With human observers or judges or changes in instrumentation and calibration, error can result from changes in their skills and levels of concentration over the course of the experiment.

- *Selection*   Bias may be introduced as a result of differences in the selection of subjects for the comparison groups or when intact classes are employed as experimental or control groups. Selection bias, moreover, may interact with other factors (history, maturation, etc.) to cloud even further the effects of the comparative treatments.
- *Experimental mortality*   The loss of subjects through dropout often occurs in long-running experiments and may result in confounding the effects of the experimental variables, for whereas initially the groups may have been randomly selected, the residue that stays the course is likely to be different from the unbiased sample that began it.
- *Instrument reactivity*   The effects that the instruments of the study exert on the people in the study (see also Vulliamy, Lewin and Stephens, 1990).
- *Selection-maturation interaction*   where there is a confusion between the research design effects and the variables' effects.

Threats to external validity

Threats to external validity are likely to limit the degree to which generalizations can be made from the particular experimental conditions to other populations or settings. Below, we summarize a number of factors (adapted from Campbell and Stanley, 1963; Bracht and Glass, 1968; Hammersley and Atkinson, 1983; Vulliamy, 1990; Lewis-Beck, 1993) that jeopardize external validity.

- *Failure to describe independent variables explicitly*   Unless independent variables are adequately described by the researcher, future replications of the experimental conditions are virtually impossible.
- *Lack of representativeness of available and target populations*   Whilst those participating in the experiment may be representative of an available population, they may not be representative of the population to which the experimenter seeks to generalize her findings, i.e. poor sampling and/or randomization.
- *Hawthorne effect*   Medical research has long recognized the psychological effects that arise out of mere participation in drug experiments, and placebos and double-blind designs are commonly employed to counteract the biasing effects of participation. Similarly, so-called Hawthorne effects threaten to contaminate experimental treatments in educational research when subjects realize their role as guinea pigs.
- *Inadequate operationalizing of dependent variables*   Dependent variables that the experimenter operationalizes must have validity in the non-experimental setting to which she wishes to generalize her findings. A paper and pencil questionnaire on career choice, for example, may have little validity in respect of the actual employment decisions made by undergraduates on leaving university.
- *Sensitization/reactivity to experimental conditions*   As with threats to internal validity, pretests may cause changes in the subjects' sensitivity to the experimental variables and thus cloud the true effects of the experimental treatment.
- *Interaction effects of extraneous factors and experimental treatments*   All of the above threats to external validity represent interactions of various clouding factors with treatments. As well as these, interaction effects may also arise as a result of any or all of those factors identified under the section on 'Threats to internal validity'.
- *Invalidity or unreliability of instruments*   The use of instruments which yield data in which confidence cannot be placed (see below on tests).
- *Ecological validity*, and its partner, the extent to which behaviour observed in one

context can be generalized to another. Hammersley and Atkinson (1983: 10) comment on the serious problems that surround attempts to relate inferences from responses gained under experimental conditions, or from interviews, to everyday life.

By way of summary, we have seen that an experiment can be said to be internally valid to the extent that within its own confines, its results are credible (Pilliner, 1973); but for those results to be useful, they must be generalizable beyond the confines of the particular experiment; in a word, they must be externally valid also. Pilliner points to a lopsided relationship between internal and external validity. Without internal validity an experiment cannot possibly be externally valid. But the converse does not necessarily follow; an internally valid experiment may or may not have external validity. Thus, the most carefully designed experiment involving a sample of Welsh-speaking children is not necessarily generalizable to a target population which includes non-Welsh-speaking subjects.

It follows, then, that the way to good experimentation in schools, or indeed any other organizational setting, lies in maximizing both internal and external validity.

Validity and reliability in questionnaires

Validity of postal questionnaires can be seen from two viewpoints according to Belson (1986). First, whether respondents who complete questionnaires do so accurately, honestly and correctly; and second, whether those who fail to return their questionnaires would have given the same distribution of answers as did the returnees. The question of accuracy can be checked by means of the intensive interview method, a technique consisting of twelve principal tactics that include familiarization, temporal reconstruction, probing and challenging. The interested reader should consult Belson (1986: 35–8).

The problem of non-response (the issue of 'volunteer bias' as Belson calls it) can, in part, be checked on and controlled for, particularly when the postal questionnaire is sent out on a continuous basis. It involves follow-up contact with non-respondents by means of interviewers trained to secure interviews with such people. A comparison is then made between the replies of respondents and non-respondents. Further, Hudson and Miller (1997) suggest several strategies for maximizing the response rate to postal questionnaires (and, thereby to increase reliability). They involve:

- including stamped addressed envelopes;
- multiple rounds of follow-up to request returns;
- stressing the importance and benefits of the questionnaire;
- stressing the importance of, and benefits to, the client group being targeted (particularly if it is a minority group that is struggling to have a voice);
- providing interim data from returns to non-returners to involve and engage them in the research;
- checking addresses and changing them if necessary;
- following up questionnaires with a personal telephone call;
- tailoring follow-up requests to individuals (with indications to them that they are personally known and/or important to the research – including providing respondents with clues by giving some personal information to show that they are known) rather than blanket generalized letters;
- features of the questionnaire itself (ease of completion, time to be spent, sensitivity of the questions asked, length of the questionnaire);
- invitations to a follow-up interview (face to face or by telephone);
- encouragement to participate by a friendly third party;
- understanding the nature of the sample population in depth, so that effective targeting strategies can be used.

The advantages of the questionnaire over interviews, for instance, are: it tends to be more reliable; because it is anonymous, it encourages greater honesty (though, of course, dishonesty and falsification might not be able to be discovered in a questionnaire); it is more economical than the interview in terms of time and money; and there is the possibility that it may be mailed. Its disadvantages, on the other hand, are: there is often too low a percentage of returns; the interviewer is able to answer questions concerning both the purpose of the interview and any misunderstandings experienced by the interviewee, for it sometimes happens in the case of the latter that the same questions have different meanings for different people; if only closed items are used, the questionnaire may lack coverage or authenticity; if only open items are used, respondents may be unwilling to write their answers for one reason or another; questionnaires present problems to people of limited literacy; and an interview can be conducted at an appropriate speed whereas questionnaires are often filled in hurriedly. There is a need, therefore, to pilot questionnaires and refine their contents, wording, length, etc. as appropriate for the sample being targeted.

One central issue in considering the reliability and validity of questionnaire surveys is that of sampling. An unrepresentative, skewed sample, one that is too small or too large, can easily distort the data, and indeed, in the case of very small samples, prohibit statistical analysis (Morrison, 1993). The issue of sampling has been covered in the preceding chapter.

Validity and reliability in observations

There are questions about two types of validity in observation-based research. In effect, comments about the subjective and idiosyncratic nature of the participant observation study are to do with its external validity. How do we know that the results of this one piece of research are applicable to other situations? Fears that observers' judgements will be affected by their close involvement in the group relate to the internal validity of the method. How do we know that the results of this one piece of

research represent the real thing, the genuine product? In the preceding chapter on sampling, we refer to a number of techniques (quota sampling, snowball sampling, purposive sampling) that researchers employ as a way of checking on the representativeness of the events that they observe and of cross-checking their interpretations of the meanings of those events.

In addition to external validity, participant observation also has to be rigorous in its internal validity checks. There are several threats to validity and reliability here, for example:

- the researcher, in exploring the present, may be unaware of important antecedent events;
- informants may be unrepresentative of the sample in the study;
- the presence of the observer might bring about different behaviours (reactivity and ecological validity);
- the researcher might 'go native', becoming too attached to the group to see it sufficiently dispassionately.

To address this Denzin suggests triangulation of data sources and methodologies. Chapter 6 discusses the principal ways of overcoming problems of reliability and validity in observational research in naturalistic inquiry. In essence it is suggested that the notion of 'trustworthiness' (Lincoln and Guba, 1985) replaces more conventional views of reliability and validity, and that this notion is devolved on issues of *credibility, confirmability, transferability* and *dependability*. Chapter 6 indicates how these areas could be addressed.

If observational research is much more structured in its nature, yielding quantitative data, then the conventions of intra- and inter-rater reliability apply. Here steps are taken to ensure that observers enter data into the appropriate categories consistently (i.e. intra- and inter-rater reliability) and accurately. Further, to ensure validity, a pilot must have been conducted to ensure that the observational categories themselves are appropriate, exhaustive, discrete, unambiguous and effectively operationalize the purposes of the research.

Validity and reliability in tests

The researcher will have to judge the place and significance of test data, not forgetting the problem of the Hawthorne effect operating negatively or positively on students who have to undertake the tests. There is a range of issues which might affect the reliability of the test – for example, the time of day, the time of the school year, the temperature in the test room, the perceived importance of the test, the degree of formality of the test situation, 'examination nerves', the amount of guessing of answers by the students (the calculation of *standard error* which the tests demonstrate feature here), the way that the test is administered, the way that the test is marked, the degree of closure or openness of test items. Hence the researcher who is considering using testing as a way of acquiring research data must ensure that it is appropriate, valid and reliable (Linn, 1993).

Wolf (1994) suggests four main factors that might affect reliability: the range of the group that is being tested, the group's level of proficiency, the length of the measure (the longer the test the greater the chance of errors), and the way in which reliability is calculated. Fitz-Gibbon (1997: 36) argues that, other things being equal, longer tests are more reliable than shorter tests. Additionally there are several ways in which reliability might be compromised in tests. Feldt and Brennan (1993) suggest four types of threat to reliability:

- *individuals* (e.g. their motivation, concentration, forgetfulness, health, carelessness, guessing, their related skills, e.g. reading ability, their usedness to solving the type of problem set, the effects of practice);
- *situational factors* (e.g. the psychological and physical conditions for the test – the context);
- *test marker factors*, e.g. idiosyncrasy and subjectivity;
- *instrument variables* (e.g. poor domain sampling, errors in sampling tasks, the realism of the tasks and relatedness to the experience of the testees, poor question items, the assump-

tion or extent of unidimensionality in item response theory, length of the test, mechanical errors, scoring errors, computer errors).

There is also a range of particular problems in conducting reliable tests, for example:

- there might be a questionable assumption of transferability of knowledge and skills from one context to another (e.g. students might perform highly in a mathematics examination, but are unable to use the same algorithm in a physics examination);
- students whose motivation, self-esteem, and familiarity with the test situation are low might demonstrate less than their full abilities;
- language and readability exert a significant influence (e.g. whether testees are using their first or second language);
- tests might have a strong cultural bias;
- instructions might be unclear and ambiguous;
- difficulty levels might be too low or too high;
- the number of operations in a single test item might be unreasonable (e.g. students might be able to perform each separate item but might be unable to perform several operations in combination).

To address reliability there is a need for moderation procedures (before and after the administration of the test) to iron out inconsistencies between test markers (Harlen, 1994), including:

- statistical reference/scaling tests;
- inspection of samples (by post or by visit);
- group moderation of grades;
- *post hoc* adjustment of marks;
- accreditation of institutions;
- visits of verifiers;
- agreement panels;
- defining marking criteria;
- exemplification;
- group moderation meetings.

Whilst moderation procedures are essentially *post hoc* adjustments to scores, agreement trials and practice-marking can be undertaken before the administration of a test, which is particularly important if there are large numbers of scripts or several markers.

The issue here is that the results as well as the instruments should be reliable. Reliability is also addressed by:

- calculating co-efficients of reliability, split half techniques, the Kuder–Richardson formula, parallel/equivalent forms of a test, test/re-test methods;
- calculating and controlling the standard error of measurement;
- increasing the sample size (to maximize the range and spread of scores in a norm-referenced test), though criterion-referenced tests recognize that scores may bunch around the high level (in mastery learning for example), i.e. that the range of scores might be limited, thereby lowering the correlation co-efficients that can be calculated;
- increasing the number of observations made and items included in the test (in order to increase the range of scores);
- ensuring effective domain sampling of items in tests based on item response theory (a particular issue in Computer Adaptive Testing introduced below (Thissen, 1990));
- ensuring effective levels of item discriminability and item difficulty.

Reliability not only has to be achieved but be seen to be achieved, particularly in 'high stakes' testing (where a lot hangs on the results of the test, e.g. entrance to higher education or employment). Hence the procedures for ensuring reliability must be transparent. The difficulty here is that the more one moves towards reliability as defined above, the more the test will become objective, the more students will be measured as though they are inanimate objects, and the more the test will become decontextualized.

An alternative form of reliability which is premissed on a more constructivist psychology, emphasizes the significance of context, the importance of subjectivity and the need to engage and involve the testee more fully than a simple test. This rehearses the tension between positivism and more interpretive approaches outlined in the first chapter of this book. Objective tests, as described in this chapter, lean strongly towards the positivist paradigm, whilst more phenomenological and interpretive paradigms of social science research will emphasize the importance of settings, of individual perceptions, of attitudes, in short, of 'authentic' testing (e.g. by using non-contrived, non-artificial forms of test data, for example portfolios, documents, course work, tasks that are stronger in realism and more 'hands on'). Though this latter adopts a view which is closer to assessment rather than narrowly 'testing', nevertheless the two overlap, both can yield marks, grades and awards, both can be formative as well as summative, both can be criterion-referenced.

With regard to validity, it is important to note here that an effective test will ensure adequate:

- *content validity* (e.g. adequate and representative coverage of programme and test objectives in the test items, a key feature of domain sampling); content validity is achieved by ensuring that the content of the test fairly samples the class or fields of the situations or subject matter in question. Content validity is achieved by making professional judgements about the relevance and sampling of the contents of the test to a particular domain. It is concerned with coverage and representativeness rather than with patterns of response or scores. It is a matter of judgement rather than measurement (Kerlinger, 1986). Content validity will need to ensure several features of a test (Wolf, 1994): (a) test coverage (the extent to which the test covers the relevant field); (b) test relevance (the extent to which the test items are taught through, or are relevant to, a particular programme); (c) programme coverage (the extent to which the programme covers the overall field in question).
- *criterion-related validity* (where a high correlation co-efficient exists between the scores on the test and the scores on other accepted tests of the same performance); criterion-related validity is achieved by comparing the

scores on the test with one or more variables (criteria) from other measures or tests that are considered to measure the same factor. Wolf (1994) argues that a major problem facing test devisers addressing criterion-related validity is the selection of the suitable criterion measure. He cites the example of the difficulty of selecting a suitable criterion of academic achievement in a test of academic aptitude. The criterion must be: (a) relevant (and agreed to be relevant); (b) free from bias (i.e. where external factors that might contaminate the criterion are removed); (c) reliable – precise and accurate; (d) capable of being measured or achieved.

- *construct validity* (e.g. the clear relatedness of a test item to its proposed construct/unobservable quality or trait, demonstrated by both empirical data and logical analysis and debate, i.e. the extent to which particular constructs or concepts can give an account for performance on the test); construct validity is achieved by ensuring that performance on the test is fairly explained by particular appropriate constructs or concepts. As with content validity, it is not based on test scores, but is more a matter of whether the test items are indicators of the underlying, latent construct in question. In this respect construct validity also subsumes content and criterion-related validity. It is argued (Loevinger, 1957) that, in fact construct validity is the queen of the types of validity because it is subsumptive and because it concerns constructs or explanations rather than methodological factors. Construct validity is threatened by (a) under-representation of the construct, i.e. the test is too narrow and neglects significant facets of a construct, (b) the inclusion of irrelevancies – excess reliable variance.
- *concurrent validity* (where the results of the test concur with results on other tests or instruments that are testing/assessing the same construct/performance – similar to predictive validity but without the time dimension. Concurrent validity can occur simultaneously with another instrument rather than after some time has elapsed);
- *face validity* (that, superficially, the test appears – at face value – to test what it is designed to test);
- *jury validity* (an important element in construct validity, where it is important to agree on the conceptions and operationalization of an unobservable construct);
- *predictive validity* (where results on a test accurately predict subsequent performance – akin to criterion-related validity);
- *consequential validity* (where the inferences that can be made from a test are sound);
- *systemic validity* (Fredericksen and Collins, 1989) (where programme activities both enhance test performance and enhance performance of the construct that is being addressed in the objective). Cunningham (1998) gives an example of systemic validity where, if the test and the objective of vocabulary performance leads to testees increasing their vocabulary, then systemic validity has been addressed.

To ensure test validity, then the test must demonstrate fitness for purpose as well as addressing the several types of validity outlined above. The most difficult for researchers to address, perhaps, is construct validity, for it argues for agreement on the definition and operationalization of an unseen, half-guessed-at construct or phenomenon. The community of scholars has a role to play here. For a full discussion of validity see Messick (1993). To conclude this chapter, we turn briefly to consider validity and reliability in life history accounts.

Validity and reliability in life histories

Three central issues underpin the quality of data generated by life history methodology. They are to do with representativeness, validity and reliability. Plummer (1983) draws attention to a frequent criticism of life history research, namely, that its cases are atypical rather than representative. To avoid this charge, he urges intending researchers to, 'work out and explicitly state the life history's relationship to a wider population' (Plummer, 1983) by way of appraising the subject on a continuum of representativeness and non-representativeness.

Reliability in life history research hinges upon the identification of sources of bias and the application of techniques to reduce them. Bias arises from the informant, the researcher, and the interactional encounter itself. Box 5.1, adapted from Plummer (1983) provides a checklist of some aspects of bias arising from these principal sources.

Several validity checks are available to intending researchers. Plummer identifies the following:

1   The subject of the life history may present an autocritique of it, having read the entire product.

2   A comparison may be made with similar written sources by way of identifying points of major divergence or similarity.

3   A comparison may be made with official records by way of imposing accuracy checks on the life history.

4   A comparison may be made by interviewing other informants.

Essentially, the validity of any life history lies in its ability to represent the informant's subjective reality, that is to say, his or her definition of the situation.

Box 5.1
Principal sources of bias in life history research

Source: Informant
Is misinformation (unintended) given?
Has there been evasion?
Is there evidence of direct lying and deception?
Is a 'front' being presented?
What may the informant 'take for granted' and hence not reveal?
How far is the informant 'pleasing you'?
How much has been forgotten?
How much may be self-deception?

Source: Researcher
Attitudes of researcher: age, gender, class, race, religion, politics etc.
Demeanour of researcher: dress, speech, body language etc.
Personality of researcher: anxiety, need for approval, hostility, warmth etc.
Scientific role of researcher: theory held (etc.), researcher expectancy

Source: The interaction
The encounter needs to be examined. Is bias coming from:
The physical setting – 'social space'?
The prior interaction?
Non-verbal communication?
Vocal behaviour?

Source Adapted from Plummer, 1983: Table 5.2, p. 103

Part three

Styles of educational research

It is important to distinguish between matters of research design, methodology and instrumentation. Too often methods are confused with methodology, and methodology is confused with design. Part Two provided an introduction to design issues and this part examines different styles or kinds of research, separating them from methods – instruments to be used for data collection and analysis. We identify eight main styles of educational research in this section. Although we recognize that these are by no means exhaustive, we suggest that this fairly covers the major styles of research methodology. The gamut of research styles is vast and this part illustrates the scope of what is available, embracing quantitative and qualitative research, together with small scale and large scale approaches. These enable the researcher to address the notion of 'fitness for purpose' in deciding the most appropriate style of research for the task in hand.

This part deliberately returns to issues introduced in Part One, and suggests that, though styles of research can be located within particular research paradigms, this does not necessitate the researcher selecting a single paradigm only, nor does it advocate paradigm-driven research. Rather, the intention here is to shed light on styles of research from the paradigmatic contexts in which they are located. To do this we have introduced considerable new material into this part, for example on naturalistic and ethnographic research (including issues in data analysis), computer usage, action research as political *praxis*, the limits of statistical significance and the importance of effect size, the burgeoning scope of meta-analysis, event history analysis, Nominal Group Technique and Delphi techniques, recent developments in case study research, and issues in correlational research. The previous edition kept separate developmental research and surveys; this edition has brought them together as they are mutually informing.

6 Naturalistic and ethnographic research

Elements of naturalistic inquiry

Chapter 1 indicated that several approaches to educational research are contained in the paradigm of qualitative, naturalistic and ethnographic research. The characteristics of that paradigm (Boas, 1943; Blumer, 1969; Lincoln and Guba, 1985; Woods, 1992; LeCompte and Preissle, 1993) include:

- humans actively construct their own meanings of situations;
- meaning arises out of social situations and is handled through interpretive processes;
- behaviour and, thereby, data are socially situated, context-related, context-dependent and context-rich. To understand a situation researchers need to understand the context because situations affect behaviour and perspectives and *vice versa*;
- realities are multiple, constructed and holistic;
- knower and known are interactive, inseparable;
- only time- and context-bound working hypotheses (idiographic statements) are possible;
- all entities-are in a state of mutual simultaneous shaping, so that it is impossible to distinguish causes from effects;
- inquiry is value-bound:
- inquiries are influenced by inquirer values as expressed in the choice of a problem, evaluand, or policy option, and in the framing, bounding, and focusing of that problem, evaluand or policy option;
- inquiry is influenced by the choice of the paradigm that guides the investigation into the problem;

- inquiry is influenced by the choice of the substantive theory utilized to guide the collection and analysis of data and in the interpretation of findings;
- inquiry is influenced by the values that inhere in the context;
- inquiry is either value-resident (reinforcing or congruent) or value-dissonant (conflicting). Problem, evaluand, or policy option, paradigm, theory, and context must exhibit congruence (value-resonance) if the inquiry is to produce meaningful results;
- research must include 'thick descriptions' (Geertz, 1973) of the contextualized behaviour;
- the attribution of meaning is continuous and evolving over time;
- people are deliberate, intentional and creative in their actions;
- history and biography intersect – we create our own futures but not necessarily in situations of our own choosing;
- social research needs to examine situations through the eyes of the participants – the task of ethnographies, as Malinowski (1922: 25) observed, is to grasp the point of view of the native [sic], his [sic] view of the world and relation to his life;
- researchers are the instruments of the research (Eisner, 1991);
- researchers generate rather than test hypotheses;
- researchers do not know in advance what they will see or what they will look for;
- humans are anticipatory beings;
- human phenomena seem to require even

more conditional stipulations than do other kinds;

- meanings and understandings replace proof;
- generalizability is interpreted as generalizability to identifiable, specific settings and subjects rather than universally;
- situations are unique;
- the processes of research and behaviour are as important as the outcomes;
- people, situations, events and objects have meaning conferred upon them rather than possessing their own intrinsic meaning;
- social research should be conducted in natural, uncontrived, real world settings with as little intrusiveness as possible by the researcher;
- social reality, experiences and social phenomena are capable of multiple, sometimes contradictory interpretations and are available to us through social interaction;
- all factors, rather than a limited number of variables, have to be taken into account;
- data are analysed inductively, with constructs deriving from the data during the research;
- theory generation is derivative – grounded (Glaser and Strauss, 1967) – the data suggest the theory rather than *vice versa*.

Lincoln and Guba (1985: 39–43) tease out the implications of these axioms:

- studies must be set in their natural settings as context is heavily implicated in meaning;
- humans are the research instrument;
- utilization of tacit knowledge is inescapable;
- qualitative methods sit more comfortably than quantitative methods with the notion of the human-as-instrument;
- purposive sampling enables the full scope of issues to be explored;
- data analysis is inductive rather than a priori and deductive;
- theory emerges rather than is pre-ordinate. A priori theory is replaced by grounded theory;
- research designs emerge over time (and as the sampling changes over time);
- the outcomes of the research are negotiated;

- the natural mode of reporting is the case study;
- nomothetic interpretation is replaced by idiographic interpretation;
- applications are tentative and pragmatic;
- the focus of the study determines its boundaries;
- trustworthiness and its components replace more conventional views of reliability and validity.

LeCompte and Preissle (1993) suggest that ethnographic research is a process involving methods of inquiry, an outcome and a resultant record of the inquiry. The intention of the research is to create as vivid a reconstruction as possible of the culture or groups being studied (p. 235). That said, there are several purposes of qualitative research, for example, description and reporting, the creation of key concepts, theory generation and testing. LeCompte and Preissle (1993) indicate several key elements of ethnographic approaches:

- phenomenological data are elicited (p. 3);
- the world view of the participants is investigated and represented – their 'definition of the situation' (Thomas, 1923);
- meanings are accorded to phenomena by both the researcher and the participants; the process of research, therefore is hermeneutic, uncovering meanings (LeCompte and Preissle, 1993: 31–2);
- the constructs of the participants are used to structure the investigation;
- empirical data are gathered in their naturalistic setting (unlike laboratories or in controlled settings as in other forms of research where variables are manipulated);
- observational techniques are used extensively (both participant and non-participant) to acquire data on real-life settings;
- the research is holistic, that is, it seeks a description and interpretation of 'total phenomena';
- there is a move from description and data to inference, explanation, suggestions of causation, and theory generation;

- methods are 'multimodal' and the ethnographer is a 'methodological omnivore' (ibid.: 232).

Hitchcock and Hughes (1989: 52–3) suggest that ethnographies involve:

- the production of descriptive cultural knowledge of a group;
- the description of activities in relation to a particular cultural context from the point of view of the members of that group themselves;
- the production of a list of features constitutive of membership in a group or culture;
- the description and analysis of patterns of social interaction;
- the provision as far as possible of 'insider accounts';
- the development of theory.

There are several key differences between this approach and that of the positivists to whom we made reference in Chapter 1. LeCompte and Preissle (ibid.: 39–44) suggest that ethnographic approaches are concerned more with description rather than prediction, induction rather than deduction, generation rather than verification of theory, construction rather than enumeration, and subjectivities rather than objective knowledge. With regard to the latter the authors distinguish between *emic* approaches (as in the term 'phonemic', where the concern is to catch the subjective meanings placed on situations by participants) and *etic* approaches (as in the term 'phonetic', where the intention is to identify and understand the objective or researcher's meaning and constructions of a situation) (p. 45).

That said, Woods (1992) argues that some differences between quantitative and qualitative research have been exaggerated. He proposes, for example (p. 381), that the 1970s witnessed an unproductive dichotomy between the two, the former being seen as strictly in the hypothetico-deductive mode (testing theories) and the latter being seen as the inductive method used for generating theory. He suggests that the epistemological contrast between the two is overstated, as qualitative techniques can be used both for generating and testing theories.

Indeed Dobbert and Kurth-Schai (1992) urge ethnographic approaches to become not only more systematic but to study and address regularities in social behaviour and social structure (pp. 94–5). The task of ethnographers is to balance a commitment to catch the diversity, variability, creativity, individuality, uniqueness and spontaneity of social interactions (e.g. by 'thick descriptions' (Geertz, 1973)) with a commitment to the task of social science to seek regularities, order and patterns within such diversity (ibid.: 150). As Durkheim noted, there are 'social facts'.

Following this line, it is possible, therefore, to suggest that ethnographic research can address issues of generalizability – a tenet of positivist research – interpreted as 'comparability' and 'translatability' (LeCompte and Preissle, 1992: 47). For comparability the characteristics of the group that is being studied need to be made explicit so that readers can compare them with other similar or dissimilar groups. For translatability the analytic categories used in the research as well as the characteristics of the groups are made explicit so that meaningful comparisons can be made to other groups and disciplines.

Spindler and Spindler (1992: 72–4) put forward several hallmarks of effective ethnographies:

- Observations have contextual relevance, both in the immediate setting in which behaviour is observed and in further contexts beyond.
- Hypotheses emerge *in situ* as the study develops in the observed setting.
- Observation is prolonged and often repetitive. Events and series of events are observed more than once to establish reliability in the observational data.
- Inferences from observation and various forms of ethnographic inquiry are used to address insiders' views of reality.
- A major part of the ethnographic task is to elicit sociocultural knowledge from participants, rendering social behaviour comprehensible.

- Instruments, schedules, codes, agenda for interviews, questionnaires, etc. should be generated *in situ*, and should derive from observation and ethnographic inquiry.
- A transcultural, comparative perspective is usually present, although often it is an unstated assumption, and cultural variation (over space and time) is natural.
- Some sociocultural knowledge that affects behaviour and communication under study is tacit/implicit, and may not be known even to participants or known ambiguously to others. It follows that one task for an ethnography is to make explicit to readers what is tacit/implicit to informants.
- The ethnographic interviewer should not frame or predetermine responses by the kinds of questions that are asked, because the informants themselves have the emic, native cultural knowledge.
- In order to collect as much live data as possible, any technical device may be used.
- The ethnographer's presence should be declared and his or her personal, social and interactional position in the situation should be described.

With 'mutual shaping and interaction' between the researcher and participants taking place (Lincoln and Guba, 1985: 155) the researcher becomes, as it were, the 'human instrument' in the research (ibid.: 187), building on her tacit knowledge in addition to her propositional knowledge, using methods that sit comfortably with human inquiry, e.g. observations, interviews, documentary analysis and 'unobtrusive' methods (ibid.: 187). The advantage of the 'human instrument' is her adaptability, responsiveness, knowledge, ability to handle sensitive matters, ability to see the whole picture, ability to clarify and summarize, to explore, to analyse, to examine atypical or idiosyncratic responses (ibid.: 193–4).

Planning naturalistic research

In many ways the issues in naturalistic research are not exclusive; they apply to other forms of research, for example: identifying the problem and research purposes; deciding the focus of the study; selecting the research design and instrumentation; addressing validity and reliability; ethical issues; approaching data analysis and interpretation. These are common to all research. More specifically Wolcott (1992: 19) suggests that naturalistic researchers should address the stages of watching, asking and reviewing, or, as he puts it, experiencing, inquiring and examining. In naturalistic inquiry it is possible to formulate a more detailed set of stages that can be addressed (Hitchcock and Hughes, 1989: 57–71; LeCompte and Preissle, 1993; Bogdan and Biklen, 1992):

Stage 1 Locating a field of study.
Stage 2 Addressing ethical issues.
Stage 3 Deciding the sampling.
Stage 4 Finding a role and managing entry into the context.
Stage 5 Finding informants.
Stage 6 Developing and maintaining relations in the field.
Stage 7 Data collection *in situ*.
Stage 8 Data collection outside the field.
Stage 9 Data analysis.
Stage 10 Leaving the field.
Stage 11 Writing the Report.

These stages – addressed later in this chapter – are shot through with a range of issues that will affect the research, for example:

- personal issues (the disciplinary sympathies of the researcher, researcher subjectivities and characteristics. Hitchcock and Hughes (1989: 56) indicate that there are several serious strains in conducting fieldwork because the researcher's own emotions, attitudes, beliefs, values, characteristics enter the research; indeed the more this happens the less will be the likelihood of gaining the participants' perspectives and meanings);
- the kinds of participation that the researcher will undertake;
- issues of advocacy (where the researcher may be expected to identify with the same emo-

tions, concerns and crises as the members of the group being studied and wishes to advance their cause, often a feature that arises at the beginning and the end of the research when the researcher is considered to be a legitimate spokesperson for the group);

- role relationships;
- boundary maintenance in the research;
- the maintenance of the balance between distance and involvement;
- ethical issues;
- reflexivity.

Reflexivity recognizes that researchers are inescapably part of the social world that they are researching, and, indeed, that this social world is an already interpreted world by the actors, undermining the notion of objective reality. Researchers are in the world and of the world. They bring their own biographies to the research situation and participants behave in particular ways in their presence. Reflexivity suggests that researchers should acknowledge and disclose their own selves in the research; they should hold themselves up to the light, echoing Cooley's (1902) notion of the 'looking glass self'. Highly reflexive researchers will be acutely aware of the ways in which their selectivity, perception, background and inductive processes and paradigms shape the research. They are research instruments. McCormick and James (1988: 191) argue that combating reactivity through reflexivity requires researchers to monitor closely and continually their own interactions with participants, their own reaction, roles, biases, and any other matters that might bias the research. This is addressed more fully in the chapter 5 on validity, encompassing issues of triangulation and respondent validity.

Lincoln and Guba (1985: 226–47) set out ten elements in research design for naturalistic studies:

1 Determining a focus for the inquiry.
2 Determining fit of paradigm to focus
3 Determining the fit of the inquiry paradigm to the substantive theory selected to guide the inquiry.

4 Determining where and from whom data will be collected.
5 Determining successive phases of the inquiry.
6 Determining instrumentation.
7 Planning data collection and recording modes.
8 Planning data analysis procedures.
9 Planning the logistics:
- prior logistical considerations for the project as a whole;
- the logistics of field excursions prior to going into the field;
- the logistics of field excursions while in the field;
- the logistics of activities following field excursions;
- the logistics of closure and termination.
10 Planning for trustworthiness.

This can be set out into a sequential, staged approach to planning naturalistic research (see, for example: Schatzman and Strauss, 1973; Delamont, 1992). Spradley (1979) sets out the stages of: (a) selecting a problem; (b) collecting cultural data; (c) analysing cultural data; (d) formulating ethnographic hypotheses; writing the ethnography. More fully, we suggest an eleven stage model.

Stage 1: locating a field of study

Bogdan and Biklen (1992: 2) suggest that research questions in qualitative research are not framed by simply operationalizing variables as in the positivist paradigm. Rather, they propose that research questions are formulated in situ and in response to situations observed, i.e. that topics are investigated in all their complexity, in the naturalistic context.

Stage 2: addressing ethical issues

Deyle, Hess and LeCompte (1992: 623) identify several critical ethical issues that need to be addressed in approaching the research:

How does one present oneself in the field? As

whom does one present oneself? How ethically defensible is it to pretend to be somebody that you are not in order to: (a) gain knowledge that you would otherwise not be able to gain; (b) gain and preserve access to places which otherwise you would be unable to gain or sustain such access?

The issues here are several. Firstly, there is the issue of *informed consent* (to participate and for disclosure), whether and how to gain participant assent (see also LeCompte and Preissle, 1993: 66). This uncovers another consideration, namely *covert* or *overt* research. On the one hand there is a powerful argument for informed consent. However, the more participants know about the research the less naturally they may behave (ibid.: 108), and naturalism is self-evidently a key criterion of the naturalistic paradigm.

Mitchell (1993) catches the dilemma for researchers in deciding whether to undertake overt or covert research. The issue of informed consent, he argues, can lead to the selection of particular forms of research – those where researchers can control the phenomena under investigation – thereby excluding other kinds of research where subjects behave in less controllable, predictable, prescribed ways, indeed where subjects may come in and out of the research over time.

He argues that in the real social world access to important areas of research is prohibited if informed consent has to be sought, for example in researching those on the margins of society or the disadvantaged. It is in the participants' own interests that secrecy is maintained as, if secrecy is not upheld, important work may not be done and 'weightier secrets' (ibid., p. 54) may be kept which are of legitimate public interest and in the participants' own interests. Mitchell makes a powerful case for secrecy, arguing that informed consent may excuse social scientists from the risk of confronting powerful, privileged, and cohesive groups who wish to protect themselves from public scrutiny. Secrecy and informed consent are moot points. The researcher, then, has to consider her loyalties and responsibilities

(LeCompte and Preissle, 1993: 106), for example what is the public's right to know and what is the individual's right to privacy? (Morrison, 1993).

In addition to the issue of overt or covert research, LeCompte and Preissle (1993) indicate that the problems of *risk* and *vulnerability* to participants must be addressed; steps must be taken to prevent risk or harm to participants (non-maleficence – the principle of *primum non nocere*). Bogdan and Biklen (1992: 54) extend this to include issues of embarrassment as well as harm to the participants. The question of vulnerability is present at its strongest when participants in the research have their freedom to choose limited, e.g. by dint of their age, by health, by social constraints, by dint of their life style (e.g. engaging in criminality), social acceptability, experience of being victims (e.g. of abuse, of violent crime) (p. 107). As the authors comment, participants rarely initiate research, so it is the responsibility of the researcher to protect participants. Relationships between researcher and the researched are rarely symmetrical in terms of power; it is often the case that those with more power, information and resources research those with less.

A standard protection is often the guarantee of *confidentiality*, withholding participants' real names and other identifying characteristics. The authors contrast this with anonymity, where identity is withheld because it is genuinely unknown (p. 106). The issues of identifiability and traceability are raised. Further, participants might be able to identify themselves in the research report though others may not be able to identify them. A related factor here is the *ownership* of the data and the results, the control of the release of data (and to whom, and when) and what rights respondents have to veto the research results. Patrick (1973) indicates this point at its sharpest, when as an ethnographer of a Glasgow gang, he was witness to a murder; the dilemma was clear – to report the matter (and thereby, also to 'blow his cover', consequently endangering his own life) or to stay as a covert researcher.

Bogdan and Biklen (1992: 54) add to this discussion the need to respect participants as subjects, not simply as research objects to be used and then discarded.

Stage 3: deciding the sampling

In an ideal world the researcher would be able to study a group in its entirety. This was the case in Goffman's (1968) work on 'total institutions' – e.g. hospitals, prisons and police forces. It was also the practice of anthropologists who were able to study specific isolated communities or tribes. That is rarely possible nowadays because such groups are no longer isolated or insular. Hence the researcher is faced with the issue of sampling, that is, deciding which people it will be possible to select to represent the wider group (however defined). The researcher has to decide the groups for which the research questions are appropriate, the contexts which are important for the research, the time periods that will be needed, and the possible artefacts of interest to the researcher. In other words decisions are necessary on the sampling of people, contexts, issues, time frames, artefacts and data sources. This takes the discussion beyond conventional notions of sampling, which are confined to issues of sampling populations.

In several forms of research sampling is fixed at the start of the study, though there may be attrition of the sample through 'mortality' (e.g. people leaving the study). Mortality is seen as problematic. Ethnographic research regards this as natural rather than a problem. People come into and go from the study. This impacts on the decision whether to have a synchronic investigation occurring at a single point in time, or a diachronic study where events and behaviour are monitored over time to allow for change, development, and evolving situations. In ethnographic inquiry sampling is recursive and *ad hoc* rather than fixed at the outset; it changes and develops over time. Let us consider how this might happen.

LeCompte and Preissle (ibid.: 82–3) point out that ethnographic methods rule out statistical sampling, for a variety of reasons:

- the characteristics of the wider population are unknown;
- there are no straightforward boundary markers (categories or strata) in the group;
- generalizability, a goal of statistical methods, is not necessarily a goal of ethnography;
- characteristics of a sample may not be evenly distributed across the sample;
- only one or two subsets of a characteristic of a total sample may be important;
- researchers may not have access to the whole population;
- some members of a subset may not be drawn from the population from which the sampling is intended to be drawn.

Hence other types of sampling are required. A criterion-based selection requires the researcher to specify in advance a set of attributes, factors, characteristics or criteria that the study must address. The task then is to ensure that these appear in the sample selected (the equivalent of a stratified sample). There are other forms of sampling (discussed in Chapter 4) that are useful in ethnographic research (Bogdan and Biklen, 1992: 70; LeCompte and Preissle, 1993: 69–83), such as:

- convenience sampling (opportunistic sampling, selecting from whoever happens to be available);
- critical-case sampling (e.g. people who display the issue or set of characteristics in their entirety or in a way that is highly significant for their behaviour);
- the norm of a characteristic is identified, then the extremes of that characteristic are located, and finally, the bearers of that extreme characteristic are selected;
- typical case-sampling (where a profile of attributes or characteristics that are possessed by an 'average', typical person or case is identified, and the sample is selected from these typical people or cases);
- unique-case sampling, where cases that are rare, unique or unusual on one or more criteria are identified, and sampling takes places within these. Here whatever other

characteristics or attributes a person might share with others, a particular attribute or characteristic sets that person apart.

- reputational-case sampling, a variant of extreme-case and unique-case sampling, is where a researcher chooses a sample on the recommendation of experts in the field;
- snowball sampling – using the first interviewee to suggest or recommend other interviewees.

Patton (1980) identifies six types of sampling that are useful in naturalistic research, including

- *sampling extreme/deviant cases* – this is done in order to gain information about unusual cases that may be particularly troublesome or enlightening;
- *sampling typical cases* – this is done in order to avoid rejecting information on the grounds that it has been gained from special or deviant cases;
- *maximum variation sampling* – this is done in order to document the range of unique changes that have emerged, often in response to the different conditions to which participants have had to adapt;
- *sampling critical cases* – this is done in order to permit maximum applicability to others – if the information holds true for critical cases (e.g. cases where all of the factors sought are present), then it is likely to hold true for others;
- *sampling politically important or sensitive cases* – this can be done to draw attention to the case;
- *convenience sampling* – this saves time and money and spares the researcher the effort of finding less amenable participants.

Lincoln and Guba (1985: 201–2) suggest an important difference between conventional and naturalistic research designs. In the former the intention is to focus on similarities and to be able to make generalizations, whereas in the latter the objective is informational, to provide such a wealth of detail that the uniqueness and individuality of each case can be represented. To the charge that naturalistic inquiry, thereby, cannot yield generalizations because of sampling flaws the writers argue that this is necessarily though trivially true. In a word, it is unimportant.

Stage 4: finding a role and managing entry into the context

This involves issues of access and permission, establishing a reason for being there, developing a role and a persona, identifying the 'gatekeepers' who facilitate entry and access to the group being investigated (see LeCompte and Preissle, 1993: 100 and 111). The issue here is complex, for the researcher will be both a member of the group and yet studying that group, so it is a delicate matter to negotiate a role that will enable the researcher to be both participant and observer. The authors comment (p. 112) that the most important elements in securing access are the willingness of researchers to be flexible and their sensitivity to nuances of behaviour and response in the participants.

A related issue is the timing of the point of entry, so that researchers can commence the research at appropriate junctures (e.g. before the start of a programme, at the start of a programme, during a programme, at the end of a programme, after the end of a programme). The issue goes further than this, for the ethnographer will need to ensure acceptance into the group, which will be a matter of her/his dress, demeanour, persona, age, colour, ethnicity, empathy and identification with the group, language, accent, argot and jargon, willingness to become involved and to take on the group's values and behaviour etc. (see Patrick's (1973) fascinating study of a Glasgow gang).

Lofland (1971) suggests that the field researcher should attempt to adopt the role of the 'acceptable incompetent', balancing intrusion with knowing when to remain apart.

Stage 5: finding informants

This involves identifying those people who have the knowledge about the society or group being studied. This places the researcher in a difficult position, for she has to be able to evaluate key informants, to decide:

- whose accounts are more important than others;
- which informants are competent to pass comments;
- which are reliable;
- what the statuses of the informants are;
- how representative are the key informants (of the range of people, of issues, of situations, of views, of status, of roles, of the group);
- how to see the informants in different settings;
- how knowledgeable informants actually are – do they have intimate and expert understanding of the situation;
- how central to the organization or situation the informant is (e.g. marginal or central);
- how to meet and select informants;
- how critical the informants are as gatekeepers to other informants, opening up or restricting entry to avenues of inquiry to people (Hammersley and Atkinson, 1983: 73);
- the relationship between the informant and others in the group or situation being studied.

The selection and/or relationships with informants is problematical; LeCompte and Preissle (1993: 95), for example, suggest that the first informants that an ethnographer meets might be self-selected people who are marginal to the group, have a low status, and who, therefore, might be seeking to enhance their own prestige by being involved with the research. Indeed Lincoln and Guba (1985: 252) argue that the researcher must be careful to use informants rather than informers, the latter possibly having 'an axe to grind'. Researchers who are working with gatekeepers, they argue, will be engaged in a constant process of bargaining and negotiation.

Stage 6: developing and maintaining relations in the field

This involves addressing interpersonal and practical issues, for example:

- building participants' confidence in the researcher;
- developing rapport, trust, sensitivity and discretion;
- handling people and issues with which the researcher disagrees or finds objectionable or repulsive;
- being attentive and empathizing;
- being discreet;
- deciding how long to stay. Spindler and Spindler (1992: 65) suggest that ethnographic validity is attained by having the researcher *in situ* long enough to see things happening repeatedly rather than just once, that is to say, observing regularities.

LeCompte and Preissle (1993: 89) suggest that fieldwork, particularly because it is conducted face-to-face, raises problems and questions that are less significant in research that is conducted at a distance, including: (a) how to communicate meaningfully with participants; (b) how they and the researcher might be affected by the emotions evoked in one another, and how to handle these; (c) differences and similarities between the researcher and the participants (e.g. personal characteristics, power, resources), and how these might affect relationships between parties and the course of the investigation; (d) the researcher's responsibilities to the participants (*qua* researcher and member of their community), even if the period of residence in the community is short; (e) how to balance responsibilities to the community with responsibilities to other interested parties. The issue here is that the data collection process is itself socially situated; it is neither a clean, antiseptic activity nor always a straightforward negotiation.

Stage 7: data collection in situ

The qualitative researcher is able to use a variety of techniques for gathering information. There is no single prescription for which data collection instruments to use; rather, the issue here is of 'fitness for purpose' because, as was mentioned earlier, the ethnographer is a methodological omnivore! That said, there are several types of data collection instruments that are used more widely in qualitative research than others. The researcher can use field notes, participant observation, journal notes, interviews, diaries, life histories, artefacts, documents, video recordings, audio recordings etc. Several of these are discussed elsewhere in this book. Lincoln and Guba (1985: 199) distinguish between 'obtrusive' (e.g. interviews, observation, non-verbal language) and 'unobtrusive' methods (e.g. documents and records), on the basis of whether another human typically is present at the point of data collection.

Field notes can be written both *in situ* and away from the situation. They contain the results of observations. The nature of observation in ethnographic research is discussed fully in Chapter 17. Accompanying observation techniques is the use of interview techniques, documentary analysis and life histories. These are discussed separately in Chapters 7, 15 and 16. The popularly used interview technique employed in qualitative interviewing is the semi-structured interview, where a schedule is prepared but it is sufficiently open-ended to enable the contents to be re-ordered, digressions and expansions made, new avenues to be included, and further probing to be undertaken. Carspecken (1996: 159–60) describes how such interviews can range from the interviewer giving bland encouragements, 'non-leading' leads, active listening and low-inference paraphrasing to medium- and high-inference paraphrasing. In interviews the researcher might wish to explore further some matters arising from the observations. In naturalistic research the canons of validity in interviews include: honesty, depth of response, richness of response, and commitment of the interviewee (Oppenheim, 1992).

Lincoln and Guba (1985: 268–70) propose several purposes for interviewing, including: *present constructions* of events, feelings, persons, organizations, activities, motivations, concerns, claims, etc.; *reconstructions* of past experiences; *projections* into the future; *verifying, amending and extending data.*

Further, Silverman (1993: 92–3) adds that interviews in qualitative research are useful for: (a) gathering facts; (b) accessing beliefs about facts; (c) identifying feelings and motives; (d) commenting on the standards of actions (what could be done about situations); (e) present or previous behaviour; (f) eliciting reasons and explanations.

Lincoln and Guba (1985) emphasize that the planning of the conduct of the interview is important, including the background preparation, the opening of the interview, its pacing and timing, keeping the conversation going and eliciting knowledge, and rounding off and ending the interview. Clearly, it is important that careful consideration be given to the several stages of the interview. For example at the planning stage of the interview attention will need to be given to the number (per person), duration, timing, frequency, setting/location, number of people in a single interview situation (e.g. individual or group interviews) and respondent styles (LeCompte and Preissle, 1993: 177). At the implementation stage the conduct of the interview will be important, for example responding to interviewees, prompting, probing, supporting, empathizing, clarifying, crystallizing, exemplifying, summarizing, avoiding censure, accepting. At the analysis stage there will be several important considerations, for example (ibid.: 195): the ease and clarity of communication of meaning; the interest levels of the participants; the clarity of the question and the response; the precision (and communication of this) of the interviewer; how the interviewer handles questionable responses (e.g. fabrications, untruths, claims made).

The qualitative interview tends to move away from the pre-structured, standardized form and toward the open-ended or semi-structured interview (see Chapter 15), as this enables respondents to project their own ways of defining the world. It permits flexibility rather than fixity of sequence of discussions, and it also enables participants to raise and pursue issues and matters that might not have been included in a pre-devised schedule (Denzin, 1970; Silverman, 1993).

In addition to interviews, Lincoln and Guba (1985) discuss data collection from non-human sources, including:

1   Documents and records (e.g. archival records, private records). These have the attraction of being always available, often at low cost, and being factual. On the other hand they may be unrepresentative, they may be selective, lack objectivity, be of unknown validity, and may possibly be deliberately deceptive (see Finnegan, 1996).
2   Unobtrusive informational residues. These include artefacts, physical traces, and a variety of other records. Whilst they frequently have face validity, and whilst they may be simple and direct, gained by non-interventional means (hence reducing the problems of reactivity), they may also be very heavily inferential, difficult to interpret, and may contain elements whose relevance is questionable.

Stage 8: data collection outside the field

In order to make comparisons and to suggest explanations for phenomena, researchers might find it useful to go beyond the confines of the groups in which they occur. That this is a thorny issue is indicated in the following example. Two students are arguing very violently and physically in a school. At one level it is simply a fight between two people. However, this is a common occurrence between these two students as they are neighbours outside school and they don't enjoy positive amicable relations as their families are frequently feuding. The two households have been placed next door to each other by the local authority because the authority has taken a decision to keep together families who are very poor at paying for their local housing rent (i.e. a 'sink'

estate). The local authority has taken this decision because of a government policy to keep together disadvantaged groups so that targeted action and interventions can be more effective, meeting the needs of whole communities as well as individuals.

The issue here is: how far out of a micro-situation does the researcher need to go to understand that micro-situation? This is an imprecise matter but it is not insignificant in educational research (e.g. it underpinned: (a) the celebrated work by Bowles and Gintis (1976) on schooling in capitalist America, in which the authors suggested that the hidden curricula of schools were preparing students for differential occupational futures that perpetuated an inegalitarian capitalist system; (b) research on the self-fulfilling prophecy (Hurn, 1978); (c) work by Pollard (1985: 110) on the social world of the primary school, where everyday interactions in school were preparing students for the individualism, competition, achievement orientation, hierarchies and self-reliance that characterize mass private consumption in wider society; (d) Delamont's (1981) advocacy that educationists should study similar but different institutions to schools (e.g. hospitals and other 'total' institutions) in order to make the familiar strange (see also Erickson, 1973).

Stage 9: data analysis

This involves organizing, accounting for, and explaining the data; in short, making sense of the data in terms of the participants' definitions of the situation, noting patterns, themes, categories and regularities. Typically in qualitative research, data analysis commences during the data collection process. There are several reasons for this, and these are discussed below.

At a practical level, qualitative research rapidly amasses huge amounts of data, and early analysis reduces the problem of data overload by selecting out significant features for future focus. Miles and Huberman (1984) suggest that careful data display is an important element of data reduction and selection. 'Progressive focussing', according to Parlett and Hamilton (1976), starts with the researcher taking a wide angle lens to gather data, and then, by sifting, sorting, reviewing and reflecting on them the salient features of the situation emerge. These are then used as the agenda for subsequent focusing. The process is akin to funnelling from the wide to the narrow.

At a theoretical level a major feature of qualitative research is that analysis commences early on in the data collection process so that theory generation can be undertaken (LeCompte and Preissle, 1993: 238). The authors (pp. 237–53) advise that researchers should set out the main outlines of the phenomena that are under investigation. They then should assemble chunks or groups of data, putting them together to make a coherent whole (e.g. through writing summaries of what has been found). Then they should painstakingly take apart their field notes, matching, contrasting, aggregating, comparing and ordering notes made. The intention is to move from description to explanation and theory generation.

Becker and Geer (1960) indicate how this might proceed:

- comparing different groups simultaneously and over time;
- matching the responses given in interviews to observed behaviour;
- an analysis of deviant and negative cases;
- calculating frequencies of occurrences and responses;
- assembling and providing sufficient data that keeps separate raw data from analysis.

For clarity, the process of data analysis can be portrayed in a sequence of seven steps:

Step 1   Establish units of analysis of the data, indicating how these units are similar to and different from each other.
Step 2   Create a 'domain analysis'.
Step 3   Establish relationships and linkages between the domains.
Step 4   Making speculative inferences.
Step 5   Summarizing.

Step 6   Seeking negative and discrepant cases.
Step 7   Theory generation.

The following pages address each of these steps.

Step 1: establish units of analysis of the data, indicating how these units are similar to and different from each other

The criterion here is that each unit of analysis (category – conceptual, actual, classification element, cluster, issue) should be as discrete as possible whilst retaining fidelity to the integrity of the whole, i.e. that each unit must be a fair rather than a distorted representation of the context and other data. The creation of units of analysis can be done by ascribing *codes* to the data (Miles and Huberman, 1984). This is akin to the process of 'unitizing' (Lincoln and Guba, 1985: 203).

Codes define categories; they are astringent, pulling together a wealth of material into some order and structure. They keep words as words; they maintain context specificity.

At this stage the codes are essentially *descriptive* and might include (Bogdan and Biklen, 1992: 167–72): situation codes; perspectives held by subjects; ways of thinking about people and objects; process codes; activity codes; event codes; strategy codes; relationship and social structure codes; methods codes. However, to be faithful to the data, the codes themselves derive from the data responsively rather than being created pre-ordinately. Hence the researcher will go through the data ascribing codes to each piece of datum. The code is a word or abbreviation that is sufficiently close to that which it is describing that the researcher can see at a glance what it means (in this respect it is unlike a number). For example, the code 'trust' might refer to a person's trustworthiness; the code ' power' might refer to the status or power of the person in the group.

Miles and Huberman advise that codes should be kept as discrete as possible and that coding should start earlier rather than later as late coding enfeebles the analysis. It is possible, they suggest, for as many as ninety codes to be held in the working memory whilst going through data, though clearly, there is a process of iteration and reiteration whereby some codes that are used in the early stages of coding might be modified subsequently and *vice versa*, necessitating the researcher to go through a data set more than once to ensure consistency, refinement, modification and exhaustiveness of coding (some codes might become redundant, others might need to be broken down into finer codes). By coding up the data the researcher is able to detect frequencies (which codes are occurring most commonly) and patterns (which codes occur together).

Hammersley and Atkinson (1983: 177–8) propose that the first activity here is to read and re-read the data to become thoroughly familiar with them, noting also any interesting patterns, any surprising, puzzling or unexpected features, any apparent inconsistencies or contradictions (e.g. between groups, within and between individuals and groups, between what people say and what they do).

Step 2: create a 'domain analysis'

This involves grouping the units into domains, clusters, groups, patterns, themes and coherent sets to form domains. A domain is any symbolic category that includes other categories (Spradley, 1979: 100). At this stage it might be useful for the researcher to recode the data into domain codes, or to review the codes used to see how they naturally fall into clusters, perhaps creating overarching codes for each cluster. Hammersley and Atkinson (1983) show how items can be assigned to more than one category, and, indeed, see this as desirable as it maintains the richness of the data. This is akin to the process of 'categorization' (Lincoln and Guba, 1985), putting 'unitized' data to provide descriptive and inferential information.

Spradley (1979) suggests that establishing domains can be achieved by four analytic tasks: (a) selecting a sample of verbatim interview and field notes; (b) looking for the names of things; (c) identifying possible terms from the sample;

(d) searching through additional notes for other items to include. He identifies six steps to achieve these tasks: (i) select a single semantic relationship; (ii) prepare a domain analysis sheet; (iii) select a sample of statements from respondents; (iv) search for possible cover terms and included terms that fit the semantic relationship identified; (v) formulate structural questions for each domain identified; (vi) list all the hypothesized domains. Domain analysis, then, strives to discover relationships between symbols (ibid.: 157).

Step 3: establish relationships and linkages between the domains

This process ensures that the data, their richness and 'context-groundedness' are retained. Linkages can be found by identifying confirming cases, by seeking 'underlying associations' (LeCompte and Preissle, 1993: 246) and connections between data subsets.

Step 4: making speculative inferences

This is an important stage, for it moves the research from description to inference. It requires the researcher, on the basis of the evidence, to posit some explanations for the situation, some key elements and possibly even their causes. It is the process of hypothesis generation or the setting of working hypotheses that feeds into theory generation.

Step 5: summarizing

By this stage the researcher will be in a position to write a summary of the main features of the situation that have been researched so far. The summary will identify key factors, key issues, key concepts and key areas for subsequent investigation. It is a watershed stage during the data collection, as it pinpoints major themes, issues and problems that have arisen from the data to date (responsively) and suggests avenues for further investigation. The concepts used will have been a combination of those derived from the data themselves and those inferred by the researcher (Hammersley and Atkinson, 1983: 178).

By this stage the researcher will have gone through the preliminary stages of theory generation. Patton (1980) sets these out for qualitative data:

- finding a focus for the research and analysis;
- organizing, processing, ordering and checking data;
- writing a qualitative description or analysis;
- inductively developing categories, typologies, and labels;
- analysing the categories to identify where further clarification and cross-clarification are needed;
- expressing and typifying these categories through metaphors (see also Pitman and Maxwell, 1992: 747);
- making inferences and speculations about relationships, causes and effects.

Bogdan and Biklen (1992: 154–63) identify several important items that researchers need to address at this stage, including: forcing yourself to take decisions that will focus and narrow the study and decide what kind of study it will be; developing analytical questions; using previous observational data to inform subsequent data collection; writing reflexive notes and memos about observations, ideas, what you are learning; trying out ideas with subjects; analysing relevant literature whilst you are conducting the field research; generating concepts, metaphors and analogies and visual devices to clarify the research.

Step 6: seeking negative and discrepant cases

In theory generation it is important to seek not only confirming cases but to weigh the significance of disconfirming cases. LeCompte and Preissle (1993: 270) suggest that because interpretations of the data are grounded in the data themselves, results that fail to support an original hypothesis are neither discarded nor discredited; rather, it is the hypotheses themselves

that must be modified to accommodate these data. Indeed Erickson (1992: 208) identifies progressive problem-solving as one key aspect of ethnographic research and data analysis. LeCompte and Preissle (1993: 250–1) define a negative case as an exemplar which disconfirms or refutes the working hypothesis, rule or explanation so far. It is the qualitative researcher's equivalent of the positivist's null hypothesis. The theory that is being developed becomes more robust if it addresses negative cases, for it sets the boundaries to the theory; it modifies the theory, it sets parameters to the applicability of the theory.

Discrepant cases are not so much exceptions to the rule (as in negative cases) as variants of the rule (ibid.: 251). The discrepant case leads to the modification or elaboration of the construct, rule or emerging hypothesis. Discrepant case analysis requires the researcher to seek out cases for which the rule, construct or explanation cannot account or with which they will not fit, i.e. they are neither exceptions nor contradictions, they are simply different!

Step 7: theory generation

Here the theory derives from the data – it is grounded in the data and emerges from it. As Lincoln and Guba (1985: 205) argue, grounded theory must fit the situation that is being researched. By going through the previous sections, particularly the search for confirming, negative and discrepant cases, the researcher is able to keep a 'running total' of these cases for a particular theory. The researcher also generates alternative theories for the phenomena under investigation and performs the same count of confirming, negative and discrepant cases. Lincoln and Guba (ibid.: 253) argue that the theory with the greatest incidence of confirming cases and the lowest incidence of negative and discrepant cases is the most robust.

There are several procedural tools for analysing qualitative data. LeCompte and Preissle (ibid.: 253) see analytic induction, constant comparison, typological analysis and enumeration (discussed above) as valuable tools for the qualitative researcher to use in analysing data and generating theory.

Analytic induction is a term and process that was introduced by Znaniecki (1934) deliberately in opposition to statistical methods of data analysis. LeCompte and Preissle (1993: 254) suggest that the process is akin to the several steps set out above, in that: (a) data are scanned to generate categories of phenomena; (b) relationships between these categories are sought; (c) working typologies and summaries are written on the basis of the data examined; (d) these are then refined by subsequent cases and analysis; (e) negative and discrepant cases are deliberately sought to modify, enlarge or restrict the original explanation/theory. Denzin (1970: 192) uses the term 'analytical induction' to describe the broad strategy of participant observation that is set out below:

- A rough definition of the phenomenon to be explained is formulated.
- A hypothetical explanation of that phenomenon is formulated.
- One case is studied in the light of the hypothesis, with the object of determining whether or not the hypothesis fits the facts in that case.
- If the hypothesis does not fit the facts, either the hypothesis is reformulated or the phenomenon to be explained is redefined, so that the case is excluded.
- Practical certainty may be attained after a small number of cases has been examined, but the discovery of negative cases disproves the explanation and requires a reformulation.
- This procedure of examining cases, redefining the phenomenon, and reformulating the hypothesis is continued until a universal relationship is established, each negative case calling for a redefinition of a reformulation.

A more deliberate seeking of disconfirming cases is advocated by Bogdan and Biklen (1992: 72) where they enumerate five main stages in analytic induction:

Step 1   In the early stages of the research a rough definition and explanation of the particular phenomenon is developed.
Step 2   This definition and explanation is examined in the light of the data that are being collected during the research.
Step 3   If the definition and/or explanation that have been generated need modification in the light of new data (e.g. if the data do not fit the explanation or definition) then this is undertaken.
Step 4   A deliberate attempt is made to find cases that may not fit into the explanation or definition.
Step 5   The process of redefinition and reformulation is repeated until the explanation is reached that embraces all the data, and until a generalized relationship has been established, which will also embrace the negative cases.

Constant comparison, LeCompte and Preissle (1993: 256) opine, combines the elements of inductive category coding (see above) with simultaneously comparing these with the other events and social incidents that have been observed and coded over time and location. This enables social phenomena to be compared across categories, where necessary, giving rise to new dimensions, codes and categories.

Glaser (1978) indicates that constant comparison can proceed from the moment of starting to collect data, to seeking key issues and categories, to discovering recurrent events or activities in the data that become categories of focus, to expanding the range of categories. This process can continue during the writing-up process (which should be continuous), so that a model or explanation of the phenomena can emerge that accounts for fundamental social processes and relationships.

In *constant comparison* data are compared across a range of situations, times, groups of people, and through a range of methods. The process resonates with the methodological notion of triangulation. Glaser and Strauss (1967: 105–6) suggest that the constant comparison method involves four stages: (1) comparing incidents and data that are applicable to each category, comparing them with previous incidents in the same category and with other data that are in the same category; (2) integrating these categories and their properties; (3) bounding the theory; (4) setting out the theory.

Typological analysis is essentially a classificatory process (LeCompte and Preissle, 1993: 257) wherein data are put into groups, subsets or categories on the basis of some clear criterion (e.g. acts, behaviour, meanings, nature of participation, relationships, settings, activities). It is the process of *secondary coding* (Miles and Huberman, 1984) where descriptive codes are then drawn together and put into subsets. Typologies are a set of phenomena that represent subtypes of a more general set or category (Lofland, 1970). Lazarsfeld and Barton (1951) suggest that a typology can be developed in terms of an underlying dimension or key characteristic. In creating typologies Lofland insists that the researcher must: (a) deliberately assemble all the data on how a participant addresses a particular issue – what strategies are being employed; (b) disaggregate and separate out the variations between the ranges of instances of strategies; (c) classify these into sets and subsets; (d) present them in an ordered, named and numbered way for the reader.

Lincoln and Guba (1985: 354–5) urge the researcher to be mindful of several issues in analysing and interpreting the data, including: (a) data overload; (b) the problem of acting on first impressions only; (c) the availability of people and information (e.g. how representative these are and how to know if missing people and data might be important); (d) the dangers of only seeking confirming rather than disconfirming instances; (e) the reliability and consistency of the data and confidence that can be placed in the results.

These are significant issues in addressing reliability, trustworthiness and validity in the research (see the discussions of reliability and validity in Chapter 5). The essence of this approach, that theory emerges from and is grounded in data, is not without its critics. For example, Silverman (1993: 47) suggests that it fails to acknowledge the implicit theories which guide research in its early stages (i.e. data are not theory neutral but theory-saturated) and that it might be strong on providing categorizations without necessarily having explanatory potential. These are caveats that should feed into the process of reflexivity in qualitative research, perhaps.

Stage 10: leaving the field

The issue here is how to terminate the research, how to terminate the roles adopted, how (and whether) to terminate the relationships that have built up over the course of the research, and how to disengage from the field in ways that bring as little disruption to the group or situation as possible (LeCompte and Preissle, 1993: 101).

Stage 11: writing the report

Delamont (1998) notes the shift in emphasis in much research literature, away from the *conduct* of the research and towards the *reporting* of the research. It is often the case that the main vehicle for writing naturalistic research is the case study (see Chapter 9), whose 'trustworthiness' (Lincoln and Guba, 1985: 189) is defined in terms of credibility, transferability, dependability and confirmability – discussed in Chapter 5. Case studies are useful in that they can provide the thick descriptions that are useful in ethnographic research, and can catch and portray to the reader what it is like to be involved in the situation (ibid.: 214). As the writers comment (p. 359), the case study is the ideal instrument for 'emic' inquiry. It also builds in and builds on the tacit knowledge that the writer and reader bring to the report, and, thereby, takes seriously their notion of the 'human instrument' in research, indicating the interactions of researcher and participants.

Lincoln and Guba provide several guidelines for writing case studies (ibid.: 365–6):

- the writing should strive to be informal and to capture informality;

- as far as possible the writing should report facts except in those sections where interpretation, evaluation and inference are made explicit;
- in drafting the report it is more advisable to opt for over-inclusion rather than under-inclusion;
- the ethical conventions of report writing must be honoured, e.g. anonymity, non-traceability;
- the case study writer should make clear the data that gave rise to the report, so the readers have a means of checking back for reliability and validity and inferences;
- a fixed completion date should be specified.

Spradley suggests nine practical steps that can be followed in writing an ethnography:

Step 1   Select the audience.
Step 2   Select the thesis.
Step 3   Make a list of topics and create an outline of the ethnography.
Step 4   Write a rough draft of each section of the ethnography.
Step 5   Revise the outline and create subheadings.
Step 6   Edit the draft.
Step 7   Write an introduction and a conclusion.
Step 8   Re-read the data and report to identify examples.
Step 9   Write the final version.

Clearly there are several other aspects of case study reporting that need to be addressed. These are set out in Chapter 9.

Critical ethnography

An emerging branch of ethnography that resonates with the critical paradigm outlined in Chapter 1 is the field of critical ethnography. Here not only is qualitative, anthropological, participant, observer-based research undertaken, but its theoretical basis lies in critical theory (Quantz, 1992: 448; Carspecken, 1996). As was outlined in Chapter 1, this paradigm is concerned with the exposure of oppression and inequality in society with a view to emancipating individuals and groups towards collective empowerment. In this respect research is an inherently political enterprise. Carspecken (1996, 4ff.) suggests several key premises of critical ethnography:

- research and thinking are mediated by power relations;
- these power relations are socially and historically located;
- facts and values are inseparable;
- relationships between objects and concepts are fluid and mediated by the social relations of production;
- language is central to perception;
- certain groups in society exert more power than others;
- inequality and oppression are inherent in capitalist relations of production and consumption;
- ideological domination is strongest when oppressed groups see their situation as inevitable, natural or necessary;
- forms of oppression mediate each other and must be considered together (e.g. race, gender, class).

Quantz (1992: 473–4) argues that research is inescapably value-laden in that it serves some interests, and that in critical ethnography the task of researchers is to expose these interests and move participants towards emancipation and freedom. The focus and process of research are thus political at heart, concerning issues of power, domination, voice and empowerment. In critical ethnography the cultures, groups and individuals being studied are located in contexts of power and interests. These contexts have to be exposed, their legitimacy interrogated, and the value base of the research itself exposed. Reflexivity is high in critical ethnography. What separates critical ethnography from other forms of ethnography is that, in the former, questions of legitimacy, power, values in society and domination and oppression are foregrounded.

How does the critical ethnographer proceed?

Carspecken and Apple (1992: 512–14) and Carspecken (1996: 41–2) identify five stages in critical ethnography:

Stage 1: compiling the primary record through the collection of monological data

At this stage the researcher is comparatively passive and unobtrusive – a participant observer. The task here is to acquire *objective* data and it is 'monological' in the sense that it concerns only the researcher writing her own notes to herself. Lincoln and Guba (1985) suggest that validity checks at this stage will include:

- using multiple devices for recording together with multiple observers;
- using a flexible observation schedule in order to minimize biases;
- remaining in the situation for a long time in order to overcome the Hawthorne effect;
- using low-inference terminology and descriptions;
- using peer-debriefing;
- using respondent validation.

Echoing Habermas's (1979, 1982, 1984) work on validity claims, validity here includes truth (the veracity of the utterance), legitimacy (rightness and appropriateness of the speaker), comprehensibility (that the utterance is comprehensible) and sincerity (of the speaker's intentions). Carspecken (1996: 104–5) takes this further in suggesting several categories of reference in objective validity: (a) that the act is comprehensible, socially legitimate and appropriate; (b) that the actor has a particular identity and particular intentions or feelings when the action takes place; (c) that objective, contextual factors are acknowledged.

Stage 2: preliminary reconstructive analysis

Reconstructive analysis attempts to uncover the taken-for-granted components of meaning or abstractions that participants have of a situation. Such analysis is intended to identify the value systems, norms, key concepts that are guiding and underpinning situations. Carspecken (ibid.: 42) suggests that the researcher goes back over the primary record from stage one to examine patterns of interaction, power relations, roles, sequences of events, and meanings accorded to situations. He asserts that what distinguishes this stage as 'reconstructive' is that cultural themes, social and system factors that are not usually articulated by the participants themselves are, in fact, reconstructed and articulated, making the undiscursive into discourse. In moving to higher level abstractions this stage can utilize high level coding (see the discussion of coding in this chapter).

In critical ethnography Carspecken (ibid.: 141) delineates several ways of ensuring validity at this stage:

- Use interviews and group discussions with the subjects themselves.
- Conduct member checks on the reconstruction in order to equalize power relations.
- Use peer debriefing (a peer is asked to review the data to suggest if the researcher is being too selective, e.g. of individuals, of data, of inference) to check biases or absences in reconstructions.
- Employ prolonged engagement to heighten the researcher's capacity to assume the insider's perspective.
- Use 'strip analysis' – checking themes and segments of extracted data with the primary data, for consistency.
- Use negative case analysis.

Stage 3: dialogical data collection

Here data are generated by, and discussed with, the participants (Carspecken and Apple, 1992). The authors argue that this is not-naturalistic in that the participants are being asked to reflect on their own situations, circumstances and lives and to begin to theorize about their lives. This is a crucial stage because it enables the participants to have a voice, to democratize the research. It may be that this stage produces new data that challenge the preceding two stages.

In introducing greater subjectivity by participants into the research at this stage Carspecken (1996: 164–5) proffers several validity checks, for example: (a) consistency checks on interviews that have been recorded; (b) repeated interviews with participants; (c) matching observation with what participants say is happening or has happened; (d) avoiding leading questions at interview, reinforced by having peer debriefers check on this; (e) respondent validation; (f) asking participants to use their own terms in describing naturalistic contexts, and to explain these terms.

Stage 4: discovering system relations

This stage relates the group being studied to other factors that impinge on that group, for example, local community groups, local sites that produce cultural products. At this stage Carspecken (ibid.: 202) notes that validity checks will include: (a) maintaining the validity requirements of the earlier stages; (b) seeking a match between the researcher's analysis and the commentaries that are provided by the participants and other researchers; (c) using peer debriefers and respondent validation.

Stage 5: using system relations to explain findings

This stage seeks to examine and explain the findings in light of macro-social theories (ibid.: 202). In part this is a matching exercise, to fit the research findings within a social theory.

In critical ethnography, therefore, the move is from describing a situation, to understanding it, to questioning it, and to changing it. This parallels the stages of ideology critique set out in Chapter 1:

Step 1 A description of the existing situation – a hermeneutic exercise.
Step 2 A penetration of the reasons that brought the situation to the form that it takes.

Step 3 An agenda for altering the situation.
Step 4 An evaluation of the achievement of the new situation.

Computer usage

LeCompte and Preissle (1993) provide a summary of ways in which information technology can be utilized in supporting ethnographic research (see also Tesch, 1990). As can be seen from the list below, the uses of information technology are diverse; as data have to be processed, and as word data are laborious to process, and as several powerful packages for data analysis and processing exist, researchers will find it useful to make full use of computing facilities. These can be used as follows (LeCompte and Preissle, 1993: 280–1):

- To store and check (e.g. proofread) data.
- To collate and segment data and to make numerous copies of data.
- To enable memoing to take place, together with details of the circumstances in which the memos were written.
- To conduct a search for words or phrases in the data and to retrieve text.
- To attach identification labels to units of text, (e.g. questionnaire responses), so that subsequent sorting can be undertaken.
- To partition data into units that have been determined either by the researcher or in response to the natural language itself.
- To enable preliminary coding of data to be undertaken.
- To sort, re-sort, collate, classify and reclassify pieces of data to facilitate constant comparison and to refine schemas of classification.
- To code memos and bring them into the same schema of classification.
- To assemble, re-assemble and recall data into categories.
- To undertake frequency counts (e.g. of words, phrases, codes).
- To cross-check data to see if they can be coded into more than one category, enabling linkages between categories to be discovered.

- To establish the incidence of data that are contained in more than one category.
- To retrieve coded data segments from subsets (e.g. by sex) in order to compare and contrast data.
- To search for pieces of data that appear in a certain (e.g. chronological) sequence.
- To establish linkages between coding categories.
- To display relationships of categories (e.g. hierarchical, temporal, relational, subsumptive, superordinate).
- To quote data in the final report.

Kelle (1995) suggests that computers are particularly effective at coping with the often-encountered problem of data overload and retrieval in qualitative research. Computers, it is argued, enable the researcher to use codes, memos, hypertext systems, selective retrieval, co-occurring codes, and to perform quantitative counts of qualitative data types (see also Seidel and Kelle, 1995). In turn, these authors suggest, this enables linkages of elements to be undertaken, the building of networks, and, ultimately, theory generation to be undertaken. Indeed Lonkila (1995) indicates how computers can assist in the generation of grounded theory through coding, constant comparison, linkages, memoing, use of diagrams, verification and, ultimately, theory building. In this process Kelle and Laurie (1995: 27) suggest that computer-aided methods can enhance: (a) validity (by the management of samples); and (b) reliability (by retrieving all the data on a given topic, thereby ensuring trustworthiness of the data).

A major feature of computer use is in the coding and compilation of data (for example, Kelle (1995: 62–104). Lonkila (1995) identifies several kinds of codes. *Open coding* generates categories and defines their properties and dimensions. *Axial coding* works within one category, making connections between subgroups of that category and makes connections between one category and another. This might be in terms of the phenomena that are being studied, the causal conditions that lead to the phenomena, the context of

the phenomena and their intervening conditions, and the actions and interactions of, and consequences for, the actors in situations. *Selective coding* identifies the core categories of text data. Seidel and Kelle (1995) suggest that codes can denote a text, passage, or fact, and can be used to construct data networks.

There are several computer packages for qualitative data (see Kelle, 1995), for example: AQUAD; ATLAS/ti; HyperQuad2; HyperRESEARCH; Hypersoft; Kwaliton; Martin; MAX; WINMAX; NUD.IST; QUALPRO; Textbase Alpha, ETHNOGRAPH, ATLAS.ti, Code-A-Text, Decision Explorer, Diction. Some of these are reviewed by Prein, Kelle and Bird (1995: 190–209).

To conclude this chapter we identify a number of difficulties that arise in the implementation of ethnographic and naturalistic research programmes.

Some problems with ethnographic and naturalistic approaches

There are several difficulties in ethnographic and natural approaches. These might affect the reliability and validity of the research, and include:

1   *The definition of the situation* – the participants are being asked for their definition of the situation, yet they have no monopoly on wisdom. They may be 'falsely conscious' (unaware of the 'real' situation), deliberately distorting or falsifying information, or highly selective. The issues of reliability and validity here are addressed in Chapter 5 (see the discussions of triangulation).

2   *Reactivity* (the Hawthorne effect) – the presence of the researcher alters the situation as participants may wish to avoid, impress, direct, deny, influence the researcher. Again, this is discussed in Chapter 5. Typically the problem of reactivity is addressed by careful negotiation in the field, remaining in the field for a considerable time, ensuring as far as possible a careful presentation of the researcher's self.

3   The *halo* effect – where existing or given information about the situation or participants might be used to be selective in subsequent data collection, or may bring about a particular reading of a subsequent situation (the research equivalent of the self-fulfilling prophecy). This is an issue of reliability, and can be addressed by the use of a wide, triangulated data base and the assistance of an external observer.

4   The *implicit conservatism* of the interpretive methodology – the kind of research described in this chapter, with the possible exception of critical ethnography, accepts the perspective of the participants and corroborates the status quo. It is focused on the past and the present rather than on the future.

5   There is the difficulty of focusing on the *familiar* – participants (and, maybe researchers too) being so close to the situation that they neglect certain, often tacit, aspects of it. The task, therefore, is to make the familiar strange. Delamont (1981) suggests that this can be done by:
   - studying unusual examples of the same issue (e.g. atypical classroom, timetabling or organizations of schools);
   - studying examples in other cultures;
   - studying other situations that might have a bearing on the situation in hand (e.g. if studying schools it might be useful to look at other similar-but-different organizations, for instance hospitals or prisons);
   - taking a significant issue and focusing on it deliberately, e.g. gendered behaviour.

6   The *open-endedness and diversity* of the situations studied. Hammersley and Atkinson (1983) counsel that the drive towards focusing on specific contexts and situations might overemphasize the difference between contexts and situations rather than their gross similarity, their routine features. Researchers, he argues, should be as aware of regularities as of differences.

7   The *neglect of wider social contexts and constraints*. In studying situations that emphasize how highly context-bound they are, this might neglect broader currents and contexts – micro-level research risks putting boundaries that exclude important macro-level factors. Wider – macro-contexts cannot be ruled out of individual situations.

8   The issue of *generalizability*. If situations are unique and non-generalizable, as many naturalistic principles would suggest, how is the issue of generalizability going to be addressed? To which contexts will the findings apply, and what is the role and nature of replication studies?

9   How to write up *multiple realities* and explanations? How will a representative view be reached? What if the researcher sees things that are not seen by the participants?

10 Who *owns* the data, the report, and who has control over the release of the data?

Naturalistic and ethnographic research, then, are important but problematical research methods in education. Their widespread use signals their increasing acceptance as legitimate and important styles of research.

7 Historical research

Introduction

Mouly (1978) states that while historical research cannot meet some of the tests of the scientific method interpreted in the specific sense of its use in the physical sciences (it cannot depend, for instance, on direct observation or experimentation, but must make use of reports that cannot be repeated), it qualifies as a scientific endeavour from the standpoint of its subscription to the same principles and the same general scholarship that characterize all scientific research.[1]

Historical research has been defined as the systematic and objective location, evaluation and synthesis of evidence in order to establish facts and draw conclusions about past events (Borg (1963). It is an act of reconstruction undertaken in a spirit of critical inquiry designed to achieve a faithful representation of a previous age. In seeking data from the personal experiences and observations of others, from documents and records, researchers often have to contend with inadequate information so that their reconstructions tend to be sketches rather than portraits. Indeed, the difficulty of obtaining adequate data makes historical research one of the most taxing kinds of inquiry to conduct satisfactorily.[2] Reconstruction implies a holistic perspective in that the method of inquiry characterizing historical research attempts to 'encompass and then explain the whole realm of man's past in a perspective that greatly accents his social, cultural, economic, and intellectual development' (Hill and Kerber, 1967).

Ultimately, historical research is concerned with a broad view of the conditions and not necessarily the specifics which bring them about, although such a synthesis is rarely achieved without intense debate or controversy, especially on matters of detail. The act of historical research involves the identification and limitation of a problem or an area of study; sometimes the formulation of a hypothesis (or set of questions); the collection, organization, verification, validation, analysis and selection of data; testing the hypothesis (or answering the questions) where appropriate; and writing a research report. This sequence leads to a new understanding of the past and its relevance to the present and future.

The values of historical research have been categorized by Hill and Kerber as follows:

- it enables solutions to contemporary problems to be sought in the past;
- it throws light on present and future trends;
- it stresses the relative importance and the effects of the various interactions that are to be found within all cultures;
- it allows for the revaluation of data in relation to selected hypotheses, theories and generalizations that are presently held about the past.

As the writers point out, the ability of history to employ the past to predict the future, and to use the present to explain the past, gives it a dual and unique quality which makes it especially useful for all sorts of scholarly study and research.[3]

The particular value of historical research in the field of education is unquestioned. It can, for example, yield insights into some educational problems that could not be achieved by any other means. Further, the historical study of an educational idea or institution can do much to help us understand how our present educational system has come about; and this kind of understanding can in turn help to establish a sound basis for further progress or change. Historical research in education can also show how and why educational theories and practices developed. It enables educationalists to use former practices to evaluate newer, emerging ones. Recurrent trends can be more easily identified and assessed from a historical standpoint – witness, for example, the various guises in which progressivism in education have appeared. And it can contribute to a fuller understanding of the relationship between politics and education, between school and society, between local and central government, and between teacher and pupil.[4]

Historical research in education may concern itself with an individual, a group, a movement, an idea or an institution. As Best (1970) points out, however, not one of these objects of historical interest and observation can be considered in isolation. No one person can be subjected to historical investigation without some consideration of his or her contribution to the ideas, movements or institutions of a particular time or place. These elements are always interrelated. The focus merely determines the point of emphasis towards which historical researchers direct their attention. Box 7.1 illustrates some of these relationships from the history of education. For example, no mat-

ter whether the historian chooses to study the Jesuit order, religious teaching orders, the Counter-Reformation or Ignatius Loyola, each of the other elements appears as a prominent influence or result, and an indispensable part of the narrative. For an example of historical research see Thomas (1992) and Gaukroger and Schwartz (1997).

Choice of subject

As with other methods we consider in this book, historical research may be structured by a flexible sequence of stages, beginning with the selection and evaluation of a problem or area of study. Then follows the definition of the problem in more precise terms, the selection of suitable sources of data, collection, classification and processing of the data, and finally, the evaluation and synthesis of the data into a balanced and objective account of the subject under investigation. There are, however, some important differences between the method of historical research and other research methods used in education. The principal difference has been highlighted by Borg:

> In historical research, it is especially important that the student carefully defines his problem and appraises its appropriateness before committing himself too fully. Many problems are not adaptable to historical research methods and cannot be adequately treated using this approach. Other problems have little or no chance of producing significant results either because of the lack of

Box 7.1
Some historical interrelations between men, movements and institutions

Men	Movements	Institutions	
		Type	Specific
Ignatius Loyola	Counter-reformation	Religious teaching order	Society of Jesus, 1534
Benjamin Franklin	Scientific movement; Education for life	Academy	Philadelphia Academy, 1751
John Dewey	Experimentalism Progressive education	Experimental school	University of Chicago Elementary School, 1896

Source Adapted from Best, 1970

pertinent data or because the problem is a trivial one.

(Borg, 1963)

One can see from Borg's observations that the choice of a problem can sometimes be a daunting business for the potential researcher. Once a topic has been selected, however, and its potential and significance for historical research evaluated, the next stage is to define it more precisely, or, perhaps more pertinently, delimit it so that a more potent analysis will result. Too broad or too vague a statement can result in the final report lacking direction or impact. Best expresses it like this: 'The experienced historian realizes that research must be a penetrating analysis of a limited problem, rather than the superficial examination of a broad area. The weapon of research is the rifle not the shotgun' (Best, 1970). Various prescriptions exist for helping to define historical topics. Gottschalk (1951) recommends that four questions should be asked in identifying a topic:

- Where do the events take place?
- Who are the people involved?
- When do the events occur?
- What kinds of human activity are involved?

As Travers (1969) suggests, the scope of a topic can be modified by adjusting the focus of any one of the four categories; the geographical area involved can be increased or decreased; more or fewer people can be included in the topic; the time span involved can be increased or decreased; and the human activity category can be broadened or narrowed. It sometimes happens that a piece of historical research can only begin with a rough idea of what the topic involves; and that delimitation of it can only take place after the pertinent material has been assembled.

In hand with the careful specification of the problem goes the need, where this is appropriate, for an equally specific and testable hypothesis (sometimes a sequence of questions may be substituted.) As in empirical research, the hypothesis gives direction and focus to data collection and analysis. It imposes a selection, a structure on what would otherwise be an overwhelming mass of information. As Borg (1963) observes:

Without hypotheses, historical research often becomes little more than an aimless gathering of facts. In searching the materials that make up the sources of historical research data, unless the student's attention is aimed at information relating to specific questions or concerned with specific hypotheses, he [sic] has little chance of extracting a body of data from the available documents that can be synthesized to provide new knowledge or new understanding of the topic studied. Even after specific hypotheses have been established, the student must exercise strict self-control in his study of historical documents or he will find himself collecting much information that is interesting but is not related to his area of inquiry. If the student's hypotheses are not sufficiently delimited or specific, it is an easy matter for him to become distracted and led astray by information that is not really related to his field of investigation.

Hill and Kerber (1967) have pointed out that the evaluation and formulation of a problem associated with historical research often involve the personality of the researcher to a greater extent than do other basic types of research. They suggest that personal factors of the investigator such as interest, motivation, historical curiosity, and educational background for the interpretation of historical facts tend to influence the selection of the problem to a great extent.

Data collection

One of the principal differences between historical research and other forms of research is that historical research must deal with data that already exist. Hockett (1955) expresses it thus:

History is not a science of *direct* observation, like chemistry and physics. The historian like the geologist interprets past events by the traces they have left; he deals with the evidence of man's past acts and thoughts. But the historian, no less than the scientist, must utilize evidence resting on reliable observation. The difference in procedure is due to the fact that the historian usually does not make his own observations, and that those upon whose observations he must depend are, or were, often if not usually untrained observers. Historical method is, strictly speaking, a process *supplementary* to observations, a process by which the historian attempts to test the truthfulness of the reports of observations made by others. Like the scientist, he [sic] examines his data and formulates hypotheses, i.e. tentative conclusions. These conjectures he must test by seeking fresh evidence or re-examining the old, and this process he must continue until, in the light of all available evidence, the hypotheses are abandoned as untenable or modified until they are brought into conformity with the available evidence.

(Hockett, 1955)

Sources of data in historical research may be classified into two main groups: *primary sources*, which are the life blood of historical research; and *secondary sources*, which may be used in the absence of, or to supplement, primary data.

Primary sources of data have been described as those items that are original to the problem under study and may be thought of as being in two categories, thus:

1   The remains or relics of a given period. Although such remains and artefacts as skeletons, fossils, weapons, tools, utensils, buildings, pictures, furniture, coins and objets d'art were not meant to transmit information to subsequent eras, nevertheless they may be useful sources providing sound evidence about the past.

2   Those items that have had a direct physical relationship with the events being reconstructed. This category would include not only the written and oral testimony provided by actual participants in, or witnesses of, an event, but also the participants themselves. Documents considered as primary sources include manuscripts, charters, laws; archives of official minutes or records, files, letters, memoranda, memoirs, biography, official publications, wills, newspapers and magazines, maps, diagrams, catalogues, films, paintings, inscriptions, recordings, transcriptions, log books and research reports. All these are, intentionally or unintentionally, capable of transmitting a first-hand account of an event and are therefore considered as sources of primary data. Historical research in education draws chiefly on the kind of sources identified in this second category.

Secondary sources are those that do not bear a direct physical relationship to the event being studied. They are made up of data that cannot be described as original. A secondary source would thus be one in which the person describing the event was not actually present but who obtained descriptions from another person or source. These may or may not have been primary sources. Other instances of secondary sources used in historical research include: quoted material, textbooks, encyclopedias, other reproductions of material or information, prints of paintings or replicas of art objects. Best (1970) points out that secondary sources of data are usually of limited worth because of the errors that result when information is passed on from one person to another.

Various commentators stress the importance of using primary sources of data where possible (Hill and Kerber, 1967). The value, too, of secondary sources should not be minimized. There are numerous occasions where a secondary source can contribute significantly to more valid and reliable historical research than would otherwise be the case.

One further point: the review of the literature in other forms of educational research is regarded as a preparatory stage to gathering data and serves to acquaint researchers with previous research on the topics they are studying (Travers, 1969). It thus enables them to continue in a tradition, to place their work in context, and to learn from earlier endeavours. The function of the review of the literature in historical research, however, is different in that it provides the data for research; the researchers' acceptance or otherwise of their hypotheses will depend on their selection of information from the review and the interpretation they put on it. Borg (1963) has identified other differences: one is that the historical researcher will have to peruse longer documents than the empirical researcher who normally studies articles very much more succinct and precise. Further, documents required in historical research often date back much further than those in empirical research. And one final point: documents in education often consist of unpublished material and are therefore less accessible than reports of empirical studies in professional journals.

For a detailed consideration of the specific problems of documentary research, the reader is referred to the articles by Platt (1981) where she considers authenticity, availability of documents, sampling problems, inference and interpretation.

Evaluation

Because workers in the field of historical research gather much of their data and information from records and documents, these must be carefully evaluated so as to attest their worth for the purposes of the particular study. Evaluation of historical data and information is often referred to as historical criticism and the reliable data yielded by the process are known as historical evidence. Historical evidence has thus been described as that body of validated facts and information which can be accepted as trustworthy, as a valid basis for the testing and interpretation of hypotheses. Historical criticism is usually undertaken in two stages: first, the authenticity of the source is appraised; and second, the accuracy or worth of the data is evaluated. The two processes are known as external and internal criticism respectively, and since they each present problems of evaluation they merit further inspection.

External criticism

External criticism is concerned with establishing the authenticity or genuineness of data. It is therefore aimed at the document (or other source) itself rather than the statements it contains; with analytic forms of the data rather than the interpretation or meaning of them in relation to the study. It therefore sets out to uncover frauds, forgeries, hoaxes, inventions or distortions. To this end, the tasks of establishing the age or authorship of a document may involve tests of factors such as signatures, handwriting, script, type, style, spelling and place-names. Further, was the knowledge it purports to transmit available at the time and is it consistent with what is known about the author or period from another source? Increasingly sophisticated analyses of physical factors can also yield clues establishing authenticity or otherwise: physical and chemical tests of ink, paper, parchment, cloth and other materials, for example. Investigations in the field of educational history are less likely to encounter deliberate forgeries than in, say, political or social history, though it is possible to find that official documents, correspondence and autobiographies have been 'ghosted', that is, prepared by a person other than the alleged author or signer.

Internal criticism

Having established the authenticity of the document, the researcher's next task is to evaluate the accuracy and worth of the data contained therein. While they may be genuine, they may not necessarily disclose the most faithful picture. In their concern to establish the meaning and reliability of data, investigators are confronted with a more difficult problem than external criticism because they have to establish the credibility of the author of the documents. Travers (1969) has listed those characteristics commonly considered in making evaluations of writers. Were they trained or untrained observers of the events? In other words, how competent were they? What were their relationships to the events? To what extent were they under pressure, from fear or vanity, say, to distort or omit facts? What were the intents of the writers of the documents? To what extent were they experts at recording those particular events? Were the habits of the authors such that they might interfere with the accuracy of recordings? Were they too antagonistic or too sympathetic to give true pictures? How long after the event did they record their testimonies? And were they able to remember accurately? Finally, are they in agreement with other independent witnesses?

Many documents in the history of education tend to be neutral in character, though it is possible that some may be in error because of these kinds of observer characteristics. A particular problem arising from the questions posed by Travers is that of bias. This can be particularly acute where life histories are being studied. The chief concern here, as Plummer (1983) reminds us, resides in examining possible sources of bias which prevent researchers from finding out what is wanted and using techniques to minimize the possible sources of bias.

Researchers generally recognize three sources of bias: those arising from the subject being interviewed, those arising from themselves as researchers and those arising from the subject-researcher interaction (Travers, 1969).[5]

Writing the research report

Once the data have been gathered and subjected to external criticism for authenticity and to internal criticism for accuracy, the researcher is next confronted with the task of piecing together an account of the events embraced by the research problem. This stage is known as the process of synthesis. It is probably the most difficult phase in the project and calls for considerable imagination and resourcefulness. The resulting pattern is then applied to the testing of the hypothesis.

The writing of the final report is equally demanding and calls for creativity and high standards of objective and systematic analysis.

Best (1970) has listed the kinds of problems occurring in the various types of historical research projects submitted by students. These include:

- Defining the problem too broadly.
- The tendency to use easy-to-find secondary sources of data rather than sufficient primary sources, which are harder to locate but usually more trustworthy.
- Inadequate historical criticism of data, due to failure to establish authenticity of sources and trustworthiness of data. For example, there is often a tendency to accept a statement as necessarily true when several observers agree. It is possible that one may have influenced the others, or that all were influenced by the same inaccurate source of information.
- Poor logical analysis resulting from:
  - oversimplification – failure to recognize the fact that causes of events are more often multiple and complex than single and simple;
  - overgeneralization on the basis of insufficient evidence, and false reasoning by analogy, basing conclusions upon superficial similarities of situations;
  - failure to interpret words and expression in the light of their accepted meaning in an earlier period;
  - failure to distinguish between significant facts in a situation and those that are irrelevant or unimportant.
- Expression of personal bias, as revealed by statements lifted out of context for purposes of persuasion, assuming too generous or uncritical an attitude towards a person or idea (or being too unfriendly or critical), excessive admiration for the past (sometimes known as the 'old oaken bucket' delusion), or an equally unrealistic admiration for the new or contemporary, assuming that all change represents progress.
- Poor reporting in a style that is dull and colourless, too flowery or flippant, too persuasive or of the 'soap-box' type, or lacking in proper usage.

Borg and Gall (1979: 400) suggest several mistakes that can be made in conducting historical research:

- The selection of a topic for which historical sources are slight, inaccessible or non-existent.
- Over-reliance on secondary sources.
- Failure to subject the historical sources to internal or external validity/criticism checks.
- Lack of reflexivity and the researcher's selectivity and bias in using sources.
- Importing concepts from other disciplines.
- Making illegitimate inferences of causality and monocausality.
- Generalizing beyond acceptable limits of the data.
- Listing facts without appropriate thematization.

In addition to these, Sutherland (1969) has brilliantly illustrated two further common errors among historians of education. These are first, projecting current battles backwards onto a historical background which leads to distortion; and second, 'description in a vacuum' which fails to illustrate the relationship of the educational system to the structure of society. To conclude on a more positive note Mouly (1978) itemizes five basic criteria for evaluating historical research:

- *Problem* Has the problem been clearly defined? It is difficult enough to conduct historical research adequately without adding to the confusion by starting out with a nebulous problem. Is the problem capable of solution? Is it within the competence of the investigator?
- *Data* Are data of a primary nature available in sufficient completeness to provide a solution, or has there been an overdependence on secondary or unverifiable sources?
- *Analysis* Has the dependability of the data been adequately established? Has the relevance of the data been adequately explored?
- *Interpretation* Does the author display adequate mastery of his [sic] data and insight into the relative significance? Does he display adequate historical perspective? Does he maintain his objectivity or does he allow personal bias to distort the evidence? Are his hypotheses plausible? Have they been adequately tested? Does he take a sufficiently broad view of the total situation? Does he see the relationship between his data and other 'historical facts'?
- *Presentation* Does the style of writing attract as well as inform? Does the report make a contribution on the basis of newly discovered data or new interpretation, or is it simply 'uninspired hack-work'? Does it reflect scholarliness?

The use of quantitative methods

By far the greater part of research in historical studies is qualitative in nature. This is so because the proper subject-matter of historical research consists to a great extent of verbal and other symbolic material emanating from a society's or a culture's past. The basic skills required of the researcher to analyse this kind of qualitative or symbolic material involve collecting, classifying, ordering, synthesizing, evaluating and interpreting. At the basis of all these acts lies sound personal judgement. In the comparatively recent past, however, attempts have been made to apply the quantitative methods of the scientist to the solution of historical problems (Travers, 1969). Of these methods, the one having greatest relevance to historical research is that of content analysis, the basic goal of which is to take a verbal, non-quantitative document and transform it into quantitative data (Bailey, 1978).

Content analysis itself has been defined as 'a multipurpose research method developed specifically for investigating a broad spectrum of problems in which the content of communication serves as a basis of inference',[6] from word counts (Travers, 1969) to categorization. Approaches to content analysis are careful to identify appropriate categories and units of analysis, both of which will reflect the nature of the document being analysed and the purpose of the research. Categories are normally determined after initial inspection of the document and will cover the main areas of content.

We can readily see how the technique of content analysis may be applied to selected aspects of historical research in education. It could be used, for instance, in the analysis of educational documents. In addition to elucidating the content of the document, the method may throw additional light on the source of the communication, its author, and on its intended recipients, those to whom the message is directed. Further, an analysis of this kind would tell us more about the social context and the kinds of factors stressed or ignored, and of the influence of political factors, for instance. It follows from this that content analysis may form the basis of comparative or cross-cultural studies. The purposes of content analysis have been identified by Holsti (1968):

- To describe trends in communication content.
- To relate known characteristics of sources to messages they produce.
- To audit communication content against standards.
- To analyse techniques of persuasion.
- To analyse style.
- To relate known attributes of the audience to messages produced for them.
- To describe patterns of communication.

Different examples of the use of content analysis in historical contexts are provided by Thomas and Znaniecki (1918)[7] and Bradburn and Berlew (1961). A further example of content analysis in historical settings is McClelland et al.'s (1953) study of the relationship between the need to achieve (n'ach, for short) among members of a society and the economic growth of the particular society in question. Finally, for a more detailed and technical consideration of the use of quantitative methods in historical research, a study which looks at the classifying and arranging of historical data and reviews basic descriptive statistics, we refer the reader to Floud (1979).

Life histories

Thomas and Znaniecki's monumental study, *The Polish Peasant in Europe and America* (1918),

serves as an appropriate introduction to this section, for their detailed account of the life and times of Wladek Wisniewski is commonly held to be the first sociological life history.

The life history, according to Plummer (1983), is frequently a full-length book about one person's life in his or her own words. Often, Plummer observes, it is gathered over a number of years, the researcher providing gentle guidance to the subject, encouraging him or her either to write down episodes of life or to tape-record them. And often as not, these materials will be backed up with intensive observations of the subject's life, with interviews of the subject's friends and acquaintances and with close scrutiny of relevant documents such as letters, diaries and photographs. Essentially, the life history is an 'interactive and co-operative technique directly involving the researcher' (Plummer, 1983).

Recent accounts of the perspectives and interpretations of people in a variety of educational settings are both significant and pertinent,[8] for they provide valuable 'insights into the ways in which educational personnel come to terms with the constraints and conditions in which they work' (Goodson, 1983). Life histories, Goodson argues, 'have the potential to make a far-reaching contribution to the problem of understanding the links between "personal troubles" and "public issues", a task that lies at the very heart of the sociological enterprise'. Their importance, he asserts, 'is best confirmed by the fact that teachers continually, most often unsolicited, import life history data into their accounts of classroom events' (Goodson, 1983).

Miller (1999) demonstrates that biographical research is a distinctive way of conceptualizing social activity. He provides outlines of the three main approaches to analysis, that is to say:

- the *realist* which is focused upon grounded-theory techniques;
- the *neo-positivist*, employing more structured interviews; and
- the *narrative* with its emphasis on using the interplay between interviewer and interviewee to actively construct life histories.

Denzin (1999) suggests that there are several varieties of biographical research methods including: biography, autobiography, story, discourse, narrative writing, personal history, oral history, case history, life history, personal experience, and case study. This is addressed further by Connelly and Clandinin (1999) who indicate several approaches to narrative inquiry:

- oral history;
- stories;
- annals and chronicles;
- photographs;
- memory boxes;
- interviews;
- journals;
- autobiography;
- letters;
- conversations;
- and documents.

In exploring the appropriateness of life history techniques to a particular research project, and with ever-present constraints of time, facilities and finance in mind, it is useful to distinguish life histories both by type and mode of presentation, both factors bearing directly upon the scope and feasibility of the research endeavour. Box 7.2 draws on an outline by Hitchcock and Hughes (1989). Readers may wish to refer to the descriptions of types and modes of presentation contained in Box 7.2 in assessing the differing demands that are made on intending researchers as they gather, analyse and present their data. Whether retrospective or contemporaneous, a life history involves five broad research processes. These have been identified and described by Plummer (1983).

Preparation

This involves the researcher both in selecting an appropriate problem and devising relevant research techniques. Questions to be asked at this stage are first, *'Who is to be the object of the study?'* – the great person, the common person, the volunteer, the selected, the coerced? Second, *'What makes a good informant?'* Plummer draws

attention to key factors such as accessibility of place and availability of time, and the awareness of the potential informant of his/her particular cultural milieu. A good informant is able and willing to establish and maintain a close, intimate relationship with the researcher. It is axiomatic that common sympathies and mutual respect are prerequisites for the sustenance and success of a life history project. Third, *'What needs clarifying in the early stages of the research?'* The motivations of the researcher need to be made explicit to the intended subject. So too, the question of remuneration for the subject's services should be clarified from the outset. The issue of anonymity must also be addressed, for unlike other research methodologies, life histories reveal intimate details (names, places, events) and provide scant cover from prying eyes. The earlier stages of the project also provide opportunities for discussing with the research subject the precise nature of

Box 7.2
A typology of life histories and their modes of presentation

> **Types**
> *Retrospective life history*
> a reconstruction of past events from the present feelings and interpretations of the individual concerned.
>
> *Contemporaneous life history*
> a description of an individual's daily life in progress, here and now.
>
> **Modes of Presentation**
> *Naturalistic*
> a first-person life history in which the life story is largely in the words of the individual subject, supported by a brief introduction, commentary and conclusion on the part of the researcher.
>
> *Thematically-edited*
> subject's words are retained intact but are presented by the researcher in terms of a series of themes, topics or headings, often in chapter-by-chapter format.
>
> *Interpreted and edited*
> the researcher's influence is most marked in his/her version of a subject's life story which the researcher has sifted, distilled, edited and interpreted.

Source Adapted from Hitchcock and Hughes, 1989

the life history study, the logistics of interview situations and modes of data recording.

Data collection

Central to the success of a life history is the researcher's ability to use a variety of interview techniques (see also Chapter 15). As the occasion demands, these may range from relatively structured interviews that serve as general guides from the outset of the study, to informal, unstructured interviews reminiscent of non-directive counselling approaches espoused by Carl Rogers (1945) and his followers. In the case of the latter, Plummer (1983) draws attention to the importance of empathy and 'non-possessive warmth' on the part of the interviewer-researcher. A third interviewing strategy involves a judicious mixture of participant observation (see Chapter 17) and casual chatting, supplemented by note-taking.

Data storage

Typically, life histories generate enormous amounts of data. Intending researchers must make early decisions about the use of tape-recordings, the how, what and when of their transcription and editing, and the development of coding and filing devices if they are to avoid being totally swamped by the materials created. Readers are referred to the discussion in Chapter 9 and to Fiedler's (1978) extensive account of methods appropriate to field studies in natural settings.

Data analysis

Three central issues underpin the quality of data generated by life history methodology. They are to do with representativeness, reliability and validity (see also Chapters 5, 9 and 15).

Plummer draws attention to a frequent criticism of life history research, namely that its cases are atypical rather than representative. To avoid this charge, he urges intending researchers to 'work out and explicitly state the life history's relationship to a wider population' (Plummer, 1983) by way of appraising the subject on a continuum of representativeness and non-representativeness.

Reliability in life history research hinges upon the identification of sources of bias and the application of techniques to reduce them. Bias arises from the informant, the researcher, and the interactional encounter itself (Plummer, 1983), and these were presented in Box 5.1. Several validity checks are available to intending researchers. Plummer identifies the following:

- The subject of the life history may present an autocritique of it, having read the entire product.
- A comparison may be made with similar written sources by way of identifying points of major divergence or similarity.
- A comparison may be made with official records by way of imposing accuracy checks on the life history.
- A comparison may be made by interviewing other informants.

Essentially, the validity of any life history lies in its ability to represent the informant's subjective reality, that is to say, his or her definition of the situation.

Data presentation

Plummer provides three points of direction for the researcher intent upon writing a life history. First, have a clear view of who you are writing for and what you wish to accomplish by writing the account. Are you aiming to produce a case history or a case study? Case histories 'tell a good story for its own sake' (Plummer, 1983). Case studies, by contrast, use personal documents for wider theoretical purposes such as the verification and/or the generation of theory. Second, having established the purpose of the life history, decide how far you should intrude upon your assembled data. Intrusion occurs both through editing and interpreting. Editing ('cutting', sequencing, disguising names, places etc.) is almost a *sine qua non* of any life history study.

Paraphrasing Plummer, editing involves getting your subject's own words, grasping them from the inside and turning them into a structured and coherent statement that uses the subject's words in places and your own, as researcher, in others, but retains their authentic meaning at all times. Third, as far as the mechanics of writing a life history are concerned, practise writing regularly. Writing, Plummer observes, needs working at, and daily drafting, revising and redrafting is necessary. For an example of life history methodology and research see Evetts (1991).

8 Surveys, longitudinal, cross-sectional and trend studies

Many educational research methods are descriptive; that is, they set out to describe and to interpret *what is*. Descriptive research, according to Best, is concerned with:

> conditions or relationships that exist; practices that prevail; beliefs, points of views, or attitudes that are held; processes that are going on; effects that are being felt; or trends that are developing. At times, descriptive research is concerned with how *what is* or *what exists* is related to some preceding event that has influenced or affected a present condition or event.
>
> (Best, 1970)

Such studies look at individuals, groups, institutions, methods and materials in order to describe, compare, contrast, classify, analyse and interpret the entities and the events that constitute their various fields of inquiry.

This chapter deals with several types of descriptive survey research, including longitudinal, cross-sectional and trend or prediction studies. Collectively longitudinal, cross-sectional and trend or prediction studies are sometimes termed developmental research because they are concerned both to describe what the present relationships are among variables in a given situation and to account for changes occurring in those relationships as a function of time. The term 'developmental' is primarily biological, having to do with the organization and life processes of living things. The concept has been appropriated and applied to diverse educational, historical, sociological and psychological phenomena. In education, for example, developmental studies often retain the original biological orientation of the term, having to do with the acquisition of motor and perceptual skills in young children. However, the designation 'developmental' has wider application in this field, for example, in connection with Piaget's studies of qualitative changes occurring in children's thinking, and Kohlberg's work on moral development.

Typically, surveys gather data at a particular point in time with the intention of describing the nature of existing conditions, or identifying standards against which existing conditions can be compared, or determining the relationships that exist between specific events. Thus, surveys may vary in their levels of complexity from those which provide simple frequency counts to those which present relational analysis.

Surveys may be further differentiated in terms of their scope. A study of contemporary developments in post-secondary education, for example, might encompass the whole of Western Europe; a study of subject choice, on the other hand, might be confined to one secondary school. The complexity and scope of surveys in education can be illustrated by reference to familiar examples. The surveys undertaken for the Plowden Committee on primary school children (Central Advisory Council on Education, 1967) collected a wealth of information on children, teachers and parents and used sophisticated analytical techniques to predict pupil attainment. By contrast, the small scale survey of Jackson and Marsden (1962) involved a detailed study of the backgrounds and values of 88 working-class adults who had achieved success through selective secondary education.

Box 8.1
Stages in the planning of a survey

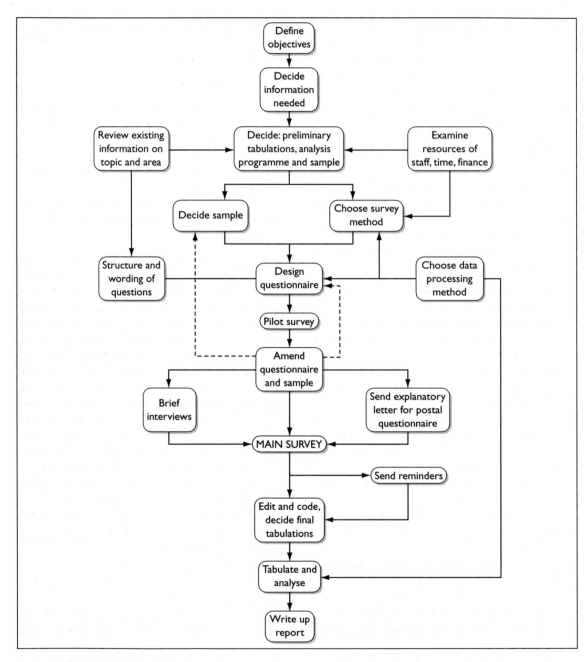

Source Adapted from Davidson, 1970

Whether the survey is large scale and undertaken by some governmental bureau or small scale and carried out by the lone researcher, the collection of information typically involves one or more of the following data-gathering techniques: structured or semi-structured interviews, self-completion or postal questionnaires, standardized tests of attainment or performance, and attitude scales. Typically, too, surveys proceed through well-defined stages, though not every stage outlined in Box 8.1 is required for the successful completion of a survey.

A survey has several characteristics and several claimed attractions; typically it is used to scan a wide field of issues, populations, programmes etc. in order to measure or describe any generalized features. It is useful (Morrison, 1993: 38–40) in that it usually:

- gathers data on a one-shot basis and hence is economical and efficient;
- represents a wide target population (hence there is a need for careful sampling, see Chapter 4);
- generates numerical data;
- provides descriptive, inferential and explanatory information;
- manipulates key factors and variables to derive frequencies (e.g. the numbers registering a particular opinion or test score);
- gathers standardized information (i.e. using the same instruments and questions for all participants);
- ascertains correlations (e.g. to find out if there is any relationship between gender and scores);
- presents material which is uncluttered by specific contextual factors;
- captures data from multiple choice, closed questions, test scores or observation schedules;
- supports or refutes hypotheses about the target population;
- generates accurate instruments through their piloting and revision;
- makes generalizations about, and observes patterns of response in, the targets of focus;

- gathers data which can be processed statistically;
- usually relies on large scale data gathering from a wide population in order to enable generalizations to be made about given factors or variables.

Examples of surveys[1] are:

- opinion polls (which refute the notion that only opinion polls can catch opinions);
- test scores (e.g. the results of testing students nationally or locally);
- students' preferences for particular courses, e.g. humanities, sciences;
- reading surveys (e.g. Southgate's *et al.* example of teaching practices in 1981 in the United Kingdom).

A researcher using these types of survey typically will be seeking to gather large scale data from as representative a sample population as possible in order to say with a measure of statistical confidence that certain observed characteristics occur with a degree of regularity, or that certain factors cluster together (see Chapter 20) or that they correlate with each other (correlation and covariance), or that they change over time and location (e.g. results of test scores used to ascertain the 'value-added' dimension of education, maybe using regression analysis and analysis of residuals to determine the difference between a predicted and an observed score), or regression analysis to use data from one variable to predict an outcome on another variable.

The attractions of a survey lie in its appeal to generalizability or universality within given parameters, its ability to make statements which are supported by large data banks and its ability to establish the degree of confidence which can be placed in a set of findings.

On the other hand, if a researcher is concerned to catch local, institutional or small scale factors and variables – to portray the specificity of a situation, its uniqueness and particular complexity, its interpersonal dynamics, and to provide explanations of why a situation occurred or why a person or group of people returned a particular set of results or behaved in a particular way in a situation, or how a programme changes and develops over time, then a survey approach is probably unsuitable. Its degree of explanatory potential or fine detail is limited; it is lost to broad brush generalizations which are free of temporal, spatial or local contexts, i.e. its appeal largely rests on the basis of positivism. The individual instance is sacrificed to the aggregated response (which has the attraction of anonymity, non-traceability and confidentiality for respondents).

Surveys typically rely on large scale data, e.g. from questionnaires, test scores, attendance rates, results of public examinations etc., all of which would enable comparisons to be made over time or between groups. This is not to say that surveys cannot be undertaken on a small scale basis, as indeed they can; rather, it is to say that the generalizability of such small scale data will be slight. In surveys the researcher is usually very clearly an outsider; indeed questions of reliability must attach themselves to researchers conducting survey research on their own subjects, e.g. participants in a course that they have been running.[2] Further, it is critical that attention is paid to rigorous sampling, otherwise the basis of its applicability to wider contexts is seriously undermined. Non-probability samples tend to be avoided in surveys if generalizability is sought; probability sampling will tend to lead to generalizability of the data collected.

Some preliminary considerations

Three prerequisites to the design of any survey are: the specification of the exact purpose of the inquiry; the population on which it is to focus; and the resources that are available. Hoinville and Jowell's (1978) consideration of each of these key factors in survey planning can be illustrated in relation to the design of an educational inquiry.

The purpose of the inquiry

First, a survey's general purpose must be translated into a specific central aim. Thus, 'to explore teachers' views about in-service work' is somewhat nebulous, whereas 'to obtain a detailed description of primary and secondary teachers' priorities in the provision of in-service education courses' is reasonably specific.

Having decided upon and specified the primary objective of the survey, the second phase of the planning involves the identification and itemizing of subsidiary topics that relate to its central purpose. In our example, subsidiary issues might well include: the types of courses required; the content of courses; the location of courses; the timing of courses; the design of courses; and the financing of courses.

The third phase follows the identification and itemization of subsidiary topics and involves formulating specific information requirements relating to each of these issues. For example, with respect to the type of courses required, detailed information would be needed about the duration of courses (one meeting, several meetings, a week, a month, a term or a year), the status of courses (non-award bearing, award bearing, with certificate, diploma, degree granted by college or university), the orientation of courses (theoretically oriented involving lectures, readings, etc., or practically oriented involving workshops and the production of curriculum materials).

As these details unfold, note Hoinville and Jowell, consideration would have to be given to the most appropriate ways of collecting items of information (interviews with selected teachers, postal questionnaires to selected schools, etc.).

The population upon which the survey is focused

The second prerequisite to survey design, the specification of the population to which the inquiry is addressed, affects decisions that researchers must make both about sampling and resources. In our hypothetical survey of in-service requirements, for example, we might specify the population as 'those primary and secondary teachers employed in schools within a 30-mile radius of Loughborough University'. In this case, the population is readily identifiable and, given sufficient resources to contact every member of the designated group, sampling decisions do not arise. Things are rarely so straightforward, however. Often the criteria by which populations are specified ('severely challenged', 'under-achievers', 'intending teachers' or 'highly anxious') are difficult to operationalize. Populations, moreover, vary considerably in their accessibility; pupils and student teachers are relatively easy to survey, gypsy children and headteachers are more elusive. More importantly, in a large survey researchers usually draw a sample from the population to be studied; rarely do they attempt to contact every member. We deal with the question of sampling shortly.

The resources available

The third important factor in designing and planning a survey is the financial cost. Sample surveys are labour-intensive (see Davidson, 1970), the largest single expenditure being the fieldwork where costs arise out of the interviewing time, travel time and transport claims of the interviewers themselves. There are additional demands on the survey budget. Training and supervising the panel of interviewers can often be as expensive as the costs incurred during the time that they actually spend in the field. Questionnaire construction, piloting, printing, posting, coding, together with computer programming – all eat into financial resources.

Proposals from intending education researchers seeking governmental or private funding are often weakest in the amount of time and thought devoted to a detailed planning of the financial implications of the projected inquiries. (In this chapter we confine ourselves from this point to a discussion of surveys based on self-completion questionnaires. A full account of the interview as a research technique is given in Chapter 15.)

From here it is possible to identify several stages to the conduct of a survey. Rosier (1997: 154–62) suggests that the planning of a survey will need to include clarification of:

- the research questions to which answers need to be provided;
- the conceptual framework of the survey, specifying in precise terms the concepts that will be used and explored;
- operationalizing the research questions (e.g. into hypotheses);
- the instruments to be used for data collection, e.g.: to chart or measure background characteristics of the sample (often nominal data), academic achievements (e.g. examination results, degrees awarded), attitudes and opinions (often using ordinal data from rating scales) and behaviour (using observational techniques);
- sampling strategies and subgroups within the sample (unless the whole population is being surveyed, e.g. through census returns or nationally aggregated test scores etc.);
- pre-piloting the survey;
- piloting the survey;
- data collection practicalities and conduct (e.g. permissions, funding, ethical considerations, response rates);
- data preparation (e.g. coding, data entry for computer analysis, checking and verification);
- data analysis (e.g. statistical processes, construction of variables and factor analysis, inferential statistics);
- reporting the findings (answering the research questions).

It is important to pilot and pre-pilot a survey. The difference between the pre-pilot and the pilot is significant. Whereas the pre-pilot is usually a series of open-ended questions that are used to generate categories for closed, typically multiple choice questions, the pilot is used to test the actual survey instrument itself (see Chapter 14).

A rigorous survey, then, formulates clear, specific objectives and research questions, ensures that the instrumentation, sampling, and data types are appropriate to yield answers to the research questions, ensures that as high a level of sophistication of data analysis is undertaken as the data will sustain (but no more!).

Survey sampling

Because questions to do with sampling arise directly from the second of our preliminary considerations, that is, defining the population upon which the survey is to focus, researchers must take sampling decisions early in the overall planning of a survey (see Box 8.1). We have already seen that due to factors of expense, time and accessibility, it is not always possible or practical to obtain measures from a population. Researchers endeavour therefore to collect information from a smaller group or subset of the population in such a way that the knowledge gained is representative of the total population under study. This smaller group or subset is a 'sample'. Notice how competent researchers start with the total population and work down to the sample. By contrast, novices work from the bottom up, that is, they determine the minimum number of respondents needed to conduct a successful survey. However, unless they identify the total population in advance, it is virtually impossible for them to assess how representative the sample is that they have drawn. There are two methods of sampling. One yields probability samples in which, as the term implies, the probability of selection of each respondent is known. The other yields non-probability samples, in which the probability of selection is unknown. We refer the reader to Chapter 4 for a discussion of sampling.

Longitudinal, cross-sectional and trend studies

The term 'longitudinal' is used to describe a variety of studies that are conducted over a period of time. Often, as we have seen, the word 'developmental' is employed in connection with longitudinal studies that deal specifically with aspects of human growth.

A clear distinction is drawn between longitudinal and cross-sectional studies.[3] The longitudinal study gathers data over an extended period of time; a short-term investigation may take several weeks or months; a long-term study can extend over many years. Where successive measures are taken at different points in time from the same respondents, the term 'follow-up study' or 'cohort study' is used in the British literature, the equivalent term in the United States being the 'panel study'. The term 'cohort' is a group of people with some common characteristic. A cohort study is sometimes differentiated from a panel study. In a cohort study a specific population is tracked over a specific period of time but selective sampling within that sample occurs (Borg and Gall, 1979: 291). This means that some members of a cohort may not be included each time. By contrast, in a panel study each same individual is tracked over time.

Where different respondents are studied at different points in time, the study is called 'cross-sectional'. Where a few selected factors are studied continuously over time, the term 'trend study' is employed. One example of regular or repeated cross-sectional social surveys is the General Household Survey, in which the same questions are asked every year though they are put to a different sample of the population each time. A well known example of a longitudinal (cohort) study is the National Child Development Study, which started in 1958, the most recent round of interviews took place in 1991. The British Household Panel Survey has interviewed individuals from a representative sample each year in the 1990s.

Cohort studies and trend studies are prospective longitudinal methods in that they are ongoing in their collection of information about individuals or their monitoring of specific events. Retrospective longitudinal studies, on the other hand, focus upon individuals who have reached some defined end-point or state. For example, a group of young people may be the researcher's particular interest (intending social workers, convicted drug offenders or university dropouts, for example), and the questions to which she will address herself are likely to include ones such as: 'Is there anything about the previous experience of these individuals that can account for their present situation?'

Retrospective analysis is not confined to longitudinal studies alone. For example Rose and Sullivan (1993: 185) suggest that cross-sectional studies can use retrospective factual questions, e.g. previous occupations, dates of birth within the family, dates of marriage, divorce, though the authors advise against collecting other types of retrospective data in cross-sectional studies, as the quality of the data diminishes the further back one asks respondents to recall previous states or even facts.

A cross-sectional study is one that produces a 'snapshot' of a population at a particular point in time. The epitome of the cross-sectional study is a national census in which a representative sample of the population consisting of individuals of different ages, different occupations, different educational and income levels, and residing in different parts of the country, is interviewed on the same day. More typically in education, cross-sectional studies involve indirect measures of the nature and rate of changes in the physical and intellectual development of samples of children drawn from representative age levels. The single 'snapshot' of the cross-sectional study provides researchers with data for either a retrospective or a prospective inquiry.

Trend or prediction studies have an obvious importance to educational administrators or planners. Like cohort studies, they may be of relatively short or long duration. Essentially, the trend study examines recorded data to establish patterns of change that have already occurred in order to predict what will be likely to occur in the future. In trend studies two or more cross-sectional studies are undertaken with identical age groups at more than one point in time in order to make comparisons over time (e.g. the Scholastic Aptitude and Achievement tests in the United States) (Keeves, 1997: 141) and the National Assessment of Educational Progress results (Lietz and Keeves, 1997: 122). A major difficulty researchers face in conducting trend analyses is the intrusion of unpredictable factors that invalidate forecasts formulated on past data. For this reason, short-term trend studies tend to be more accurate than long-term analyses. The distinctions we have drawn between the various terms used in developmental research are illustrated in Box 8.2.

Box 8.2
Types of developmental research

TREND STUDY

Recorded data on factors a, b, c → Predicted patterns → *Observations on a, b, c.*

1 2 3 4 5 6 *n*

COHORT STUDY

Sample A Observation 1 → Sample A Observation 2 → Sample A Observation 3 → Sample A Observation 4 → Sample A Observation 5

CROSS-SECTIONAL STUDY

Sample A ← Sample B ← Sample C → Sample D → Sample E

SOCIAL PROCESSES

Retrospective ←——————————————————————→ Prospective

OVER TIME

Strengths and weaknesses of cohort and cross-sectional studies

Longitudinal studies of the cohort analysis type have an important place in the research armoury of educational investigators. Cohort studies of human growth and development conducted on representative samples of populations are uniquely able to identify typical patterns of development and to reveal factors operating on those samples which elude other research designs. They permit researchers to examine individual variations in characteristics or traits, and to produce individual growth curves. Cohort studies, too, are particularly appropriate when investigators attempt to establish causal relationships, for this task involves identifying changes in certain characteristics that result in changes in others. Cross-sectional designs are inappropriate in causal research. Cohort analysis is especially useful in sociological research because it can show how changing properties of individuals fit together into changing properties of social systems as a whole. For example, the study of staff morale and its association with the emerging organizational climate of a newly opened school would lend itself to this type of developmental research. A further strength of cohort studies in schools is that they provide longitudinal records whose value derives in part from the known fallibility of any single test or assessment (see Davie, 1972). Finally, time, always a limiting factor in experimental and interview settings, is generally more readily available in cohort studies, allowing the researcher greater opportunity to observe trends and to distinguish 'real' changes from chance occurrences (see Bailey, 1978).

Longitudinal studies suffer several disadvantages (though the gravity of these weaknesses is challenged by supporters of cohort analysis). The disadvantages are first, that they are time-consuming and expensive, because the researcher is obliged to wait for growth data to accumulate. Second, there is the difficulty of sample mortality. Inevitably during the course of a long-term cohort study, subjects drop out, are lost or refuse further co-operation. Such attrition makes it unlikely that those who remain in the study are as representative of the population as the sample that was originally drawn. Sometimes attempts are made to lessen the effects of sample mortality by introducing aspects of cross-sectional study design, that is, 'topping up' the original cohort sample size at each time of retesting with the same number of respondents drawn from the same population. The problem here is that differences arising in the data from one survey to the next may then be accounted for by differences in the persons surveyed rather than by genuine changes or trends. A third difficulty has been termed 'control effect' (sometimes referred to as 'measurement effect'). Often, repeated interviewing results in an undesired and confusing effect on the actions or attitudes under study, influencing the behaviour of subjects, sensitizing them to matters that have hitherto passed unnoticed, or stimulating them to communication with others on unwanted topics (see Riley, 1963). Fourth, cohort studies can suffer from the interaction of biological, environmental and intervention influences. Finally, cohort studies in education pose considerable problems of organization due to the continuous changes that occur in pupils, staff, teaching methods and the like. Such changes make it highly unlikely that a study will be completed in the way that it was originally planned.

Cohort studies, as we have seen, are particularly appropriate in research on human growth and development. Why then are so many studies in this area cross-sectional in design? The reason is that they have a number of advantages over cohort studies; they are less expensive; they produce findings more quickly; they are less likely to suffer from control effects; and they are more likely to secure the co-operation of respondents on a 'one-off' basis. Generally, cross-sectional designs are able to include more subjects than are cohort designs.

The strengths of cohort analysis are the weaknesses of the cross-sectional design. The cross-sectional study is a less effective method for the researcher who is concerned to identify individual variations in growth or to establish causal relationships between variables. Sampling in the cross-sectional study is complicated because different subjects are involved at each age level and may not be comparable. Further problems arising out of selection effects and the obscuring of irregularities in growth weaken the cross-sectional study so much that one observer dismisses the method as a highly unsatisfactory way of obtaining developmental data except for the crudest purposes. Douglas (1976),[4] who pioneered the first national cohort study to be undertaken in any country, makes a spirited defence of the method against the common criticisms that are levelled against it – that it is expensive and time-consuming. His account of the advantages of cohort analysis over cross-sectional designs is summarized in Box 8.3.

The comparative strengths and weaknesses of longitudinal studies (including retrospective studies), cross-section analysis and trend studies are summarized in Box 8.4 (see also Rose and Sullivan (1993: 184–8)). Several of the strengths and weaknesses of retrospective longitudinal studies share the same characteristics as those of *ex post facto* research, discussed in Chapter 11.

Event history analysis

Recent developments in longitudinal studies include the use of 'event history analysis' (e.g. von Eye, 1990; Rose and Sullivan, 1993: 189–90; Plewis, 1997). This is a set of statistical techniques whose key concepts include: *a risk set* (a set of participants who have yet to experience a particular event or situation); a *survivor function* or *survivor curve* (the decline in the size of risk over time); the *hazard* or *hazard rate* (the rate at which particular events occur, or the risk of a particular event occurring at a particular time). Event-history analysis suggests that it is possible to consider the dependent variable in (e.g. marriage, employment changes, redundancy, further and higher education, moving house, death) as predictable within certain time frames for individuals. The rationale for this derives from life-table analysis used by demographers to calculate survival and mortality rates in a given population over time. For example if x number of the population are alive at time t, then it may be possible to predict the survival rate of that population at time $t + 1$. In a sense it is akin to a prediction study. Life-table studies are straightforward in that they are concerned with specific,

Box 8.3
Advantages of cohort over cross-sectional designs

1 Some types of information, for example, on attitudes or assessment of potential ability, are only meaningful if collected contemporaneously. Other types are more complete or more accurate if collected during the course of a longitudinal survey, though they are likely to have some value even if collected retrospectively, for example, length of schooling, job history, geographical movement.

2 In cohort studies, no duplication of information occurs, whereas in cross-sectional studies the same type of background information has to be collected on each occasion. This increases the interviewing costs.

3 The omission of even a single variable, later found to be important, from a cross-sectional study is a disaster, whereas it is usually possible in a cohort study to fill the gap, even if only partially, in a subsequent interview.

4 A cohort study allows the accumulation of a much larger number of variables, extending over a much wider area of knowledge than would be possible in a cross-sectional study. This is of course because the collection can be spread over many interviews. Moreover, information may be obtained at the most appropriate time, for example, information on job entry may be obtained when it occurs even if this varies from one member of the sample to another.

5 Starting with a birth cohort removes later problems of sampling and allows the extensive use of subsamples. It also eases problems of estimating bias and reliability.

6 Longitudinal studies are free of one of the major obstacles to causal analysis, namely, the re-interpretation of remembered information so that it conforms with conventional views on causation. It also provides the means to assess the direction of effect.

Source Adapted from Douglas, 1976

Box 8.4

The characteristics, strengths and weaknesses of longitudinal, cross-sectional, trend analysis, and retrospective longitudinal studies

Study type	Features	Strengths	Weaknesses
Longitudinal studies (cohort/ panel studies)	1 Single sample over extended period of time. 2 Enables the same individuals to be compared over time (diachronic analysis). 3 Micro-level analysis.	1 Useful for establishing causal relationships and for making reliable inferences. 2 Shows how changing properties of individuals fit into systemic change. 3 Operates within the known limits of instrumentation employed. 4 Separates real trends from chance occurrence. 5 Brings the benefits of extended time frames. 6 Useful for charting growth and development. 7 Gathers data contemporaneously rather than retrospectively, thereby avoiding the problems of selective or false memory. 8 Economical in that a picture of the sample is built up over time. 9 In-depth and comprehensive coverage of a wide range of variables, both initial and emergent – individual specific effects and population heterogeneity. 10 Enables change to be analysed at the *individual/ micro* level. 11 Enables the dynamics of change to be caught, the flows into and out of particular states and the transitions between states. 12 Individual level data are more accurate than macro-level, cross-sectional data. 13 Sampling error reduced as the study remains with the same sample over time. 14 Enables clear recommendations for intervention to be made.	1 Time-consuming – it takes a long time for the studies to be conducted and the results to emerge. 2 Problems of sample mortality heighten over time and diminish initial representativeness. 3 Control effects – repeated interviewing of the same sample influences their behaviour. 4 Intervening effects attenuate the initial research plan. 5 Problem of securing participation as it involves repeated contact. 6 Data, being rich at an individual level, are typically complex to analyse.

continued

Box 8.4
continued

Study type	Features	Strengths	Weaknesses
Cross-sectional studies	1 Snapshot of different samples at one or more points in time (synchronic analysis). 2 Large-scale and representative sampling. 3 Macro-level analysis. 4 Enables different groups to be compared. 5 Can be retrospective and/or prospective.	1 Comparatively quick to conduct. 2 Comparatively cheap to administer. 3 Limited control effects as subjects only participate once. 4 Stronger likelihood of participation as it is for a single time. 5 Charts aggregated patterns. 6 Useful for charting population-wide features at one or more single points in time. 7 Enable researchers to identify the proportions of people in particular groups or states. 8 Large samples enable inferential statistics to be used, e.g. to compare subgroups within the sample.	1 Do not permit analysis of causal relationships. 2 Unable to chart individual variations in development or changes, and their significance. 3 Sampling not entirely comparable at each round of data collection as different samples are used. 4 Can be time-consuming as background details of each sample have to be collected each time. 5 Omission of a single variable can undermine the results significantly. 6 Unable to chart changing social processes over time. 7 They only permit analysis of overall, *net* change at the macro-level through aggregated data.
Trend analysis	1 Selected factors studied continuously over time. 2 Uses recorded data to predict future trends.	1 Maintains clarity of focus throughout the duration of the study. 2 Enables prediction and projection on the basis of identified and monitored variables and assumptions.	1 Neglects influence of unpredicted factors. 2 Past trends are not always a good predictor of future trends. 3 Formula-driven, i.e. could be too conservative or initial assumptions might be erroneous. 4 Neglects the implications of chaos and complexity theory, e.g. that long-range forecasting is dangerous. 5 The criteria for prediction may be imprecise.

continued

Box 8.4
continued

Study type	Features	Strengths	Weaknesses
Retrospective longitudinal studies	1 Retrospective analysis of history of a sample. 2 Individual- and micro-level data.	1 Useful for establishing causal relationships. 2 Clear focus (e.g. how did this particular end state or set of circumstances come to be?) 3 Enables data to be assembled that are not susceptible to experimental analysis.	1 Remembered information might be faulty, selective and inaccurate. 2 People might forget, suppress or fail to remember certain factors. 3 Individuals might interpret their own past behaviour in light of their subsequent events, i.e. the interpretations are not contemporaneous with the actual events. 4 The roots and causes of the end state may be multiple, diverse, complex, unidentified and unstraightforward to unravel. 5 Simple causality is unlikely. 6 A cause may be an effect and *vice versa*. 7 It is difficult to separate real from perceived or putative causes. 8 It is seldom easily falsifiable or confirmable.

non-repeatable events (e.g. death); in this case the calculation of life expectancy does not rely on distinguishing various causes of death (Rose and Sullivan, 1993: 189). However, in event-history analysis the parameters become much more complex as multiple factors come into the equation, requiring some form of multivariate analysis to be undertaken.

In event-history analysis the task is to calculate the 'hazard rate' – the probability of a dependent variable occurring to an individual within a specified time frame. The approach is mathematical, using log-linear analysis to compute the relative size of each of several factors (independent variables), e.g. by calculating co-efficients in cross-tabulations, that will have an effect on the hazard rate, the likelihood of an event occurring to an individual within a specific time frame (Rose and Sullivan, 1993: 190).[5]

Event-history analysis also addresses the problem of attrition, as members leave a study over time. Plewis (1997: 117) suggests that many longitudinal studies suffer from sample loss over time, and attempts to address the issue of *censoring* – the adjustments necessary in a study in order to take account of the accretion of missing data. *Right censoring* occurs when we know when a particular event commences but not when it finishes; *left censoring* occurs when we know of the existence of a particular event or situation, but not when it began. Plewis (ibid.: 118) suggests that censored events and episodes (where attrition has taken place) last longer than uncensored events and episodes, and, hence, hazard rates that are based on uncensored observations will usually be too high. Event-history is a valuable, and increasingly used technique for research.

9 Case studies

Introduction

How can knowledge of the ways in which children learn and the means by which schools achieve their goals be verified, built upon and extended? This is a central question for educational research. The problem of verification and cumulation of educational knowledge is implicit in our discussion of the nature of educational inquiry in the opening chapter of the book. There, we outline three broad approaches to educational research. The first, based on the 'scientific' paradigm, rests upon the creation of theoretical frameworks that can be tested by experimentation, replication and refinement. The second approach seeks to understand and interpret the world in terms of its actors and consequently may be described as interpretive and subjective. A third, emerging, approach that takes account of the political and ideological contexts of much educational research is that of critical educational research.

The paradigm most naturally suited to case study research, the subject of this chapter, is the second one, with its emphasis on the interpretive and subjective dimensions. The first paradigm, the 'scientific', is reflected in our examples of quantitative case study research. The use of critical theory in case study research is at a comparatively embryonic stage but offers rich potential. Our broad treatment of case study techniques follows directly from a typology of observation studies that we develop shortly. We begin with a brief description of the case study itself.

What is a case study?

A case study is a specific instance that is frequently designed to illustrate a more general principle (Nisbet and Watt, 1984: 72), it is 'the study of an instance in action' (Adelman *et al.*, 1980). The single instance is of a bounded system, for example a child, a clique, a class, a school, a community. It provides a unique example of real people in real situations, enabling readers to understand ideas more clearly than simply by presenting them with abstract theories or principles. Indeed a case study can enable readers to understand how ideas and abstract principles can fit together (ibid.: 72–3). Case studies can penetrate situations in ways that are not always susceptible to numerical analysis.

Case studies can establish cause and effect, indeed one of their strengths is that they observe effects in real contexts, recognizing that context is a powerful determinant of both causes and effects. As Nisbet and Watt remark (p. 78), the whole is more than the sum of its parts. Sturman (1999: 103) argues that a distinguishing feature of case studies is that human systems have a wholeness or integrity to them rather than being a loose connection of traits, necessitating in-depth investigation. Further, contexts are unique and dynamic, hence case studies investigate and report the complex dynamic and unfolding interactions of events, human relationships and other factors in a unique instance. Hitchcock and Hughes (1995: 316) suggest that case studies are distinguished less by the methodologies that they employ than by the subjects/objects of their inquiry (though, as indicated below, there is frequently a resonance between case studies and interpretive methodologies). Hitchcock and Hughes (1995: 322) further suggest that the case study approach is particularly valuable when the researcher has little control over events. They consider (p. 317) that a case study has several hallmarks:

- It is concerned with a rich and vivid description of events relevant to the case.
- It provides a chronological narrative of events relevant to the case.
- It blends a description of events with the analysis of them.
- It focuses on individual actors or groups of actors, and seeks to understand their perceptions of events.
- It highlights specific events that are relevant to the case.
- The researcher is integrally involved in the case.
- An attempt is made to portray the richness of the case in writing up the report.

Case studies, they suggest (ibid.: 319): (a) are set in temporal, geographical, organizational, institutional and other contexts that enable boundaries to be drawn around the case; (b) can be defined with reference to characteristics defined by individuals and groups involved; and (c) can be defined by participants' roles and functions in the case. They also point out that case studies:

- will have temporal characteristics which help to define their nature;
- will have geographical parameters allowing for their definition;
- will have boundaries which allow for definition;
- may be defined by an individual in a particular context, at a point in time;
- may be defined by the characteristics of the group;
- may be defined by role or function;
- may be shaped by organizational or institutional arrangements.

Case studies strive to portray 'what it is like' to be in a particular situation, to catch the close-up reality and 'thick description' (Geertz, 1973) of participants' lived experiences of, thoughts about and feelings for, a situation. Hence it is important for events and situations to be allowed to speak for themselves rather than to be largely interpreted, evaluated or judged by the researcher. In this respect the case study is akin to the television documentary.

This is not to say that case studies are unsystematic or merely illustrative; case study data are gathered systematically and rigorously. Indeed Nisbet and Watt (ibid.: 91) specifically counsel case study researchers to avoid:

- journalism (picking out more striking features of the case, thereby distorting the full account in order to emphasize these more sensational aspects);
- selective reporting (selecting only that evidence which will support a particular conclusion, thereby misrepresenting the whole case);
- an anecdotal style (degenerating into an endless series of low-level banal and tedious illustrations that take over from in-depth, rigorous analysis); one is reminded of Stake's (1978) wry comment that 'our scrapbooks are full of enlargements of enlargements', alluding to the tendency of some case studies to over-emphasize detail to the detriment of seeing the whole picture;
- pomposity (striving to derive or generate profound theories from low-level data, or by wrapping up accounts in high-sounding verbiage);
- blandness (unquestioningly accepting only the respondents' views, or only including those aspects of the case study on which people agree rather than areas on which they might disagree).

Case studies can make theoretical statements, but, like other forms of research and human sciences, these must be supported by the evidence presented. This requires the nature of generalization in case study to be clarified. Generalization can take various forms, for example:

- from the single instance to the class of instances that it represents (for example a single-sex selective school might act as a case study to catch significant features of other single-sex selective schools);

- from features of the single case to a multiplicity of classes with the same features;
- from the single features of part of the case to the whole of that case.

More recently Simons (1996) has argued that case study needs to address six paradoxes; it needs to:

- reject the subject–object dichotomy, regarding all participants equally;
- recognize the contribution that a genuine creative encounter can make to new forms of understanding education;
- regard different ways of seeing as new ways of knowing;
- approximate the ways of the artist;
- free the mind of traditional analysis;
- embrace these paradoxes, with an overriding interest in people.

There are several types of case study. Yin (1984) identifies three such types in terms of their outcomes: (a) exploratory (as a pilot to other studies or research questions); (b) descriptive (providing narrative accounts); (c) explanatory (testing theories). Exploratory case studies that act as a pilot can be used to generate hypotheses that are tested in larger scale surveys, experiments or other forms of research, e.g. observational. However Adelman *et al.* (1980) caution against using case studies solely as preliminaries to other studies, e.g. as pre-experimental or pre-survey; rather, they argue, case studies exist in their own right as a significant and legitimate research method.

Yin's (1984) classification accords with Merriam (1988) who identifies three types: (a) descriptive (narrative accounts); (b) interpretative (developing conceptual categories inductively in order to examine initial assumptions); (c) evaluative (explaining and judging). Merriam also categorizes four common domains or kinds of case study: ethnographic, historical, psychological and sociological. Sturman (1999: 107),

echoing Stenhouse (1985), identifies four kinds of case study: (a) an ethnographic case study – single in-depth study; (b) action research case study; (c) evaluative case study; and (d) educational case study. Stake (1994) identifies three main types of case study: (a) intrinsic case studies (studies that are undertaken in order to understand the particular case in question); (b) instrumental case studies (examining a particular case in order to gain insight into an issue or a theory); (c) collective case studies (groups of individual studies that are undertaken to gain a fuller picture). Because case studies provide fine grain detail they can also be used to complement other, more coarsely grained – often large scale – kinds of research. Case study material in this sense can provide powerful human-scale data on macro-political decision-making, fusing theory and practice, for example the work of Ball (1990), Bowe *et al.* (1992) and Ball (1994a) on the impact of government policy on specific schools.

Case studies have several claimed strengths and weaknesses. These are summarized in Box 9.1 (Adelman *et al.*, 1980) and Box 9.2 (Nisbet and Watt, 1984). From the preceding analysis it is becoming clear that case studies frequently follow the interpretive tradition of research – seeing the situation through the eyes of participants – rather than the quantitative paradigm, though this need not always be the case. Its sympathy to the interpretive paradigm has rendered case study an object of criticism, treating peculiarities rather than regularities (Smith, 1991: 375). Smith (1991: 375) suggests that:

> The case study method . . . is the logically weakest method of knowing. The study of individual careers, communities, nations, and so on has become essentially passé. Recurrent patterns are the main product of the enterprise of historic scholarship.

This is prejudice and ideology rather than critique, but signifies the problem of respectability and legitimacy that case study has to conquer amongst certain academics. Like other research methods, case study has to demonstrate

Box 9.1
Possible advantages of case study

Case studies have a number of advantages that make them attractive to educational evaluators or researchers. Thus:

1 Case study data, paradoxically, is 'strong in reality' but difficult to organize. In contrast, other research data is often 'weak in reality' but susceptible to ready organization. This strength in reality is because case studies are down-to-earth and attention-holding, in harmony with the reader's own experience, and thus provide a 'natural' basis for generalization.
2 Case studies allow generalizations either about an instance or from an instance to a class. Their peculiar strength lies in their attention to the subtlety and complexity of the case in its own right.
3 Case studies recognize the complexity and 'embeddedness' of social truths. By carefully attending to social situations, case studies can represent something of the discrepancies or conflicts between the viewpoints held by participants. The best case studies are capable of offering some support to alternative interpretations.
4 Case studies, considered as products, may form an archive of descriptive material sufficiently rich to admit subsequent reinterpretation. Given the variety and complexity of educational purposes and environments, there is an obvious value in having a data source for researchers and users whose purposes may be different from our own.
5 Case studies are 'a step to action'. They begin in a world of action and contribute to it. Their insights may be directly interpreted and put to use; for staff or individual self-development, for within-institutional feedback; for formative evaluation; and in educational policy making.
6 Case studies present research or evaluation data in a more publicly accessible form than other kinds of research report, although this virtue is to some extent bought at the expense of their length. The language and the form of the presentation is hopefully less esoteric and less dependent on specialized interpretation than conventional research reports. The case study is capable of serving multiple audiences. It reduces the dependence of the reader upon unstated implicit assumptions . . . and makes the research process itself accessible. Case studies, therefore, may contribute towards the 'democratization' of decision-making (and knowledge itself). At its best, they allow readers to judge the implications of a study for themselves.

Source Adapted from Adelman *et al.*, 1980

Box 9.2
Nisbet and Watt's (1984) strengths and weaknesses of case study

Strengths
1 The results are more easily understood by a wide audience (including non-academics) as they are frequently written in everyday, non-professional language.
2 They are immediately intelligible; they speak for themselves.
3 They catch unique features that may otherwise be lost in larger scale data (e.g. surveys); these unique features might hold the key to understanding the situation.
4 They are strong on reality.
5 They provide insights into other, similar situations and cases, thereby assisting interpretation of other similar cases.
6 They can be undertaken by a single researcher without needing a full research team.
7 They can embrace and build in unanticipated events and uncontrolled variables.

Weaknesses
1 The results may not be generalizable except where other readers/researchers see their application.
2 They are not easily open to cross-checking, hence they may be selective, biased, personal and subjective.
3 They are prone to problems of observer bias, despite attempts made to address reflexivity.

reliability and validity. This can be difficult, for given the uniqueness of situations, they may be, by definition, inconsistent with other case studies or unable to demonstrate this positivist view of reliability. Even though case studies do not have to demonstrate this form of reliability, nevertheless there are important questions to be faced in undertaking case studies, for example

(Adelman *et al.*, 1980; Nisbet and Watt, 1984; Hitchcock and Hughes, 1995):

What exactly is a case?

How are cases identified and selected?

What kind of case study is this (what is its purpose)?

What is reliable evidence?

What is objective evidence?

What is an appropriate selection to include from the wealth of generated data?

What is a fair and accurate account?

Under what circumstances is it fair to take an exceptional case (or a critical event – see the discussion of observation in Chapter 17)?

What kind of sampling is most appropriate?

To what extent is triangulation required and how will this be addressed?

What is the nature of the validation process in case studies?

How will the balance be struck between uniqueness and generalization?

What is the most appropriate form of writing up and reporting the case study?

What ethical issues are exposed in undertaking a case study?

A key issue in case study research is the selection of information. Though it is frequently useful to record typical, representative occurrences, the researcher need not always adhere to criteria of representativeness. For example, it may be that infrequent, unrepresentative but critical incidents or events occur that are crucial to the understanding of the case. For example, a subject might only demonstrate a particular behaviour once, but it is so important as not to be ruled out simply because it occurred once; sometimes a single event might occur which sheds a hugely important insight into a person or situation (see the discussion of critical incidents in the chapter on observation); it can be a key to understanding a situation (Flanagan, 1949).

For example, it may be that a psychological case study might happen upon a single instance of child abuse earlier in an adult's life, but the effects of this were so profound as to constitute a turning point in understanding that adult. A child might suddenly pass a single comment that indicates complete frustration with or complete fear of a teacher, yet it is too important to overlook. Case studies, in not having to seek frequencies of occurrences, can replace quantity with quality and intensity, separating the *significant few* from the *insignificant many* instances of behaviour. Significance rather than frequency is a hallmark of case studies, offering the researcher an insight into the real dynamics of situations and people.

Types of case study

Unlike the experimenter who manipulates variables to determine their causal significance or the surveyor who asks standardized questions of large, representative samples of individuals, the case study researcher typically observes the characteristics of an individual unit – a child, a clique, a class, a school or a community. The purpose of such observation is to probe deeply and to analyse intensively the multifarious phenomena that constitute the life cycle of the unit with a view to establishing generalizations about the wider population to which that unit belongs.

Antipathy among researchers towards the statistical-experimental paradigm has created something of a boom industry in case study research. Delinquents (Patrick, 1973), dropouts (Parker, 1974) and drug-users (Young, 1971) to say nothing of studies of all types of schools (King, 1979),[1] attest to the wide use of the case study in contemporary social science and educational research. Such wide use is marked by an equally diverse range of techniques employed in the collection and analysis of both qualitative and quantitative data. Whatever the problem or the approach, at the heart of every case study lies a method of observation. Box 9.3 sets out a typology of observation studies.

Acker's (1990) study is an ethnographic account that is based on several hundred hours of participant observational material, whilst Boulton's (1992) work, by contrast, is based on highly structured, non-participant observation

Box 9.3
A typology of observation studies

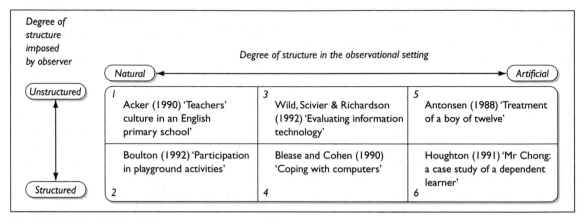

Source Adapted from Bailey, 1978

conducted over five years. The study by Wild, Scivier and Richardson (1992) used participant observation, loosely structured interviews that yielded simple frequency counts. Bleace and Cohen's (1990) study of coping with computers used highly structured observation schedules, undertaken by non-participant observers, with the express intention of obtaining precise, quantitative data on the classroom use of a computer programme. This was part of a longitudinal study in primary classrooms, and yielded typical profiles of individual behaviour and group interaction in students' usage of the computer programme. Antonsen's (1988) study was of a single child undergoing psychotherapy at a Child Psychiatric Unit, and uses unstructured observation within the artificial setting of a psychiatric clinic and is a record of the therapist's non-directive approach. Finally Houghton's (1991) study uses data from structured sets of test materials together with focused interviews with those with whom this international student had contact. Together these case studies provide a valuable insight into the range and types of case study.

There are two principal kinds of observation in case study – participant observation and non-participant observation. In the former, observers engage in the very activities they set out to observe. Often, their 'cover' is so complete that

as far as the other participants are concerned, they are simply one of the group. In the case of Patrick for example, born and bred in Glasgow, his researcher role remained hidden from the members of the Glasgow gang in whose activities he participated for a period of four months (see Patrick, 1973). Such complete anonymity is not always possible, however. Thus in Parker's study of downtown Liverpool adolescents, it was generally known that the researcher was waiting to take up a post at the university. In the meantime, 'knocking around' during the day with the lads and frequenting their pub at night rapidly established that he was 'OK':

> I was a drinker, a hanger-arounder, and had been tested in illegal 'business' matters and could be relied on to say nothing since I 'knew the score'.
>
> (Parker, 1974)

Cover is not necessarily a prerequisite of participant observation. In an intensive study of a small group of working-class boys during their last two years at school and their first months in employment, Willis (1977) attended all the different subject classes at school – 'not as a teacher, but as a member of the class' – and worked alongside each boy in industry for a short period.

Non-participant observers, on the other hand,

stand aloof from the group activities they are investigating and eschew group membership – no great difficulty for King (1979), an adult observer in infant classrooms. Listen to him recounting how he firmly established his non-participant status with young children:

I rapidly learnt that children in infants' classrooms define any adult as another teacher or teacher surrogate. To avoid being engaged in conversation, being asked to spell words or admire pictures, I evolved the following technique.

To begin with, I kept standing so that physical height created social distance . . . Next, I did not show immediate interest in what the children were doing, or talk to them. When I was talked to I smiled politely and if necessary I referred the child asking a question to the teacher. Most importantly, I avoided eye contact: if you do not look you will not be seen.

(King, 1979)

The best illustration of the non-participant observer role is perhaps the case of the researcher sitting at the back of a classroom coding up every three seconds the verbal exchanges between teacher and pupils by means of a structured set of observational categories.

It is frequently the case that the type of observation undertaken by the researcher is associated with the type of setting in which the research takes place. In Box 9.3 we identify a continuum of settings ranging from the 'artificial' environments of the counsellor's and the therapist's clinics (cell 5 and 6) to the 'natural' environments of school classrooms, staffrooms and playgrounds (cells 1 and 2). Because our continuum is crude and arbitrary we are at liberty to locate studies of an information technology audit and computer usage (cells 3 and 4) somewhere between the 'artificial' and the 'natural' poles.

Although in theory each of the six examples of case studies in Box 9.3 could have been undertaken either as a participant or as a non-participant observation study, a number of factors intrude to make one or other of the observational strategies the dominant mode of

inquiry in a particular type of setting. Bailey explains as follows:

In a natural setting it is difficult for the researcher who wishes to be covert not to act as a participant. If the researcher does not participate, there is little to explain his presence, as he is very obvious to the actual participants . . . Most studies in a natural setting are unstructured participant observation studies . . . Much the opposite is true in an artificial environment. Since there is no natural setting, in a sense none of the persons being studied are really participants of long standing, and thus may accept a non-participant observer more readily . . . Laboratory settings also enable a non-participant observer to use sophisticated equipment such as videotape and tape recordings . . . Thus most studies in an artificial laboratory setting will be structured and will be non-participant studies.

(Bailey, 1978)

What we are saying is that the unstructured, ethnographic account of teachers' work (cell 1) is the most typical method of observation in the natural surroundings of the school in which that study was conducted. Similarly, the structured inventories of study habits and personality employed in the study of Mr Chong (cell 6) reflect a common approach in the artificial setting of a counsellor's office.

Why participant observation?

The natural scientist, Schutz (1962) points out, explores a field that means nothing to the molecules, atoms and electrons therein. By contrast, the subject matter of the world in which the educational researcher is interested is composed of people and is essentially meaningful to them. That world is subjectively structured, possessing particular meanings for its inhabitants. The task of the educational investigator is very often to explain the means by which an orderly social world is established and maintained in terms of its shared meanings. How do participant observation techniques assist the researcher in this task? Bailey (1978) identifies some inherent advantages in the participant observation approach:

- Observation studies are superior to experiments and surveys when data are being collected on non-verbal behaviour.
- In observation studies, investigators are able to discern ongoing behaviour as it occurs and are able to make appropriate notes about its salient features.
- Because case study observations take place over an extended period of time, researchers can develop more intimate and informal relationships with those they are observing, generally in more natural environments than those in which experiments and surveys are conducted.
- Case study observations are less reactive than other types of data-gathering methods. For example, in laboratory-based experiments and in surveys that depend upon verbal responses to structured questions, bias can be introduced in the very data that researchers are attempting to study.

Recording observations

I filled thirty-two notebooks with about half a million words of notes made during nearly six hundred hours [of observation].

(King, 1979)

The recording of observations is a frequent source of concern to inexperienced case study researchers. How much ought to be recorded? In what form should the recordings be made? What does one do with the mass of recorded data? Lofland (1971) gives a number of useful suggestions about collecting field notes:

- Record the notes as quickly as possible after observation, since the quantity of information forgotten is very slight over a short period of time but accelerates quickly as more time passes.
- Discipline yourself to write notes quickly and reconcile yourself to the fact that although it may seem ironic, recording of

field notes can be expected to take as long as is spent in actual observation.

- Dictating rather than writing is acceptable if one can afford it, but writing has the advantage of stimulating thought.
- Typing field notes is vastly preferable to handwriting because it is faster and easier to read, especially when making multiple copies.
- It is advisable to make at least two copies of field notes and preferable to type on a master for reproduction. One original copy is retained for reference and other copies can be used as rough draft to be cut up, reorganized and rewritten.
- The notes ought to be full enough adequately to summon up for one again, months later, a reasonably vivid picture of any described event. This probably means that one ought to be writing up, at the very minimum, at least a couple of single space typed pages for every hour of observation.[2]

The sort of note-taking recommended by Lofland and actually undertaken by King (1979) and Wolcott (1973)[3] in their ethnographic accounts grows out of the nature of the unstructured observation study. Note-taking, confessed Wolcott, helped him fight the acute boredom that he sometimes felt when observing the interminable meetings that are the daily lot of the school principal. Occasionally, however, a series of events would occur so quickly that Wolcott had time only to make cursory notes which he supplemented later with fuller accounts. One useful tip from this experienced ethnographer is worth noting: never resume your observations until the notes from the preceding observation are complete. Until your observations and impressions from one visit are a matter of record, there is little point in returning to the classroom or school and reducing the impact of one set of events by superimposing another and more recent set. Indeed, when to record one's data is but one of a number of practical problems identified by Walker, which are listed in Box 9.4 (Walker, 1980).

Box 9.4

The case study and problems of selection

Among the issues confronting the researcher at the outset of his case study are the problems of selection. The following questions indicate some of the obstacles in this respect:

1   How do you get from the initial idea to the working design (from the idea to a specification, to usable data)?
2   What do you lose in the process?
3   What unwanted concerns do you take on board as a result?
4   How do you find a site which provides the best location for the design?
5   How do you locate, identify and approach key informants?
6   How they see you creates a context within which you see them. How can you handle such social complexities?
7   How do you record evidence? When? How much?
8   How do you file and categorize it?
9   How much time do you give to thinking and reflecting about what you are doing?
10 At what points do you show your subjects what you are doing?
11 At what points do you give them control over who sees what?
12 Who sees the reports first?

Source Adapted from Walker, 1980

Planning a case study

In planning a case study there are several issues that researchers may find useful to consider (e.g. Adelman *et al.*, 1980):

- The particular circumstances of the case, including: (a) the possible disruption to individual participants that participation might entail; (b) negotiating access to people; (c) negotiating ownership of the data; (d) negotiating release of the data;
- The conduct of the study including: (a) the use of primary and secondary sources; (b) the opportunities to check data; (c) triangulation (including peer examination of the findings, respondent validation and reflexivity); (d) data collection methods – in the interpretive paradigm case studies tend to use certain

data collection methods, e.g. semi-structured and open interviews, observation, narrative accounts and documents, diaries, maybe also tests, rather than other methods, e.g. surveys, experiments. Nisbet and Watt (1984) suggest that, in conducting interviews, it may be wiser to interview senior people later rather than earlier so that the most effective use of discussion time can be made, the interviewee having been put into the picture fully before the interview; (e) data analysis and interpretation, and, where appropriate, theory generation; (f) the writing of the report – Nisbet and Watt (ibid.) suggest that it is important to separate conclusions from the evidence, with the essential evidence included in the main text, and to balance illustration with analysis and generalization;

- The consequences of the research (for participants). This might include the anonymizing of the research in order to protect participants, though such anonymization might suggest that a primary goal of case study is generalization rather than the portrayal of a unique case, i.e. it might go against a central feature of case study. Anonymizing reports might render them anodyne, and Adelman *et al.* suggest that the distortion that is involved in such anonymization – to render cases unrecognizable might be too high a price to pay for going public.

Nisbet and Watt (1984: 78) suggest three main stages in undertaking a case study. Because case studies catch the dynamics of unfolding situations it is advisable to commence with a very wide field of focus, an open phase, without selectivity or prejudgement. Thereafter progressive focusing enables a narrower field of focus to be established, identifying key foci for subsequent study and data collection. At the third stage a draft interpretation is prepared which needs to be checked with respondents before appearing in the final form. Nisbet and Watt (ibid.: 79) advise against the generation of hypotheses too early in a case study; rather, they suggest, it is important to gather data openly. Respondent validation can

Box 9.5
Continua of data collection, types and analysis in case study research

```
┌─────────────────────────────────────────────┐
│                 Data collection              │
│  Unstructured    ◄─────►      Structured     │
│  (field notes)   (interviews – (survey, census│
│                  open to closed) data)       │
│                                              │
│                   Data types                 │
│  Narrative       ◄─────►      Numeric        │
│  (field notes)   (coded       (ratio scale data)│
│                  qualitative data            │
│                  and non-                    │
│                  parametric                  │
│                  statistics)                 │
│                                              │
│                  Data analysis               │
│  Journalistic    ◄─────►      Statistical    │
│  (impressionistic) (content   (inferential   │
│                  analysis)    statistics)    │
└─────────────────────────────────────────────┘
```

Source Adapted from Sturman, 1997

be particularly useful as respondents might suggest a better way of expressing the issue or may wish to add or qualify points.

There is a risk in respondent validation, however, that they may disagree with an interpretation. Nisbet and Watt (ibid.: 81) indicate the need to have negotiated rights to veto. They also recommend that researchers: (a) promise that respondents can see those sections of the report that refer to them (subject to controls for confidentiality, e.g. of others in the case study); (b) take full account of suggestions and responses made by respondents and, where possible, to modify the account; (c) in the case of disagreement between researchers and respondents, promise to publish respondents' comments and criticisms alongside the researchers' report.

Sturman (1997) places on a set of continua the nature of data collection, types and analysis techniques in case study research. These are presented in summary form (Box 9.5). At one pole we have unstructured, typically qualitative data, whilst at the other we have structured, typically quantitative data. Researchers using case study approaches will need to decide which methods of data collection, which type of data and techniques of analysis to employ.

Conclusion

The different strategies we have illustrated in our six examples of case studies in a variety of educational settings suggest that participant observation is best thought of as a generic term that describes a methodological approach rather than one specific method.[4] What our examples have shown is that the representativeness of a particular sample often relates to the observational strategy open to the researcher. Generally speaking, the larger the sample, the more representative it is, and the more likely that the observer's role is of a participant nature.

10 Correlational research

Introduction

Human behaviour at both the individual and social level is characterized by great complexity, a complexity about which we understand comparatively little, given the present state of social research. One approach to a fuller understanding of human behaviour is to begin by teasing out simple relationships between those factors and elements deemed to have some bearing on the phenomena in question. The value of correlational research is that it is able to achieve this end.

Much of social research in general, and educational research more particularly, is concerned at our present stage of development with the first step in this sequence – establishing interrelationships among variables. We may wish to know, for example, how delinquency is related to social class background; or whether an association exists between the number of years spent in full-time education and subsequent annual income; or whether there is a link between personality and achievement. Numerous techniques have been devised to provide us with numerical representations of such relationships and they are known as 'measures of association'. We list the principal ones in Box 10.1. The interested reader is referred to Cohen and Holliday (1982, 1996), texts containing worked examples of the appropriate use (and limitations) of the correlational techniques outlined in Box 10.1, together with other measures of association such as Kruskal's *gamma*, Somer's *d*, and Guttman's *lambda*.

Look at the words used at the top of the Box to explain the nature of variables in connection with the measure called the Pearson product

moment, r. The variables, we learn, are 'continuous' and at the 'interval' or the 'ratio' scale of measurement. A continuous variable is one that, theoretically at least, can take any value between two points on a scale. Weight, for example, is a continuous variable; so too is time, so also is height. Weight, time and height can take on any number of possible values between nought and infinity, the feasibility of measuring them across such a range being limited only by the variability of suitable measuring instruments.

A ratio scale includes an absolute zero and provides equal intervals. Using weight as our example, we can say that no mass at all is a zero measure and that 1,000 grams is 400 grams heavier than 600 grams and twice as heavy as 500. In our discussion of correlational research that follows, we refer to a relationship as a 'correlation' rather than an 'association' whenever that relationship can be further specified in terms of an increase or a decrease of a certain number of units in the one variable (IQ for example) producing an increase or a decrease of a related number of units of the other (e.g. mathematical ability).

Turning again to Box 10.1, we read in connection with the second measure shown there (Rank order or Kendall's tau) that the two continuous variables are at the 'ordinal' scale of measurement. An ordinal scale is used to indicate rank order; that is to say, it arranges individuals or objects in a series ranging from the highest to the lowest according to the particular characteristic being measured. In contrast to the interval scale discussed earlier, ordinal numbers assigned to such a series do not indicate absolute quantities

Box 10.1
Common measures of relationship

Measure	Nature of Variables	Comment
Pearson product moment r	Two continuous variables; interval or ratio scale	Relationship linear
Rank order or Kendall's tau	Two continuous variables; ordinal scale	
Correlation ratio, η (eta)	One variable continuous, other either continuous or discrete	Relationship nonlinear
Intraclass	One variable continuous; other discrete; interval or ratio scale	Purpose: to determine within-group similarity
Biserial, r_{bis} Point biserial, $r_{pt\ bis}$	One variable continuous; other (a) continuous but dichotomized. r_{bis} or (b) true dichotomy, $r_{pt\ bis}$	Index of item discrimination (used in item analysis)
Phi co-efficient, Φ	Two true dichotomies; nominal or ordinal series	
Partial correlation $r_{12.3}$	Three or more continuous variables	Purpose: to determine relationship between two variables, with effect of third held constant
Multiple correlation $r_{1.234}$	Three or more continuous variables	Purpose: to predict one variable from a linear weighted combination of two or more independent variables
Kendall's co-efficient of concordance, (W)	Three or more continuous variables; ordinal series	Purpose: to determine the degree of (say, interrater) agreement

Source Mouly, 1978

nor can one assume that the intervals between the numbers are equal. For example, in a class of children rated by a teacher on the degree of their co-operativeness and ranged from highest to lowest according to that attribute, it cannot be assumed that the difference in the degree of co-operativeness between subjects ranked 1 and 2 is the same as that obtaining between subjects 9 and 10; nor can it be taken that subject 1 possesses 10 times the quantity of co-operativeness of subject 10.

The variables involved in connection with the phi co-efficient measure of association (halfway down Box 10.1) are described as 'true dichotomies' and at the 'nominal' scale of measurement. Truly dichotomous variables (such as sex or driving test result) can take only two values (male or female; pass or fail). The nominal scale is the most elementary scale of measurement. It does no more than identify the categories into which individuals, objects or events may be classified. Those categories have to be mutually exclusive of course, and a nominal scale should also be complete; that is to say it should include all possible classifications of a particular type.

To conclude our explanation of terminology, readers should note the use of the phrase 'discrete variable' in the description of the third correlation ratio (eta) in Box 10.1. We said earlier that a continuous variable can take on any value between two points on a scale. A discrete variable, however, can only take on numerals or values that are specific points on a scale. The number of players in a football team is a discrete variable. It is usually 11; it could be fewer than 11, but it could never be 7¼!

Explaining correlation and significance

Correlational techniques are generally intended to answer three questions about two variables or two sets of data. First, 'Is there a relationship between the two variables (or sets of data)?' If the answer to this question is 'yes', then two other questions follow: 'What is the direction of the relationship?' and 'What is the magnitude?'

Relationship in this context refers to any tendency for the two variables (or sets of data) to vary consistently. Pearson's product moment coefficient of correlation, one of the best-known measures of association, is a statistical value ranging from -1.0 to $+1.0$ and expresses this relationship in quantitative form. The coefficient is represented by the symbol r.

Where the two variables (or sets of data) fluctuate in the same direction, i.e. as one increases so does the other, or as one decreases so does the other, a positive relationship is said to exist. Correlations reflecting this pattern are prefaced with a plus sign to indicate the positive nature of the relationship. Thus, $+1.0$ would indicate perfect positive correlation between two factors, as with the radius and diameter of a circle, and $+0.80$ a high positive correlation, as between academic achievement and intelligence, for example. Where the sign has been omitted, a plus sign is assumed.

A negative correlation or relationship, on the other hand, is to be found when an increase in one variable is accompanied by a decrease in the other variable. Negative correlations are prefaced with a minus sign. Thus, -1.0 would represent perfect negative correlation, as between the number of errors children make on a spelling test and their score on the test, and -0.30 a low negative correlation, as between absenteeism and intelligence, say.

Generally speaking, researchers tend to be more interested in the magnitude of an obtained correlation than they are in its direction. Correlational procedures have been developed so that no relationship whatever between two variables is represented by zero (or 0.00), as between body weight and intelligence, possibly. This means that a person's performance on one variable is totally unrelated to her performance on a second variable. If she is high on one, for example, she is just as likely to be high or low on the other. Perfect correlations of $+1.00$ or -1.00 are rarely found. The correlation co-efficient may be seen then as an indication of the predictability of one variable given the other: it is an indication of covariation. The relationship between two variables can be examined visually by plotting the paired measurements on graph paper with each pair of observations being represented by a point. The resulting arrangement of points is known as a 'scatter diagram' and enables us to assess graphically the degree of relationship between the characteristics being measured. Box 10.2 gives some examples of 'scatter diagrams' in the field of educational research.

Let us imagine we observe that many people with large hands also have large feet and that people with small hands also have small feet (see Morrison, 1993: 136–40). We decide to conduct an investigation to see if there is any correlation or degree of association between the size of feet and the size of hands, or whether it was just chance that led some people to have large hands and large feet. We measure the hands and the feet of 100 people and observe that 99 times out of 100 those people with large feet also have large hands. That seems to be more than mere

Box 10.2
Correlation scatter diagrams

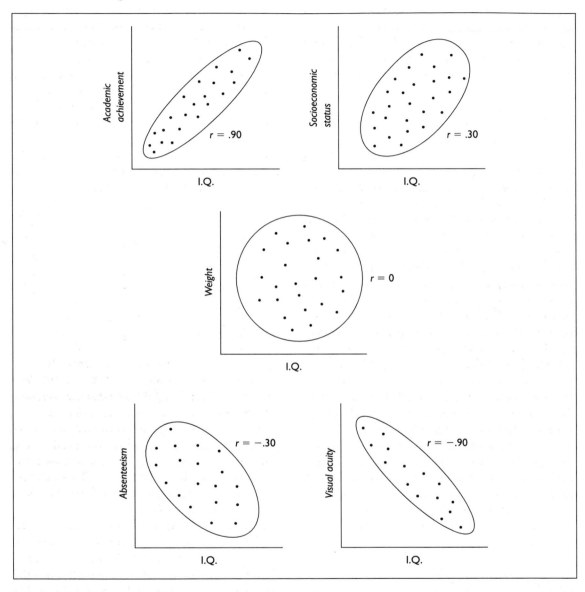

Source Tuckman, 1972

coincidence; it would seem that we could say with some certainty that if a person has large hands then she will also have large feet. How do we know when we can make that assertion? When do we know that we can have confidence in this prediction?

For statistical purposes, if we can observe this relationship occurring 95 times out of 100 i.e. that chance only accounted for 5 per cent of the difference, then we could say with some confidence that there seems to be a high degree of association between the two variables hands and feet; it would only occur by chance in 5 people in every 100, reported as the 0.05 level of significance (0.05 being five-hundredths). If we can observe this relationship occurring 99 times out of every 100 (as in the example of hands and feet), i.e. that chance only accounted for 1 per cent of the difference, then we could say with even greater confidence that there seems to be a very high degree of association between the two variables; it would only occur by chance once in every hundred, reported as the 0.01 level of significance (0.01 being one-hundredth). We begin with a null hypothesis, which states that there is no relationship between the size of hands and the size of feet. The task is to disprove or reject the hypothesis – the burden of responsibility is to reject the null hypothesis. If we can show that the hypothesis is untrue for 95 per cent or 99 per cent of the population, then we have demonstrated that there is a statistically significant relationship between the size of hands and the size of feet at the 0.05 and 0.01 levels of significance respectively. These two levels of significance – the 0.05 and 0.01 levels – are the levels at which statistical significance is frequently taken to have been demonstrated. The researcher would say that the null hypothesis (that there is no significant relationship between the two variables) had been rejected and that the level of significance observed (ρ) was either at the 0.05 or 0.01 level.

Let us take a second example. Let us say that we have devised a scale of 1–8 which can be used to measure the sizes of hands and feet. Using the scale we make the following calculations for eight people, and set out the results thus:

	Hand size	Foot size
Subject A	1	1
Subject B	2	2
Subject C	3	3
Subject D	4	4
Subject E	5	5
Subject F	6	6
Subject G	7	7
Subject H	8	8

We can observe a perfect correlation between the size of the hands and the size of feet, from the person who has a size 1 hand and a size 1 foot to the person who has a size 8 hand and also a size 8 foot. There is a perfect positive correlation (as one variable increases, e.g. hand size, so the other variable – foot size – increases, and as one variable decreases so does the other). Using a mathematical formula (a correlation statistic, available in most statistics books) we would calculate that this perfect correlation yields an index of association – a co-efficient of correlation – which is + 1.00.

Suppose that this time we carried out the investigation on a second group of eight people and reported the following results:

	Hand size	Foot size
Subject A	1	8
Subject B	2	7
Subject C	3	6
Subject D	4	5
Subject E	5	4
Subject F	6	3
Subject G	7	2
Subject H	8	1

This time the person with a size 1 hand has a size 8 foot and the person with the size 8 hand has a size 1 foot. There is a perfect negative correlation (as one variable increases, e.g. hand size, the other variable – foot size – decreases, and as one variable decreases, the other increases). Using the same mathematical formula we would calculate that this perfect negative correlation yielded an index of association – a co-efficient of correlation – which is – 1.00.

Now, clearly it is very rare to find a perfect positive or a perfect negative correlation; the truth of the matter is that looking for correlations will yield co-efficients of correlation which lie somewhere between – 1.00 and + 1.00. How do we know whether the co-efficients of correlation are significant or not?

Let us say that we take a third sample of eight people and undertake an investigation into their hand and foot size. We enter the data case by case (Subject A to Subject H), indicating their rank order for hand size and then for foot size. This time the relationship is less clear because the rank ordering is more mixed, for example, Subject A has a hand size of 2 and 1 for foot size, Subject B has a hand size of 1 and a foot size of 2 etc.:

	Hand size	Foot size
Subject A	2	1
Subject B	1	2
Subject C	3	3
Subject D	5	4
Subject E	4	5
Subject F	7	6
Subject G	6	7
Subject H	8	8

Using the mathematical formula for calculating the correlation statistic, we find that the co-efficient of correlation for the eight people is 0.7857. Is it statistically significant? From a table of significance (commonly printed in appendices to books on statistics or research methods), we read off whether the co-efficient is statistically significant or not for a specific number of cases, for example:

Number of cases	Level of significance	
	0.05	0.01
6	0.93	0.96
7	0.825	0.92
8	0.78	0.875
9	0.71	0.83
10	0.65	0.795
20	0.455	0.595
30	0.36	0.47

We see that for eight cases in an investigation the correlation co-efficient has to be 0.78 or higher, if it is to be significant at the 0.05 level, and 0.875 or higher, if it is to be significant at the 0.01 level of significance. As the correlation co-efficient in the example of the third experiment with eight subjects is 0.7857 we can see that it is higher than that required for significance at the 0.05 level (0.78) but not as high as that required for significance at the 0.01 level (0.875). We are safe, then, in stating that the degree of association between the hand and foot sizes rejects the null hypothesis and demonstrates statistical significance at the 0.05 level.

The first example above of hands and feet (see p. 193) is very neat because it has 100 people in the sample. If we have more or less than 100 people how do we know if a relationship between two factors is significant? Let us say that we have data on 30 people; in this case, because our sample size is so small, we might hesitate to say that there is a strong association between the size of hands and size of feet if we observe that in 27 people (i.e. 90 per cent of the population). On the other hand, let us say that we have a sample of 1,000 people and we observe the association in 700 of them. In this case, even though only 70 per cent of the sample demonstrate the association of hand and foot size, we might say that because the sample size is so large we can have greater confidence in the data than on the small sample.

Statistical significance varies according to the size of the population in the sample (as can be seen also in the section of the table of significance reproduced above). In order to be able to determine significance we need to have two facts in our possession: the size of the sample and the co-efficient of correlation. As the selection from the table of significance reproduced above shows, the co-efficient of correlation can decrease and still be statistically significant as long as the sample size increases. (This resonates with Krejcie and Morgan's (1970) principles for sampling, observed in chapter 4, viz. as the population increases the sample size increases at a diminishing rate in addressing randomness.)

To ascertain significance from a table, then, it is simply a matter of reading off the significance level from a table of significance according to the sample size, or processing data on a computer programme to yield the appropriate statistic. In the selection from the table of significance for the third example above concerning hand and foot size, the first column indicates the number of people in the sample and the other two columns indicate significance at the two levels. Hence, if we have 30 people in the sample then, for the correlation to be significant at the 0.05 level, we would need a correlation co-efficient of 0.36, whereas, if there were only 10 people in the sample, we would need a correlation co-efficient of 0.65 for the correlation to be significant at the same 0.05 level.

In addition to the types of purpose set out above, the calculation of a correlation co-efficient is also used in determining the item discriminability of a test (see Chapter 18), e.g. using a point bi-serial calculation, and in determining split-half reliability in test items (see Chapter 5) using the Spearman rank order correlation statistic.

More recently statistical significance on its own has been seen as an unacceptable index of effect (Thompson, 1994, 1996, 1998; Thompson and Snyder, 1997; Rozeboom, 1997: 335; Fitz-Gibbon, 1997: 43) because it depends on sample size. What is also required to accompany significance is information about *effect size* (American Psychological Association, 1994: 18). Indeed effect size is seen as much more important than significance (see also Chapter 12). Statistical significance is seen as arbitrary and unhelpful – a 'corrupt form of the scientific method' (Carver, 1978), being an obstacle rather than a facilitator in educational research. It commands slavish adherence rather than addressing the subtle, sensitive and helpful notion of effect size (see Fitz-Gibbon, 1997: 118). Indeed commonsense should tell the researcher that a differential measure of effect size is more useful than the blunt edge of statistical significance.

Whilst correlations are widely used in research, and they are straightforward to calculate and to interpret, the researcher must be aware of four caveats in undertaking correlational analysis:

1   Do not assume that correlations imply causal relationships (Mouly, 1978) (i.e. simply because having large hands appears to correlate with having large feet does not imply that having large hands causes one to have large feet).

2   There is a need to be alert to a Type I error – rejecting the null hypothesis when it is in fact true (a particular problem as the sample increases, as the chances of finding a significant association increase, irrespective of whether a true association exists (Rose and Sullivan, 1993: 168), requiring the researcher, therefore to set a higher limit (e.g. 0.01 or 0.001) for statistical significance to be achieved).

3   There is a need to be alert to a Type II error – accepting the null hypothesis when it is in fact not true (often the case if the levels of significance are set too stringently, i.e. requiring the researcher to lower the level of significance (e.g. 0.1 or 0.2) required).

4   Statistical significance must be accompanied by an indication of effect size.

Identifying and resolving issues (2) and (3) are addressed in Chapter 5.

Curvilinearity

The correlations discussed so far have assumed linearity, that is, the more we have of one property, the more (or less) we have of another property, in a direct positive or negative relationship. A straight line can be drawn through the points on the scatter diagrams (scatterplots). However, linearity cannot always be assumed. Consider the case, for example, of stress: a little stress might enhance performance ('setting the adrenalin running') positively, whereas too much stress might lead to a downturn in performance. Where stress enhances performance there is a positive correlation, but when stress debilitates performance there is a negative correlation. The result is not a straight line of correlation (indicating linearity) but a curved line (indicating curvilinearity). This can be shown graphically (Box 10.3). It is assumed here, for the purposes of the example, that muscular strength can be measured on a single scale. It is clear from the graph that muscular strength increases from birth until 50 years, and thereafter it declines as muscles degenerate. There is a positive correlation between age and muscular strength on the left hand side of the graph and a negative correlation on the right hand side of the graph, i.e. a curvilinear correlation can be observed.

Hopkins, Hopkins and Glass (1996: 92) provide

Box 10.3
A line diagram to indicate curvilinearity

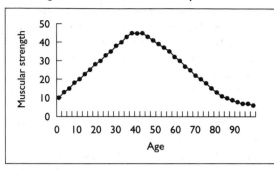

another example of curvilinearity: room temperature and comfort. Raising the temperature a little can make for greater comfort – a positive correlation – whilst raising it too greatly can make for discomfort – a negative correlation. Many correlational statistics assume linearity (e.g. the Pearson product-moment correlation). However, rather than using correlational statistics arbitrarily or blindly, the researcher will need to consider whether, in fact, linearity is a reasonable assumption to make, or whether a curvilinear relationship is more appropriate (in which case more sophisticated statistics will be needed, e.g. η ('eta') (Glass and Hopkins, 1996, section 8.7; Cohen and Holliday, 1996: 84) or mathematical procedures will need to be applied to transform non-linear relations into linear relations). Examples of curvilinear relationships might include:

- Pressure from the principal and teacher performance;
- Pressure from the teacher and student achievement;
- Degree of challenge and student achievement;
- Assertiveness and success;
- Age and muscular strength;
- Age and physical control;
- Age and concentration;
- Age and sociability;
- Age and cognitive abilities.

Hopkins, Hopkins and Glass (ibid.) suggest that the variable 'age' frequently has a curvilinear

relationship with other variables. The authors also point out (p. 92) that poorly constructed tests can give the appearance of curvilinearity if the test is too easy (a 'ceiling effect' where most students score highly) or if it is too difficult, but that this curvilinearity is, in fact, spurious, as the test does not demonstrate sufficient item difficulty or discriminability.

In planning correlational research, then, attention will need to be given to whether linearity or curvilinearity is to be assumed.

Co-efficients of correlation

The co-efficient of correlation, then, tells us something about the relations between two variables. Other measures exist, however, which allow us to specify relationships when more than two variables are involved. These are known as measures of 'multiple correlation' and 'partial correlation'.

Multiple correlation measures indicate the degree of association between three or more variables simultaneously. We may want to know, for example, the degree of association between delinquency, social class background and leisure facilities. Or we may be interested in finding out the relationship between academic achievement, intelligence and neuroticism. Multiple correlation, or 'regression' as it is sometimes called, indicates the degree of association between n variables. It is related not only to the correlations of the independent variables with the dependent variables, but also to the intercorrelations between the dependent variables.

Partial correlation aims at establishing the degree of association between two variables after the influence of a third has been controlled or partialled out. Studies involving complex relationships utilize multiple and partial correlations in order to provide a clearer picture of the relationships being investigated. Guilford and Fruchter (1973) define a partial correlation between two variables as:

one that nullifies the effects of a third variable (or a number of variables) upon both the variables being correlated. The correlation between height and weight of boys in a group where age is permitted to vary would be higher than the correlation between height and weight in a group at constant age. The reason is obvious. Because certain boys are older, they are both heavier and taller. Age is a factor that enhances the strength of correspondence between height and weight. With age held constant, the correlation would still be positive and significant because at any age, taller boys tend to be heavier.

(Guilford and Fruchter, 1973)

Correlational research is particularly useful in tackling problems in education and the social sciences because it allows for the measurement of a number of variables and their relationships simultaneously. The experimental approach, by contrast, is characterized by the manipulation of a single variable, and is thus appropriate for dealing with problems where simple causal relationships exist. In educational and behavioural research, it is invariably the case that a number of variables contribute to a particular outcome. Experimental research thus introduces a note of unreality into research, whereas correlational approaches, while less rigorous, allow for the study of behaviour in more realistic settings. Where an element of control is required, however, partial correlation achieves this without changing the context in which the study takes place. However, correlational research is less rigorous than the experimental approach because it exercises less control over the independent variables; it is prone to identify spurious relation patterns; it adopts an atomistic approach; and the correlation index is relatively imprecise, being limited by the unreliability of the measurements of the variables.

Characteristics of correlational studies

Correlational studies may be broadly classified as either 'relational studies' or as 'prediction studies'. We now look at each a little more closely.

In the case of the first of these two categories, correlational research is mainly concerned with

achieving a fuller understanding of the complexity of phenomena or, in the matter of behavioural and educational research, behavioural patterns, by studying the relationships between the variables which the researcher hypothesizes as being related. As a method, it is particularly useful in exploratory studies into fields where little or no previous research has been undertaken. It is often a shot in the dark aimed at verifying hunches a researcher has about a presumed relationship between characteristics or variables. Take a complex notion like 'teacher effectiveness', for example. This is dependent upon a number of less complex factors operating singly or in combination. Factors such as intelligence, motivation, person perception, verbal skills and empathy come to mind as possibly having an effect on teaching outcomes. A review of the research literature will confirm or reject these possibilities. Once an appropriate number of factors have been identified in this way, suitable measures may then be chosen or developed to assess them. They are then given to a representative sample and the scores obtained are correlated with a measure of the complex factor being investigated, namely, teacher effectiveness. As it is an exploratory undertaking, the analysis will consist of correlation co-efficients only, though if it is designed carefully, we will begin to achieve some understanding of the particular behaviour being studied. The investigation and its outcomes may then be used as a basis for further research or as a source of additional hypotheses.

Exploratory relationship studies may also employ partial correlational techniques. Partial correlation is a particularly suitable approach when a researcher wishes to nullify the influence of one or more important factors upon behaviour in order to bring the effect of less important factors into greater prominence. If, for example, we wanted to understand more fully the determinants of academic achievement in a comprehensive school, we might begin by acknowledging the importance of the factor of intelligence and establishing a relationship between intelligence and academic achievement.

The intelligence factor could then be held constant by partial correlation, thus enabling the investigator to clarify other, lesser factors such as motivation, parental encouragement or vocational aspiration. Clearly, motivation is related to academic achievement but if a pupil's motivation score is correlated with academic achievement without controlling the intelligence factor, it will be difficult to assess the true effect of motivation on achievement because the pupil with high intelligence but low motivation may possibly achieve more than pupils with lower intelligence but higher motivation. Once intelligence has been nullified, it is possible to see more clearly the relationship between motivation and achievement. The next stage might be to control the effects of both intelligence and motivation and then to seek a clearer idea of the effects of other selected factors – parental encouragement or vocational aspiration, for instance. Finally, exploratory relationship studies may employ sophisticated, multivariate techniques in teasing out associations between dependent and independent variables.

In contrast to exploratory relationship studies, prediction studies are usually undertaken in areas having a firmer and more secure knowledge base. Prediction through the use of correlational techniques is based on the assumption that at least some of the factors that will lead to the behaviour to be predicted are present and measurable at the time the prediction is made (see Borg, 1963). If, for example, we wanted to predict the probable success of a group of salespeople on an intensive training course, we would start with variables that have been found in previous research to be related to later success in saleswork. These might include enterprise, verbal ability, achievement motivation, emotional maturity, sociability and so on. The extent to which these predictors correlate with the particular behaviour we wish to predict, namely, successful selling, will determine the accuracy of our prediction. Clearly, variables crucial to success cannot be predicted if they are not present at the time of making the prediction. A salesperson's ability to fit in with a team of his or her

fellows cannot be predicted where these future colleagues are unknown.

In order to be valuable in prediction, the magnitude of association between two variables must be substantial; and the greater the association, the more accurate the prediction it permits. In practice, this means that anything less than perfect correlation will permit errors in predicting one variable from a knowledge of the other.

Borg recalls that much prediction research in the United States has been carried out in the field of scholastic success. Some studies in this connection have been aimed at short-term prediction of students' performance in specific courses of study, while other studies have been directed at long-term prediction of general academic success. Sometimes, short-term academic prediction is based upon a single predictor variable. Most efforts to predict future behaviours, however, are based upon scores on a number of predictor variables, each of which is useful in predicting a specific aspect of future behaviour. In the prediction of college success, for example, a single variable such as academic achievement is less effective as a predictor than a combination of variables such as academic achievement together with, say, motivation, intelligence, study habits, etc. More complex studies of this kind, therefore, generally make use of multiple correlation and multiple regression equations.

Predicting behaviours or events likely to occur in the near future is easier and less hazardous than predicting behaviours likely to occur in the more distant future. The reason is that in short-term prediction, more of the factors leading to success in predicted behaviour are likely to be present. In addition, short-term prediction allows less time for important predictor variables to change or for individuals to gain experience that would tend to change their likelihood of success in the predicted behaviour.

One further point: correlation, as Mouly and Borg observe, is a group concept, a generalized measure that is useful basically in predicting group performance. Whereas, for instance, it can be predicted that gifted children as a group will succeed at school, it cannot be predicted with certainty that one particular gifted child will excel. Further, low co-efficients will have little predictive value, and only a high correlation can be regarded as valid for individual prediction.

Interpreting the correlation co-efficient

Once a correlation co-efficient has been computed, there remains the problem of interpreting it. A question often asked in this connection is how large should the co-efficient be for it to be meaningful. The question may be approached in three ways: by examining the strength of the relationship; by examining the statistical significance of the relationship (discussed earlier); and by examining the square of the correlation co-efficient.

Inspection of the numerical value of a correlation co-efficient will yield clear indication of the strength of the relationship between the variables in question. Low or near zero values indicate weak relationships, while those nearer to +1 or −1 suggest stronger relationships. Imagine, for instance, that a measure of a teacher's success in the classroom after five years in the profession is correlated with her final school experience grade as a student and that it was found that $r = +0.19$. Suppose now that her score on classroom success is correlated with a measure of need for professional achievement and that this yielded a correlation of 0.65. It could be concluded that there is a stronger relationship between success and professional achievement scores than between success and final student grade.

Exploratory relationship studies are generally interpreted with reference to their statistical significance, whereas prediction studies depend for their efficacy on the strength of the correlation co-efficients. These need to be considerably higher than those found in exploratory relationship studies and for this reason rarely invoke the concept of significance.

The third approach to interpreting a co-efficient is provided by examining the square of the co-efficient of correlation, r^2. This shows the proportion of variance in one variable that can be attributed to its linear relationship with the second variable. In other words, it indicates the amount the two variables have in common. If, for example, two variables A and B have a correlation of 0.50, then $(0.50)^2$ or 0.25 of the variation shown by the B scores can be attributed to the tendency of B to vary linearly with A. Box 10.4 shows graphically the common variance between reading grade and arithmetic grade having a correlation of 0.65.

There are three cautions to be borne in mind when one is interpreting a correlation co-efficient. First, a co-efficient is a simple number and must not be interpreted as a percentage. A correlation of 0.50, for instance, does not mean 50 per cent relationship between the variables. Further, a correlation of 0.50 does not indicate twice as much relationship as that shown by a correlation of 0.25. A correlation of 0.50 actually indicates more than twice the relationship shown by a correlation of 0.25. In fact, as co-efficients approach + 1 or − 1, a difference in the absolute values of the co-efficients becomes more important than the same numerical difference between lower correlations would be.

Second, a correlation does not necessarily imply a cause-and-effect relationship between two factors, as we have previously indicated. Third, a correlation co-efficient is not to be interpreted in any absolute sense. A correlational value for a given sample of a population may not necessarily be the same as that found in another sample from the same population.

Box 10.4

Visualization of correlation of 0.65 between reading grade and arithmetic grade

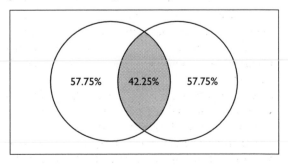

Source Fox, 1969

Chapter 10

Many factors influence the value of a given correlation co-efficient and if researchers wish to extrapolate to the populations from which they drew their samples they will then have to test the significance of the correlation.

We now offer some general guidelines for interpreting correlation co-efficients. They are based on Borg's (1963) analysis and assume that the correlations relate to a hundred or more subjects.

Correlations ranging from 0.20 to 0.35

Correlations within this range show only very slight relationship between variables although they may be statistically significant. A correlation of 0.20 shows that only 4 per cent of the variance is common to the two measures. Whereas correlations at this level may have limited meaning in exploratory relationship research, they are of no value in either individual or group prediction studies.

Correlations ranging from 0.35 to 0.65

Within this range, correlations are statistically significant beyond the 1 per cent level. When correlations are around 0.40, crude group prediction may be possible. As Borg notes, correlations within this range are useful, however, when combined with other correlations in a multiple regression equation. Combining several correlations in this range can in some cases yield individual predictions that are correct within an acceptable margin of error. Correlations at this level used singly are of little use for individual prediction because they yield only a few more correct predictions than could be accomplished by guessing or by using some chance selection procedure.

Correlations ranging from 0.65 to 0.85

Correlations within this range make possible group predictions that are accurate enough for most purposes. Nearer the top of the range, group predictions can be made very accurately,

usually predicting the proportion of successful candidates in selection problems within a very small margin of error. Near the top of this correlation range individual predictions can be made that are considerably more accurate than would occur if no such selection procedures were used.

Correlations over 0.85

Correlations as high as this indicate a close relationship between the two variables correlated. A correlation of 0.85 indicates that the measure used for prediction has about 72 per cent variance in common with the performance being predicted. Prediction studies in education very rarely yield correlations this high. When correlations at this level are obtained, however, they are very useful for either individual or group prediction.

Examples of correlational research

To conclude this chapter, we illustrate the use of correlation co-efficients in a small-scale study of young children's attainments and self-images, and, by contrast, we report some of the findings of a very large scale, longitudinal survey of the outcomes of truancy that uses special techniques for controlling intruding variables in looking at the association between truancy and occupational prospects. Finally, we show how partial correlational techniques can clarify the strength and direction of associations between variables.

Small-scale study of attainment and self-image

A study by Crocker and Cheeseman (1988) investigated young children's ability to assess the academic worth of themselves and others. Specifically, the study posed the following three questions:

1   Can children in their first years at school assess their own academic rank relative to their peers?

2   What level of match exists between self-estimate, peer-estimate, teacher-estimate of academic rank?

3   What criteria do these children use when making these judgements?

Using three infant schools in the Midlands the age range of which was from 5 to 7 years, the researchers selected a sample of 141 children from 5 classes. Observations took place on 20 half-day visits to each class and the observer was able to interact with individual children. Notes on interactions were taken. Subsequently, each child was given pieces of paper with the names of all his or her classmates on them and was then asked to arrange them in 2 piles – those the child thought were 'better than me' at school work and those the child thought were 'not as good as me'. No child suggested that the task was one which he or she could not do. The relative self-rankings were converted to a percentage of children seen to be 'better than me' in each class.

Correspondingly, each teacher was asked to rank all the children in her class without using any standardized test. Spearman's rank order correlations were calculated between self-teacher, self-peer, and peer-teacher rankings. The table below indicates there was a high degree of agreement between self estimates of rank position, peer estimate and teacher estimate. The correlations appeared to confirm earlier researches in which there was broad agreement between self, peer and teacher ratings (see Box 10.5).

Box 10.5
Correlations between the various estimates of academic rank

Class	Self–peer	Self–teacher	Peer–teacher
1	0.68	0.62	0.82
2	0.72	0.74	0.80
3	0.59	0.55	0.86
4	0.83	0.59	0.65
5	0.70	0.68	0.82

Note All correlations are significant beyond the 0.01 level
Source Crocker and Cheeseman, 1988

The researchers conclude that the youngest schoolchildren quickly acquire a knowledge of those academic criteria that teachers use to evaluate pupils. The study disclosed a high degree of agreement between self, peers and teacher as to the rank order of children in a particular classroom. It seemed that only the youngest used nonacademic measures to any great extent and that this had largely disappeared by the time the children were 6 years old.

Large-scale study of truancy

Drawing on the huge database of the National Child Development Study (a longitudinal survey of all people in Great Britain born in the week 3–9 March, 1958), Hibbett and her associates (1990) were able to explore the association between reported truancy at school, based on information obtained during the school years, and occupational, financial and educational progress, family formation and health, based on interview at the age of 23 years. We report here on some occupational outcomes of truancy.

Whereas initial analyses demonstrated a consistent relationship between truancy and dropping out of secondary education, less skilled employment, increased risk of unemployment and a reduced chance of being in a job involving further training, these associations were derived from comparisons between truants and all other members of the 1958 cohort. In brief, they failed to take account of the fact that truants and non-truants differed in respect of such vital factors as family size, father's occupation, and poorer educational ability and attainment before truancy commenced. Using sophisticated statistical techniques, the investigators went on to control for these initial differences, thus enabling them to test whether or not the outcomes for truants differed once they were being compared with people who were similar in these respects. The multivariate techniques used in the analyses need not concern us here. Suffice it to say that by and large, the differences that were noted before controlling for the intruding variables persisted even when those controls were introduced. That is to say, truancy was found to correlate with:

- unstable job history;
- a shorter mean length of jobs;
- higher total number of jobs;
- greater frequency of unemployment;
- greater mean length of unemployment spells;
- lower family income.

Thus, by sequentially controlling for such variables as family size, father's occupation, measured ability and attainment at 11 years, etc., the researchers were able to ascertain how much each of these independent variables contributed to the relationship between truancy and the outcome variables that we identify above.

The investigators report their findings in terms such as:

- truants were 2.4 times more likely than non-truants to be unemployed rather than in work;
- truants were 1.4 times more likely than non-truants to be out of the labour force;
- truants experienced, on average, 4.2 months more unemployment than non-truants;
- truants were considerably less well off than non-truants in net family income per week.

The researchers conclude that their study challenges a commonly held belief that truants simply outgrow school and are ready for the world of work. On the contrary, truancy is often a sign of more general and long-term difficulties and a predictor of unemployment problems of a more severe kind than will be the experience of others who share the disadvantaged backgrounds and the low attainments that typify truants.

Partial correlation and associations between variables

The ability of partial correlational techniques to clarify the strength and direction of associations between variables is demonstrated in a study by Halpin, Croll and Redman (1990). In an exploration of teachers' perceptions of the effects of in-service education, the authors report correlations between Teaching (T), Organization and Policy (OP), Attitudes and Knowledge (AK) and the dependent variable, Pupil Attainment (PA).

The strength of these associations suggests that there is a strong tendency ($r = 0.68$) for teachers who claim a higher level of 'INSET effect' on the Teaching dimension to claim also a higher level of effect on Pupil Attainment and *vice versa*. The correlations between the Organization and Policy (OP) and Pupil Attainment (PA), and Attitudes and Knowledge (AK) and Pupil Attainment (PA), however, are much weaker ($r = 0.27$ and $r = 0.23$ respectively). When the researchers calculated the partial correlation between Teaching and Pupil Attainment, controlling for (a) Organization and Policy and (b) Attitudes and Knowledge, the results showed little difference in respect of Teaching and Pupil Attainment ($r = 0.66$ as opposed to 0.68 above). However there was a noticeably reduced association with regard to Pupil Attainment and Organization and Policy (0.14 as opposed to 0.27 above) and Attitudes and Knowledge (0.09 as opposed to 0.23 above) when the association between Teaching and Pupil Attainment is partialled out. The authors conclude that improved teaching is seen as improving Pupil Attainment, regardless of any positive effects on Organization and Policy and Attitudes and Knowledge.

Ex post facto research

Introduction

When translated literally, *ex post facto* means 'from what is done afterwards'. In the context of social and educational research the phrase means 'after the fact' or 'retrospectively' and refers to those studies which investigate possible cause-and-effect relationships by observing an existing condition or state of affairs and searching back in time for plausible causal factors. In effect, researchers ask themselves what factors seem to be associated with certain occurrences, or conditions, or aspects of behaviour. *Ex post facto* research, then, is a method of teasing out possible antecedents of events that have happened and cannot, therefore, be engineered or manipulated by the investigator. The following example will illustrate the basic idea. Imagine a situation in which there has been a dramatic increase in the number of fatal road accidents in a particular locality. An expert is called in to investigate. Naturally, there is no way in which she can study the actual accidents because they have happened; nor can she turn to technology for a video replay of the incidents. What she can do, however, is attempt a reconstruction by studying the statistics, examining the accident spots, and taking note of the statements given by victims and witnesses. In this way the expert will be in a position to identify possible determinants of the accidents. These may include excessive speed, poor road conditions, careless driving, frustration, inefficient vehicles, the effects of drugs or alcohol and so on. On the basis of her examination, she can formulate hypotheses as to the likely causes and submit them to the appropriate authority in the form of recommendations. These may include improving road conditions, or lowering the speed limit, or increasing police surveillance, for instance. The point of interest to us is that in identifying the causes retrospectively, the expert adopts an *ex post facto* perspective.

Kerlinger (1970) has defined *ex post facto* research more formally as that in which the independent variable or variables have already occurred and in which the researcher starts with the observation of a dependent variable or variables. She then studies the independent variable or variables in retrospect for their possible relationship to, and effects on, the dependent variable or variables. The researcher is thus examining retrospectively the effects of a naturally occurring event on a subsequent outcome with a view to establishing a causal link between them. Interestingly, some instances of *ex post facto* designs correspond to experimental research in reverse, for instead of taking groups that are equivalent and subjecting them to different treatments so as to bring about differences in the dependent variables to be measured, an *ex post facto* experiment begins with groups that are already different in some respect and searches in retrospect for the factor that brought about the difference. Indeed Spector (1993: 42) suggests that *ex post facto* research is a procedure that is intended to transform a non-experimental research design into a pseudo-experimental form.

Two kinds of design may be identified in *ex post facto* research – the co-relational study and the criterion group study. The former is sometimes termed 'causal research' and the latter, 'causal-comparative research'. A co-relational (or causal) study is concerned with identifying the antecedents of a present condition. As its name suggests, it involves the collection of two sets of data, one of which will be retrospective, with a view to determining the relationship between them. The basic design of such an experiment may be represented thus:[1]

An example of this kind of design can be seen in the study by Borkowsky (1970). Where a strong relationship is found between the independent and dependent variables, three possible interpretations are open to the researcher:

1   that the variable X has caused O;
2   that the variable O has caused X; or
3   that some third unidentified, and therefore unmeasured, variable has caused X and O.

It is often the case that a researcher cannot tell which of these is correct.

The value of co-relational or causal studies lies chiefly in their exploratory or suggestive character for, as we have seen, while they are not always adequate in themselves for establishing causal relationships among variables, they are a useful first step in this direction in that they do yield measures of association.

In the criterion-group (or causal-comparative) approach, the investigator sets out to discover possible causes for a phenomenon being studied, by comparing the subjects in which the variable is present with similar subjects in whom it is absent. The basic design in this kind of study may be represented thus:

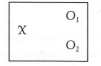

If, for example, a researcher chose such a design to investigate factors contributing to teacher effectiveness, the criterion group O_1, the effective teachers, and its counterpart O_2, a group *not* showing the characteristics of the criterion group, are identified by measuring the differential effects of the groups on classes of children. The researcher may then examine X, some variable or event, such as the background, training, skills and personality of the groups, to discover what might 'cause' only some teachers to be effective.

Criterion-group or causal-comparative studies may be seen as bridging the gap between descriptive research methods on the one hand and true experimental research on the other.

Characteristics of *ex post facto research*

In *ex post facto* research the researcher takes the effect (or dependent variable) and examines the data retrospectively to establish causes, relationships or associations, and their meanings.

Other characteristics of *ex post facto* research become apparent when it is contrasted with true experimental research. Kerlinger (1970) describes the *modus operandi* of the experimental researcher. ('If *x*, then *y*' in Kerlinger's usage. We have substituted X for *x* and O for *y* to fit in with Campbell and Stanley's (1963) conventions throughout the chapter.) Kerlinger hypothesizes: if X, then O; if frustration, then aggression. Depending on circumstances and his own predilections in research design, he uses some method to manipulate X. He then observes O to see if concomitant variation, the variation expected or predicted from the variation in X, occurs. If it does, this is evidence for the validity of the proposition, X–O, meaning 'If X, then O'. Note that the scientist here predicts from a controlled X to O. To help him achieve control, he can use the principle of randomization and active manipulation of X and can assume, other things being equal, that O is varying as a result of the manipulation of X.

In *ex post facto* designs, on the other hand, O is observed. Then a retrospective search for X ensues. An X is found that is plausible and agrees with the hypothesis. Due to lack of control of X and other possible Xs, the truth of the hypothesized relation between X and O cannot be asserted with the confidence of the experimental researcher. Basically, then, *ex post facto* investigations have, so to speak, a built-in weakness: lack of control of the independent variable or variables. As Spector (1993: 43) suggests, it is impossible to isolate and control every possible variable, or to know with absolute certainty which are the most crucial variables.

This brief comparison highlights the most important difference between the two designs – control. In the experimental situation, investigators at least have manipulative control; they have as a minimum one active variable. If an experiment is a 'true' experiment, they can also exercise control by randomization. They can assign subjects to groups randomly; or, at the very least, they can assign treatments to groups at random. In the *ex post facto* research situation, this control of the independent variable is not possible, and what is perhaps more important, neither is randomization. Investigators must take things as they are and try to disentangle them, though having said this, we must point out that they can make use of selected procedures that will give them an element of control in this research. These we shall touch upon shortly.

By their very nature, *ex post facto* experiments can provide support for any number of different, perhaps even contradictory, hypotheses; they are so completely flexible that it is largely a matter of postulating hypotheses according to one's personal preference. The investigator begins with certain data and looks for an interpretation consistent with them; often, however, a number of interpretations may be at hand. Consider again the hypothetical increase in road accidents in a given town. A retrospective search for causes will disclose half a dozen plausible ones. Experimental studies, by contrast, begin with a specific interpretation and then determine whether it is congruent with externally derived data. Frequently, causal relationships seem to be established on nothing more substantial than the premise that any related event occurring prior to the phenomenon under study is assumed to be its cause – the classical *post hoc, ergo propter hoc* fallacy.[2] Overlooked is the fact that even when we do find a relationship between two variables, we must recognize the possibility that both are individual results of a common third factor rather than the first being necessarily the cause of the second. And as we have seen earlier, there is also the real possibility of reverse causation, e.g. that a heart condition promotes obesity rather than the other way around, or that they encourage each other. The point is that the evidence simply illustrates the hypothesis; it does not test it, since hypotheses cannot be tested on the same data from which they were derived. The relationship noted may actually exist, but it is not necessarily the only relationship, or perhaps the crucial one. Before we can accept that smoking is the primary cause of lung cancer, we have to rule out alternative hypotheses.

We must not conclude from what has just been said that *ex post facto* studies are of little value; many of our important investigations in education and psychology are *ex post facto* designs. There is often no choice in the matter: an investigator cannot cause one group to become failures, delinquent, suicidal, brain-damaged or dropouts. Research must of necessity rely on existing groups. On the other hand, the inability of *ex post facto* designs to incorporate the basic need for control (e.g. through manipulation or randomization) makes them vulnerable from a scientific point of view and the possibility of their being misleading should be clearly acknowledged. *Ex post facto* designs are probably better conceived more circumspectly, not as experiments with the greater certainty that these denote, but more as surveys, useful as sources of hypotheses to be tested by more conventional experimental means at a later date.

Occasions when appropriate

It would follow from what we have said in the preceding section that *ex post facto* designs are appropriate in circumstances where the more powerful experimental method is not possible. These would arise when, for example, it is not possible to select, control and manipulate the factors necessary to study cause-and-effect relationships directly; or when the control of all variables except a single independent variable may be unrealistic and artificial, preventing the normal interaction with other influential variables; or when laboratory controls for many research purposes would be impractical, costly or ethically undesirable.

Ex post facto research is particularly suitable in social, educational and – to a lesser extent – psychological contexts where the independent variable or variables lie outside the researcher's control. Examples of the method abound in these areas: the research on cigarette smoking and lung cancer, for instance; or studies of teacher characteristics; or studies examining the relationship between political and religious affiliation and attitudes; or investigations into the relationship between school achievement and independent variables such as social class, race, sex and intelligence. Many of these may be divided into large-scale or small-scale *ex post facto* studies, for example Stables's (1990) large scale study of differences between pupils from mixed and single-sex schools and Arnold's and Atkins's (1991) small scale study of the social and emotional adjustment of hearing-impaired children.[3]

Advantages and disadvantages of ex post facto *research*

Among the advantages of the approach we may identify the following:

- *Ex post facto* research meets an important need of the researcher where the more rigorous experimental approach is not possible. In the case of the alleged relationship between smoking and lung cancer, for instance, this cannot be tested experimentally (at least as far as human beings are concerned).
- The method yields useful information concerning the nature of phenomena – what goes with what and under what conditions. In this way, *ex post facto* research is a valuable exploratory tool.
- Improvements in statistical techniques and general methodology have made *ex post facto* designs more defensible.

- In some ways and in certain situations the method is more useful than the experimental method, especially where the setting up of the latter would introduce a note of artificiality into research proceedings.
- *Ex post facto* research is particularly appropriate when simple cause-and-effect relationships are being explored.
- The method can give a sense of direction and provide a fruitful source of hypotheses that can subsequently be tested by the more rigorous experimental method.

Among the limitations and weaknesses of *ex post facto* designs the following may be mentioned:

- There is the problem of lack of control in that the researcher is unable to manipulate the independent variable or to randomize her subjects.
- One cannot know for certain whether the causative factor has been included or even identified.
- It may be that no single factor is the cause.
- A particular outcome may result from different causes on different occasions.
- When a relationship has been discovered, there is the problem of deciding which is the cause and which the effect; the possibility of reverse causation has to be considered.
- The relationship of two factors does not establish cause and effect.
- Classifying into dichotomous groups can be problematic.
- There is the difficulty of interpretation and the danger of the *post hoc* assumption being made, that is, believing that because X precedes O, X causes O.
- It often bases its conclusions on too limited a sample or number of occurrences.
- It frequently fails to single out the really significant factor or factors, and fails to recognize that events have multiple rather than single causes.
- As a method it is regarded by some as too flexible.

- It lacks nullifiability and confirmation.
- The sample size might shrink massively with multiple matchings (Spector, 1993: 43).

Designing an ex post facto *investigation*

We earlier referred to the two basic designs embraced by *ex post facto* research – the co-relational (or causal) model and the criterion group (or causal-comparative) model. We return to them again here in order to consider designing both types of investigation. As we saw, the causal model attempts to identify the antecedent of a present condition and may be represented thus:

Although one variable in an *ex post facto* study

| Independent variable | Dependent variable |
| X | O |

cannot be confidently said to depend upon the other as would be the case in a truly experimental investigation, it is nevertheless usual to designate one of the variables as independent (X) and the other as dependent (O). The left to right dimension indicates the temporal order, though having established this, we must not overlook the possibility of reverse causality.

The second model, the causal-comparative, may be represented schematically as:

Group	Independent variable	Dependent variable
E	X	O_1
C		O_2

Using this model, the investigator hypothesizes the independent variable and then compares two groups, an experimental group (E) which has been exposed to the presumed independent variable X and a control group (C) which has not. (The dashed line in the model shows that the comparison groups E and C are not equated by random assignment.) Alternatively, she may examine two groups that are different in some way or ways and then try to account for the difference or differ-

ences by investigating possible antecedents. These two examples reflect two types of approach to causal-comparative research: the 'cause-to-effect' kind and the 'effect-to-cause' kind.

The basic design of causal-comparative investigations is similar to an experimentally designed study. The chief difference resides in the nature of the independent variable, X. In a truly experimental situation, this will be under the control of the investigator and may therefore be described as manipulable. In the causal-comparative model (and also the causal model), however, the independent variable is beyond her control, having already occurred. It may therefore be described in this design as non-manipulable.

Procedures in ex post facto *research*

We now examine the steps involved in implementing a piece of *ex post facto* research. We may begin by identifying the problem area to be investigated. This stage will be followed by a clear and precise statement of the hypothesis to be tested or questions to be answered. The next step will be to make explicit the assumptions on which the hypothesis and subsequent procedures will be based. A review of the research literature will follow. This will enable the investigator to ascertain the kinds of issues, problems, obstacles and findings disclosed by previous studies in the area. There will then follow the planning of the actual investigation and this will consist of three broad stages – identification of the population and samples; the selection and construction of techniques for collecting data; and the establishment of categories for classifying the data. The final stage will involve the description, analysis and interpretation of the findings.

It was noted earlier that the principal weakness of *ex post facto* research is the absence of control over the independent variable influencing the dependent variable in the case of causal designs or affecting observed differences between dependent variables in the case of causal-comparative designs. (We take up the question of control in experimental research in greater detail in the next chapter.) Although the *ex post facto* researcher is denied not only this kind of control but also the principle of randomization, she can nevertheless utilize procedures that will give her some measure of control in her investigation. And it is to some of these that we now turn.

One of the commonest means of introducing control into this type of research is that of matching the subjects in the experimental and control groups where the design is causal-comparative. One group of writers explain it thus:

> The matching is usually done on a subject-to-subject basis to form matched pairs. For example, if one were interested in the relationship between scouting experiences and delinquency, he could locate two groups of boys classified as delinquent and non-delinquent according to specified criteria. It would be wise in such a study to select pairs from these groups matched on the basis of socio-economic status, family structure, and other variables known to be related to both scouting experience and delinquency. Analysis of the data from the matched samples could be made to determine whether or not scouting characterized the non-delinquent and was absent in the background of the delinquent.
>
> (Ary *et al.*, 1972)

There are difficulties with this procedure, however, for it assumes that the investigator knows what the relevant factors are, that is, the factors that may be related to the dependent variable. Further, there is the possibility of losing those subjects who cannot be matched, thus reducing one's sample.

As an alternative procedure for introducing a degree of control into *ex post facto* research, Ary and his colleagues suggest building the extraneous independent variables into the design and using an analysis of variance technique. They explain:

> Assume that intelligence is a relevant extraneous variable and it is not feasible to control it through matching or other means. In this case, intelligence could be added to the design as another independent variable and the subjects of the study classified in terms of intelligence levels. The dependent variable measures would then be analyzed through an analysis of variance and the main and interaction effects of intelligence might be determined. Such a procedure would reveal any significant differences among the groups on the dependent variable, but no causal relationship between intelligence and the dependent variable could be assumed. Other extraneous variables could be operating to produce both the main effect and any interaction effects.
>
> (Ary *et al.*, 1972)

Yet another procedure which may be adopted for introducing a measure of control into *ex post facto* design is that of selecting samples that are as homogeneous as possible on a given variable. The writers quoted above illustrate the procedure with the following example.

> If intelligence were a relevant extraneous variable, its effects could be controlled by using subjects from only one intelligence level. This procedure serves the purpose of disentangling the independent variable in which the investigator may be interested from other variables with which it is commonly associated, so that any effects that are found can justifiably be associated with the independent variable.
>
> (Ary *et al.*, 1972)

Finally, control may be introduced into an *ex post facto* investigation by stating and testing any alternative hypotheses that might be plausible explanations for the empirical outcomes of the study. A researcher has thus to beware of accepting the first likely explanation of relationships in an *ex post facto* study as necessarily the only or final one. A well-known instance to which reference has already been made is the presumed relationship between cigarette smoking and lung cancer. Government health officials have been quick to seize on the explanation that smoking causes lung cancer. Tobacco firms, however, have put forward an alternative hypothesis – that both smoking and lung cancer are possibly the result of a third, as yet unspecified, factor. In other words, the possibility that both the independent and dependent variables are simply two separate results of a single common cause cannot be ignored.

12 Experiments, quasi-experiments and single-case research

Introduction

The issue of *causality* and, hence, predictability has exercised the minds of researchers considerably (Smith, 1991: 177). One response to the problem has been in qualitative research that defines causality in the terms of the participants (Chapter 6). Another response has been in the operation of *control*, and it finds its apotheosis in the experimental design. If rival causes or explanations can be eliminated from a study then, it is argued, clear causality can be established, the model can *explain* outcomes. Smith (1991: 177) claims the high ground for the experimental approach, arguing that it is the *only* method that directly concerns itself with causality; this, clearly is contestable, as we show in Chapters 6–9, and 13 of this book.

In Chapter 11, we described *ex post facto* research as experimentation in reverse in that *ex post facto* studies start with groups that are already different with regard to certain characteristics and then proceed to search, in retrospect, for the factors that brought about those differences. We then went on to cite Kerlinger's description of the experimental researcher's approach:

> If *x*, then *y*; if frustration, then aggression . . . the researcher uses some method to measure *x* and then observes *y* to see if concomitant variation occurs.
>
> (Kerlinger, 1970)

The essential feature of experimental research is that investigators deliberately control and manipulate the conditions which determine the events in which they are interested. At its simplest, an experiment involves making a change in the value of one variable – called the independent variable – and observing the effect of that change on another variable – called the dependent variable.

Imagine that we have been transported to a laboratory to investigate the properties of a new wonder-fertilizer that farmers could use on their cereal crops, let us say wheat (Morrison, 1993: 44–5). The scientist would take the bag of wheat seed and randomly split it into two equal parts. One part would be grown under normal existing conditions – controlled and measured amounts of soil, warmth, water and light and no other factors. This would be called the control group. The other part would be grown under the same conditions – the same controlled and measured amounts of soil, warmth, water and light as the control group, *but*, additionally, the new wonder-fertilizer. Then, four months later, the two groups are examined and their growth measured. The control group has grown half a metre and each ear of wheat is in place but the seeds are small. The experimental group, by contrast, has grown half a metre as well but has significantly more seeds on each ear, the seeds are larger, fuller and more robust.

The scientist concludes that, because both groups came into contact with nothing other than measured amounts of soil, warmth, water and light, then it could not have been anything else but the new wonder-fertilizer that caused the experimental group to flourish so well. The key factors in the experiment were:

- the random allocation of the whole bag of wheat into two matched groups (the control and the experimental group), involving the initial measurement of the size of the wheat to ensure that it was the same for both groups (i.e. the pretest);

- the identification of key variables (soil, warmth, water, and light);
- the control of the key variables (the same amounts to each group);
- the exclusion of any other variables;
- the giving of the special treatment (the intervention) to the experimental group whilst holding every other variable constant for the two groups;
- the final measurement of yield and growth (the post-test);
- the comparison of one group with another;
- the stage of generalization – that this new wonder-fertilizer improves yield and growth under a given set of conditions.

This model, premised on notions of isolation and control of variables in order to establish causality, may be appropriate for a laboratory, though whether, in fact a social situation either ever *could become* the antiseptic, artificial world of the laboratory or *should become* such a world is both an empirical and a moral question respectively. Further, the ethical dilemmas of treating humans as manipulable, controllable and inanimate are considerable (see Chapter 2). However, let us pursue the experimental model further.

Frequently in learning experiments in classroom settings the independent variable is a stimulus of some kind, a new method in arithmetical computation for example, and the dependent variable is a response, the time taken to do twenty problems using the new method. Most empirical studies in educational settings, however, are quasi-experimental rather than experimental. The single most important difference between the quasi-experiment and the true experiment is that in the former case, the researcher undertakes his study with groups that are intact, that is to say, the groups have been constituted by means other than random selection. We begin by identifying the essential features of pre-experimental, true experimental and quasi-experimental designs, our intention being to introduce the reader to the meaning and purpose of control in educational experimentation.

Designs in educational experimentation

In the outline of research designs that follows we use symbols and conventions from Campbell and Stanley (1963):

1   X represents the exposure of a group to an experimental variable or event, the effects of which are to be measured.
2   O refers to the process of observation or measurement.
3   Xs and Os in a given row are applied to the same persons.
4   Left to right order indicates temporal sequence.
5   Xs and Os vertical to one another are simultaneous.
6   R indicates random assignment to separate treatment groups.
7   Parallel rows unseparated by dashes represent comparison groups equated by randomization, while those separated by a dashed line represent groups not equated by random assignment.

A pre-experimental design: the one group pretest–post-test

Very often, reports about the value of a new teaching method or interest aroused by some curriculum innovation or other reveal that a researcher has measured a group on a dependent variable (O_1), for example, attitudes towards minority groups, and then introduced an experimental manipulation (X), perhaps a ten-week curriculum project designed to increase tolerance of ethnic minorities. Following the experimental treatment, the researcher has again measured group attitudes (O_2) and proceeded to account for differences between pretest and post-test scores by reference to the effects of X.

The one group pretest–post-test design can be represented as:

Experimental	O_1	X	O_2

Suppose that just such a project has been undertaken and that the researcher finds that O_2 scores indicate greater tolerance of ethnic minorities than O_1 scores. How justified is she in attributing the cause of O_1–O_2 differences to the experimental treatment (X), that is, the term's project work? At first glance the assumption of causality seems reasonable enough. The situation is not that simple, however. Compare for a moment the circumstances represented in our hypothetical educational example with those which typically obtain in experiments in the physical sciences. A physicist who applies heat to a metal bar can confidently attribute the observed expansion to the rise in temperature that she has introduced because within the confines of her laboratory she has excluded (i.e. controlled) all other extraneous sources of variation (this example is suggested by Pilliner, 1973).

The same degree of control can never be attained in educational experimentation. At this point readers may care to reflect upon some possible influences other than the ten-week curriculum project that might account for the O_1–O_2 differences in our hypothetical educational example.

They may conclude that factors to do with the pupils, the teacher, the school, the classroom organization, the curriculum materials and their presentation, the way that the subjects' attitudes were measured, to say nothing of the thousand and one other events that occurred in and about the school during the course of the term's work, might all have exerted some influence upon the observed differences in attitude. These kinds of extraneous variables which are outside the experimenters' control in one-group pretest–post-test designs threaten to invalidate their research efforts. We identify a number of such threats to the validity of educational experimentation in Chapter 5.

A 'true' experimental design: the pretest–post-test control group design

A complete exposition of experimental designs is beyond the scope of this chapter. In the brief outline that follows, we have selected one design from the comprehensive treatment of the subject by Campbell and Stanley (1963) in order to identify the essential features of what they term a 'true experimental' and what Kerlinger (1970) refers to as a 'good' design. Along with its variants, the chosen design is commonly used in educational experimentation.

The pretest–post-test control group design can be represented as:

Experimental	RO_1	X	O_2
Control	RO_3		O_4

It differs from the pre-experimental design that we have just described in that it involves the use of two groups which have been constituted by randomization. As Kerlinger observes, in theory, random assignment to E and C conditions controls all possible independent variables. In practice, of course, it is only when enough subjects are included in the experiment that the principle of randomization has a chance to operate as a powerful control. However, the effects of randomization even with a small number of subjects is well illustrated in Box 12.1.

Randomization, then, ensures the greater likelihood of equivalence, that is, the apportioning[1] out between the experimental and control groups of any other factors or characteristics of the subjects which might conceivably affect the experimental variables in which the researcher is interested. It is, as Kerlinger (1970) notes, the addition of the control group in our present example and the random assignment of subjects to E and C groups that radically alters the situation from that which obtains in the pre-experimental design outlined earlier. For if the groups are made equivalent, then any so-called 'clouding' effects should be present in both groups.

Box 12.1
The effects of randomization

Select twenty cards from a pack, ten red and ten black. Shuffle and deal into two ten-card piles. Now count the number of red cards and black cards in either pile and record the results. Repeat the whole sequence many times, recording the results each time.

You will soon convince yourself that the most likely distribution of reds and blacks in a pile is five in each: the next most likely, six red (or black) and four black (or red); and so on. You will be lucky (or unlucky for the purposes of the demonstration!) to achieve one pile of red and the other entirely of black cards. The probability of this happening is 1 in 92,378! On the other hand, the probability of obtaining a 'mix' not more than 6 of one colour and 4 of the other is about 82 in 100.

If you now imagine the red cards to stand for the 'better' ten children and the black cards for the 'poorer' ten children in a class of twenty, you will conclude that the operation of the laws of chance alone will almost probably give you close equivalent 'mixes' of 'better' and 'poorer' children in the experimental and control groups.

Source Adapted from Pilliner, 1973

If the mental ages of the children of the experimental group increase, so should the mental ages of the children of the control group . . . If something happens to affect the experimental subjects between the pretest and the post-test, this something should also affect the subjects of the control groups.

(Kerlinger, 1970)

So strong is this simple and elegant true experimental design, that all the threats to internal validity identified by Campbell and Stanley (1963) are controlled in the pretest–post-test control group design.

One problem that has been identified with this particular experimental design is the interaction effect of testing. Good (1963) explains that whereas the various threats to the validity of the experiments listed in Chapter 5 can be thought of as main effects, manifesting themselves in mean differences independently of the presence of other variables, interaction effects, as their name implies, are joint effects and may occur even when no main effects are present.[2] For example, an interaction effect may occur as a result of the pretest measure sensitizing the subjects to the experimental variable.[3] Interaction effects can be controlled for by adding to the pretest–post-test control group design two more groups that do not experience the pretest measures. The result is a four-group design, as suggested by Solomon. Later in the chapter, we describe an educational study which built into a pretest–post-test group design a further control group to take account of the possibility of pretest sensitization.

A quasi-experimental design: the non-equivalent control group design

Often in educational research, it is simply not possible for investigators to undertake true experiments. At best, they may be able to employ something approaching a true experimental design in which they have control over what Campbell and Stanley (1963) refer to as 'the who and to whom of measurement' but lack control over 'the when and to whom of exposure', or the randomization of exposures – essential if true experimentation is to take place. These situations are quasi-experimental and the methodologies employed by researchers are termed quasi-experimental designs. (Kerlinger (1970) refers to quasi-experimental situations as 'compromise designs', an apt description when applied to much educational research where the random selection or random assignment of schools and classrooms is quite impracticable.)

One of the most commonly used quasi-experimental designs in educational research can be represented as:

Experimental	O_1	X	O_2
Control	O_3		O_4

The dashed line separating the parallel rows in the diagram of the non-equivalent control group indicates that the experimental and control groups have not been equated by randomization – hence the term 'non-equivalent'. The addition of a control group makes the present design a decided improvement over the one group pretest–post-test design, for to the degree that experimenters can make E and C groups as equivalent as possible, they can avoid the equivocality of interpretations that plague the pre-experimental design discussed earlier. The equivalence of groups can be strengthened by matching, followed by random assignment to E and C treatments.

Where matching is not possible, the researcher is advised to use samples from the same population or samples that are as alike as possible (Kerlinger, 1970). Where intact groups differ substantially, however, matching is unsatisfactory due to regression effects which lead to different group means on post-test measures. Campbell and Stanley put it this way:

> If [in the non-equivalent control group design] the means of the groups are substantially different, then the process of matching not only fails to provide the intended equation but in addition insures the occurrence of unwanted regression effects. It becomes predictably certain that the two groups will differ on their post-test scores altogether independently of any effects of X, and that this difference will vary directly with the difference between the total populations from which the selection was made and inversely with the test–retest correlation.
> (Campbell and Stanley, 1963)

Procedures in conducting experimental research

In Chapter 11, we identified a sequence of steps in carrying out an *ex post facto* study. An experimental investigation must also follow a set of logical procedures. Those that we now enumerate, however, should be treated with some circumspection. It is extraordinarily difficult (and indeed, foolhardy) to lay down clear-cut rules as

guides to experimental research. At best, we can identify an ideal route to be followed, knowing full well that educational research rarely proceeds in such a systematic fashion. (For a detailed discussion of the practical issues in educational experimentation, see Evans (1978), Chapter 4, 'Planning experimental work', Riecken and Boruch (1974), and Bennett and Lumsdaine (1975).)

First, the researcher must identify and define the research problem as precisely as possible, always supposing that the problem is amenable to experimental methods.

Second, she must formulate hypotheses that she wishes to test. This involves making predictions about relationships between specific variables and at the same time making decisions about other variables that are to be excluded from the experiment by means of controls. Variables, remember, must have two properties. First, they must be measurable. Physical fitness, for example, is not directly measurable until it has been operationally defined. Making the variable 'physical fitness' operational means simply defining it by letting something else that is measurable stand for it – a gymnastics test, perhaps. Second, the proxy variable must be a valid indicator of the hypothetical variable in which one is interested. That is to say, a gymnastics test probably is a reasonable proxy for physical fitness; height on the other hand most certainly is not.

Third, the researcher must select appropriate levels at which to test the independent variables in order for differences to be observed. The experimenter will vary the stimuli at such levels as are of practical interest in the real-life situation. For example comparing reading periods of forty-four minutes, or forty-six minutes, with timetabled reading lessons of forty-five minutes is scarcely likely to result in observable differences in attainment.

Fourth, in planning the design of the experiment, the researcher must take account of the population to which she wishes to generalize her results. This involves her in decisions over sample sizes and sampling methods.

Fifth, with problems of validity in mind, the

researcher must select instruments, choose tests and decide upon appropriate methods of analysis.

Sixth, before embarking upon the actual experiment, the researcher must pilot test the experimental procedures to identify possible snags in connection with any aspect of the investigation (Simon, 1978).

Seventh, during the experiment itself, the researcher must endeavour to follow tested and agreed-on procedures to the letter. The standardization of instructions, the exact timing of experimental sequences, the meticulous recording and checking of observations – these are the hallmark of the competent researcher.

With her data collected, the researcher faces the most important part of the whole enterprise. Processing data, analysing results and drafting reports are all extremely demanding activities, both in intellectual effort and time.

Borg and Gall (1979: 547) set out a useful series of steps in the planning and conduct of an experiment:

Step 1   Carry out a measure of the dependent variable.

Step 2   Assign participants to matched pairs, based on the scores and measures established from Step 1.

Step 3   Randomly assign one person from each pair to the control group and the other to the experimental group.

Step 4   Administer the experimental treatment/ intervention to the experimental group and, if appropriate, a placebo to the control group. Ensure that the control group is not subject to the intervention.

Step 5   Carry out a measure of the dependent variable with both groups and compare/measure them in order to determine the effect and its size on the dependent variable.

Borg and Gall indicate that difficulties arise in the close matching of the sample of the control and experimental groups. This involves careful identification of the variables on which the matching must take place. They suggest (p. 547) that matching on a number of variables that correlate with the dependent variable is more likely to reduce errors than matching on a single variable. The problem, of course, is that the greater the number of variables that have to be matched, the harder it is actually to find the sample of people who are matched. Hence the balance must be struck between having too few variables such that error can occur, and having so many variables that it is impossible to draw a sample.

Further, the authors draw attention to the need to specify the degree of exactitude (or variance) of the match. For example, if the subjects were to be matched on, say, linguistic ability as measured in a standardized test, it is important to define the limits of variability that will be used to define the matching (e.g. ± 3 points). As before, the greater the degree of precision in the matching here, the closer will be the match, but the greater the degree of precision the harder it will be to find an exactly matched sample.

One way of addressing this issue is to place all the subjects in rank order on the basis of the scores or measures of the dependent variable. Then the first two subjects become one matched pair (which one is allocated to the control group and which to the experimental group is done randomly, e.g. by tossing a coin), subjects three and four become the next matched pair, subjects five and six become the next matched pair, and so on until the sample is drawn. Here the loss of precision is counterbalanced by the avoidance of the loss of subjects.

The alternative to matching that has been discussed earlier in the chapter is randomization. Smith (1991: 215) suggests that matching is most widely used in quasi-experimental and non-experimental research, and is a far inferior means of ruling out alternative causal explanations than randomization. Randomization, he argues, produces equivalence over a whole range of variables, whereas matching produces equivalence over only a few named variables. The use of randomized controlled trials (RCTs), a method used in medicine, is a putative way of establishing causality and generalizability (though, in medicine, the sample sizes for some RCTs are necessarily so small – there being limited sufferers from a particular complaint – that randomization is seriously compromised).

A powerful advocacy of RCTs for planning and evaluation is provided by Boruch (1997). Indeed he argues (p. 69) that the problem of poor experimental controls has led to highly questionable claims being made about the success of programmes. Examples of the use of RCTs can be seen in Maynard and Chalmers (1997).

Mitchell and Jolley (1988: 103) pose three important questions that researchers need to consider when comparing two groups:

- Are the two groups equal at the commencement of the experiment?
- Would the two groups have grown apart naturally, regardless of the intervention?
- To what extent has initial measurement error of the two groups been a contributory factor in differences between scores?

Examples from educational research

Example 1: a pre-experimental design

A pre-experimental design was used in a study involving the 1991–2 Postgraduate Diploma in Education group following a course of training to equip them to teach social studies in senior secondary schools in Botswana. The researcher wished to find out whether the programme of studies he had devised would effect changes in the students' orientations towards social studies teaching. To that end, he employed a research instrument, the Barth/Shermis Studies Preference Scale (BSSPS).

The BSSPS provides measures of what purport to be three social studies traditions or philosophical orientations, the oldest of which, Citizenship Transmission, involves indoctrination of the young in the basic values of a society. The second orientation, called the Social Science, is held to relate to the acquisition of knowledge-gathering skills based on the mastery of social science concepts and processes. The third tradition, Reflective Inquiry, emphasizes the process of inquiry. Forty-eight Postgraduate Diploma students were administered the BSSPS during the first session of their one-year course of study. At the end of the programme, the

BSSPS was again completed in order to determine whether changes had occurred in students' philosophical orientations. Briefly, the 'preferred orientation' in the pretest and post-test was the criterion measure, the two orientations least preferred being ignored. Broadly speaking, students tended to move from a majority holding a Citizenship Transmission orientation at the beginning of the course to a greater affirmation of the Social Science and the Reflective Inquiry traditions. Using the symbols and conventions adopted earlier to represent research designs, we can illustrate the Botswana study as:

| Experimental | O_1 | X | O_2 |

The briefest consideration reveals inadequacies in the design. Indeed, Campbell and Stanley describe the one group pretest–post-test design as 'a "bad example" to illustrate several of the confounded extraneous variables that can jeopardize internal validity. These variables offer plausible hypotheses explaining an O_1–O_2 difference, rival to the hypothesis that caused the difference' (Campbell and Stanley, 1963). The investigator is rightly cautious in his conclusions: 'it is possible to say that the social studies course *might* be responsible for this phenomenon, although other extraneous variables might be operating' (Adeyemi, 1992, emphasis added). Somewhat ingenuously he puts his finger on one potential explanation, that the changes could have occurred among his intending teachers because the shift from 'inculcation to rational decision-making was in line with the recommendation of the Nine Year Social Studies Syllabus issued by the Botswana Ministry of Education in 1989' (Adeyemi, 1992).

Example 2: a quasi-experimental design

Mason, Mason and Quayle's longitudinal study took place between 1984 and 1992. Its principal aim was to test whether the explicit teaching of linguistic features of GCSE textbooks, coursework and examinations would produce an improvement in performance across the secondary curriculum. The design adopted in the study may be represented as:

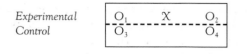

This is, of course, the non-equivalent control group design outlined earlier in this chapter in which parallel rows separated by dashed lines represent groups that have not been equated by random assignment.

In brief, the researchers adopted a methodology akin to teaching English as a foreign language and applied this to Years 7–9 in the study school and two neighbouring schools, monitoring the pupils at every stage and comparing their performance with control groups drawn both from the three schools. Inevitably, because experimental and control groups were not randomly allocated, there were significant differences in the performance of some groups on pre-treatment measures such as the York Language Aptitude Test. Moreover, because no standardized reading tests of sufficient difficulty were available as post-treatment measures, tests had to be devised by the researchers, who provide no details as to their validity or reliability. These difficulties notwithstanding, pupils in the experimental groups taking public examinations in 1990 and 1991 showed substantial gains in respect of the percentage increases of those obtaining GCSE Grades AC. The researchers note that during the three years 1989 to 1991, 'no other significant change in the policy, teaching staff or organization of the school took place which could account for this dramatic improvement of 50 per cent' (Mason *et al.*, 1992).

Although the researchers attempted to control extraneous variables, readers may well ask whether threats to internal and external validity (see Chapter 5) were sufficiently met as to allow such a categorical conclusion as, 'the pupils . . . achieved greater success in public examinations as a result of taking part in the project' (Mason *et al.*, 1992).

Example 3: a 'true' experimental design

Another investigation (Bhadwal and Panda, 1991) concerned with effecting improvements in students' performance as a consequence of changing teaching strategies used a more robust experimental design. In rural India, the researchers drew a sample of seventy-eight pupils, matched by socio-economic backgrounds and non-verbal IQs, from three primary schools that were themselves matched by location, physical facilities, teachers' qualifications and skills, school evaluation procedures and degree of parental involvement. Twenty-six pupils were randomly selected to comprise the experimental group, the remaining fifty-two being equally divided into two control groups. Before the introduction of the changed teaching strategies to the experimental group, all three groups completed questionnaires on their study habits and attitudes. These instruments were specifically designed for use with younger children and were subjected to the usual item analyses, test–retest and split-half reliability inspections. Bhadwal and Panda's research design can be represented as:

Experimental	RO_1	X	RO_2
First control	RO_3		RO_4
Second control	RO_5		RO_6

Recalling Kerlinger's discussion of a 'good' experimental design, the version of the pretest–post-test control design employed here (unlike the design used in Example 2 above) resorted to randomization which, in theory, controls all possible independent variables. Kerlinger adds, however, '*in practice*, it is only when enough subjects are included in the experiment that the principle of randomization has a chance to operate as a powerful control' (Kerlinger, 1970). It is doubtful whether twenty-six pupils in each of the three groups in Bhadwal and Panda's study constituted 'enough subjects'.

In addition to the matching procedures in drawing up the sample, and the random allocation of pupils to experimental and control groups, the researchers also used analysis of covariance, as a further means of controlling for initial differences between E and C groups on their pretest mean scores on the independent variables, study habits and attitudes.

The experimental programme[4] involved improving teaching skills, classroom organization, teaching aids, pupil participation, remedial help, peer-tutoring, and continuous evaluation. In addition, provision was also made in the experimental group for ensuring parental involvement and extra reading materials. It would be startling if such a package of teaching aids and curriculum strategies did not effect significant changes in their recipients and such was the case in the experimental results. The Experimental Group made highly significant gains in respect of its level of study habits as compared with Control Group 2 where students did not show a marked change. What did surprise the investigators, we suspect, was the significant increase in levels of study habits in Control Group 1. Maybe, they opine, this unexpected result occurred because Control Group 1 pupils were tested immediately prior to the beginning of their annual examinations. On the other hand, they concede, some unaccountable variables might have been operating. There is, surely, a lesson here for all researchers!

Single-case research: ABAB design

Increasingly, in recent years, single-case research as an experimental methodology has extended to such diverse fields as clinical psychology, medicine, education, social work, psychiatry, and counselling. Most of the single-case studies carried out in these (and other) areas share the following characteristics:

- they involve the continuous assessment of some aspect of human behaviour over a period of time, requiring on the part of the researcher the administration of measures on multiple occasions within separate phases of a study.

- they involve 'intervention effects' which are replicated in the same subject(s) over time.

Continuous assessment measures are used as a basis for drawing inferences about the effectiveness of intervention procedures.

The characteristics of single-case research studies are discussed by Kazdin (1982) in terms of ABAB designs, the basic experimental format in most single-case researches. ABAB designs, Kazdin observes, consist of a family of procedures in which observations of performance are made over time for a given client or group of clients. Over the course of the investigation, changes are made in the experimental conditions to which the client is exposed. The basic rationale of the ABAB design is illustrated in Box 12.2. What it does is this. It examines the effects of an intervention by alternating the baseline condition (the A phase), when no intervention is in effect, with the intervention condition (the B phase). The A and B phases are then repeated to complete the four phases. As Kazdin says, the effects of the intervention are clear if performance improves during the first intervention phase, reverts to or approaches original baseline levels of performance when the treatment is withdrawn, and improves again when treatment is recommenced in the second intervention phase.

An example of the application of the ABAB design in an educational setting is provided by Dietz (1977)[5] whose single-case study sought to measure the effect that a teacher could have upon the disruptive behaviour of an adolescent boy whose persistent talking disturbed his fellow classmates in a special education class.

In order to decrease the unwelcome behaviour, a reinforcement programme was devised in which the boy could earn extra time with the teacher by decreasing the number of times he called out. The boy was told that when he made three (or fewer) interruptions during any 55-minute class period the teacher would spend extra time working with him. In the technical language of behaviour modification theory, the pupil would receive reinforcing consequences

Box 12.2
The ABAB design

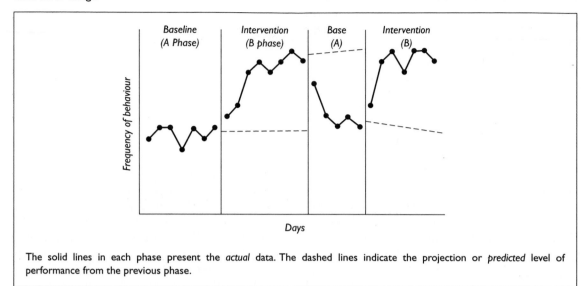

The solid lines in each phase present the *actual* data. The dashed lines indicate the projection or *predicted* level of performance from the previous phase.

Source Adapted from Kazdin, 1982

when he was able to show a low rate of disruptive behaviour (in Box 12.3 this is referred to as 'differential reinforcement of low rates' or DRL).

When the boy was able to desist from talking aloud on fewer than three occasions during any timetabled period, he was rewarded by the teacher spending fifteen minutes with him helping him with his learning tasks. The pattern of results displayed in Box 12.3 shows the considerable changes that occurred in the boy's behaviour when the intervention procedures were carried out and the substantial increases in disruptions towards baseline levels when the teacher's rewarding strategies were withdrawn. Finally, when the intervention was reinstated, the boy's behaviour is seen to improve again.

By way of conclusion, the single-case research design is uniquely able to provide an experimental technique for evaluating interventions for the individual subject. Moreover, such interventions can be directed towards the particular subject or group and replicated over time or across behaviours, situations, or persons. Single-case research

offers an alternative strategy to the more usual methodologies based on between-group designs. There are, however, a number of problems that arise in connection with the use of single-case designs having to do with ambiguities introduced by trends and variations in baseline phase data and with the generality of results from single-case research. The interested reader is directed to Kazdin (1982), Borg (1981) and Vasta (1979).[6]

Meta-analysis in educational research

The study by Bhadwal and Panda (1991) is typical of research undertaken to explore the effectiveness of classroom methods. Often as not, such studies fail to reach the light of day, particularly when they form part of the research requirements for a higher degree. Meta-analysis is, simply, the analysis of other analyses. It involves aggregating the results of other studies into a coherent account. Among the advantages of using meta-analysis, Fitz-Gibbon cites the following:

Box 12.3
An ABAB design in an educational setting

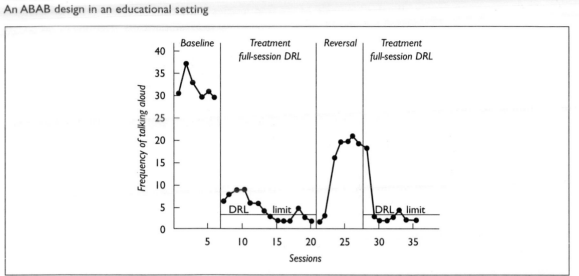

Source Kazdin, 1982

– Humble, small-scale reports which have simply been gathering dust may now become useful.

– Small-scale research conducted by individual students and lecturers will be valuable since meta-analysis provides a way of coordinating results drawn from many studies without having to co-ordinate the studies themselves.

– For historians, a whole new genre of studies is created – the study of how *effect sizes* vary over time, relating this to historical changes.

(Fitz-Gibbon, 1985: 46)

McGaw (1997: 371) suggests that *quantitative* meta-analysis replaces intuition, which is frequently reported narratively (Wood, 1995: 389), as a means of synthesizing different research studies transparently and explicitly (a *desideratum* in many synthetic studies (Jackson, 1980)), particularly when they differ very substantially. Narrative reviews, suggest Jackson (1980), Cook *et al.* (1992: 13) and Wood (1995: 390) are prone to:

- lack comprehensiveness, being selective and only going to subsets of studies;
- misrepresentation and crude representation of research findings;

- over-reliance on significance tests as a means of supporting hypotheses, thereby overlooking the point that sample size exerts a major effect on significance levels, and overlooking effect size;
- reviewers' failure to recognize that random sampling error can play a part in creating variations in findings amongst studies;
- overlook differing and conflicting research findings;
- reviewers' failure to examine critically the evidence, methods and conclusions of previous reviews;
- overlook the extent to which findings from research are mediated by the characteristics of the sample;
- overlook the importance of intervening variables in research;
- unreplicability because the procedures for integrating the research findings have not been made explicit.

Over the past few years a quantitative method for synthesizing research results has been developed by Glass *et al.* (1978; 1981) and others (e.g. Hedges and Olkin, 1985; Hedges, 1990;

Rosenthal, 1991) to supersede narrative intuition. Meta-analysis, essentially the 'analysis of analysis', is a means of quantitatively (a) identifying generalizations from a range of separate and disparate studies, and (b) discovering inadequacies in existing research such that new emphases for future research can be proposed. It is simple to use and easy to understand, though the statistical treatment that underpins it is somewhat complex. It involves the quantification and synthesis of findings from separate studies on some common measure, usually an aggregate of effect size estimates, together with an analysis of the relationship between effect size and other features of the studies being synthesized. Statistical treatments are applied to attenuate the effects of other contaminating factors, e.g. sampling error, measurement errors, and range restriction. Research findings are coded into substantive categories for generalizations to be made (Glass *et al.*, 1981), such that consistency of findings is discovered that, through the traditional means of intuition and narrative review, would have been missed.

Fitz-Gibbon (1985: 45) explains the technique by suggesting that in *meta-analysis* the effects of variables are examined in terms of their *effect size*, that is to say, in terms of *how much* difference they make rather than only in terms of whether or not the effects are statistically significant at some arbitrary level such as 5 percent. Because, with *effect sizes*, it becomes easier to concentrate on the educational significance of a finding rather than trying to assess its importance by its statistical significance, we may finally see statistical significance kept in its place as just one of many possible threats to internal validity. The move towards elevating effect size over significance levels is hugely important (see also Chapter 10), and signals an emphasis on 'fitness for purpose' (the size of the effect having to be suitable for the researcher's purposes) over arbitrary cut-off points in significance levels as determinants of utility.

The term 'meta-analysis' originated in 1976 (Glass, 1976) and early forms of meta-analysis used calculations of combined probabilities and frequencies with which results fell into defined categories (e.g. statistically significant at given levels), though problems of different sample sizes confounded rigour (e.g. large samples would yield significance in trivial effects, whilst important data from small samples would not be discovered because they failed to reach statistical significance) (Light and Smith, 1971; Glass *et al.*, 1981; McGaw, 1997: 371). Glass (1976) and Glass *et al.* (1981) suggested three levels of analysis: (a) primary analysis of the data; (b) secondary analysis, a re-analysis using different statistics; (c) meta-analysis analysing results of several studies statistically in order to integrate the findings. Glass *et al.* (1981) and Hunter *et al.* (1982) suggest several stages in the procedure:

Step 1   Identify the variables for focus (independent and dependent).

Step 2   Identify all the studies which feature the variables in which the researcher is interested.

Step 3   Code each study for those characteristics that might be predictors of outcomes and effect sizes. (e.g. age of participants, gender, ethnicity, duration of the intervention).

Step 4   Estimate the effect sizes through calculation for each pair of variables (dependent and independent variable) (see Glass, 1977), weighting the effect size by the sample size.

Step 5   Calculate the mean and the standard deviation of effect sizes across the studies, i.e. the variance across the studies.

Step 6   Determine the effects of sampling errors, measurement errors and range of restriction.

Step 7   If a large proportion of the variance is attributable to the issues in Step 6, then the average effect size can be considered an accurate estimate of relationships between variables.

Step 8   If a large proportion of the variance is not attributable to the issues in Step 6, then review those characteristics of interest which correlate with the study effects.

Cook *et al.* (1992: 7–12) set out a five stage model for an integrative review as a research process, covering:

- problem formulation (where a high quality meta-analysis must be rigorous in its attention to the design, conduct and analysis of the review);
- data collection (where sampling of studies for review has to demonstrate fitness for purpose);
- data retrieval and analysis (where threats to validity in non-experimental research – of which integrative review is an example – are addressed). Validity here must demonstrate fitness for purpose, reliability in coding, and attention to the methodological rigour of the original pieces of research;
- analysis and interpretation (where the accumulated findings of several pieces of research should be regarded as complex data points that have to be interpreted by meticulous statistical analysis).

Fitz-Gibbon (1984: 141–2) sets out four steps in conducting a meta-analysis:

Step 1 Finding studies (e.g. published, unpublished, reviews) from which effect sizes can be computed.

Step 2 Coding the study characteristics (e.g. date, publication status, design characteristics, quality of design, status of researcher).

Step 3 Measuring the effect sizes (e.g. locating the experimental group as a z-score in the control group distribution) so that outcomes can be measured on a common scale, controlling for 'lumpy data' (non-independent data from a large data set).

Step 4 Correlating effect sizes with context variables (e.g. to identify differences between well-controlled and poorly controlled studies).

Wood (1995: 393) suggests that effect-size can be calculated by dividing the significance level by the sample size. Glass et al. (1981: 29, 102) calculate the effect size as:

$$\frac{(\overline{X} \text{ of experimental group} - \overline{X} \text{ of control group})}{\text{Standard deviation of the control group}}$$

Hedges (1981) and Hunter et al., (1982) suggest alternative equations to take account of differential weightings due to sample size variations.

The two most frequently used indices of effect sizes are standardized mean differences and correlations (ibid.: 373), though nonparametric statistics, e.g. the median, can be used. Lipsey (1992: 93–100) sets out a series of statistical tests for working on effect sizes, effect size means and homogeneity. It is clear from this that Glass and others assume that meta-analysis can only be undertaken for a particular kind of research – the experimental type – rather than for all types of research; this might limit its applicability.

Glass et al. (1981) suggest that meta-analysis is particularly useful when it uses unpublished dissertations, as these often contain weaker correlations than those reported in published research, and hence act as a brake on misleading, more spectacular generalizations. Meta-analysis, it is claimed (Cooper and Rosenthal, 1980), is a means of avoiding Type II errors (discussed in Chapter 5 – failing to find effects that really exist), synthesizing research findings more rigorously and systematically, and generating hypotheses for future research. However Hedges and Olkin (1980) and Cook et al. (1992: 297) show that Type II errors become more likely as the number of studies included in the sample increases.

Further, Rosenthal (1991) has indicated a method for avoiding Type I errors (finding an effect that, in fact, does not exist) that is based on establishing how many unpublished studies that average a null result would need to be undertaken to offset the group of published statistically significant studies. For one example he shows a ratio of 277:1 of unpublished to published research, thereby indicating the limited bias in published research.

Meta-analysis is not without its critics. Since so much depends upon the quality of the results that are to be synthesized, there is the danger that adherents may simply multiply the inadequacies of the data base and the limits of the sample (e.g. trying to compare the incomparable). Hunter et al. (1982) suggest that sampling error and the influence of other factors has to be addressed, and that it should account for less than 75 per cent of the variance in observed effect sizes if the results are to be acceptable and able to be coded into categories. The issue is clear here: coding categories have to declare their level of precision, their reliability (e.g. inter-coder reliability – the equivalent of inter-rater reliability, see Chapter 5) and validity (McGaw, 1997: 376–7).

To the charge that selection bias will be as strong in meta-analysis – which embraces both published and unpublished research – as in solely published research, Glass *et al.* (1981: 226–9) argue that it is necessary to counter gross claims made in published research with more cautious claims found in unpublished research.

Because the quantitative mode of (many) studies demands only a few common variables to be measured in each case, argues Tripp (1985),[7] cumulation of the studies tends to increase sample size much more than it increases the complexity of the data in terms of the number of variables. Meta-analysis risks attempting to synthesize studies which are insufficiently similar to each other to permit this with any legitimacy (Glass *et al.*, 1981: 22; McGaw, 1997: 372) other than at an unhelpful level of generality. The analogy here might be to try to keep together oil and water as 'liquids'; meta-analysts would argue that differences between studies and their relationships to findings can be coded and addressed in meta-analysis. Eysenck (1978) suggests that early meta-evaluation studies mixed apples with oranges! Though Glass *et al.* (1981: 218–20) refute this charge, it remains the case (McGaw, 1997) that there is a risk in meta-analysis of dealing indiscriminately with a large and sometimes incoherent body of research literature.

It is unclear, too, how meta-analysis differentiates between 'good' and 'bad' research – e.g. between methodologically rigorous and poorly constructed research (Cook *et al.*, 1992: 297). Smith and Glass (1977) suggest that it is possible to use study findings, regardless of their methodological quality, though Glass and Smith (1978) and Slavin (1984a, 1984b), in a study of the effects of class size, indicate that methodological quality does make a difference. Glass *et al.* (1981: 220–6) effectively address the charge of using data from 'poor' studies, arguing, amongst other points, that many weak studies can add up to a strong conclusion (p. 221) and that the differences in the size of experimental effects between high-validity and low-validity studies are surprisingly small (p. 226).

Further, Wood (1995: 296) suggests that meta-analysis oversimplifies results by concentrating on overall effects to the neglect of the interaction of intervening variables. To the charge that, because meta-analyses are frequently conducted on large data sets where multiple results derive from the same study (i.e. that the data are non-independent) and are therefore unreliable, Glass *et al.* (1981) indicate how this can be addressed by using sophisticated data analysis techniques (pp. 153–216). Finally, a practical concern is the time required not only to use the easily discoverable studies (typically large-scale published studies) but to include the smaller-scale unpublished studies; the effect of neglecting the latter might be to build in bias in the meta-analysis.

It is the traditional pursuit of generalizations from each quantitative study which has most hampered the development of a data base adequate to reflect the complexity of the social nature of education. The cumulative effects of 'good' and 'bad' experimental studies is graphically illustrated in Box 12.4.

An example of meta-analysis in educational research

Glass and Smith (1978) and Glass *et al.* (1981: 35–44) identified seventy-seven empirical studies of the relationship between class size and pupil learning.[8] These studies yielded 725 comparisons of the achievements of smaller and larger classes, the comparisons resting on data accumulated from nearly 900,000 pupils of all ages and aptitudes studying all manner of school subjects. Using regression analysis, the 725 comparisons were integrated into a single curve showing the relationship between class size and achievement in general. This curve revealed a definite inverse relationship between class size and pupil learning. When the

Box 12.4

Class size and learning in well-controlled and poorly-controlled studies

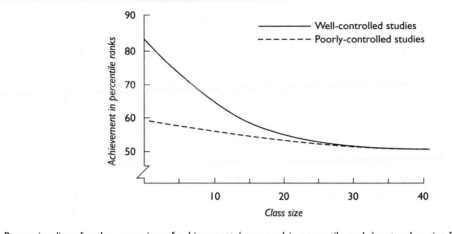

Regression lines for the regression of achievement (expressed in percentile ranks) onto class-size for studies that were well-controlled and poorly-controlled in the assignment of pupils to classes.

Source Adapted from Glass and Smith, 1978

researchers derived similar curves for a variety of circumstances that they hypothesized would alter the basic relationship (for example, grade level, subject taught, pupil ability etc.), virtually none of these special circumstances altered the basic relationship. Only one factor substantially affected the curve – whether the original study controlled adequately in the experimental sense for initial differences among pupils and teachers in smaller and larger classes. Adequate and inadequate control curves are set out in Box 12.4.[9]

13 Action research

Introduction

One of the founding figures of action research, Kurt Lewin (1948) remarked that research which produced nothing but books is inadequate. The task, as Marx suggests in his *Theses on Feuerbach*, is not merely to understand and interpret the world but to change it. Action research is a powerful tool for change and improvement at the local level. Indeed Lewin's own work was deliberately intended to change the life chances of disadvantaged groups in terms of housing, employment, prejudice, socialization, and training. Its combination of *action* and *research* has contributed to its attraction to researchers, teachers and the academic and educational community alike, demolishing Hodgkinson's (1957) corrosive criticism of action research as easy hobby games for little engineers!

The scope of action research as a method is impressive. Action research may be used in almost any setting where a problem involving people, tasks and procedures cries out for solution, or where some change of feature results in a more desirable outcome. It can be undertaken by the individual teacher, a group of teachers working co-operatively within one school, or a teacher or teachers working alongside a researcher or researchers in a sustained relationship, possibly with other interested parties like advisers, university departments and sponsors on the periphery (Holly and Whitehead, 1986). Action research can be used in a variety of areas, for example:

- *teaching methods* – replacing a traditional method by a discovery method;
- *learning strategies* – adopting an integrated approach to learning in preference to a single-subject style of teaching and learning;
- *evaluative procedures* – improving one's methods of continuous assessment;
- *attitudes and values* – encouraging more positive attitudes to work, or modifying pupils' value systems with regard to some aspect of life;
- *continuing professional development of teachers* – improving teaching skills, developing new methods of learning, increasing powers of analysis, of heightening self-awareness;
- *management and control* – the gradual introduction of the techniques of behaviour modification;
- *administration* – increasing the efficiency of some aspect of the administrative side of school life.

These examples do not mean, however, that action research can be typified straightforwardly; that is to distort its complex and multifaceted nature. Indeed Kemmis (1997) suggests that there are several schools of action research.[1]

Defining action research

The different conceptions of action research can be revealed in some typical definitions of action research, for example Hopkins (1985: 32) and Ebbutt (1985: 156) suggest that the combination of action and research renders that action a form of disciplined inquiry, in which a personal attempt is made to understand, improve and reform practice. Cohen and Manion (1994: 186) define it as 'a small-scale intervention in the

functioning of the real world and a close examination of the effects of such an intervention'.
The rigour of action research is attested by
Corey (1953: 6) who argues that it is a process in
which practitioners study problems *scientifically*
(our italics) so that they can evaluate, improve
and steer decision-making and practice. Indeed
Kemmis and McTaggart (1992: 10) argue that 'to
do action research is to plan, act, observe and
reflect more carefully, more systematically, and
more rigorously than one usually does in everyday life'.

A more philosophical stance on action
research, one that echoes the work of Habermas,
is taken by Carr and Kemmis (1986: 162), who
regard it as a form of 'self-reflective inquiry' by
participants, undertaken in order to improve
understanding of their practices in context with
a view to maximizing social justice. Grundy
(1987: 142) regards action research as concerned
with improving the 'social conditions of existence'. Kemmis and McTaggart (1992) suggest
that:

> Action research is concerned equally with chang-
> ing *individuals*, on the one hand, and, on the other,
> the *culture* of the groups, institutions and societies
> to which they belong. The culture of a group can
> be defined in terms of the characteristic substance
> and forms of the language and discourses, activities
> and practices, and social relationships and organi-
> zation which constitute the interactions of the
> group.
>
> (Kemmis and McTaggart, 1992: 16)

It can be seen that action research is designed to
bridge the gap between research and practice
(Somekh, 1995: 340), thereby striving to overcome the perceived persistent failure of research
to impact on, or improve, practice (see also
Rapoport, 1970: 499; and McCormick and
James, 1988: 339). Stenhouse (1979) suggests that
action research should contribute not only to
practice but to a theory of education and teaching which is accessible to other teachers, making
educational practice more reflective (Elliott,
1991: 54).

Action research combines diagnosis with

reflection, focusing on practical issues that have
been identified by participants and which are
somehow both problematic yet capable of being
changed (Elliott, 1978: 355–6; 1991: 49). Zuber-
Skerritt (1996b: 83) suggests that 'the aims of
any action research project or program are to
bring about practical improvement, innovation,
change or development of social practice, and
the practitioners' better understanding of their
practices'.

The several strands of action research are
drawn together by Kemmis and McTaggart
(1988) in their all-encompassing definition:

> Action research is a form of *collective* self-reflective
> inquiry undertaken by participants in social situa-
> tions in order to improve the rationality and justice
> of their own social or educational practices, as well as
> their understanding of these practices and the situ-
> ations in which these practices are carried out . . .
> The approach is only action research when it is *col-
> laborative*, though it is important to realize that the
> action research of the group is achieved through
> the *critically examined action* of individual group
> members.
>
> (Kemmis and McTaggart, 1988: 5)

Kemmis and McTaggart (1992) distinguish action
research from the everyday actions of teachers:

- It is *not* the usual thinking teachers do when
  they think about their teaching. Action
  research is more systematic and collaborative in
  collecting evidence on which to base rigorous
  group reflection.

- It is *not* simply problem-solving. Action
  research involves problem-posing, not just
  problem-solving. It does not start from a view
  of 'problems' as pathologies. It is motivated by
  a quest to improve and understand the world
  by changing it and learning how to improve it
  from the effects of the changes made.

- It is *not* research done on other people. Action
  research is research by particular people on
  their own work, to help them improve what
  they do, including how they work with and for
  others . . .

- Action research is *not* 'the scientific method'

applied to teaching. There is not just one view of 'the scientific method'; there are many.

(Kemmis and McTaggart, 1992: 21–2)

Noffke and Zeichner (1987) make several claims for action research with teachers, *viz.* that it:

- brings about changes in their definitions of their professional skills and roles;
- increases their feelings of self-worth and confidence;
- increases their awareness of classroom issues;
- improves their dispositions toward reflection;
- changes their values and beliefs;
- improves the congruence between practical theories and practices;
- broadens their views on teaching, schooling and society.

A significant feature here is that action research lays claim to the professional development of teachers; action research for professional development is a frequently heard maxim (e.g. Nixon, 1981; Oja and Smulyan, 1989; Somekh, 1995: 343; Winter, 1996). It is 'situated learning'; learning *in* the workplace and *about* the workplace (Collins and Duguid, 1989). The claims for action research, then are several. Arising from these claims and definitions are several principles.

Principles and characteristics of action research

Hult and Lennung (1980: 241–50) and McKernan (1991: 32–3) suggest that action research:

- makes for practical problem solving as well as expanding scientific knowledge;
- enhances the competencies of participants;
- is collaborative;
- is undertaken directly *in situ*;
- uses feedback from data in an ongoing cyclical process;
- seeks to understand particular complex social situations;
- seeks to understand the processes of change within social systems;

- is undertaken within an agreed framework of ethics;
- seeks to improve the quality of human actions;
- focuses on those problems that are of immediate concern to practitioners;
- is participatory;
- frequently uses case study;
- tends to avoid the paradigm of research that isolates and controls variables;
- is formative, such that the definition of the problem, the aims and methodology may alter during the process of action research;
- includes evaluation and reflection;
- is methodologically eclectic;
- contributes to a science of education;
- strives to render the research usable and shareable by participants;
- is dialogical and celebrates discourse;
- has a critical purpose in some forms;
- strives to be emancipatory.

Zuber-Skerritt (1996b: 85) suggests that action research is:

critical (and self-critical) collaborative inquiry by *reflective* practitioners being
accountable and making results of their inquiry public
self-evaluating their practice and engaged in
participatory problem-solving and continuing professional development.

This latter view is echoed in Winter's (1996: 13–14) six key principles of action research:

- *reflexive critique*, which is the process of becoming aware of our own perceptual biases;
- *dialectical critique*, which is a way of understanding the relationships between the elements that make up various phenomena in our context;
- *collaboration*, which is intended to mean that everyone's view is taken as a contribution to understanding the situation;
- *risking disturbance*, which is an understanding of our own taken-for-granted processes and willingness to submit them to critique;

- *creating plural structures*, which involves developing various accounts and critiques, rather than a single authoritative interpretation;
- *theory and practice internalized*, which is seeing theory and practice as two interdependent yet complementary phases of the change process.

The several features that the definitions at the start of this chapter have in common suggest that action research has key principles. These are summarized by Kemmis and McTaggart (1992: 22–5):

- Action research is an approach to *improving education* by *changing* it and learning from the consequences of changes.
- Action research is *participatory*: it is research through which people work towards the improvement of *their own practices* (and only secondarily on other people's practices).
- Action research develops through *the self-reflective spiral*: a spiral of cycles of *planning, acting* (implementing plans), *observing* (systematically), *reflecting* . . . and then re-planning, further implementation, observing and reflecting.
- Action research is *collaborative*: it involves those responsible for action in improving it.
- Action research establishes *self-critical communities* of people participating and collaborating in all phases of the research process: the planning, the action, the observation and the reflection; it aims to build communities of people committed to *enlightening* themselves about the relationship between circumstance, action and consequence in their own situation, and *emancipating* themselves from the institutional and personal constraints which limit their power to live their own legitimate educational and social values.
- Action research is a *systematic learning process* in which people act deliberately, though remaining open to surprises and responsive to opportunities.
- Action research involves people in *theorizing* about their practices – being *inquisitive* about

circumstances, action and consequences and coming to *understand* the relationships between circumstances, actions and consequences in their own lives.

- Action research requires that people put their practices, ideas and assumptions about institutions to the *test* by gathering *compelling evidence* which could convince them that their previous practices, ideas and assumptions were wrong or wrong-headed.
- Action research is open-minded about what counts as evidence (or data) – it involves not only *keeping records* which describe what is happening as accurately as possible . . . but also *collecting and analyzing our own judgements, reactions and impressions* about what is going on.
- Action research involves keeping a *personal journal* in which we record our progress and our reflections about two parallel sets of learning: our learnings about the practices we are studying . . . and our learnings about the process (the practice) of studying them.
- Action research is a *political process* because it involves us in making changes that will affect others.
- Action research involves people in making *critical analyses* of the situations (classrooms, schools, systems) in which they work: these situations are *structured* institutionally.
- Action research *starts small*, by working through changes which even a single person (myself) can try, and works towards extensive changes – even critiques of ideas or institutions which in turn might lead to more general reforms of classroom, school or system-wide policies and practices.
- Action research starts with *small cycles* of planning, acting, observing and reflecting which can help to define issues, ideas and assumptions more clearly so that those involved can define more *power questions* for themselves as their work progresses.
- Action research starts with *small groups* of collaborators at the start, but widens the community of participating action researchers so that it gradually includes more

and more of those involved and affected by the practices in question.

- Action research allows us to build *records* of our improvements: (a) records of our changing *activities and practices*, (b) records of the changes in the *language and discourse* in which we describe, explain and justify our practices, (c) records of the changes in the *social relationships and forms of organization* which characterize and constrain our practices, and (d) records of the development in mastery of *action research*.
- Action research allows us to give a *reasoned justification* of our educational work to others because we can show how the evidence we have gathered and the critical reflection we have done have helped us to create a *developed, tested and critically-examined rationale* for what we are doing.

Though these principles find widespread support in the literature on action research, they require some comment. For example, there is a strong emphasis in these principles on action research as a co-operative, collaborative activity (e.g. Hill and Kerber, 1967). Kemmis and McTaggart locate this in the work of Lewin himself, commenting on his commitment to group decision-making (p. 6). They argue, for example, that 'those affected by planned changes have the primary responsibility for deciding on courses of critically informed action which seem likely to lead to improvement, and for evaluating the results of strategies tried out in practice'. *Action research is a group activity* (p. 6) and that *action research is not individualistic*. To lapse into individualism is to destroy the critical dynamic of the group (p. 15) (italics in original).

The view of action research solely as a group activity, however, might be too restricting. It is possible for action research to be an individualistic matter as well, relating action research to the 'teacher-as-researcher' movement (Stenhouse 1975). Whitehead (1985: 98) explicitly writes about action research in individualistic terms, and we can take this to suggest that a teacher can ask herself or himself : 'What do I see as my

problem?' 'What do I see as a possible solution?' 'How can I direct the solution?' 'How can I evaluate the outcomes and take subsequent action?'

The adherence to action research as a group activity derives from several sources. *Pragmatically*, Oja and Smulyan (1989: 14), in arguing for collaborative action research, suggest that teachers are more likely to change their behaviours and attitudes if they have been involved in the research that demonstrates not only the need for such change but that it can be done – the issue of 'ownership' and 'involvement' that finds its parallel in management literature that suggests that those closest to the problem are in the best position to identify it and work towards its solution (e.g. Morrison, 1998).

Ideologically, there is a view that those experiencing the issue should be involved in decision-making, itself hardly surprising given Lewin's own work with disadvantaged and marginalized groups, i.e. groups with little voice. That there is a coupling of the ideological and political debate here has been brought more up to date with the work of Freire (1970) and Torres (1992: 56) in Latin America, the latter setting out several principles of participatory action research:

- It commences with explicit social and political intentions that articulate with the dominated and poor classes and groups in society.
- It must involve popular participation in the research process, i.e. it must have a social basis.
- It regards knowledge as an agent of social transformation as a whole, thereby constituting a powerful critique of those views of knowledge (theory) as somehow separate from practice.
- Its epistemological base is rooted in critical theory and its critique of the subject/object relations in research.
- It must raise the consciousness of individuals, groups, and nations.

Participatory action research recognizes a role for the researcher as facilitator, guide, formulator and summarizer of knowledge, and raiser of issues (e.g. the possible consequences of actions, the awareness of structural conditions) (Weiskopf and Laske (1996: 132–3).

What is being argued here is that action research is a democratic activity (Grundy, 1987: 142). This form of democracy is participatory (rather than, for example, representative), a key feature of critical theory (discussed below, see also Aronowitz and Giroux, 1986; Giroux, 1989). Action research is seen as an empowering activity. Elliott (1991: 54) argues that such empowerment has to be at a collective rather than individual level as individuals do not operate in isolation from each other, but are shaped by organizational and structural forces.

The issue is important, for it begins to separate action research into different camps (Kemmis, 1997: 177). On the one hand are long-time advocates of action research such as Elliott (e.g. 1978; 1991) who are in the tradition of Schwab and Schön and who emphasize reflective practice; this is a particularly powerful field of curriculum research with notions of the 'teacher-as-researcher' (Stenhouse, 1975, and the reflective practitioner, Schön, 1983, 1987). On the other are advocates in the 'critical' action research model, e.g. Carr and Kemmis (1986).

Action research as critical praxis

Much of the writing in this field of action research draws on the Frankfurt School of critical theory (discussed in Chapter 1), in particular the work of Habermas. Indeed Weiskopf and Laske (1996: 123) locate action research, in the German tradition, squarely as a 'critical social science'. Using Habermas's early writing on knowledge-constitutive interests (1972, 1974) a three-fold typification of action research can be constructed; the classification was set out in Chapter 1.

Grundy (1987: 154) argues that 'technical' action research is designed to render an existing situation more efficient and effective. In this respect it is akin to Argyris's notion of 'single-loop learning' (Argyris, 1990), being functional, often short-term and technical. It is akin to Schön's (1987) notion of 'reflection-in-action'

(Morrison, 1995a). Elliott (1991: 55) suggests that this view is limiting for action research since it is too individualistic and neglects wider curriculum structures, regarding teachers in isolation from wider factors.

By contrast, 'practical' action research is designed to promote teachers' professionalism by drawing on their informed judgement (Grundy, 1987: 154). It is akin to Schön's 'reflection-on-action' and is a hermeneutic activity of understanding and interpreting social situations with a view to their improvement. Grundy suggests (p. 148) that it is this style that characterizes much action research in the UK.

Emancipatory action research has an explicit agenda which is as political as it is educational. Grundy (1987) provides a useful introduction to this view. She argues (pp. 146–7) that emancipatory action research seeks to develop in participants their understandings of illegitimate structural and interpersonal constraints that are preventing the exercise of their autonomy and freedom. These constraints, she argues, are based on illegitimate repression, domination and control. When participants develop a consciousness of these constraints, she suggests, they begin to move from unfreedom and constraint to freedom, autonomy and social justice.

Action research, then, aims to empower individuals and social groups to take control over their lives within a framework of the promotion, rather than the suppression of generalizable interests (Habermas, 1976). It commences with a challenge to the illegitimate operation of power, hence in some respects (albeit more politicized because it embraces the dimension of power) it is akin to Argyris's (1990) notion of 'double-loop learning' in that it requires participants to question and challenge given value systems. For Grundy, praxis fuses theory and practice within an egalitarian social order, and action research is designed with the political agenda of improvement towards a more just, egalitarian society. This accords to some extent with Lewin's view that action research leads to equality and co-operation, an end to exploitation and the furtherance of democracy (see also Hopkins, 1985:

32; Carr and Kemmis, 1986: 163). Zuber-Skerritt (1996a) suggests that:

> emancipatory action research . . . is collaborative, critical and self-critical inquiry by practitioners . . . into a major problem or issue or concern in their own practice. They own the problem and feel responsible and accountable for solving it through teamwork and through following a cyclical process of:
>
> 1 strategic *planning*;
> 2 *action*, i.e. implementing the plan;
> 3 *observation*, evaluation and self-evaluation;
> 4 critical and self-critical *reflection* on the results of points 1–3 and making decisions for the next cycle of action research.
>
> Zuber-Skerritt (1996a: 3)

Action research, she argues (p. 5) is *emancipatory* when it aims not only at technical and practical improvement and the participants' better understanding, along with transformation and change within the existing boundaries and conditions, but also at changing the system itself or those conditions which impede desired improvement in the system/organization . . . There is no hierarchy, but open and 'symmetrical communication'.

The emancipatory interest is based on the notion of action researchers as participants in a community of equals. This, in turn is premised on Habermas's notion of the 'ideal speech situation' which can be summarized thus (Morrison, 1996b: 171):

- orientation to a common interest ascertained without deception;
- freedom to enter a discourse and equal opportunity for discussion;
- freedom to check questionable claims and evaluate explanations;
- freedom to modify a given conceptual framework;
- freedom to reflect on the nature of knowledge;
- freedom to allow commands or prohibitions to enter discourse when they can no longer be taken for granted;

- freedom to assess justifications;
- freedom to alter norms;
- freedom to reflect on the nature of political will;
- mutual understanding between participants;
- recognition of the legitimacy of each subject to participate in the dialogue as an autonomous and equal partner;
- discussion to be free from domination and distorting or deforming influences;
- the consensus resulting from discussion derives from the force of the better argument alone, and not from the positional power of the participants;
- all motives except the co-operative search for truth are excluded;
- the speech act validity claims of truth, legitimacy, sincerity and comprehensibility are all addressed.

This formidable list, characterized, perhaps, by the opacity of Habermas's language itself (see Morrison, 1995b) is problematical, though this will not be discussed in this volume (for a full analysis of this see Morrison (1995b)). What is important to note, perhaps, is that:

- action research here is construed as reflective practice with a political agenda;
- all participants (and action research is participatory) are equal 'players';
- action research, in this vein, is necessarily dialogical – interpersonal – rather than monological (individual); and
- communication is an intrinsic element, with communication being amongst the community of equals (Grundy and Kemmis, 1988: 87, term this 'symmetrical communication');
- because it is a community of equals, action research is necessarily democratic and promotes democracy;
- that the search is for consensus (and consensus requires more than one participant), hence it requires collaboration and participation.

In this sense emancipatory action research fulfils the requirements of action research set out by Kemmis and McTaggart above; indeed it could be argued that *only* emancipatory action research (in the three-fold typology) has the potential to do this.

Kemmis (1997: 177) suggests that the distinction between the two camps (the reflective practitioners and the critical theorists) lies in their interpretation of action research. For the former, action research is an improvement to professional practice at the local, perhaps classroom level, within the capacities of individuals and the situations in which they are working; for the latter, action research is part of a broader agenda of changing education, changing schooling and changing society.

A key term in action research is 'empowerment'; for the former camp, empowerment is largely a matter of the professional sphere of operations, achieving professional autonomy through professional development. For the latter, empowerment concerns taking control over one's life within a just, egalitarian, democratic society. Whether the latter is realizable or utopian is a matter of critique of this view. Where is the evidence that critical action research either empowers groups or alters the macro-structures of society? Is critical action research socially transformative? At best the jury is out; at worst the jury simply has gone away as capitalism overrides egalitarianism worldwide. The point at issue here is the extent to which the notion of emancipatory action research has attempted to hijack the action research agenda, and whether, in so doing (if it has), it has wrested action research away from practitioners and into the hands of theorists and the academic research community only.

More specifically, several criticisms have been levelled at this interpretation of emancipatory action research (Gibson, 1985; Morrison, 1995a, 1995b; Somekh, 1995; Melrose, 1996; Grundy, 1996; Weiskopf and Laske, 1996; Webb, 1996; McTaggart, 1996; Kemmis, 1997), including the views that:

- it is utopian and unrealizable;
- it is too controlling and prescriptive, seeking to capture and contain action research within

a particular mould – it moves towards conformity;
- it adopts a narrow and particularistic view of emancipation and action research, and how to undertake the latter;
- it undermines the significance of the individual teacher-as-researcher in favour of self-critical communities. Kemmis and McTaggart (1992: 152) pose the question 'why *must* action research consist of a *group* process?';
- the three-fold typification of action research is untenable;
- it assumes that rational consensus is achievable, that rational debate will empower all participants (i.e. it understates the issue of power, wherein the most informed are already the most powerful – Grundy (1996: 111) argues that the better argument derives from the one with the most evidence and reasons, and that these are more available to the powerful, thereby rendering the conditions of equality suspect);
- it overstates the desirability of consensus-oriented research (which neglects the complexity of power);
- power cannot be dispersed or rearranged simply by rationality;
- action research as critical theory reduces its practical impact and confines it to the commodification of knowledge in the academy;
- is uncritical and self-contradicting;
- will promote conformity through slavishly adhering to its orthodoxies;
- is naïve in its understanding of groups and celebrates groups over individuals, particularly the 'in-groups' rather than the 'out-groups';
- privileges its own view of science (rejecting objectivity) and lacks modesty;
- privileges the authority of critical theory;
- is elitist whilst purporting to serve egalitarianism;
- assumes an undifferentiated view of action research;
- is attempting to colonize and redirect action research.

This seemingly devastating critique serves to remind the reader that critical action research, even though it has caught the high ground of recent coverage, is highly problematical. It is just as controlling as those controlling agendas that it seeks to attack (Morrison, 1995b). Indeed Melrose (1996: 52) suggests that, because critical research is, itself, value laden it abandons neutrality; it has an explicit social agenda that, under the guise of examining values, ethics, morals and politics that are operating in a particular situation, is actually aimed at transforming the *status quo*.

Procedures for action research

Nixon offers several principles for considering action research in schools (Box 13.1). There are several ways in which the steps of action research have been analysed. Blum (National Education Association of the United States, 1959) casts action research into two simple stages: a diagnostic stage in which the problems are analysed and the hypotheses developed; and a therapeutic stage in which the hypotheses are tested by a consciously directed intervention or experiment *in situ*. Lewin (1946, 1948) codified the action research process into four main stages: planning, acting, observing and reflecting.

He suggests that action research commences with a general idea and data are sought about the presenting situation. The successful outcome of this examination is the production of a plan of action to reach an identified objective, together with a decision on the first steps to be taken. Lewin acknowledges that this might involve modifying the original plan or idea. The next stage of implementation is accompanied by ongoing fact-finding to monitor and evaluate the intervention, i.e. to act as a formative evaluation. This feeds forward into a revised plan and set of procedures for implementation, themselves accompanied by monitoring and evaluation. Lewin (1948: 205) suggests that such 'rational social management' can be conceived of as a spiral of planning, action and fact-finding about the outcomes of the actions taken.

Box 13.1
Action research in classroom and school

1   All teachers possess certain skills which can contribute to the research task. The important thing is to clarify and define one's own particular set of skills. Some teachers, for example, are able to collect and interpret statistical data; others to record in retrospective accounts the key moments of a lesson. One teacher may know something about questionnaire design; another have a natural flair for interviewing. It is essential that teachers work from their own particular strengths when developing the research.

2   The situations within which teachers work impose different kinds of constraints. Some schools, for example, are equipped with the most up-to-date audio-visual equipment, others cannot even boast a cassette tape-recorder. Some have spare rooms in which interviews could be carried out, others hardly have enough space to implement the existing time-table. Action research must be designed in such a way as to be easily implemented within the pattern of constraints existing within the school.

3   Any initial definition of the research problem will almost certainly be modified as the research proceeds. Nevertheless, this definition is important because it helps to set limits to the inquiry. If, for example, a teacher sets out to explore through action research the problem of how to start a lesson effectively, the research will tend to focus upon the first few minutes of the lesson. The question of what data to collect is very largely answered by a clear definition of the research problem.

Source Nixon, 1981

The legacy of Lewin's work, though contested (e.g. Elliott, 1978, 1991; McTaggart, 1996: 248) is powerful in the steps of action research set out by Kemmis and McTaggart (1981: 2):

> In practice, the process begins with a *general idea* that some kind of improvement or change is desirable. In deciding just where to begin in making improvements, one decides on a *field of action* . . . where the battle (not the whole war) should be fought. It is a decision on where it is possible to have an impact. The general idea prompts a '*reconnaissance*' of the circumstances of the field, and fact-finding about them. Having decided on the

field and made a preliminary reconnaissance, the action researcher decides on a *general plan* of action. Breaking the general plan down into achievable steps, the action researcher settles on the *first action step*. Before taking this first step the action researcher becomes more circumspect, and devises a way of *monitoring* the effects of the first action step. When it is possible to maintain fact-finding by monitoring the action, the first step is taken. As the step is implemented, new data start coming in and the effect of the action can be described and *evaluated*. The general plan is then revised in the light of the new information about the field of action and the second action step can be planned along with appropriate monitoring procedures. The second step is then implemented, monitored and evaluated; and the spiral of action, monitoring, evaluation and replanning continues.

McKernan (1991: 17) suggests that Lewin's model of action research is a series of spirals, each of which incorporates a cycle of analysis, reconnaissance, reconceptualization of the problem, planning of the intervention, implementation of the plan, evaluation of the effectiveness of the intervention. Ebbutt (1985) adds to this the view that feedback within and between each cycle is important, facilitating reflection (see also McNiff, 1988). This is reinforced in the model of action research by Altricher and Gstettner (1993) where, though they have four steps (p. 343): (a) finding a starting point, (b) clarifying the situation, (c) developing action strategies and putting them into practice, (d) making teachers' knowledge public – they suggest that steps (b) and (c) need not be sequential, thereby avoiding the artificial divide that might exist between data collection, analysis and interpretation.

Zuber-Skerritt (1996b: 84) sets emancipatory (critical) action research into a cyclical process of: '(1) strategic planning, (2) implementing the plan (action), (3) observation, evaluation and self-evaluation, (4) critical and self-critical reflection on the results of (1)–(3) and making decisions for the next cycle of research'. In an imaginative application of action research to organizational change theory she takes the

famous work of Lewin (1952) on forcefield analysis and change theory (unfreezing → moving → refreezing) and the work of Beer *et al.* (1990) on task alignment, and sets them into an action research sequence that clarifies the steps of action research very usefully (Box 13.2).

In our earlier editions we set out an eight-stage process of action research that attempts to draw together the several strands and steps of the action research undertaking. The first stage will involve the identification, evaluation and formulation of the problem perceived as critical in an everyday teaching situation. 'Problem' should be interpreted loosely here so that it could refer to the need to introduce innovation into some aspect of a school's established programme.

The second stage involves preliminary discussion and negotiations among the interested parties – teachers, researchers, advisers, sponsors, possibly – which may culminate in a draft proposal. This may include a statement of the questions to be answered (e.g. 'Under what conditions can curriculum change be best effected?' 'What are the limiting factors in bringing about effective curriculum change?' 'What strong points of action research can be employed to bring about curriculum change?'). The researchers in their capacity as consultants (or sometimes as programme initiators) may draw upon their expertise to bring the problem more into focus, possibly determining causal factors or recommending alternative lines of approach to established ones. This is often the crucial stage for, unless the objectives, purposes and assumptions are made perfectly clear to all concerned, and unless the role of key concepts is stressed (e.g. feedback), the enterprise can easily miscarry.

The third stage may involve a review of the research literature to find out what can be learned from comparable studies, their objectives, procedures and problems encountered.

The fourth stage may involve a modification or redefinition of the initial statement of the problem at stage one. It may now emerge in the form of a testable hypothesis; or as a set of guiding objectives. Sometimes change agents deliberately

Box 13.2
A model of emancipatory action research for organizational change

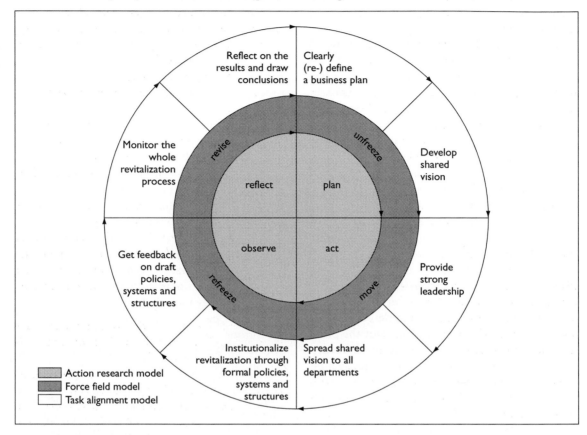

Reflect on the results and draw conclusions

Clearly (re-) define a business plan

Monitor the whole revitalization process

Develop shared vision

revise

unfreeze

reflect

plan

observe

act

Get feedback on draft policies, systems and structures

Provide strong leadership

refreeze

move

Institutionalize revitalization through formal policies, systems and structures

Spread shared vision to all departments

Action research model
Force field model
Task alignment model

Source Zuber-Skerritt, 1996b: 99

decide against the use of objectives on the grounds that they have a constraining effect on the process itself. It is also at this stage that assumptions underlying the project are made explicit (e.g. in order to effect curriculum changes, the attitudes, values, skills and objectives of the teachers involved must be changed).

The fifth stage may be concerned with the selection of research procedures – sampling, administration, choice of materials, methods of teaching and learning, allocation of resources and tasks, deployment of staff and so on.

The sixth stage will be concerned with the choice of the evaluation procedures to be used and will need to take into consideration that evaluation in this context will be continuous.

The seventh stage embraces the implementation of the project itself (over varying periods of time). It will include the conditions and methods of data collection (e.g. fortnightly meetings, the keeping of records, interim reports, final reports, the submission of self-evaluation and group-evaluation reports, etc.); the monitoring of tasks and the transmission of feedback to the research team; and the classification and analysis of data.

The eighth and final stage will involve the interpretation of the data; inferences to be drawn; and overall evaluation of the project (see Woods, 1989). Discussions on the findings will take place in the light of previously agreed evaluative criteria. Errors, mistakes and problems will be considered. A general summing-up may follow this, in which the outcomes of the project are reviewed, recommendations made, and arrangements for dissemination of results to interested parties decided.

As we stressed, this is a basic framework; much activity of an incidental and possibly *ad hoc* nature will take place in and around it. This may comprise discussions among teachers, researchers and pupils; regular meetings among teachers or schools to discuss progress and problems, and to exchange information; possibly regional conferences; and related activities, all enhanced by the range of current hardware – tapes, video recordings and transcripts.

Hopkins (1985), McNiff (1988), Edwards (1990) and McNiff, Lomax and Whitehead (1996) offer much practical advice on the conduct of action research, including 'getting started', operationalization, planning, monitoring and documenting the intervention, collecting data and making sense of them, using case studies, evaluating the action research, ethical issues and reporting. We urge readers to go to these helpful sources. These are essentially both introductory sources and manuals for practice.

Kemmis and McTaggart (1992: 25–7) offer a useful series of observations for beginning action research:

- Get an action research group together and *participate* yourself – be a model learner about action research.
- Be content to start to work with a *small group*.
- *Get organized.*
- *Start small.*
- *Establish a time line.*
- Arrange for *supportive work-in-progress discussions* in the action research group.
- Be tolerant and supportive – expect people to learn from experience.
- Be persistent about monitoring.
- Plan for a long haul on the bigger issues of changing classroom practices and school structures.
- Work to involve (in the research process) those who are involved (in the action), so

that they share responsibility for the whole action research process.
- Remember that *how you think about things* – the language and understandings that shape your action – may need changing just as much as the specifics of what you do.
- *Register progress* not only with the participant group but also with the whole staff and other interested people.
- If necessary arrange *legitimizing rituals* – involving consultants or other outsiders.
- Make time to *write* throughout your project.
- Be explicit about what you have achieved by *reporting progress*.
- Throughout, keep in mind *the distinction between education and schooling*.
- Throughout, ask yourself whether your action research project is helping you (and those with whom you work) to improve the extent to which you are *living your educational values* (italics in original).

It is clear from this list that action research is a blend of practical and theoretical concerns, it is both action and research.

In conducting action research the participants can be both methodologically eclectic and can use a variety of instruments for data collection: questionnaires, diaries, interviews, case studies, observational data, experimental design, field notes, photography, audio and video recording, sociometry, rating scales, biographies and accounts, documents and records, in short the full *gamut* of techniques (for a discussion of these, see Hopkins, 1985; McKernan, 1991, and the chapters in our own book here).

Additionally a useful way of managing to gain a focus within a group of action researchers is through the use of Nominal Group Technique (Morrison, 1993). The administration is straightforward and is useful for gathering information in a single instance. In this approach one member of the group provides the group with a series of questions, statements or issues. A four-stage model can be adopted:

Stage 1 A short time is provided for individuals to write down without interruption or discussion with anybody else their own answers, views, reflections and opinions in response to questions/statements/issues provided by the group leader (e.g. problems of teaching or organizing such-and-such, or an identification of issues in the organization of a piece of the curriculum etc.).

Stage 2   The responses are entered onto a sheet of paper which is then displayed for others to view. The leader invites *individual* comments on the displayed responses to the questions/statements/issue, but no group discussion, i.e. the data collection is still at an individual level, and then notes these comments on the display sheet on which the responses have been collected. The process of inviting individual comments/contributions which are then displayed for everyone to see is repeated until no more comments are received.

Stage 3   At this point the leader asks the respondents to identify *clusters* of displayed comments and responses, i.e. to put some structure, order and priority into the displayed items. It is here that control of proceedings moves from the leader to the participants. A group discussion takes place since a process of clarification of meanings and organizing issues and responses into coherent and cohesive bundles is required which then moves to the identification of priorities.

Stage 4   Finally the leader invites any further group discussion about the material and its organization.

The process of the Nominal Group Technique enables individual responses to be included within a group response, i.e. the individual's contribution to the group delineation of significant issues is maintained. This technique is very useful in gathering data from individuals and putting them into some order which is shared by the group (and action research is largely, though not exclusively, a group matter), e.g. of priority, of similarity and difference, of generality and specificity. It also enables individual disagreements to be registered and to be built into the group responses and identification of significant issues to emerge. Further, it gives equal status to all respondents in the situation, for example, the voice of the new entrant to the teaching profession is given equal consideration to the voice of the headteacher of several years' experience. The attraction of this process is that it balances writing with discussion, a divergent phase with a convergent phase, space for individual comments and contributions to group interaction. It is a useful device for developing collegiality. All participants have a voice and are heard.

The written partner to the Nominal Group Technique is the Delphi technique. This has the advantage that it does not *require* participants to meet together as a whole group. This is particularly useful in institutions where time is precious and where it is difficult to arrange a whole group meeting. The process of data collection resembles that of the nominal group technique in many respects: it can be set out in a three-stage process:

Stage 1   The leader asks participants to respond to a series of questions and statements in writing. This may be done on an individual basis or on a small group basis – which enables it to be used flexibly, e.g. within a department, within an age phase.

Stage 2   The leader collects the written responses and collates them into clusters of issues and responses (maybe providing some numerical data on frequency of response). This analysis is then passed back to the respondents for comment, further discussion and identification of issues, responses and priorities. At this stage the respondents are presented with a *group response* (which may reflect similarities or record differences) and the respondents are asked to react to this *group response*. By adopting this procedure the individual has the opportunity to agree with the group response (i.e. to move from a possibly small private individual disagreement to a general group agreement) or to indicate a more substantial disagreement with the group response.

Stage 3   This process is repeated as many times as it is necessary. In saying this, however, the leader will need to identify the most appropriate place to stop the re-circulation of responses. This might be done at a group meeting which, it is envisaged, will be the plenary session for the participants, i.e. an endpoint of data collection will be in a whole group forum.

By presenting the group response back to the participants, there is a general progression in the technique towards a polarizing of responses, i.e. a clear identification of areas of consensus and dissensus (and emancipatory action research strives for consensus). The Delphi technique brings advantages of clarity, privacy, voice and collegiality. In doing so it engages the issues of confidentiality, anonymity and disclosure of relevant information whilst protecting participants' rights to privacy. It is a very useful means of undertaking behind-the-scenes data collection which can then be brought to a whole group meeting; the price that this exacts is that the leader has much more work to do in collecting, synthesizing, collating, summarizing, prioritizing and re-circulating data than in the Nominal Group Technique, which is immediate. As participatory techniques both the Nominal Group Technique and Delphi techniques are valuable for data collection and analysis in action research. A fully worked example of the use of Delphi techniques for an international study is Cogan and Derricot (1998), a study of citizenship education.

Reflexivity in action research

The analysis so far has made much of the issue of reflection, be it reflection-in-action, reflection-on-action, or critical reflection (Morrison, 1995a). Reflection, it has been argued, occurs at every stage of action research. Beyond this, the notion of *reflexivity* is central to action research, because the researchers are also the participants and practitioners in the action research – they are part of the social world that they are studying (Hammersley and Atkinson, 1983: 14). Hall (1996: 29) suggests that reflexivity is an integral element and epistemological basis of emancipatory action research because it takes as its pre-

miss the view of the construction of knowledge in which: (a) data are authentic and reflect the experiences of all participants; (b) democratic relations exist between all participants in the research; the researcher's views (which may be theory-laden) do not hold precedence over the views of participants.

What is being required in the notion of reflexivity is a self-conscious awareness of the effects that the participants-as-practitioners-and-researchers are having on the research process, how their values, attitudes, perceptions, opinions, actions, feelings etc. are feeding into the situation being studied (akin, perhaps, to the notion of counter-transference in counselling). The participants-as-practitioners-and-researchers need to apply to themselves the same critical scrutiny that they are applying to others and to the research. This issue is discussed in Chapter 5.

Some practical and theoretical matters

Much has been made in this chapter of the democratic principles that underpin a considerable amount of action research. The ramifications of this are several. For example, there must be a free flow of information between participants and communication must be extensive (Elliott, 1978: 356) and, echoing the notion of the ideal speech situation discussed earlier, communication must be open, unconstrained and unconstraining – the force of the better argument. That this might be problematic in some organizations has been noted by Holly (1984: 100), as action research and schools are often structured differently, schools being hierarchical, formal and bureaucratic whilst action research is collegial, informal, open, collaborative and crosses formal boundaries. In turn this suggests that, for action research to be successful, the conditions of collegiality have to be present, for example (Morrison, 1998: 157–8):

- participatory approaches to decision-making;
- democratic and consensual decision-making;
- shared values, beliefs and goals;

- equal rights of participation in discussion;
- equal rights to determine policy;
- equal voting rights on decisions;
- the deployment of sub-groups who are accountable to the whole group;
- shared responsibility and open accountability;
- an extended view of expertise;
- judgements and decisions based on the power of the argument rather than the positions power of the advocates;
- shared ownership of decisions and practices.

It is interesting, perhaps, that these features, derived from management theory, can apply so well to action research – action research nests comfortably within certain management styles. Indeed Zuber-Skerritt (1996b: 90) suggests that the main barriers to emancipatory action research are: (a) single-loop learning (rather than double-loop learning (Argyris, 1990)); (b) overdependence on experts or seniors to the extent that independent thought and expression are stifled; (c) an orientation to efficiency rather than to research and development (one might add here 'rather than to reflection and problem posing'); (d) a preoccupation with operational rather than strategic thinking and practice.

Zuber-Skerritt (1996a: 17) suggests four practical problems that action researchers might face:

- How can we formulate a method of work which is sufficiently economical as regards the amount of data gathering and data processing for a practitioner to undertake it alongside a normal workload, over a limited time scale?
- How can action research techniques be sufficiently specific that they enable a small-scale investigation by a practitioner to lead to genuinely new insights, and avoid being accused of being either too minimal to be valid, or too elaborate to be feasible?
- How can these methods, given the above, be readily available and accessible to anyone who wishes to practise them, building on the competencies which practitioners already possess?
- How can these methods contribute a genuine improvement of understanding and skill,

beyond prior competence, in return for the time and energy expended – that is, a more rigorous process than that which characterizes positivist research?

She also suggests that the issue of the audience of action research reports is problematic:

> The answer to the question 'who are action research reports written for?' is that there are three audiences – each of equal importance. One audience comprises those colleagues with whom we have collaborated in carrying out the research reported ... It is important to give equal importance to the second audience. These are interested colleagues in other institutions, or in other areas of the same institution, for whom the underlying structure of the work presented may be similar to situations in which they work ... But the third, and perhaps most important audience, is ourselves. The process of writing involves clarifying and exploring ideas and interpretations (p. 26).
>
> Action research reports, argues Somekh (1995: 347), unlike many 'academic' papers, are typically written in the first person, indeed, she argues, not to do so is hard to defend (given, perhaps, the significance of participation, collaboration, reflexivity and individuality). They have to be written in the everyday, commonsense language of the participants.
>
> (Elliott, 1978: 356)

We have already seen that the participants in a change situation may be either a teacher, a group of teachers working internally, or else teachers and researchers working on a collaborative basis. It is this last category, where action research brings together two professional bodies each with its own objectives and values, that we shall consider further at this point because of its inherent problematic nature. Both parties share the same interest in an educational problem, yet their respective orientations to it differ. It has been observed (Halsey, 1972, for instance) that research values precision, control, replication and attempts to generalize from specific events. Teaching, on the other hand, is concerned with action, with doing things, and translates generalizations into specific acts. The incompatibility between action and research in these respects, therefore, can be a source of problems (Marris and Rein, 1967).

Another issue of some consequence concerns headteachers' and teachers' attitudes to the possibility of change as a result of action research. Hutchinson and Whitehouse (1986), for example, having monitored teachers' efforts to form collaborative groups within their schools, discovered one source of difficulty to be not only resistance from heads but also, and in their view more importantly, from some teachers themselves to the action researcher's efforts to have them scrutinize individual and social practice, possibly with a view to changing it, e.g. in line with the head teacher's policies.

Finally, Winter draws attention to the problem of interpreting data in action research. He writes:

> The action research/case study tradition does have a methodology for the *creation* of data, but not (as yet) for the interpretation of data. We are shown how the descriptive journal, the observer's field notes, and the open-ended interview are utilized to create accounts of events which will *confront* the practitioner's current pragmatic assumptions and definitions; we are shown the potential value of this process (in terms of increasing teachers' sensitivity) and the problem it poses for individual and collective professional equilibrium. What we are *not* shown is *how* the teacher can or should handle the data thus collected.
>
> (Winter, 1982)

The problem for Winter is how to carry out an interpretive analysis of restricted data, that is, data which can make no claim to be generally representative. In other words, the problem of validity cannot be side-stepped by arguing that the contexts are unique.

Conclusion

Action research is an expanding field which is commanding significant education attention and which has its own centres (e.g. at the Universities of Cambridge and East Anglia in the UK and Deakin University in Australia) and its own journals (e.g. *Educational Action Research*). It has been seen as a significant vehicle for empowering teachers, though this chapter has questioned the extent of this. As a research device it combines six notions:

1 a straightforward cycle of: identifying a problem, planning an intervention, implementing the intervention, evaluating the outcome;
2 reflective practice;
3 political emancipation;
4 critical theory;
5 professional development; and
6 participatory practitioner research.

It is a flexible, situationally responsive methodology that offers rigour, authenticity and voice. That said, this chapter has tried to expose both the attractions and problematic areas of action research. In its thrust towards integrating action and research one has to question whether this is an optimistic way of ensuring that research impacts on practice for improvement, or whether it is a recessive hybrid.

Part four

Strategies for data collection and researching

This section moves to a closer-grained account of instruments for collecting data, how they can be used, and how they can be constructed. We identify eight kinds of instrument for data collection in what follows, and have expanded on the previous edition of the book by new chapters on testing (including recent developments in item response theory and computer-adaptive testing), questionnaire design and observation, together with material on focus groups, statistical significance, multilevel modelling, laddering in personal constructs, telephone interviewing, and speech act theory (echoing elements of critical theory that were introduced in Part One).

The intention of this part is to enable researchers to decide on the most appropriate instruments for data collection, and to design such instruments. The strengths and weaknesses of these instruments are set out, so that decisions on their suitability avoid being arbitrary and the criterion of fitness for purpose is held high. To that end, the intention is to introduce underlying issues of principle in instrumentation as well as to ensure that practical guidelines are provided for researchers. For each instrument the purpose is to ensure that researchers can devise appropriate data collection instruments for themselves, and are aware of the capabilities of such instruments to provide useful and usable data.

14 Questionnaires

The field of questionnaire design is vast, and this chapter is intended to provide a straightforward introduction to its key elements, indicating the main issues to be addressed, some important problematical considerations and how they can be resolved. The chapter follows a sequence in designing a questionnaire that, it is hoped, will be useful for researchers. The sequence is:

ethical issues;
approaching the planning of a questionnaire;
operationalizing the questionnaire;
structured, semi-structured and unstructured questionnaires;
avoiding pitfalls in question writing;
dichotomous questions;
multiple choice questions;
rank ordering;
rating scales;
open-ended questions;
asking sensitive questions;
sequencing the questions;
questionnaires containing few verbal items;
the layout of the questionnaire;
covering letters/sheets and follow-up letters;
piloting the questionnaire;
practical considerations in questionnaire design;
postal questionnaires;
processing questionnaire data.

It is suggested that the researcher may find it useful to work through these issues in sequence, though, clearly, a degree of recursion is desirable.

The questionnaire is a widely used and useful instrument for collecting survey information, providing structured, often numerical data,

being able to be administered without the presence of the researcher, and often being comparatively straightforward to analyze (Wilson and McLean, 1994).[1] These attractions have to be counterbalanced by the time taken to develop, pilot and refine the questionnaire, by the possible unsophistication and limited scope of the data that are collected, and from the likely limited flexibility of response, though, as Wilson and McLean (ibid.: 3) observe, this can frequently be an attraction. The researcher will have to judge the appropriateness of using a questionnaire for data collection, and, if so, what kind of questionnaire it will be.

Ethical issues

The questionnaire will always be an intrusion into the life of the respondent, be it in terms of time taken to complete the questionnaire, the level of threat or sensitivity of the questions, or the possible invasion of privacy. Questionnaire respondents are not passive data providers for researchers; they are subjects not objects of research. There are several sequiturs that flow from this.

Respondents cannot be coerced into completing a questionnaire. They might be strongly encouraged, but the decision whether to become involved and when to withdraw from the research is entirely theirs. Their involvement in the research is likely to be a function of:

- their *informed consent* (see Chapter 2 on the ethics of educational research);
- their *rights to withdraw* at any stage or *not*

to complete particular items in the questionnaire;

- the potential of the research to improve their situation (the issue of *beneficence*);
- the guarantees that the research will not harm them (the issue of *non-maleficence*);
- the guarantees of *confidentiality, anonymity* and *non-traceability* in the research;
- the degree of *threat* or *sensitivity* of the questions (which may lead to respondents' over-reporting or under-reporting (Sudman and Bradburn, 1982: 32 and Chapter 3);
- factors in the questionnaire itself (e.g. its coverage of issues, its ability to catch what respondents want to say rather than to promote the researcher's agenda), i.e. the avoidance of bias and the assurance of validity and reliability in the questionnaire – the issues of *methodological rigour and fairness*. Methodological rigour is an ethical, not simply a technical, matter (Morrison, 1996c), and respondents have a right to expect reliability and validity;
- the *reactions* of the respondent, for example respondents will react if they consider an item to be offensive, intrusive, misleading, biased, misguided, irritating, inconsiderate, impertinent or abstruse.

These factors impact on every stage of the use of a questionnaire, to suggest that attention has to be given to the questionnaire itself, the approaches that are made to the respondents, the explanations that are given to the respondents, the data analysis and the data reporting.

Approaching the planning of a questionnaire

At this preliminary stage of design, it can sometimes be helpful to use a flow chart technique to plan the sequencing of questions. In this way, researchers are able to anticipate the type and range of responses that their questions are likely to elicit. In Box 14.1 we illustrate a flow chart employed in a commercial survey based upon an interview schedule, though the application of the method to a self-completion questionnaire is self-evident.

Operationalizing the questionnaire

The process of operationalizing a questionnaire is to take a general purpose or set of purposes and turn these into concrete, researchable fields about which actual data can be gathered. Firstly, a questionnaire's general purposes must be clarified and then translated into a specific, concrete aim or set of aims. Thus, 'to explore teachers' views about in-service work' is somewhat nebulous, whereas 'to obtain a detailed description of primary and secondary teachers' priorities in the provision of in-service education courses' is reasonably specific.

Having decided upon and specified the primary objective of the questionnaire, the second phase of the planning involves the identification and itemizing of subsidiary topics that relate to its central purpose. In our example, subsidiary issues might well include: the types of courses required; the content of courses; the location of courses; the timing of courses; the design of courses; and the financing of courses.

The third phase follows the identification and itemization of subsidiary topics and involves formulating specific information requirements relating to each of these issues. For example, with respect to the type of courses required, detailed information would be needed about the duration of courses (one meeting, several meetings, a week, a month, a term or a year), the status of courses (non-award bearing, award bearing, with certificate, diploma, degree granted by college or university), the orientation of courses (theoretically oriented involving lectures, readings, etc., or practically oriented involving workshops and the production of curriculum materials).

What we have in the example, then, is a move from a generalized area of interest or purpose to a very specific set of features about which direct data can be gathered. Wilson and McLean (ibid.: 8–9) suggest an alternative approach which is to identify the research prob-

Box 14.1
A flow chart technique for question planning

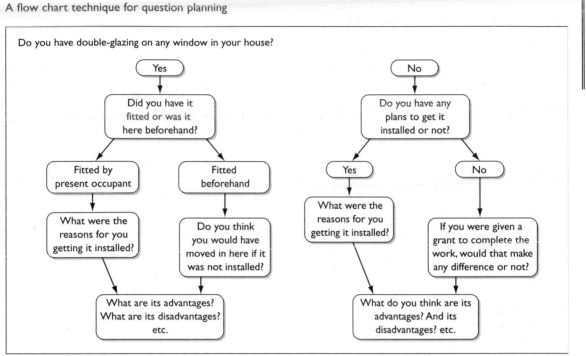

Source Social and Community Planning Research, 1972

lem, then to clarify the relevant concepts or constructs, then to identify what kinds of measures (if appropriate) or empirical indicators there are of these, i.e. the kinds of data required to give the researcher relevant evidence about the concepts or constructs, e.g. their presence, their intensity, their main features and dimensions, their key elements etc.

What unites these two approaches is their recognition of the need to ensure that the questionnaire: (a) is clear on its purposes; (b) is clear on what needs to be included or covered in the questionnaire in order to meet the purposes; (c) is exhaustive in its coverage of the elements of inclusion; (d) asks the most appropriate *kinds* of question (discussed below); (e) elicits the most appropriate *kinds* of data to answer the research purposes and sub-questions; (f) asks for empirical data.

Structured, semi-structured and unstructured questionnaires

Though there is a large range of types of questionnaire, there is a simple rule of thumb: the larger the size of the sample, the more structured, closed and numerical the questionnaire may have to be, and the smaller the size of the sample, the less structured, more open and word-based the questionnaire may be. Highly structured, closed questions are useful in that they can generate frequencies of response amenable to statistical treatment and analysis. They also enable comparisons to be made across groups in the sample (Oppenheim, 1992: 115). Indeed it would be almost impossible, as well as unnecessary, to try to process vast quantities of word-based data in a short time frame. If a site-specific case study is required, then qualitative, less structured, word-based and open-ended questionnaires may be more appropriate as they can capture the specificity of a particular situation. Where measurement is sought then a quantitative approach is required; where rich and personal data are sought, then a word-based qualitative approach might be more suitable.

The researcher can select several types of questionnaire, from highly structured to unstructured. If a closed and structured questionnaire is used, enabling patterns to be observed and comparisons to be made, then the questionnaire will need to be piloted and refined so that the final version contains as full a range of possible responses as can be reasonably foreseen. Such a questionnaire is heavy on time early in the research; however, once the questionnaire has been 'set up' then the mode of analysis might be comparatively rapid. For example, it may take two or three months to devise a survey questionnaire, pilot it, refine it and set it out in a format that will enable the data to be processed and statistics to be calculated. However, the 'trade-off' from this is that the data analysis can be undertaken fairly rapidly – we already know the response categories, the nature of the data and the statistics to be used; it is simply a matter of processing the data – often using computer analysis. Indeed there are several computer packages available for paperless, on-line questionnaire completion, e.g. Results for Research™, SphinxSurvey.

It is perhaps misleading to describe a questionnaire as being 'unstructured', as the whole devising of a questionnaire requires respondents to adhere to some form of given structure. That said, between a completely open questionnaire that is akin to an open invitation to 'write what one wants' and a totally closed, completely structured questionnaire, there is the powerful tool of the semi-structured questionnaire. Here a series of questions, statements or items are presented and the respondent is asked to answer, respond to or comment on them in a way that she or he thinks best. There is a clear structure, sequence, focus, but the format is open-ended, enabling the respondent to respond in her/his own terms. The semi-structured questionnaire

sets the agenda but does not presuppose the nature of the response.

Types of questionnaire items

There are several kinds of question and response modes in questionnaires, including, for example: dichotomous questions; multiple choice questions; rating scales; and open-ended questions. These are considered below (see also Wilson, 1996). Closed questions prescribe the range of responses from which the respondent may choose. In general closed questions (dichotomous, multiple choice and rating scales) are quick to complete and straightforward to code (e.g. for computer analysis), and do not discriminate unduly on the basis of how articulate the respondents are (Wilson and McLean, 1994: 21). On the other hand they do not enable respondents to add any remarks, qualifications and explanations to the categories, and there is a risk that the categories might not be exhaustive and that there might be bias in them (Oppenheim, 1992: 115).

Open questions, on the other hand, enable respondents to write a free response in their own terms, to explain and qualify their responses and avoid the limitations of pre-set categories of response. On the other hand the responses are difficult to code and to classify. The issue for researchers is one of 'fitness for purpose'.

Avoiding pitfalls in question writing

Though there are several kinds of questions that can be used (discussed below), there are several caveats about the framing of questions in a questionnaire:

1   Avoid leading questions, that is, questions which are worded (or their response categories presented) in such a way as to suggest to respondents that there is only one acceptable answer, and that other responses might or might not gain approval or disapproval respectively. For example:

Do you prefer abstract, academic-type

courses, or down-to-earth, practical courses that have some pay-off in your day-to-day teaching?

The guidance here is to check the 'loadedness' or possible pejorative overtones of terms or verbs.

2   Avoid highbrow questions even with sophisticated respondents. For example:

> What particular aspects of the current positivistic/interpretive debate would you like to see reflected in a course of developmental psychology aimed at a teacher audience?

Where the sample being surveyed is representative of the whole adult population, misunderstandings of what researchers take to be clear, unambiguous language are commonplace.

3   Avoid complex questions. For example:

> Would you prefer a short, non-award bearing course (3,4 or 5 sessions) with part-day release (e.g. Wednesday afternoons) and one evening per week attendance with financial reimbursement for travel, or a longer, non-award bearing course (6, 7 or 8 sessions) with full-day release, or the whole course designed on part-day release without evening attendance?

4   Avoid irritating questions or instructions. For example:

> Have you ever attended an in-service course of any kind during your entire teaching career?

> If you are over forty, and have never attended an in-service course, put one tick in the box marked *NEVER* and another in the box marked *OLD*.

5   Avoid questions that use negatives and double negatives (Oppenheim, 1992: 128). For example:

> How strongly do you feel that no teacher should enrol on the in-service, award-bearing course who has not completed at least two years full-time teaching?

6   Avoid too many open-ended questions on self-completion questionnaires. Because self-completion questionnaires cannot probe respondents to find out just what they mean by particular responses, open-ended questions are a less satisfactory way of eliciting information. (This caution does not hold in the interview situation, however.) Open-ended questions, moreover, are too demanding of most respondents' time. Nothing can be more off-putting than the following format which might appear in a questionnaire:

> Use pages 5, 6 and 7 respectively to respond to each of the questions about your attitudes to in-service courses in general and your beliefs about their value in the professional life of the serving teacher.

The problem of ambiguity in words is intractable; at best it can be minimized rather than eliminated altogether. The most innocent of questions is replete with ambiguity (Youngman, 1984: 158–9; Morrison, 1993: 71–2). Take the following examples:

Does your child regularly do homework?

What does 'regularly' mean – once a day; once a year; once a term; once a week?

How many students are there in the school?

What does this mean: on roll, on roll but absent; marked as present but out of school on a field trip; at this precise moment or this week (there being a difference in attendance between a Monday and a Friday), or between the first term of an academic year and the last term of the academic year for secondary school students as some of them will have left school to go into employment and others will be at home revising for examinations or have completed them?

How many computers do you have in school?

What does this mean: present but broken; including those out of school being repaired; the property of the school or staffs' and students' own computers; on average or exactly in school today?

Have you had a French lesson this week?

What constitutes a 'week': the start of the school week (i.e. from Monday to a Friday), since last Sunday (or Saturday depending on one's religion), or, if the question were put on a Wednesday, since last Wednesday; how representative of all weeks is this week – there being public examinations in the school for some of the week?

> How far do you agree with the view that without a Parent–Teacher Association you cannot talk about the progress of your children?

The double negative ('without' and 'cannot') makes this question a difficult one to answer. If I wanted to say that I believe that Parent–Teacher Associations are necessary for adequate consultation between parents and teachers, do I answer with a 'yes' or a 'no'?

> How old are you?
> 15–20
> 20–30
> 30–40
> 40–50
> 50–60

The categories are not discrete; will an old-looking 40-year-old flatter himself and put himself in the 30–40 category, or will an immature 20-year-old seek the maturity of being put into the 20–30 category? The rule in questionnaire design is to avoid any overlap of categories.

> Vocational education is only available to the lower ability students but it should be open to every student.

This is, in fact, a double question. What does the respondent do who agrees with the first part of the sentence – 'vocational education is only available to the lower ability students' – but disagrees with the latter part of the sentence, or *vice versa*? The rule in questionnaire design is to ask only one question at a time.

Though it is impossible to legislate for the respondents' interpretation of wording, the researcher, of course, has to adopt a common-sense approach to this, recognizing the inherent ambiguity but nevertheless still feeling that it is possible to live with this ambiguity.

An ideal questionnaire possesses the same properties as a good law:

> It is clear, unambiguous and uniformly workable. Its design must minimize potential errors from respondents . . . and coders. And since people's participation in surveys is voluntary, a questionnaire has to help in engaging their interest, encouraging their co-operation, and eliciting answers as close as possible to the truth.
>
> (Davidson, 1970)

Dichotomous questions

A highly structured questionnaire will ask closed questions. These can take several forms. *Dichotomous* questions require a 'yes'/'no' response, e.g. 'have you ever had to appear in court?', 'do you prefer didactic methods to child-centred methods'? The dichotomous question is useful, for it compels respondents to 'come off the fence' on an issue. Further, it is possible to code responses quickly, there being only two categories of response. A dichotomous question is also useful as a funnelling or sorting device for subsequent questions, for example: 'if you answered "yes" to question X, please go to question Y; if you answered "no" to question X, please go to question Z'. Sudman and Bradburn (1982: 89) suggest that if dichotomous questions are being used, then it is desirable to use several to gain data on the same topic, in order to reduce the problems of respondents' 'guessing' answers.

On the other hand, the researcher must ask, for instance, whether a 'yes'/'no' response actually provides any useful information. Requiring respondents to make a 'yes'/'no' decision may be inappropriate; it might be more appropriate to have a range of responses, for example in a rating scale. There may be comparatively few complex or subtle questions which can be answered with a simple 'yes' or 'no'. A 'yes' or a 'no' may be inappropriate for a situation whose complexity is better served by a series of questions which catch that complexity. Further, Youngman (1984: 163) suggests that it is a natural human tendency to agree with a statement rather than to disagree with it; this suggests that a simple dichotomous question might build in respondent bias.

In addition to dichotomous questions ('yes'/'no' questions) a piece of research might ask for information about dichotomous variables, for example gender (male/female), type of school (elementary/secondary), type of course (vocational/non-vocational). In these cases only one of two responses can be selected. This enables nominal data to be gathered, which can then be processed using the chi-square statistic, the binomial test, the G-test, and cross-tabulations (see Cohen and Holliday (1996) for examples).

Multiple choice questions

To try to gain some purchase on complexity, the researcher can move towards *multiple choice* questions, where the range of choices is designed to capture the likely range of responses to given statements. For example, the researcher might ask a series of questions about a new Chemistry scheme in the school; a statement precedes a set of responses thus:

The New Intermediate Chemistry Education (NICE) is:

(a) a waste of time;
(b) an extra burden on teachers;
(c) not appropriate to our school;
(d) a useful complementary scheme;
(e) a useful core scheme throughout the school;
(f) well-presented and practicable.

The categories would have to be discrete (i.e. having no overlap and being mutually exclusive) and would have to exhaust the possible range of responses. Guidance would have to be given on the completion of the multiple-choice, clarify-

ing, for example, whether respondents are able to tick only *one* response (a *single answer* mode) or *several* responses (*multiple answer* mode) from the list. Like dichotomous questions, multiple choice questions can be quickly coded and quickly aggregated to give frequencies of response. If that is appropriate for the research, then this might be a useful instrument.

Just as dichotomous questions have their parallel in dichotomous variables, so multiple choice questions have their parallel in *multiple elements of a variable*. For example, the researcher may be asking to which form a student belongs – there being up to, say, forty forms in a large school, or the researcher may be asking which post-16 course a student is following (e.g. academic, vocational, manual, non-manual). In these cases only one response may be selected. As with the dichotomous variable, the listing of several categories or elements of a variable (e.g. form membership and course followed) enables nominal data to be collected and processed using the chi-square statistic, the G-test, and cross-tabulations (Cohen and Holliday, 1996).

The multiple choice questionnaire seldom gives more than a crude statistic, for words are inherently ambiguous. In the example above the notion of 'useful' is unclear, as are 'appropriate', 'practicable' and 'burden'. Respondents could interpret these words differently in their own contexts, thereby rendering the data ambiguous. One respondent might see the utility of the chemistry scheme in one area and thereby say that it is useful – ticking (d). Another respondent might see the same utility in that same one area but, because it is only useful in that single area, may see this as a flaw and therefore not tick category (d). With an anonymous questionnaire this difference would be impossible to detect.

This is the heart of the problem of questionnaires – that different respondents interpret the same words differently. 'Anchor statements' can be provided to allow a degree of discrimination in response (e.g. 'strongly agree', 'agree' etc.) but there is no guarantee that respondents will always interpret them in the way that was intended. In the example above this might not be a problem as the researcher might only be seeking an index of utility – without wishing to know the areas of utility or the reasons for that utility. The evaluator might only be wishing for a crude statistic (which might be very useful statistically in making a decisive judgement about a program) in which case this rough and ready statistic might be perfectly acceptable.

What one can see in the example above is not only ambiguity in the wording but a very incomplete set of response categories which is hardly capable of representing all aspects of the chemistry scheme. That this might be politically expedient cannot be overlooked, for if the choice of responses is limited, then those responses might enable bias to be built into the research. For example, if the responses were limited to statements about the *utility* of the chemistry scheme, then the evaluator would have little difficulty in establishing that the scheme was useful. By avoiding the inclusion of negative statements or the opportunity to record a negative response the research will surely be biased. The issue of the wording of questions has been discussed earlier.

Rank ordering

The rank order question is akin to the multiple choice question in that it identifies options from which respondents can choose, yet it moves beyond multiple choice items in that it asks respondents to identify priorities. This enables a *relative* degree of preference, priority, intensity etc. to be charted.

In the rank ordering exercise a list of factors is set out and the respondent is required to place them in a rank order, for example:

Please indicate your priorities by placing numbers in the boxes to indicate the ordering of your views, 1 = the highest priority, 2 = the second highest, and so on.

The proposed amendments to the mathematics scheme might be successful if the following factors are addressed:

- the appropriate material resources are in school ☐
- the amendments are made clear to all teachers ☐
- the amendments are supported by the mathematics team ☐
- the necessary staff development is assured ☐
- there are subsequent improvements to student achievement ☐
- the proposals have the agreement of all teachers ☐
- they improve student motivation ☐
- parents approve of the amendments ☐
- they will raise the achievements of the brighter students ☐
- the work becomes more geared to problem-solving ☐

In this example ten items are listed. Whilst this might be enticing for the researcher, enabling fine distinctions possibly to be made in priorities, it might be asking too much of the respondents to make such distinctions. They genuinely might not be able to differentiate their responses, or they simply might not feel strongly enough to make such distinctions. The inclusion of too long a list might be overwhelming. Indeed Wilson and McLean (1994: 26) suggest that it is unrealistic to ask respondents to arrange priorities where there are more than five ranks that have been requested. In the case of the list of ten points above, the researcher might approach this problem in one of two ways. The list in the questionnaire item can be reduced to five items only, in which case the *range* and comprehensiveness of responses that fairly catches what the respondent feels is significantly reduced. Alternatively, the list of ten items can be retained, but the request can be made to the respondents only to rank their first five priorities, in which case the range is retained and the task is not overwhelming (though the problem of sorting the data for analysis is increased).

Rankings are useful in indicating *degrees* of response. In this respect they are like rating scales, discussed below.

Rating scales

One way in which degrees of response, intensity of response, and the move away from dichotomous questions has been managed can be seen in the notion of *rating scales* – Likert scales, semantic differential scales, Thurstone scales, Guttman scaling. These are very useful devices for the researcher, as they build in a degree of sensitivity and differentiation of response whilst still generating numbers. This chapter will focus on the first two of these, though readers will find the others discussed in Oppenheim (1992). A Likert scale (named after its deviser, Rensis Likert, 1932) provides a range of responses to a given question or statement, for example:

How important do you consider work placements to be for secondary school students?
1 = not at all
2 = very little
3 = a little
4 = a lot
5 = a very great deal

All students should have access to free higher education.

1 = strongly disagree
2 = disagree
3 = neither agree nor disagree
4 = agree
5 = strongly agree

In these examples the categories need to be discrete and to exhaust the range of possible responses which respondents may wish to give. Notwithstanding the problems of interpretation which arise as in the previous example – one respondent's 'agree' may be another's 'strongly agree', one respondent's 'very little' might be another's 'a little' – the greater subtlety of response which is built into a rating scale renders this a very attractive and widely used instrument in research.

These two examples both indicate an important feature of an attitude scaling instrument, *viz.* the assumption of *unidimensionality* in the scale; the scale should only be measuring one thing at a time (Oppenheim, 1992: 187–8). Indeed this is a cornerstone of Likert's own thinking (1932).

It is a very straightforward matter to convert a dichotomous question into a multiple choice question. For example, instead of asking the 'do you?', 'have you?', 'are you?', 'can you?' type questions in a dichotomous format, a simple addition to wording will convert it into a much more subtle rating scale, by substituting the words 'to what extent?', 'how far?', 'how much?' etc.

A semantic differential is a variation of a rating scale which operates by putting an adjective at one end of a scale and its opposite at the other, for example:

How informative do you consider the new set of history text books to be?

	1	2	3	4	5	6	7	
useful	–	–	–	–	–	–	–	useless

The respondent indicates on the scale by circling or putting a mark on that position which most represents what she or he feels.

Osgood *et al.* (1957), the pioneers of this technique, suggest that semantic differential scales are useful in three contexts: *evaluative* (e.g. valuable–valueless, useful–useless, good–bad); *potency* (e.g. large–small, weak–strong, light–heavy); and *activity* (e.g. quick–slow, active–passive, dynamic–lethargic).

Rating scales are widely used in research, and rightly so, for they combine the opportunity for a flexible response with the ability to determine frequencies, correlations and other forms of quantitative analysis. They afford the researcher the freedom to fuse measurement with opinion, quantity and quality.

Though rating scales are powerful and useful in research, the researcher, nevertheless, needs to be aware of their limitations. For example, the researcher may not be able in infer a degree of sensitivity and subtlety from the data that they cannot bear. There are other cautionary factors about rating scales, be they Likert scales or semantic differential scales:

- There is no assumption of equal intervals between the categories, hence a rating of 4 indicates neither that it is twice as powerful as 2 nor that it is twice as strongly felt; one cannot infer that the intensity of feeling in the Likert scale between 'strongly disagree' and 'disagree' somehow matches the intensity of feeling between 'strongly agree' and 'agree'. These are illegitimate inferences. The problem of equal intervals has been addressed in Thurstone scales (Thurstone and Chave, 1929; Oppenheim, 1992: 190–5).
- We have no check on whether the respondents are telling the truth. Some respondents may be deliberately falsifying their replies.
- We have no way of knowing if the respondent might have wished to add any other comments about the issue under investigation. It might have been the case that there was something far more pressing about the issue than the rating scale included but which was condemned to silence for want of a category. A straightforward way to circumvent this issue is to run a pilot and also to include a category entitled 'other (please state)'.
- Most of us would not wish to be called extremists; we often prefer to appear like each other in many respects. For rating scales this means that we might wish to avoid the two extreme poles at each end of the continuum of the rating scales, reducing the number of positions in the scales to a choice of three (in a five-point scale). That means that *in fact* there could be very little choice for us. The way round this is to create a larger scale than a five-point scale, for example a seven-point scale. To go beyond a seven-point scale is to invite a degree of detail and precision which might be inappropriate for the item in question, particularly if the argument set out above is accepted, *viz.* that one respondent's scale point three might be another's scale point four.
- On the scales so far there have been mid-points; on the five-point scale it is category three, and on the seven-point scale it is category four. The use of an odd number of points on a scale enables this to occur. However, choosing an even number of scale points, for example a six-point scale, might *require* a decision on rating to be indicated.

For example, suppose a new staffing structure has been introduced into a school and the head-teacher is seeking some guidance on its effectiveness. A six-point rating scale might ask respondents to indicate their response to the statement:

> The new staffing structure in the school has enabled teamwork to be managed within a clear model of line management.

(Circle one number)

	1	2	3	4	5	6	
strongly agree	–	–	–	–	–	–	strongly disagree

Let us say that one member of staff circled 1, eight staff circled 2, twelve staff circled 3, nine staff circled 4, two staff circled 5, and seven staff circled 6. There being no mid-point on this continuum, the researcher could infer that those respondents who circled 1, 2, or 3 were in some measure of agreement, whilst those respondents who circled 4, 5, or 6 were in some measure of disagreement. That would be very useful for, say, a headteacher, in publicly displaying agreement, there being twenty-one staff (1 + 8 + 12) agreeing with the statement and eighteen (9 + 2 + 7) displaying a measure of disagreement. However, one could point out that the measure of 'strongly disagree' attracted seven staff – a very strong feeling – which was not true for the 'strongly agree' category, which only attracted one member of staff. The extremity of the voting has been lost in a crude aggregation.

Further, if the researcher were to aggregate the scoring around the two mid-point categories (3 and 4) there would be twenty-one members of staff represented, leaving nine (1 + 8) from categories 1 and 2 and nine (2 + 7) from categories 5 and 6; adding together categories 1, 2, 5 and 6, a total of 18 is reached, which is less than the twenty-one total of the two categories 3 and 4. It seems on this scenario that it is far from clear that there was agreement with the statement from the staff; indeed taking the high incidence of 'strongly disagree', it could be argued that those staff who were perhaps ambivalent (categories 3 and 4), coupled with those who registered a 'strongly disagree' indicate not agreement but disagreement with the statement.

The interpretation of data has to be handled very carefully; ordering them to suit a researcher's own purposes might be very alluring but illegitimate. The golden rule here is that crude data can only yield crude interpretation; subtle statistics require subtle data. The interpretation of data must not distort the data unfairly.

It has been suggested that the attraction of rating scales is that they provide more opportunity than dichotomous questions for rendering data more sensitive and responsive to respondents. This makes rating scales particularly useful for tapping attitudes, perceptions and opinions of respondents. The need for a pilot to devise and refine categories, making them exhaustive and discrete, has been suggested as a necessary part of this type of data collection.

Questionnaires that are going to yield numerical or word-based data can be analyzed using computer programmes (for example SPSS, SphinxSurvey or Ethnograph respectively). If the researcher intends to process the data using a computer package it is essential that the layout and coding system of the questionnaire is appropriate for the computer package. Instructions for layout in order to facilitate data entry are contained in manuals that accompany such packages.

Rating scales are more sensitive instruments than dichotomous scales. Nevertheless they are limited in their usefulness to researchers by their fixity of response caused by the need to select from a given choice. A questionnaire might be tailored even more to respondents by including *open-ended* questions to which respondents can reply in their own terms and own opinions, and these we now consider.

Open-ended questions

The open-ended question is a very attractive device for smaller scale research or for those sec-

tions of a questionnaire that invite an honest, personal comment from the respondents in addition to ticking numbers and boxes. The questionnaire simply puts the open-ended questions and leaves a space (or draws lines) for a free response. It is the open-ended responses that might contain the 'gems' of information that otherwise might not have been caught in the questionnaire. Further, it puts the responsibility for and ownership of the data much more firmly into the respondents' hands.

This is not to say that the open-ended question might well not frame the answer, just as the stem of a rating scale question might frame the response given. However, an open-ended question can catch the authenticity, richness, depth of response, honesty and candour which, as is argued elsewhere in this book, are the hallmarks of qualitative data.

Oppenheim (1992: 56–7) suggests that a sentence-completion item is a useful adjunct to an open-ended question, for example:

Please complete the following sentence in your own words:

An effective teacher . . .

or

The main things that I find annoying with disruptive students are . . .

Open-endedness also carries problems of data handling. For example, if one tries to convert opinions into numbers (e.g. so many people indicated some degree of satisfaction with the new principal's management plan), then it could be argued that the questionnaire should have used rating scales in the first place. Further, it might well be that the researcher is in danger of violating one principle of word-based data, which is that they are not validly susceptible to aggregation, i.e. that it is trying to bring to word-based data the principles of numerical data, borrowing from one paradigm (quantitative methodology) to inform another paradigm (qualitative methodology).

Further, if a genuinely open-ended question is

being asked, it is perhaps unlikely that responses will bear such a degree of similarity to each other to enable them to be aggregated too tightly. Open-ended questions make it difficult for the researcher to make comparisons between respondents, as there may be little in common to compare. Moreover, to complete an open-ended questionnaire takes much longer than placing a tick in a rating scale response box; not only will time be a constraint here, but there is an assumption that respondents will be sufficiently or equally capable of articulating their thoughts and committing them to paper.

Despite these cautions, the space provided for an open-ended response is a window of opportunity for the respondent to shed light on an issue or course. Thus, an open-ended questionnaire has much to recommend it.

Asking sensitive questions

Sudman and Bradburn (1982: Chapter 3) draw attention to the important issue of including sensitive items in a questionnaire. Whilst the anonymity of a questionnaire and, frequently, the lack of face-to-face contact between the researcher and the respondents in a questionnaire might facilitate responses to sensitive material, the issues of sensitivity and threat cannot be avoided, as they might lead to under-reporting and over-reporting by participants. Sudman and Bradburn (1982: 55–6) identify several important considerations in addressing potentially threatening or sensitive issues, for example socially undesirable behaviour (e.g. drug abuse, sexual offences, violent behaviour, criminality, illnesses, employment and unemployment, physical features, sexual activity, behaviour and sexuality, gambling, drinking, family details, political beliefs, social taboos). They suggest that:

- Open rather than closed questions might be more suitable to elicit information about socially undesirable behaviour, particularly frequencies.
- Long rather than short questions might be

more suitable for eliciting information about socially undesirable behaviour, particularly frequencies.
- Using familiar words might increase the number of reported frequencies of socially undesirable behaviour.
- Using data gathered from informants, where possible, can enhance the likelihood of obtaining reports of threatening behaviour.
- Deliberately loading the question so that overstatements of socially desirable behaviour and understatements of socially undesirable behaviour are reduced might be a useful means of eliciting information.
- With regard to socially undesirable behaviour, it might be advisable, firstly, to ask whether the respondent has engaged in that behaviour previously, and then move to asking about his or her current behaviour. By contrast, when asking about socially acceptable behaviour the reverse might be true, i.e. asking about current behaviour before asking about everyday behaviour.
- In order to defuse threat, it might be useful to locate the sensitive topic within a discussion of other more or less sensitive matters, in order to suggest to respondents that this issue might not be too important.
- Use alternative ways of asking standard questions, for example sorting cards, or putting questions in sealed envelopes, or repeating questions over time (this has to be handled sensitively, so that respondents do not feel that they are being 'checked'), and in order to increase reliability.
- Ask respondents to keep diaries in order to increase validity and reliability.
- At the end of an interview ask respondents their views on the sensitivity of the topics that have been discussed questions.
- If possible find ways of validating the data.

Indeed the authors suggest (ibid.: 86) that, as the questions become more threatening and sensitive, it is wise to expect greater bias and unreliability. They draw attention to the fact (ibid.: 208) that several nominal, demographic details might be considered threatening by respondents. This has implications for their location within the questionnaire (discussed below). The issue here is that sensitivity and threat are to be viewed through the eyes of respondents rather than the questionnaire designer; what might appear innocuous to the researcher might be highly sensitive or offensive to the respondent.

Sequencing the questions

The order of the questions in a questionnaire, to some extent, is a function of the target sample (e.g. how they will react to certain questions), the purposes of the questionnaire (e.g. to gather facts or opinions), the sensitivity of the research (e.g. how personal and potentially disturbing the issues are that will be addressed), and the overall balance of the questionnaire (e.g. where best to place sensitive questions in relation to less threatening questions, and how many of each to include).

The ordering of the questionnaire is important, for early questions may set the tone of, or the mind-set of the respondent to, the later questions. For example, a questionnaire that makes a respondent irritated or angry early on is unlikely to have managed to enable that respondent's irritation or anger to subside by the end of the questionnaire. As Oppenheim remarks (1992: 121) one covert purpose of each question is to ensure that the respondent will continue to co-operate.

Further, a respondent might 'read the signs' in the questionnaire, seeking similarities and resonances between statements, so that responses to early statements will affect responses to later statements and *vice versa*. Whilst multiple items may act as a cross-check, this very process might be irritating for some respondents.

The key principle, perhaps, is to avoid creating a mood-set or a mind-set early on in the questionnaire. For this reason it is important to commence the questionnaire with non-threatening questions that they can readily answer. After that it might be possible to move towards more personalized questions.

Completing a questionnaire can be seen as a learning process in which respondents become more at home with the task as they proceed. Initial questions should therefore be simple, have high interest value, and encourage participation. This will build up the confidence and motivation of the respondent. The middle section of the questionnaire should contain the difficult questions; the last few questions should be of high interest in order to encourage respondents to return the completed schedule.

A common sequence of a questionnaire is:

1   to commence with unthreatening factual questions (that, perhaps, will give the researcher some nominal data about the sample, e.g. age group, sex, occupation, years in post, qualifications etc.);
2   to move to closed questions (e.g. dichotomous, multiple choice, rating scales) about given statements or questions, eliciting responses that require opinions, attitudes, perceptions, views;
3   to move to more open-ended questions (or, maybe, to intersperse these with more closed questions) that seek responses on opinions, attitudes, perceptions and views, together with reasons for the responses given. These responses and reasons might include sensitive or more personal data.

The move is from objective facts to subjective attitudes and opinions through justifications and to sensitive, personalized data. Clearly the ordering is neither as discrete nor as straightforward as this. For example, an apparently innocuous question about age might be offensive to some respondents, a question about income is unlikely to go down well with somebody who has just become unemployed, and a question about religious belief might be seen as an unwarranted intrusion into private matters.

The issue here is that the questionnaire designer has to anticipate the sensitivity of the topics in terms of the respondents, and this has a large socio-cultural dimension. What is being argued here is that the *logical* ordering of a questionnaire has to be mediated by its *psychological* ordering. The instrument has to be viewed through the eyes of the respondent as well as the designer.

In addition to the *overall* sequencing of the questionnaire, Oppenheim (1992: Chapter 7) suggests that the sequence *within* sections of the questionnaire is important. He indicates that the questionnaire designer can use *funnels* and *filters* within the question. A funnelling process moves from the general to the specific, asking questions about the general context or issues and then moving toward specific points within that. A filter is used to include and exclude certain respondents, i.e. to decide if certain questions are relevant or irrelevant to them, and to instruct respondents about how to proceed (e.g. which items to jump to or proceed to). For example, if a respondent indicates a 'yes'; or a 'no' to a certain question, then this might exempt her/him from certain other questions in that section or subsequently.

Questionnaires containing few verbal items

The discussion so far has assumed that questionnaires are entirely word-based. This might be off-putting for many respondents, particularly children. In these circumstances a questionnaire might include visual information and ask participants to respond to this (e.g. pictures, cartoons, diagrams) or might include some projective visual techniques (e.g. to draw a picture or diagram, to join two related pictures with a line, to write the words or what someone is saying or thinking in a 'bubble' picture), to tell the story of a sequence of pictures together with personal reactions to it. The issue here is that, in tailoring the format of the questionnaire to the characteristics of the sample, a very wide embrace might be necessary to take in non word-based techniques. This is not only a matter of *appeal* to respondents, but, perhaps more significantly, is a matter of *accessibility* of the questionnaire to the respondents, i.e. a matter of reliability and validity.

The layout of the questionnaire

The appearance of the questionnaire is vitally important. It must look easy, attractive and interesting rather than complicated, unclear, forbidding and boring. A compressed layout is uninviting and it clutters everything together; a larger questionnaire with plenty of space for questions and answers is more encouraging to respondents. Verma and Mallick (1999: 120) also suggest the use of high quality paper if funding permits.

It is important, perhaps, for respondents to be introduced to the purposes of each section of a questionnaire, so that they can become involved in it and maybe identify with it. If space permits, it is useful to tell the respondent the purposes and foci of the sections/of the questionnaire, and the reasons for the inclusion of the items.

Clarity of wording and simplicity of design are essential. Clear instructions should guide respondents: 'Put a tick', for example, invites participation, whereas complicated instructions and complex procedures intimidate respondents. Putting ticks in boxes by way of answering a questionnaire is familiar to most respondents, whereas requests to circle precoded numbers at the right-hand side of the questionnaire can be a source of confusion and error. In some cases it might also be useful to include an example of how to fill in the questionnaire (e.g. ticking a box, circling a statement), though, clearly, care must be exercised to avoid leading the respondents to answering questions in a particular way by dint of the example provided (e.g. by suggesting what might be a desired answer to the subsequent questions). Verma and Mallick (1999: 121) suggest the use of emboldening to draw the respondent's attention to significant features.

Ensure that short, clear instructions accompany each section of the questionnaire. Repeating instructions as often as necessary is good practice in a postal questionnaire. Since everything hinges on respondents knowing exactly what is required of them, clear, unambiguous instructions, boldly and attractively displayed, are essential.

Clarity and presentation also impact on the numbering of the questions. For example a four-page questionnaire might contain sixty questions, broken down into four sections. It might be off-putting to respondents to number each question (1–60) as the list will seem interminably long, whereas to number each section (1–4) makes the questionnaire look manageable.

Hence it is useful, in the interests of clarity and logic to break down the questionnaire into subsections with section headings. This will also indicate the overall logic and coherence of the questionnaire to the respondents, enabling them to 'find their way' through the questionnaire. It might be useful to preface each subsection with a brief introduction that tells them the purpose of that section.

The practice of sectionalizing and sublettering questions (e.g. Q9 (a) (b) (c) . . .) is a useful technique for grouping together questions to do with a specific issue. It is also a way of making the questionnaire look smaller than it actually is!

This previous point also requires the questionnaire designer to make it clear if respondents are exempted from completing certain questions or sections of the questionnaire (discussed earlier in the section on filters). If so, then it is vital that the sections or questions are numbered so that the respondent knows exactly where to move to next. Here the instruction might be, for example: 'if you have answered "yes" to question 10 please go to question 15, otherwise continue with question 11', or, for example: 'if you are the school principal please answer this section, otherwise proceed to section three'.

Arrange the contents of the questionnaire in such a way as to maximize co-operation. For example, include questions that are likely to be of general interest. Make sure that questions which appear early in the format do not suggest to respondents that the inquiry is not intended for them. Intersperse attitude questions throughout the schedule to allow respondents to air their views rather than merely describe their behaviour. Such questions relieve boredom and frustration as well as providing valuable information in the process.

Coloured pages can help to clarify the overall structure of the questionnaire and the use of different colours for instructions can assist respondents.

It is important to include in the questionnaire, perhaps at the beginning, assurances of confidentiality, anonymity, and non-traceability, for example by indicating that they need not give their name, that the data will be aggregated, that individuals will not be able to be identified through the use of categories or details of their location etc. (i.e. that it will not be possible to put together a traceable picture of the respondents through the compiling of nominal, descriptive data about the respondents). In some cases, however, the questionnaire might ask respondents to put their name so that they can be traced for follow-up interviews in the research (Verma and Mallick, 1999: 121); here the guarantee of eventual anonymity and non-traceability will still need to be given.

Finally, a brief note at the very end of the questionnaire can: (a) ask respondents to check that no answer has been inadvertently missed out; (b) solicit an early return of the completed schedule; (c) thank respondents for their participation and co-operation, and offer to send a short abstract of the major findings when the analysis is completed.

Covering letters/sheets and follow-up letters

The purpose of the covering letter/sheet is to indicate the aim of the research, to convey to respondents its importance, to assure them of confidentiality, and to encourage their replies. The covering letter/sheet should:

- provide a title to the research;
- introduce the researcher, her/his name, address, organization, contact telephone/ fax/e-mail address, together with an invitation to feel free to contact the researcher for further clarification or details;

- indicate the purposes of the research;
- indicate the importance and benefits of the research;
- indicate any professional backing, endorsement, or sponsorship of, or permission for, the research (e.g. professional associations, government departments);
- set out how to return the questionnaire (e.g. in the accompanying stamped, addressed envelope, in a collection box in a particular institution, to a named person; whether the questionnaire will be collected – and when, where and by whom);
- indicate the address to which to return the questionnaire;
- indicate what to do if questions or uncertainties arise ;
- indicate a return-by date;
- indicate any incentives for completing the questionnaire;
- provide assurances of confidentiality, anonymity and non-traceability;
- thank respondents in advance for their co-operation.

Verma and Mallick (1999: 122) also suggest that, where possible, it is useful to personalize the letter, avoiding 'Dear colleague', 'Dear Madam/ Ms/Sir' etc., and replacing these with exact names.

With these intentions in mind, the following practices are to be recommended:

- The appeal in the covering letter must be tailored to suit the particular audience. Thus, a survey of teachers might stress the importance of the study to the profession as a whole.
- Neither the use of prestigious signatories, nor appeals to altruism, nor the addition of handwritten postscripts affect response levels to postal questionnaires.
- The name of the sponsor or the organization conducting the survey should appear on the letterhead as well as in the body of the covering letter.
- A direct reference should be made to the confidentiality of respondents' answers and

the purposes of any serial numbers and codings should be explained.
- A pre-survey letter advising respondents of the forthcoming questionnaire has been shown to have substantial effect on response rates.
- A short covering letter is most effective; aim at no more than one page.

Piloting the questionnaire

It bears repeating that the wording of questionnaires is of paramount importance and that pretesting is crucial to its success. A pilot has several functions, principally to increase the reliability, validity and practicability of the questionnaire (Oppenheim, 1992; Morrison, 1993; Wilson and McLean, 1994: 47), it thus serves:

- to check the clarity of the questionnaire items, instructions and layout;
- to gain feedback on the validity of the questionnaire items, the operationalization of the constructs and the purposes of the research;
- to eliminate ambiguities or difficulties in wording;
- to gain feedback on the *type* of question and its format (e.g. rating scale, multiple choice, open, closed etc.);
- to gain feedback on response categories for closed questions, and for the appropriateness of specific questions or stems of questions;
- to gain feedback on the attractiveness and appearance of the questionnaire;
- to gain feedback on the layout, sectionalizing, numbering and itemization of the questionnaire;
- to check the time taken to complete the questionnaire;
- to check whether the questionnaire is too long or too short, too easy or too difficult, too unengaging, too threatening, too intrusive, too offensive;
- to generate categories from open-ended responses to use as categories for closed response-modes (e.g. rating scale items);
- to identify redundant questions (e.g. those

questions which consistently gain a total 'yes' or 'no' response (Youngman, 1984: 172)), i.e. those questions with little discriminability;

- to identify commonly misunderstood or non-completed items (e.g. by studying common patterns of unexpected response and non-response (Verma and Mallick, 1999: 120));
- to try out the coding/classification system for data analysis.

In short, as Oppenheim (1992: 48) remarks, *everything* about the questionnaire should be piloted; nothing should be excluded, not even the type face or the quality of the paper!

Practical considerations in questionnaire design

Taking the issues discussed so far in questionnaire design, a range of practical implications for designing a questionnaire can be highlighted:

- Operationalize the purposes of the questionnaire carefully.
- Decide on the most appropriate *type* of question – dichotomous, multiple choice, rank orderings, rating scales, closed, open.
- Ensure that every issue has been explored exhaustively and comprehensively; decide on the content and explore it in depth and breadth.
- Ensure that the data acquired will answer the research questions.
- Ask, for ease of analysis (particularly of a large sample), more closed than open questions.
- Balance comprehensiveness and exhaustive coverage of issues with the demotivating factor of having respondents complete several pages of a questionnaire.
- Ask only one thing at a time in a question.
- Strive to be unambiguous and clear in the wording.
- Be simple, clear and brief wherever possible.
- Balance brevity with politeness (Oppenheim, 1992: 122). It might be advantageous to

replace a staccato phrase like 'marital status' with a gentler 'please indicate whether you are married, living with a partner, or single . . .' or 'I would be grateful if would tell me if you are married, living with a partner, or single'.

- Ensure a balance of questions which ask for facts and opinions (this is especially true if statistical correlations and cross-tabulations are required).
- Avoid leading questions.
- Try to avoid threatening questions.
- Do not assume that respondents know the answer, or have information to answer the questions, or will always tell the truth (wittingly or not). Therefore include 'don't know', 'not applicable', 'unsure', 'neither agree nor disagree' and 'not relevant' categories.
- Avoid making the questions too hard.
- Consider the readability levels of the questionnaire and the reading and writing abilities of the respondents (which may lead the researcher to conduct the questionnaire as a structured interview).
- Put sensitive questions later in the questionnaire in order to avoid creating a mental set in the mind of respondents, but not so late in the questionnaire that boredom and lack of concentration have occurred.
- Be very clear on the layout of the questionnaire so that it is clear and attractive (this is particularly the case if a computer program is going to be used for data analysis).
- Avoid, where possible, splitting an item over more than one page, as the respondent may think that the item from the previous page is finished.
- Ensure that the respondent knows how to enter a response to each question, e.g. by underlining, circling, ticking, writing; provide the instructions for introducing, completing and returning (or collection of) the questionnaire (provide a stamped addressed envelope if it is to be a postal questionnaire).
- Pilot the questionnaire, using a group of respondents who are drawn from the possible sample but who will not receive the final, refined version.

- Decide how to avoid falsification of responses (e.g. introduce a checking mechanism into the questionnaire responses to another question on the same topic or issue).
- Be satisfied if you receive a 50 per cent response to the questionnaire; decide what you will do with missing data and what is the significance of the missing data (that might have implications for the strata of a stratified sample targeted in the questionnaire), and why the questionnaires have not been completed and returned (e.g. were the questions too threatening?, was the questionnaire too long? – this might have been signalled in the pilot).
- Include a covering explanation, giving thanks for anticipated co-operation, indicating the purposes of the research, how anonymity and confidentiality will be addressed, who you are and what position you hold, and who will be party to the final report.
- If the questionnaire is going to be administered by someone other than the researcher, ensure that instructions for administration are provided and that they are clear.

A key issue that runs right through this lengthy list is for the reader to pay considerable attention to respondents, and to see the questionnaire through their eyes, and how they will regard it (e.g. from hostility to suspicion to apathy to grudging compliance to welcome; from easy to difficult, from motivating to boring, from straightforward to complex etc.).

Postal questionnaires

Frequently, the postal questionnaire is the best form of survey in an educational inquiry. Take, for example, the researcher intent on investigating the adoption and use made of a new curriculum series in secondary schools. An interview survey based upon some sampling of the population of schools would be both expensive and time-consuming. A postal questionnaire, on the other hand, would have several distinct advantages. Moreover, given the usual constraints over finance and resources, it might well prove the only viable way of carrying through such an inquiry.

What evidence we have about the advantages and disadvantages of postal surveys derives from settings other than educational. Many of the findings, however, have relevance to the educational researcher. Here, we focus upon some of the ways in which educational researchers can maximize the response level that they obtain when using postal surveys.

Research shows that a number of myths about postal questionnaires are not borne out by the evidence (see Hoinville and Jowell, 1978). Response levels to postal surveys are not invariably less than those obtained by interview procedures; frequently they equal, and in some cases surpass, those achieved in interviews. Nor does the questionnaire necessarily have to be short in order to obtain a satisfactory response level. With sophisticated respondents, for example, a short questionnaire might appear to trivialize complex issues with which they are familiar. Hoinville and Jowell identify a number of factors in securing a good response rate to a postal questionnaire.

Initial mailing

- Use good-quality envelopes, typed and addressed to a named person wherever possible.
- Use first-class – rapid – postage services, with stamped rather than franked envelopes wherever possible.
- Enclose a stamped envelope for the respondent's reply.
- In surveys of the general population, Thursday is the best day for mailing out; in surveys of organizations, Monday or Tuesday are recommended.
- Avoid at all costs a December survey (questionnaires will be lost in the welter of Christmas postings in the western world).

Follow-up letter

Of the four factors that Hoinville and Jowell discuss in connection with maximizing response levels, the follow-up letter has been shown to be the most productive. The following points should be borne in mind in preparing reminder letters:

- All of the rules that apply to the covering letter apply even more strongly to the follow-up letter.
- The follow-up should re-emphasize the importance of the study and the value of the respondents' participation.
- The use of the second person singular, the conveying of an air of disappointment at non-response and some surprise at non-cooperation have been shown to be effective ploys.
- Nowhere should the follow-up give the impression that non-response is normal or that numerous non-responses have occurred in the particular study.
- The follow-up letter must be accompanied by a further copy of the questionnaire together with a stamped addressed envelope for its return.
- Second and third reminder letters suffer from the law of diminishing returns, so how many follow-ups are recommended and what success rates do they achieve? It is difficult to generalize, but the following points are worth bearing in mind. A well-planned postal survey should obtain at least a 40 per cent response rate and with the judicious use of reminders, a 70 per cent to 80 per cent response level should be possible. A preliminary pilot survey is invaluable in that it can indicate the general level of response to be expected. The main survey should generally achieve at least as high as and normally a higher level of return than the pilot inquiry. The Government Social Survey (now the Office of Population Censuses and Surveys) recommends the use of three reminders which, they say, can increase the original return by as much as 30 per cent in surveys

of the general public. A typical pattern of responses to the three follow-ups is as follows:

Original despatch	40 per cent
First follow-up	+20 per cent
Second follow-up	+10 per cent
Third follow-up	+5 per cent
Total	75 per cent

Incentives

An important factor in maximizing response rates is the use of incentives. Although such usage is comparatively rare in British surveys, it can substantially reduce non-response rates particularly when the chosen incentives accompany the initial mailing rather than being mailed subsequently as rewards for the return of completed schedules. The explanation of the effectiveness of this particular ploy appears to lie in the sense of obligation that is created in the recipient. Care is needed in selecting the most appropriate type of incentive. It should clearly be seen as a token rather than a payment for the respondent's efforts and, according to Hoinville and Jowell, should be as neutral as possible. In this respect, they suggest that books of postage stamps or ballpoint pens are cheap, easily packaged in the questionnaire envelopes, and appropriate to the task required of the respondent.

The preparation of a flow chart can help the researcher to plan the timing and the sequencing of the various parts of a postal survey. One such flow chart suggested by Hoinville and Jowell (1978) is shown in Box 14.2. The researcher might wish to add a chronological chart alongside it to help plan the exact timing of the events shown here.

Validity

Our discussion, so far, has concentrated on ways of increasing the response rate of postal questionnaires; we have said nothing yet about the validity of this particular technique.

Validity of postal questionnaires can be seen

Box 14.2

A flow chart for the planning of a postal survey

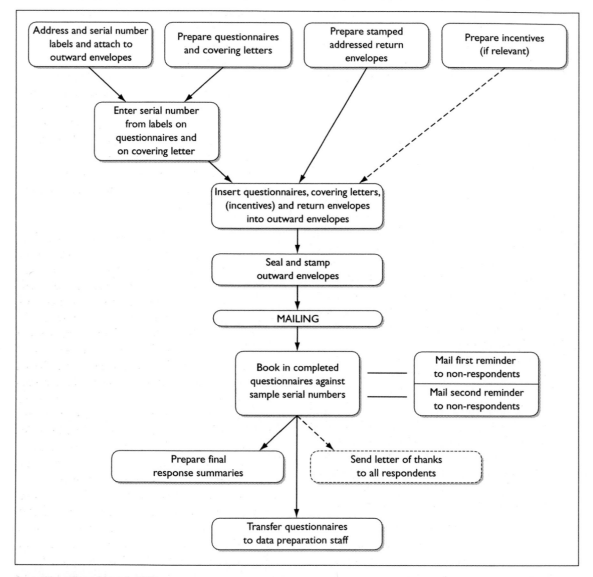

Source Hoinville and Jowell, 1978

from two viewpoints according to Belson (1986). First, whether respondents who complete questionnaires do so accurately and, second, whether those who fail to return their questionnaires would have given the same distribution of answers as did the returnees.

The question of accuracy can be checked by means of the intensive interview method, a technique consisting of twelve principal tactics that include familiarization, temporal reconstruction, probing and challenging.

The interested reader should consult Belson (1986: 35–8).

The problem of non-response (the issue of

'volunteer bias' as Belson calls it) can, in part, be checked on and controlled for, particularly when the postal questionnaire is sent out on a continuous basis. It involves follow-up contact with non-respondents by means of interviewers trained to secure interviews with such people. A comparison is then made between the replies of respondents and non-respondents.

Processing questionnaire data

Let us assume that researchers have followed the advice we have given about the planning of postal questionnaires and have secured a high response rate to their surveys. Their task is now to reduce the mass of data they have obtained to a form suitable for analysis. 'Data reduction', as the process is called, generally consists of coding data in preparation for analysis – by hand in the case of small surveys; by computers when numbers are larger. First, however, prior to coding, the questionnaires have to be checked. This task is referred to as *editing*.

Editing questionnaires is intended to identify and eliminate errors made by respondents. (In addition to the clerical editing that we discuss in this section, editing checks are also performed by the computer, e.g. SphinxSurvey, HyperRE-SEARCH, Results for Research™. For an account of computer-run structure checks and valid coding range checks, see also Hoinville and Jowell (1978) pp. 150–5. Moser and Kalton (1977) point to three central tasks in editing:

1   *Completeness*   A check is made that there is an answer to every question. In most surveys, interviewers are required to record an answer to every question (a 'not applicable' category always being available). Missing answers can sometimes be cross-checked from other sections of the survey. At worst, respondents can be contacted again to supply the missing information.

2   *Accuracy*   As far as is possible a check is made that all questions are answered accurately. Inaccuracies arise out of carelessness on the part of either interviewers or respondents. Sometimes a deliberate attempt is made to mislead. A tick in the wrong box, a ring round the wrong code, an error in simple arithmetic – all can reduce the validity of the data unless they are picked up in the editing process.

3   *Uniformity*   A check is made that interviewers have interpreted instructions and questions uniformly. Sometimes the failure to give explicit instructions over the interpretation of respondents' replies leads to interviewers recording the same answer in a variety of answer codes instead of one. A check on uniformity can help eradicate this source of error.

The primary task of data reduction is *coding*, that is, assigning a code number to each answer to a survey question. Of course, not all answers to survey questions can be reduced to code numbers. Many open-ended questions, for example, are not reducible in this way for computer analysis. Coding can be built into the construction of the questionnaire itself. In this case, we talk of precoded answers. Where coding is developed after the questionnaire has been administered and answered by respondents, we refer to post-coded answers. Precoding is appropriate for closed-ended questions – male 1, female 0, for example; or single 0, married 1, separated 2, divorced 3. For questions such as those whose answer categories are known in advance, a coding frame is generally developed before the interviewing commences so that it can be printed into the questionnaire itself. For open-ended questions (Why did you choose this particular in-service course rather than XYZ?), a coding frame has to be devised after the completion of the questionnaire. This is best done by taking a random sample of the questionnaires (10 per cent or more, time permitting) and generating a frequency tally of the range of responses as a preliminary to coding classification. Having devised the coding frame, the researcher can make a further check on its validity by using it to code up a further sample of the questionnaires. It is vital to get coding frames right from the outset –

extending them or making alterations at a later point in the study is both expensive and wearisome.

There are several computer packages that will process questionnaire survey data. At the time of writing one such is SphinxSurvey. This package, like others of its type, assists researchers in the design, administration and processing of questionnaires, either for paper-based or for on-screen administration. Responses can be entered rapidly, and data can be examined automatically, producing graphs and tables, as well as a wide range of statistics. (The Plus[2] edition offers lexical analysis of open-ended text, and the Lexica Edition has additional functions for qualitative data analysis.) A website for previewing a demonstration of this program can be found at *http://www.scolari.co.uk* and is typical of several of its kind.

Whilst coding is usually undertaken by the researcher, Sudman and Bradburn (1982: 149) also make the case for coding by the respondents themselves, to increase validity. This is particularly valuable in open-ended questionnaire items, though, of course, it does assume not only the willingness of respondents to become involved *post hoc* but, also, that the researcher can identify and trace the respondents, which, as was indicated earlier, is an ethical matter.

Introduction

The use of the interview in research marks a move away from seeing human subjects as simply manipulable and data as somehow external to individuals, and towards regarding knowledge as generated between humans, often through conversations (Kvale, 1996: 11). Regarding an interview, as Kvale (ibid.: 14) remarks, as an *interview*, an interchange of views between two or more people on a topic of mutual interest, sees the centrality of human interaction for knowledge production, and emphasizes the social situatedness of research data. As we suggested in Chapter 2, knowledge should be seen as constructed between participants, generating *data* rather than *capta* (Laing, 1967: 53). As such, the interview is not exclusively either subjective or objective, it is intersubjective (ibid.: 66). Interviews enable participants – be they interviewers or interviewees – to discuss their interpretations of the world in which they live, and to express how they regard situations from their own point of view. In these senses the interview is not simply concerned with collecting data about life: it is part of life itself, its human embeddedness is inescapable.

Conceptions of the interview

Kitwood (1977) lucidly contrasts three conceptions of it. The first conception is that of a potential means of pure information transfer and collection. A second conception of the interview is that of a transaction which inevitably has bias, which is to be recognized and controlled. According to this viewpoint, Kitwood explains that 'each participant in an interview will define the situation in a particular way. This fact can be best handled by building controls into the research design, for example by having a range of interviewers with different biases'. The interview is best understood in terms of a theory of motivation which recognizes a range of non-rational factors governing human behaviour, like emotions, unconscious needs and interpersonal influences. Kitwood points out that both these views of the interview regard the inherent features of interpersonal transactions as if they were 'potential obstacles to sound research, and therefore to be removed, controlled, or at least harnessed in some way'.

The third conception of the interview sees it as an encounter necessarily sharing many of the features of everyday life (see for example, Box 15.1). What is required, according to this view, is not a technique for dealing with bias, but a theory of everyday life that takes account of the relevant features of interviews. These may include role-playing, stereotyping, perception and understanding. One of the strongest advocates of this viewpoint is Cicourel (1964) who lists five of the unavoidable features of the interview situation that would normally be regarded as problematic:

1   There are many factors which inevitably differ from one interview to another, such as mutual trust, social distance and the interviewer's control.
2   The respondent may well feel uneasy and adopt avoidance tactics if the questioning is too deep.
3   Both interviewer and respondent are bound

Box 15.1
Attributes of ethnographers as interviewers

Trust   There would have to be a relationship between the interviewer and interviewee that transcended the research, that promoted a bond of friendship, a feeling of togetherness and joint pursuit of a common mission rising above personal egos.

Curiosity   There would have to be a desire to know, to learn people's views and perceptions of the facts, to hear their stories, discover their feelings. This is the motive force, and it has to be a burning one, that drives researchers to tackle and overcome the many difficulties involved in setting up and conducting successful interviews.

Naturalness   As with observation one endeavours to be unobtrusive in order to witness events as they are, untainted by one's presence and actions, so in interviews the aim is to secure what is within the minds of interviewees, uncoloured and unaffected by the interviewer.

Source Adapted from Woods, 1986

to hold back part of what it is in their power to state.

4   Many of the meanings which are clear to one will be relatively opaque to the other, even when the intention is genuine communication.

5   It is impossible, just as in everyday life, to bring every aspect of the encounter within rational control.

The message here is that no matter how hard an interviewer may try to be systematic and objective, the constraints of everyday life will be a part of whatever interpersonal transactions she initiates. Barker and Johnson (1998: 230) argue that the interview is a particular medium for enacting or displaying people's knowledge of cultural forms, as questions, far from being neutral, are couched in the cultural repertoires of all participants, indicating how people make sense of their social world and of each other.[1]

Purposes of the interview

The purposes of the interview are many and varied, for example:

- to evaluate or assess a person in some respect;
- to select or promote an employee;
- to effect therapeutic change, as in the psychiatric interview;
- to test or develop hypotheses;
- to gather data, as in surveys or experimental situations;
- to sample respondents' opinions, as in doorstep interviews.

Although in each of these situations the respective roles of the interviewer and interviewee may vary and the motives for taking part may differ, a common denominator is the transaction that takes place between seeking information on the part of one and supplying information on the part of the other.

The research interview may serve three purposes. First, it may be used as the principal means of gathering information having direct bearing on the research objectives. As Tuckman describes it, 'By providing access to what is "inside a person's head", [it] makes it possible to measure what a person knows (knowledge or information), what a person likes or dislikes (values and preferences), and what a person thinks (attitudes and beliefs)' (Tuckman, 1972). Second, it may be used to test hypotheses or to suggest new ones; or as an explanatory device to help identify variables and relationships. And third, the interview may be used in conjunction with other methods in a research undertaking. In this connection, Kerlinger (1970) suggests that it might be used to follow up unexpected results, for example, or to validate other methods, or to go deeper into the motivations of respondents and their reasons for responding as they do.

We limit ourselves here to the use of the interview as a specific research tool. Interviews in this sense range from the formal interview in which set questions are asked and the answers recorded on a standardized schedule; through less formal interviews in which the interviewer is free to modify the sequence of questions, change the wording, explain them or add to them; to the completely informal interview where the interviewer may have a number of key issues which she raises in conversational style. Beyond this point is located the non-directive interview in which the interviewer takes on a subordinate role.

The research interview has been defined as 'a two-person conversation initiated by the interviewer for the specific purpose of obtaining research-relevant information, and focused by him [sic] on content specified by research objectives of systematic description, prediction, or explanation' (Cannell and Kahn, 1968: 527). It involves the gathering of data through direct verbal interaction between individuals. In this sense it differs from the questionnaire where the respondent is required to record in some way her responses to set questions.

As the interview has some things in common with the self-administered questionnaire, it is frequently compared with it. Each has advantages over the other in certain respects. The advantages of the questionnaire, for instance, are: it tends to be more reliable; because it is anonymous, it encourages greater honesty; it is more economical than the interview in terms of time and money; and there is the possibility that it may be mailed. Its disadvantages, on the other hand, are: there is often too low a percentage of returns; the interviewer is able to answer questions concerning both the purpose of the interview and any misunderstandings experienced by the interviewee, for it sometimes happens in the case of the latter that the same questions have different meanings for different people; if only closed items are used, the questionnaire will be subject to the weaknesses already discussed; if only open items are used, respondents may be unwilling to write their answers for one reason or another; questionnaires present problems to people of limited literacy; and an interview can be conducted at an appropriate speed whereas questionnaires are often filled in hurriedly.

By way of interest, we illustrate the relative merits of the interview and the questionnaire in Box 15.2. It has been pointed out that the direct interaction of the interview is the source of both its advantages and disadvantages as a research technique (Borg, 1963). One advantage, for example, is that it allows for greater depth than is the case with other methods of data collection. A disadvantage, on the other hand, is that it is prone to subjectivity and bias on the part of the interviewer. Oppenheim (1992: 81–2) suggests that interviews have a higher response rate than questionnaires because respondents become more involved and, hence, motivated; they enable more to be said about the research than is usually mentioned in a covering letter to

Box 15.2
Summary of relative merits of interview versus questionnaire

Consideration		Interview	Questionnaire
1	Personal need to collect data	Requires interviewers	Requires a secretary
2	Major expense	Payment to interviewers	Postage and printing
3	Opportunities for response-keying (personalization)	Extensive	Limited
4	Opportunities for asking	Extensive	Limited
5	Opportunities for probing	Possible	Difficult
6	Relative magnitude of data reduction	Great (because of coding)	Mainly limited to rostering
7	Typically, the number of respondents who can be reached	Limited	Extensive
8	Rate of return	Good	Poor
9	Sources of error	Interviewer, instrument, coding, sample	Limited to instrument and sample
10	Overall reliability	Quite limited	Fair
11	Emphasis on writing skill	Limited	Extensive

Source Tuckman, 1972

a questionnaire, and they are better than questionnaires for handling more difficult and open-ended questions.

Types of interview

The number of types of interview given is frequently a function of the sources one reads! For example LeCompte and Preissle (1993) give six types: (a) standardized interviews; (b) in-depth interviews; (c) ethnographic interviews; (d) elite interviews; (e) life history interviews; (f) focus groups. Bogdan and Biklen (1992) add to this: (g) semi-structured interviews; (h) group interviews. Lincoln and Guba (1985) add: (i) structured interviews; and Oppenheim (1992: 65) adds to this: (j) exploratory interviews. Patton (1980: 206) outlines four types: (k) informal conversational interviews; (l) interview guide approaches; (m) standardized open-ended interviews; (n) closed quantitative interviews. Patton sets these out clearly thus (Box 15.3):

How is the researcher to comprehend the range of these various types? Kvale (1996: 126–7) sets the several types of interview along a series of continua, arguing that interviews differ in the openness of their purpose, their degree of structure, the extent to which they are exploratory or hypothesis-testing, whether they seek description or interpretation, whether they are largely cognitive-focused or emotion-focused. A major difference lies in the degree of structure in the interview, which, itself, reflects the purposes of the interview, for example, to generate numbers of respondents' feelings about a given issue or to indicate unique, alternative feelings about a particular matter. Lincoln and Guba (1985: 269) suggest that the structured interview is useful when the researcher is aware of what she does not know and therefore is in a position to frame questions that will supply the knowledge required, whereas the unstructured interview is useful when the researcher is not aware of what she does not know, and therefore, relies on the respondents to tell her!

The issue here is of 'fitness for purpose'; the more one wishes to gain comparable data – across people, across sites – the more standardized and quantitative one's interview tends to become; the more one wishes to acquire unique, non-standardized, personalized information about how individuals view the world, the more one veers towards qualitative, open-ended, unstructured interviewing. Indeed this is true not simply of interviews but of their written counterpart – questionnaires. Oppenheim (1992: 86) indicates that standardization should refer to *stimulus equivalence*, i.e. that every respondent should *understand* the interview question in the same way, rather than replicating the exact wording, as some respondents might have difficulty with, or interpret very differently, and perhaps irrelevantly, particular questions. (He also adds, that, as soon as the wording of a question is altered, however minimally, it becomes, in effect, a different question!)

Exploratory interviews (Oppenheim, 1992: 65) are designed to be essentially heuristic and seek to develop hypotheses rather than to collect facts and numbers. As these frequently cover emotionally loaded topics they require skill on the part of the interviewer to handle the interview situation, enabling respondents to talk freely and emotionally and to have candour, richness, depth, authenticity, honesty about their experiences.

Morrison (1993: 34–6) sets out five continua of different ways of conceptualizing interviews. At one end of the first continuum are numbers, statistics, objective facts, quantitative data; at the other end are transcripts of conversations, comments, subjective accounts, essentially word-based qualitative data.

At one end of the second continuum are closed questions, multiple choice questions where respondents have to select from a given, predetermined range of responses that particular response which most accurately represents what they wish to have recorded for them; at the other end of the continuum are open-ended questions which do not require the selection from a given range of responses – respondents can answer the questions in their own way and in their own words, i.e. the research is responsive to participants' own frames of reference.

Box 15.3
Strengths and weaknesses of different types of interview

Type of interview	Characteristics	Strengths	Weaknesses
1 Informal conversational interview	Questions emerge from the immediate context and are asked in the natural course of things; there is no predetermination of question topics or wording.	Increases the salience and relevance of questions; interviews are built on and emerge from observations; the interview can be matched to individuals and circumstances.	Different information collected from different people with different questions. Less systematic and comprehensive if certain questions don't arise 'naturally'. Data organization and analysis can be quite difficult.
2 Interview guide approach	Topics and issues to be covered are specified in advance, in outline form; interviewer decides sequence and working of questions in the course of the interview.	The outline increases the comprehensiveness of the data and makes data collection somewhat systematic for each respondent. Logical gaps in data can be anticipated and closed. Interviews remain fairly conversational and situational.	Important and salient topics may be inadvertently omitted. Interviewer flexibility in sequencing and wording questions can result in substantially different responses, thus reducing the comparability of responses.
3 Standardized open-ended interviews	The exact wording and sequence of questions are determined in advance. All interviewees are asked the same basic questions in the same order.	Respondents answer the same questions, thus increasing comparability of responses; data are complete for each person on the topics addressed in the interview. Reduces interviewer effects and bias when several interviewers are used. Permits decision-makers to see and review the instrumentation used in the evaluation. Facilitates organization and analysis of the data.	Little flexibility in relating the interview to particular individuals and circumstances; standardized wording of questions may constrain and limit naturalness and relevance of questions and answers.
4 Closed quantitative interviews	Questions and response categories are determined in advance. Responses are fixed; respondent chooses from among these fixed responses.	Data analysis is simple; responses can be directly compared and easily aggregated; many short questions can be asked in a short time.	Respondents must fit their experiences and feelings into the researcher's categories; may be perceived as impersonal, irrelevant, and mechanistic. Can distort what respondents really mean or experienced by so completely limiting their response choices.

Source Patton, 1980: 206

At one end of the third continuum is a desire to measure responses, to compare one set of responses with another, to correlate responses, to see how many people said this, how many rated a particular item as such-and-such; at the other end of the continuum is a desire to capture the uniqueness of a particular situation, person, or programme – what makes it different from others, i.e. to record the quality of a situation or response.

At one end of the fourth continuum is a desire for formality and the precision of numbers and prescribed categories of response where the researcher knows in advance what is being sought; at the other end is a more responsive, informal intent where what is being sought is more uncertain and pre-determined. The researcher goes into the situation and responds to what emerges.

At one end of the fifth continuum is the attempt to find regularities – of response, opinions etc. – in order to begin to make generalizations from the data, to describe what is happening; at the other end is the attempt to portray and catch uniqueness, the quality of a response, the complexity of a situation, to understand why respondents say what they say, and all of this in their own terms.

One can cluster the sets of poles of the five continua thus:

Quantitative approaches	Qualitative approaches
Numbers	Words
predetermined, given	open-ended, responsive
measuring	capturing uniqueness
short-term, intermittent	long-term, continuous
comparing	capturing particularity
correlating	valuing quality
frequencies	individuality
formality	informality
looking at regularities	looking for uniqueness
description	explanation
objective facts	subjective facts
describing	interpreting
looking in from the outside	looking from the inside
structured	unstructured
statistical	ethnographic, illuminative

The left hand column is much more formal and pre-planned to a high level of detail, whilst the right hand column is far less formal and the fine detail only emerges once the researcher is *in situ*. Interviews in the left hand column are front-loaded, that is, they require all the categories and multiple choice questions to be worked out in advance. This usually requires a pilot to try out the material and refine it. Once the detail of this planning is completed the analysis of the data is relatively straightforward because the categories for analysing the data have been worked out in advance, hence data analysis is rapid.

The right hand column is much more end-loaded, that is, it is quicker to commence and gather data because the categories do not have to be worked out in advance, they emerge once the data have been collected. However, in order to discover the issues that emerge and to organize the data presentation, the analysis of the data takes considerably longer.

Kvale (1996: 30) sets out key characteristics of qualitative research interviews:

- *Life world* The topic of the qualitative research interview is the lived world of the subjects and their relation to it.
- *Meaning* The interview seeks to interpret the meaning of central themes in the life world of the subject. The interviewer registers and interprets the meaning of what is said as well as how it is said.
- *Qualitative* The interview seeks qualitative knowledge expressed in normal language, it does not aim at quantification.
- *Descriptive* The interview attempts to obtain open nuanced descriptions of different aspects of the subjects' life worlds.
- *Specificity* Descriptions of specific situations and action sequences are elicited, not general opinions.
- *Deliberate naiveté* The interviewer exhibits an openness to new and unexpected phenomena, rather than having ready-made categories and schemes of interpretation.
- *Focused* The interview is focused on particular themes; it is neither strictly structured with standardized questions, nor entirely 'non-directive'.
- *Ambiguity* Interviewee statements can some-

times be ambiguous, reflecting contradictions in the world the subject lives in.

- *Change* The process of being interviewed may produce new insights and awareness, and the subject may in the course of the interview come to change his or her descriptions and meanings about a theme.
- *Sensitivity* Different interviewers can produce different statements on the same themes, depending on their sensitivity to and knowledge of the interview topic.
- *Interpersonal relations* The knowledge obtained is produced through the interpersonal interaction in the interview.
- *Positive experience* A well carried-out research interview can be a rare and enriching experience for the interviewee, who may obtain new insights into his or her life situation.

There are four main kinds of interview that we discuss here that may be used specifically as research tools: (a) the structured interview; (b) the unstructured interview; (c) the non-directive interview; and (d) the focused interview. The structured interview is one in which the content and procedures are organized in advance. This means that the sequence and wording of the questions are determined by means of a schedule and the interviewer is left little freedom to make modifications. Where some leeway is granted her, it too is specified in advance. It is therefore characterized by being a closed situation. In contrast to this, the unstructured interview is an open situation, having greater flexibility and freedom. As Kerlinger (1970) notes, although the research purposes govern the questions asked, their content, sequence and wording are entirely in the hands of the interviewer. This does not mean, however, that the unstructured interview is a more casual affair, for in its own way it also has to be carefully planned.

The non-directive interview as a research technique derives from the therapeutic or psychiatric interview. The principal features of it are the minimal direction or control exhibited by the interviewer and the freedom the respondent has to express her subjective feelings as fully and as spontaneously as she chooses or is able. As Moser and Kalton (1977) put it:

> The informant is encouraged to talk about the subject under investigation (usually himself) and the course of the interview is mainly guided by him. There are no set questions, and usually no predetermined framework for recorded answers. The interviewer confines himself to elucidating doubtful points, to rephrasing the respondent's answers and to probing generally. It is an approach especially to be recommended when complex attitudes are involved and when one's knowledge of them is still in a vague and unstructured form.
>
> (Moser and Kalton, 1977)

The need to introduce rather more interviewer control into the non-directive situation led to the development of the focused interview. The distinctive feature of this type is that it focuses on a respondent's subjective responses to a known situation in which she has been involved and which has been analysed by the interviewer prior to the interview. She is thereby able to use the data from the interview to substantiate or reject previously formulated hypotheses. As Merton and Kendall (1946) explain,

> In the usual depth interview, one can urge informants to reminisce on their experiences. In the focused interview, however, the interviewer can, when expedient, play a more active role: he can introduce more explicit verbal cues to the stimulus pattern or even *represent* it. In either case this usually activates a concrete report of responses by informants.
>
> (Merton and Kendall, 1946)

We examine the non-directive interview and the focused interview in more detail later in the chapter.

Planning interview-based research procedures

Kvale (1996: 88) sets out seven stages of an interview investigation that can be used to plan this type of research:

- *Thematizing* Formulate the purpose of an investigation and describe the concept of the topic to be investigated before the interviews start. The *why* and *what* of the investigation should be clarified before the question of *how* – method – is posed.
- *Designing* Plan the design of the study, taking into consideration all seven stages of the investigation, before the interviewing starts.
- *Interviewing* Conduct the interviews based on an interview guide and with a reflective approach to the knowledge sought and the interpersonal relation of the interview situation.
- *Transcribing* Prepare the interview material for analysis, which commonly includes a transcription from oral speech to written text.
- *Analysing* Decide, on the basis of the purpose and topic of the investigation, and on the nature of the interview material, which methods of analysis are appropriate for the interviews.
- *Verifying* Ascertain the generalizability, reliability, and validity of the interview findings.
- *Reporting* Communicate the findings of the study and the methods applied in a form that lives up to scientific criteria, takes the ethical aspects of the investigation into consideration, and that results in a readable product.

We use these to structure our comments here about the planning of interview-based research.

Thematizing

The preliminary stage of an interview study will be the point where the purpose of the research is decided. It may begin by outlining the theoretical basis of the study, its broad aims, its practical value and the reasons why the interview approach was chosen. There may then follow the translation of the general goals of the research into more detailed and specific objectives. This is the most important step, for only careful formulation of objectives at this point will eventually produce the right kind of data necessary for satisfactory answers to the research problem.

Designing

There follows the preparation of the interview schedule itself. This involves translating the research objectives into the questions that will make up the main body of the schedule. This needs to be done in such a way that the questions adequately reflect what it is the researcher is trying to find out. It is quite usual to begin this task by writing down the variables to be dealt with in the study. As one commentator says, 'The first step in constructing interview questions is to *specify your variables by name*. Your variables are what you are trying to measure. They tell you where to begin' (Tuckman, 1972).

Before the actual interview items are prepared, it is desirable to give some thought to the question format and the response mode. The choice of question format, for instance, depends on a consideration of one or more of the following factors:

- the objectives of the interview;
- the nature of the subject matter;
- whether the interviewer is dealing in facts, opinions or attitudes;
- whether specificity or depth is sought;
- the respondent's level of education;
- the kind of information she can be expected to have;
- whether or not her thought needs to be structured; some assessment of her motivational level;
- the extent of the interviewer's own insight into the respondent's situation;
- the kind of relationship the interviewer can expect to develop with the respondent.

Having given prior thought to these matters, the researcher is in a position to decide whether to use open and/or closed questions, direct and/or indirect questions, specific and/or non-specific questions, and so on.

Construction of schedules

Three kinds of items are used in the construction of schedules used in research interviews (see Kerlinger, 1970). First, 'fixed-alternative' items allow the respondent to choose from two or more alternatives. The most frequently used is the dichotomous item which offers two alternatives only: 'yes-no' or 'agree-disagree', for instance. Sometimes a third alternative such as 'undecided' or 'don't know' is also offered.

> *Example*: Do you feel it is against the interests of a school to have to make public its examination results?
> Yes
> No
> Don't know

Kerlinger has identified the chief advantages and disadvantages of fixed-alternative items. They have, for example, the advantage of achieving greater uniformity of measurement and therefore greater reliability; of making the respondents answer in a manner fitting the response category; and of being more easily coded.

Disadvantages include their superficiality; the possibility of irritating respondents who find none of the alternatives suitable; and the possibility of forcing responses that are inappropriate, either because the alternative chosen conceals ignorance on the part of the respondent or because she may choose an alternative that does not accurately represent the true facts. These weaknesses can be overcome, however, if the items are written with care, mixed with open-ended ones, and used in conjunction with probes on the part of the interviewer.

Second, 'open-ended items' have been succinctly defined by Kerlinger as 'those that supply a frame of reference for respondents' answers, but put a minimum of restraint on the answers and their expression' (Kerlinger, 1970). Other than the subject of the question, which is determined by the nature of the problem under investigation, there are no other restrictions on either the content or the manner of the interviewee's reply.

> *Example*: What kind of television programmes do you most prefer to watch?

Open-ended questions have a number of advantages: they are flexible; they allow the interviewer to probe so that she may go into more depth if she chooses, or to clear up any misunderstandings; they enable the interviewer to test the limits of the respondent's knowledge; they encourage co-operation and help establish rapport; and they allow the interviewer to make a truer assessment of what the respondent really believes. Open-ended situations can also result in unexpected or unanticipated answers which may suggest hitherto unthought-of relationships or hypotheses. A particular kind of open-ended question is the 'funnel' to which reference has been made earlier. This starts, the reader will recall, with a broad question or statement and then narrows down to more specific ones. Kerlinger (1970) quotes an example from the study by Sears, Maccoby and Levin (1957):

> All babies cry, of course. Some mothers feel that if you pick up a baby every time it cries, you will spoil it. Others think you should never let a baby cry for very long. How do you feel about this? What did you do about it? How about the middle of the night?
> (Sears, Maccoby and Levin, 1957)

Third, the 'scale' is, as we have already seen, a set of verbal items to each of which the interviewee responds by indicating degrees of agreement or disagreement. The individual's response is thus located on a scale of fixed alternatives. The use of this technique along with open-ended questions is a comparatively recent development and means that scale scores can be checked against data elicited by the open-ended questions.

> *Example*: Attendance at school after the age of 14 should be voluntary:
> Strongly agree Agree Undecided Disagree Strongly disagree

It is possible to use one of a number of scales in this context: attitude scales, rank-order scales, rating scales, and so on. We touch upon this subject again subsequently.

Question formats

We now look at the kinds of questions and modes of response associated with interviewing. First, the matter of question format: how is a question to be phrased or organized? (see Wilson, 1996). Tuckman (1972) has listed four such formats that an interviewer may draw upon. Questions may, for example, take a direct or indirect form. Thus an interviewer could ask a teacher whether she likes teaching: this would be a direct question. Or else she could adopt an indirect approach by asking for the respondent's views on education in general and the ways schools function. From the answers proffered, the interviewer could make inferences about the teacher's opinions concerning her own job. Tuckman suggests that by making the purpose of questions less obvious, the indirect approach is more likely to produce frank and open responses.

There are also those kinds of questions which deal with either a general or specific issue. To ask a child what she thought of the teaching methods of the staff as a whole would be a general or non-specific question. To ask her what she thought of her teacher as a teacher would be a specific question. There is also the sequence of questions designated the funnel in which the movement is from the general and non-specific to the more specific. Tuckman comments, 'Specific questions, like direct ones, may cause a respondent to become cautious or guarded and give less-than-honest answers. Non-specific questions may lead circuitously to the desired information but with less alarm by the respondents' (Tuckman, 1972).

A further distinction is that between questions inviting factual answers and those inviting opinions. Both fact and opinion questions can yield less than the truth, however: the former do not always produce factual answers; nor do the latter necessarily elicit honest opinions. In both instances, inaccuracy and bias may be minimized by careful structuring of the questions.

There are several ways of categorizing questions, for example (Spradley, 1979; Patton, 1980):

- descriptive questions;
- experience questions;
- behaviour questions;
- knowledge questions;
- construct-forming questions;
- contrast questions (asking respondents to contrast one thing with another);
- feeling questions;
- sensory questions;
- background questions;
- demographic questions.

These concern the *substance* of the question. Kvale (1996: 133–5) adds to these what might be termed the *process* questions, i.e. questions that:

- introduce a topic or interview;
- follow-up on a topic or idea;
- probe for further information or response;
- ask respondents to specify and provide examples;
- directly ask for information;
- indirectly ask for information;
- interpret respondents' replies.

We may also note that an interviewee may be presented with either a question or a statement. In the case of the latter she will be asked for her response to it in one form or another.

> *Example question*: Do you think homework should be compulsory for all children between 11 and 16?
> *Example statement*: Homework should be compulsory for all children between 11 and 16 years old.
> Agree Disagree Don't know

Response modes

If there are varied ways of asking questions, it follows there will be several ways in which they may be answered. It is to the different response modes that we now turn. In all, Tuckman (1972) lists seven such modes.

The first of these is the 'unstructured response'. This allows the respondent to give her answer in whatever way she chooses.

Example: Why did you not go to university?

A 'structured response', by contrast, would limit her in some way.

Example: Can you give me two reasons for not going to university?

Although the interviewer has little control over the unstructured response, it does ensure that the respondent has the freedom to give her own answer as fully as she chooses rather than being constrained in some way by the nature of the question. The chief disadvantage of the unstructured response concerns the matter of quantification. Data yielded in the unstructured response are more difficult to code and quantify than data in the structured response.

A 'fill-in response' mode requires the respondent to supply rather than choose a response, though the response is often limited to a word or phrase.

Example:

What is your present occupation? or

How long have you lived at your present address?

The differences between the fill-in response and the unstructured response is one of degree.

A 'tabular response' is similar to a fill-in response though more structured. It may demand words, figures or phrases, so example:

University	Subject	Degree	Dates	
			From	To

It is thus a convenient and short-hand way of recording complex information.

A 'scaled response' is one structured by means of a series of gradations. The respondent is required to record her response to a given statement by selecting from a number of alternatives.

Example: What are your chances of reaching a top managerial position within the next five years?

Excellent Good Fair Poor Very poor

Tuckman draws our attention to the fact that, unlike an unstructured response which has to be coded to be useful as data, a scaled response is collected in the form of usable and analysable data.

A 'ranking response' is one in which a respondent is required to rank-order a series of words, phrases or statements according to a particular criterion.

Example: Rank order the following people in terms of their usefulness to you as sources of advice and guidance on problems you have encountered in the classroom. Use numbers 1 to 5, with 1 representing the person most useful.

Education tutor

Subject tutor

Classteacher

Headteacher

Other student

Ranked data can be analysed by adding up the rank of each response across the respondents, thus resulting in an overall rank order of alternatives.

A 'checklist response' requires that the respondent selects one of the alternatives presented to her. In that they do not represent points on a continuum, they are nominal categories.

Example: I get most satisfaction in college from:

the social life

studying on my own

attending lectures

college societies

giving a paper at a seminar

This kind of response tends to yield less information than the other kinds considered.

Finally, the 'categorical response' mode is similar to the checklist but simpler in that it offers respondents only two possibilities.

Example: Material progress results in greater happiness for people

True False

or

In the event of another war, would you be prepared to fight for your country?

Yes No

Summing the numbers of respondents with the same responses yields a nominal measure.

As a general rule, the kind of information sought and the means of its acquisition will determine the choice of response mode. Data analysis, then, ought properly to be considered alongside the choice of response mode so that the interviewer can be confident that the data will serve her purposes and analysis of them can be duly prepared. Box 15.4 summarizes the relationship between response mode and type of data.

Once the variables to be measured or studied have been identified, questions can be constructed so as to reflect them. It is important to bear in mind that more than one question format and more than one response mode may be employed when building up a schedule. The final mixture will depend on the kinds of factors mentioned earlier – the objectives of the research, and so on.

Where an interview schedule is to be used by a number of trained interviewers, it will of course be necessary to include in it appropriate instructions for both interviewer and interviewees.

The framing of questions for a semi-structured interview will also need to consider *prompts* and *probes* (Morrison, 1993: 66). Prompts enable the interviewer to clarify topics or questions, whilst probes enable the interviewer to ask respondents to extend, elaborate, add to, provide detail for, clarify or qualify their response, thereby addressing richness, depth of response, comprehensiveness and honesty that are some of the hallmarks of successful interviewing (see also Patton, 1980: 238).

Hence an interview schedule for a semi-structured interview (i.e. where topics and open-ended questions are written but the exact sequence and wording does not have to be followed with each respondent) might include:

- the topic to be discussed;
- the specific possible questions to be put for each topic;
- the issues within each topic to be discussed, together with possible questions for each issue;
- a series of prompts and probes for each topic, issue and question.

'How many interviews do I need to conduct?' is a frequent question of novice researchers, asking both about the numbers of people and the number of interviews with each person. The advice here echoes that of Kvale (1996: 101) that one conducts interviews with as many people as necessary in order to gain the information sought. There is no simple rule of thumb, as this depends on the purpose of the interview, for example, whether it is to make generalizations, to provide in-depth, individual data, to gain a range of responses. Though the reader is directed to the chapter on sampling for fuller treatment of these matters, the issue here is that the interviewer must ensure that the interviewees

Box 15.4
The selection of response mode

Response mode	Type of data advantages	Chief advantages	Chief disadvantages
Fill-in	Nominal	Less biasing; greater response flexibility	More difficult to score
Scaled	Interval	Easy to score	Time consuming; can be biasing
Ranking	Ordinal	Easy to score; forces discrimination	Difficult to complete
Checklist or categorical	Nominal (may be interval when totalled)	Easy to score; easy to respond	Provides less data and fewer options

Source Tuckman, 1972

selected will be able to furnish the researcher with the information required.

Interviewing

Setting up and conducting the interview will make up the next stage in the procedure. Where the interviewer is initiating the research herself, she will clearly select her own respondents; where she is engaged by another agent, then she will probably be given a list of people to contact. Tuckman (1972) has succinctly reviewed the procedures to adopt at the interview itself. He writes,

> At the meeting, the interviewer should brief the respondent as to the nature or purpose of the interview (being as candid as possible without biasing responses) and attempt to make the respondent feel at ease. He should explain the manner in which he will be recording responses, and if he plans to tape record, he should get the respondent's assent. At all times, an interviewer must remember that he is a data collection instrument and try not to let his own biases, opinions, or curiosity affect his behaviour. It is important that the interviewer should not deviate from his format and interview schedule although many schedules will permit some flexibility in choice of questions. The respondent should be kept from rambling away from the essence of a question, but not at the sacrifice of courtesy.
>
> (Tuckman, 1972)

It is crucial to keep uppermost in one's mind the fact that the interview is a social, interpersonal encounter, not merely a data collection exercise. Indeed Kvale (1996: 125) suggests that an interview follows an unwritten script for interactions, the rules for which only surface when they are transgressed. Hence the interviewer must be at pains to conduct the interview carefully and sensitively. Kvale (1996: 147) adds that, as the researcher is the research instrument, the effective interviewer is not only knowledgeable about the subject matter but is also an expert in interaction and communication. The interviewer will need to establish an appropriate atmosphere such that the participant can feel secure to talk freely. This operates at several levels.

For example there is the need to address the *cognitive* aspect of the interview, ensuring that the interviewer is sufficiently knowledgeable about the subject matter that she or he can conduct the interview in an informed manner, and that the interviewee does not feel threatened by lack of knowledge. That this is a particular problem when interviewing children has been documented by Simons (1982) and Lewis (1992), who indicate that children will tend to say anything rather than nothing at all, thereby limiting the possible reliability of the data.

Further, the *ethical* dimension of the interview needs to be borne in mind, ensuring, for example, informed consent, guarantees of confidentiality, beneficence and non-maleficence (i.e. that the interview may be to the advantage of the respondent and will not harm her). The issue of ethics also needs to take account of what is to count as data, for example it is often after the cassette recorder or video camera has been switched off that the 'gems' of the interview are revealed, or people may wish to say something 'off the record'; the status of this kind of information needs to be clarified before the interview commences. The ethical aspects of interviewing are more fully discussed later in the chapter.

Then there is a need to address the *interpersonal, interactional, communicative and emotional* aspects of the interview. For example, the interviewer and interviewee communicate nonverbally, by facial and bodily expression. Something as slight as a shift in position in a chair might convey whether the researcher is interested, angry, bored, agreeing, disagreeing and so on. Here the interviewer has to be adept at 'active listening'.

The interviewer is also responsible for considering the *dynamics* of the situation, for example, how to keep the conversation going, how to motivate participants to discuss their thoughts, feelings and experiences, and how to overcome the problems of the likely asymmetries of power in the interview (where the interviewer typically defines the situation, the topic, the conduct, the introduction, the course of the interview, and the closing of the interview) (Kvale, 1996: 126).

As Kvale suggests, the interview is not usually a reciprocal interaction between two equal participants. It is important to keep the interview moving forward, and how to achieve this needs to be anticipated by the interviewer, for example by being clear on what one wishes to find out, asking those questions that will elicit the kinds of data sought, giving appropriate verbal and non-verbal feedback to the respondent during the interview. It extends even to considering when the interviewer should keep silent (ibid.: 135).

The 'directiveness' of the interviewer has been scaled by Whyte (1982), where a six-point scale was devised (1 = the least directive, and 6 = the most directive):

1   Making encouraging noises.
2   Reflecting on remarks made by the informant.
3   Probing on the last remark made by the informant.
4   Probing an idea preceding the last remark by the informant.
5   Probing an idea expressed earlier in the interview.
6   Introducing a new topic.

This is not to say that the interviewer should avoid being too directive or not directive enough; indeed on occasions a confrontational style might yield much more useful data than a non-confrontational style. Further, it may be in the interests of the research if the interview is sometimes quite tightly controlled, as this might facilitate the subsequent analysis of the data. For example, if the subsequent analysis will seek to categorize and classify the responses, then it might be useful for the interviewer to clarify meaning and even suggest classifications during the interview (see Kvale, 1996: 130).

Patton (1980: 210) suggests that it is important to maintain the interviewee's motivation, hence the interviewer must keep boredom at bay, for example by keeping to a minimum demographic and background questions. The issue of the *interpersonal* and *interactional* elements reaches further, for the language of all speakers has to be considered, for example, translating the academic language of the researcher into the everyday, more easy-going and colloquial language of the interviewee, in order to generate rich descriptions and authentic data. Patton (1980: 225) goes on to underline the importance of clarity in questioning, and suggests that this entails the interviewer finding out what terms the interviewees use about the matter in hand, what terms they use amongst themselves, and avoiding the use of academic jargon. The issue here is not only that the language of the interviewer must be understandable to interviewees but that it must be part of their frame of reference, such that they feel comfortable with it.

This can be pursued even further, suggesting that the age, gender, race, class, dress, language of the interviewers and interviewees will all exert an influence on the interview itself. This is discussed fully in Chapter 5 on reliability and validity.

The *sequence* and *framing* of the interview questions will also need to be considered, for example ensuring that easier and less threatening, non-controversial questions are addressed earlier in the interview in order to put respondents at their ease (see Patton, 1980: 210–11). This might mean that the 'what' questions precede the more searching and difficult 'how' and 'why' questions (though, as Patton reminds us (ibid.: 211), knowledge questions – 'what' - type questions – can be threatening). The interviewer's questions should be straightforward and brief, even though the responses need not be (Kvale, 1996: 132). It will also need to consider the *kinds* of questions to be put to interviewees, discussed earlier.

There are several problems in the actual conduct of an interview that can be anticipated and, possibly, prevented, ensuring that the interview proceeds comfortably, for example (see Field and Morse, 1989):

- avoiding interruptions from outside (e.g. telephone calls, people knocking on the door);
- minimizing distractions;
- minimizing the risk of 'stage fright' in interviewees and interviewers;

- avoiding asking embarrassing or awkward questions;
- jumping from one topic to another;
- giving advice or opinions (rather than active listening);
- summarizing too early or closing off an interview too soon;
- being too superficial;
- handling sensitive matters (e.g. legal matters, personal matters, emotional matters).

There is also the issue of how to record the interview as it proceeds. For example, an audio-tape recorder might be unobtrusive but might constrain the respondent; a videotape might yield more accurate data but might be even more constraining, with its connotation of sur-veillance. Merton *et al.* (1956) comment on the tendency of taping to 'cool things down'. It might be less threatening not to have any mechanical means of recording the interview, in which case the reliability of the data might rely on the memory of the interviewer. An alterna-tive might be to have the interviewer make notes *during* the interview, but this could be highly off-putting for some respondents. The issue here is that there is a trade-off between the need to catch as much data as possible and yet to avoid having so threatening an environ-ment that it impedes the potential of the inter-view situation.

What is being suggested here is that the inter-view, as a social encounter, has to take account of, and plan for, the whole range of other, possi-bly non-cognitive, factors that form part of everyday conduct. The 'ideal' interview, then, meets several 'quality criteria' (Kvale, 1996: 145):

- The extent of spontaneous, rich, specific, and relevant answers from the interviewee.
- The shorter the interviewer's questions and the longer the subject's answers, the better.
- The degree to which the interviewer follows up and clarifies the meanings of the relevant aspects of the answers.
- The ideal interview is to a large extent inter-preted throughout the interview.
- The interviewer attempts to verify his or her interpretations of the subject's answers in the course of the interview.
- The interview is 'self-communicating' – it is a story contained in itself that hardly requires much extra descriptions and explanations.

Transcribing

This is a crucial step, for there is the potential for massive data loss, distortion and the reduction of complexity. We have suggested throughout that the interview is a social encounter, not merely a data collection exercise; the problem with much transcription is that it becomes solely a record of data rather than a record of a social encounter. Indeed this problem might have begun at the data collection stage; for example, an audiotape is selective, it filters out important contextual factors, neglecting the visual and non-verbal aspects of the interview (Mishler, 1986). Indeed it is frequently the non-verbal communi-cation that gives more information than the verbal communication. Morrison (1993: 63) recounts the incident of an autocratic head-teacher extolling the virtues of collegiality and democratic decision-making whilst shaking her head vigorously from side to side and pressing the flat of her hand in a downwards motion away from herself as if to silence discussion! To replace audio recording with video recording might make for richer data and catch non-verbal communication, but this then becomes very time-consuming to analyse.

Transcriptions inevitably lose data from the original encounter. This problem is com-pounded, for a transcription represents the translation from one set of rule systems (oral and interpersonal) to another very remote rule system (written language). As Kvale (1996: 166) suggests the prefix *trans* indicates a change of state or form; transcription is selective transfor-mation. Therefore it is unrealistic to pretend that the data on transcripts are anything but *already interpreted* data. As Kvale (ibid.: 167) remarks, the transcript can become an opaque screen between the researcher and the original live interview situation.

There can be no single 'correct' transcription; rather the issue becomes whether, to what extent, and how a transcription is useful for the research. Transcriptions are decontextualized, abstracted from time and space, from the dynamics of the situation, from the live form, and from the social, interactive, dynamic and fluid dimensions of their source; they are frozen.

The words in transcripts are not necessarily as solid as they were in the social setting of the interview. Scheurich (1995: 240) suggests that even conventional procedures for achieving reliability are inadequate here, for holding constant the questions, the interviewer, the interviewee, the time and place does not guarantee stable, unambiguous data. Indeed Mishler (1991: 260) suggests that data and the relationship between meaning and language are contextually situated; they are unstable, changing and capable of endless reinterpretation.

We are not arguing against transcriptions, rather, we are cautioning against the researcher believing that they tell everything that took place in the interview. This might require the researcher to ensure that different *kinds* of data are recorded in the transcript of the audiotape, for example:

- what was being said;
- the tone of voice of the speaker(s) (e.g. harsh, kindly, encouraging);
- the inflection of the voice (e.g. rising or falling, a question or a statement, a cadence or a pause, a summarizing or exploratory tone, opening or closing a line of inquiry);
- emphases placed by the speaker;
- pauses (short to long) and silences (short to long);
- interruptions;
- the mood of the speaker(s) (e.g. excited, angry, resigned, bored, enthusiastic, committed, happy, grudging);
- the speed of the talk (fast to slow, hurried or unhurried, hesitant to confident);
- how many people were speaking simultaneously;
- whether a speaker was speaking continuously or in short phrases;
- who is speaking to whom;
- indecipherable speech;
- any other events that were taking place at the same time that the researcher can recall.

If the transcript is of videotape, then this enables the researcher to comment on all of the non-verbal communication that was taking place in addition to the features noted from the audiotape. The issue here is that it is often inadequate to transcribe only spoken words; other data are important. Of course, as soon as other data are noted, this becomes a matter of interpretation (what is a long pause, what is a short pause, was the respondent happy or was it just a 'front', what gave rise to such-and-such a question or response, why did the speaker suddenly burst into tears?). As Kvale (1996: 183) notes, interviewees' statements are not simply collected by the interviewer, they are, in reality, co-authored.

Analysing

Once data from the interview have been collected, the next stage involves analysing them, often by some form of coding or scoring. In qualitative data the data analysis here is almost inevitably interpretive, hence the data analysis is less a completely accurate representation (as in the numerical, positivist tradition) but more of a reflexive, reactive interaction between the researcher and the decontextualized data that are already interpretations of a social encounter. The great tension in data analysis is between maintaining a sense of the holism of the interview and the tendency for analysis to atomize and fragment the data – to separate them into constituent elements, thereby losing the synergy of the whole, and in interviews often the whole is greater than the sum of the parts. There are several stages in analysis, for example:

- generating natural units of meaning;
- classifying, categorizing and ordering these units of meaning;
- structuring narratives to describe the interview contents;
- interpreting the interview data.

These are comparatively generalized stages. Miles and Huberman (1994) suggest twelve tactics for generating meaning from transcribed and interview data:

- counting frequencies of occurrence (of ideas, themes, pieces of data, words);
- noting patterns and themes (Gestalts), which may stem from repeated themes and causes or explanations or constructs;
- seeing plausibility – trying to make good sense of data, using informed intuition to reach a conclusion;
- clustering – setting items into categories, types, behaviours and classifications;
- making metaphors – using figurative and connotative language rather than literal and denotative language, bringing data to life, thereby reducing data, making patterns, decentring the data, and connecting data with theory;
- splitting variables to elaborate, differentiate and 'unpack' ideas, i.e. to move away from the drive towards integration and the blurring of data;
- subsuming particulars into the general (akin to Glaser's (1978) notion of 'constant comparison' – see Chapter 6 in this book) – a move towards clarifying key concepts;
- factoring – bringing a large number of variables under a smaller number of (frequently) unobserved hypothetical variables;
- identifying and noting relations between variables;
- finding intervening variables – looking for other variables that appear to be 'getting in the way' of accounting for what one would expect to be strong relationships between variables;
- building a logical chain of evidence – noting causality and making inferences;
- making conceptual/theoretical coherence – moving from metaphors to constructs to theories to explain the phenomena.

This progression, though perhaps positivist in its tone, is a useful way of moving from the specific to the general in data analysis. Miles and Huberman (1994) attach much importance to coding of interview responses, partially as a way of reducing what is typically data overload from qualitative data.

Coding has been defined by Kerlinger (1970) as the translation of question responses and respondent information to specific categories for the purpose of analysis. As we have seen, many questions are precoded, that is, each response can be immediately and directly converted into a score in an objective way. Rating scales and checklists are examples of precoded questions. Coding is the ascription of a category label to a piece of data, with the category label either decided in advance or in response to the data that have been collected.

In coding a piece of transcription the researcher systematically goes through the data, typically line by line, and writes a descriptive code by the side of each piece of datum, for example:

Text	Code
The students will undertake problem-solving in science	PROB
I prefer to teach mixed ability classes	MIXABIL

One can see here that the codes are frequently abbreviations, enabling the researcher to understand immediately the issue that they are describing because they resemble that issue (rather than, for example, ascribing a number as a code for each piece of datum, where the number provides no clue as to what the datum or category concerns). Miles and Huberman (1994) suggest that the coding label should bear sufficient resemblance to the original data so that the researcher can know, by looking at the code, what the original piece of datum concerned. There are several computer packages that can help the coder here (e.g. Ethnograph, NUD.IST), though they require the original transcript to be entered onto the computer. One such, Code-A-Text, is particularly useful for analysing dialogues both quantitatively and qualitatively (the system also accepts sound and video input).

Having performed the first round of coding

the researcher is able to detect patterns, themes and begin to make generalizations (e.g. by counting the frequencies of codes). The researcher can also group codes into more general clusters, each with a code, i.e. begin the move towards factoring the data.

Miles and Huberman suggest that it is possible to keep as many as ninety codes in the working memory at any one time, though they indicate that data might be recoded on a second or third reading, as codes that were used early on might have to be refined in light of codes that are used later, either to make the codes more discriminating or to conflate codes that are unnecessarily specific. There is also the danger that early codes might influence too strongly the later codes. Codes, they argue, should be kept as discrete as possible, and they should enable the researcher to catch the complexity and comprehensiveness of the data. They recommend earlier rather than later coding, as late coding, they suggest, enfeebles the analysis.

Perhaps the biggest problem concerns the coding and scoring of open-ended questions. Two solutions are possible here. Even though a response is open-ended, the interviewer may precode her interview schedule so that while an interviewee is responding freely, the interviewer is assigning the content of her responses, or parts of it, to predetermined coding categories. Classifications of this kind may be developed during pilot studies.

Example:
Q. What is it that you like least about your job?
A. Mostly the way the place is run – and the long hours; and the prospects aren't too good.
Coding:
colleagues
organization   X
the work
conditions   X
other
future prospects   X

Alternatively, data may be postcoded. Having recorded the interviewee's response, either by summarizing it during or after the interview itself, or verbatim by tape recorder, the researcher may subject it to content analysis and submit it to one of the available scoring procedures – scaling, scoring, rank scoring, response counting, etc.

Content analysis involves reading and judgement; Brenner *et al.* (1985) set out several steps in undertaking a content analysis of open-ended data:

Step 1 Briefing (understanding the problem and its context in detail).
Step 2 Sampling (of people, including the types of sample sought, see Chapter 4).
Step 3 Associating (with other work that has been done).
Step 4 Hypothesis development.
Step 5 Hypothesis testing.
Step 6 Immersion (in the data collected, to pick up all the clues).
Step 7 Categorizing (in which the categories and their labels must: (a) reflect the purpose of the research; (b) be exhaustive; (c) be mutually exclusive).
Step 8 Incubation (e.g. reflecting on data and developing interpretations and meanings).
Step 9 Synthesis (involving a review of the rationale for coding and an identification of the emerging patterns and themes).
Step 10 Culling (condensing, excising and even reinterpreting the data so that they can be written up intelligibly).
Step 11 Interpretation (making meaning of the data).
Step 12 Writing, including (pp. 140–3): giving clear guidance on the incidence of occurrence; proving an indication of direction and intentionality of feelings; being aware of what is not said as well as what it said – silences; indicating salience (to the readers and respondents).
Step 13 Rethinking.

This process, the authors suggest (ibid.: 144), requires researchers to address several factors:

- Understand the research brief thoroughly.
- Evaluate the relevance of the sample for the research project.

- Associate their own experiences with the problem, looking for clues from the past.
- Develop testable hypotheses as the basis for the content analysis (the authors name this the 'Concept Book').
- Test the hypotheses throughout the interviewing and analysis process.
- Stay immersed in the data throughout the study.
- Categorize the data in the Concept Book, creating labels and codes.
- Incubate the data before writing up.
- Synthesize the data in the Concept Book, looking for key concepts.
- Cull the data, being selective is important because it is impossible to report everything that happened.
- Interpret the data, identifying its meaning and implication.
- Write up the report.
- Rethink and rewrite: have the research objectives been met?

Hycner (1985) sets out procedures that can be followed when phenomenologically analysing interview data. In summary, the guidelines are as follows:

- *Transcription* Having the interview tape transcribed, noting not only the literal statements but also non-verbal and paralinguistic communication.
- *Bracketing and phenomenological reduction* for Hycner this means, 'suspending (bracketing) as much as possible the researcher's meaning and interpretations and entering into the world of the unique individual who was interviewed' (Hycner, 1985). The researcher thus sets out to understand what the interviewee is saying rather than what she expects that person to say.
- *Listening to the interview for a sense of the whole* This involves listening to the entire tape several times and reading the transcription a number of times in order to provide a context for the emergence of specific units of meaning and themes later on.
- *Delineating units of general meaning* This

entails a thorough scrutiny of both verbal and non-verbal gestures to elicit the participant's meaning. Hycner says, 'It is a crystallization and condensation of what the participant has said, still using as much as possible the literal words of the participant' (Hycner, 1985).

- *Delineating units of meaning relevant to the research question* Once the units of general meaning have been noted, they are then reduced to units of meaning relevant to the research question.
- *Training independent judges to verify the units of relevant meaning* Findings can be verified by using other researchers to carry out the above procedures.
- *Eliminating redundancies* At this stage, the researcher checks the lists of relevant meaning and eliminates those clearly redundant to others previously listed.
- *Clustering units of relevant meaning* The researcher now tries to determine if any of the units of relevant meaning naturally cluster together; whether there seems to be some common theme or essence that unites several discrete units of relevant meaning.
- *Determining themes from clusters of meaning* The researcher examines all the clusters of meaning to determine if there is one (or more) central theme(s) which expresses the essence of these clusters.
- *Writing a summary of each individual interview* It is useful at this point, the author suggests, to go back to the interview transcription and write up a summary of the interview incorporating the themes that have been elicited from the data.
- *Return to the participant with the summary and themes, conducting a second interview* This is a check to see whether the essence of the first interview has been accurately and fully captured.
- *Modifying themes and summary* With the new data from the second interview, the researcher looks at all the data as a whole and modifies or adds themes as necessary.
- *Identifying general and unique themes for all the*

interviews   The researcher now looks for the themes common to most or all of the interviews as well as the individual variations. The first step is to note if there are themes common to all or most of the interviews. The second step is to note when there are themes that are unique to a single interview or a minority of the interviews.

- *Contextualization of themes*   At this point it is helpful to place these themes back within the overall contexts or horizons from which these themes emerged.
- *Composite summary*   The author considers it useful to write up a composite summary of all the interviews which would accurately capture the essence of the phenomenon being investigated. The author concludes, 'Such a composite summary describes the "world" in general, as experienced by the participants. At the end of such a summary the researcher might want to note significant individual differences' (Hycner, 1985).

Verifying

Chapter 5 has discussed at length the issues of reliability, validity and generalizability of the data from interviews, and so these issues will not be repeated here. The reader is advised to explore not only that section of Chapter 5, but, indeed the whole chapter. Kvale (1996: 237) makes the point that validation must take place at all seven stages of the interview-based investigation:

Stage 1   *Thematizing*. The theoretical underpinnings of the research must be sound and the link between theory and research questions must be logical.
Stage 2   *Designing*. The research design must be adequate and sound in terms of methodology, operationalization, sampling, and ethical defensibility.
Stage 3   *Interviewing*. The data must be trustworthy and the interview must be conducted to the highest standards, with validity and reliability checks being made as it unfolds.

Stage 4   *Transcribing*. The translation from oral and social media to a written medium should be faithful to key features of the original media.
Stage 5   *Analysing*. The methods of analysis and interpretations of the data are faithful to the data.
Stage 6   *Validating*. Decisions are reached on the most appropriate forms of validity for the study, and who the validators might be.
Stage 7   *Reporting*. The report fairly reflects the study and can be seen to be fair by the readers.

One main issue here is that there is no single canon of validity; rather, the notion of fitness for purpose within an ethically defensible framework should be adopted, giving rise to different kinds of validity for different kinds of interview-based research (e.g. structured to unstructured, qualitative to quantitative, nomothetic to idiographic, generalizable to unique, descriptive to explanatory, positivist to ethnographic, preordinate to responsive).

Reporting

The nature of the reporting will be decided to some extent by the nature of the interviewing. For example a standardized, structured interview may yield numerical data that may be reported succinctly in tables and graphs, whilst a qualitative, word-based, open-ended interview will yield word-based accounts that take up considerably more space.

Kvale (1996: 263–6) suggests several elements of a report: (a) an introduction that includes the main themes and contents; (b) an outline of the methodology and methods (from designing to interviewing, transcription and analysis); (c) the results (the data analysis, interpretation and verification); (d) a discussion.

If the report is largely numerical then figures and tables might be appropriate; if the interview is more faithfully represented in words rather than numbers then this presents the researcher with the issue of how to present particular quotations. Here Kvale (ibid.: 266) suggests that direct quotations should: (a) illuminate and relate to the general text whilst maintaining a balance with the main text; (b) be contextualized and be accompanied by a commentary and interpretation; (c) be particularly clear, useful, and the 'best' of the data (the 'gems'!); (d) should include an indication of how they have been edited; and (e) be incorporated into a natural written style of the report.

Group interviewing

Group interviewing is a useful way of conducting interviews. Watts and Ebbutt (1987) set out the advantages and disadvantages of group interviewing as a means of collecting data in educational research. The advantages include the potential for discussions to develop, thus yielding a wide range of responses. They explain, 'such interviews are useful . . . where a group of people have been working together for some time or common purpose, or where it is seen as important that everyone concerned is aware of what others in the group are saying' (Watts and Ebbutt, 1987). For example, Lewis (1992) found that 10-year-olds' understanding of severe learning difficulties was enhanced in group interview situations, the children challenging and extending each other's ideas and introducing new ideas into the discussion. The group interview, the paper argues, can generate a wider range of responses than in individual interviews. Bogdan and Biklen (1992: 100) add that group interviews might be useful for gaining an insight into what might be pursued in subsequent individual interviews. There are practical and organizational advantages, too. Group interviews are often quicker than individual interviews and hence are timesaving and involve minimal disruption. The group interview can also bring together people with varied opinions, or as representatives of different collectivities. Group interviews of children might also be less intimidating for them than individual interviews. Simons (1982) and Lewis (1992) chart some difficulties in interviewing children, for example how to:

- overcome children being easily distracted;
- avoid the researcher being seen as an authority figure;
- keep the interview relevant;
- interview inarticulate, hesitant and nervous children;
- get the children's teacher away from the children;
- respond to the child who says something then immediately wishes she hadn't said it;
- elicit genuine responses from children rather than simply responses to the interview situation;
- get beyond the institutional, headteacher's, or 'expected' response;
- keep children to the point;
- avoid children being too extreme or destructive of each other's views;
- pitch language at the appropriate level;
- avoid the interview being an arduous bore;
- overcome children's poor memories;
- avoid children being too focused on particular features or situations;
- overcome the problem that some children will say anything rather than feel they do not have 'the answer';
- overcome the problem that some children dominate the conversation;
- avoid the problem of children feeling very exposed in front of their friends;
- avoid children feeling uncomfortable or threatened (addressed, perhaps, by placing children with their friends);
- avoid children telling lies.

Clearly these problems are not exclusive to children; they apply equally well to some adult group interviews. Group interviews require skilful chairing and attention to the physical layout of the room so that everyone can see everyone else. Group size is also an issue; too few and it can put pressure on individuals, too large and the group fragments and loses focus. Lewis (1992) summarizes research to indicate that a group of around six or seven is an optimum size, though it can be smaller for younger children.

As regards the disadvantages of group interviews,

Watts and Ebbutt note that they are of little use in allowing personal matters to emerge, or where the researcher has to aim a series of follow-up questions at one specific member of the group. As they explain, 'the dynamic of a group denies access to this sort of data' (Watts and Ebbutt, 1987). Further, Lewis (1992) comments on the problem of coding up the responses of group interviews. For further guidance on this topic and the procedures involved, we refer the reader to Simons (1982), Watts and Ebbutt (1987), Hedges (1985), Breakwell (1990), Spencer and Flin (1990) and Lewis (1992).

Focus groups

As an adjunct to group interviews, the use of focus groups is growing in educational research, albeit more slowly than, for instance, in business and political circles. Focus groups are a form of group interview, though not in the sense of a backwards and forwards between interviewer and group. Rather, the reliance is on the interaction within the group who discuss a topic supplied by the researcher (Morgan, 1988: 9). Hence the participants interact with each other rather than with the interviewer, such that the views of the participants can emerge – the participants' rather than the researcher's agenda can predominate. It is from the *interaction* of the group that the data emerge. Focus groups are contrived settings, bringing together a specifically chosen sector of the population to discuss a particular given theme or topic, where the interaction with the group leads to data and outcomes. Their contrived nature is both their strength and their weakness: they are unnatural settings yet they are very focused on a particular issue and, therefore, will yield insights that might not otherwise have been available in a straightforward interview; they are economical on time, producing a large amount of data in a short period of time, but they tend to produce less data than interviews with the same number of individuals on a one-to-one basis (ibid.: 19).

Focus groups (Morgan, 1988; Krueger, 1988) are useful for:

- orientation to a particular field of focus;
- developing themes, topic, and schedules for subsequent interviews and/or questionnaires;
- generating hypotheses that derive from the insights and data from the group;
- generating and evaluating data from different sub-groups of a population;
- gathering feedback from previous studies.

Focus groups might be useful to triangulate with more traditional forms of interviewing, questionnaire, observation etc. There are several issues to be addressed in running focus groups, for example (Morgan, 1988: 41–8):

- deciding the number of focus groups for a single topic (one group is insufficient, as the researcher will be unable to know whether the outcome is unique to the behaviour of the group);
- deciding the size of the group (too small and intra-group dynamics exert a disproportionate effect, too large and the group becomes unwieldy and hard to manage; it fragments). Morgan (ibid.: 43) suggests between four and twelve people per group;
- how to allow for people not 'turning up' on the day. Morgan (ibid.: 44) suggests the need to over-recruit by as much as 20 per cent;
- taking extreme care with the sampling, so that *every* participant is the bearer of the particular characteristic required or that the group has homogeneity of background in the required area, otherwise the discussion will lose focus or become unrepresentative. Sampling is a major key to the success of focus groups;
- ensuring that participants have something to say and feel comfortable enough to say it;
- chairing the meeting so that a balance is struck between being too directive and veering off the point, i.e. keeping the meeting open-ended but to the point.

Unlike group interviewing with children, discussed above, focus groups operate more successfully if they are composed of relative strangers rather than friends, unless friendship, of course, is an important criterion for the focus (e.g. that the group will discuss something that is usually only discussed amongst friends).

Although its potential is considerable, the focus group, as a particular kind of group interviewing, still has to find its way into educational circles to the extent that it has in other areas of life.

The non-directive interview and the focused interview

Originating from psychiatric and therapeutic fields, the non-directive interview is characterized by a situation in which the respondent is responsible for initiating and directing the course of the encounter and for the attitudes she expresses in it (in contrast to the structured or research interview we have already considered, where the dominating role assumed by the interviewer results in, to use Kitwood's phrase, 'an asymmetry of commitment' (Kitwood, 1977)). It is a particularly valuable technique in that it gets at the deeper attitudes and perceptions of the person being interviewed in such a way as to leave them free from interviewer bias. We shall examine briefly the characteristics of the therapeutic interview and then consider its usefulness as a research tool in the social and educational sciences.

The non-directive interview as it is currently understood grew out of the pioneering work of Freud and subsequent modifications to his approach by later analysts. His basic discovery was that if one can arrange a special set of conditions and have a patient talk about his/her difficulties in a certain way, behaviour changes of many kinds can be accomplished. The technique developed was used to elicit highly personal data from patients in such a way as to increase their self-awareness and improve their skills in self-analysis (Madge, 1965). By these means they became better able to help themselves.

The present-day therapeutic interview has its most persuasive advocate in Carl Rogers. Basing his analysis on his own clinical studies, he has identified a sequence of characteristic stages in the therapeutic process, beginning with the client's decision to seek help. He/she is met by a counsellor who is friendly and receptive, but not didactic. The next stage is signalled when the client begins to give vent to hostile, critical and destructive feelings, which the counsellor accepts, recognizes and clarifies. Subsequently, and invariably, these antagonistic impulses are used up and give way to the first expressions of positive feeling. The counsellor likewise accepts these until suddenly and spontaneously 'insight and self-understanding come bubbling through' (Rogers, 1942). With this insight comes the realization of possible courses of action and also the power to make decisions. It is in translating these into practical terms that clients free themselves from dependence on the counsellor.

Rogers (1945) subsequently identified a number of qualities in the interviewer which he deemed essential: that she bases her work on attitudes of acceptance and permissiveness; that she respects the client's responsibility for his own situation; that she permits the client to explain his problem in his own way; and that she does nothing that would in any way arouse the client's defences.

There are a number of features of the therapeutic interview which are peculiar to it and may well be inappropriate in other settings: for example, as we have seen, the interview is initiated by the respondent; his/her motivation is to obtain relief from a particular symptom; the interviewer is primarily a source of help, not a procurer of information; the actual interview is part of the therapeutic experience; the purpose of the interview is to change the behaviour and inner life of the person and its success is defined in these terms; and there is no restriction on the topics discussed.

A researcher has a different order of priorities however, e.g. focus, economics of time; what appear as advantages in a therapeutic context may be decided limitations when the technique is used for research purposes, even though she may be sympathetic to the spirit of the non-directive interview (Madge, 1965).

One attempt to meet this need is reported by

Merton and Kendall (1946) in which the focused interview was developed. While seeking to follow closely the principle of non-direction, the method did introduce rather more interviewer control in the kinds of questions used and sought also to limit the discussion to certain parts of the respondent's experience.

The focused interview differs from other types of research interview in certain respects (Merton and Kendall, 1946):

- The persons interviewed are known to have been involved in a particular situation: they may, for example, have watched a TV programme; or seen a film; or read a book or article; or have been a participant in a social situation.
- By means of the techniques of content analysis, elements in the situation which the researcher deems significant have previously been analysed by her. She has thus arrived at a set of hypotheses relating to the meaning and effects of the specified elements.
- Using her analysis as a basis, the investigator constructs an interview guide. This identifies the major areas of inquiry and the hypotheses which determine the relevant data to be obtained in the interview.
- The actual interview is focused on the subjective experiences of the people who have been exposed to the situation. Their responses enable the researcher both to test the validity of her hypotheses, and to ascertain unanticipated responses to the situation, thus giving rise to further hypotheses.

From this it can be seen that the distinctive feature of the focused interview is the prior analysis by the researcher of the situation in which subjects have been involved. The advantages of this procedure have been cogently explained by Merton and Kendall:

> Fore-knowledge of the situation obviously reduces the task confronting the investigator, since the interview need not be devoted to discovering the objective nature of the situation. Equipped in advance with a content analysis, the interviewer can readily distinguish the objective facts of the case from the subjective definitions of the situation. He [sic] thus becomes alert to the entire field of 'selective response'. When the interviewer, through his familiarity with the objective situation, is able to recognize symbolic or functional silences, 'distortions', avoidances, or blockings, he is the more prepared to explore their implications.
>
> (Merton and Kendall, 1946)

In the quest for what Merton and Kendall term 'significant data', the interviewer must develop the ability to evaluate continuously the interview while it is in progress. To this end, they established a set of criteria by which productive and unproductive interview material can be distinguished. Briefly, these are:

- *Non-direction* Interviewer guidance should be minimal.
- *Specificity* Respondents' definitions of the situation should find full and specific expression.
- *Range* The interview should maximize the range of evocative stimuli and responses reported by the subject.
- *Depth and personal context* The interview should bring out the affective and value-laden implications of the subjects' responses, to determine whether the experience had central or peripheral significance. It should elicit the relevant personal context, the idiosyncratic associations, beliefs and ideas.

By way of example of productive interview material, Ashton (1994) used focused interviews to ascertain the strengths of beliefs and the personal reactions of principals of further education colleges to various changes being pressed upon them by central government and local agencies.

Telephone interviewing

Telephone interviewing is an important method of data collection and is common practice in survey research.[2] Dicker and Gilbert (1988), Nias (1991), Oppenheim (1992) and Borg and Gall (1996) suggest several attractions to telephone interviewing:

- It is sometimes cheaper than face-to-face interviewing.
- It enables researchers to select respondents from a much more dispersed population than if they have to travel to meet the interviewees.
- It is useful for gaining rapid responses to a structured questionnaire.
- Monitoring and quality control are undertaken more easily since interviews are undertaken and administered centrally, indeed there are greater guarantees that the researcher actually carries out the interview as required.
- Call-back costs are so slight as to enable frequent call-backs possible, enhancing reliability and contact.
- Many groups, particularly of busy people, can be reached at times more convenient to them than if a visit were to be made.
- They are safer to undertake than, for example, having to visit dangerous neighbourhoods.
- They can be used to collect sensitive data, as possible feelings of threat of face-to-face questions about awkward, embarrassing or difficult matters is absent.
- Response rate is higher than, for example, questionnaires.

Clearly this issue is not as cut-and-dried as the claims made for it, as there are several potential problems with telephone interviewing, for example (see also Chapter 5):

- It is very easy for respondents simply to hang up on the caller.
- There is a chance of skewed sampling, as not all of the population have a telephone (often those lower income households – perhaps the very people that the researcher wishes to target) or can hear (e.g. the old and second language speakers in addition to those with hearing difficulties).
- There is a lower response rate at weekends.
- Some people have a deep dislike of telephones, that sometimes extends to a phobia, and this inhibits their responses or willingness to participate.

- Respondents may not disclose information because of uncertainty about actual (even though promised) confidentiality.
- Many respondents (up to 25 per cent, Oppenheim, 1992: 97) will be 'ex-directory' and so their numbers will not be available in telephone directories.
- Respondents may withhold important information or tell lies, as the non-verbal behaviour that frequently accompanies this is not witnessed by the interviewer.
- It is often more difficult for complete strangers to communicate by telephone than face-to-face, particularly as non-verbal cues are absent.
- Respondents are naturally suspicious (e.g. of the caller trying to sell a product).
- One telephone might be shared by several people.
- Responses are difficult to write down or record during the interview.

That said, Sykes and Hoinville (1985) and also Borg and Gall (1996) suggest that telephone interviewing reaches nearly the same proportion of many target populations as 'standard' interviews, that it obtains nearly the same rate of response, and produces comparable information to 'standard' interviews, sometimes at a fraction of the cost.

Harvey (1988), Oppenheim (1992) and Miller (1995) consider that: (a) telephone interviews need careful arrangements for timing and duration (typically that they are shorter and quicker than face-to-face interviews) – a preliminary call may be necessary to fix a time when a longer call is to be made; (b) the interviewer will need to have ready careful prompts and probes, including more than usual closed questions and less complex questions, in case the respondent 'dries up' on the telephone; (c) both interviewer and interviewee need to be prepared in advance of the interview if its potential is to be realized; and (d) sampling requires careful consideration, using, for example, random numbers or some form of stratified sample. In general, however, many of the issues from 'standard' forms of interviewing apply equally well to telephone interviewing (see also Chapter 4).

Ethical issues in interviewing

Interviews have an ethical dimension; they concern interpersonal interaction and produce information about the human condition. One can identify three main areas of ethical issues here – informed consent, confidentiality, and the consequences of the interviews; each is problematic (Kvale, 1996: 111–20). For instance, who should give the informed consent (e.g. participants, their superiors), and for whom and what? How much information should be given, and to whom? What is legitimate private and public knowledge? How might the research help or harm the interviewees? Does the interviewer have a duty to point out the possible harmful consequences of the research data or will this illegitimately steer the interview?

It is difficult to lay down hard and fast ethical rules, as, by definition, ethical matters are contestable. Nevertheless, it is possible to raise some ethical questions to which answers need to be given before the interviews commence:

- Has the informed consent of the interviewees been gained?
- Has this been obtained in writing or orally?
- How much information should be given in advance of the study?
- How can adequate information be provided if the study is exploratory?
- Have the possible consequences of the research been made clear to the participants?
- Has care been taken to prevent any harmful effects of the research to the participants (and to others)?
- To what extent do any potential benefits outweigh the potential harm done by the research, and how justifiable is this for conducting the research?
- How will the research benefit the participants?
- Who will benefit from the research?
- To what extent is there reciprocity between what participants give to and receive from the research?
- Have confidentiality, anonymity, non-identifiability and non-traceability been guaranteed? Should participants' identities be disguised?
- How does the Data Protection Act (1984) operate in interview situations?
- Who will have access to the data?
- What has been done to ensure that the interview is conducted in an appropriate, non-stressful, non-threatening, manner?
- How will the data and transcriptions be verified, and by whom?
- Who will see the results of the research? Will some parts be withheld? Who own the data? At what stage does ownership of the data pass from interviewees to interviewers? Are there rights of veto for what appears? To whom should sensitive data be made available (e.g. should interview data on child abuse or drug taking be made available with or without consent to parents and the police)?
- How far should the researcher's own agenda and views predominate? What if the researcher makes a different interpretation from the interviewee? Should the interviewees be told, even if they have not asked for these interpretations?

These issues, by no means an exhaustive list, are not exclusive to the research interview, though they are highly applicable here. For further reading on ethical issues we refer readers to Chapter 2.

16 Accounts

The rationale of much of this chapter is located in the interpretive, ethnographic paradigm which strives to view situations through the eyes of participants, to catch their intentionality and their interpretations of frequently complex situations, their meaning systems and the dynamics of the interaction as it unfolds. This is akin to the notion of 'thick description' from Geertz (1973) and his predecessor Ryle (1949). The chapter proceeds in several stages: firstly, we set out the characteristics of the ethogenic approach; secondly, we set out procedures in eliciting, analysing and authenticating accounts; thirdly, we provide an introduction to handling qualitative accounts and their related fields of: (a) network analysis; (b) discourse analysis; fourthly, we provide an introduction to accounts; finally, we review the strengths and weaknesses of ethogenic approaches. We recognize that the field of language and language use is vast, and to try to do justice to it here is the 'optimism of ignorance' (Edwards, 1976). Rather, we attempt to indicate some important ways in which researchers can use accounts in collecting data for their research.

The field also owes a considerable amount to the communication theory and speech act theory of Austin (1962), Searle (1969) and, more recently, Habermas (e.g. 1979, 1984). In particular, the notion that there are three kinds of speech act (locutionary – saying something; illocutionary – doing something whilst saying something; and perlocutionary – achieving something by saying something) might commend itself for further study.

Introduction

Although each of us sees the world from our own point of view, we have a way of speaking about our experiences which we share with those around us. Explaining our behaviour towards one another can be thought of as accounting for our actions in order to make them intelligible and justifiable to our fellows. Thus, saying 'I'm terribly sorry, I didn't mean to bump into you', is a simple case of the explication of social meaning, for by locating the bump outside any planned sequence and neutralizing it by making it intelligible in such a way that it is not warrantable, it ceases to be offensive in that situation (Harré, 1978).

Accounting for actions in those larger slices of life called social episodes is the central concern of a participatory psychology which focuses upon actors' intentions, their beliefs about what sorts of behaviour will enable them to reach their goals, and their awareness of the rules that govern those behaviours. Studies carried out within this framework have been termed 'ethogenic', an adjective which expresses a view of the human being as a person, that is, a plan-making, self-monitoring agent, aware of goals and deliberately considering the best ways to achieve them. Ethogenic studies represent another approach to the study of social behaviour and their methods stand in bold contrast to those commonly employed in much of the educational research which we describe in Chapter 12. Before discussing the elicitation and analysis of accounts we need to outline the ethogenic approach in more detail. This we do by reference to the work of one of its foremost exponents, Rom Harré (1974, 1976, 1977a, 1977b, 1978).

The ethogenic approach

Harré (1978) identifies five main principles in the ethogenic approach. They are set out in Box 16.1.

Characteristics of accounts and episodes

The discussion of accounts and episodes that now follows develops some of the ideas contained in the principles of the ethogenic approach outlined in Box 16.1.

We have already noted that accounts must be seen within the context of social episodes. The idea of an episode is a fairly general one. The concept itself may be defined as any coherent fragment of social life. Being a natural division of life, an episode will often have a recognizable beginning and end, and the sequence of actions that constitute it will have some meaning for the participants. Episodes may thus vary in duration and reflect innumerable aspects of life. A pupil entering primary school at seven and leaving at eleven would be an extended episode. A two-minute television interview with a political celebrity would be another. The contents of an episode which interest the ethogenic researcher include not only the perceived behaviour such as gesture and speech, but also the thoughts, the feelings and the intentions of those taking part. And the 'speech' that accounts for those thoughts, feelings and intentions must be conceived of in the widest connotation of the word. Thus, accounts may be personal records of the events we experience in our day-to-day lives, our conversations with neighbours, our letters to friends, our entries in diaries. Accounts serve to explain our past, present and future oriented actions.

Providing that accounts are authentic, it is argued, there is no reason why they should not be used as scientific tools in explaining people's actions.

Procedures in eliciting, analysing and authenticating accounts

The account-gathering method proposed by Brown and Sime (1977) is summarized in Box 16.2. It involves attention to informants, the

Box 16.1
Principles in the ethogenic approach

---

1   An explicit distinction is drawn between *synchronic analysis*, that is, the analysis of social practices and institutions as they exist at any one time, and *diachronic analysis*, the study of the stages and the processes by which social practices and institutions are created and abandoned, change and are changed. Neither type of analysis can be expected to lead directly to the discovery of universal social psychological principles or laws.

2   In social interactions, it is assumed that action takes place through endowing intersubjective entities with meaning; the ethogenic approach therefore concentrates upon the *meaning system*, that is, the whole sequence by which a social act is achieved in an episode. Consider, for example, the action of a kiss in the particular episodes of (a) leaving a friend's house; (b) the passing-out parade at St Cyr; and (c) the meeting in the garden of Gethsemane.

3   The ethogenic approach is concerned with speech which accompanies action. That speech is intended to make the action intelligible and justifiable in occurring at the time and the place it did in the whole sequence of unfolding and co-ordinated action. Such speech is *accounting*. In so far as accounts are socially meaningful, it is possible to derive *accounts of accounts*.

4   The ethogenic approach is founded upon the belief that a human being tends to be the kind of person his language, his traditions, his tacit and explicit knowledge tell him he is.

5   The skills that are employed in ethogenic studies therefore make use of commonsense understandings of the social world. As such the activities of the poet and the playwright offer the ethogenic researcher a better model than those of the physical scientist.

Source Adapted from Harré, 1978

Box 16.2
Account gathering

Research strategy	Control procedure
1 **Informants**	
Definition of episode and role groups representing domain of interest	Rationale for choice of episode and role groups
Identification of exemplars	Degree of involvement of potential informants
Selection of individual informants	Contact with individuals to establish motive for participation, competence and performance
2 **Account gathering situation**	
Establishing venue	Contextual effects of venue
Recording the account	Appropriateness and accuracy in documenting account
Controlling relevance of account	Accounts agenda
Authenticating account	Negotiation and internal consistency
Establishing role of interviewer and interviewee	Degree of direction
Post account authentication	Corroboration
3 **Transformation of accounts**	
Provision of working documents	Transcription reliability; coder reliability
Data reduction techniques	Appropriateness of statistical and content analyses
4 **Researchers' accounts**	
Account of the account – summary, overview, interpretation	Description of research operations, explanatory scheme and theoretical background

Source Brown and Sime, 1981

account-gathering situation, the transformation of accounts, and researchers' accounts, and sets out control procedures for each of these elements.

Problems of eliciting, analysing and authenticating accounts are further illustrated in the following outlines of two educational studies. The first is concerned with valuing among older boys and girls; the second is to do with the activities of pupils and teachers in using computers in primary classrooms. In a study of adolescent values, Kitwood (1977) developed an experience-sampling method, that is, a qualitative technique for gathering and analysing accounts based upon tape-recorded interviews that were themselves prompted by the fifteen situations listed in Box 16.3.

Because the experience-sampling method avoids interrogation, the material which emerges is less organized than that obtained from a tightly structured interview. Successful handling of individual accounts therefore requires the researcher to know the interview content extremely well and to work toward the gradual

emergence of tentative interpretive schemata which she then modifies, confirms or falsifies as the research continues. Kitwood identifies eight methods for dealing with the tape-recorded accounts. Methods 1–4 are fairly close to the approach adopted in handling questionnaires; and methods 5–8 are more in tune with the ethogenic principles that we identified earlier:

1   *The total pattern of choice*   The frequency of choice of various items permits some surface generalizations about the participants, taken as a group. The most revealing analyses may be those of the least and most popular items.

2   *Similarities and differences*   Using the same technique as in method 1, it is possible to investigate similarities and differences within the total sample of accounts according to some characteristic(s) of the participants such as age, sex, level of educational attainment, etc.

3   *Grouping items together*   It may be convenient for some purposes to fuse together

Box 16.3
Experience sampling method

Below are listed fifteen types of situation which most people have been in at some time. Try to think of something that has happened in your life in the last year or so, or perhaps something that keeps on happening, which fits into each of the descriptions. Then choose the ten of them which deal with the things that seem to you to be most important, which cover your main interests and concerns, and the different parts of your life. When we meet we will talk together about the situations you have chosen. Try beforehand to remember as clearly as you can what happened, what you and others did, and how you yourself felt and thought. Be as definite as you can. If you like, write a few notes to help you keep the situation in mind.

1   When there was a misunderstanding between you and someone else (or several others) . . .
2   When you got on really well with people . . .
3   When you had to make an important decision . . .
4   When you discovered something new about yourself . . .
5   When you felt angry, annoyed or resentful . . .
6   When you did what was expected of you . . .
7   When your life changed direction in some way . . .
8   When you felt you had done something well . . .
9   When you were right on your own, with hardly anyone taking your side . . .
10 When you 'got away with it', or were not found out . . .
11 When you made a serious mistake . . .
12 When you felt afterwards that you had done right . . .
13 When you were disappointed with yourself . . .
14 When you had a serious clash or disagreement with another person . . .
15 When you began to take seriously something that had not mattered much to you before . . .

Source Adapted from Kitwood, 1977

categories that cover similar subject matter. For example, items 1, 5 and 14 in Box 16.3 relate to conflict; items 4, 7 and 15, to personal growth and change.

4   *Categorization of content*   The content of a particular item is inspected for the total sample and an attempt is then made to develop some categories into which all the material will fit. The analysis is most effective when two or more researchers work in collaboration, each initially proposing a category system independently and then exchanging views to negotiate a final category system.

5   *Tracing a theme*   This type of analysis transcends the rather artificial boundaries which the items themselves imply. It aims to collect as much data as possible relevant to a particular topic regardless of where it occurs in the interview material. The method is exacting because it requires very detailed knowledge of content and may entail going through taped interviews several times. Data so collected may be further analysed along the lines suggested in method 4 above.

6   *The study of omissions*   The researcher may well have expectations about the kind of issues likely to occur in the interviews. When some of these are absent, that fact may be highly significant. The absence of an anticipated topic should be explored to discover the correct explanation of its omission.

7   *Reconstruction of a social life-world*   This method can be applied to the accounts of a number of people who have part of their lives in common, for example, a group of friends who go around together. The aim is to attempt some kind of reconstruction of the world which the participants share in analysing the fragmentary material obtained in an interview. The researcher seeks to understand the dominant modes of orient-

ing to reality, the conceptions of purpose and the limits to what is perceived.

8   *Generating and testing hypotheses*   New hypotheses may occur to the researcher during the analysis of the tape-recordings. It is possible to do more than simply advance these as a result of tentative impressions; one can loosely apply the hypothetico-deductive method to the data. This involves putting the hypothesis forward as clearly as possible, working out what the verifiable inferences from it would logically be, and testing these against the account data. Where these data are too fragmentary, the researcher may then consider what kind of evidence and method of obtaining it would be necessary for more thorough hypothesis testing. Subsequent sets of interviews forming part of the same piece of research might then be used to obtain relevant data.

In the light of the weaknesses in account gathering and analysis (discussed later), Kitwood's suggestions of safeguards are worth mentioning. First, he calls for cross-checking between researchers as a precaution against consistent but unrecognized bias in the interviews themselves. Second, he recommends member tests, that is, taking hypotheses and unresolved problems back to the participants themselves or to people in similar situations to them for their comments. Only in this way can researchers be sure that they understand the participants' own grounds for action. Since there is always the possibility that an obliging participant will readily confirm the researcher's own speculations, every effort should be made to convey to the participant that one wants to know the truth as he or she sees it, and that one is as glad to be proved wrong as right.

A study by Blease and Cohen (1990) used cross-checking as a way of validating the classroom observation records of co-researchers, and member tests to authenticate both quantitative and qualitative data derived from teacher and pupil informants. Thus, in the case of cross-checking, the classroom observation schedules of research assistants and researchers were compared and discussed, to arrive at definitive accounts of the range and duration of specific computer activities occurring within observation sessions. Member tests arose when interpretations of interview data were taken back to participating teachers for their comments. Similarly, pupils' scores on certain self-concept scales were discussed individually with respondents in order to ascertain why children awarded themselves high or low marks in respect of a range of skills in using computer programmes.

Network analyses of qualitative data

Another technique that has been successfully employed in the analysis of qualitative data is described by its originators as 'systematic network analysis' (Bliss, Monk and Ogborn, 1983). Drawing upon developments in artificial intelligence, Bliss and her colleagues employed the concept of 'relational network' to represent the content and structuring of a person's knowledge of a particular domain.

Essentially, network analysis involves the development of an elaborate system of categories by way of classifying qualitative data and preserving the essential complexity and subtlety of the materials under investigation. A notational technique is employed to generate network-like structures that show the interdependencies of the categories as they are developed. Network mapping is akin to cognitive mapping,[1] an example of which can be seen in the work of Bliss *et al.* (1983).

What makes a good network?

Bliss *et al.* (1983) point out that there cannot be one overall account of criteria for judging the merits of a particular network. They do, however, attempt to identify a number of factors that ought to feature in any discussion of the standards by which a network might fairly be judged as adequate.

First, any system of description needs to be valid and reliable: valid in the sense that it is appropriate in kind and, within that kind, sufficiently complete and faithful; reliable in the sense that there exists an acceptable level of agreement between people as to how to use the network system to describe data.

Second, there are properties that a network description should possess such as clarity, completeness and self-consistency. These relate to a further criterion of 'network utility', the sufficiency of detail contained in a particular network. A third property that a network should possess is termed 'learnability'. Communicating the terms of the analysis to others, say the authors, is of central importance. It follows therefore that much hinges on whether networks are relatively easy or hard to teach to others. A fourth aspect of network acceptability has to do with its 'testability'. Bliss *et al.* identify two forms of testability, the first having to do with testing a network as a 'theory' against data, the second with testing data against a 'theory' or expectation via a network.

Finally, the terms 'expressiveness' and 'persuasiveness' refer to qualities of language used in developing the network structure. And here, the authors proffer the following advice. 'Helpful as the choice of an expressive coding mood or neat use of indentation or brackets may be, *the code actually says no more than the network distinguishes*' (our italics).

To conclude, network analysis would seem to have a useful role to play in educational research by providing a technique for dealing with the bulk and the complexity of the accounts that are typically generated in qualitative studies.

Discourse analysis

Discourse researchers explore the organization of ordinary talk and everyday explanations and the social actions performed in them. Collecting, transcribing and analysing discourse data constitutes a kind of psychological 'natural history' of the phenomena in which discourse analysts are interested (Edwards and Potter, 1993). Discourses can be regarded as sets of linguistic material that are coherent in organization and content and enable people to construct meaning in social contexts (Coyle, 1995: 245). The emphasis on the *construction* of meaning indicates the action perspective of discourse analysis (ibid.) and this resonates with the notion of speech acts mentioned at the start of this chapter: locutions, illocutions and perlocutions.

Further, the focus on discourse and speech acts links this style of research to Habermas's critical theory set out at the start of this book. Habermas argues that utterances are never simply sentences (Habermas, 1970: 368) that are disembodied from context, but, rather, their meaning derives from the intersubjective contexts in which they are set. A speech situation has a double structure, the propositional content (the locutionary aspect – what is being said) and the performatory content (the illocutionary and perlocutionary aspect – what is being done or achieved through the utterance). For Habermas (1979, 1984) each utterance has to abide by the criteria of legitimacy, truth, rightness, sincerity and comprehensibility. His concept of the 'ideal speech situation' argues that speech – and, for our purposes here – discourse, should seek to be empowering and not subject to repression or ideological distortion. His ideal speech situation is governed by several principles, not the least of which are: mutual understanding between participants, freedom to enter a discourse, an equal opportunity to use speech acts, discussion to be free from domination, the movement towards consensus resulting from the discussion alone and the force of the argument alone (rather than the position power of speakers). For Habermas, then, discourse analysis would seek to uncover, through ideology critique (see Chapter 1) the repressive forces which 'systematically distort' communication. For our purposes, we can take from Habermas the need to expose and interrogate the dominatory influences that not only thread through the discourses which researchers are studying, but the discourses that the research itself produces.

Recent developments in discourse analysis have made important contributions to our understanding of children's thinking, challenging views (still common in educational circles) of 'the child as a lone organism, constructing a succession of general models of the world as each new stage is mastered' (Edwards, 1991). Rather than treating children's language as representative of an inner cognitive world to be explored experimentally by controlling for a host of intruding variables, discourse analysts treat that language as action, as 'situated discursive practice'.[2]

By way of example, Edwards (1993) explores discourse data emanating from a visit to a greenhouse by 5-year-old pupils and their teacher, to see plants being propagated and grown. His analysis shows how children take understandings of adults' meanings from the words they hear and the situations in which those words are used. And in turn, adults (in this case, the teacher) take from pupils' talk, not only what

they might mean but also what they could and should mean. What Edwards describes as 'the discursive appropriation of ideas' (Edwards 1991) is illustrated in Box 16.4.

Discourse analysis requires a careful reading and interpretation of textual material, with interpretation being supported by the linguistic evidence. The inferential and interactional aspects of discourse and discourse analysis suggest the need for the researcher to be highly sensitive to the nuances of language (Coyle, 1995: 247). In discourse analysis, as in qualitative data analysis generally (Miles and Huberman, 1984), the researcher can use coding at an early stage of analysis, assigning codes to the textual material being studied (Parker, 1992; Potter and Wetherell, 1987). This enables the researcher to discover patterns and broad areas in the

Box 16.4
Concepts in children's talk

81	Sally	Cuttings can grow to plants.
82	Teacher	[writing] 'Cuttings can grow –,' instead of saying 'to
83		plants' you can say 'grow, = [in:] to plants.'
84	Sally	= You wrote Chris [tina.]
85	Teacher	Oops. Thank you. I'll do this again. 'Cuttings can
86		grow into plants'. That's also good. What is a cutting,
87		Christina?
88	Christina	A cutting is, umm, I don't know.
89	Teacher	Who knows what a cutting is besides Sally? Sam.
90	Sam	It's when you cut off a –, it's when you cut off a piece
91		of a plant.
92	Teacher	Exactly, and when you cut off a piece of a plant, what do
93		you then do with it to make it grow? If you leave
94		[it –,]
95	X	[Put it in soil.]
96	Teacher	Well, sometimes you can put it in soil.
97	Y	And [plant it,]
98	Teacher	[But what –,] wait, what else could you put it in?
99	Sam	Put it in a pot?
100	Teacher	Pot, with soil, or . . . ? There's another way.
101	Sally	I know another way. =
102	Teacher	= Wait. Sam, do you know? No? =
103	Sam	= Dirt.
104	Teacher	No, it doesn't have to do with s –, it's not a solid, it's
105		a liquid. What [liquid –,]
106	Meredith	[Water.]
107	Teacher	Right. [. . .]

Source Edwards, 1993

discourse; computer programmes such as Code-A-Text and Ethnograph can assist here. With this achieved the researcher can then re-examine the text to discover intentions, functions and consequences of the discourse (examining the speech act functions of the discourse, e.g. to impart information, to persuade, to accuse, to censure, to encourage etc). By seeking *alternative explanations* and the *degree of variability* in the discourse, it is possible to rule out rival interpretations and arrive at a fair reading of what was actually taking place in the discourse in its social context.

The application of discourse analysis to our understanding of classroom learning processes is well exemplified in a study by Edwards and Mercer (1987). Rather than taking the classroom talk as evidence of children's thought processes, the researchers explore it as 'contextualized dialogue with the teacher. The discourse itself is the educational reality and the issue becomes that of examining how teacher and children construct a shared account, a common interpretative framework for curriculum knowledge and for what happens in the classroom' (Edwards, 1991).

Overriding asymmetries between teachers and pupils, Edwards concludes, both cognitive (in terms of knowledge) and interactive (in terms of power), impose different discursive patterns and functions. Indeed Edwards (1980) suggests that teachers control classroom talk very effectively, reproducing asymmetries of power in the classroom by telling the students when to talk, what to talk about, and how well they have talked.

Discourse analysis has been criticized for its lack of systematicity (Coyle, 1995: 256), for its emphasis on the linguistic construction of a social reality, and the impact of the analysis in shifting attention away from what is being analysed and towards the analysis itself, i.e. the risk of losing the independence of phenomena. Discourse analysis risks reifying discourse. One must not lose sight of the fact that the discourse analysis itself is a text, a discourse that in turn can be analysed for its meaning and inferences, rendering the need for reflexivity to be high (Ashmore, 1989).[3]

Edwards and Westgate (1987) show what substantial strides have been made in recent years in the development of approaches to the investigation of classroom dialogue. Some methods encourage participants to talk; others wait for talk to emerge and sophisticated audio/video techniques record the result by whatever method it is achieved. Thus captured, dialogue is reviewed, discussed and reflected upon; moreover, that reviewing, discussing and reflecting is usually undertaken by researchers. It is they, generally, who read 'between the lines' and 'within the gaps' of classroom talk by way of interpreting the intentionality of the participating discussants.[4]

Analysing social episodes

A major problem in the investigation of that natural unit of social behaviour, the 'social episode', has been the ambiguity that surrounds the concept itself and the lack of an acceptable taxonomy by which to classify an interaction sequence on the basis of empirically quantifiable characteristics. Several quantitative studies have been undertaken in this field. For example Magnusson (1971), Ekehammer and Magnusson (1973) and McQuitty (1957) use factor analysis and linkage analysis respectively, whilst Forgas (1976, 1978), Peevers and Secord (1973) and Secord and Peevers (1974) use multidimensional scaling and cluster analysis.

Account gathering in educational research: an example

The 'free commentary' method that Secord and Peevers (1974) recommend as a way of probing for explanations of people's behaviour lies at the very heart of the ethnographer's skills. In the example of ethnographic research that follows, one can detect the researcher's attempts to get below the surface data and to search for the deeper, hidden patterns that are only revealed when attention is directed to the ways that group members interpret the flow of events in their lives.

Heath: 'Questioning at home and at school' (1982)

Heath's study of misunderstandings existing between black children and their white teachers in classrooms in the south of the United States brought to light teachers' assumptions that pupils would respond to language routines and the uses of language in building knowledge and skills just as other children (including their own) did (Heath, 1982).[5] Specifically, she sought to understand why these particular children did *not* respond just as others did. Her research involved eliciting explanations from both the children's parents and teachers. 'We don't talk to our children like you folks do', the parents observed when questioned about their children's behaviour. Those children, it seemed to Heath, were not regarded as information givers or as appropriate conversational partners for adults. That is not to say that the children were excluded from language participation. They did, in fact, participate in a language that Heath describes as rich in styles, speakers and topics. Rather, it seemed to the researcher that the teachers' characteristic mode of questioning was 'to pull attributes of things out of context, particularly out of the context of books and name them – queens, elves, police, red apples' (Heath, 1982). The parents did *not* ask these kinds of questions of their children, and the children themselves had their own ways of deflecting such questions, as the example in Box 16.5 well illustrates.

Heath elicited both parents' and teachers' accounts of the children's behaviour and their apparent communication 'problems' (see Box 16.6). Her account of accounts arose out of periods of participation and observation in classrooms and in some of the teachers' homes. In particular, she focused upon the ways in which 'the children learned to use language to satisfy their needs, ask questions, transmit information, and convince those around them that they were competent communicators' (Heath, 1982). This involved her in a much wider and more intensive study of the total fabric of life in Trackton, the southern community in which the research was located.

> Over five years . . . I was able to collect data across a wide range of situations and to follow some children longitudinally as they acquired communicative competence in Trackton. Likewise, at various periods during these years, I observed Trackton adults in public service encounters and on their jobs . . . The context of language use, including setting, topic, and participants (both those directly involved in the talk and those who only listened) determined in large part how community members, teachers, public service personnel, and fellow workers judged the communicative competence of Trackton residents.
>
> (Heath, 1982)[6]

Box 16.5

'Ain't nobody can talk about things being about theirselves'

This comment by a 9-year-old boy was directed to his teacher when she persisted in interrogating him about the story he had just completed in his reading group.

Teacher:	What is the story about?
Children:	(silence)
Teacher:	Uh . . . Let's . . . Who is it the story talks about?
Children:	(silence)
Teacher:	*Who* is *the* main character? . . . Um . . . What *kind* of story is it?
Child:	Ain't nobody can talk about things being about theirselves.

The boy was saying 'There's no way anybody can talk (and ask) about things being about themselves'.

Source Adapted from Spindler, 1982

Box 16.6
Parents and teachers: divergent viewpoints on children's communicative competence

---

Parents
The teachers won't listen. My kid, he too scared to talk, 'cause nobody play by the rules he know. At home, I can't shut 'im up.

Miss Davis, she complain 'bout Ned not answerin' back. He say she asks dumb questions she already know 'bout.

Teachers
They don't seem to be able to answer even the simplest questions.

I would almost think some of them have a hearing problem; it is as though they don't hear me ask a question. I get blank stares to my questions. Yet when I am making statements or telling stories which interest them, they always seem to hear me.

The simplest questions are the ones they can't answer in the classroom; yet on the playground, they can explain a rule for a ballgame or describe a particular kind of bait with no problem. Therefore, I know they can't be as dumb as they seem in my class.

I sometimes feel that when I look at them and ask a question I'm staring at a wall I can't break through. There's something there; yet in spite of all the questions I ask, I'm never sure I've gotten through to what's inside that wall.

Source Adapted from Spindler, 1982

Problems in gathering and analysing accounts

The importance of the meaning of events and actions to those who are involved in them is now generally recognized in social research. The implications of the ethogenic stance in terms of actual research techniques, however, remain problematic. Menzel (1978)[7] discusses a number of ambiguities and shortcomings in the ethogenic approach, arising out of the multiplicity of meanings that may be held for the same behaviour. Most behaviour, Menzel observes, can be assigned meanings and more than one of these may very well be valid simultaneously. It is fallacious therefore, he argues, to insist upon determining 'the' meaning of an act. Nor can it be said that the task of interpreting an act is done when one has identified one meaning of it, or the one meaning that the researcher is pleased to designate as the true one.

A second problem that Menzel raises is to do with actors' meanings as sources of bias. How central a place, he asks, ought to be given to actors' meanings in formulating explanations of events? Should the researcher exclusively and invariably be guided by these considerations? To do so would be to ignore a whole range of potential explanations which few researchers would wish to see excluded from consideration.

These are far-reaching, difficult issues though by no means intractable. What solutions does Menzel propose? First we must specify 'to whom' when asking what acts and situations mean. Second, researchers must make choices and take responsibility in the assignment of meanings to acts; moreover, problem formulations must respect the meaning of the act to us, the researchers. And third, explanations should respect the meanings of acts to the actors themselves but need not invariably be centred on these meanings.

Menzel's plea is for the usefulness of an outside observer's account of a social episode alongside the explanations that participants themselves may give of that event. A similar argument is implicit in McIntyre and McLeod's (1978) justification of objective, systematic observation in classroom settings. Their case is set out in Box 16.7.

Strengths of the ethogenic approach

The advantages of the ethogenic approach to the educational researcher lie in the distinctive insights that are made available to her through

Box 16.7
Justification of objective systematic observation in classroom settings

When Smith looks at Jones and says, 'Jones, why does the blue substance spread through the liquid?' (probably with a particular kind of voice inflection), and then silently looks at Jones (probably with a particular kind of facial expression), the observer can unambiguously categorize the event as 'Smith asks Jones a question seeking an explanation of diffusion in a liquid.' Now Smith might describe the event as 'giving Jones a chance to show he knows something', and Jones might describe the event as 'Smith trying to get at me'; but if either of them denied the validity of the observer's description, they would be simply wrong, because the observer would be describing at least part of what the behaviour which occurred means in English in Britain. No assumptions are made here about the effectiveness of classroom communication; but the assumption is made that . . . communication is dependent on the system of conventional meanings available within the wider culture. More fundamentally, this interpretation implies that the systematic observer is concerned with an objective reality (or, if one prefers, a shared intersubjective reality) of classroom events. This is not to suggest that the subjective meanings of events to participants are not important, but only that these are not accessible to the observer and that *there is an objective reality to classroom activity which does not depend on these meanings* [our emphasis].

Source McIntyre and McLeod, in McAleese and Hamilton, 1978

the analysis of accounts of social episodes. The benefits to be derived from the exploration of accounts are best seen by contrasting[8] the ethogenic approach with a more traditional educational technique such as the survey which we discussed in Chapter 8.

There is a good deal of truth in the assertion of the ethogenically oriented researcher that approaches which employ survey techniques such as the questionnaire take for granted the very things that should be treated as problematic in an educational study. Too often, the phenomena that ought to be the focus of attention are taken as given, that is, they are treated as the starting point of the research rather than becoming the centre of the researcher's interest and effort to discover how the phenomena arose or came to be important in the first place. Numerous educational studies, for example, have identified the incidence and the duration of disciplinary infractions in school; only relatively recently, however, has the meaning of classroom disorder, as opposed to its frequency and type, been subjected to intensive investigation.[9] Unlike the survey, which is a cross-sectional technique that takes its data at a single point in time, the ethogenic study employs an ongoing observational approach that focuses upon processes rather than products. Thus it is the process of becoming deviant in school which would capture the attention of the ethogenic

researcher rather than the frequency and type of misbehaviour among k types of ability in children located in n kinds of school.

A note on stories

A comparatively neglected area in educational research is the field of stories and storytelling. Bauman (1986: 3) suggests that stories are oral literature whose meanings, forms and functions are situationally rooted in cultural contexts, scenes and events which give meaning to action. This recalls Bruner (1986) who, echoing the interpretive mode of educational research, regards much action as 'storied text', with actors making meaning of their situations through narrative. Stories have a legitimate place as an inquiry method in educational research (Parsons and Lyons, 1979), and, indeed, Jones (1990), Crow (1992), Dunning (1993) and Thody (1997) place them on a par with interviews as sources of evidence for research. Thody (1997: 331) suggests that, as an extension to interviews, stories – like biographies – are rich in authentic, live data; they are, she avers, an 'unparalleled method of reaching practitioners' mindsets'. She provides a fascinating report on stories as data sources for educational management research as well as for gathering data from young children (pp. 333–4).

Thody indicates (p. 331) how stories can be

analysed, using, for example, conventional techniques such as: categorizing and coding of content; thematization; concept building. In this respect stories have their place alongside other sources of primary and secondary documentary evidence (e.g. case studies, biographies). They can be used in *ex post facto* research, historical research, as accounts or in action research; in short they are part of the everyday battery of research instruments that are available to the researcher. The rise in the use of oral history as a legitimate research technique in social research can be seen here to apply to educational research. Though they might be problematic in that verification is difficult (unless other people were present to verify events reported), stories, being rich in the subjective involvement of the storyteller, offer an opportunity for the researcher to gather authentic, rich and 'respectable' data (Bauman, 1986).

17 Observation

Observational data are attractive as they afford the researcher the opportunity to gather 'live' data from 'live' situations. The researcher is given the opportunity to look at what is taking place *in situ* rather than at second hand (Patton, 1990: 203–5). This enables researchers to understand the context of programmes, to be open-ended and inductive, to see things that might otherwise be unconsciously missed, to discover things that participants might not freely talk about in interview situations, to move beyond perception-based data (e.g. opinions in interviews), and to access personal knowledge. Because observed incidents are less predictable there is a certain freshness to this form of data collection that is often denied in other forms, e.g. a questionnaire or a test.

Observations, it is argued (Morrison, 1993: 80), enable the researcher to gather data on:

- the *physical setting* (e.g. the physical environment and its organization);
- the *human setting* (e.g. the organization of people, the characteristics and make up of the groups or individuals being observed, for instance gender, class);
- the *interactional setting* (e.g. the interactions that are taking place, formal, informal, planned, unplanned, verbal, non-verbal etc.);
- the *programme setting* (e.g. the resources and their organization, pedagogic styles, curricula and their organization).

Patton (1990: 202) suggests that observational data should enable the researcher to enter and understand the situation that is being described. The kind of observations available to the researcher lie on a continuum from unstructured to structured, responsive to pre-ordinate. A *highly structured* observation will know in advance what it is looking for (i.e. pre-ordinate observation) and will have its observation categories worked out in advance. A *semi-structured observation* will have an agenda of issues but will gather data to illuminate these issues in a far less pre-determined or systematic manner. An *unstructured observation* will be far less clear on what it is looking for and will therefore have to go into a situation and observe what is taking place before deciding on its significance for the research. In a nutshell, a structured observation will already have its hypotheses decided and will use the observational data to conform or refute these hypotheses. On the other hand, a semi-structured and, more particularly, an unstructured observation, will be hypothesis-generating rather than hypothesis-testing. The semi-structured and unstructured observations will review observational data before suggesting an explanation for the phenomena being observed.

Though it is possible to argue that all research is some form of participant observation since we cannot study the world without being part of it (Adler and Adler, 1994), nevertheless Gold (1958) offers a well-known classification of researcher roles in observation, that lie on a continuum. At one end is the *complete participant*, moving to the *participant-as-observer*, thence to the *observer-as-participant*, and finally to the *complete observer*. The move is from complete participation to complete detachment. The mid-points of this continuum strive to balance involvement with detachment, closeness with distance, familiarity with strangeness. The role of the complete observer is typified in the one-way mirror, the video cassette, the audio-cassette and the photograph, whilst complete participation involves researchers taking on membership roles (overt or covert).

Traditionally observation has been characterized as non-interventionist (Adler and Adler, 1994: 378), where researchers do not seek to manipulate the situation or subjects, they do not pose questions for the subjects, nor do they deliberately create 'new provocations' (ibid.: 378). Quantitative research tends to have a small field of focus, fragmenting the observed into minute chunks that can subsequently be aggregated into a variable. Qualitative research, on the other hand, draws the researcher into the phenomenological complexity of participants' worlds; here situations unfold, and connections, causes and correlations can be observed as they occur over time. The qualitative researcher seeks to catch the dynamic nature of events, to seek intentionality, and to seek large trends and patterns over time.

If we know in advance what we wish to observe, i.e. if the observation is concerned to chart the *incidence, presence* and *frequency* of elements of the four settings referred to earlier (Morrison, 1993: 80), and maybe wishes to compare one situation with another, then it may be more efficient in terms of time to go into a situation with an already designed observation schedule. If, on the other hand, we want to go into a situation and let the elements of the situation speak for themselves, perhaps with no concern with how one situation compares with another, then it may be more appropriate to opt for a less structured observation.

The former, structured observation, takes much time to prepare but the data analysis is fairly rapid, the categories having already been established, whilst the latter, less structured approach, is quicker to prepare but the data take much longer to analyse. The former approach operates within the agenda of the researcher and hence might neglect aspects of the four settings above if they do not appear on the observation schedule, i.e. it looks selectively at situations. On the other hand, the latter operates within the agenda of the participants, i.e. it is responsive to what it finds and therefore, by definition, is honest to the situation which it finds. Here selectivity derives from the *situation* rather than from the *researcher* in the sense that key issues emerge from, follow from the observation, rather than the researcher knowing in advance what those key issues will be.

Structured observation

A structured observation is very systematic and enables the researcher to generate numerical data from the observations. Numerical data, in turn, facilitate the making of comparisons between settings and situations, and frequencies, patterns and trends to be noted or calculated. The observer adopts a passive, non-intrusive role, merely noting down the incidence of the factors being studied. Observations are entered on an observational schedule. An example of this is shown in Box 17.1 This is an example of a schedule used to monitor student and teacher conversations over a ten minute period. The upper seven categories indicate who is speaking to whom, whilst the lower four categories indicate the nature of the talk. Looking at the example of the observation schedule, several points can be noted:

- The categories for the observation are discrete, i.e. there is no overlap between them. For this to be the case requires a pilot to have been developed and tested in order to iron out any problems of overlap of categories.
- Each column represents a thirty second time interval, i.e. the movement from left to right represents the chronology of the sequence, and the researcher has to enter data in the appropriate cell of the matrix every thirty seconds (see below: instantaneous sampling).
- Because there are so many categories which have to be scanned at speed (every thirty seconds), the researcher will need to practise completing the schedule until he or she

becomes proficient and consistent in entering data (i.e. the observed behaviours, settings etc. are entered into the same categories consistently), achieving reliability. This can be done either through practising with video material or through practising in a live situation with participants who will not subsequently be included in the research. If there is to be more than one researcher then it may be necessary to provide training sessions so that the team of researchers proficiently, efficiently and consistently enter the same sort of data in the same categories, i.e. that there is inter-rater reliability.

• The researcher will need to decide what entry is to be made in the appropriate category, for example: a tick (✓), a forward slash (/), a backward slash (\), a figure (1, 2, 3 etc.), a letter (a, b, c etc.), a tally mark (|). Whatever code or set of codes is used, it must be understood by all the researchers (if there is a team) and must be simple and quick to enter (i.e. symbols rather than words). Bearing in mind that every thirty seconds one or more entries must be made in each column,

the researcher will need to become proficient in fast and accurate data entry of the appropriate codes.[1]

The need to pilot a structured observation schedule, as in the example, cannot be overemphasized. Categories must be mutually exclusive and must be comprehensive. The researcher, then, will need to decide:

1 the foci of the observation (e.g. people as well as events);
2 the frequency of the observations (e.g. every thirty seconds, every minute, every two minutes);
3 the length of the observation period (e.g. one hour, twenty minutes);
4 the nature of the entry (the coding system).

The criterion of 'fitness for purpose' is used for making decisions on these four matters. Structured observation will take much time in preparation but the analysis of the data should be rapid as the categories for analysis will have been built into the schedule itself. So, for example, if close, detailed scrutiny is required then the time

Box 17.1
A structured observation schedule

Student to student	/	/	/	/															
Student to students					/	/													
Student to teacher											/	/	/	/					
Students to teacher							/	/	/	/	/								
Teacher to student															/	/			
Teacher to students																	/	/	/
Student to self																			
Task in hand					✓	✓					✓	✓	✓	✓	✓	✓	✓	✓	✓
Previous task							✓	✓	✓	✓	✓								
Future task																			
Non-task	✓	✓	✓	✓															

Notes
/ = participants in the conversation
✓ = nature of the conversation

intervals will be very short, and if less detail is required then the intervals may be longer.

There are four principal ways of entering data onto a structured observation schedule: event sampling, instantaneous sampling, interval recording, and rating scales.

Event sampling

Event sampling, also known as a sign system, requires a tally mark to be entered against each statement each time it is observed, for example:

teacher shouts at the child	/////
child shouts at the teacher	///
parent shouts at the teacher	//
teacher shouts at the parent	//

The researcher will need to devise statements that yield the data that answer the research questions. This method is useful for finding out the frequencies or incidence of observed situations or behaviours, so that comparisons can be made; we can tell that the teacher does most shouting and that the parent shouts least of all. However, whilst these data enable us to chart the incidence of observed situations or behaviours, the difficulty with them is that we are unable to determine the chronological order in which they occurred. For example, two different stories could be told from these data if the sequence of events were known. If the data were presented in a chronology, one story could be seen as follows, where the numbers 1–7 are the different periods over time (e.g. every thirty seconds):

	1	2	3	4	5	6	7
teacher shouts at the child		/	/	/	/		/
child shouts at the teacher	/	/					/
parent shouts at the teacher		/			/		
teacher shouts at the parent						/	/

Imagine the scene: a parent and his child arrive late for school one morning and the child slips into the classroom; an event quickly occurs which prompts the child to shout at the teacher, the exasperated teacher is very cross when thus provoked by the child; the teacher shouts at the child who then brings in the parent (who has not

yet left the premises); the parent shouts at the teacher for unreasonable behaviour and the teacher shouts back at the child. It seems in this version that the teacher only shouts when provoked by the child or parent.

If the same number of tally marks were distributed in a different order, a very different story might emerge, for example:

	1	2	3	4	5	6	7
teacher shouts at the child	/	/	/	/		/	
child shouts at the teacher					/	/	/
parent shouts at the teacher					/		/
teacher shouts at the parent	/	/					

In this scene it is the teacher who is the instigator of the shouting, shouting at the child and then at the parent; the child and the parent only shout back when they have been provoked!

Instantaneous sampling

If it is important to know the chronology of events, then it is necessary to use instantaneous sampling, sometimes called time sampling. Here the researcher enters what she observes at standard intervals of time, for example every twenty seconds, every minute. On the stroke of that interval she notes what is happening at that precise moment and enters it into the appropriate category on the schedule. For example, imagine that the sampling will take place every thirty seconds; numbers 1–7 represent each thirty second interval thus:

	1	2	3	4	5	6	7
teacher smiles at the child	/	/	/	/			
child smiles at the teacher				/	/	/	/
teacher smiles at the parent	/	/	/	/			
parent smiles at the teacher				/	/	/	/

In this scene the researcher notes down what is happening on the thirty second point and notices from these precise moments that the teacher initiates the smiling but that all parties seem to be doing quite a lot of smiling, with the parent and the child doing the same amount of smiling each! Instantaneous sampling involves recording what is happening on the instant and entering it on the appropriate category. The chronology of events is thus preserved.

Interval recording

This method charts the chronology of events to some extent and, like instantaneous sampling, requires the data to be entered in the appropriate category at fixed intervals. However, instead of charting what is happening on the instant, it charts what has happened during the preceding interval. So, for example, if recording were to take place every thirty seconds, then the researcher would note down in the appropriate category what had happened during the preceding thirty seconds. Whilst this enables frequencies to be calculated, simple patterns to be observed and an approximate sequence of events to be noted, because it charts what has taken place in the preceding interval of time, some elements of the chronology might be lost. For example, if three events took place in the preceding thirty seconds of the example, then the order of the three events would be lost; we would know simply that they had occurred.

Rating scales

In this method the researcher is asked to make some judgement about the events being observed, and to enter responses onto a rating scale. For example, Wragg (1994) suggests that observed teaching behaviour might be entered onto rating scales by placing the observed behaviour onto a continuum:

	1	2	3	4	5	
Warm	—	—	—	—	—	Aloof
Stimulating	—	—	—	—	—	Dull
Businesslike	—	—	—	—	—	Slipshod

An observer might wish to enter a rating according to a five point scale of observed behaviour, for example:

1 = not at all   2 = very little   3 = a little   4 = a lot
5 = a very great deal

	1	2	3	4	5
Child seeks teacher's attention					
Teacher praises the child					
Teacher intervenes to stop misbehaviour					

What is required here is for the researcher to move from low inference (simply reporting observations) to a higher degree of inference (making judgements about events observed). This might introduce a degree of unreliability into the observation (for example through: (a) the halo effect; (b) the central tendency wherein observers will avoid extreme categories; (c) recency – where observers are influenced by more recent events than less recent events). That said, this might be a helpful summary way of gathering observational data.

Whilst structured observation can provide useful numerical data (e.g. Bennett *et al.*, 1984; Galton *et al.*, 1980), there are several concerns which must be addressed in this form of observation, for example:

- the method is behaviourist, excluding any mention of the intentions or motivations of the people being observed;
- the individual's subjectivity is lost to an aggregated score;
- there is an assumption that the observed behaviour provides evidence of underlying feelings, i.e. that concepts or constructs can be crudely measured in observed occurrences.

This latter point is important, for it goes to the very heart of the notion of validity, since it requires researchers to satisfy themselves that it is valid to infer that a particular behaviour indicates a particular state of mind or particular intention or motivation. The thirst to operationalize concepts and constructs can easily lead researchers to provide simple indicators of complex concepts.

Further, structured observation neglects the

significance of contexts – temporal and spatial – thereby overlooking the fact that behaviours may be context specific. In their concern for the overt and the observable, researchers may overlook unintended outcomes which may have significance; they may be unable to show how significant are the behaviours of the participants being observed in their own terms. If we accept that behaviour is developmental, that interactions evolve over time and, therefore, are, by definition, fluid, then the three methods of structured observation outlined above appear to take a series of 'freeze-frame' snapshots of behaviour, thereby violating the principle of fluidity of action. Captured for an instant in time, it is difficult to infer a particular meaning to one or more events (Stubbs and Delamont, 1976), just as it is impossible to say with any certainty what is taking place when we study a single photograph or a set of photographs of a particular event. Put simply, if structured observation is to hold water, then the researcher may need to gather additional data from other sources to inform the interpretation of observational data.

This latter point is a matter not only for structured observation but, equally, for unstructured observation, for what is being suggested here is the notion that *triangulation* (of methods, of observers, of time and space) can assist the researcher to generate reliable evidence. There is a risk that observations will be selective, and the effects of this can be attenuated by triangulation. One way of gathering more reliable data (for example about a particular student or group of students) is by *tracking* them through the course of a day or a week, following them from place to place, event to event. It is part of teaching folklore that students will behave very differently for one teacher than for another, and a full picture of students' behaviour might require the observer to see the students in different contexts.

Critical incidents

There will be times when reliability as consistency in observations is not always necessary.

For example, a student might only demonstrate a particular behaviour once, but it is so important as not to be ruled out simply because it occurred once. One only has to commit a single murder to be branded a murderer! Sometimes one event can occur which reveals an extremely important insight into a person or situation. Critical incidents (Flanagan, 1949) and critical events (Wragg, 1994) are particular events or occurrences that might typify or illuminate very starkly a particular feature of a teacher's behaviour or teaching style for example. Wragg (1994: 64) writes that these are events that appear to the observer to have more interest than other ones, and therefore warrant greater detail and recording than other events; they have an important insight to offer. For example, a child might unexpectedly behave very aggressively when asked to work with another child – that might reveal an insight into the child's social tolerance; a teacher might suddenly overreact when a student produces a substandard piece of work – the straw that breaks the camel's back – that might indicate a level of frustration tolerance or intolerance and the effects of that threshold of tolerance being reached. These events are critical in that they may be non-routine but very revealing; they offer the researcher an insight that would not be available by routine observation. They are frequently unusual events.[2]

Naturalistic observation

There are degrees of participation in observation (LeCompte and Preissle, 1993: 93–4). The 'complete participant' is a researcher who takes on an insider role in the group being studied, and maybe who does not even declare that she is a researcher (echoing the comments above about the ethics of covert research). The 'participant-as-observer', as its name suggests, is part of the social life of participants and documents and records what is happening for research purposes. The 'observer-as-participant', like the participant-as-observer, is known as a researcher to the group, and maybe has less extensive contact with the group. With the 'complete observer' participants do not realize that they are being observed (e.g. using a one-way mirror), hence this is another form of covert research. Hammersley and Atkinson (1983: 93–5) suggest that comparative involvement may come in the forms of the complete participant and the participant-as-observer, with a degree of subjectivity and sympathy, whilst comparative detachment may come in the forms of the observer-as-participant and the complete observer, where objectivity and sympathy are key characteristics. Both complete participation and complete detachment are as limiting as each other. As a complete participant the researcher dare not go outside the confines of the group for fear of revealing her identity (in covert research), and as a complete observer there is no contact with the observed, so inference is dangerous. That said, both complete participation and complete detachment minimize reactivity, though in the former there is the risk of 'going native' – where the researcher adopts the values, norms and behaviours of the group as her own, i.e. ceases to be a researcher and becomes a member of the group.

In participant observational studies the researcher stays with the participants for a substantial period of time to reduce reactivity effects (the effects of the researcher on the researched), recording what is happening, whilst taking a role in that situation. In schools this might be taking on some particular activities, sharing supervisions, participating in school life, recording impressions, conversations, observations, comments, behaviour, events and activities and the views of all participants in a situation. Participant observation is often combined with other forms of data collection that, together, elicit the participants' definitions of the situation and their organizing constructs in accounting for situations and behaviour. By staying in a situation over a long period the researcher is also able to see how events evolve over time, catching the dynamics of situations, the people, personalities, contexts, resources, roles etc.

Morrison (1993: 88) argues that by 'being immersed in a particular context over time not only will the salient features of the situation emerge and present themselves but a more holistic view will be gathered of the interrelationships of factors'. Such immersion facilitates the generation of 'thick descriptions' which lend themselves to accurate explanation and interpretation of events rather than relying on the researcher's own inferences.

Components of 'thick descriptions' involve (Carspecken, 1996: 47), for example, recording: speech acts; non-verbal communication; descriptions in low-inference vocabulary; careful and frequent recording of the time and timing of events; the observer's comments that are placed into categories; detailed contextual data.

Observations are recorded in field notes; these can be written at several levels. At the level of *description* they might include, for example (Spradley, 1980; Bogdan and Biklen, 1992: 120–1; LeCompte and Preissle, 1993: 224):

- quick, fragmentary jottings of key words/symbols;
- transcriptions and more detailed observations written out fully;
- descriptions that, when assembled and written out, form a comprehensive and comprehensible account of what has happened;
- pen portraits of participants;
- reconstructions of conversations;
- descriptions of the physical settings of events;
- descriptions of events, behaviour and activities;
- description of the researcher's activities and behaviour.

Lincoln and Guba (1985: 273) suggest a variety of elements or types of observations that include:

- ongoing notes, either verbatim or categorized *in situ*;
- logs or diaries of field experiences (similar to field notes though usually written after some time has elapsed since the observations were made);
- notes that are made on specific, predetermined themes (e.g. that have arisen from grounded theory);

- 'chronologs', where each separate behavioural episode is noted, together with the time at which it occurred, or recording an observation at regular time intervals, e.g. every two or three minutes;
- context maps—maps, sketches, diagrams or some graphic display of the context (usually physical) within which the observation takes place, such graphics enabling movements to be charted;
- entries on pre-determined schedules (including rating scales, checklists and structured observation charts), using taxonomic or categoric systems, where the categories derive from previous observational or interview data;
- sociometric diagrams indicating social relationships, e.g. isolates (whom nobody chooses), stars (whom everyone chooses); and dyads (who choose each other);
- debriefing questionnaires from respondents that are devised for, and by, the observer only, to be used for reminding the observer of main types of information and events once she or he has left the scene;
- data from debriefing sessions with other researchers, again as an *aide-memoire*.

LeCompte and Preissle (1993: 199–200) provide a useful set of guidelines for directing observations of specific activities, events or scenes, suggesting that they should include answers to the following questions:

- who is in the group/scene/activity – who is taking part?
- how many people are there, their identities and their characteristics?
- how do participants come to be members of the group/event/activity?
- what is taking place?
- how routine, regular, patterned, irregular and repetitive are the behaviours observed?
- what resources are being used in the scene?
- how are activities being described, justified, explained, organized, labelled?
- how do different participants behave towards each other?

- what are the statuses and roles of the participants?
- who is making decisions, and for whom?
- what is being said, and by whom?
- what is being discussed frequently/infrequently?
- what appears to be the significant issues that are being discussed?
- what non-verbal communication is taking place?
- who is talking and who is listening?
- where does the event take place?
- when does the event take place?
- how long does the event take?
- how is time used in the event?
- how are the individual elements of the event connected?
- how are change and stability managed?
- what rules govern the social organization of, and behaviour in, the event?
- why is this event occurring, and occurring in the way that it is?
- what meanings are participants attributing to what is happening?
- what are the history, goals, and values of the group in question?

That this list is long (and by no means exhaustive) reflects the complexity of even the apparently most mundane activity!

Spradley (1980) suggests a checklist of the content of field notes:

- *Space*   the physical setting;
- *Actors*   the people in the situation;
- *Activities*   the sets of related acts that are taking place;
- *Objects*   the artifacts and physical things that are there;
- *Acts*   the specific actions that participants are doing;
- *Events*   the sets of activities that are taking place;
- *Time*   the sequence of acts, activities and events;
- *Goals*   what people are trying to achieve;
- *Feelings*   what people feel and how they express this.

At the level of *reflection*, field notes might include (Bogdan and Biklen, 1992: 122):

- reflections on the descriptions and analyses that have been done;
- reflections on the methods used in the observations and data collection and analysis;
- ethical issues, tensions, problems and dilemmas;
- the reactions of the observer to what has been observed and recorded – attitude, emotion, analysis etc.;
- points of clarification that have been and/or need to be made;
- possible lines of further inquiry.

Lincoln and Guba (1985: 327) indicate three main types of item that might be included in a journal:

1   a daily schedule, including practical matters, e.g. logistics;
2   a personal diary, for reflection, speculation and catharsis;
3   notes on and a log of methodology.

For the level of *analysis* see the discussion of Stage 9 below.

What is being suggested through these comments is that the data should be comprehensive enough to enable the reader to reproduce the analysis that was performed. It should focus on the observable and make explicit the inferential, and that the construction of abstractions and generalizations might commence early but should not starve the researcher of novel channels of inquiry (Sacks, 1992).

Observations include both oral and visual data. In addition to the observer writing down details in field notes, a powerful recording device is through audio-visual recording (Erickson, 1992: 209–10). Comprehensive audio-visual recording can overcome the partialness of the observer's view of a single event and can overcome the tendency towards only recording the frequently occurring events. Audio-visual data collection has the capacity for completeness of analysis and comprehensiveness of material, reducing both the dependence on prior interpre-

tations by the researcher, and the possibility again of only recording events which happen frequently. Of course, one has to be cautious here, for installing video cameras might bring the problem of reactivity. If fixed they might be as selective as participant observers, and if movable, they might still be highly selective (Morrison, 1993: 91).

The context of observation is important (Silverman, 1993: 146). Indeed Spradley (1979) and Kirk and Miller (1986) suggest that observers should keep four sets of observational data to include:

- notes made *in situ*;
- expanded notes that are made as soon as possible after the initial observations;
- journal notes to record issues, ideas, difficulties etc. that arise during the field-work;
- a developing, tentative running record of ongoing analysis and interpretation.

The intention here is to introduce some systematization into observations in order to increase their reliability. In this respect Silverman (1993) reminds us of the important distinction between *etic* and *emic* analysis. *Etic* analysis uses the conceptual framework of the researcher, whilst *emic* approaches use the conceptual frameworks of those being researched. Structured observation uses *etic* approaches, with predefined frameworks that are adhered to unswervingly, whilst *emic* approaches sit comfortably within qualitative approaches, where the definitions of the situations are captured through the eyes of the observed.

Participant observation studies are not without their critics. The accounts that typically emerge from participant observations echo the criticisms of qualitative data outlined earlier, being described as subjective, biased, impressionistic, idiosyncratic and lacking in the precise quantifiable measures that are the hallmark of survey research and experimentation. Whilst it is probably true that nothing can give better insight into the life of a gang of juvenile delinquents than going to live with them for an extended period of time, critics of participant observation studies will point to the dangers of 'going native' as a result of playing a role within such a group. How do we know that observers do not lose their perspective and become blind to the peculiarities that they are supposed to be investigating?

Adler and Adler (1994: 380) suggest several stages in an observation. Commencing with the selection of a setting on which to focus, the observer then seeks a means of gaining entry to the situation (for example, taking on a role in it). Having gained entry the observer can then commence the observation proper, be it structured or unstructured, focused or unfocused. If quantitative observation is being used then data are gathered to be analysed *post hoc*; if more ethnographic techniques are being used then *progressive focusing* requires the observer to undertake analysis *during* the period of observation itself (discussed earlier).

The question that researchers frequently ask is 'how much observation to do', or 'when do I stop observation?'. Of course, there is no hard and fast rule here, though it may be appropriate to stop when 'theoretical saturation' has been reached (Adler and Adler, 1994: 380), i.e. when the situations that are being observed appear to be repeating data that have already been collected. Of course, it may be important to carry on collecting data at this point, to indicate overall frequencies of observed behaviour, enabling the researcher to find the most to the least common behaviours observed over time. Further, the greater the number of observations, the greater the reliability of the data might be, enabling emergent categories to be verified. What is being addressed here is the reliability of the observations (see the earlier discussion of triangulation).

Ethical considerations

Though observation frequently claims neutrality by being non-interventionist, there are several ethical considerations that surround it. There is a well-documented literature on the dilemma surrounding overt and covert observation. Whereas in overt research the subjects know that they are being observed, in covert research they do not. On the one hand this latter form of research appears to violate the principle of informed consent, invades the privacy of subjects and private space, treats the participants instrumentally – as research objects – and places the researcher in a position of misrepresenting her/his role (Mitchell, 1993), or rather, of denying it. However, on the other hand, it is argued (ibid.) that there are some forms of knowledge that are legitimately in the public domain but access to which is only available to the covert researcher (see, for example, the fascinating account of the lookout 'watch queen' in the homosexual community (Humphreys, 1975)). Covert research might be necessary to gain access to marginalized and stigmatized groups, or groups who would not willingly accede to the requests of a researcher to become involved in research. This might include those groups in sensitive positions, for example drug users and suppliers, HIV sufferers, political activists, child abusers, police informants, and racially motivated attackers. Mitchell makes a powerful case for covert research, arguing that not to undertake covert research is to deny access to powerful groups who operate under the protection of silence, to neglect research on sensitive but important topics, and to reduce research to mealy-mouthed avoidance of difficult but strongly held issues and beliefs, i.e. to capitulate when the going gets rough! In a series of examples from research undertaken covertly, he makes the case that not to have undertaken this kind of research would be to deny the public access to areas of legitimate concern, the agendas of the powerful (who can manipulate silence and denial of access to their advantage), and the public knowledge of poorly understood groups or situations.

That covert research can be threatening is well documented from Patrick's (1973) study of a Glasgow gang, where the researcher had to take extreme care not to 'blow his cover' when witness to a murder, to Mitchell's (1993) account of the careful negotiation of role required to undertake covert research into a group of 'millennialists' – ultra-right-wing armed political groups in America who were bound by codes of secrecy, and to his research on mountaineers, where membership of the group involved initiation into the rigours and pains of mountaineering (the researcher had to become a fully fledged mountaineer himself to gain acceptance by the group).

The ethical dilemmas are numerous, charting the tension between invasion and protection of privacy and the public's legitimate 'right to know', between informed consent and its violation in the interests of a wider public, between observation as a superficial, perhaps titillating, spectator sport and as important social research. At issue is the dilemma that arises between protecting the individual and protecting the wider public, posing the question 'whose beneficence?' – whom does the research serve, whom does the research protect, is the greater good the protection and interests of the individual or the protection and interests of the wider public, will the research harm already damaged or vulnerable people, will the research improve their lot, will the research have to treat the researched instrumentally in the interests of gathering otherwise unobtainable yet valuable research data? The researcher has inescapable moral obligations to consider, and, whilst codes of ethical conduct abound, each case might have to be judged on its own merits.

Further, the issue of non-intervention is, itself, problematical. Whilst the claim for observation as being non-interventionist was made at the start of this chapter, the issue is not as clean as this, for researchers inhabit the world that they are researching, and their influence may not be neutral (the Hawthorne and halo effects discussed in Chapter 5). This is clearly an issue in, for example, school inspections, where the presence of an inspector in the classroom exerts a powerful influence on what takes place; it is disingenuous to pretend otherwise. Observer effects can be considerable.

Moreover, the non-interventionist observer has to consider her/his position very closely. In the example of Patrick's witness to a murder above, should the researcher have 'blown his cover' and reported the murder? What if not acting on the witnessed murder might have yielded access to further sensitive data? Should a researcher investigating drug or child abuse, report the first incident, or 'hang back' in order to gain access to further, more sensitive data? Should a witness to abuse simply report it or take action about it? If I see an incident of racial abuse, or bullying, do I maintain my non-interventionist position? Is the observer merely a journalist, providing data for others to judge? When does non-intervention become morally reprehensible? These are issues for which one cannot turn to codes of conduct for a clear adjudication.

Conclusion

Observation methods are powerful tools for gaining insight into situations.[3] As with other data collection techniques, they are beset by issues of validity and reliability. Even low inference observation, perhaps the safest form of observation, is itself highly selective, just as perception is selective. Higher forms of inference, whilst moving towards establishing causality, rely on greater levels of interpretation by the observer, wherein the observer makes judgements about intentionality and motivation. In this respect it has been suggested that additional methods of gathering data might be employed, to provide corroboration and triangulation, in short, to ensure that reliable inferences are derived from reliable data.

This chapter has outlined several different types of observation and the premises that underlie them, the selection of the method to be used depending on 'fitness for purpose'. Overriding the issues of which specific method of observation to use, this chapter has suggested that observation places the observer into the moral domain, that it is inadequate simply to describe observation as a non-intrusive, non-interventionist technique and thereby to abrogate responsibility for the participants involved. Like other forms of data collection in the human sciences, observation is not a morally neutral enterprise. Observers, like other researchers, have obligations to participants as well as to the research community.

18 Tests

Tests and testing have a long and venerable history. Since the spelling test of Rice (1897), the fatigue test of Ebbinghaus (1897) and the intelligence scale of Binet (1905) the growth of tests has proceeded at an extraordinary pace in terms of volume, variety, scope and sophistication. The field of testing is extensive, so extensive in fact that the comments that follow must needs be of an introductory nature and the reader seeking a deeper understanding will have to refer to specialist texts and sources on the subject. Limitations of space permit no more than a brief outline of a small number of key issues to do with tests and testing. Readers wishing to undertake studies to greater depth will need to pursue their interests elsewhere.

In tests, researchers have at their disposal a powerful method of data collection, an impressive array of tests for gathering data of a numerical rather than verbal kind. In considering testing for gathering research data, several issues need to be borne in mind:

- Are we dealing with parametric or non-parametric tests?
- Are they achievement potential or aptitude tests?
- Are they norm-referenced or criterion-referenced?
- Are they available commercially for researchers to use or will researchers have to develop home produced tests?
- Do the test scores derive from a pretest and post-test in the experimental method?
- Are they group or individual tests?

Let us unpack some of these issues.

Parametric and non–parametric tests

Parametric tests are designed to represent the wide population – e.g. of a country or age group. They make assumptions about the wider population and the characteristics of that wider population, i.e. the parameters of abilities are known. They assume (Morrison, 1993):

- that there is a normal curve of distribution of scores in the population (the bell-shaped symmetry of the Gaussian curve of distribution seen, for example, in standardized scores of IQ or the measurement of people's height or the distribution of achievement on reading tests in the population as a whole);
- that there are continuous and equal intervals between the test scores (so that, for example, a score of 80 per cent could be said to be double that of 40 per cent; this differs from the ordinal scaling of rating scales discussed earlier in connection with questionnaire design where equal intervals between each score could not be assumed).

Parametric tests will usually be published as standardized tests which are commercially available and which have been piloted on a large and representative sample of the whole population. They usually arrive complete with the backup data on sampling, reliability and validity statistics which have been computed in the devising of the tests. Working with these tests enables the researcher to use statistics applicable to interval and ratio levels of data.

On the other hand, non-parametric tests make few or no assumptions about the distribution of the population (the parameters of the scores) or the characteristics of that population. The tests do not assume a regular bell-shaped curve of distribution in the wider population; indeed the wider population is perhaps irrelevant as these tests are designed for a given specific population – a class in school, a chemistry group, a primary school year group. Because they make no assumptions about the wider population, the researcher is confined to working with non-parametric statistics appropriate to nominal and ordinal levels of data.

The attraction of non-parametric statistics is their utility for small samples because they do not make any assumptions about how normal, even and regular the distributions of scores will be. Furthermore, computation of statistics for non-parametric tests is less complicated than that for parametric tests. It is perhaps safe to assume that a home-devised test (like a home-devised questionnaire) will probably be non-parametric unless it deliberately contains interval and ratio data. Non-parametric tests are the stock-in-trade of classroom teachers – the spelling test, the mathematics test, the end-of-year examination, the mock-examination. They have the advantage of being tailored to particular institutional, departmental and individual circumstances. They offer teachers a valuable opportunity for quick, relevant and focused feedback on student performance.

Parametric tests are more powerful than non-parametric tests because they not only derive from standardized scores but enable the researcher to compare sub-populations with a whole population (e.g. to compare the results of one school or local education authority with the whole country, for instance in comparing students' performance in norm-referenced or criterion-referenced tests against a national average score in that same test). They enable the researcher to use powerful statistics in data processing (e.g. means, standard deviations, t-tests, Pearson product moment correlations, factor analysis, analysis of variance), and to make *inferences* about the results. Because non-parametric tests make no assumptions about the wider population a different set of statistics is available to the researcher (e.g. modal scores, rankings, the chi-square statistic, a Spearman correlation). These can be used in very specific situations – one class of students, one year group, one style of teaching, one curriculum area – and hence are valuable to teachers.

Norm-referenced, criterion-referenced and domain-referenced tests

A norm-referenced test compares students' achievements relative to other students' achievements (e.g. a national test of mathematical performance or a test of intelligence which has been standardized on a large and representative sample of students between the ages of six and sixteen). A criterion-referenced test does not compare student with student but, rather, requires the student to fulfil a given set of criteria, a predefined and absolute standard or outcome (Cunningham, 1998). For example, a driving test is usually criterion-referenced since to pass it requires the ability to meet certain test items – reversing round a corner, undertaking an emergency stop, avoiding a crash, etc. *regardless* of how many others have or have not passed the driving test. Similarly many tests of playing a musical instrument require specified performances – e.g. the ability to play a particular scale or arpeggio, the ability to play a Bach fugue without hesitation or technical error. If the student meets the criteria, then he or she passes the examination.

The link between criterion referenced tests and mastery learning is strong, for both emphasize the achievement of objectives *per se* rather than in comparison to other students. Both place an emphasis on learning outcomes. Further, Cunningham (1998) has indicated the link between criterion referencing, the minimum competency testing and measurement driven instruction in the US; all of them share the concern for measuring predetermined and specific outcomes and objectives. Though this use of criterion-referencing declined in the closing decade of the twentieth century, the use of criterion-referencing to set standards burgeoned in the same period. What we have, then, is the move away from criterion-referencing as measurement of the achievement of detailed and specific behavioural objectives and towards a testing of what a student has achieved that is not so specifically framed.

A criterion-referenced test provides the researcher with information about exactly what a student has learned, what she can do, whereas a norm-referenced test can only provide the researcher with information on how well one student has achieved in comparison to another, enabling rank orderings of performance and achievement to be constructed. Hence a major feature of the norm-referenced test is its ability to discriminate between students and their achievements – a well constructed norm-referenced test enables differences in achievement to be measured acutely, i.e. to provide variability or a great range of scores. For a criterion-referenced test this is less of a problem, the intention here is to indicate whether students have achieved a set of given criteria, regardless of how many others might or might not have achieved them, hence variability or range is less important here.

The question of the politics in the use of data from criterion-referenced examination results arises when such data are used in a norm-referenced way to compare student with student, school with school, local authority with local authority, region with region (as has been done in the United Kingdom with the publication of 'league tables' of local authorities' successes in the achievement of their students when tested at the age of seven – a process which is envisaged to develop into the publication of achievements at several ages and school by school).

More recently an outgrowth of criterion-referenced testing has been the rise of domain-referenced tests (Gipps, 1994: 81). Here considerable significance is accorded to the careful and detailed specification of the content or the domain which will be assessed. The domain is the particular field or area of the subject that is being tested, for example, light in science, two-part counterpoint in music, parts of speech in English language. The domain is set out very clearly and very fully, such that the full depth and breadth of the content is established. Test items are then selected from this very full field, with careful attention to sampling procedures so that representativeness of the wider field is ensured in the test items. The student's achievements on that test are computed to yield a proportion of the maximum score possible, and this, in turn, is used as an index of the proportion of the overall domain that she has grasped. So, for example, if a domain has 1,000 items and the test has 50 items, and the student scores 30 marks from the possible 50 then it is inferred that she has grasped 60 per cent ($\{30 \div 50\} \times 100$) of the domain of 1,000 items. Here inferences are being made from a limited number of items to the student's achievements in the whole domain; this requires careful and representative sampling procedures for test items.

Commercially produced tests and researcher-produced tests

There is a battery of tests in the public domain which cover a vast range of topics and which can be used for evaluative purposes. Most schools will have used published tests at one time or another: diagnostic tests, aptitude tests, achievement tests, norm-referenced tests, readiness tests, subject-specific tests, skills tests, criterion-referenced tests, reading tests, verbal reasoning tests, non-verbal reasoning tests, tests of social adjustment, tests of intelligence, tests of critical thinking; the list is colossal.

There are several attractions to using published tests:

- They are objective;
- They have been piloted and refined;
- They have been standardized across a named population (e.g. a region of the country, the whole country, a particular age group or various age groups) so that they represent a wide population;
- They declare how reliable and valid they are (mentioned in the statistical details which are

usually contained in the manual of instructions for administering the test);

- They tend to be parametric tests, hence enabling sophisticated statistics to be calculated;
- They come complete with instructions for administration;
- They are often straightforward and quick to administer and to mark;
- Guides to the interpretation of the data are usually included in the manual;
- Researchers are spared the task of having to devise, pilot and refine their own test.

Several commercially produced tests have restricted release or availability, hence the researcher might have to register with a particular association before being given clearance to use the test or before being given copies of it. For example, the Psychological Corporation Ltd and McGraw-Hill publishers not only hold the rights to a world-wide battery of tests of all kinds but require registration before releasing tests. In this example the Psychological Corporation also has different levels of clearance, so that certain parties or researchers may not be eligible to have a test released to them because they do not fulfil particular criteria for eligibility.

Published tests by definition are not tailored to institutional or local contexts or needs; indeed their claim to objectivity is made on the grounds that they are deliberately supra-institutional. The researcher wishing to use published tests must be certain that the purposes, objectives and content of the published tests match the purposes, objectives and content of the evaluation. For example, a published diagnostic test might not fit the needs of the evaluation to have an achievement test; a test of achievement might not have the predictive quality which the researcher seeks in an aptitude test, a published reading test might not address the areas of reading that the researcher is wishing to cover, a verbal reading test written in English might contain language which is difficult for a student whose first language is not English. These are important considerations. A much-cited text on evaluating the utility for researchers of commercially available tests is produced by the American Psychological Association (1974) in the *Standards for Educational and Psychological Testing*.

The golden rule for deciding to use a published test is that it must demonstrate *fitness for purpose*. If it fails to demonstrate this, then tests will have to be devised by the researcher. The attraction of this latter point is that such a 'homegrown' test will be tailored to the local and institutional context very tightly, i.e. that the purposes, objectives and content of the test will be deliberately fitted to the *specific* needs of the researcher in a specific, given context. In discussing 'fitness for purpose' (Cronbach, 1949; Gronlund and Linn, 1990) set out a range of criteria against which a commercially produced test can be evaluated for its suitability for specific research purposes.

Against these advantages of course there are several important considerations in devising a 'home-grown' test. Not only might it be time-consuming to devise, pilot, refine and then administer the test but, because much of it will probably be non-parametric, there will be a more limited range of statistics which may be applied to the data than in the case of parametric tests.

The scope of tests and testing is far-reaching; it is as if no areas of educational activity are untouched by them. Achievement tests, largely summative in nature, measure achieved performance in a given content area. Aptitude tests are intended to predict capability, achievement potential, learning potential and future achievements. However, the assumption that these two constructs – achievement and aptitude – are separate has to be questioned (Cunningham, 1998); indeed it is often the case that a test of aptitude for, say, geography, at a particular age or stage will be measured by using an achievement test at that age or stage. Cunningham (1998) has suggested that an achievement test might include more straightforward measures of basic skills whereas aptitude tests might put these in combination, e.g. combining reasoning (often abstract) and particular knowledge, i.e. that achievement and aptitude tests differ according to what they are testing. Not only do the tests differ according to what they measure, but, since both can be used predictively, they differ according to what they might be able to predict. For example, because an achievement test is more specific and often tied to a specific content area, it will be useful as a predictor of future performance in that content area but will be largely unable to predict future performance out of that content area. An aptitude test tends to test more generalized abilities (e.g. aspects of 'intelligence', skills and abilities that are common to several areas of knowledge or curricula), hence it is able to be used as a more generalized predictor of achievement. Achievement tests, Gronlund (1985) suggests, are more linked to school experiences whereas aptitude tests encompass out-of-school learning and wider experiences and abilities. However Cunningham (1998), in arguing that there is a considerable overlap between the two types, is suggesting that the difference is largely cosmetic. An achievement test tends to be much more specific and linked to instructional programmes and cognate areas than an aptitude test, which looks for more general aptitudes (Hanna, 1993) (e.g. intelligence or intelligences, Gardner, 1993).[1]

Constructing a test

The opportunity to devise a test is exciting and challenging, and in doing so the researcher will have to consider:

- the *purposes* of the test (for answering evaluation questions and ensuring that it tests what it is supposed to be testing, e.g. the achievement of the objectives of a piece of the curriculum);
- the *type* of test (e.g. diagnostic, achievement, aptitude, criterion-referenced, norm-referenced);
- the *objectives* of the test (cast in very specific terms so that the content of the test items can be seen to relate to specific objectives of a programme or curriculum);
- the *content* of the test;

- the *construction* of the test, involving *item analysis* in order to clarify the *item discriminability* and *item difficulty* of the test (see below);
- the *format* of the test – its layout, instructions, method of working and of completion (e.g. oral instructions to clarify what students will need to write, or a written set of instructions to introduce a practical piece of work);
- the nature of the *piloting* of the test;
- the *validity and reliability* of the test;
- the provision of a *manual of instructions* for the administration, marking and data treatment of the test (this is particularly important if the test is not to be administered by the researcher or if the test is to be administered by several different people, so that reliability is ensured by having a standard procedure).

In planning a test the researcher can proceed thus:

1 Identify the purposes of the test

The purposes of a test are several, for example to *diagnose* a student's strengths, weaknesses and difficulties, to measure *achievement*, to measure *aptitude* and *potential*, to identify *readiness* for a programme. Gronlund and Linn (1990) term this 'placement testing' and it is usually a form of pretest, normally designed to discover whether students have the essential prerequisites to begin a programme (e.g. in terms of knowledge, skills, understandings). These types of tests occur at different stages. For example the placement test is conducted prior to the commencement of a programme, and will identify starting abilities and achievements – the initial or 'entry' abilities in a student. If the placement test is designed to assign students to tracks, sets or teaching groups (i.e. to place them into administrative or teaching groupings), then the entry test might be criterion-referenced or norm-referenced; if it is designed to measure detailed starting points, knowledge, abilities and skills then the test might be more criterion-referenced as it requires a high level of detail. It has its equivalent in 'baseline assessment' and is an important feature if one is to measure the 'value-added' component of teaching and learning: one can only assess how much a set of educational experiences has added value to the student if one knows that student's starting point and starting abilities and achievements.

- *Formative* testing is undertaken during a programme, and is designed to monitor students' progress during that programme, to measure achievement of sections of the programme, and to diagnose strengths and weaknesses. It is typically criterion-referenced.
- *Diagnostic* testing is an in-depth test to discover particular strengths, weaknesses and difficulties that a student is experiencing, and is designed to expose causes and specific areas of weakness or strength. This often requires the test to include several items about the same feature, so that, for example, several types of difficulty in a student's understanding will be exposed; the diagnostic test will need to construct test items that will focus on each of a range of very specific difficulties that students might be experiencing, in order to identify the exact problems that they are having from a range of possible problems. Clearly this type of test is criterion-referenced.
- *Summative* testing is the test given at the end of the programme, and is designed to measure achievement, outcomes, or 'mastery'. This might be criterion-referenced or norm-referenced, depending to some extent on the use to which the results will be put (e.g. to award certificates or grades, to identify achievement of specific objectives).

2 Identify the test specifications

The test specifications include:

- which programme objectives and student learning outcomes will be addressed;
- which content areas will be addressed;
- the relative weightings, balance and coverage of items;
- the total number of items in the test;
- the number of questions required to address a particular element of a programme or learning outcomes;
- the exact items in the test.

To ensure validity in a test it is essential to ensure that the objectives of the test are fairly addressed in the test items. Objectives, it is argued (Mager, 1962; Wiles and Bondi, 1984), should: (a) be specific and be expressed with an appropriate degree of precision; (b) represent intended learning outcomes; (c) identify the actual and observable behaviour which will demonstrate achievement; (d) include an active verb; (e) be unitary (focusing on one item per objective).

One way of ensuring that the objectives are fairly addressed in test items can be done through a matrix frame that indicates the *coverage* of content areas, the coverage of *objectives* of the programme, and the *relative weighting* of the items on the test. Such a matrix is set out in Box 18.1 taking the example from a secondary school history syllabus.

Box 18.1 indicates the main areas of the programme to be covered in the test (*content areas*); then it indicates which objectives or detailed content areas will be covered (1a–3c) – these numbers refer to the identified specifications in the syllabus; then it indicates the marks/percentages to be awarded for each area. This indicates several points:

- the least emphasis is given to the build-up to and end of the war (10 marks each in the 'total' column);
- the greatest emphasis is given to the invasion of France (35 marks in the 'total' column);
- there is fairly even coverage of the objectives specified (the figures in the 'total' row only vary from 9–13);
- greatest coverage is given to objectives 2a and 3a, and least coverage is given to objective 1c;
- some content areas are not covered in the test items (the blanks in the matrix).

Box 18.1
A matrix of test items

Content areas	Objective/area of programme content			Objective/area of programme content			Objective/area programme content			Total
Aspects of the 1939–45 war	1a	1b	1c	2a	2b	2c	3a	3b	3c	
The build-up to the 1939–45 world war	1	2		2	1	1	1	1	1	10
The invasion of Poland	2	1	1	3	2	2	3	3	3	20
The invasion of France	3	4	5	4	4	3	4	4	4	35
The allied invasion	3	2	3	3	4	3	3	2	2	25
The end of the conflict	2	1		1	1	1	2	2		10
Total	11	10	9	13	12	10	13	12	10	100

Hence we have here a test scheme that indicates relative weightings, coverage of objectives and content, and the relation between these two latter elements. Gronlund and Linn (1990) suggest that relative weightings should be addressed by firstly assigning percentages at the foot of each column, then by assigning percentages at the end of each row, and then completing each cell of the matrix within these specifications. This ensures that appropriate sampling and coverage of the items are achieved. The example of the matrix refers to specific objectives as column headings; of course these could be replaced by factual knowledge, conceptual knowledge and principles, and skills for each of the column headings. Alternatively they could be replaced with specific aspects of an activity, for example (Cohen, Manion and Morrison, 1996: 416): designing a crane, making the crane, testing the crane, evaluating the results, improving the design. Indeed these latter could become content (row) headings as shown in Box 18.2. Here one can see that

practical skills will carry fewer marks than recording skills (the column totals), and that making and evaluating carry equal marks (the row totals).

This exercise also enables some indication to be gained on the number of items to be included in the test, for instance in the example of the history test above the matrix is 5 × 9 = 45 possible items, and in the 'crane' activity below the matrix is 5 × 4 = 20 possible items. Of course, there could be considerable variation in this, for example more test items could be inserted if it were deemed desirable to test one cell of the matrix with more than one item (possible for cross-checking), or indeed there could be fewer items if it were possible to have a single test item that serves more than one cell of the matrix. The difficulty in matrix construction is that it can easily become a runaway activity, generating very many test items and, hence, leading to an unworkably long test – typically the greater the degree of specificity required, the greater the

Box 18.2
Compiling elements of test items

Content area	Identifying key concepts and principles	Practical skills	Evaluative skills	Recording results	Total
Designing a crane	2	1	1	3	7
Making the crane	2	5	2	3	12
Testing the crane	3	3	1	4	11
Evaluating the results	3		5	4	12
Improving the design	2	2	3	1	8
Total	12	11	12	15	50

number of test items there will be. One skill in test construction is to be able to have a single test item that provides valid and reliable data for more than a single factor.

Having undertaken the test specifications, the researcher should have achieved clarity on (a) the exact test items that test certain aspects of achievement of objectives, programmes, contents etc.; (b) the coverage and balance of coverage of the test items; and (c) the relative weightings of the test items.

3 Select the contents of the test

Here the test is subject to *item analysis*. Gronlund and Linn (1990) suggest that an item analysis will need to consider:

- the suitability of the format of each item for the (learning) objective (appropriateness);
- the ability of each item to enable students to demonstrate their performance of the (learning) objective (relevance);
- the clarity of the task for each item;
- the straightforwardness of the task;
- the unambiguity of the outcome of each item, and agreement on what that outcome should be;
- the cultural fairness of each item;
- the independence of each item (i.e. where the influence of other items of the test is minimal and where successful completion of one item is not dependent on successful completion of another);
- the adequacy of coverage of each (learning) objective by the items of the test.

In moving to test construction the researcher will need to consider how each element to be tested will be *operationalized*: (a) what indicators and kinds of evidence of achievement of the objective will be required; (b) what indicators of high, moderate and low achievement there will be; (c) what the students will be doing when they are working on each element of the test; (d) what the outcome of the test will be (e.g. a written response, a tick in a box of multiple choice items, an essay, a diagram, a computation).

Indeed the Task Group on Assessment and Testing in the UK (1988) took from the work of the UK's Assessment of Performance Unit the suggestion that attention will have to be given to the *presentation*, *operation* and *response* modes of a test: (a) how the task will be introduced (e.g. oral, written, pictorial, computer, practical demonstration); (b) what the students will be doing when they are working on the test (e.g. mental computation, practical work, oral work, written); and (c) what the outcome will be – how they will show achievement and present the outcomes (e.g. choosing one item from a multiple choice question, writing a short response, open-ended writing, oral, practical outcome, computer output). Operationalizing a test from objectives can proceed by stages:

- identify the objectives/outcomes/elements to be covered;
- break down the objectives/outcomes/elements into constituent components or elements;
- select the components that will feature in the test, such that, if possible, they will represent the larger field (i.e. domain referencing, if required);
- recast the components in terms of specific, practical, observable behaviours, activities and practices that fairly represent and cover that component;
- specify the kinds of data required to provide information on the achievement of the criteria;
- specify the success criteria (performance indicators) in practical terms, working out marks and grades to be awarded and how weightings will be addressed;
- write each item of the test;
- conduct a pilot to refine the language/readability and presentation of the items, to gauge item discriminability, item difficulty and distractors (discussed below), and to address validity and reliability.

Item analysis, Gronlund and Linn aver (p. 255), is designed to ensure that: (a) the items function as they are intended, for example, that criterion-referenced items fairly cover the fields and criteria and that norm-referenced items demonstrate *item discriminability* (discussed below); (b) the level of difficulty of the items is appropriate (see below: *item difficulty*); (c) the test is reliable (free of distractors – unnecessary information and irrelevant cues, see below: *distractors*) (see Millmann and Greene (1993)). An item analysis will consider the accuracy levels available in the answer, the item difficulty, the importance of the knowledge or skill being tested, the match of the item to the programme, and the number of items to be included.

The basis of item analysis can be seen in *item response theory* (see Hambleton, 1993). Item response theory (IRT) is based on the principle that it is possible to measure single, specific latent traits, abilities, attributes that, themselves, are not observable, i.e. to determine observable quantities of unobservable quantities. The theory model assumes a relationship between a person's possession or level of a particular attribute, trait or ability and his/her response to a test item. IRT is also based on the view that it is possible:

- to identify objective levels of difficulty of an item, e.g. the Rasch model (Wainer and Mislevy, 1990);
- to devise items that will be able to discriminate effectively between individuals;
- to describe an item independently of any particular sample of people who might be responding to it, i.e. is not group dependent (i.e. the item difficulty and item discriminability are independent of the sample);
- to describe a testee's proficiency in terms of his or her achievement on an item of a known difficulty level;
- to describe a person independently of any sample of items that has been administered to that person (i.e. a testee's ability does not depend on the particular sample of test items);
- to specify and predict the properties of a test before it has been administered;
- for traits to be unidimensional (single traits are specifiable, e.g. verbal ability, mathematical proficiency) and to account for test outcomes and performance;
- for a set of items to measure a common trait or ability;
- for a testee's response to any one test item not to affect his or her response to another test item;
- that the probability of the correct response to an item does not depend on the number of testees who might be at the same level of ability;
- that it is possible to identify objective levels of difficulty of an item;
- that a statistic can be calculated that indicates the precision of the measured ability for each testee, and that this statistic depends on the ability of the testee and the number and properties of the test items.

In constructing a test the researcher will need to undertake an item analysis to clarify the item discriminability and item difficulty of each item of the test. *Item discriminability* refers to the potential of the item in question to be answered correctly by those students who have a lot of the particular quality that the item is designed to measure and to be answered incorrectly by those students who have less of the particular quality that the same item is designed to measure. In other words, how effective is the test item in showing up differences between a group of students? Does the item enable us to discriminate between students' abilities in a given field? An item with high discriminability will enable the researcher to see a potentially wide variety of scores on that item; an item with low discriminability will show scores on that item poorly differentiated. Clearly a high measure of discriminability is desirable.

Suppose the researcher wishes to construct a test of mathematics for eventual use with thirty students in a particular school (or with class A in a particular school). The researcher devises a test and *pilots* it in a different school or class B respectively, administering the test to thirty students of the same age (i.e. she matches the sample of the pilot school or class to the sample in the school which eventually will be used). The scores of the thirty pilot children are then split into three groups of ten students each (high, medium and low scores). It would be reasonable to assume that there will be more correct answers to a particular item amongst the high scorers than amongst the low scorers. For each item compute the following:

$$\frac{A - B}{\frac{1}{2}(N)}$$

where

A = the number of *correct* scores from the high scoring group;

B = the number of *correct* scores from the low scoring group;

N = the *total* number of students in the two groups.

Suppose all ten students from the high scoring group answered the item correctly and two students from the low scoring group answered the item correctly. The formula would work out thus:

$$\frac{8}{\frac{1}{2}(10 + 10)} = 0.80 \text{ (index of item discriminability).}$$

The maximum index of discriminability is 1.00. Any item whose index of discriminability is less than 0.67, i.e. is too undiscriminating, should be reviewed firstly to find out whether this is due to ambiguity in the wording or possible clues in the wording. If this is not the case, then whether the researcher uses an item with an index lower than 0.67 is a matter of judgement. It would appear, then, that the item in the example would be appropriate to use in a test. For a further discussion of item discriminability see Linn (1993).

One can use the discriminability index to examine the effectiveness of *distractors*. This is based on the premise that an effective distractor should attract more students from a low scoring group than from a high scoring group. Consider the following example, where low and high scoring groups are identified:

	A	B	C
Top 10 students	10	0	2
Bottom 10 students	8	0	10

In example A, the item discriminates positively in that it attracts more correct responses (10) from the top 10 students than the bottom 10 (8) and hence is a poor distractor; here, also, the discriminability index is 0.20, hence is a poor discriminator and is also a poor distractor. Example B is an ineffective distractor because nobody was included from either group. Example C is an effective distractor because it includes far more students from the bottom 10 students (10) than the higher group (2). However, in this case any ambiguities must be ruled out before the discriminating power can be improved.

Distractors are the stuff of multiple choice items, where incorrect alternatives are offered, and students have to select the correct alternatives. Here a simple frequency count of the number of times a particular alternative is selected will provide information on the effectiveness of the distractor: if it is selected many times then it is working effectively; if it is seldom or never selected then it is not working effectively and it should be replaced.

If we wished to calculate the *item difficulty* of a test, we could use the following formula:

$$\frac{A}{N} \times 100$$

where

A = the number of students who answered the item correctly

N = the *total* number of students who attempted the item

Hence if 12 students out of a class of 20 answered the item correctly, then the formula would work out thus:

$$\frac{12}{20} \times 100 = 60\%$$

The maximum index of difficulty is 100 per cent. Items falling below 33 per cent and above 67 per cent are likely to be too easy and too difficult respectively. It would appear, then, that this item would be appropriate to use in a test. Here, again, whether the researcher uses an item with an index of difficulty below or above the cut-off points is a matter of judgement. In a norm-referenced test the item difficulty should be around 50 per cent (Frisbie, 1981). For further discussion of item difficulty see Linn (1993) and Hanna (1993).

Given that the researcher can only know the degree of item discriminability and difficulty once the test has been undertaken, there is an unavoidable need to pilot home-grown tests. Items with limited discriminability and limited difficulty must be weeded out and replaced, those items with the greatest discriminability and the most appropriate degrees of difficulty can be retained; this can only be undertaken once data from a pilot have been analysed.

Item discriminability and item difficulty take on differential significance in norm-referenced and criterion-referenced tests. In a norm-referenced test we wish to compare students with each other, hence item discriminability is very important. In a criterion-referenced test, on the other hand, it is not important *per se* to be able to compare or discriminate between students' performance. For example, it may be the case that we wish to discover whether a group of students has learnt a particular body of knowledge, that is the objective, rather than, say, finding out how many have learned it better than others. Hence it may be that a criterion-referenced test has very low discriminability if all the students achieve very well or achieve very poorly, but the discriminability is less important than the fact that the students have or have not learnt the material. A norm-referenced test would regard such a poorly discriminating item as unsuitable for inclusion, whereas a criterion-referenced test would regard such an item as providing useful information (on success or failure).

With regard to item difficulty, in a criterion-referenced test the level of difficulty is that which is appropriate to the task or objective. Hence if an objective is easily achieved then the test item should be easily achieved; if the objective is difficult then the test item should be correspondingly difficult. This means that, unlike a norm-referenced test where an item might be reworked in order to increase its discriminability index, this is less of an issue in criterion-referencing. Of course, this is not to deny the value of undertaking an item difficulty analysis, rather, it is to question the centrality of such a concern. Gronlund and Linn (1990: 265) suggest that where instruction has been effective the item difficulty index of a criterion-referenced test will be high.

In addressing the item discriminability, item difficulty and distractor effect of particular test items, it is advisable, of course, to pilot these tests and to be cautious about placing too great a store on indices of difficulty and discriminability that are computed from small samples.

In constructing a test with item analysis, item discriminability, item difficulty and distractor effects in mind, it is important also to consider the actual requirements of the test (Nuttall, 1987; Cresswell and Houston, 1991), for example:

- are all the items in the test equally difficult?;
- which items are easy, moderately hard, hard, very hard?;
- what kinds of task each item is addressing (e.g. is it (a) a practice item – repeating known knowledge, (b) an application item – applying known knowledge, (c) a synthesis item – bringing together and integrating diverse areas of knowledge)?;
- if not, what makes some items more difficult than the rest?;
- whether the items are sufficiently within the experience of the students;
- how motivated students will be by the contents of each item (i.e. how relevant they perceive the item to be, how interesting it is).

The contents of the test will also need to take account of the notion of *fitness for purpose*, for example in the types of test items. Here the researcher will need to consider whether the kinds of data to demonstrate ability, understanding and achievement will be best demonstrated in, for example (Lewis, 1974; Cohen, Manion and Morrison, 1996):

- an open essay;
- a factual and heavily directed essay;
- short answer questions;
- divergent thinking items;
- completion items;
- multiple choice items (with one correct answer or more than one correct answer);
- matching pairs of items or statements;
- inserting missing words;
- incomplete sentences or incomplete, unlabelled diagrams;
- true/false statements;
- open-ended questions where students are given guidance on how much to write (e.g. 300 words, a sentence, a paragraph);
- closed questions.

These items can test recall, knowledge, comprehension, application, analysis, synthesis, and evaluation, i.e. different orders of thinking. These take their rationale from Bloom (1956) on hierarchies of thinking – from low order (comprehension, application), through middle order thinking (analysis, synthesis) to higher order thinking (evaluation, judgement, criticism). Clearly the selection of the form of the test item will be based on the principle of gaining the maximum amount of information in the most economical way. More recently this is evidenced in the explosive rise of machine-scorable multiple choice completion tests, where optical mark readers and scanners can enter and process large scale data rapidly.

4 Consider the form of the test

Much of the discussion in this chapter assumes that the test is of the pen-and-paper variety. Clearly this need not be the case, for example tests can be written, oral, practical, interactive, computer-based, dramatic, diagrammatic, pictorial, photographic, involve the use of audio and video material, presentational and role-play, simulations. This does not negate the issues discussed in this chapter, for the form of the test will still need to consider, for example, reliability and validity, difficulty, discriminability, marking

and grading, item analysis, timing. Indeed several of these factors take on an added significance in non-written forms of testing; for example: (a) reliability is a major issue in judging live musical performance or the performance of a gymnastics routine – where a 'one-off' event is likely; (b) reliability and validity are significant issues in group performance or group exercises – where group dynamics may prevent a testee's true abilities from being demonstrated. Clearly the researcher will need to consider whether the test will be undertaken individually, or in a group, and what form it will take.

5 Write the test item

The test will need to address the intended and unintended clues and cues that might be provided in it, for example (Morris et al., 1987):

- the number of blanks might indicate the number of words required;
- the number of dots might indicate the number of letters required;
- the length of blanks might indicate the length of response required;
- the space left for completion will give cues about how much to write;
- blanks in different parts of a sentence will be assisted by the reader having read the other parts of the sentence (anaphoric and cataphoric reading cues).

Hanna (1993: 139–41) and Cunningham (1998) provide several guidelines for constructing short-answer items to overcome some of these problems:

- make the blanks close to the end of the sentence;
- keep the blanks the same length;
- ensure that there can be only a single correct answer;
- avoid putting several blanks close to each other (in a sentence or paragraph) such that the overall meaning is obscured;
- only make blanks of key words or concepts, rather than of trivial words;

- avoid addressing only trivial matters;
- ensure that students know exactly the kind and specificity of the answer required;
- specify the units in which a numerical answer is to be given;
- use short-answers for testing knowledge recall.

With regard to multiple choice items there are several potential problems:

- the number of choices in a single multiple choice item (and whether there is one or more right answer(s));
- the number and realism of the distractors in a multiple-choice item (e.g. there might be many distractors but many of them are too obvious to be chosen – there may be several redundant items);
- the sequence of items and their effects on each other;
- the location of the correct response(s) in a multiple choice item.

Gronlund and Linn (1990), Hanna (1993: 161–75) and Cunningham (1998) set out several suggestions for constructing effective multiple choice test items:

- ensure that they catch significant knowledge and learning rather than low-level recall of facts;
- frame the nature of the issue in the stem of the item, ensuring that the stem is meaningful in itself (e.g. replace the general 'sheep: (a) are graminivorous, (b) are cloven footed, (c) usually give birth to one or two calves at a time' with 'how many lambs are normally born to a sheep at one time?');
- ensure that the stem includes as much of the item as possible, with no irrelevancies;
- avoid negative stems to the item;
- keep the readability levels low;
- ensure clarity and unambiguity;
- ensure that all the options are plausible so that guessing of the only possible option is avoided;
- avoid the possibility of students making the correct choice through incorrect reasoning;

- include some novelty to the item if it is being used to measure understanding;
- ensure that there can only be a single correct option (if a single answer is required) and that it is unambiguously the right response;
- avoid syntactical and grammatical clues by making all options syntactically and grammatically parallel and by avoiding matching the phrasing of a stem with similar phrasing in the response;
- avoid including in the stem clues as to which may be the correct response;
- ensure that the length of each response item is the same (e.g. to avoid one long correct answer from standing out);
- keep each option separate, avoiding options which are included in each other;
- ensure that the correct option is positioned differently for each item (e.g. so that it is not always option 2);
- avoid using options like 'all of the above' or 'none of the above';
- avoid answers from one item being used to cue answers to another item – keep items separate.

Morris *et al.* (1987: 161), Gronlund and Linn (1990), Hanna (1993: 147) and Cunningham (1998) also indicate particular problems in true-false questions:

- ambiguity of meaning;
- some items might be partly true or partly false;
- items that polarize – being too easy or too hard;
- most items might be true or false under certain conditions;
- it may not be clear to the student whether facts or opinions are being sought;
- as this is dichotomous, students have an even chance of guessing the correct answer;
- an imbalance of true to false statements;
- some items might contain 'absolutes' which give powerful clues, e.g. 'always', 'never', 'all', 'none'.

To overcome these problems the authors suggest several points that can be addressed:

- avoid generalized statements (as they are usually false);
- avoid trivial questions;
- avoid negatives and double negatives in statements;
- avoid over-long and over-complex statements;
- ensure that items are rooted in facts;
- ensure that statements can be either only true or false;
- write statements in everyday language;
- decide where it is appropriate to use 'degrees' – 'generally', 'usually', 'often' – as these are capable of interpretation;
- avoid ambiguities;
- ensure that each statement only contains one idea;
- if an opinion is to be sought then ensure that it is attributable to a named source;
- ensure that true statements and false statements are equal in length and number.

Morris *et al.* (1987), Hanna (1993: 150–2) and Cunningham (1998) also indicate particular potential difficulties in matching items:

- it might be very clear to a student which items in a list simply *cannot* be matched to items in the other list (e.g. by dint of content, grammar, concepts), thereby enabling the student to complete the matching by elimination rather than understanding;
- one item in one list might be able to be matched to several items in the other;
- the lists might contain unequal numbers of items, thereby introducing distractors – rendering the selection as much a multiple choice item as a matching exercise.

The authors suggest that difficulties in matching items can be addressed thus:

- ensure that the items for matching are homogeneous – similar – over the whole test (to render guessing more difficult);
- avoid constructing matching items to answers that can be worked out by elimination (e.g. by ensuring that: (a) there are different numbers of items in each column so that there are more options to be matched than there are items; (b) students can avoid being able to reduce the field of options as they increase the number of items that they have matched; (c) the same option may be used more than once);
- decide whether to mix the two columns of matched items (i.e. ensure, if desired, that each column includes both items and options);
- sequence the options for matching so that they are logical and easy to follow (e.g. by number, by chronology);
- avoid over-long columns and keep the columns on a single page;
- make the statements in the options columns as brief as possible;
- avoid ambiguity by ensuring that there is a clearly suitable option that stands out from its rivals;
- make it clear what the nature of the relationship should be between the item and the option (on what terms they relate to each other);
- number the items and letter the options.

With regard to essay questions, there are several advantages that can be claimed. For example, an essay, as an open form of testing, enables complex learning outcomes to be measured, it enables the student to integrate, apply and synthesize knowledge, to demonstrate the ability for expression and self-expression, and to demonstrate higher order and divergent cognitive processes. Further, it is comparatively easy to construct an essay title. On the other hand, essays have been criticized for yielding unreliable data (Gronlund and Linn, 1990; Cunningham, 1998), for being prone to unreliable (inconsistent and variable) scoring, neglectful of intended learning outcomes and prone to marker bias and preference (being too intuitive, subjective, holistic, and time-consuming to mark). To overcome these difficulties the authors suggest that:

- the essay question must be restricted to those learning outcomes that are unable to be measured more objectively;

- the essay question must ensure that it is clearly linked to desired learning outcomes; that it is clear what behaviours the students must demonstrate;
- the essay question must indicate the field and tasks very clearly (e.g. 'compare', 'justify', 'critique', 'summarize', 'classify', 'analyse', 'clarify', 'examine', 'apply', 'evaluate', 'synthesize', 'contrast', 'explain', 'illustrate');
- time limits are set for each essay;
- options are avoided, or, if options are to be given, ensure that, if students have a list of titles from which to choose, each title is equally difficult and equally capable of enabling the student to demonstrate achievement, understanding etc.
- marking criteria are prepared and are explicit, indicating what must be included in the answers and the points to be awarded for such inclusions or ratings to be scored for the extent to which certain criteria have been met;
- decisions are agreed on how to address and score irrelevancies, inaccuracies, poor grammar and spelling;
- the work is double marked, blind, and, where appropriate, without the marker knowing (the name of) the essay writer.

Clearly these are issues of reliability (see Chapter 5 on reliability and validity). The following issue is that layout can exert a profound effect on the test.

6 Consider the layout of the test

This will include (Gronlund and Linn, 1990; Hanna, 1993; Linn, 1993; Cunningham, 1998):

- the nature, length and clarity of the instructions (e.g. what to do, how long to take, how much to do, how many items to attempt, what kind of response is required (e.g. a single word, a sentence, a paragraph, a formula, a number, a statement etc.), how and where to enter the response, where to show the 'working out' of a problem, where to start new answers, e.g. in a separate booklet), is one answer only required to a multiple choice item, or is more than one answer required;
- the spreading of the instructions through the test, avoiding overloading students with too much information at first, and providing instructions for each section as they come to it;
- what marks are to be awarded for which parts of the test;
- minimizing ambiguity and taking care over the readability of the items;
- the progression from the easy to the more difficult items of the test (i.e. the location and sequence of items);
- the visual layout of the page, for example, avoiding overloading students with visual material or words;
- the grouping of items – keeping together items that have the same contents or the same format;
- the setting out of the answer sheets/locations so that they can be entered onto computers and read by optical mark readers and scanners (if appropriate).

The layout of the text should be such that it supports the completion of the test and that this is done as efficiently and as effectively as possible for the student.

7 Consider the timing of the test

This refers to two areas: (a) when the test will take place (the day of the week, month, time of day) and (b) the time allowances to be given to the test and its component items. With regard to the former, in part this is a matter of reliability, for the time of day, week etc. might influence how alert, motivated, capable a student might be. With regard to the latter, the researcher will need to decide what time restrictions are being imposed and why (for example, is the pressure of a time constraint desirable – to show what a student can do under time pressure – or an unnecessary impediment, putting a time boundary around something that need not be bounded –

was Van Gogh put under a time pressure to produce the painting of sunflowers?).

Though it is vital that the student knows what the overall time allowance is for the test, clearly it might be helpful to a student to indicate notional time allowances for different elements of the test; if these are aligned to the relative weightings of the test (see the discussions of weighting and scoring) they enable a student to decide where to place emphasis in the test – she may want to concentrate her time on the high scoring elements of the test. Further, if the items of the test have exact time allowances, this enables a degree of standardization to be built into the test, and this may be useful if the results are going to be used to compare individuals or groups.

8 Plan the scoring of the test

The awarding of scores for different items of the test is a clear indication of the relative significance of each item – the weightings of each item are addressed in their scoring. It is important to ensure that easier parts of the test attract fewer marks than more difficult parts of it, otherwise a student's results might be artificially inflated by answering many easy questions and fewer more difficult questions (Gronlund and Linn, 1990). Additionally, there are several attractions to making the scoring of tests as detailed and specific as possible (Cresswell and Houston, 1991; Gipps, 1994), awarding specific points for each item and sub-item, for example:

- it enables partial completion of the task to be recognized – students gain marks in proportion to how much of the task they have completed successfully (an important feature of domain referencing);
- it enables a student to compensate for doing badly in some parts of a test by doing well in other parts of the test;
- it enables weightings to be made explicit to the students;
- it enables the rewards for successful comple-

tion of parts of a test to reflect considerations such as the length of the item, the time required to complete it, its level of difficulty, its level of importance;
- it facilitates moderation because it is clear and specific;
- it enables comparisons to be made across groups by item;
- it enables reliability indices to be calculated (see discussions of reliability);
- scores can be aggregated and converted into grades straightforwardly.

Ebel (1979) argues that the more marks that are available to indicate different levels of achievement (e.g. for the awarding of grades), the greater the reliability of the grades will be, though, clearly this could make the test longer. Scoring will also need to be prepared to handle issues of poor spelling, grammar and punctuation – is it to be penalized, and how will consistency be assured here? Further, how will issues of omission be treated, e.g. if a student omits the units of measurement (miles per hour, dollars or pounds, metres or centimetres)?

Related to the scoring of the test is the issue of reporting the results. If the scoring of a test is specific then this enables variety in reporting to be addressed, for example, results may be reported item by item, section by section, or whole test by whole test. This degree of flexibility might be useful for the researcher, as it will enable particular strengths and weaknesses in groups of students to be exposed.

The desirability of some of the above points is open to question. For example, it could be argued that the strength of criterion-referencing is precisely its specificity, and that to aggregate data (e.g. to assign grades) is to lose the very purpose of the criterion-referencing (Gipps, 1994: 85). For example, if I am awarded a grade E for spelling in English, and a grade A for imaginative writing, this could be aggregated into a C grade as an overall grade of my English language competence, but what does this C grade mean? It is meaningless, it has no frame of reference or clear criteria, it loses the useful specificity of the A and E grades, it is a compromise that actually tells us nothing. Further, aggregating such grades assumes equal levels of difficulty of all items.

Of course, raw scores are still open to interpretation – which is a matter of judgement rather than exactitude or precision (Wiliam, 1996). For example, if a test is designed to assess 'mastery' of a subject, then the researcher is faced with the issue of deciding what constitutes 'mastery' – is it an absolute (i.e. very high score) or are there gradations, and if the latter, then where do these gradations fall? For published tests the scoring is standardized and already made clear, as are the conversions of scores into, for example, percentiles and grades.

Underpinning the discussion of scoring is the need to make it unequivocally clear exactly what the marking criteria are – what will and will not score points. This requires a clarification of whether there is a 'checklist' of features that must be present in a student's answer.

Clearly criterion-referenced tests will have to declare their lowest boundary – a cut-off point – below which the student has been deemed to fail to meet the criteria. A compromise can be seen in those criterion-referenced tests which award different grades for different levels of performance of the same task, necessitating the clarification of different cut-off points in the examination. A common example of this can be seen in the GCSE examinations for secondary school pupils in the United Kingdom, where students can achieve a grade between A and F for a criterion-related examination.

The determination of cut-off points has been addressed by Nedelsky (1954), Angoff (1971), Ebel (1972) and Linn (1993). Angoff (1971) suggests a method for dichotomously scored items. Here judges are asked to identify the proportion of minimally acceptable persons who would answer each item correctly. The sum of these proportions would then be taken to represent the minimally acceptable score.

An elaborated version of this principle comes from Ebel (1972). Here a difficulty by relevance matrix is constructed for all the items. Difficulty might be assigned three levels (e.g. easy, medium and hard), and relevance might be assigned three levels (e.g. highly relevant, moderately relevant, barely relevant). When each and every test item has been assigned to the cells of the matrix the judges estimate the proportion of items in each cell that minimally acceptable persons would answer correctly, with the standard for each judge being the weighted average of the proportions in each cell (which are determined by the number of items in each cell). In this method judges have to consider two factors – relevance and difficulty (unlike Angoff, where only difficulty featured). What characterizes these approaches is the trust that they place in experts in making judgements about levels (e.g. of difficulty, or relevance, or proportions of successful achievement), i.e. they are based on fallible human subjectivity.

Ebel (1979) argues that one principle in assignation of grades is that they should represent equal intervals on the score scales. Reference is made to median scores and standard deviations, median scores because it is meaningless to assume an absolute zero on scoring, and standard deviations as the unit of convenient size for inclusion of scores for each grade (see also Cohen and Holliday, 1996). One procedure is thus:

Step 1   Calculate the median and standard deviation of the scores.
Step 2   Determine the lower score limits of the mark intervals using the median and the standard deviation as the unit of size for each grade.

However, the issue of cut-off scores is complicated by the fact that they may vary according to the different purposes and uses of scores (e.g. for diagnosis, for certification, for selection, for programme evaluation), as these purposes will affect the number of cut-off points and grades, and the precision of detail required. For a full analysis of determining cut-off grades see Linn (1993).

The issue of scoring takes in a range of factors, for example: grade norms, age norms, percentile norms and standard score norms (e.g. z-scores, T-scores, stanine scores, percentiles).

These are beyond the scope of this book to discuss, but readers are referred to Cronbach (1970), Gronlund and Linn (1990), Cohen and Holliday (1996), Hopkins *et al.* (1996).

Devising a pretest and post-test

The construction and administration of tests is an essential part of the experimental model of research, where a pretest and a post-test have to be devised for the control and experimental groups. The pretest and post-test must adhere to several guidelines:

- The pretest may have questions which differ in form or wording from the post-test, though the two tests must test the same content, i.e. they will be alternate forms of a test for the same groups.
- The pretest must be the same for the control and experimental groups.
- The post-test must be the same for both groups.
- Care must be taken in the construction of a post-test to avoid making the test easier to complete by one group than another.
- The level of difficulty must be the same in both tests.

Test data feature centrally in the experimental model of research; additionally, they may feature as part of a questionnaire, interview and documentary material.

Reliability and validity of tests

Chapter 5 covers issues of reliability and validity. Suffice it here to say that reliability concerns the degree of confidence that can be placed in the results and the data, which is often a matter of statistical calculation and subsequent test redesigning. Validity, on the other hand, concerns the extent to which the test tests what it is supposed to test! This devolves on content, construct, face, criterion-related, and concurrent validity.

Ethical issues in preparing for tests

A major source of unreliability of test data derives from the extent and ways in which students have been prepared for the test. These can be located on a continuum from direct and specific preparation, through indirect and general preparation, to no preparation at all. With the growing demand for test data (e.g. for selection, for certification, for grading, for employment, for tracking, for entry to higher education, for accountability, for judging schools and teachers) there is a perhaps understandable pressure to prepare students for tests. This is the 'high-stakes' aspect of testing (Harlen, 1994), where much hinges on the test results. At one level this can be seen in the backwash effect of examinations on curricula and syllabuses; at another level it can lead to the direct preparation of students for specific examinations. Preparation can take many forms (Mehrens and Kaminski, 1989; Gipps, 1994):

- ensuring coverage, amongst other programme contents and objectives, of the objectives and programme that will be tested;
- restricting the coverage of the programme content and objectives to those only that will be tested;
- preparing students with 'exam technique';
- practice with past/similar papers;
- directly matching the teaching to specific test items, where each piece of teaching and contents is the same as each test item;
- practice on an exactly parallel form of the test;
- telling students in advance what will appear on the test;
- practice on, and preparation of, the identical test itself (e.g. giving out test papers in advance) without teacher input;
- practice on, and preparation of, the identical test itself (e.g. giving out the test papers in advance), with the teacher working through the items, maybe providing sample answers.

How ethical it would be to undertake the final four of these is perhaps questionable, or indeed any apart from the first on the list. Are they cheating or legitimate test preparation? Should one teach to a test; is not to do so a dereliction of duty (e.g. in criterion- and domain-referenced tests) or giving students an unfair advantage and thus reducing the reliability of the test as a true and fair measure of ability or achievement? In high stakes assessment (e.g. for public account-ability and to compare schools and teachers) there is even the issue of not entering for tests students whose performance will be low (see, for example, Haladyna, Nolen and Hass, 1991). There is a risk of a correlation between the 'stakes' and the degree of unethical practice – the greater the stakes, the greater the incidence of unethical practice. Unethical practice, observes Gipps (1994) occurs where scores are inflated but reliable inference on performance or achievement is not, and where different groups of students are prepared differentially for tests, i.e. giving some students an unfair advantage over others. To overcome such problems, she suggests, it is ethical and legitimate for teachers to teach to a broader domain than the test, that teachers should not teach directly to the test, and the situation should only be that better instruction rather than test preparation is accept-able (Cunningham, 1998).

One can add to this list of considerations (Cronbach, 1970; Hanna, 1993; Cunningham, 1998) the view that:

- tests must be valid and reliable (see the chap-ter on reliability and validity);
- the administration, marking and use of the test should only be undertaken by suitably competent/qualified people (i.e. people and projects should be vetted);
- access to test materials should be controlled, for instance: test items should not be repro-duced apart from selections in professional publication; the tests should only be released to suitably qualified professionals in connec-tion with specific professionally acceptable projects;
- tests should benefit the testee (beneficence);
- clear marking and grading protocols should

exist (the issue of transparency is discussed in the chapter on reliability and validity);
- test results are only reported in a way that cannot be misinterpreted;
- the privacy and dignity of individuals should be respected (e.g. confidentiality, anonymity, non-traceability);
- individuals should not be harmed by the test or its results (non-maleficence);
- informed consent to participate in the test should be sought.

Computerized adaptive testing

A recent trend in testing is towards computer-ized adaptive testing (Wainer, 1990). This is par-ticularly useful for large-scale testing, where a wide range of ability can be expected. Here a test must be devised that enables the tester to cover this wide range of ability; hence it must include some easy to some difficult items – too easy and it does not enable a range of high ability to be charted (testees simply getting all the answers right), too difficult and it does not enable a range of low ability to be charted (testees simply get-ting all the answers wrong). We find out very lit-tle about a testee if we ask a battery of questions which are too easy or too difficult for her. Fur-ther, it is more efficient and reliable if a test can avoid the problem for high ability testees of hav-ing to work through a mass of easy items in order to reach the more difficult items and for low ability testees of having to try to guess the answers to more difficult items. Hence it is use-ful to have a test that is flexible and that can be adapted to the testees. For example, if a testee found an item too hard the next item could adapt to this and be easier, and, conversely, if a testee was successful on an item the next item could be harder.

Wainer indicates that in an adaptive test the first item is pitched in the middle of the assumed ability range; if the testee answers it correctly then it is followed by a more difficult item, and if the testee answers it incorrectly then it is fol-lowed by an easier item. Computers here provide an ideal opportunity to address the flexibility, discriminability and efficiency of testing. Testees can work at their own pace, they need not be discouraged but can be challenged, the test is scored instantly to provide feedback to the testee, a greater range of items can be included in the test and a greater degree of precision and reliability of measurement can be achieved; indeed test security can be increased and the problem of understanding answer sheets is avoided.

Clearly the use of computer adaptive testing has several putative attractions. On the other hand it requires different skills from traditional tests, and these might compromise the reliability of the test, for example:

- the mental processes required to work with a computer screen and computer programme differ from those required for a pen and paper test;
- motivation and anxiety levels increase or decrease when testees work with computers;
- the physical environment might exert a significant difference, e.g. lighting, glare from the screen, noise from machines, loading and running the software;
- reliability shifts from an index of the variability of the test to an index of the standard error of the testee's performance. The usual formula for calculating standard error assumes that error variance is the same for all scores, whereas in item response theory it is assumed that error variance depends on each testee's ability. The conventional statistic of error variance calculates a single average variance of summed scores, whereas in item response theory this is, at best very crude, and at worst misleading as variation is a function of ability rather than test variation and cannot fairly be summed (see Thissen, 1990, for an analysis of how to address this issue);
- having so many test items increases the chance of inclusion of poor items.

Computer adaptive testing requires a large item pool for each area of content domain to be developed (Flaugher, 1990), with sufficient numbers, variety and spread of difficulty. The items have to be pretested and validated, their difficulty and discriminability calculated, the effect of distractors reduced, the capability of the test to address unidimensionality and/or multidimensionality to be clarified, and the rules for selecting items to be enacted.

19 Personal constructs

Introduction

One of the most interesting theories of personality to have emerged this century and one that has had an increasing impact on educational research is 'personal construct theory'. Personal constructs are the basic units of analysis in a complete and formally stated theory of personality proposed by George Kelly in a book entitled *The Psychology of Personal Constructs* (1955). Kelly's own experiences were intimately related to the development of his imaginative theory. He began his career as a school psychologist dealing with problem children referred to him by teachers. As his experiences widened, instead of merely corroborating a teacher's complaint about a pupil, Kelly tried to understand the complaint in the way the teacher construed it. This change of perspective constituted a significant reformulation of the problem. In practical terms it resulted in an analysis of the teacher making the complaint as well as the problem pupil. By viewing the problem from a wider perspective Kelly was able to envisage a wider range of solutions.

The insights George Kelly gained from his clinical work led him to the view that there is no objective, absolute truth and that events are only meaningful in relation to the ways that are construed by individuals. Kelly's primary focus is upon the way individuals perceive their environment, the way they interpret what they perceive in terms of their existing mental structure, and the way in which, as a consequence, they behave towards it. In *The Psychology of Personal Constructs*, Kelly proposes a view of people actively engaged in making sense of and extending their experience of the world. Personal constructs are the dimensions that we use to conceptualize

aspects of our day-to-day world. The constructs that we create are used by us to forecast events and rehearse situations before their actual occurrence. According to Kelly, we take on the role of scientist seeking to predict and control the course of events in which we are caught up. For Kelly, the ultimate explanation of human behaviour 'lies in scanning man's undertakings, the questions he asks, the lines of inquiry he initiates and the strategies he employs' (Kelly, 1969). Education, in Kelly's view, is necessarily experimental. Its ultimate goal is individual fulfilment and the maximizing of individual potential. In emphasizing the need of each individual to question and explore, construct theory implies a view of education that capitalizes upon the child's natural motivation to engage in spontaneous learning activities. It follows that the teacher's task is to facilitate children's ongoing exploration of the world rather than impose adult perspectives upon them. Kelly's ideas have much in common with those to be found in Rousseau's *Emile*.

The central tenets of Kelly's theory are set out in terms of a fundamental postulate and a number of corollaries. It is not proposed here to undertake a detailed discussion of his theoretical propositions. Good commentaries are available in Bannister (1970) and Ryle (1975). Instead, we look at the method suggested by Kelly of eliciting constructs and assessing the mathematical relationships between them, that is, repertory grid technique.

Characteristics of the method

Kelly proposes that each person has access to a limited number of 'constructs' by means of which she evaluates the phenomena that constitute her world. These phenomena – people, events, objects, ideas, institutions and so on – are known as 'elements'. He further suggests that the constructs that each of us employs may be thought of as bi-polar, that is, capable of being defined in terms of polar adjectives (good–bad) or polar phrases (makes me feel happy – makes me feel sad).

A number of different forms of repertory grid technique have been developed since Kelly's first formulation. All have the two essential characteristics in common that we have already identified, that is, constructs – the dimensions used by a person in conceptualizing aspects of her world; and elements – the stimulus objects that a person evaluates in terms of the constructs she employs. In Box 19.1, we illustrate the empirical technique suggested by Kelly for eliciting constructs and identifying their relationship with elements in the form of a repertory grid.

Since Kelly's original account of what he called 'The Role Construct Repertory Grid Test', several variations of repertory grid have been developed and used in different areas of research. It is the flexibility and adaptability of repertory grid technique that has made it such an attractive tool to researchers in psychiatric, counselling, and more recently, educational settings. We now review a number of developments in the form and the use of the technique. Alban-Metcalf (1997: 318) suggests that the use of repertory grids is largely twofold: in their 'static' form they elicit perceptions that people hold of others at a single point in time; in their 'dynamic' form, repeated application of the method indicates changes in perception over time; the latter is useful for charting development and change.

'Elicited' versus 'provided' constructs

A central assumption of this 'standard' form of repertory grid is that it enables the researcher to elicit constructs that subjects customarily use in

Box 19.1
Eliciting constructs and constructing a repertory grid

A person is asked to name a number of people who are significant to him. These might be, for example, mother, father, wife, friend, employer, priest. These constitute the *elements* in the repertory grid.

The subject is then asked to arrange the elements into groups of threes in such a manner that two are similar in some way but at the same time different from the third. The ways in which the elements may be alike or different are the *constructs*, generally expressed in bi-polar form (quiet – talkative; mean – generous; warm – cold). The way in which two of the elements are similar is called the *similarity pole* of the construct; and the way in which two of the elements are different from the third, the *contrast pole* of the construct.

A grid can now be constructed by asking the subject to place each element at either the *similarity* or the *contrast* pole of each construct. Let × = one pole of the construct, and blank = the other. The result can be set out as follows:

CONSTRUCTS   ELEMENTS

	A	B	C	D	E	F
1 quiet – talkative	×	×	×			×
2 mean – generous	×			×	×	
3 warm – cold		×			×	

It is now possible to derive different kinds of information from the grid. By studying each *row*, for example, we can get some idea of how a person defines each construct in terms of significant people in his life. From each *column*, we have a personality profile of each of the significant people in terms of the constructs selected by the subjects. More sophisticated treatments of grid data are discussed in examples presented in the text.

Source Adapted from Kelly, 1969

interpreting and predicting the behaviour of those people who are important in their lives. Kelly's method of eliciting personal constructs required the subject to complete a number of cards, 'each showing the name of a person in [his/her] life'. Similarly, in identifying elements, the subject was asked, 'Is there an important way in which two of [the elements] – any two – differ from the third?', i.e. triadic elicitation (see, for example, Nash, 1976). This insistence upon important persons and important ways that they are alike or differ, where both constructs and elements are nominated by the subjects themselves, is central to Personal Construct Theory. Kelly gives it precise expression in his Individuality Corollary – 'Persons differ from each other in their construction of events.'

Several forms of repertory grid technique now in common use represent a significant departure from Kelly's individuality corollary in that they provide constructs to subjects rather than elicit constructs from them.

One justification for the use of provided constructs is implicit in Ryle's commentary on the individuality corollary: 'Kelly paid rather little attention to developmental and social processes', Ryle observes, 'his own concern was with the personal and not the social'. Ryle believes that the individuality corollary would be strengthened by the additional statement that 'persons *resemble* each other in their construction of events' (Ryle, 1975).

Can the practice of providing constructs to subjects be reconciled with the individuality corollary assumptions? A review of a substantial body of research suggests a qualified 'yes':

[While] it seems clear in the light of research that individuals prefer to use their own elicited constructs rather than provided dimensions to describe themselves and others ... the results of several studies suggest that normal subjects, at least, exhibit approximately the same degree of differentiation in using carefully selected supplied lists of adjectives as when they employ their own elicited personal constructs.

(Adams-Webber, 1970)

However, see Fransella and Bannister (1977) on elicited versus supplied constructs as a 'grid-generated' problem.

Bannister and Mair (1968) support the use of supplied constructs in experiments where hypotheses have been formulated and in those involving group comparisons. The use of elicited constructs alongside supplied ones can serve as a useful check on the meaningfulness of those that are provided, substantially lower inter-correlations between elicited and supplied constructs suggesting, perhaps, the lack of relevance of those provided by the researcher. The danger with supplied constructs, Bannister and Mair argue, is that the researcher may assume that the polar adjectives or phrases she provides are the verbal equivalents of the psychological dimensions in which she is interested.

Allotting elements to constructs

When a subject is allowed to classify as many or as few elements at the similarity or the contrast pole, the result is often a very lopsided construct with consequent dangers of distortion in the estimation of construct relationships. Bannister and Mair (1968) suggest two methods for dealing with this problem which we illustrate in Box 19.2. The first, the 'split-half form', requires the subject to place half the elements at the similarity pole of each construct, by instructing her to decide which element most markedly shows the characteristics specified by each of the constructs. Those elements that are left are allocated to the contrast pole. As Bannister observes, this technique may result in the discarding of constructs (for example, male–female) which cannot be summarily allocated. A second method, the 'rank order form', as its name suggests, requires the subject to rank the elements from the one which most markedly exhibits the particular characteristic (shown by the similarity pole description) to the one which least exhibits it. As the second example in Box 19.2 shows, a rank order correlation co-efficient can be used to estimate the extent to which there is similarity in the allotment of elements on any two constructs.

Box 19.2
Allotting elements to constructs: three methods

Example 1: Split-half form

Elements   Constructs

1	2	3	4	5	6	7	8	9	10
×		×	×		×		×			1 fast–slow
	×	×		×		×			×	2 late–early
		×	×		×			×	×	3 dangerous–safe

Since the subject is forced to allocate half of the elements to one pole, the chance expectancy of matchings occurring on 10 elements when two constructs are compared is 5. Deviation scores can be computed from chance level. Thus 5 matchings = 0; in constructs 1 and 2, matchings = −3; in constructs 1 and 3, matchings = +1; and in constructs 2 and 3, matchings = −1. The probability of particular matching scores being obtained can be had by reference to statistical tables.

Example 2: Rank-order form

Elements   Constructs

1	2	3	4	5	6	7	8	9	10
10	1	2	5	8	7	3	4	9	6	1 fast–slow
9	4	10	1	6	8	5	2	3	7	2 late–early
7	9	5	6	10	2	1	4	8	3	3 dangerous–safe

Spearman's rho (r_s)   Relationship scores
Constructs 1 and 2 = .15 $(0.15)^2 \times 100 = +23$
Constructs 1 and 3 = .24 $(0.24)^2 \times 100 = +58$
Constructs 2 and 3 = −.16 $(-0.16)^2 \times 100 = -26$

Example 3: Rating form

Elements   Constructs

1	2	3	4	5	6	7	8	9	10
4	4	2	1	4	3	5	1	5	2	1 fast
1	1	3	5	1	3	2	2	5	5	2 late
5	1	3	2	2	1	4	5	1	2	3 dangerous

A 5-point rating scale is shown in which, in this example, single poles of the constructs are rated as follows:

Not at all like		Average		Very much like
1	2	3	4	5

Bannister and Mair suggest several methods for calculating relationships between constructs from the rating form (pp. 63–5). For a detailed discussion of measures of construct relationships, see Fransella and Bannister (1977, pp. 60–72).

Source Adapted from Bannister and Mair, 1968

Following Bannister, a 'construct relationship' score can be calculated by squaring the correlation co-efficient and multiplying by 100. (Because correlations are not linearly related they cannot be used as scores.) The construct relationship score gives an estimate of the percentage variance that the two constructs share in common in terms of the rankings on the two grids.

A third method of allotting elements is the 'rating form'. Here, the subject is required to judge each element on a 7-point or a 5-point scale, for example, absolutely beautiful (7) to absolutely ugly (1). Commenting on the advantages of the rating form, Bannister and Mair (1968) note that it offers the subject greater latitude in distinguishing between elements than that provided for in the original form proposed by Kelly. At the same time the degree of differentiation asked of the subject may not be as great as that demanded in the ranking method. As with the rank order method, the rating form approach also allows the use of most correlation techniques. The rating form is the third example illustrated in Box 19.2.

Alban-Metcalf (1997: 317) suggests that there are two principles that govern the selection of elements in the repertory grid technique. The first is that the elements must be relevant to that part of the construct system that is being investigated, and the second is that the selected elements must be representative. The greater the number of elements (typically between 10 and 25) or constructs that are elicited, the greater is the chance of representativeness. Constructs can be psychological (e.g. anxious), physical (e.g. tall), situational (e.g. from this neighbourhood), and behavioural (e.g. is good at sport).

Laddering and pyramid constructions

The technique known as laddering arises out of Hinkle's (1965) important revision of the theory of personal constructs and the method employed in his research. Hinkle's concern was for the location of any construct within an individual's construct system, arguing that a construct has differential implications within a given hierarchical context. Here a construct is selected by the interviewer, and the respondent is asked which pole applies to a particular, given element (Alban-Metcalf, 1997: 316). The constructs that are elicited are a sequence that has a logic for the individual and that can be arranged in a hierarchical manner of subordinate and superordinate constructs (ibid.: 317). That is 'laddering up', where there is a progression from subordinate to superordinate constructs. The reverse process (superordinate to subordinate) is 'laddering down', asking, for example, how the respondent knows that such and such a construct applies to a particular person.

Hinkle (1965) went on to develop an Implication Grid or Impgrid, in which the subject is required to compare each of his constructs with every other to see which implies the other. The question 'why?' is asked over and over again to identify the position of any construct in an individual's hierarchical construct system. Box 19.3 illustrates Hinkle's laddering technique with an example from educational research reported by Fransella (1975).

In pyramid construction respondents are asked to think of a particular 'element', a person, and then to specify an attribute which is characteristic of that person. Then the respondent is asked to identify a person who displays the opposite characteristic. This sets out the two poles of the construct. Finally, laddering down of each of the opposite poles is undertaken, thereby constructing a pyramid of relationships between the constructs (Alban-Metcalf, 1997: 317).

Grid administration and analysis

The example of grid administration and analysis outlined below employs the split-half method of allocating elements to constructs and a form of 'anchor analysis' devised by Bannister. We assume that 16 elements and 15 constructs have already been elicited by means of a technique such as the one illustrated in Box 19.1.

Procedures in grid administration

Draw up a grid measuring 16 (elements) by 15 (constructs) as in Box 19.1, writing along the top the names of the elements, but first inserting the additional element, 'self'. Alongside the rows write in the construct poles.

You now have a grid in which each intersection or cell is defined by a particular column

Box 19.3
Laddering

Constructs		Elements teachers							
		A	B	C	D	E	F	G	H
masculine		2	1	5	4	3	6	8	7
serious		6	2	1	3	8	4	5	7
good teacher									
authoritarian									
sexy									
old									
gets on with others									
lonely									
like me in character									
like I hope to become									

A matrix of rankings for a repertory grid with teachers as elements

You may decide to stop when you have elicited seven or eight constructs from the teacher elements. But you could go on to 'ladder' two or three of them. This process of laddering is in effect asking yourself (or someone else) to abstract from one conceptual level to another. You could ladder from *man–woman*, but it might be easier to start off with *serious–light-hearted*. Ask yourself which you would prefer to be – *serious* or *light-hearted*. You might reply *light-hearted*. Now pose the question 'why'. Why would you rather be a *light-hearted* person than a *serious* person? Perhaps the answer would be that *light-hearted* people *get on better with others* than do *serious* people. Ask yourself 'why' again. Why do you want to be the sort of person who gets on better with others? Perhaps it transpires that you think that people who do not get on well with others are *lonely*. In this way you elicit more constructs but ones that stand on the shoulders of those previously elicited. Whatever constructs you have obtained can be put into the grid.

Source Adapted from Fransella, 1975

(element) and a particular row (construct). The administration takes the form of allocating every element on every construct. If, for example, your first construct is 'kind–cruel', allocate each element in turn on that dimension, putting a cross in the appropriate box if you consider that person (element) kind, or leaving it blank if you consider that person cruel. Make sure that half of the elements are designated kind and half cruel.

Proceed in this way for each construct in turn, always placing a cross where the construct pole to the left of the grid applies, and leaving it blank if the construct pole to the right is applicable. Every element must be allocated in this way, and half of the elements must always be allocated to the left-hand pole.

Procedures in grid analysis

The grid may be regarded as a reflection of conceptual structure in which constructs are linked by virtue of their being applied to the same persons (elements). This linkage is measured by a process of matching construct rows.

To estimate the linkage between constructs 1 and 2 in Box 19.4, for example, count the number of matches between corresponding boxes in each row. A match is counted where the same element has been designated with a cross (or a blank) on both constructs. So, for constructs 1 and 2 in Box 19.4, we count 6 such matches. By chance we would expect 8 (out of 16) matches, and we may subtract this from the observed value to arrive at an estimate of such deviation from chance.

Constructs	Match	Difference score
1–2	6	6–8 = –2

By matching construct 1 against all remaining constructs (3 . . . 15), we get a score for each comparison. Beginning then with construct 2, and comparing this with every other construct (3 . . . 15), and so on, every construct on the grid is matched with every other one and a difference score for each obtained. This is recorded in matrix form, with the reflected half of the table also filled in (see difference score for constructs 1–2 in Box 19.5). The sign of the difference score is retained. It indicates the direction of the linkage. A positive sign shows that the constructs are positively associated, a negative sign that they are negatively associated.

Now add up (without noting sign) the sum of the difference scores for each column (construct) in the matrix. The construct with the largest difference score is the one which, statistically, accounts for the greatest amount of variance in

the grid. Note this down. Now look in the body of the matrix for that construct which has the largest non-significant association with the one which you have just noted (in the case of a 16-element grid as in Box 19.4, this will be a difference score of ± 3 or less). This second construct can be regarded as a dimension which is orthogonal to the first, and together they may form the axes for mapping the person's psychological space.

If we imagine the construct with the highest difference score to be 'kind–cruel' and the highest non-significant associated construct to be 'confident–unsure', then every other construct in the grid may be plotted with reference to these two axes. The co-ordinates for the map are provided by the difference scores relating to the matching of each construct with the two used to form the axes of the graph. In this way a pictorial representation of the individual's 'personal construct space' can be obtained, and inferences made from the spatial relationships between plotted constructs (see Box 19.6).

Box 19.4
Elements

Construct	Self	1	2	3	4	5	6	7	8	9	10	11	12	13	14	15	Construct
KIND	×		×				×	×			×	×	×			×	CRUEL
CONFIDENT	×	×		×	×		×			×		×		×			UNSURE
‾‾‾‾																	‾‾‾‾
‾‾‾‾																	‾‾‾‾
‾‾‾‾																	‾‾‾‾

Box 19.5
Difference score for constructs

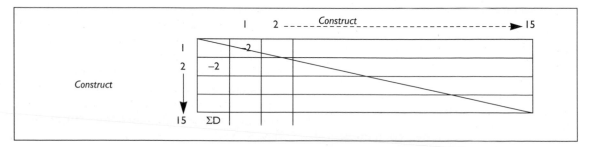

Box 19.6
Grid matrix

	+8	Kind	
Confident			Unsure
−8		0	+8
	−8	Cruel	

By rotating the original grid 90 degrees and carrying out the same matching procedure on the columns (figures), a similar map may be obtained for the people (figures) included in the grid. Grid matrices can be subjected to analyses of varying degrees of complexity. We have illustrated one of the simplest ways of calculating relationships between constructs in Box 19.5. For the statistically minded researcher, a variety of programmes exist in GAP, the Grid Analysis Package developed by Slater and described by Chetwynd (1974).[1] GAP programmes analyse the single grid, pairs of grids and grids in groups. Grids may be aligned either by construct, by element or both. A fuller discussion of metric factor analysis is given in Fransella and Bannister (1977: 73–81) and Pope and Keen (1981: 77–91).

Non-metric methods of grid analysis make no assumptions about the linearity of relationships between the variables and the factors. Moreover, where the researcher is primarily interested in the relationships between elements, multidimensional scaling may prove a more useful approach to the data than principal components analysis.

The choice of one method rather than another must ultimately rest both upon what is statistically correct and what is psychologically desirable. The danger in the use of advanced computer programmes, as Fransella and Bannister point out, is being caught up in the numbers game. Their plea is that grid users should have at least an intuitive grasp of the processes being so competently executed by their computers!

Strengths of repertory grid technique

It is in the application of interpretive perspectives in social research, where the investigator seeks to understand the meaning of events to those participating, that repertory grid technique offers exciting possibilities. It is particularly able to provide the researcher with an abundance and a richness of interpretable material. Repertory grid is, of course, especially suitable for the exploration of relationships between an individual's personal constructs as the studies of Foster (1992)[2] and Neimeyer (1992), for example, show. Foster employed a Grids Review and Organizing Workbook (GROW), a structured exercise based on personal construct theory, to help a 16-year-old boy articulate constructs relevant to his career goals. Neimeyer's career counselling used a Vocational Reptest with a 19-year-old female student who compared and contrasted various vocational elements (occupations), laddering techniques being employed to determine construct hierarchies. Repertory grid is equally adaptable to the problem of identifying changes in individuals that occur as a result of some educational experience. By way of example, Burke, Noller and Caird (1992)[3] identified changes in the constructs of a cohort of technical teacher trainees during the course of their two-year studies leading to qualified status.

In modified formats (the 'dyad' and the 'double dyad') repertory grid has employed relationships between people as elements, rather than people themselves, and demonstrated the increased sensitivity of this type of grid in identifying problems of adjustment in such diverse fields as family counselling (Alexander and Neimeyer, 1989) and sports psychology (Feixas, Marti and Villegas, 1989).

Finally, repertory grid can be used in studying the changing nature of construing and the patterning of relationships between constructs in groups of children from relatively young ages as the work of Epting *et al.* (1971), Salmon (1969) and Applebee (1976) have shown.

Difficulties in the use of repertory grid technique

Fransella and Bannister (1977) point to a number of difficulties in the development and use of grid technique, the most important of which is, perhaps, the widening gulf between technical advances in grid forms and analyses and the theoretical basis from which these are derived. There is, it seems, a rapidly expanding grid industry. Small wonder, then, as Fransella and Bannister wryly observe, that studies such as a one-off analysis of the attitudes of a group of people to asparagus, which bears little or no relation to personal construct theory, are on the increase.

A second difficulty relates to the question of bi-polarity in those forms of the grid in which customarily only one pole of the construct is used. Researchers may make unwarranted inferences about constructs' polar opposites. Yorke's illustration of the possibility of the researcher obtaining 'bent' constructs suggests the usefulness of the opposite method (Epting *et al.*, 1971) in ensuring the bi-polarity of elicited constructs.

A third caution is urged with respect to the elicitation and laddering of constructs. Laddering, note Fransella and Bannister, is an art, not a science. Great care must be taken not to impose constructs. Above all, the researcher must learn to listen to her subject(s).

A number of practical problems commonly experienced in rating grids are identified by Yorke.[4] These are:

- Variable perception of elements of low personal relevance.
- Varying the context in which the elements are perceived during the administration of the grid.
- Halo effect intruding into the ratings where the subject sees the grid matrix building up.
- Accidental reversal of the rating scale (mentally switching from 5 = high to 1 = high, perhaps because 'five points' and 'first' are both ways of describing high quality). This can happen both within and between constructs, and is particularly likely where a neg-
ative or implicitly negative property is ascribed to the pair during triadic elicitation.
- Failure to follow the rules of the rating procedure. For example, where the pair has had to be rated at the high end of a 5-point scale, triads have been found in a single grid rated as 5, 4, 4; 1, 1, 2; 1, 2, 4 which must call into question the constructs and their relationship with the elements.

More fundamental criticism of the repertory grid, however, argues that it exhibits a nomothetic positivism that is discordant with the very theory on which it is based. Whatever the method of rating, ranking or dichotomous allocation of elements on constructs, is there not an implicit assumption, asks Yorke, that the construct is stable across all of the elements being rated? Similar to scales of measurement in the physical sciences, elements are assigned to positions on a fixed scale of meaning as though the researcher were dealing with length or weight. But meaning, Yorke reminds us, is 'anchored in the shifting sands of semantics'. This he ably demonstrates by means of a hypothetical problem of rating four people on the construct 'generous–mean'. Yorke shows that it would require a finely wrought grid of enormous proportions to do justice to the nuances of meaning that could be elicited in respect of the chosen construct. The charge that the rating of elements on constructs and the subsequent statistical analyses retain a positivistic core in what purports to be a non-positivistic methodology is difficult to refute.

Finally, increasing sophistication in computer-based analyses of repertory grid forms leads inevitably to a burgeoning number of concepts by which to describe the complexity of what can be found within matrices. It would be ironic, would it not, Fransella and Bannister ask, if repertory grid technique were to become absorbed into the traditions of psychological testing and employed in terms of the assumptions which underpin such testing. From measures to traits is but a short step, they warn.

Some examples of the use of repertory grid in educational research

Our first two examples of the use of personal constructs in education have to do with course evaluation, albeit one less directly than the other. The first study employs the triadic sorting procedure that Kelly originally suggested; the second illustrates the use of sophisticated interactive software in the elicitation and analysis of personal constructs. Kremer-Hayon's (1991) study sought to answer two questions: first, 'What are the personal constructs by which headteachers relate to their staff?' and second, 'To what extent can those constructs be made more "professional"?' The subjects of her research were thirty junior school headteachers participating in an in-service university programme on school organization and management, educational leadership and curriculum development. The broad aim of the course was to improve the professional functioning of its participants. Headteachers' personal constructs were elicited through the triadic sorting procedure in the following way:

1 Participants were provided with ten cards which they numbered 1 to 10. On each card they wrote the name of a member of staff with whom they worked at school.
2 They were then required to arrange the cards in threes, according to arbitrarily-selected numbers provided by the researcher.
3 Finally, they were asked to suggest one way in which two of the three named teachers in any one triad were similar and one way in which the third member was different.

During the course of the two-year in-service programme, the triadic sorting procedure was undertaken on three occasions: Phase 1 at the beginning of the first year, Phase 2 at the beginning of the second year, and Phase 3 two months later, after participants had engaged in a workshop aimed at enriching and broadening their perspectives as a result of analysing personal constructs elicited during Phases 1 and 2.

The analysis of the personal construct data generated categories derived directly from the headteachers' sortings. Categories were counted separately for each and for all headteachers, thus yielding personal and group profiles. This part of the analysis was undertaken by two judges working independently, who had previously attained 85 per cent agreement on equivalent data. In classifying categories as 'professional' Kremer-Hayon (1991) drew on a research literature which included the following attributes of a profession: 'a specific body of knowledge and expertise, teaching skill, theory and research, accountability, commitment, code of ethics, solidarity and autonomy'. Descriptors were further differentiated as 'cognitive' and 'affective'. By way of example, the first three attributes of professionalism listed above, (specific body of knowledge, teaching skills and theory and research) were taken to connote cognitive aspects; the next four, affective. Thus, the data were classified into the following categories:

professional features (cognitive and affective)
general features (cognitive and affective)
background data (professional and non-professional)
miscellaneous

At the onset of the in-service programme, the group of head-teachers related to their teaching staff by general rather than professional descriptors, and by affective rather than cognitive descriptors. The overall group profile at Phase 1 appeared to be non-professional and affective. This patterning changed at the onset of the second year when, as far as professional descriptors were concerned, a more balanced picture emerged. Upon the completion of the workshop (Phase 3), there was a substantial change towards a professional direction.

Kremer-Hayon concludes that the growth in the number of descriptors pertaining to professional features bears some promise for professional staff development.

The research report of Fisher et al. (1991) arose out of an evaluation of a two-year diploma course in a college of further and higher education. Repertory grid was chosen as a particularly suitable means of helping students chart their way through the course of study and reveal to them aspects of their personal and professional growth. At the same time, it was felt that repertory grid would provide tutors and course directors with important feedback about teaching, examining and general management of the course as a whole.

'Flexigrid', the interactive software used in the study, was chosen to overcome what the authors identify as the major problem of grid production and subsequent exploration of emerging issues – the factor of time. During the diploma course, five three-hour sessions were set aside for training and the elicitation of grids. Students were issued with a booklet containing exact instructions on using the computer. They were asked to identify six items they felt important in connection with their diploma course. These six elements, along with the constructs arising from the triads selected by the software were entered into the computer. Students worked singly using the software and then discussed their individual findings in pairs, having already been trained how to interpret the 'maps' that appeared on the printouts. Individuals' and partners' interpretations were then entered in the students' booklets. Tape-recorders were made available for recording conversations between pairs. The analysis of the data in the research report derives from a series of computer printouts accompanied by detailed student commentaries, together with field notes made by the researchers and two sets of taped discussions.

From a scrutiny of all diploma student grids and commentaries, Fisher, Russell and McSweeney drew the following conclusions about students' changing reactions to their studies as the course progressed.

1   The over-riding student concerns were to do with anxiety and stress connected with the completion of assignments; such concerns, moreover, linked directly to the role of assessors.

2   Extrinsic factors took over from intrinsic ones, that is to say, finishing the course became more important than its intrinsic value.

3   Tutorial support was seen to provide a cushion against excessive stress and fear of failure. There was some evidence that tutors had not been particularly successful at defusing problems to do with external gradings.

The researchers were satisfied with the potential of 'Flexigrid' as a tool for course evaluation. Particularly pleasing was the high level of internal validity shown by the congruence of results from the focused grids and the content analysis of students' commentaries.

For further examples of repertory grid technique we refer the reader to: (a) Harré and Rosser's (1975) account of ethogenically oriented research into the rules governing disorderly behaviour among secondary school leavers, which parallels both the spirit and the approach of an extension of repertory grid described by Ravenette (1977); (b) a study of student teachers' perceptions of the teaching practice situation (Osborne, 1977) which uses 13×13 matrices to elicit elements (significant role incumbents) and provides an example of Smith's and Leach's (1972) use of hierarchical structures in repertory grids.

Grid technique and audio/video lesson recording

Parsons et al. (1983) show how grid technique and audio/video recordings of teachers' work in classrooms can be used to make explicit the 'implicit models' that teachers have of how children learn.

Fourteen children were randomly selected and, on the basis of individual photographs, triadic comparisons were made to elicit constructs concerning one teacher's ideas about the similarities and differences in the manner in which these children learned. In addition, extensive observations of the teacher's classroom behaviour were undertaken under naturalistic conditions and verbatim recordings (audio and video) were made for future review and discussion between the teacher and the researchers at the end of each recording session.

What very soon became evident in these ongoing complementary analyses was the clear distinction that Mrs C (the teacher) held for high and low achievers. The analysis of the children in class as shown in the video tapes revealed that not only did high and low achievers sit in separate groups but the teacher's whole approach to these two groupings differed:

> With high achievers, Mrs. C would often adopt a 'working with' approach, i.e. verbalizing what children had done, with their help. When confronted with low achievers, Mrs. C would more often ask 'why' they had tackled problems in a certain manner, and wait for an answer.
>
> (Parsons *et al.*, 1983)

Focused grids, non-verbal grids, exchange grids and sociogrids

A number of developments have been reported in the use of computer programmes in repertory grid research.[5] We briefly identify these as follows:

1   Focusing a grid assists in the interpretation of raw grid data. Each element is compared with every other element and the ordering of elements in the grid is changed so that those most alike are clustered most closely together. A similar rearrangement is made in respect of each construct.

2   Physical objects can be used as elements and grid elicitation is then carried out in non-verbal terms. Thomas (1978) claims that this approach enhances the exploration of sensory and perceptual experiences.

3   Exchange grids are procedures developed to enhance the quality of conversational exchanges. Basically, one person's construing provides the format for an empty grid which is offered to another person for completion. The empty grid consists of the first person's verbal descriptions from which his ratings have been deleted. The second person is then invited to test his comprehending of the first person's point of view by filling in the grid as he believes the other has already completed it. Various computer programmes ('Pairs', 'Cores' and 'Difference') are available to assist analysis of the processes of negotiation elicited in exchange grids.

4   In the 'Pairs' analysis, all constructs in one grid are compared with all constructs in the other grid and a measure of commonality in construing is determined. 'Pairs' analysis leads on to 'Sociogrids' in which the pattern of relationships between the grids of one group can be identified. In turn, 'Sociogrids' can provide a mode grid for the whole group or a number of mode grids identifying cliques. 'Socionets' which reveal the pattern of shared construing can also be derived.

With these brief examples, the reader will catch something of the flavour of what can be achieved using the various manifestations of repertory grid techniques in the field of educational research.[6]

20 Multi-dimensional measurement

Introduction

However limited our knowledge of astronomy, most of us have learned to pick out certain clusterings of stars from the infinity of those that crowd the northern skies and to name them as the familiar Plough, Orion, and the Great Bear. Few of us would identify constellations in the southern hemisphere that are instantly recognizable by those in Australia.

Our predilection for reducing the complexity of elements that constitute our lives to a more simple order doesn't stop at star gazing. In numerous ways, each and every one of us attempts to discern patterns or shapes in seemingly unconnected events in order to better grasp their significance for us in the conduct of our daily lives. The educational researcher is no exception.

As research into a particular aspect of human activity progresses, the variables being explored frequently turn out to be more complex than was first realized. Investigation into the relationship between teaching styles and pupil achievement is a case in point. Global distinctions between behaviour identified as progressive or traditional, informal or formal, are vague and woolly and have led inevitably to research findings that are at worse inconsistent, at best, inconclusive. In reality, epithets such as informal or formal in the context of teaching and learning relate to 'multi-dimensional concepts', that is, concepts made up of a number of variables. 'Multi-dimensional scaling', on the other hand, is a way of analysing judgements of similarity between such variables in order that the dimensionality of those judgements can be assessed (Bennett and Bowers, 1977). As regards research into teaching styles and pupil achievement, it has been suggested that multi-dimensional typologies of teacher behaviour should be developed. Such typologies, it is believed, would enable the researcher to group together similarities in teachers' judgements about specific aspects of their classroom organization and management, and their ways of motivating, assessing and instructing pupils.

Techniques for grouping such judgements are many and various. What they all have in common is that they are methods for 'determining the number and nature of the underlying variables among a large number of measures', a definition which Kerlinger (1970) uses to describe one of the best-known grouping techniques, 'factor analysis'. We begin the chapter by illustrating a number of methods of grouping or clustering variables ranging from elementary linkage analysis which can be undertaken by hand, to factor analysis, which is best left to the computer. We then outline one way of analysing data cast into multi-dimensional tables. Finally, we append a brief note on a recent, sophisticated technique for exploring multivariate data.

Elementary linkage analysis: an example

Seven constructs were elicited from an infant school teacher who was invited to discuss the ways in which she saw the children in her class (see Chapter 19). She identified favourable and unfavourable constructs as follows: 'intelligent' (+), 'sociable' (+), 'verbally good' (+), 'well-behaved' (+), 'aggressive' (−), 'noisy' (−) and 'clumsy' (−).

Four boys and six girls were then selected at random from the class register and the teacher was asked to place each child in rank order under each of the seven constructs, using rank position 1 to indicate the child most like the particular construct, and rank position 10, the child least like the particular construct. The teacher's rank ordering is set out in Box 20.1. Notice that on three constructs, the rankings have been reversed in order to maintain the consistency of favourable 1, unfavourable 10.

Elementary linkage analysis (McQuitty, 1957) is one way of exploring the relationship between the teacher's personal constructs, that is, of assessing the dimensionality of the judgements that she makes about her pupils. It seeks to identify and define the clusterings of certain variables within a set of variables. Like factor analysis which we shortly illustrate, elementary linkage analysis searches for interrelated groups of correlation co-efficients. The objective of the search is to identify 'types'. By type, McQuitty refers to 'a category of people or other objects (personal constructs in our example) such that the members are internally self-contained in being like one another'. Box 20.2 sets out the intercorrelations between the seven personal construct ratings shown in Box 20.1 (Spearman's *rho* is the method of correlation used in this example).

Steps in elementary linkage analysis

1   In Box 20.2, underline the strongest, that is the highest, correlation co-efficient in each column of the matrix. Ignore negative signs.
2   Identify the highest correlation co-efficient in the entire matrix. The two variables having this correlation constitute the first two of Cluster 1.
3   Now identify all those variables which are most like the variables in Cluster 1. To do this, read along the rows of the variables which emerged in Step 2, selecting any of the co-efficients which are underlined in the rows. Box 20.3 illustrates diagramatically the ways in which these new cluster members

Box 20.1
Rank ordering of ten children on seven constructs

	INTELLIGENT		SOCIABLE
(favourable)	1 Heather	(favourable)	1 Caroline
	2 Richard		2 Richard
	3 Caroline		3 Sharon
	4 Tim		4 Jane
	5 Patrick		5 Tim
	6 Sharon		6 Janice
	7 Janice		7 Heather
	8 Jane		8 Patrick
	9 Alex		9 Karen
(unfavourable)	10 Karen	(unfavourable)	10 Alex
	AGGRESSIVE		NOISY
(unfavourable)	10 Alex	(unfavourable)	10 Alex
	9 Patrick		9 Patrick
	8 Tim		8 Karen
	7 Karen		7 Tim
	6 Richard		6 Caroline
	5 Caroline		5 Richard
	4 Heather		4 Heather
	3 Jane		3 Janice
	2 Sharon		2 Sharon
(favourable)	1 Janice	(favourable)	1 Jane
	VERBALLY-GOOD		CLUMSY
(favourable)	1 Richard	(unfavourable)	10 Alex
	2 Caroline		9 Patrick
	3 Heather		8 Karen
	4 Janice		7 Tim
	5 Patrick		6 Richard
	6 Tim		5 Sharon
	7 Alex		4 Jane
	8 Sharon		3 Janice
	9 Jane		2 Caroline
(unfavourable)	10 Karen	(favourable)	1 Heather
	WELL-BEHAVED		
(favourable)	1 Janice		
	2 Jane		
	3 Sharon		
	4 Caroline		
	5 Heather		
	6 Richard		
	7 Tim		
	8 Karen		
	9 Patrick		
(unfavourable)	10 Alex		

Source Cohen, 1977

are related to the original pair which initially constituted Cluster 1.

4   Now identify any variables which are most like the variables elicited in Step 3. Repeat

Box 20.2

Intercorrelations between seven personal constructs

		(1)	(2)	(3)	(4)	(5)	(6)	(7)
Intelligent	(1)		53	−10	−16	83	−52	13
Sociable	(2)	53		−50	−59	44	−56	61
Aggressive	(3)	−10	−50		91	−07	79	−96
Noisy	(4)	−16	−59	91		−01	73	−93
Verbally-good	(5)	83	44	−07	−01		−43	12
Clumsy	(6)	−52	−56	79	73	−43		−81
Well-behaved	(7)	13	61	−96	−93	12	−81	
(decimal points omitted)								

Source Cohen, 1977

Box 20.3

The structuring of relationships among the seven personal constructs

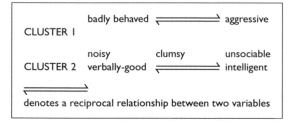

denotes a reciprocal relationship between two variables

Source Cohen, 1977

this procedure until no further variables are identified.

5   Excluding all those variables which belong within Cluster 1, repeat Steps 2 to 4 until all the variables have been accounted for.

Cluster analysis: an example[1]

Elementary linkage analysis is one method of grouping or clustering together correlation co-efficients which show similarities among a set of variables. We now illustrate another method of clustering which was used by Bennett (1976)[2] in his study of teaching styles and pupil progress. His starting point was a disaffection for global descriptions such as 'progressive' and 'traditional' as applied to teaching styles in junior school classrooms. A more adequate theoretical and experimental conceptualization of the elements constituting teaching styles was attempted through the construction of a questionnaire

containing twenty-eight statements illustrating six major areas of teacher classroom behaviour: classroom management and control; teacher control and sanctions; curriculum content and planning; instructional strategies; motivational techniques; and assessment procedures.

Bennett constructed a typology of teaching styles from the responses of 468 top-junior-school classteachers to the questionnaire. His cluster analysis of their responses involved calculating co-efficients of similarity between subjects across all the variables that constituted the final version of the questionnaire. This technique involves specifying the number of clusters of subjects to which the researcher wishes the data to be reduced. Examination of the central profiles of all solutions from twenty-two to three clusters, showed that at the twelve-cluster solution level, between-cluster differences were maximized in relation to within-cluster error (see Bennett, 1976). An essential prerequisite to the clustering technique employed in this study was the use of factor analysis to ensure that the variables were relatively independent of one another and that groups of variables were not over-weighted in the analysis. Principal Components analysis followed by varimax rotation reduced the twenty-eight variables in Bennett's original questionnaire to the nineteen shown in Box 20.4. For purposes of exposition, Bennett ordered the types of teaching style shown in Box 20.4, from the most progressive cluster (Type 1) to the most traditional cluster (Type 12), noting

Box 20.4

Central profiles (percentage occurrence) at 12-cluster levels

Item							Type						
		1	2	3	4	5	6	7	8	9	10	11	12
1	Pupils have choice in where to sit	**63**	**66**	**17**	**46**	**50**	18	7	17	3	7	**77**	**00**
2	Pupils allocated to seating by ability	**14**	**16**	25	**0**	**12**	**45**	20	7	**81**	**58**	**3**	50
3	Pupils not allowed freedom of movement in the classroom	49	**38**	**83**	76	100	84	87	100	86	97	97	100
4	Teacher expects pupils to be quiet	**31**	**34**	**92**	61	**23**	55	56	90	81	74	**90**	**100**
5	Pupils taken out of school regularly as normal teaching activity	51	50	**83**	49	**81**	45	17	47	31	**19**	26	42
6	Pupils given homework regularly	9	22	**8**	27	**65**	3	**13**	43	36	29	21	**56**
	Teaching emphasis												
7	(i) Above average teacher talks to whole class	**29**	**16**	**79**	58	**30**	74	83	73	33	**94**	85	70
8	(ii) Above average pupils working in groups on teacher tasks	46	**13**	**83**	**12**	77	**92**	3	3	22	**68**	**10**	8
9	(iii) Above average pupils working in groups of own choice	**89**	3	29	**94**	19	32	13	3	**0**	23	0	0
10	(iv) Above average pupils working individually on teacher tasks	**9**	**97**	**0**	**3**	42	**0**	73	83	100	**0**	72	92
11	(v) Above average pupils working individually on work of own choice	**94**	**9**	42	**85**	42	**18**	57	57	8	**3**	**8**	28
12	Pupils' work marked and graded	**3**	**3**	**13**	**15**	31	**16**	33	33	8	32	31	97
13	Stars given to pupils who produce best work	**9**	31	38	55	**8**	**18**	17	**73**	17	**87**	**69**	75
14	Arithmetic tests given at least once a week	**9**	**9**	71	88	100	**8**	10	70	50	**94**	56	81
15	Spelling tests given at least once a week	**23**	**19**	67	**94**	**92**	**18**	7	73	**92**	**94**	87	92
16	Teacher smacks for persistent disruptive behaviour	34	34	**96**	24	31	45	**80**	**93**	42	68	64	58
17	Teacher sends pupil out of room for persistent disruptive behaviour	**11**	25	**13**	6	**8**	3	7	10	**25**	0	**33**	**11**
18	Allocation of teaching time (i) Above average separate subject teaching	**20**	**31**	**4**	82	81	95	**100**	47	81	**100**	**100**	92
19	(ii) Above average integrated subject teaching	97	91	100	24	65	8	10	93	14	7	0	0
	N in cluster	35	32	24	33	26	38	30	30	36	31	39	36

Source Bennett 1976

however, that whilst the extreme types could be described in these terms, the remaining types all contained elements of both progressive and traditional teaching styles. The figures in heavy typeface show percentage response levels that were considered significantly different from the total population distribution.

Bennett described the twelve types of teacher styles as follows:

1 These teachers favour integration of subject matter, and, unlike most other groups, allow pupils choice of work, whether undertaken individually or in groups. Most allow pupils

choice of seating. Less than half curb movement and talk. Assessment in all its forms, tests, grading and homework, appears to be discouraged. Intrinsic motivation is favoured.

2   These teachers also prefer integration of subject matter. Teacher control appears to be low, but less pupil choice of work is offered. However, most allow pupils choice of seating, and only one-third curb movement and talk. Few test or grade work.

3   The main teaching mode of this group is class teaching and group work. Integration of subject matter is preferred, associated with taking pupils out of school. They appear to be strict, most curbing movement and talk, and offenders are smacked. The amount of testing is average, but the amount of grading and homework is below average.

4   These teachers prefer separate subject teaching but a high proportion allow pupil choice both in group and individual work. None seat their pupils by ability. They test and grade more than average.

5   A mixture of separate subject and integrated subject teaching is characteristic of this group. The main teaching mode is pupils working in groups of their own choice on tasks set by the teacher. Teacher talk is lower than average. Control is high with regard to movement but not to talk. Most give tests every week and many give homework regularly. Stars are rarely used, and pupils are taken out of school regularly.

6   These teachers prefer to teach subjects separately with emphasis on groups working on teacher-specified tasks. The amount of individual work is small. These teachers appear to be fairly low on control, and are below average on assessment and the use of extrinsic motivation.

7   This group is separate subject oriented, with a high level of class teaching together with individual work. Teacher control appears to be tight, few allow movement or choice of seating, and offenders are smacked. Assessment, however, is low.

8   This group of teachers has very similar characteristics to those in Type 3, the difference being that these prefer to organize the work on an individual rather than group basis. Freedom of movement is restricted, and most expect pupils to be quiet.

9   These teachers favour separate subject teaching, the predominant teaching mode being individuals working on tasks set by the teacher. Teacher control appears to be high; most curb movement and talk, and seat by ability. Pupil choice is minimal. Regular spelling tests are given, but few mark or grade work or use stars.

10   All these teachers favour separate subject teaching. The teaching mode favoured is teacher talk to whole class, and pupils working in groups determined by the teacher on tasks set by the teacher. Most curb movement and talk, and over two-thirds smack for disruptive behaviour. There is regular testing and most give stars for good work.

11   All members of this group stress separate subject teaching by way of class teaching and individual work. Pupil choice of work is minimal, although most teachers allow choice of seating. Movement and talk are curbed, and offenders are smacked.

12   This is an extreme group in a number of respects. None favour an integrated approach. Subjects are taught separately by class teaching and individual work. None allow pupils' choice of seating, and every teacher curbs movement and talk. These teachers are above average on all assessment procedures, and extrinsic motivation predominates.

Bennett's typology of teacher styles and his analysis of pupil performance based on the typology aroused considerable debate. Readers may care to follow up critical comments on the cluster analysis procedures we have outlined here.[3] It is important to note, perhaps, how times have changed since this study was undertaken — many of the practices that Bennett describes would be considered illegal today!

Factor analysis: an example

Factor analysis, we said earlier, is a way of determining the nature of underlying patterns among a large number of variables. It is particularly appropriate in research where investigators aim to impose an 'orderly simplification' (Child, 1970) upon a number of interrelated measures. We illustrate the use of factor analysis in a study of occupational stress among teachers (McCormick and Solman, 1992).

Despite a decade or so of sustained research, the concept of occupational stress still causes difficulties for researchers intent upon obtaining objective measures in such fields as the physiological and the behavioural, because of the wide range of individual differences. Moreover, subjective measures such as self-reports, by their very nature, raise questions about the external validation of respondents' revelations. This latter difficulty notwithstanding, McCormick and Solman (1992) chose the methodology of self-report as the way into the problem, dichotomizing it into first, the teacher's view of self, and second, the external world as it is seen to impinge upon the occupation of teaching. Stress, according to the researchers, is considered as 'an unpleasant and unwelcome emotion' whose negative effect for many is 'associated with illness of varying degree' (McCormick and Solman, 1992). They began their study on the basis of the following premises:

1   Occupational stress is an undesirable and negative response to occupational experiences.
2   To be responsible for one's own occupational stress can indicate a personal failing.

Drawing on attribution theory, McCormick and Solman consider that the idea of blame is a key element in a framework for the exploration of occupational stress. The notion of blame for occupational stress, they assert, fits in well with tenets of attribution theory, particularly in terms of attribution of responsibility having a self-serving bias.[4] Taken in concert with organizational facets of schools, the researchers hypothesized that teachers would 'externalize responsibility for their stress increasingly to increasingly distant and identifiable domains' (McCormick and Solman, 1992). Their selection of dependent and independent variables in the research followed directly from this major hypothesis.

McCormick and Solman developed a questionnaire instrument that included thirty-two items to do with occupational satisfaction. These were scored on a continuum ranging from 'strongly disagree' to 'strongly agree'. Thirty-eight further items had to do with possible sources of occupational stress. Here, respondents rated the intensity of the stress they experienced when exposed to each source. Stress items were judged on a scale ranging from 'no stress' to 'extreme stress'. In yet another section of the questionnaire, respondents rated how responsible they felt certain nominated persons or institutions were for the occupational stress that they, the respondents, experienced. These entities included self, pupils, superiors, the Department of Education, the Government and society itself. Finally, the teacher-participants were asked to complete a fourteen-item Locus of Control scale, giving a measure of internality/externality. 'Internals' are people who see outcomes as a function of what they themselves do; 'externals' see outcomes as a result of forces beyond their control. The items included in this lengthy questionnaire arose partly from statements about teacher stress used in earlier investigations, but mainly as a result of hunches about blame for occupational stress that the researchers derived from attribution theory. As Child (1970) observes:

> In most instances, the factor analysis is preceded by a hunch as to the factors that might emerge. In fact, it would be difficult to conceive of a manageable analysis which started in an empty-headed fashion . . . Even the 'let's see what happens' approach is pretty sure to have a hunch at the back of it somewhere. It is this testing and the generation of hypotheses which forms the principal concern of most factor analysts.
>
> (Child, 1970)

The 90-plus-item inventory was completed by 387 teachers. Separate correlation matrices composed of the inter-correlations of the 32 items on the satisfaction scale, the 8 items in the persons/institutions responsibility measure and the 38 items on the stress scale were factor analysed.

The technical details of factor analysis are beyond the scope of this book. Briefly, however, the procedures followed by McCormick and Solman involved a method called Principal Components, by means of which factors or groupings are extracted. These are rotated to produce a more meaningful interpretation of the underlying structure than that provided by the Principal Components method. (Readable accounts of factor analysis may be found in Kerlinger (1970) and Child (1970).)

In the factor analysis of the eight-item responsibility for stress measure, the researchers identified three factors. Box 20.5 shows those three factors with what are called their 'factor loadings'. These are like correlation co-efficients, ranging from −1.0 to +1.0 and are interpreted similarly. That is to say they indicate the correlation between the person/institution responsibility items shown in Box 20.5, and the factors.

Box 20.5
Factor analysis of responsibility for stress items

Factor groupings of responsibility items with factor loadings and (rounded) percentages of teachers responding in the two most extreme categories of *much stress* and *extreme stress*.		
	Loading	Percentage
Factor 1: School structure		
Superiors	0.85	29
School Organization	0.78	31
Peers	0.77	13
Factor 2: Bureaucratic authority		
Department of Education	0.89	70
Government	0.88	66
Factor 3: Teacher–student relationships		
Students	0.85	45
Society	0.60	60
Yourself	0.50	20

Source McCormick and Solman, 1992

Looking at Factor 1, 'School structure', for example, it can be seen that in the three items loading there are, in descending order of weight, superiors (0.85), school organization (0.78) and peers (0.77). 'School structure' as a factor, the authors suggest, is easily identified and readily explained. But what of Factor 3, 'Teacher–student relationships', which includes the variables students, society and yourself? McCormick and Solman (1992) proffer the following tentative interpretation:

> An explanation for the inclusion of the variable 'yourself' in this factor is not readily at hand. Clearly, the difference between the variable 'yourself' and the 'students' and 'society' variables is that only 20% of these teachers rated themselves as very or extremely responsible for their own stress, compared to 45% and 60% respectively for the latter two. Possibly the degree of responsibility which teachers attribute to themselves for their occupational stress is associated with their perceptions of their part in controlling student behaviour. This would seem a reasonable explanation, but requiring further investigation.
>
> (McCormick and Solman, 1992)

Box 20.6 shows the factors derived from the analysis of the thirty-eight occupational stress items. Five factors were extracted. They were named: 'Student domain', 'External (to school) domain', 'Time demands', 'School domain' and 'Personal domain'. Whilst a detailed discussion of the factors and their loadings is inappropriate here, we draw readers' attention to one or two interesting findings. Notice, for example, how the second factor, 'External (to school) domain', is consistent with the factoring of the responsibility for stress items reported in Box 20.5. That is to say, the variables to do with the Government and the Department of Education have loaded on the same factor. The researchers venture this further elaboration of the point:

> when a teacher attributes occupational stress to the Department of Education, it is not as a member of the Department of Education, although such, in fact is the case. In this context, the Department of

Box 20.6

Factor analysis of the occupational stress items

Factor groupings of stress items with factor loadings and (rounded) percentages of teachers responding to the two extremes of *much stress* and *extreme stress*

	Loading	Percentage
Factor 1: Student domain		
Poor work attitudes of students	0.79	49
Difficulty in motivating students	0.75	44
Having to deal with students who constantly misbehave	0.73	57
Inadequate discipline in the school	0.70	47
Maintaining discipline with difficult classes	0.64	55
Difficulty in setting and maintaining standards	0.63	26
Verbal abuse by students	0.62	39
Students coming to school without necessary equipment	0.56	23
Deterioration of society's control over children	0.49	55
Factor 2: External (to school) domain		
The Government's education policies	0.82	63
The relationship which the Department of Education has with its schools	0.80	55
Unrealistic demands from the Department of Education	0.78	63
The conviction that the education system is getting worse	0.66	49
Media criticism of teachers	0.64	52
Lack of respect in society for teachers	0.63	56
Having to implement Departmental policies	0.59	38
Feeling of powerlessness	0.55	44
Factor 3: Time demands		
Insufficient time for personal matters	0.74	43
Just not enough time in the school day	0.74	51
Difficulty of doing a good job in the classroom because of other delegated responsibilities	0.73	43
Insufficient time for lesson preparation and marking	0.69	50
Excessive curriculum demands	0.67	49
Difficulty in covering the syllabus in the time available	0.61	37
Demanding nature of the job	0.58	64
Factor 4: School domain		
Lack of support from the principal	0.83	21
Not being appreciated by the principal	0.83	14
Principal's reluctance to make tough decisions	0.77	30
Lack of opportunity to participate in school decision-making	0.74	16
Lack of support from other colleagues	0.57	11
Lack of a supportive and friendly atmosphere	0.55	17
Things happen at school over which you have no control	0.41	36
Factor 5: Personal domain		
Personal failings	0.76	13
Feeling of not being suited to teaching	0.72	10
Having to teach a subject for which you are not trained	0.64	23

Source McCormick and Solman, 1992

Education is outside 'the system to which the teacher belongs', namely the school. A similar argument can be posed for the nebulous concept of Society. The Government is clearly a discrete political structure.

(McCormick and Solman, 1992)

'School domain', Factor 4 in Box 20.6, consists of items concerned with support from the school principal and colleagues as well as the general nurturing atmosphere of the school. Of particular interest here is that teachers report relatively low levels of stress for these items. Box 20.7 reports the factor analysis of the thirty-two items to do with occupational satisfaction. Five factors were extracted and named as 'Supervision', 'Income', 'External demands', 'Advancement' and 'School culture'. Again, space precludes a full outline of the results set out in Box 20.7. Notice, however, an apparent anomaly in the first factor, 'Supervision'. Responses to items to do with teachers' supervisors and recognition seem to indicate that in general, teachers are satisfied with their supervisors, but feel that they receive too little recognition. Box 20.7 shows that 21 per cent of teacher-respondents agree or strongly agree that they receive too little recognition, yet 52 per cent agree or strongly agree that they do receive recognition from their immediate supervisors. McCormick and Solman offer the following explanation:

The difference can be explained, in the first instance, by the degree or amount of recognition given. That is, immediate supervisors give recognition, but not enough. Another interpretation is that superiors other than the immediate supervisor do not give sufficient recognition for their work.

(McCormick and Solman, 1992)

Here is a clear case for some form of respondent validation (see Chapter 5).

Having identified the underlying structures of occupational stress and occupational satisfaction, the researchers then went on to explore the relationships between stress and satisfaction by using a technique called 'canonical correlation analysis'. The technical details of this procedure are beyond the scope of this book. Interested readers are referred to Levine, who suggests that 'the most acceptable approach to interpretation of canonical variates is the examination of the correlations of the original variables with the canonical variate' (Levine, 1984). This is the procedure adopted by McCormick and Solman.

From Box 20.8 we see that factors having high correlations with Canonical Variate 1 are Stress: Student domain (-0.82) and Satisfaction: External demands (0.72). The researchers offer the following interpretation of this finding:

[This] indicates that teachers perceive that 'non-teachers' or outsiders expect too much of them (*External demands*) and that stress results from poor student attitudes and behaviour (*Student domain*). One interpretation might be that for these teachers, high levels of stress attributable to the Student domain are associated with low levels of satisfaction in the context of demands from outside the school, and vice versa. It may well be that, for some teachers, high demand in one of these is perceived as affecting their capacity to cope or deal with the demands of the other. Certainly, the teacher who is experiencing the urgency of a struggle with student behaviour in the classroom, is unlikely to think of the requirements of persons and agencies outside the school as important.

(McCormick and Solman, 1992)

The outcomes of their factor analyses frequently puzzle researchers. Take, for example, one of the loadings on the third canonical variate. There, we see that the stress factor 'Time demands' correlates negatively (-0.52). One might have supposed, the authors say, that stress attributable to the external domain would have correlated with the variate in the same direction. But this is not so. It correlates positively at 0.80. One possible explanation, they suggest, is that an increase in stress experienced because of time demands coincides with a lowering of stress attributable to the external domain, as time is expended in meeting demands from the external domain. The researchers concede, however, that this explanation would need close examination before it could be accepted.

Box 20.7
Factor analysis of the occupational satisfaction items

Factor groupings of satisfaction items with factor loadings and (rounded) percentages of teacher responses in the two positive extremes of 'strongly agree' and 'agree' for positive statements, or 'strongly disagree' and 'disagree' for statements of a negative nature; the latter items were reversed for analysis and are indicated by*

	Loading	Percentage
Factor 1: Supervision		
My immediate supervisor does not back me up*	0.83	70
I receive recognition from my immediate supervisor	0.80	52
My immediate supervisor is not willing to listen*	0.78	68
My immediate supervisor makes me feel uncomfortable*	0.78	66
My immediate supervisor treats everyone equitably	0.68	62
My superiors do not appreciate what a good job I do*	0.66	39
I receive too little recognition*	0.51	21
Factor 2: Income		
My income is less than I deserve*	0.80	10
I am well paid in proportion to my ability	0.78	8
My income from teaching is adequate	0.78	19
My pay compares well with other non-teaching jobs	0.66	6
Teachers' income is barely enough to live on*	0.56	24
Factor 3: External demands		
Teachers have an excessive workload*	0.72	5
Teachers are expected to do too many non-teaching tasks*	0.66	4
People expect too much of teachers*	0.56	4
There are too many changes in education*	0.53	10
I am satisfied with the Department of Education as an employer	0.44	12
People who aren't teachers do not understand the realities in schools*	0.34	1
Factor 4: Advancement		
Teaching provides me with an opportunity to advance professionally	0.76	37
I am not getting ahead in my present position*	0.67	16
The Government is striving for a better education system	0.54	22
The Department of Education is concerned for teachers' welfare	0.52	6
Factor 5: School culture		
I am happy to be working at this particular school	0.77	73
Working conditions in my school are good	0.64	46
Teaching is very interesting work	0.60	78

Source McCormick and Solman, 1992

McCormick and Solman's questionnaire also elicited biographical data from the teacher-respondents in respect of sex, number of years teaching, type and location of school and position held in school. By rescoring the stress items on a scale ranging from 'No stress' (1) to 'Extreme stress' (5) and using the means of the factor scores, the researchers were able to explore associations between the degree of perceived occupational stress and the biographical data supplied by participants. Space precludes a full account of McCormick and Solman's findings. We illustrate two or three significant results in Box 20.9. In the *School domain* more stress was

Box 20.8
Correlations between (dependent) stress and (independent) satisfaction factors and canonical variates

	Canonical variates		
	1	2	3
Stress factors			
Student domain	−0.82	−0.47	0.05
External (to school) domain	−0.15	−0.04	0.80
Time	−0.43	0.17	−0.52
School domain	−0.34	0.86	0.16
Personal domain	0.09	−0.05	−0.25
Satisfaction factors			
Supervision	0.23	−0.91	0.32
Income	0.45	0.13	0.12
External demands	0.72	0.33	0.28
Advancement	0.48	−0.04	−0.71
School culture	0.06	−0.28	−0.54

Source Adapted from McCormick and Solman, 1992

reported by secondary school teachers than by their colleagues teaching younger pupils, not really a very surprising result, the researchers observe, given that infant/primary schools are generally much smaller than their secondary counterparts and that teachers are more likely to be part of a smaller, supportive group. In the domain of *Time demands*, females experienced more stress than males, a finding consistent with that of other research. In the *Personal domain*, a significant difference was found in respect of the school's location, the level of occupational stress increasing from the rural setting, through the country/city to the metropolitan area. To conclude, factor analysis techniques are ideally suited to studies such as that of McCormick and Solman in which lengthy questionnaire-type data are elicited from a large number of participants and where researchers are concerned to explore underlying structures and relationships between dependent and independent variables. Inevitably, such tentative explorations raise as many questions as they answer.[5]

Box 20.9
Biographical data and stress factors

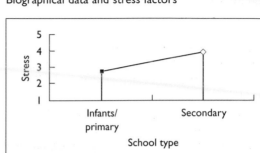

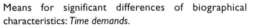

Means for significant differences of biographical characteristics: *External to school domain.*

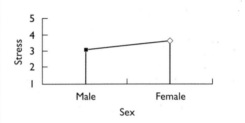

Means for significant differences of biographical characteristics: *Time demands.*

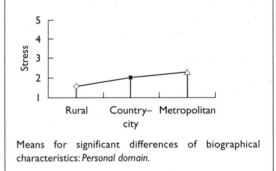

Means for significant differences of biographical characteristics: *Personal domain.*

Source McCormick and Solman, 1992

Examples of studies using factor analysis and linkage analysis

The use of factor analysis and linkage analysis in studies of children's judgements of educational situations is illustrated in the work of Magnusson (1971) and Ekehammar and Magnusson (1973). In the latter study, pupils were required to rate descriptions of various educational episodes on a scale of perceived similarity ranging from '0 = not at all similar' to '4 = identical'. Twenty different situations were presented, two at a time, in the same randomized order for all subjects. For example, 'listening to a lecture but do not understand a thing' would be judged against 'sitting at home writing an essay'. Product moment correlation co-efficients between pairs of similarity matrices calculated for all subjects varied between 0.57 and 0.79, with a median value of 0.71. No individual matrix deviated markedly from any of the others. A factor analysis of the total correlation matrix showed that the descriptions of situations had very clear structures for the children involved. Moreover, judgements of perceived similarity between situations had a considerable degree of consistency over time. Ekehammar and Magnusson (1973) compared their dimensional analysis with a categorical approach to the data using elementary linkage (McQuitty, 1957). They reported that this latter approach gave a result which was entirely in agreement with the result of the dimensional analysis. Five categories of situations were obtained with the same situations distributed in categories in the same way as they were distributed in factors in the dimensional analysis.

Examples of studies using multi-dimensional scaling and cluster analysis

Forgas (1976) studied housewives' and students' perceptions of typical social episodes in their lives, the episodes having been elicited from the respective groups by means of a diary technique. Subjects were required to supply two adjectives to describe each of the social episodes they had recorded as having occurred during the previous twenty-four hours. From a pool of some 146 adjectives thus generated, ten (together with their antonyms) were selected on the basis of their salience, their diversity of usage and their independence of one another. Two more scales from speculative taxonomies were added to give twelve unidimensional scales purporting to describe the underlying episode structures. These scales were used in the second part of the

study to rate twenty-five social episodes in each group, the episodes being chosen as follows. An 'index of relatedness' was computed on the basis of the number of times a pair of episodes was placed in the same category by respective housewife and student judges. Data were aggregated over the total number of subjects in each of the two groups. The twenty-five 'top' social episodes in each group were retained. Forgas's analysis is based upon the ratings of twenty-six housewives and twenty-five students of their respective twenty-five episodes on each of the twelve unidimensional scales. Box 20.10 shows a three-dimensional configuration of twenty-five social episodes rated by the student group on three of the scales. For illustrative purposes some of the social episodes numbered in Box 20.10 are identified by specific content.

In another study, Forgas examined the social environment of a university department consisting of tutors, students and secretarial staff, all of whom had interacted both inside and outside the department for at least six months prior to the research and thought of themselves as an intensive and cohesive social unit. Forgas's interest was in the relationship between two aspects of the social environment of the department — the perceived structure of the group and the perceptions that were held of specific social episodes. Participants were required to rate the similarity between each possible pairing of group members on a scale ranging from '1 = extremely similar' to '9 = extremely dissimilar'. An individual differences multi-dimensional scaling procedure (INDSCAL) produced an optimal three-dimensional configuration of group structure accounting for 68 per cent of the variance, group members being differentiated along the dimensions of sociability, creativity and competence.

A semi-structured procedure requiring participants to list typical and characteristic interaction situations was used to identify a number of social episodes. These in turn were validated by participant observation of the ongoing activities of the department. The most commonly occurring social episodes (those mentioned by nine or

Box 20.10
Students' perceptions of social episodes

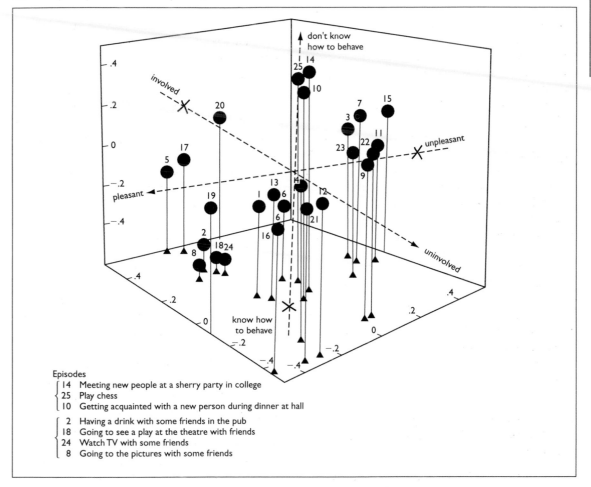

Episodes

⌈ 14 Meeting new people at a sherry party in college
⟨ 25 Play chess
⌊ 10 Getting acquainted with a new person during dinner at hall

⌈ 2 Having a drink with some friends in the pub
⎮ 18 Going to see a play at the theatre with friends
⟨ 24 Watch TV with some friends
⌊ 8 Going to the pictures with some friends

Source Adapted from Forgas, 1976

more members) served as the stimuli in the second stage of the study. Bi-polar scales similar to those reported by Forgas (1976) and elicited in like manner were used to obtain group members' judgements of social episodes.

An interesting finding reported by Forgas was that formal status differences exercised no significant effect upon the perception of the group by its members, the absence of differences being attributed to the strength of the department's cohesiveness and intimacy. In Forgas's analysis of the group's perceptions of social episodes,

the INDSCAL scaling procedure produced an optimal four-dimensional solution accounting for 62 per cent of the variance, group members perceiving social episodes in terms of anxiety, involvement, evaluation and social-emotional versus task orientation. Box 20.11 illustrates how an average group member would see the characteristics of various social episodes in terms of the dimensions by which the group commonly judged them.

Finally we outline a classificatory system that has been developed to process materials elicited

Box 20.11
Perception of social episodes

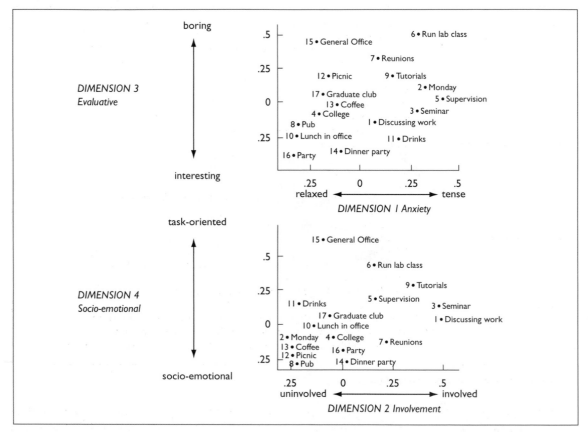

Source Adapted from Forgas, 1978

in a rather structured form of account gathering. Peevers and Secord's study of developmental changes in children's use of descriptive concepts of persons, illustrates the application of quantitative techniques to the analysis of one form of account.

In individual interviews, children of varying ages were asked to describe three friends and one person whom they disliked, all four people being of the same sex as the interviewee. Interviews were tape-recorded and transcribed. A person-concept coding system was developed, the categories of which are illustrated in Box 20.12. Each person-description was divided into items, each item consisting of one discrete piece of infor-

mation. Each item was then coded on each of four major dimensions. Detailed coding procedures are set out in Peevers and Secord (1973).

Tests of interjudge agreement on descriptiveness, personal involvement and evaluative consistency in which two judges worked independently on the interview transcripts of twenty-one boys and girls aged between five and sixteen years resulted in interjudge agreement on those three dimensions of 87 per cent, 79 per cent and 97 per cent respectively.

Peevers and Secord also obtained evidence of the degree to which the participants themselves were consistent from one session to another in their use of concepts to describe other people.

Chapter 20

Box 20.12
Person concept coding system

Dimension	Levels of descriptiveness
Descriptiveness	1 *Undifferentiating . . .*
	(person not differentiated from his environment)
	2 *Simple differentiating . . .*
	(person differentiated in simple global terms)
	3 *Differentiating . . .*
	(person differentiated in specific characteristics)
	4 *Dispositional . . .*
	(person differentiated in terms of traits)
Personal involvement	*Degrees of involvement*
	1 *Egocentric . . .*
	(other person described in self-oriented terms)
	2 *Mutual . . .*
	(other person described in terms of his relationship to perceiver)
	3 *Other oriented . . .*
	(no personal involvement expressed by perceiver)
Evaluative consistency	*Amount of consistency*
	1 *Consistent . . .*
	(nothing favourable about 'disliked', nothing unfavourable about 'liked')
	2 *Inconsistent . . .*
	(some mixture of favourableness and unfavourableness)
Depth	*Levels of depth*
	Level 1 (includes all undifferentiated and simple differentiated descriptions)
	Level 2 (includes differentiated and some dispositional descriptions)
	Level 3 (includes explanation-type differentiated and dispositional descriptions)

Source Adapted from Peevers and Secord, 1973

Children were reinterviewed between one week and one month after the first session on the pretext of problems with the original recordings. Indices of test-retest reliability were computed for each of the major coding dimensions. Separate correlation co-efficients (eta) were obtained for younger and older children in respect of their descriptive concepts of liked and disliked peers. Reliability co-efficients are as set out in Box 20.13. Secord and Peevers (1974) conclude that their approach offers the possibility of an exciting line of inquiry into the depth of insight that individuals have into the personalities of their acquaintances. Their 'free commentary' method is a modification of the more structured interview, requiring the interviewer to probe for

Box 20.13
Reliability co-efficients for peer descriptions

Dimension	Liked peers		Disliked peers	
	Younger subjects	Older subjects	Younger subjects	Older subjects
Descriptiveness	0.83	0.91	0.80	0.84
Personal involvement	0.76	0.80	0.84	0.77
Depth	0.65	0.71	0.65	0.75
Evaluative consistency	0.69	0.92	0.76	0.69

Source Peevers and Secord, 1973

explanations of why a person behaves the way he or she does or why a person is the kind of person he or she is. Peevers and Secord found that older children in their sample readily volunteered this sort of information. Harré (1977b) observes that this approach could also be extended to elicit commentary upon children's friends and enemies and the ritual actions associated with the creation and maintenance of these categories.

Multi-dimensional tables

A frequently used statistic for a 2 × 2 contingency table is the chi-square (χ^2) statistic. The chi-square statistic measures the difference between a statistically generated expected and an actual result to see if there is a significant difference between them, i.e. to see if the frequencies observed are significant; it is a measure of 'goodness of fit' between an expected and an actual result or set of results. The expected result is based on a statistical process discussed below. The chi-square statistic addresses the notion of statistical significance, itself based on notions of probability.

For a chi-square statistic data are set into a contingency table, an example of which can be seen below, a 2 × 3 contingency table, i.e. two horizontal rows and three columns (contingency tables may contain more than this number of variables). The example in this figure presents data concerning sixty students' entry into science, arts and humanities, in a college, and whether the students were male or female (Morrison, 1993: 132 − 4). The lower of the two figures in each cell is the number of actual students who have opted for the particular subjects (sciences, arts, humanities). The upper of the two figures in each cell is what might be expected purely by chance to be the number of students opting for each of the particular subjects. The figure is arrived at by statistical computation, hence the decimal fractions for the figures. What is of interest to the researcher is whether the actual distribution of subject choice by males and females differs significantly from that which

could occur by chance variation in the population of college entrants.

	Science subjects	Arts subjects	Humanities subjects	
Males	7.6 / 14	8 / 4	8.4 / 6	24
Females	11.4 / 5	12 / 16	12.6 / 15	36
	19	20	21	60

The researcher begins with the hypothesis that there is no significant difference between the actual results noted and what might be expected to occur by chance in the wider population (the null hypothesis). When the chi-square statistic is calculated, if the observed, actual distribution differs from that which might be expected to occur by chance alone, then the researcher has to determine whether that difference is statistically significant, i.e. to reject the null hypothesis.

Our example using sixty students, using a chi-square formula (available in most books on statistics) yields a final chi-square figure of 14.64; this is the figure computed from the sample of 60 college entrants. The researcher then refers to tables of the distribution of chi-square (given in most books on social science statistics) and looks up the figure to see if it indicates a statistically significant difference from that occurring by chance. Part of the chi-square distribution table is shown here:

Degrees of freedom	Level of significance	
	0.05	0.01
3	7.81	11.34
4	9.49	13.28
5	11.07	15.09
6	12.59	16.81

The researcher will see that the 'degrees of freedom' (a mathematical construct that is related to the number of restrictions that have been placed on the data) have to be identified. In many cases, to establish the degrees of freedom, one simply takes 1 away from the total number of rows of the contingency table and 1 away from the total number of columns and adds them; in this case it is $(2-1) + (3-1) = 3$ degrees of freedom. Degrees of freedom are discussed later in this chapter. (Other formulae for ascertaining degrees of freedom hold that the number is the total number of cells minus one − this is the method set out later in this chapter.) In our example above, the researcher looks along the table from the entry for the three degrees of freedom and notes that the figure calculated − of 14.64 − is statistically significant at the 0.01 level, i.e. is higher than the required 11.34, indicating that the results obtained − the distributions of the actual data − could not have occurred simply by chance. The null hypothesis is rejected at the 0.01 level of significance. Interpreting the specific figures of the contingency table in educational rather than statistical terms, noting (a) the low incidence of females in the science subjects and the high incidence of females in the arts and humanities subjects, and (b) the high incidence of males in the science subjects and low incidence of males in the arts and humanities, the researcher would say that this distribution is significant − suggesting, perhaps, that the college needs to consider action possibly to encourage females into science subjects and males into arts and humanities.

There are numerous statistical packages available for computer use that will process the calculations for most researchers; they will simply need to enter the raw data and the computer will process the data and indicate the level of statistical significance of the distributions. A much-used package is the Statistical Package for Social Sciences (SPSS) which will process these data using the CROSSTABS command sequence.

The chi-square test requires at least 80 per cent of the cells of a contingency table to contain at least five cases if confidence is to be placed in the results. This means that it may not be feasible to calculate the chi-square statistic if only a small sample is being used. Hence the researcher would tend to use this statistic for larger-scale survey data. Other approaches could be used if the problem of low cell frequencies obtains (Cohen and Holliday, 1996).

Methods of analyzing data cast into 2×2 contingency tables by means of the chi square test are generally well covered in research methods books. Increasingly, however, educational data are classified in multiple rather than two-dimensional formats. Everitt (1977) provides a useful account of methods for analyzing multi-dimensional tables and has shown, incidentally, the erroneous conclusions that can result from the practice of analyzing multi-dimensional data by summing over variables to reduce them to two-dimensional formats. In this section we too illustrate the misleading conclusions that can arise when the researcher employs bivariate rather than multivariate analysis. The outline that follows draws closely on an exposition by Whiteley (1983).

Multi-dimensional data: some words on notation

The hypothetical data in Box 20.14 refer to a survey of voting behaviour in a sample of men and women in Britain:

the row variable (sex) is represented by i;
the column variable (voting preference) is represented by j;
the layer variable (social class) is represented by k.

The number in any one cell in Box 20.14 can be represented by the symbol n_{ijk} that is to say, the score in row category i column category j, and layer category k, where:

$i = 1$ (men), 2 (women)
$j = 1$ (Conservative), 2 (Labour)
$k = 1$ (middle-class), 2 (working-class)

Box 20.14
Sex, voting preference and social class: a three-way classification table

	Middle-class		Working-class	
	Conservative	Labour	Conservative	Labour
Men	80	30	40	130
Women	100	20	40	110

Source Adapted from Whiteley, 1983

It follows therefore that the numbers in Box 20.14 can also be represented as in Box 20.15. Thus,

$$n_{121} = 30 \text{ (men, Labour, middle-class)}$$

Box 20.15

Sex, voting preference and social class: a three-way notational classification

	Middle-class		Working-class	
	Conservative	Labour	Conservative	Labour
Men	n_{111}	n_{121}	n_{112}	n_{122}
Women	n_{211}	n_{221}	n_{212}	n_{222}

and

$$n_{212} = 40 \text{ (women, Conservative, working-class)}$$

Three types of marginals can be obtained from Box 20.15 by:

1 Summing over two variables to give the marginal totals for the third. Thus:

n_{++k} = summing over sex and voting preference to give social class, for example:

$$n_{111} + n_{121} + n_{211} + n_{221} = 230 \text{ (middle-class)}$$

$$n_{112} + n_{122} + n_{212} + n_{222} = 320 \text{ (working-class)}$$

n_{+j+} = summing over sex and social class to give voting preference

n_{i++} = summing over voting preference and social class to give sex.

2 Summing over one variable to give the marginal totals for the second and third variables. Thus:

n_{+11} = 180 (middle-class Conservative)
n_{+21} = 50 (middle-class Labour)
n_{+12} = 80 (working-class Conservative)
n_{+22} = 240 (working-class Labour)

3 Summing over all three variables to give the grand total. Thus:

$$n_{+++} = 550 = N$$

Using the chi square test in a three-way classification table

Whiteley (1983) shows how easy it is to extend the 2×2 chi square test to the three-way case. The probability that an individual taken from the sample at random in Box 20.14 will be a woman is:

$$p_{2++} = \frac{n_{2++}}{n_{+++}} = \frac{270}{550} = 0.49$$

and the probability that a respondent's voting preference will be Labour is:

$$p_{+2+} = \frac{n_{+2+}}{n_{+++}} = \frac{290}{550} = 0.53$$

and the probability that a respondent will be working-class is:

$$p_{++2} = \frac{n_{++2}}{n_{+++}} = \frac{320}{550} = 0.58$$

To determine the expected probability of an individual being a woman, Labour supporter and working-class we assume that these variables are statistically independent (that is to say, there is no relationship between them) and simply apply the multiplication rule of probability theory:

$$p_{222} = (p_{2++})(p_{+2+})(p_{++2}) = (0.49)(0.53)(0.58) = 0.15$$

This can be expressed in terms of the expected frequency in cell n_{222} as:

$$N(p_{2++})(p_{+2+})(p_{++2}) = 550(0.49)(0.53)(0.58) = 82.8$$

Similarly, the expected frequency in cell n_{112} is:

$$N(p_{1++})(p_{+1+})(p_{++2}) \text{ where:}$$

$$p_{1++} = \frac{n_{1++}}{n_{+++}} = \frac{280}{550} = 0.51$$

and

$$p_{+1+} = \frac{n_{+1+}}{n_{+++}} = \frac{260}{550} = 0.47$$

and

$$p_{++2} = \frac{n_{++2}}{n_{+++}} = \frac{320}{550} = 0.58$$

Box 20.16
Expected frequencies in sex, voting preference and social class

	Middle-class		Working-class	
	Conservative	Labour	Conservative	Labour
Men	55.4	61.7	77.0	85.9
Women	53.4	59.5	74.3	82.8

Source Adapted from Whiteley, 1983

Thus $N (p_{1++}) (p_{+1+}) (p_{++2}) = 550 (0.51) (0.47) (0.58) = 77.0$

Box 20.16 gives the expected frequencies for the data shown in Box 20.14.

With the observed frequencies and the expected frequencies to hand, chi square is calculated in the usual way:

$$\chi^2 = \sum \frac{(O - E)^2}{E} = 159.41$$

Degrees of freedom

As Whiteley observes, degrees of freedom in a three-way contingency table are more complex than in a 2×2 classification. Essentially, however, degrees of freedom refer to the freedom with which the researcher is able to assign values to the cells, given fixed marginal totals. This can be computed by first determining the degrees of freedom for the marginals.

Each of the variables in our example (sex, voting preference, and social class) contains two categories. It follows therefore that we have $(2 - 1)$ degrees of freedom for each of them, given that the marginal for each variable is fixed. Since the grand total of all the marginals (i.e. the sample size) is also fixed, it follows that one more degree of freedom is also lost. We subtract these fixed numbers from the total number of cells in our contingency table. In general therefore:

degrees of freedom (df) = the number of cells in the table − 1 (for N) − the number of cells fixed by the hypothesis being tested.

Thus; where r = rows, c = columns and l = layers:

$$df = rcl (r - 1) - (c - 1) - (l - 1) - 1$$
$$= rcl - r - c - l + 2$$

that is to say $df = rcl - r - c - l + 2$ when we are testing the hypothesis of the mutual independence of the three variables.

In our example:

$$df = (2) (2) (2) - 2 - 2 - 2 + 2 = 4$$

From chi square tables we see that the critical value of χ^2 with four degrees of freedom is 9.49 at $p = 0.05$. Our obtained value greatly exceeds that number. We reject the null hypothesis and conclude that sex, voting preference, and social class are significantly interrelated.

Having rejected the null hypothesis with respect to the mutual independence of the three variables, the researcher's task now is to identify which variables cause the null hypothesis to be rejected. We cannot simply assume that because our chi-square test has given a significant result, it therefore follows that there are significant associations between all three variables. It may be the case, for example, that an association exists between two of the variables whilst the third is completely independent. What we need now is a test of 'partial independence'. Whiteley shows the following three such possible tests in respect of the data in Box 20.14. First, that sex is independent of social class and voting preference:

(1) $p_{ijk} = (p_i) (p_{jk})$

Second, that voting preference is independent of sex and social class:

(2) $p_{ijk} = (p_j) (p_{ik})$

And third, that social class is independent of sex and voting preference:

(3) $p_{ijk} = (p_k) (p_{ij})$

The following example shows how to construct the expected frequencies for the first hypothesis.

We can determine the probability of an individual being, say, woman, Labour, and working-class, assuming hypothesis (1), as follows:

$$p_{222} = (p_{2++}) (p_{+22}) = \frac{(n_{2++})}{(N)} \frac{(n_{+22})}{(N)}$$

$$p_{222} = \frac{(270)}{(550)} \frac{(240)}{(550)} = 0.214$$

$$E_{222} = N(p_{2++}) (p_{+22}) = 550 \frac{(270)}{(550)} \frac{(240)}{(550)} = 117.8$$

That is to say, assuming that sex is independent of social class and voting preference, the expected number of female, working class Labour supporters is 117.8.

When we calculate the expected frequencies for each of the cells in our contingency table in respect of our first hypothesis $(p_{ijk}) = (p_i)(p_{jk})$, we obtain the results shown in Box 20.17.

Box 20.17
Expected frequencies assuming that sex is independent of social class and voting preference

	Middle-class		Working-class	
	Conservative	Labour	Conservative	Labour
Men	91.6	25.5	40.7	122.2
Women	88.4	24.5	39.3	117.8

Source Adapted from Whiteley, 1983

$$\chi^2 = \sum \frac{(O - E)^2}{E} = 5.71$$

Degrees of freedom are given by:

$$d.f. = rcl - (cl - 1) - (r - 1) - 1$$
$$= rcl - cl - r + 1 = 8 - 4 - 2 + 1 = 3$$

Whiteley observes:

> Note that we are assuming c and l are interrelated so that once, say, p_{+11} is calculated, then p_{+12}, p_{+21} and p_{+22} are determined, so we have only 1 degree of freedom; that is to say, we lose $(cl - 1)$ degrees of freedom in calculating that relationship.
>
> (Whiteley, 1983)

From chi square tables we see that the critical value of χ^2 with three degrees of freedom is 7.81 at $p = 0.05$. Our obtained value is less than this. We therefore accept the null hypothesis and conclude that *there is no relationship between sex on the one hand and voting preference and social class on the other.*

Suppose now that instead of casting our data into a three-way classification as shown in Box 20.14, we had simply used a 2×2 contingency table and that we had sought to test the null hypothesis that *there is no relationship between sex and voting preference.* The data are shown in Box 20.18.

Box 20.18
Sex and voting preference: a two-way classification table

	Conservative	Labour
Men	120	160
Women	140	130

Source Adapted from Whiteley, 1983

When we compute chi square from the above data our obtained value is $\chi^2 = 4.48$. Degrees of freedom are given by $(r - 1) (c - 1) = (2 - 1) (2 - 1) = 1$.

From chi square tables we see that the critical value of χ^2 with 1 degree of freedom is 3.84 at $p = 0.05$. Our obtained value exceeds this. We reject the null hypothesis and conclude that *sex is significantly associated with voting preference.*

But how can we explain the differing conclusions that we have arrived at in respect of the data in Boxes 20.14 and 20.18? These examples illustrate an important and general point, Whiteley observes. In the bivariate analysis (Box 20.18) we concluded that there was a significant relationship between sex and voting preference. In the multivariate analysis (Box 20.14) that relationship was found to be non-significant when we controlled for social class. The lesson is plain: use a multivariate approach to the analysis of contingency tables wherever the data allow.

A note on multilevel modelling

Multilevel modelling (also known as multilevel regression) is a statistical method that recognizes that it is uncommon to be able to assign students in schools randomly to control and experimental groups, or indeed to conduct an experiment that requires an intervention with one group whilst maintaining a control group (Keeves and Sellin, 1997: 394).

Typically in most schools, students are brought together in particular groupings for specified purposes and each group of students has its own different characteristics which renders it different from other groups. Multilevel modelling addresses the fact that, unless it can be shown that different groups of students are, in fact, alike, it is generally inappropriate to aggregate groups of students or data for the purposes of analysis. Indeed multilevel modelling provides a striking critique of Bennett's (1976) research on teaching styles that we report earlier in this chapter (Aitken, Anderson and Hinde, 1981). Multilevel models avoid the pitfalls of aggregation and the *ecological fallacy* (Plewis, 1997: 35), i.e. making inferences about individual students and behaviour from aggregated data.

Data and variables exist at individual and group levels, indeed Keeves and Sellin (1997) break down analysis further into three main levels: (a) between students over all groups; (b) between groups; and (c) between students within groups. One could extend the notion of levels, of course, to include individual, group, class, school, local, regional, national and international levels (Paterson and Goldstein, 1991). This has been done using multilevel regression and hierarchical linear modelling. Multilevel models enable researchers to ask questions hitherto unanswered, e.g. about variability between and within schools, teachers and curricula (Plewis, 1997: 34–5), in short about the *processes* of teaching and learning.[6] Useful overviews of multilevel modelling can be found in Goldstein (1987), Fitz-Gibbon (1997) and Keeves and Sellin (1997).

Multilevel analysis avoids statistical treatments associated with experimental methods (e.g. analysis of variance and covariance); rather, it uses regression analysis and, in particular, multilevel regression. Regression analysis, argues Plewis (1997: 28), assumes *homoscedasticity* (where the residuals demonstrate equal scatter), that the residuals are independent of each other, and finally, that the residuals are normally distributed.

The whole field of multilevel modelling has proliferated rapidly in the 1990s, and is the basis of much research that is being undertaken on the 'value added' component of education and the comparison of schools in public 'league tables' of results (Fitz-Gibbon, 1991, 1997). However Fitz-Gibbon (1997: 42–4) provides important evidence to question the value of some forms of multilevel modelling. She demonstrates that residual gain analysis provides answers to questions about the value-added dimension of education which differ insubstantially from those answers that are given by multilevel modelling (the lowest correlation co-efficient being 0.93 and 71.4 per cent of the correlations computed correlating between 0.98 and 1). The important point here is that residual gain analysis is a much more straightforward technique than multilevel modelling. Her work strikes at the heart of the need to use complex multilevel modelling to assess the 'value-added' component of education. In her work (Fitz-Gibbon, 1997: 5) the value-added score – the difference between a statistically predicted performance and the actual performance – can be computed using residual gain analysis rather than multilevel modelling. Nonetheless, multilevel modelling now attracts worldwide interest. Whereas ordinary regression models do not make allowances, for example, for different schools (Paterson and Goldstein, 1991), multilevel regression can include school differences, and, indeed other variables, for example: socio-economic status (Willms, 1992), single and co-educational schools (Daly, 1996; Daly and Shuttleworth, 1997), location (Garner and Raudenbush, 1991), size of school (Paterson, 1991) and teaching styles (Zuzovsky and Aitken, 1991). Indeed Plewis (1991a) indicates how multilevel modelling can be used in longitudinal studies, linking educational progress with curriculum coverage.

21 | Role-playing

Introduction

Much current discussion of role-playing has occurred within the context of a protracted debate over the use of deception in experimental social psychology. Inevitably therefore, the following account of role-playing as a research tool involves some detailed comment on the 'deception' versus 'honesty' controversy. But role-playing has a much longer history of use in the social sciences than as a substitute for deceit. It has been employed for decades in assessing personality, in business training and in psychotherapy (Ginsburg, 1978).[1] In this latter connection, role-playing was introduced to the United States as a therapeutic procedure by Moreno in the 1930s. His group therapy sessions were called 'psychodrama', and in various forms they spread to the group dynamics movement which was developing in America in the 1950s. Current interest in encounter sessions and sensitivity training can be traced back to the impact of Moreno's pioneering work in role-taking and role-enactment.

The focus of this chapter is on the use of role-playing as a technique of educational research. Role-playing is defined as participation in simulated social situations that are intended to throw light upon the role/rule contexts governing 'real' life social episodes. The present discussion aims to extend some of the ideas set out in Chapter 16 which dealt with account gathering and analysis. We begin by itemizing a number of role-playing methods that have been reported in the literature.

Various role-play methods have been identified by Hamilton (1976) and differentiated in terms of a passive–active distinction. Thus, an individual may role-play merely by reading a description of a social episode and filling in a questionnaire about it; on the other hand, a person may role-play by being required to improvise a characterization and perform it in front of an audience. This passive–active continuum, Hamilton notes, glosses over three important analytical distinctions.

First, the individual may be asked simply to imagine a situation or actually to perform it. Hamilton terms this an 'imaginary-performed' situation. Second, in connection with performed role-play, he distinguishes between structured and unstructured activities, the difference depending upon whether the individual is restricted by the experimenter to present forms or lines. This Hamilton calls a 'scripted-improvised' distinction. And third, the participant's activities may be verbal responses, usually of the paper and pencil variety, or behavioural, involving something much more akin to acting. This distinction is termed 'verbal-behavioural'. Turning next to the content of role-play, Hamilton distinguishes between relatively involving or uninvolving contents, that is, where a subject is required to act or to imagine herself in a situation or, alternatively, to react as she believes another person would in those circumstances, the basic issue here being what person the subject is supposed to portray. Furthermore, in connection with the role in which the person is placed, Hamilton differentiates between studies that assign the individual to the role of laboratory subject and those that place her in any other role. Finally, the content of the role-play is seen to include the context of the acted or the imagined performance, that is, the elaborateness of the scenario, the involvement of other actors, and the presence or absence of an audience. The various dimensions of role-play methods identified by Hamilton are set out in Box 21.1.

To illustrate the extremes of the range in the role-playing methods identified in Box 21.1 we have selected two studies, the first of which is passive, imaginary and verbal, typical of the way in which role-playing is often introduced to pupils; the second is active, performed and behavioural, involving an elaborate scenario and the participation of numerous other actors.

In a lesson designed to develop empathizing skills (Rogers and Atwood, 1974), a number of magazine pictures were selected. The pictures included easily observed clues that served as the basis for inferring an emotion or a situation. Some pictures showed only the face of an individual, others depicted one or more persons in a particular social setting. The pictures exhibited a variety of emotions such as anger, fear, compassion, anxiety and joy. Pupils were asked to look carefully at a particular picture and then to respond to questions like:

- How do you think the individual(s) is (are) feeling?
- Why do you think this is? (Encourage students to be specific about observations from which they infer emotions. Distinguish between observations and inferences.)
- Might the person(s) be feeling a different emotion than the one you inferred? Give an example.
- Have you ever felt this way? Why?
- What do you think might happen next to this person?
- If you inferred an unpleasant emotion, what possible action might the person(s) take in order to feel better?

The second example of a role-playing study is the well-known Stanford Prison experiment carried out by Haney *et al*. (1973), a brief overview of which is given in Box 21.2. Enthusiasts of role-playing as a research methodology cite experiments such as the Stanford Prison study to support their claim that where realism and

Box 21.1
Dimensions of role-play methods

	FORM	CONTENT
Set:	imaginary v performed	*Person:* self v other
Action:	scripted v improvised	*Role:* subject v another role
Dependent variables:	verbal v behavioural	*Context:* scenario other actors audience

Source Adapted from Hamilton, 1976

spontaneity can be introduced into role-play, then such experimental conditions do, in fact, simulate both symbolically and phenomenologically, the real-life analogues that they purport to represent. Advocates of role-play would concur with the conclusions of Haney and his associates that the simulated prison developed into a psychologically compelling prison environment and they, too, would infer that the dramatic differences in the behaviour of prisoners and guards arose out of their location in different positions within the institutional structure of the prison and the social psychological conditions that prevailed there, rather than from personality differences between the two groups of subjects (see Banuazizi and Movahedi, 1975).

On the other hand, the passive, imaginary role-play required of subjects taking part in the lesson cited in the first example has been the focus of much of the criticism levelled at role-playing as a research technique. Ginsburg (1978) summarizes the argument against role-playing as a device for generating scientific knowledge:

- Role-playing is unreal with respect to the variables under study in that the subject reports what she *would do*, and that is taken as though she did do it.[2]
- The behaviour displayed is not spontaneous even in the more active forms of role-playing.
- The verbal reports in role-playing are very

Box 21.2
The Stanford Prison experiment

The study was conducted in the summer of 1971 in a mock prison constructed in the basement of the psychology building at Stanford University. The subjects were selected from a pool of 75 respondents to a newspaper advertisement asking for paid volunteers to participate in a psychological study of prison life. On a random basis half of the subjects were assigned to the role of guard and half to the role of prisoner. Prior to the experiment subjects were asked to sign a form, agreeing to play either the prisoner or the guard role for a maximum of two weeks. Those assigned to the prisoner role should expect to be under surveillance, to be harassed, but not to be physically abused. In return, subjects would be adequately fed, clothed and housed and would receive 15 dollars per day for the duration of the experiment.

The outcome of the study was quite dramatic. In less than two days after the initiation of the experiment, violence and rebellion broke out. The prisoners ripped off their clothing and their identification numbers and barricaded themselves inside the cells while shouting and cursing at the guards. The guards, in turn, began to harass, humiliate and intimidate the prisoners. They used sophisticated psychological techniques to break the solidarity among the inmates and to create a sense of distrust among them. In less than 36 hours one of the prisoners showed severe symptoms of emotional disturbance, uncontrollable crying and screaming and was released. On the third day, a rumour developed about a mass escape plot. The guards increased their harassment, intimidation and brutality towards the prisoners. On the fourth day, two prisoners showed symptoms of severe emotional disturbance and were released. On the fifth day, the prisoners showed symptoms of individual and group disintegration. They had become mostly passive and docile, suffering from an acute loss of contact with reality. The guards on the other hand, had kept up their harassment, some behaving sadistically. Because of the unexpectedly intense reactions generated by the mock prison experience, the experimenters terminated the study at the end of the sixth day.

Source Adapted from Banuazizi and Movahedi, 1975

susceptible to artefactual influence such as social desirability.

- Role-playing procedures are not sensitive to complex interactions whereas deception designs are.

In general, Ginsburg concludes, critics of role-playing view science as involving the discovery of natural truths and they contend that role-playing simply cannot substitute for deception – a sad but unavoidable state of affairs.

Role-playing versus deception: the argument

As we shall shortly see, those who support role-playing as a legitimate scientific technique for systematic research into human social behaviour reject such criticisms by offering role-playing alternatives to deception studies of phenomena such as destructive obedience to authority and to conventional research in, for example, the area of attitude formation and change.

The objections to the use of deception in experimental research are articulated as follows:

- Lying, cheating and deceiving contradict the norms that we typically try to apply in our everyday social interactions. The use of deception in the study of interpersonal relations is equally reprehensible. In a word, deception is unethical.

- The use of deception is epistemologically unsound because it rests upon the acceptance of a less than adequate model of the subject as a person. Deception studies generally try to exclude the human capacities of the subject for choice and self-presentation. They tend therefore to focus upon 'incidental' social behaviour, that is, behaviours that are outside of the subject's field of choice, intention and self-presentation that typically constitute the main focus of social activity among human actors (see Forward *et al.*, 1976).

- The use of deception is methodologically unsound. Deception research depends upon a continuing supply of subjects who are naive to the intentions of the researchers. But word soon gets round and potential subjects come to expect that they will be deceived. It is a fair guess that most subjects are suspicious and distrustful of psychological research despite the best intentions of deception researchers.

Finally, advocates of role-playing methods deplore the common practice of comparing the outcomes of role-playing replications against the standard of their deception study equivalents as a means of evaluating the relative validity of the two methods. The results of role-playing and deception, it is argued, are not directly comparable since role-playing introduces a far wider range of human behaviour into experiments (see Forward *et al.*, 1976). If comparisons are to be made, then role-playing results should provide the yardstick against which deception study data are measured and not the other way round as is generally the case. We invite readers to follow this last piece of advice and to judge the well-known experiments of Milgram (1974) on destructive obedience to authority against their role-playing replications by Mixon (1972; 1974). A more sustained discussion of ethical problems involved in deception is given in Chapter 2.

Role-playing versus deception: the evidence

Milgram's obedience-to-authority experiments

In a series of studies from 1963 to 1974, Milgram carried out numerous variations on a basic obedience experiment which involved individuals acting, one at a time, as 'teachers' of another subject (who was, in reality, a confederate of the experimenter). Teachers were required to administer electric shocks of increasing severity every time the learner failed to make a correct response to a verbal learning task. Over the years, Milgram involved more than 1,000 subjects in the experiment – subjects, incidentally, who were drawn from all walks of life rather than from undergraduate psychology classes. Summarizing his findings, Milgram (1974) reported that typically some 67 per cent of his teachers delivered the maximum electric shock

to the learner despite the fact that such a degree of severity was clearly labelled as highly dangerous to the physical well-being of the person on the receiving end. Milgram's explanation of destructive obedience to authority is summarized by Brown and Herrnstein (1975).

Mixon's starting point was a disaffection for the deceit that played such an important part in generating emotional stress in Milgram's subjects, and a desire to explore alternative approaches to the study of destructive obedience to authority. Since Milgram's dependent variable was a rule-governed action, Mixon reasoned (Mixon, 1974) the rule-governed behaviour of Milgram's subjects could have been uniform or predictable. But it was not. Why, then, did some of Milgram's subjects obey and some defy the experimenter's instructions? The situation, Mixon notes, seemed perfectly clear to most commentators; the command to administer an electric shock appeared to be obviously immoral and all subjects should therefore have disobeyed the experimenter. If defiance was so obviously called for when looking at the experiment from the outside, why, asks Mixon, was it not obvious to those taking part on the inside?

Mixon found a complete script of Milgram's experiment and proceeded to transform it into an active role-playing exercise. He writes:

> Previous interpretations [of the Milgram data] have rested on the assumption that obedient subjects helplessly performed an obviously immoral act. From the outside the situation seemed clear. It was otherwise to the actors. The actors in my role playing version could not understand why the experimenter behaved as if feedback from the 'victim' was unimportant. The feedback suggested that something serious had occurred, that something had gone badly wrong with the experiment. The experimenter behaved as if nothing serious had or could happen. The experimenter in effect contradicted the evidence that otherwise seemed so clearly to suggest that the 'victim' was in serious trouble. . . . Using the 'all-or-none' method I found that when it became perfectly clear that the experimenter believed the 'victim' was being seriously

harmed all actors indicated defiance to experimental commands. Briefly summarized, the 'all-or-none' analysis suggests that people will obey seemingly inhumane experimental commands so long as there is no good reason to think experimental safeguards have broken down; people will defy seemingly inhumane experimental commands when it becomes clear that safeguards have broken down – when consequences may indeed be what they appear to be. *When the experimental situation is confusing and mystifying as in Milgram's study, some people will obey and some will defy experimental commands.*

(Mixon, 1974, emphasis added)

We leave readers to compare Mixon's explanations with Milgram's account set out by Brown and Herrnstein (1975).

In summary, sophisticated role-playing methods such as those used by Mixon offer exciting possibilities to the educational researcher. They avoid the disadvantages of deception designs yet are able to incorporate many of the standard features of experiments such as constructing experimental conditions across factors of interest (in the Mixon studies for example, using scripts that vary the states of given role/rule contexts), randomly assigning actors to conditions as a way of randomizing out individual differences, using repeated-measures designs, and standardizing scripts and procedures to allow for replication of studies (Forward *et al.*, 1976).

Despite what has just been said about the possibilities of incorporating experimental role-playing methodologies in exploratory rather than experimental settings, Harré and Secord (1972) distinguish between 'exploration' and 'experiment' as follows. Whereas the experiment is employed to test the authenticity of what is known, exploration serves quite a different purpose:

In exploratory studies, a scientist has no very clear idea of what will happen, and aims to find out. He has a feeling for the direction in which to go . . . but no clear expectations of what to expect. He is not confirming or refuting hypotheses.

(Harré and Secord, 1972)

Increasingly, exploratory (as opposed to experimental) research into human social behaviour is turning to role-playing methodologies. The reason is plain enough. Where the primary objective of such research is the identification and elucidation of the role/rule frameworks governing social interaction, informed rather than deceived subjects are essential if the necessary data on how they genuinely think and feel are to be made available to the researcher. Contrast the position of the fully participating, informed subject in such research with that of the deceived subject under the more usual experimental conditions.

It can be argued that many of the more pressing social problems that society faces today arise out of our current ignorance of the role/rule frameworks governing human interactions in diverse social settings. If this is the case, then role-playing techniques could offer the possibility of a greater insight into the natural episodes of human behaviour that they seek to elucidate than the burgeoning amount of experimental data already at hand. The danger may lie in too much being expected of role-playing as a key to such knowledge. Ginsburg (1978) offers a timely warning. Role-playing, he urges, should be seen as a complement to conventional experiments, survey research and field observations. That is, it is an important addition to our investigative armamentarium, not a replacement.

Role-playing in educational settings

Role-playing, gaming and machine or computer simulation are three strands of development in simulation studies that have found their way into British classrooms (Taylor and Walford, 1972). Their discovery and introduction into primary and secondary schools as late as the 1960s is somewhat surprising in view of the unqualified support that distinguished educational theorists from Plato onwards have accorded to the value of play and games in education (Megarry, 1978).

The distinction between these three types of simulation – role-playing, games and machines/computers – is by no means clear-cut; for example, simulation games often contain role-playing activities and may be designed with computer back-up services to expedite their procedures (see Taylor and Walford, 1972).

In this section we focus particularly upon role-playing aspects of simulation, beginning with some brief observations on the purposes of role-playing in classroom settings and some practical suggestions directed towards the less experienced practitioners of role-playing methods.

The uses of role-playing

The uses of role-playing are classified by van Ments (1978) as:

- *Developing sensitivity and awareness.* The definitions of positions such as mother, teacher, policeman and priest, for example, explicitly or implicitly incorporate various role characteristics which often lead to the stereotyping of position occupants. Role-playing provides a means of exploring such stereotypes and developing a deeper understanding of the point of view and feelings of someone who finds herself in a particular role.
- *Experiencing the pressures which create roles.* Role-playing provides study material for group members on the ways in which roles are created in, for example, a committee. It enables subjects to explore the interactions of formal structure and individual personalities in role taking.
- *Testing out for oneself possible modes of behaviour.* In effect, this is the rehearsal syndrome: the trying out in one's mind in advance of some new situation that one has to face. Role-playing can be used for a wide variety of situations where the subject, for one reason or another, needs to learn to cope with the rituals and conventions of social intercourse and to practise them so that they can be repeated under stress.
- *Simulating a situation for others (and possibly oneself) to learn from.* Here, the role-player provides materials for others to use and work

Box 21.3
A flow chart for using role-play

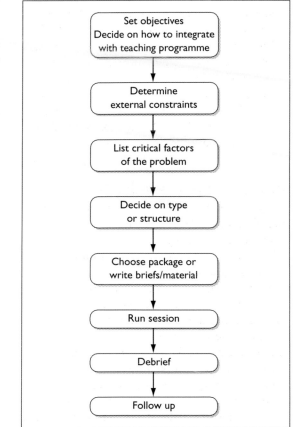

Source van Ments, 1983

upon. In the simplest situation, there is just one role-player acting out a specific role. In more complex situations such as the Stanford Prison study discussed in Box 21.2, role-playing is used to provide an environment structured on the interactions of numerous role incumbents. Suggestions for running role-play sessions are set out in Box 21.3. They are particularly appropriate to teachers intent upon using role-play in classroom settings.

Setting objectives

The first observation made by van Ments is that teachers must begin by asking themselves what

Box 21.4
Critical factors in a role-play: smoking and young people

Roles involved:	young people, parents, teachers, doctors, youth leaders, shopkeeper, cigarette manufacturer.
Critical issues:	responsibility for health, cost of illness, freedom of action, taxation revenue, advertising, effects on others.
Key communication channels:	advertisements, school contacts, family, friends.

Source Adapted from van Ments, 1983

exactly their intentions are in teaching by means of role-play. Is it, for example, to teach facts, or concepts, or skills, or awareness, or sensitivity? Depending on the specific nature of the teacher's objective, role-play can be fitted into the timetable in several ways. Van Ments identifies the following:

- as an introduction to the subject;
- as a means of supplementing or following on from a point that is being explored;
- as the focal point of a course or a unit of work;
- as a break from the routine of the classroom or the workshop;
- as a way of summarizing or integrating diverse subject matter;
- as a way of reviewing or revising a topic;
- as a means of assessing work.

Determining external constraints

Role-play can be extremely time consuming. It is vital therefore that from the outset, teachers should be aware of the following factors that may inhibit or even preclude the running of a role-play (see van Ments, 1978):

- suitable room or space (size, layout, furniture, etc.);
- sufficient time for warm up, running the actual role-play and debriefing;
- availability of assistance to help run the session.

Critical factors

The teacher, van Ments advises, must look at the critical issues involved in the problem area encompassed by the role-play and decide who has the power to influence those issues as well as who is affected by the decisions to be taken. By way of example, Box 21.4 identifies some of the principal protagonists in a role-play session to do with young people smoking.

Choosing or writing the role-play

The choice lies with teachers either to buy or borrow a ready-made role-play or to write their own. In practice, van Ments observes, most role-plays are written for specific needs and with the intention of fitting into a particular course programme. Existing role-plays can, of course, be adapted by teachers to their own particular circumstances and needs. On balance it is probably better to write the role-play oneself in order to ensure that the background is familiar to the intended participants; they can then see its relevance to the specific problem that concerns them.

Running the role-play

The counsel of perfection, van Ments reminds us, is always to pilot test the role-play material that one is going to use, preferably with a similar audience. In reality, pilot testing can be as time consuming as the play itself and may therefore be totally impracticable given timetable pressures. But however difficult the circumstances, any form of piloting, says van Ments, is better than none at all, even if it is simply a matter of talking procedures through with one or two colleagues.

Once the materials are prepared, then the role-play follows its own sequence: introduction, warm up, running, and ending. One final word of caution. It is particularly important to time the ending of the role-play in such a way as to fit into the whole programme. One method of ensuring this is to write the mechanism for ending into the role-play itself. Thus: 'You must have reached agreement on all five points before 11.30 a.m. when you have to attend a meeting of the board of directors.'

Debriefing

Debriefing is more than simply checking that the right lesson has been learnt and feeding this information back to the teacher. Rather, van Ments reminds us, it is a two-way process, during which the consequences of actions arising in the role-play can be analysed and conclusions drawn. It is at this point in the role-play sequence when mistakes and misunderstandings can be rectified. Most important of all, it is from well-conducted debriefing sessions that the teacher can draw out the implications of what the pupils have been experiencing and can then plan the continuation of their learning about the topic at hand.

Follow-up

To conclude, van Ments notes the importance of the follow-up session in the teacher's planning of the ways in which the role-play exercise will lead naturally into the next learning activity. Thus, when the role-play session has attempted to teach a skill or rehearse a novel situation, then it may be logical to repeat it until the requisite degree of competence has been reached. Conversely, if the purpose of the exercise has been to raise questions, then a follow-up session should be arranged to answer them. 'Whatever the objectives of using role play', van Ments advises, 'one must always consider the connection between it and the next learning activity' (van Ments, 1983). Above all else, avoid leaving the role-play activity in a vacuum.[3]

Strengths and weaknesses of role-playing and other simulation exercises

Taylor and Walford (1972) identify two prominent themes in their discussion of some of the possible advantages and disadvantages in the use of classroom simulation exercises. They are, first, the claimed enhancement of pupil motivation and, second, the role of simulation in the provision of relevant learning materials. The motivational advantages of simulation are said to include:

- a heightened interest and excitement in learning;
- a sustained level of freshness and novelty arising out of the dynamic nature of simulation tasks;
- a transformation in the traditional pupil-teacher subordinate-superordinate relationship;
- the fact that simulation is a universal behavioural mode.

As to the learning gains arising out of the use of simulation, the authors identify:

- the learning that is afforded at diverse levels (cognitive, social and emotional);
- the decision-making experiences that participants acquire;
- an increased role awareness;
- the ability of simulation to provide a vehicle for free interdisciplinary communication;
- the success with which the concrete approach afforded by simulation exercises bridges the gap between 'schoolwork' and 'the real world'.

What reservations are there in connection with simulation exercises? Taylor and Walford (1972) identify the following:

- Simulations, however interesting and attractive, are time-demanding activities and ought therefore to justify fully the restricted timetabling allotted to competing educational approaches.
- Many simulation exercises are in the form of game kits and these can be quite expensive.
- Simulation materials may pose problems of

logistics, operation and general acceptance as legitimate educational techniques particularly by parent associations.

Our discussion of the strengths and weaknesses of role-playing has focused upon its application in pupil groups. To illustrate Taylor and Walford's point that simulation is a universal behavioural mode, Robson and Coller's (1991) example of a role-play with students in further education deserves attention.

Role-playing in an educational setting: an example

Our example of role-play in an educational setting illustrates the fourth use of this approach that van Ments identifies, namely, simulating a situation from which others may learn. As part of a study of secondary school pupils' perceptions of teacher racism, Naylor (1995) produced four five-minute video presentations of actual classroom events reconstructed for the purposes of the research. The films were scripted and role-played by twenty-one comprehensive school pupils, each video focusing on the behaviour of a white, female teacher towards pupils of visible ethnic minority groups. A gifted teacher of drama elicited performances from the pupils and faithfully interpreted their directions in her portrayal of their devised teachers' roles. The four parts she played consisted of a supply teacher of Geography, a teacher of French, a teacher of English and a Mathematics teacher.

In an opportunity sample drawn throughout England, Naylor (1995) showed the videos to over 1,000 adolescents differentiated by age, sex, ability and ethnicity. Pupils' written responses to the four videos were scored 0 to 5 on the Kohlberg-type scale set out in Box 21.5. *Inter alia*, the analysis of scripts from a stratified sample of some 480 pupils suggested that older, high-ability girls of visible ethnic minority group membership were most perceptive of teacher racism and younger, low-ability boys of indigenous white group membership, least perceptive. For further examples of role play in an educational setting see Bolton and Heathcote (1999).

Box 21.5
Categorization of responses to the four video extracts

Level (Score)	Description
0	No response or nothing which is intelligibly about the 'ways in which people treat one another' in the extract. Alternatively this level of response may be wrong in terms of fact and/or in interpretation.
1	No reference to racism (i.e. unfairness towards visible ethnic minority pupils) either by the teacher or by pupils, either implicitly or explicitly.
2	Either some reference to pupils' racism (see level 1 above) but not to the teacher's, or, reference to racism is left unspecified as to its perpetrator. Such reference is likely to be implied and may relate to one or more examples drawn from the extract without any generalization or synthesizing statement(s). The account is at a superficial level of analysis, understanding and explanation.
3	There is some reference to the teacher's racist behaviour and actions. Such reference is, however, implied rather than openly stated. There may also be implied condemnation of the teacher's racist behaviour/actions. There will not be any generalized statement(s) about the teacher's racism supported with examples drawn from the extract.
4	At this level the account will explicitly discuss and illustrate the teacher's racism but the analysis will show a superficial knowledge and understanding of the deeper issues.
5	At this level the account will explicitly discuss the teacher's racism as a generalization and this will be well illustrated with examples drawn from the extract. One or more of these examples may well be of the less obvious and more subtle types of racist behaviour/action portrayed in the extract.

Source Naylor (unpublished)

Evaluating role-playing and other simulation exercises

Because the use of simulation methods in classroom settings is growing, there is increasing need to evaluate claims concerning the advantages and effectiveness of these newer approaches against more traditional methods. Yet here lies a major problem. To date, as Megarry observes, a high proportion of evaluation effort has been directed towards the comparative experiment involving empirical comparisons between simulation-type exercises and more traditional teaching techniques in terms of specified learning pay-offs. One objection to this approach to evaluation has been detailed earlier but is worth repeating here:

> the limitations [of the classical, experimental method] as applied to evaluating classroom simulation and games are obvious: not only are the inputs multiple, complex, and only partly known, but the outputs are disputed, difficult to isolate, detect or measure and the interaction among participants is considerable. Interacting forms, in some views, a major part of what simulation and gaming is about; it is *not* merely a source of 'noise' or experimental error.
>
> (Megarry, 1978)

What alternatives are there to the traditional type of evaluative effort? Megarry lists the following promising approaches to simulation evaluation:

- using narrative reports;
- using checklists gathered from students' recollections of outstanding positive and negative learning experiences;
- encouraging players to relate ideas and concepts learned in games to other areas of their lives;
- using the instructional interview, a form of tutorial carried out earlier with an individual learner or a small group in which materials and methods are tested by an instructor who is versed not only in the use of the materials, but also in the ways in which pupils learn.

(See also Percival's (1978) discussion of observational and self-reporting techniques.) Notice how each of the above evaluative techniques is primarily concerned with the process rather than the product of simulation.

By way of summary, simulation methods provide a means of alleviating a number of problems inherent in laboratory experiments. At the same time, they permit the retention of some of their virtues. Simulations, notes Palys (1978), share with the laboratory experiment the characteristic that the experimenter has complete manipulative control over every aspect of the situation. At the same time, the subjects' humanity is left intact in that they are given a realistic situation in which to act in whatever way they think appropriate. The inclusion of the time dimension is another important contribution of the simulation, allowing the subject to take an active role in interacting with the environment, and the experimenter the opportunity of observing a social system in action with its feedback loops, multidirectional causal connections and so forth. Finally, Palys observes, the high involvement normally associated with participation in simulations shows that the self-consciousness usually associated with the laboratory experiment is more easily dissipated.

Part five

Recent Developments in educational research

With respect to the fifth edition, the book so far has brought the 'story' of educational research up to date on very many issues, and in the concluding part that follows we outline some important developments which, we suggest, will feature prominently over the coming years. Although what we say is speculative, these initiatives, we believe, will become fruitful avenues of approach; nevertheless, the message that educational research is developing and metamorphosing is one that cannot be ignored.

It is notable that none of the developments that we include here began life in the world of education, but elsewhere. The Internet had its origins in military intelligence, whilst simulations and fuzzy logic have their origins largely in the natural sciences and mathematics. Simulations have spilled over into all walks of life, from economic forecasting to navigating ships; and fuzzy logic is prevalent in the manufacture of white goods and controlling traffic flow. Geographical Information Systems, another line of development we consider, have been brought into education, being already established in social welfare analysis and health provision. And needs analysis derives from social policy formation, housing and welfare reforms. Although it has featured in education for some time, it is emerging from recent relative neglect to assume an important role, not least because, with the impact of the introduction of industrial management systems into education, it

is premised on the belief redolent of Japanese business practice that the best people to identify a problem are the ones who are closest to it! Finally, evidence-based education, building on the subject of meta-analysis that we discussed in Part Three, has been prominent in the world of medicine for many years, and the worldwide Cochrane Collaboration – a group that collates the results of stringent experimental testing of treatments typically through randomized controlled trials, preparing, maintaining and promoting the accessibility of systematic reviews of the effects of health care interventions – testifies to this.

This mixed pedigree of emerging developments signals that educational research is eclectic in its paradigms, traditions, methodologies, instrumentation and data analysis. Further, it is important to recognize that educational research is integrative; it steps over the traditional boundaries of different disciplines; its epistemological basis being, in part, derivative, and suggestive of a need to cross such boundaries and protected territories. Educational research is both modern and postmodern! Just as new knowledge crosses traditional epistemological boundaries, is at the frontiers of traditional disciplines and creates new ones, so research, in its endeavour to create new knowledge, need not be hidebound by tradition. Education opens minds; educational research should be open to new developments.

22 Recent developments

As we saw in the introduction to this fifth part of the book, what can be observed in recent developments in educational research is the importation of ideas and methods from spheres outside education, furthering the notion that interdisciplinary inquiry is both a developing trend and, indeed, the way forward at the cutting edge of research. The frontiers of new knowledge are no longer hidebound by disciplines (for example in the discussions of needs analysis and needs assessment in this chapter). This trend can be coupled with the use of information technology for research activity (for example the discussions of simulations and modelling as we shall see). In this chapter these examples, in turn, draw on the disciplines of mathematics (e.g. chaos theory, complexity theory and fuzzy logic) and geography (Geographical Information Systems). The role of information technology has enabled researchers to break out of disciplinary boundaries and move forward with speed and success. Previous chapters have indicated the role that information technology software can play at all stages of research. This chapter discusses four such applications: the Internet, simulations, fuzzy logic, and Geographical Information Systems (GIS).

The Internet

The storage and retrieval of research data on the Internet play an important role not only in keeping researchers abreast of developments across the world, but also in providing access to data which can inform literature searches to establish construct and content validity in their own research. Indeed some kinds of research

are essentially large-scale literature searches (e.g. the research papers published in the journal *Review of Educational Research*). On-line journals, abstracts and titles enable researchers to identify the cutting edge of research and to initiate a literature search of relevant material on their chosen topic. Websites and e-mail correspondence enable networks and information to be shared. For example, researchers wishing to gain instantaneous global access to literature and recent developments in research associations can reach Australia, East Asia, the UK and America in a matter of seconds through such websites as:

http://www.aera.net (the website of the American Educational Research Association);

http://www.lalc.k12.ca.us/catalog/providers/185.html (also the website of the American Educational Research Association);

http://www.acer.edu.au/index2.html (the website of the Australian Council for Educational Research);

http://www.bera.ac.uk (the website of the British Educational Research Association);

http://scre.ac.uk (the website of the Scottish Council for Research in Education);

http://www.eera.ac.uk/index.html (the website of the European Educational Research Association);

http://www.cem.dur.ac.uk (the website of the Curriculum Evaluation and Management Centre, probably the largest monitoring centre of its kind in the world);

http://www.nfer.ac.uk (the website of the National Foundation for Educational Research in the UK);

http://www.fed.cuhk.edu.hk/~hkera (the website of the Hong Kong Educational Research Association);

http://www2.hawaii.edu.hera (the website of the Hawaii Educational Research Association);

http://www.wera-web.org/index.html (the website of the Washington Educational Research Association);

http://www.ttu.eedu/~edupsy/regis.html (the website of the Chinese American Educational Research Association);

http://www.msstate.edu/org/msera/msera.html (the website of the mid-South Educational Research Association, a very large regional association in the USA);

http://www.esrc.ac.uk (the website of the Economic and Social Research Council in the UK);

http://www.asanet.org (the website of the American Sociological Association);

Researchers wishing to access on-line journal indices and references for published research results (rather than to specific research associations as in the websites above) have a variety of websites which they can visit, for example:

http://www.leeds.ac.uk/bei (to gain access to the British Education Index);

http://www.routledge.com:9996/routledge/journal/er.html (the website of an international publisher that provides information on all its research articles);

http://www.carfax.co.uk (a service provided by a UK publisher to gain access to the Scholarly Articles Research Alerting network in the UK);

http://ericir.syr.edu/Eric/ (a service to access the international Eric educational research index);

http://ericir.syr.edu/Eric/index.html (the index to the Eric database);

http://ericir.syr.edu/ (a further website for searching Eric);

http://www.tandf.co.uk/era (the website for educational research abstracts;

http://www.leeds.ac.uk/educol/index.html (the website for Education-line, a service for electronic texts in education);

http://bubl.ac.uk (a national information service in the UK, provided for the higher education community);

http://www.sosig.ac.uk (the Social Science Information Gateway, providing access to worldwide resources and information);

http://www.carfax.co.uk/ber-ad.htm (the website of the British Educational Research Journal);

http://wos.mimas.ac.uk (the website of the Web of Science, that, amongst other functions, provides access to the Social Science Citation Index, the Science Citation Index and the Arts and Humanities Citation Index);

http://pinkerton.bham.ac.uk/era/main.htm (the website of Educational Research Abstracts Online);

http://www.socresonline.org.uk (the website of Sociological Research Online).

Researchers who do not possess website addresses have at their disposal a variety of search engines to locate them. At the time of writing some widely used engines are: Alta Vista; Euro-Ferret; Excite; GoTo; HotBot; InfoSeek Net Search; Infoseek Ultra; Lycos; Magellan; OpenTextIndex; PlanetSearch; Webcrawler; What-U-Seek; WWW Worm; Yahoo; Yahoo UK. All of these search engines enable researchers to conduct searches by *keywords* and some of them (e.g. Excite; Magellan) also enable searches to be undertaken by *concepts*. Whilst all of these are single search engines, there are also several parallel search engines (which will search several single search engines at a time), and file search engines (which will search files across the world).

Finding research information, where not available from databases and indices on CD-ROMs, is often done through the Internet by trial-and-error and serendipity, identifying the key words to unlock the doors to websites. For example, keying in such terms as 'educational research uk', 'educational research usa', 'American educational research association', or 'British educational research association' to a search engine will reveal a plethora of websites that are useful. The system of 'bookmarking' websites enables rapid retrieval of these websites for future reference; this is perhaps essential, as some Internet connections are slow, and a vast amount of material on it is, at best, unhelpful! We provide some websites and keywords that may be helpful in researching the subsequent topics in this chapter.

Simulations

The advent of computer technology has opened up powerful new vistas for research. Virtual technology, as used, for example, in air flight simulations (e.g. training new pilots) and ship piloting simulations, seeks to ensure high reliability of performance and the avoidance of failure or system breakdown. In the field of education this has spawned research into schools as high reliability organizations (Morrison, 1998: 76–8) – institutions where failure is avoided for fear of disastrous consequences, for example nuclear power plants, air traffic control, electricity supply companies (Reynolds, 1995; Stringfield, 1997: 152–7). Outside the world of education the practice of simulation is used extensively in order to identify problems and weaknesses so that action can be taken (i.e. focus is on the 'trailing edge' of weaknesses rather than to the successful aspects of the organization and its operation). The practice proceeds on the premise that, unchecked, minor flaws and errors could escalate into huge failures at a systems level (the view of chaos theory discussed below). Simulations have two main components: a *system* in which the researcher is interested and that lends itself to be modelled or simulated, and a *model* of that system (Wilcox, 1997). The system comprises any set of interrelated features, whilst the model, that is, the analogue of the system, is usually mathematical.

Wilcox (1997) has indicated two forms of simulation. In *deterministic* simulations all the mathematical and logical relationships between the components of a system are known and fixed. In *stochastic* simulations, typically the main types used in educational research, at least one variable is random.

The use of simulations has grown considerably with the increase in mathematical modelling. Computers can handle very rapidly data that would take humans several years to process. Simulations based on mathematical modelling (e.g. multiple iterations of the same formula) provide researchers with a way of imitating behaviours and systems, and extrapolating what might happen if the system runs over time or if the same mathematical calculations are repeated over and over again, where data are fed back – formatively – into the next round of calculation of the same formula. Hopkins, Hopkins and Glass (1996: 159–62) report such a case in proving the Central Limit Theorem (discussed in Chapter 4), where the process of calculation of means was repeated 10,000 times. Such modelling has its roots in chaos theory and complexity theory (Morrison, 1998: 3–5).

For Laplace and Newton, the universe was rationalistic, deterministic and of clockwork order; effects were functions of causes, small causes (minimal initial conditions) produced small effects (minimal and predictable) and large causes (multiple initial conditions) produced large (multiple) effects. Predictability, causality, patterning, universality and 'grand' overarching theories, linearity, continuity, stability, objectivity, all contributed to the view of the universe as an ordered and internally harmonistic mechanism in an albeit complex equilibrium, a rational, closed and deterministic system susceptible to comparatively straightforward scientific discovery and laws.

From the 1960s this view has been increasingly challenged with the rise of theories of chaos and complexity. Central to chaos theory are several principles (e.g. Gleick, 1987; Morrison, 1998):

- Small-scale changes in initial conditions can produce massive and unpredictable changes in outcome (e.g. a butterfly's wing beat in the Caribbean can produce a hurricane in America).
- Very similar conditions can produce very dissimilar outcomes (e.g. using simple mathematical equations (Stewart, 1990)).
- Regularity and conformity break down to irregularity and diversity.
- Even if differential equations are very simple, the behaviour of the system that they are modelling may not be simple.
- Effects are not straightforward continuous functions of causes.
- The universe is largely unpredictable.
- If something works once there is no guarantee that it will work in the same way a second time.
- Determinism is replaced by indeterminism; deterministic, linear and stable systems are replaced by 'dynamical', changing, evolving systems and non-linear explanations of phenomena.
- Continuity is replaced by discontinuity, turbulence and irreversible transformation.
- Grand, universal, all-encompassing theories and large-scale explanations provide inadequate accounts of localized and specific phenomena.
- Long-term prediction is impossible.

More recently theories of chaos have been extended to complexity theory – 'the edge of chaos' (Waldrop, 1992; Lewin, 1993) – in analysing systems, with components at one level acting as the building blocks for components at another. A complex system comprises independent elements which, themselves, might be made up of complex systems. These interact and give rise to patterned behaviour in the system as a whole. Order is not totally predetermined and fixed, but the universe (however defined) is creative, emergent (through iteration, learning and recursion), evolutionary and changing, transformative and turbulent. Order emerges in complex systems that are founded on simple rules (perhaps formulae) for interacting organisms (Kauffmann, 1995: 24).

Through feedback, recursion, perturbance, autocatalysis, connectedness and self-organization, higher and greater levels of complexity are differentiated, new forms arise from lower levels of complexity and existing forms. These complex forms derive from often comparatively simple sets of rules – local rules and behaviours generating complex global order and diversity (Waldrop, 1992: 16–17; Lewin, 1993: 38). Dynamical systems (Peak and Frame, 1994: 122) are a product of initial conditions and often simple rules for change. General laws can govern adaptive, dynamical processes (Kauffmann, 1995: 27). There are laws of emergent order, and complex behaviours and systems do not need to have complex roots (Waldrop, 1992: 270). Importantly, given these simple rules, behaviour and systems can be modelled in computer simulations.

Simulations are an emerging field in educational research, though they have been used in the natural sciences and economic forecasting for several decades. For example, Lewin (1993) and Waldrop (1992), in the study of the rise and fall of species and their behaviour, indicate how the consecutive iteration – repeated calculation – of simple formulae to express the iteration of a limited number of variables (initial conditions), wherein the data from one round of calculations are used in the next round of calculation of the same formula and so on (i.e. building in continuous feedback), can give rise to a huge diversity of outcomes (e.g. of species, of behaviour) such that it beggars simple prediction or simple cause-and-effect relationships. Waldrop (1992: 241–2) provides a fascinating example of this in the computer programme Boids, where just three initial conditions are built into a mathematical formula that catches the actuality of the diverse patterns of flight of a flock of birds. These are: (a) the boids (birds) strive to keep a minimum distance from other objects (including other boids); (b) the boids strive to keep to the same speed as other boids; (c) each boid strives to move towards the centre of the flock.

The key features of simulations are:

- The computer can model and imitate the behaviour of systems and their major attributes.
- Computer use can help us to understand the system that is being imitated by testing the simulation in a range of simulated, imitated environments (e.g. enabling researchers to see 'what happens if' the system is allowed to run its course or if variables are manipulated, i.e. to be able to predict).
- The mathematical formula models and interprets – represents and processes – key features of the reality rather than catching and manipulating the fine grain of reality.
- Mathematical relationships are assumed to be acting over and over again deterministically in controlled, bounded and clearly defined situations, on occasions giving rise to unanticipated, emergent and unexpected, wide-ranging outcomes (Tymms, 1996: 124).
- Feedback and multiple, continuous iteration are acceptable procedures for understanding the emergence of phenomena and behaviours.
- Complex and wide-ranging phenomena and behaviours derive from the repeated interplay of initial conditions/variables.
- Deterministic laws (the repeated calculation of a formula) lead to unpredictable outcomes (chaos).

In the field of education what is being suggested is that schools and classrooms, whilst being complex, non-linear, dynamical systems, can be understood in terms of the working out of simple mathematical modelling. This may be at the level of analogy only, but, as Tymms (1996: 130) remarks, if the analogue fits the reality then researchers have a powerful tool for understand-

ing such complexity in terms of the interplay of key variables or initial conditions and a set of simple rules. Further, if the construct validity of such initial conditions or key variables can be demonstrated then researchers have a powerful means of predicting what might happen over time.

Three immediate applications of simulations have been in the field of educational change (Ridgway, 1998), inspections (Tymms, 1997) and school effectiveness (Tymms, 1996). In the first, Ridgway argues that the complexity of the change process might be best understood as a complex, emergent system (see also Fullan, 1999). In the second, Tymms exposes some major flaws in the inspection process. In the third, he indicates the limitations of linear (input and output) or multi-level modelling to understand or explain why schools are effective or why there is such a range of variation between and within schools. He puts forward the case for using simulations based on mathematical modelling to account for such diversity and variation between schools; as he argues in his provocative statement: 'the world is too complicated for words' (ibid.: 131) (of course, similarly, for qualitative researchers the world may be even too complicated for numbers!).

Tymms indicates the limitations of existing school effectiveness research that is based on linear premises, however sophisticated. Instead, pouring cold water on much present school effectiveness research, he argues (pp. 132–3) that 'simulation models would suggest that even if it were possible to arrange for exactly the same classes to have exactly the same teacher for two years in the same classroom living through the same two years that the outcomes would not be the same'. For him, it is little surprise that school effectiveness research has failed to account effectively for variance between schools, because such research is based on the wrong principles. Rather, he argues, such variance is the natural outcome of the interplay of key – common – variables.

There are several potential concerns about and criticisms of simulations. To the charges that they artificially represent the world and that they are a *reductio ad absurdum*, it can be stated that researchers, like theorists, strive to construct the best fit with reality, to provide the most comprehensive explanation, and that the closer the analogy – the simulation – fits reality, the better (Tymms, 1996: 130). That is an argument for refining rather than abandoning simulations. We only need to know key elements to be able to construct an abstraction, we do not need complete, fine-grain detail.

To the charges that a simulation can never tell us anything that we do not already know, that it is no better than the assumptions on which it is built, and that a computer can only do what it is programmed to do (rendering human agency and freedom insignificant), it can be stated that: (a) simulations can reveal behaviours that occur 'behind the backs' of social actors – there are social facts (Durkheim, 1956) and patterns; (b) simulations can tell us what we do not know (Simon, 1996) – we may know premises and starting points but not where they might lead to or what they imply; (c) we do not need to know all the workings of the system to be able to explain it, only those parts that are essential for the model.

Other concerns can be voiced about simulations, for example:

- complexity and chaos theory that underpin many mathematical simulations might explain diverse, variable outcomes (as in school effectiveness research), but how do they enable developers to intervene to promote improvement?, e.g. in schools – explanation here is retrospective rather than prospective;
- how does one ascertain the key initial conditions to build into the simulation (i.e. construct validity) and how do simulations from these lead to prescriptions for practice?
- How acceptable is it to regard systems as the recurring iteration and reiteration of the same formula/model?
- In understanding chaotic complexity (in the scientific sense), how can researchers work

back from this to identify the first principles or elements or initial conditions that are important? – the complex outcomes might be due to the interaction of completely different sets of initial conditions. This is akin to Chomsky's (1959) withering critique of Skinner's behaviourism – it is impossible to infer a particular stimulus from an observation of behaviour; we cannot infer a cause from an observation or putative effect;

- Simulations work out and assume only the interplay of initial conditions, thereby neglecting the introduction of additional factors 'on the way', i.e. the process is too deterministic;
- What is being argued here is common sense, *viz.* that the interaction of people produces unpredicted and unpredictable behaviour. That is also its greatest attraction – it celebrates agency;
- Planned interventions might work at first but ultimately do not work (a reiteration, perhaps, of the Hawthorne effect); all we can predict is that we cannot predict;
- Manipulating human variables is technicist;
- There is more to behaviour than the repeated iteration of the same mathematical model;
- Whilst they may enable us to understand why there are variations in effects, simulations do not help us to establish causes or interventions;
- There will always be a world of difference between the real world and the simulated world other than at an unhelpfully simplistic level;
- As with other numerical approaches, simulations might combine refinement of process with crudity of concept (Ruddock, 1981: 49);
- Reducing the world to numbers, however sophisticated, is quite simply wrong-headed; the world is too complicated for numbers.

These criticisms are serious, and indicate that this emergent new field of research has much to do to gain legitimacy. This is not to dismiss this important and growing area; rather it is to seek its advance. These reservations – at conceptual and practical levels – do not argue against simulations but, rather, for their development and refinement. They promise much and in areas of the sciences apart from education have already yielded much of value. For further information on complexity theory and simulations we suggest that readers visit Internet websites such as:

http://www/santafe.edu/ (the website of the Santa Fe Institute – a major institute for the study of complexity theory);

http://www.brint.com/Systems.htm (a website that provides an index of material on complexity theory);

http://journals.wiley.com/1076-2787/ tocs/ (the website of the journal *Complexity*);

http://life.csu.edu.au/vl_complex/all. html (a website that provides access to the listings on complexity theory on the World-Wide Web Virtual Library).

Further, simply by keying in 'complexity theory', 'education simulations', or 'Santa Fe Institute' to a search engine on the Internet the reader will be able to access a wealth of references and information about the topics in this section.

Fuzzy logic

Computer simulations can be extended to include the developing field of 'fuzzy logic'. Here the researcher sets out to ascertain the extent to which a particular measure conforms to a semantic ideal (Fourali, 1997). Fuzzy logic recognizes that properties (e.g. fast, slow, tall, low, high, moderate, adequate, mature, developed, competent) have continuously varying values, and that we partition these values comparatively and arbitrarily into semantic categories or sections (e.g. on a rating scale). Within each category there is variation. Fuzzy logic enables us to gain a more precise measurement of the variance *within* and *between* these semantic categories; it recognizes that imprecision, rather than bivalence (*either* something is *or* is not the case) is a characteristic of many phenomena.

Fuzzy logic opts for shades of greyness rather than black-or-white (Kosko, 1994: 102)! In the field of education Fourali (1997) has shown how fuzzy logic is particularly useful in assessment. Fuzzy logic builds in feedback: systems constantly modify themselves in response to feedback, resonating with complexity theory. Kosko (1994: 63) illustrates this with the example of a washing machine whose sensors adjust the machine to the weight of washing, the amount of dirt, the texture of the washing etc. For a fuller analysis of the principles and practice of fuzzy logic see Smithson (1988), Cox (1994), Kosko (1994) and Fourali (1997). Readers wishing to research fuzzy logic in education will find a huge amount of material on the Internet, accessed by keying in 'education fuzzy logic' or 'fuzzy logic' to a search engine. Two useful websites are:

http://www.ang-physik.uni-kiel.de/ ~hoefi/fuzzy.www.english.html (a website that provides a world wide server about fuzzy logic);

http://www.fuzzytech.com/e_uni.htm (a website that provides other addresses for information).

Geographical Information Systems

The role of computer technology for educational research purposes has extended the boundaries of discipline-based research. An example of this is the use of Geographical Information Systems which are being used in the health services as well as in education.

Educational policy frequently has geographical implications and dimensions, e.g. catchment areas, school closures, open enrolment and school choice, the distribution of resources and financial expenditure, the distribution of assessment scores and examination results. Geographical Information Systems (GIS) is a computer-based system for capturing, storing, validating, analysing and displaying spatial data, both large scale and small scale, integrating several types of data from different sources (Worrall, 1990; Parsons, Chalkley and Jones, 1996).

This is useful for teasing out the implications and outcomes of policy initiatives, for example: 'What is the effect of parental choice on school catchments?'; 'What is the spread of examination scores in a particular region?'; 'How effective is the provision of secondary schools for a given population?'; 'How can a transport system be made more effective for taking students to and from school?'; 'What is the evidence for the creation of "magnet" and "sink" schools in a particular city?'. Examples of the data presented here are given in Boxes 22.1 and 22.2.

Clearly the political sensitivity and significance of these kinds of data are immense, indicating how research can inform policy-making and its effects very directly. Parsons, Chalkley and Jones (1996) provide a straightforward, fully-referenced introduction to this field of research in education, and they present case studies of catchment areas and examination performance, the redistribution of school catchments, and the pattern of movements in catchments.[1]

Readers wishing to research Geographical Information Systems on the Internet can access several sites by keying in 'education research Geographical Information Systems' on a search engine for the Internet or by visiting the following website:

http://geo.ifaran.ru/resources/giswww.html (a GIS World-Wide Web resource list).

Needs analysis

The notion of needs analysis (also called needs assessment) has existed in the world of education for over a decade, coming from social welfare (e.g. housing, employment, crime prevention and poverty reduction programmes), health programmes and social policy research. Its pedigree in education is rooted in evaluation studies and research (Suarez, 1994). Needs analysis can be used, for example, to:

- identify students' instructional needs;
- identify programme provision needs (and gaps in present provision);
- ascertain weaknesses in students' achievements or provision;
- provide information on in-service needs;
- determine where deficits exist so that they can be addressed;

Box 22.1
Geographical Information Systems in secondary schools

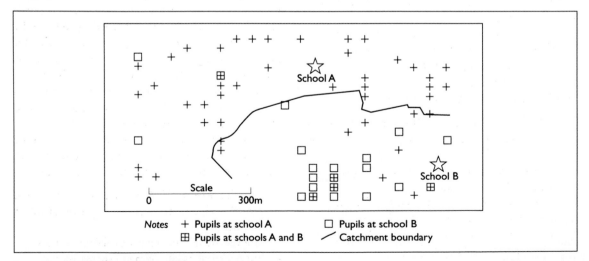

Notes   + Pupils at school A   □ Pupils at school B
        ⊞ Pupils at schools A and B   ╱ Catchment boundary

Source Parsons, Chalkley and Jones, 1996

Box 22.2
Location of home postcodes using Geographical Information Systems

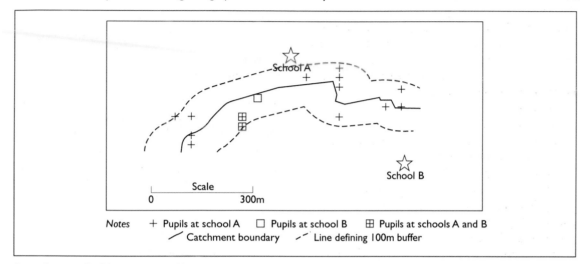

Notes   + Pupils at school A   □ Pupils at school B   ⊞ Pupils at schools A and B
         ⟋ Catchment boundary   ⟋⟋ Line defining 100m buffer

Source Parsons, Chalkley and Jones, 1996

- identify areas for expenditure and educational development.

It can be argued that needs assessment has similarities to the cause-and-effect quality models used in industry (Morrison, 1998), where the intention is to find the 'real causes' of problems rather than, for example, putative sources, so that causes rather than symptoms of problems, deficits and weaknesses can be addressed in subsequent planning.

Much hangs on the definition of 'needs' that is adopted. For example, a need can be defined in several ways (Scriven and Roth, 1978; Lund and McGechan, 1981; Stufflebeam *et al.*, 1985; Rossi and Freeman, 1993; Suarez, 1994):

- a discrepancy or underachievement (a difference between what is and what should be the case);
- wants and preferences (e.g. for future planning), reflecting values;
- anticipated requirements for the future;
- anticipated problems for the future;
- a deficit (where the absence of a feature under review is harmful).

Here the concept of a need swings between, on the one hand, deficit or shortfall, and, on the other hand, future planning and programming. The first is essentially reactive – a measure of achievement (or underachievement) which is useful in accountability studies – whilst the second is more proactive and linked to future developments: the first concerns remediation whilst the second concerns forward planning and forecasting (for example by using trend analysis, discussed in Chapter 8). Both, however, concern the process of diagnosis for subsequent planning; both are strongly in the vein of evaluative research (discussed in Chapter 1); and both are concerned with gathering information on the problem, for problem and need definition. Needs analysis is research designed to render decision-making informed rather than conjectural and speculative.

There are several components of a needs analysis. In relation to the operationalization of the term it is necessary to address key issues:

- the definition of need that is being used, e.g. the operationalization of the problem or need;
- the nature of the actual problem or need;
- the indicators of the need or problem;
- the size of the need or problem;

- the type of need or problem;
- the scope, complexity and range of the problem or need;
- the sub-elements of the need or problem;
- the priorities of aspects of the need;
- the severity or intensity of the need or problem;
- the causes of the need;
- forecasting needs;
- the consequences if the need is not addressed;
- the consequences of addressing the need.

In terms of the population concerned it is necessary to address several factors:

- the target population for an intervention;
- the number of people affected or concerned (e.g. the proportion of a total population);
- the location of the need or problem;
- the clarification of whose problem it is;
- the density and distribution of the problem;
- the incidence of the problem or need;
- how widespread is the need.

In terms of a proposed intervention there are several important factors to address:

- the identification of the exact conditions, problems and needs that the intervention is designed to address;
- the appropriateness of the programme intended to address the need;
- the purposes of the proposed intervention;
- the boundaries of the target population for an intervention (i.e. the criteria to be used for defining the target population);
- the present and estimated future size of the target population;
- the feasibility of the proposed intervention;
- responsibility for interventions (which people have to take action).

The intention is to ensure that interventions are appropriately matched to perceived problems or needs, indeed that competing and alternative proposed interventions are evaluated.

The data required for needs analysis can be derived from several sources, for example:

1   *quantitative data* from: structured surveys; 'key person' (informants) surveys; structured interviews (Rossi and Freeman, 1993); data from official public sources and documents (e.g. census returns, test and examination data, and other surveys); simulations and prediction analyses; test, assessment and examination data; application, attendance, retention, withdrawal and success rates;

2   *qualitative data* from: semi-structured interviews with individuals and groups; focus groups; case studies; critical incidents and events; public meetings; nominal group technique and Delphi techniques (Morrison, 1993); Ishikawa cause-and-effect diagrams (Morrison, 1998).

Clearly, the success of needs analysis could depend on the careful and appropriate sampling and targeting of parties concerned. Rossi and Freeman (1993: 84) suggest that qualitative data are useful for determining the nature of the need, whilst quantitative data are necessary for determining the extent of the need. The issue of sampling and targeting is not unproblematic, for issues of inclusion in, and exclusion from, the sample or target population might be highly sensitive, for example: a needs analysis of children at risk of abuse or poor parenting, or the criteria to be used for defining students who are developmentally delayed.

Further, it is possible that a need or problem will be reconceptualized as more data are obtained, the sample is widened, the number of stakeholders increase, and further evaluation studies are undertaken. For example, a problem which might be perceived initially as the incidence of noisy students in a school corridor might turn out to be a manifestation of a deeper set of problems (e.g. poor timetabling that causes all students to have to move around the school simultaneously; poor layout of corridors which leads to inevitable congestion; poor quality facilities that have noisy floors instead of carpeted floors; and poor organizational matters that result in many students having to move rooms or walk great distances).

Chapter 22

A needs analysis, then, identifies the problem or need and then proceeds to identify the aims, content, implementation, target population and outcome of an intervention. In this respect it is akin to planning action research. Suarez (1994) suggests that needs analysis for the purpose of future planning and development will tend to focus on aims and goals, whilst needs analysis that is undertaken to identify discrepancies will tend to focus on content, implementation and outcome.

It is important, then, for the researcher to be clear on the purposes of the needs analysis being undertaken, for this will determine the focus, methodology and outcome of the assessment. Consequent to this, it is necessary for the needs analysis to be clear on its remit, focus, sampling, methodology, data collection, and prescription for intervention.

The issue of prioritization of the problems, needs and aspects of the intervention is also critical, particularly because budgetary constraints will affect the conduct of the needs assessment and its subsequent recommendation. Witkin (1984) identifies several quantitative methods for identifying priorities (including, for example, ratings, amount of discrepancy between actual and intended practices or incidence). Lund and McGechan (1981) suggest that the process of prioritization will need to focus on such issues as: (a) the consequences of not meeting the need; (b) the number of people affected; (c) the meeting of the need by the parties identified (e.g. whether the problem is solely a matter for educationists or whether it involves other service sectors); (d) the criticality and severity of the needs; (e) the sequencing of the need (the order in which the needs must be addressed, and whether the addressing of some needs logically and empirically precedes the addressing of others); (f) the resource implications of meeting the needs (e.g. people, financial and budgetary, time, materials and equipment, administrative support); (g) the scope of the outcome and the utility of the intervention.

Suarez (1994) underlines the importance in needs assessment for the dissemination of the research findings to be planned and to be exten-sive. The critical factor of a needs assessment, like many evaluation studies, is the *utility* of the findings. The outcomes of needs assessment should feed into decision-making and policy-formation. Hence all stakeholders need to be involved in and informed of the research.

In planning a needs analysis, then, four main steps can be followed:

Step 1   Decide the purposes of the needs analysis and the definitions of needs that are to be used.
Step 2   Identify the focus of the needs analysis.
Step 3   Decide the methodology, sampling, instrumentation, data collection and analysis procedures and criteria to be used to judge the size, scope, extent, severity etc. of the need.
Step 4   Decide the reporting and dissemination of the results.

It can be seen that the planning of a needs analysis follows a typical plan of an evaluation or of evaluative research. For an extended example of a needs analysis see Kshir's (1999) analysis of in-service needs for staff development and curriculum change. Internet material on needs analysis in education can be found by keying in 'education needs analysis' or 'education needs evaluation' on a search engine. However, it must be stated that the overwhelming amount of Internet material here concerns business and financial needs assessment, management training needs, and IT needs assessment, though there are isolated instance of educational materials, often of an advertising nature and often concerning special educational needs. Two examples of educational entries can be found at:

http://www.metagifted.org/ (the website of the Metagifted Organisation);

http://www.metagifted.org/topics/ MultipleIntelligences/ (the section of the Metagifted Organisation that focuses on the work of Howard Gardner).

The amount of *research* data on the Internet about needs assessment in education, at the time of writing, appears limited.

Evidence-based education

This is a term that has been coined to cover the growth in interest in particular types of data and research in education. The need for practice and decision-making to be informed by the best evidence available is undeniable. In evidence-based education the evidence in question is of a particular nature or type, *viz.* that acquired from well-controlled experimental trials which indicate the effects and effect sizes of an intervention. In this respect the move towards evidence-based education resonates with the use of meta-analysis, which was discussed in Chapter 12, and with the importance of examining effect size, that was discussed in Chapters 10 and 12. More specifically, it is suggested that the evidence is strongest when it derives from randomized controlled trials (RCTs).

The roots of evidence-based practice lie in medicine, where the advocacy by Cochrane (1972) for randomized controlled trials together with their systematic review and documentation led to the foundation of the Cochrane Collaboration (Maynard and Chalmers, 1997), which is now worldwide. The careful, quantitative-based research studies that can contribute to the accretion of an evidential base is seen to be a powerful counter to the often untried and under-tested schemes that are injected into practice.

More recently evidence-based education has entered the worlds of social policy, social work (MacDonald, 1997) and education (Fitz-Gibbon, 1997). At the forefront of educational research in this area are Fitz-Gibbon (1996; 1997; 1999) and Tymms (1996), who, at the Curriculum, Evaluation and Management Centre at the University of Durham, have established one of the world's largest monitoring centres in education. Fitz-Gibbon's work is critical of multilevel modelling and, instead, suggests how indicator systems can be used with experimental methods to provide clear evidence of causality and a ready answer to her own question: how do we know what works? (Fitz-Gibbon, 1999: 33).

Echoing Anderson and Biddle (1991), Fitz-Gibbon suggests that *policy makers* shun evidence in the development of policy and that *practitioners*, in the hurly-burly of everyday activity, call upon tacit knowledge rather than the knowledge which is derived from RCTs. However, in a compelling argument (1997: 35–6), she suggests that evidence-based approaches are necessary in order to: (a) challenge the imposition of unproven practices; (b) solve problems and avoid harmful procedures; (c) create improvement that leads to more effective learning. Further, such evidence, she contends, should examine effect sizes rather than statistical significance.

Whilst the nature of evidence in evidence-based education might be contested by researchers whose sympathies (for whatever reason) lie outside randomized controlled trials, the message from Fitz-Gibbon will not go away: the educational community needs evidence on which to base its judgements and actions. The development of indicator systems worldwide attests to the importance of this, be it through assessment and examination data, inspection findings, national and international comparisons of achievement, or target setting. Rather than being a shot in the dark, evidence-based education suggests that policy formation should be informed, and policy decision-making should be based on the best information to date rather than on hunch, ideology or political will. It is bordering on the unethical to implement untried and untested recommendations in educational practice, just as it is unethical to use untested products and procedures on hospital patients without their consent.

The Internet material on evidence-based education is largely concerned with medical education at the time of writing, and this can be accessed through the keywords 'education evidence based' on a search engine. However, the following website provides some useful material for researchers:

http://www.dur.ac.uk/edeuk/ (this contains a manifesto for evidence-based education and a listing of other websites about the topic).

We close this chapter and end the book by returning to a key issue: that research is necessary to inform practice, and in doing so needs to be rigorous, circumspect and self-aware. To this extent we echo the opening words of Zen Master Sun Yat Sen that preface this fifth edition: 'To understand is hard; once one understands, action is easy.' When he made this comment he was reacting to the earlier Chinese nostrum that doing is harder than learning, i.e.: to learn is easy; to put into practice is hard. This book has tried to make the learning easier and the doing more informed.

Chapter 22

Notes

I THE NATURE OF INQUIRY

1   Parts of this chapter are taken from Cohen, L. and Manion, L. (1981) *Perspectives on Classrooms and Schools* with permission from Holt, Rinehart & Winston.

2   We are not here recommending, nor would we wish to encourage, exclusive dependence on rationally derived and scientifically provable knowledge for the conduct of education – even if this were possible. There is a rich fund of traditional and cultural wisdom in teaching (as in other spheres of life) which we would ignore to our detriment. What we are suggesting, however, is that total dependence on the latter has tended in the past to lead to an impasse: and that for further development and greater understanding to be achieved education must needs resort to the methods of science and research.

3   Primarily associated with the Vienna Circle of the 1920s whose most famous members included Schlick, Carnap, Neurath and Waisman.

4   A classic statement opposing this particular view of science is that of Kuhn, T. S. (1962) *The Structure of Scientific Revolutions*, Chicago: University of Chicago Press. Kuhn's book, acknowledged as an intellectual *tour de force*, makes the point that science is not the systematic accumulation of knowledge as presented in text books; that it is a far less rational exercise than generally imagined. In effect, it is 'a series of peaceful interludes punctuated by intellectually violent revolutions . . . in each of which one conceptual world view is replaced by another.'

5   For a straightforward overview of the discussions here see Chalmers, A. F. (1982) *What Is This Thing Called Science?* (second edition), Milton Keynes: Open University Press.

6   For a later study that examines the influence of science and objectivity on the secularization of consciousness, see the same author's *Where the Wasteland Ends*, London: Faber & Faber, 1972.

7   The formulation of scientific method outlined earlier has come in for strong and sustained criticism. Mishler for example, describes it as a 'sto-rybook image of science', out of tune with the actual practices of working scientists who turn out to resemble craftpersons rather than logicians. By craftpersons, Mishler is at pains to stress that competence depends upon 'apprenticeship training, continued practice and experienced-based, contextual knowledge of the specific methods applicable to a phenomenon of interest rather than an abstract "logic of discovery" and application of formal "rules" '. The knowledge base of scientific research, Mishler contends, is largely tacit and unexplicated; moreover, scientists learn it through a process of socialization into a 'particular form of life'. The discovery, testing and validation of findings is embedded in cultural and linguistic practices and experimental scientists proceed in pragmatic ways, learning from their errors and failures, adapting procedures to their local contexts, making decisions on the basis of their accumulated experiences. See for example, Mishler, E. G. (1990) Validation in inquiry-guided research: the role of exemplars in narrative studies, *Harvard Educational Review*, 60 (4): 415–42.

8   See, for example, Rogers, C. R. (1969) *Freedom to Learn*, Columbus, OH: Merrill Pub. Co.; and also Rogers, C. R. and Stevens, B. (1967) *Person to Person: the Problem of Being Human*, London: Souvenir Press.

9   Investigating social episodes involves analysing the accounts of what is happening from the points of view of the actors and the participant spectator(s)/investigator(s). This is said to yield three main kinds of interlocking material: images of the self and others, definitions of situations, and rules for the proper development of the action. See Harré, R. (1976) The constructive role of models, in L. Collins (ed.), *The Use of Models in the Social Sciences*, London: Tavistock Publications.

10 It may seem paradoxical to some readers that, although we have just described interpretive theories as anti-positivist, they are nevertheless conventionally regarded as 'scientific' (and hence

part of 'social science') in that they are concerned ultimately with describing and explaining human behaviour by means of methods that are in their own way every bit as rigorous as the ones used in positivist research.

11   It is not our intention here to outline philosophical challenges to paradigm theory enunciated by coherence theorists who argue for the epistemological unity of educational research. One version of unity theory is succinctly articulated by Walker and Evers (1988: 28–36).

12   See also Verma, G. K. and Beard, R. M. (1981) *What is Educational Research?* Aldershot: Gower, for further information on the nature of educational research and also a historical perspective on the subject.

2   THE ETHICS OF EDUCATIONAL AND SOCIAL RESEARCH

1   For example, American Psychological Association (1982); American Sociological Association (1971); British Sociological Association (1982); Social Research Association (1986); and the British Educational Research Association (1989). Comparable developments may be found in other fields of endeavour. For an examination of key ethical issues in medicine, business and journalism together with reviews of common ethical themes across these areas, see Serafini, A. (ed.) (1989) *Ethics and Social Concern*, New York: Paragon House. The book also contains an account of principal ethical theories from Socrates to R. M. Hare.

2   US Dept of Health, Education and Welfare, Public Health Service and National Institute of Health (1971) *The Institutional Guide to D.H.E.W. Policy on Protecting Human Subjects*, DHEW Publication (NIH): December 2, 72–102.

3   See also, Reynolds, P. D. (1979) *Ethical Dilemmas and Social Science Research*, San Francisco: Jossey-Bass.

4   As regards judging researchers' behaviour, perhaps the only area of educational research where the term ethical absolute can be unequivocally applied and where subsequent judgement is unquestionable is that concerning researchers' relationship with their data. Should they choose to abuse their data for whatever reason, the behaviour is categorically wrong; no place here for moral relativism. For once, a clear dichotomy is relevant: if there is such a thing as clearly ethical behaviour, such abuse is clearly unethical. It can take the form of first, falsifying data to support a preconceived, often favoured, hypothesis; second, manipulating data, often statistically, for

the same reason (or manipulating techniques used – deliberately including leading questions, for example); third, using data selectively, that is, ignoring or excluding the bits that don't fit one's hypothesis; and fourth, going beyond the data, in other words, arriving at conclusions not warranted by them (or over-interpreting them). But even malpractice as serious as these examples cannot be controlled by fiat: ethical injunctions would hardly be appropriate in this context, let alone enforceable. The only answer (in the absence of professional monitoring) is for the researcher to have a moral code that is 'rationally derived and intelligently applied', to use the words of the philosopher, R. S. Peters, and to be guided by it consistently. Moral competence, like other competencies, can be learned. One way of acquiring it is to bring interrogative reflection to bear on one's own code and practice, e.g. did I provide suitable feedback, in the right amounts, to the right audiences, at the right time? In sum, ethical behaviour depends on the concurrence of ethical thinking which in turn is based on fundamentally thought-out principles. Readers wishing to take the subject of data abuse further should read Peter Medawar's (1991) elegant and amusing essay, 'Scientific fraud', in D. Pike (ed.) *The Threat and the Glory: Reflections on Science and Scientists*, Oxford: Oxford University Press; and also Broad, W. and Wade, N. (1983) *Betrayers of Truth: Fraud and Deceit in the Halls of Science*, New York: Century.

5   We would see the term 'a sense of rightness' as approximately equivalent to the word 'conscience' as used in the religious tradition, or to Carl Rogers' term 'internal locus of evaluation' as used in a humanistic context. Some writers (e.g. Benstead and Constantine, 1998) distinguish between *acquired conscience* and *true conscience*. The former conforms to social ideas as to what is right and wrong and is acquired through social conditioning; the latter, *true conscience*, is a latent, innate 'sense of rightness' made manifest by heightened awareness, the consequence of which is that people know the difference between right and wrong *for themselves*. Therefore, as awareness is heightened, as sensitivity is refined, so conscience develops. Ethical problems can arise through lack of such sensitivity, and, *a fortiori*, from the ego taking over the conscience and using it for its own ends. Indeed, the competing demands of ego and conscience are often at the heart of ethical or moral dilemmas. The reader can tease out for himself or herself the implications of all this for educational research. It may be, for example, that a code of conduct

ultimately becomes unnecessary: a researcher will know intuitively whether a course of action is appropriate or not.

6   This idea of a personal code of practice may be complemented by a distinctive view from the east. For eastern teachers, 'right doing' is a consequence of 'right being'. As Guy Claxton (1981) says: 'what makes an action good is the quality of the doer, not the objective nature of the act'. This echoes Pirsig's (1976: 318) famous view in his *Zen and the Art of Motorcycle Maintenance* that to paint a perfect painting is easy: first one makes oneself perfect and then one just paints naturally.

7   Readers seeking guidance on this matter are referred to Reynolds (1979), where the author has assembled a composite code of ethics based on statements appearing in twenty-four codes related to the conduct of social science research in the United States. The seventy-eight statements listed by him cover general issues related to the code of ethics: the decision to conduct the research; the actual conduct of the research; informed consent; protection of rights and welfare of participants; deception; confidentiality and anonymity; benefits to participants; effects on aggregates or communities; and the interpretation and reporting of the results of the research. The composite code is reprinted in Frankfort-Nachmias and Nachmias (1992) and a selection of items from it may be found in Box 2.9. As we pointed out in the text, codes of practice are not a universal panacea, in spite of our advocacy, and their efficacy will vary with method and context. Some researchers, for example, have reported difficulties in working with codes of practice when doing field work. For the appropriate references to these cases, see Burgess, R. G. (1989b) Grey areas: ethical dilemmas in educational ethnography, in R. G. Burgess (ed.) (1989a) *The Ethics of Educational Research*, Lewes: Falmer Press.

3   RESEARCH DESIGN ISSUES: PLANNING RESEARCH

1   For a discussion of the nature, strengths and weaknesses of models see Morrison (1993: 37–8). He suggests that, whilst models usefully reduce the world to manageable proportions, simplifying for the sake of clarity, care has to be taken not to oversimplify complexity to the point of reductionism *ad absurdum*.

4   SAMPLING

1   This table is also reproduced in Dunham, R. B. and Smith, F. J. (1979) *Organizational Surveys: an Internal Assessment of Organizational Health*, Glenview, Ill.: Scott, Foreman and Co., 68.

5   VALIDITY AND RELIABILITY

1   For a critique of a survey, from conceptualization to reporting, see Morrison (1997).

7   HISTORICAL RESEARCH

1   See also the opening chapters in Gardiner, P. (1961) *The Nature of Historical Explanation*, Oxford: Oxford University Press, reprinted 1978.

2   By contrast, the historian of the modern period, i.e. the nineteenth and twentieth centuries, is more often faced in the initial stages with the problem of selecting from too much material, both at the stage of analysis and writing. Here the two most common criteria for such selection are (1) the degree of significance to be attached to data, and (2) the extent to which a specific detail may be considered typical of the whole.

3   However, historians themselves usually reject such a direct application of their work and rarely indulge in it on the grounds that no two events or contextual circumstances, separated geographically and temporally, can possibly be equated. As the popular sayings go, 'History never repeats itself' and so, 'The only thing we can learn from History is that we can learn nothing from History.'

4   The status of the history of education as an academic discipline is well summarized and illustrated in Sutherland, G. (1969) The study of the history of education, *History*, 54 (180).

5   See also the Social Science Research Council's (1971) *Research in Economic and Social History*, London: Heinemann, Chapters 2 and 3.

6   Holsti, O. R. (1968) Content analysis, in G. Lindzey and E. Aronson (eds), *The Handbook of Social Psychology*. Vol. 2: *Research Methods*, Reading, MA: Addison-Wesley. For a detailed account of the methods and problems involved in establishing the reliability of the content analysis of written data, see: Everett, M. (1984) The Scottish comprehensive school: its function and the roles of its teachers with special reference to the opinions of pupils and student teachers, Unpublished Ph.D. dissertation, School of Education, University of Durham.

7   Thomas, W. I. and Znaniecki, F. (1918) *The Polish Peasant in Europe and America*, Chicago: University of Chicago Press. For a fuller discussion of the monumental work of Thomas and Znaniecki,

the reader is referred to Plummer, K. (1983) *Documents of Life: an Introduction to the Problems and Literature of a Humanistic Method*, London: George Allen & Unwin, especially Chapter 3, The making of a method; and to Madge, J. (1963) *The Origin of Scientific Sociology*, London: Tavistock. For a critique of Thomas and Znaniecki, see Riley, M. W. (1963) *Sociological Research: a Case Approach*, New York: Harcourt, Brace & World, Inc.

8   Sikes, P., Measor, L. and Woods, P. (1985) *Teacher Careers*, Lewes: Falmer Press; see also: Acker, S. (1989) *Teachers, Gender and Careers*, Lewes: Falmer Press; Blease, D. and Cohen, L. (1990) *Coping with Computers: an Ethnographic Study in Primary Classrooms*, London: Paul Chapman Publishers; Evetts, J. (1990) *Women in Primary Teaching*, London: Unwin Hyman; Evetts, J. (1991) The experience of secondary headship selection: continuity and change, *Educational Studies*, 17(3), 285–94; Goodson, I. (1990) *The Making of Curriculum*, Lewes: Falmer Press; Smith, L. M. (1987) *Kensington Revisited*, Lewes: Falmer Press; Goodson, I. and Walker, R. (1988) Putting life into educational research, in R. R. Sherman and R. B. Webb (eds) *Qualitative Research in Education: Focus and Methods*, Lewes: Falmer Press; Sikes, P. and Troyna, B. (1991) True stories: a case study in the use of life histories in teacher education, *Educational Review*, 43 (1) 3–16; Winkley, D. (1995) *Diplomats and Detectives: LEA Advisers and Work*, London: Robert Royce.

8 SURVEYS, LONGITUDINAL, CROSS-SECTIONAL AND TREND STUDIES

1   There are several examples of surveys, including: Borg, M. G. (1998) Secondary school teachers' perceptions of pupils' undesirable behaviours, *British Journal of Educational Psychology*, 68, 67–79; Boulton, M. J. (1997) Teachers' views on bullying: definitions, attitudes and abilities to cope, *British Journal of Educational Psychology*, 67, 223–33; Cline, T. and Ertubney, C. (1997) The impact of gender on primary teachers' evaluations of children's difficulties in school, *British Journal of Educational Psychology*, 67, 447–56; Dosanjh, J. S. and Ghuman, P. A. S. (1997) Asian parents and English education – 20 years on: a study of two generations, *Educational Studies*, 23 (3), 459–472; Foskett, N. H. and Hesketh, A. J. (1997) Constructing choice in continuous and parallel markets: institutional and school leavers' responses to the new post-16 marketplace, *Oxford Review of Education*, 23 (3), 299–319; Gallagher, T., McEwen, A. and Knip, D. (1997) Science edu-

cation policy: a survey of the participation of sixth-form pupils in science and the subjects over a 10-year period, 1985–95, *Research Papers in Education*, 12 (2), 121–42; Hall, K. and Nuttall, W. (1999) The *relative* importance of class size to infant teachers in England, *British Educational Research Journal*, 25 (2), 245–58; Jules, V. and Kutnick, P. (1997) Student perceptions of a good teacher: the gender perspective, *British Journal of Educational Psychology*, 67, 497–511; Millan, R., Gallagher, M. and Ellis, R. (1993) Surveying adolescent worries: development of the 'Things I Worry About' scale, *Pastoral Care in Education*, 11 (1), 43–57; Papasolomoutos, C. and Christie, T. (1998) Using national surveys: a review of secondary analyses with special reference to schools, *Educational Research*, 40 (3), 295–310; Rigby, K. (1999) Peer victimisation at school and the health of secondary school students, *British Journal of Educational Psychology*, 69, 95–104; Strand, S. (1999) Ethnic group, sex and economic disadvantage: associations with pupils' educational progress from Baseline to the end of Key Stage 1, *British Educational Research Journal*, 25 (2), 179–202; Tatar, M. (1998) Teachers as significant others: gender differences in secondary school pupils' perceptions, *British Journal of Educational Psychology*, 68, 255–68; Terry, A. A. (1998) Teachers as targets of bullying by their pupils: a study to investigate incidence, *British Journal of Educational Psychology*, 68, 255–68.

Examples of different kinds of survey studies are as follows: (a) Francis's (1992) 'true cohort' study of patterns of reading development, following a group of 54 young children for two years at six monthly intervals; (b) Blatchford's 1992 cohort/cross-sectional study of 133–175 children (two samples) and their attitudes to work at 11 years of age; (c) a large scale/cross-sectional study by Munn, Johnstone and Holligan (1990) into pupils' perceptions of effective disciplinarians, with a sample size of 543; (d) a trend/prediction study of school building requirements by a government department (Department of Education and Science, 1977), identifying building and improvement needs based on estimated pupil populations from births during the decade 1976–86; (e) a survey study by Belson (1975) of 1,425 teenage boys' theft behaviour; (f) a survey by Hannan and Newby (1992) of 787 student teachers (with a 46 per cent response rate) and their views on government proposals to increase the amount of time spent in schools during the training period.

2   For a critique of a survey conducted by course leaders see Morrison (1997).

3 Examples of longitudinal and cross-sectional studies include: Busato, V. V., Prins, F. J., Elshant, J. J. and Hamaker, C. (1998) Learning styles: a cross-sectional and longitudinal study in higher education, *British Journal of Educational Psychology*, 68, 427–41; Davenport, E. C. Jr, Davison, M. L., Kuang, H., Ding, S., Kin, S.-K. and Kwak, N. (1998) High school mathematics course-taking by gender and ethnicity, *American Educational Research Journal*, 35 (3), 497–514; Davies, J. and Brember, I (1997) Monitoring reading standards in year 6: a 7-year cross-sectional study, *British Educational Research Journal*, 23 (5), 615–22; Davies, J. and Brember, I. (1998) Standards in reading at key stage 1 – a cross-sectional study, *Educational Research*, 40 (2), 153–60; Galton, M., Hargreaves, L, Comber, C., Wall, D. and Pell, T. (1999) Changes in patterns in teacher interaction in primary classrooms, 1976–1996, *British Educational Research Journal*, 25 (1), 23–37; Marsh, H. W. and Yeung, A. S. (1998) Longitudinal structural equation models of academic self-concept and achievement: gender differences in the development of math and English constructs, *American Educational Research Journal*, 35 (4), 705–38; Noack, P. (1998) School achievement and adolescents' interactions with their fathers, mothers, and friends, *European Journal of Psychology of Education*, 13 (4), 503–13; Preisler, G. M., and Ahström, M. (1997) Sign language for hard of hearing children – a hindrance or a benefit for their development? *European Journal of Psychology of Education*, 12 (4), 465–77.

4 For an account of the National Child Development Study of a cohort of 15,000 children (now adults), see Fogelman, K. (ed.) (1983) *Growing Up in Great Britain: Papers from the National Child Development Study*, London: Macmillan. The third national cohort study (the 1970 cohort) is a detailed account of the health and behaviour of Britain's 5-year-olds. See, Butler, N. R. and Golding, J. (1986) *From Birth to Five*, Oxford: Pergamon Press. .

5 For further information on event history analysis and hazard rates we refer readers to Allison, 1984; Hakim, 1987; Plewis, 1985; von Eye, 1990; Rose and Sullivan, 1993.

9 CASE STUDIES

1 King, R. (1979) *All Things Bright and Beautiful?* Chichester: John Wiley; King's study as a whole is based upon unstructured observations in infant classrooms. For a more structured inquiry into the activities of young children, see Dunn, S.

and Morgan, V. (1987) Nursery and infant school play patterns: sex-related differences, *British Educational Research Journal*, 13 (3), 271–81. An earlier study that raised questions about the so-called progressive practices in primary education is provided by Sharp, R. and Green, A. (1975) *Education and Social Control: a Study in Progressive Primary Education*, London: Routledge & Kegan Paul.

2 For a text dealing with techniques of observation, see Croll, P. (1985) *Systematic Observation*, Lewes: Falmer Press. For analysing case records (indexing, structuring, restructuring, sequencing, classification and cross-classification, coordinating and reducing) see Bromley, D. B. (1986) *The Case Study Method in Psychology and Related Disciplines*, Chichester: John Wiley.

3 For a British study employing ethnographic techniques and looking, *inter alia*, at the leadership of the head teacher, see Burgess, R. G. (1983) *Experiencing Comprehensive Education*, London: Methuen. For other case studies of schools the reader is referred to Ball, S. J. (1981) *Beachside Comprehensive*, Cambridge: Cambridge University Press; Ball, S. J. (1985) School politics, teachers' careers and educational change: a case study of becoming a comprehensive school, in L. Barton and S. Walker (eds) *Education and Social Change*, Beckenham: Croom Helm; Beynon, J. (1985a) Career histories in a comprehensive school, in S. J. Ball and I. F. Goodson (eds) *Teachers' Lives and Careers*, Lewes: Falmer Press; Beynon, J. (1985b) *Initial Encounters in the Secondary School*, Lewes: Falmer Press; and Davies, L. (1984) *Pupil Power: Deviance and Gender in School*, Lewes: Falmer Press.

4 For further examples of case studies see: Bates, I. and Dutson, J. (1995) A Bermuda triangle? A case study of the disappearance of competence-based vocational training policy in the context of practice, *British Journal of Education and Work*, 8 (2), 41–59; Jacklin, A. and Lacey, C. (1997) Gender integration in the infant classroom: a case study, *British Educational Research Journal*, 23 (5), 623–40; Woods, P. (1993) Managing marginality: teacher development through grounded life history, *British Educational Research Journal*, 19 (5), 447–88.

11 *EX POST FACTO* RESEARCH

1 In Chapters 11 and 12 we adopt the symbols and conventions used in Campbell, D. T. and Stanley, J. C. (1963) Experimental and quasi-experimental designs for research on teaching, in N. L. Gage

(ed.) *Handbook of Research on Teaching*, Chicago: Rand McNally. These are presented fully in Chapter 12.

2 For further information on logical fallacies, see Cohen, M. R. and Nagel, E. (1961) *An Introduction to Logic and Scientific Method*, London: Routledge and Kegan Paul. The example of the *post hoc, ergo propter hoc* fallacy given by the authors concerns sleeplessness, which may *follow* drinking coffee, but sleeplessness may not occur because coffee was drunk.

3 Stables's *ex post facto* design separated more than 2,300 pupils by type of school (mixed or single-sex), and then compared their perceptions of the importance of all their school subjects by means of a specially designed questionnaire. At the same time, participants were given an 'Attitudes to Physics, Chemistry and Biology' scale consisting of 64 statements to which they responded on a continuum ranging from 'strongly agree' to 'strongly disagree'. Stables's results showed that boys' and girls' attitudes in mixed schools were more strongly polarized than in single-sex schools. Drama, Biology and Languages were significantly more highly rated by boys in single-sex schools than by their fellows in mixed establishments. On the other hand, boys in mixed schools recorded greater support for Physics and Physical Sciences than boys in single-sex schools. As far as girls were concerned, Physics was better liked in single-sex schools than in mixed. Overall, the effect of being educated in a single-sex or a mixed school seemed to have greater effect on pupils' feelings towards Sciences, Modern Languages, Craft, Drama and Music. The most consistent finding in Stables's investigation was in connection with the 'Attitude to Physics, Chemistry and Biology' scale. Stables reports, 'On every section of the scale the sex difference was greater among co-educated pupils.' He concludes, 'The danger is that subject interest and specialisation may be guided to a greater extent by a desire to conform to a received sexual stereotype in mixed schools than in single-sex schools, thus effectively narrowing career choice for co-educated pupils.'

Arnold and Atkins's study consisted of twenty-three hearing-impaired children and twenty-three normally hearing pupils acting as controls. The causal-comparative design was used to ask the following questions: 'Are hearing-impaired children more maladjusted than non hearing-impaired children?', and if so, 'Are they differently maladjusted as revealed by two widely-used measures of maladjustment?' Their research used the 'Bristol Social Adjustment Guide' and 'Rutter's Children's Behaviour Ques-

tionnaire' to obtain ratings of their sample. They report that the hearing-impaired were no more maladjusted than the age-matched hearing controls, although there were high levels of maladjustment in both groups.

For further examples of *ex post facto* we refer the reader to three examples. Ben-Peretz and Kremer-Hayon (1990) studied the context and content of professional dilemmas using in-depth and open-ended interviews that were transcribed for subsequent analysis, i.e. an example of a qualitative study. Pierce and Molloy (1990) used a quantitative methodology in studying psychological and biographical differences in teachers who were experiencing burnout. McLaughlin *et al.* (1992) studied the schoolchild as a health educator, using quantitative and qualitative data; this study is a very useful example of the practice of coding addressed in Chapter 6 (Miles and Huberman, 1984; Strauss, 1987).

12 EXPERIMENTS, QUASI-EXPERIMENTS AND SINGLE-CASE RESEARCH

1 Randomization is one way of apportioning out or controlling for extraneous variables (see Riecken and Boruch, 1974; Bennett and Lumsdaine, 1975; Boruch, 1997). Alternatively, the experimenter may use matched cases, that is, subjects are matched in pairs in terms of some other variable thought likely to affect scores on the dependent variable and pairs are then allocated randomly to E and C conditions in such a way that the means and variances of the two groups are as nearly equal as possible. Finally, analysis of covariance is a powerful statistical procedure which uses pretest mean scores as covariates to control for initial differences between E and C groups on a number of independent variables.

2 See also the discussion of validity and reliability in educational research, in Hammersley, M. (1987) Some notes on the terms 'validity' and 'reliability', *British Educational Research Journal*, 13 (1), 73–81.

3 Questions have been raised about the authenticity of both definitions and explanations of the Hawthorne effect. See Diaper, G. (1990) The Hawthorne Effect: a fresh examination, *Educational Studies*, 16 (3), 261–7.

4 Ethical considerations arising out of such gross differentiation in educational provision to impoverished pupils is a matter of ethical concern.

5 The interested reader is referred to the following studies that draw upon single case designs in British schools: Gersch, I. (1984) Behaviour

modification and systems analysis in a secondary school: combining two approaches, *Behavioural Approaches with Children*, 8, 83–91; McNamara, E. (1986) The effectiveness of incentive and sanction systems used in secondary schools: a behavioural analysis, *Durham and Newcastle Research Review*, 10, 285–90; Merrett, F., Wilkins, J., Houghton, S. and Wheldall, K. (1988) Rules, sanctions and rewards in secondary schools, *Educational Studies*, 14 (2), 139–49; Sharpe, P. (1985) Behaviour modification in the secondary school: a survey of students' attitudes to rewards and praise, *Behavioural Approaches with Children*, 9, 109–12; and Wheldall, K. and Panagopoulou-Stamatelatou, A. (1991) The effects of pupil self-recording of on-task behaviour in primary school children, *British Educational Research Journal*, 17 (2), 113–27.

6   Examples of experimental research can be seen in: Alfassi, M. (1998) Reading for meaning: the efficacy of reciprocal teaching in fostering reading comprehension in high school students in remedial reading classes, *American Educational Research Journal*, 35 (2), 309–22; Bijstra, J. O. and Jackson, S. (1998) Social skills training with early adolescents: effects on social skills, well-being, self-esteem and coping, *European Journal of Psychology of Education*, 13 (4), 569–83; Bryant, P., Devine, M., Ledward, A., and Nunes, T. (1997) Spelling with apostrophes and understanding possession, *British Journal of Educational Psychology*, 67, 91–110; Cline, T., Proto, A., Raval, P. D., and Paolo, T. (1998) The effects of brief exposure and of classroom teaching on attitudes children express towards facial disfigurement in peers, *Educational Research*, 40 (1), 55–68; Didierjean, A. and Cauzinille-Marmèche, E. (1998) Reasoning by analogy: is it schema-mediated or case-based? *European Journal of Psychology of Education*, 13 (3), 385–98; Dugard, P. and Todman, J. (1995) Analysis of pretest and post-test control group designs in educational research, *Educational Psychology*, 15 (2), 181–98; Hall, E., Hall, C., and Abaci, R. (1997) The effects of human relations training on reported teacher stress, pupil control ideology and locus of control, *British Journal of Educational Psychology*, 67, 483–96; Littleton, K., Ashman, H., Light, P., Artis, J., Roberts, T. and Oosterwegel, A. (1999) Gender, task contexts, and children's performance on a computer-based task, *European Journal of Psychology of Education*, 14 (1), 129–39; Marcinkiewicz, H. R. and Clariana, R. B. (1997) The performance effects of headings within multi-choice tests, *British Journal of Edu-*

cational Psychology, 67, 111–17; Overett, S. and Donald, D. (1998) Paired reading: effects of a parental involvement programme in a disadvantaged community in South Africa, *British Journal of Educational Psychology*, 68, 347–56; Sainsbury, M., Whetton, C., Mason, K. and Schagen, I. (1998) Fallback in attainment on transfer at age 11: evidence from the summer literacy schools evaluation, *Educational Research*, 40 (1), 73–81; Tones, K. (1997) Beyond the randomized controlled trial: a case for 'judicial review', *Health Education Research*, 12 (2) i–iv.

7   See also, Hamilton, D. (1981) Generalisation in the educational sciences: problems and purposes, in T. S. Popkewitz and R. S. Tabachnick (eds) *The Study of Schooling*, New York: Praeger.

8   Criteria for selecting from a larger pool of studies those deemed to be well-controlled are set out in Cohen, P. A., Kulik, J. A. and Kulik, C. L. (1982) Educational outcomes of tutoring: a meta-analysis of findings, *American Educational Research Journal*, 19 (2), 237–48. See also Kumar, D. D. (1991) A meta-analysis of the relationship between science instruction and student engagement, *Educational Review*, 43 (1), 49–56.

9   An example of meta-analysis in educational research can be seen in Severiens, S. and ten Dam, G. (1998) A multilevel meta-analysis of gender differences in learning orientations, *British Journal of Educational Psychology*, 68, 595–618. The use of meta-analysis is widespread, indeed the Cochrane Collaboration is a pioneer in this field, focusing on meta-analyses of randomized controlled trials; see Maynard and Chalmers (1997).

13 ACTION RESEARCH

1   Examples of action research include: McFee, G. (1993) Reflections on the nature of action research, *Cambridge Journal of Education*, 23 (2) 173–83; Postlethwaite, K. and Haggarty, L. (1998) Towards effective and transferable learning in secondary school: the development of an approach based on mastery learning, *British Educational Research Journal*, 24 (3), 333–53.

14 QUESTIONNAIRES

1   Examples of questionnaires in educational research include: Hannan and Newby (1992); Black, D. R. and Scott, W. A. H. (1997) Factors affecting the employment of teachers returning to the United Kingdom after teaching abroad, *Educational Research*, 39 (1), 37–63; Pithers, R. T.

and Soden, R. (1999) Person–environment fit and teacher stress, *Educational Research*, 41, 51–61.

15 INTERVIEWS

1   Examples of interviews in educational research include: Carroll, S. and Walford, G. (1997) Parents' responses to the school quasi-market, *Research Papers in Education*, 12 (1) 3–26; Cicognani, C. (1998) Parents' educational styles and adolescent autonomy, *European Journal of Psychology of Education*, 13 (4), 485–502; Cullen, K. (1997) Headteacher appraisal: a view from the inside, *Research Papers in Education*, 12 (2), 177–204; Ferris, J. and Gerber, R. (1996) Mature-age students' feelings of enjoying learning in a further education context, *European Journal of Psychology of Education*, 11 (1), 79–96; Robinson, P. and Smithers, A. (1999) Should the sexes be separated for secondary education – comparisons of single-sex and co-educational schools? *Research Papers in Education*, 14 (1), 23–49; Van Etten, S., Pressley, M., Freebern, G. and Echevarria, M. (1998) An interview study of college freshmen's beliefs about their academic motivation, *European Journal of Psychology of Education*, 13 (1), 105–30.

2   Examples of telephone interviews include: Jones, J. L. (1998) Managing the induction of newly appointed governors, *Educational Research*, 40 (3) 329–51.

16 ACCOUNTS

1   For an example of concept mapping in educational research see: Lawless, L., Smee, P. and O'Shea, T. (1998) Using concept sorting and concept mapping in business and public administration, and education: an overview, *Educational Research*, 40 (2), 219–35.

2   See also: Edwards, D. and Mercer, N. M. (1989) Reconstructing context: the conventionalization of classroom knowledge, *Discourse Processes*, 12, 91–104; Potter, J. and Wetherall, M. (1987) *Discourse and Social Psychology: Beyond Attitudes and Behaviour*, London: Sage; Walkerdine, V. (1988) *The Mastery of Reason: Cognitive Development and the Production of Rationality*, London: Routledge.

3   For further examples of discourse analysis see: Butzkamm, W. (1998) Code-switching in a bilingual history lesson: the mother tongue as a conversational lubricant, *Bilingual Education and Bilingualism*, 1 (2): 81–99; Mercer, N., Wegerif, R. and Dawes, L. (1999) Children's talk and the development of reasoning in the classroom, *British Educational Research Journal*, 25 (1) 95–111; Ramsden, C. and Reason, D. (1997) Conversation – discourse analysis in library and information services, *Education for Information*, 15 (4), 283–95.

4   Our account draws on the outline contained in O'Neill, B. and McMahon, H. (1990) *Opening New Windows with Bubble Dialogue*, Language Development and Hypermedia Research Group, Faculty of Education, University of Ulster at Coleraine. See also the taxonomies for the analysis of social episodes by Windisch, V. (1990) *Speech and Reasoning in Everyday Life*, Cambridge: Cambridge University Press; Schonbach, P. (1990) *Account Episodes: the Management or Escalation of Conflict*, Cambridge: Cambridge University Press; Semin, G. R. and Manstead, A. S. R. (1983) *The Accountability of Conduct: a Social Psychological Analysis*, London: Academic Press. Bubble dialogue was born out of children's comic strips. Cunningham *et al.* (1991) have extended and powerfully transformed the comic strip in their computer-based application. Four icons, representing a speech bubble and a thought bubble per character are presented alongside two characters on the screen. Clicking on an icon brings up an empty 'say' or 'think' bubble for the chosen character. The comic genre is so well established, the authors opine, that even very young children when presented with empty bubbles, feel compelled to speak for the characters, playing out their roles. Sometimes the authors write in a first speech or thought (an 'opener' as they call it) to get a dialogue started. When pupils are more familiar with the tool, they readily create their own scenes and openers. In bubble dialogue, *characters* are set against a *backdrop*, the presence of which is considered crucial. A *prologue* helps set the *scene* in which the *dialogue* takes place. From the researcher's vantage point, bubble dialogue permits perceived relationships to be varied (by backdrop, prologue, openers). Bubble dialogue, its creators conclude, 'is a powerful methodology for users to make public those perceptions of context, content and interaction which might otherwise remain unformed and unsaid as well as unwritten' (O'Neill and McMahon, 1990). Bubble dialogue (in comic script format rather than computer-based application) has been used by Cohen (1993) to explore perceptions and interpretations of racist behaviour in secondary school classrooms.

5   Heath, S. B. (1982) Questioning at home and at school: a comparative study, in G. Spindler (ed.) *Doing the Ethnography of Schooling*, New York:

Holt, Rinehart & Winston. Interesting ethnographic studies of children in classrooms and playgrounds appear in the Routledge & Kegan Paul series, Social Worlds of Childhood: Davies, B. (1982) *Life in the Classroom and Playground: the Accounts of Primary School Children*, London: Routledge & Kegan Paul; and Sluckin, A. (1981) *Growing up in the Playground: the Social Development of Children*, London: Routledge & Kegan Paul. See also: Troyna, B. and Hatcher, R. (1992) *Racism in Children's Lives: a Study in Mainly-White Primary Schools*, London: Routledge; Woods, P. and Hammersley, M. (1993) *Gender and Ethnicity in Schools: Ethnographic Accounts*, London: Routledge.

6   For further similar examples see: Bates, I. and Dutson, J. (1995) A Bermuda triangle? A case study of the disappearance of competence-based vocational training policy in the context of practice, *British Journal of Education and Work*, 8 (2), 41–59; Ziegahn, L. and Hinchman, K. A. (1999) Liberation or reproduction: explaining meaning in college tutors' adult literacy tutoring, *International Journal of Qualitative Studies in Education*, 12 (1), 85–101.

7   Menzel, H. (1978) Meaning – who needs it? in M. Brenner, P. Marsh and M. Brenner (eds) *The Social Context of Method*, London: Croom Helm. For a further discussion of the problem, see Gilbert, G. N. (1983) Accounts and those accounts called actions, in G. N. Gilbert and P. Abell, *Accounts and Action*, Aldershot: Gower.

8   The discussion at this point draws on that in Bailey, K. D. (1978) *Methods of Social Research*, London: Collier-Macmillan, 261.

9   See, for example: Hargreaves, D. H., Hester, S. K. and Mellor, F. J. (1975) *Deviance in Classrooms*, London: Routledge & Kegan Paul; Marsh, P., Rosser, E. and Harré, R. (1978) *The Rules of Disorder*, London: Routledge & Kegan Paul.

17   OBSERVATION

1   For an example of time-sampling see: Childs, G. (1997) A concurrent validity study of teachers' ratings for nominated 'problem' children, *British Journal of Educational Psychology*, 67, 457–74.

2   For an example of critical incidents see: Tripp, D. (1994) Teachers' lives, critical incidents and professional practice, *International Journal of Qualitative Studies in Education*, 7 (1) 65–72.

3   For an example of an observational study see: Sideris, G. (1998) Direct classroom observation, *Research in Education*, 59, 19–28.

18   TESTS

1   For an example of a test-based piece of research see: Bielinski, J. and Davison, M. L. (1998) Gender differences by item difficulty interactions in multiple choice mathematics items, *American Educational Research Journal*, 35 (3), 455–76.

19   PERSONAL CONSTRUCTS

1   See also University of Manchester Regional Computing Centre (UMRCC) (1981) *GAP: Grid Analysis Package*, Manchester: University of Manchester Regional Computing Centre.

2   See also: Slater, P. (1977) *The Measurement of Interpersonal Space*, Vol. 2, Chichester: Wiley.

3   See also the following applications of personal construct theory to research on teachers and teacher groups: Cole, A. L. (1991) Personal theories of teaching: development in the formative years, *Alberta Journal of Educational Research*, 37 (2), 119–32; Corporal, A. H. (1991) Repertory grid research into cognitions of prospective primary school teachers, *Teaching and Teacher Education*, 36, 315–29; Lehrer, R. and Franke, M. L. (1992) Applying personal construct psychology to the study of teachers' knowledge of fractions, *Journal for Research in Mathematical Education*, 23 (3), 223–41; Shapiro, B. L. (1990) A collaborative approach to help novice science teachers reflect on changes in their construction of the role of the science teacher, *Alberta Journal of Educational Research*, 36 (3), 203–22; Shaw, E. L. (1992) The influence of methods instruction on the beliefs of preservice elementary and secondary science teachers: preliminary comparative analyses, *School Science and Mathematics*, 92, 14–22.

4   See also Yorke, D. M. (1985) Indexes of stability in repertory grids: a small-scale comparison, *British Educational Research Journal*, 11(3), 221–5.

5   See also Pope, M. L. and Keen, T. R. (1981) *Personal Construct Psychology and Education*, London: Academic Press, especially Chapters 8 and 9; Shaw, M. L. G. (ed.) (1981) *Recent Advances in Personal Construct Technology*, London: Academic Press; Thomas, L. F. and Harri-Augstein, E. S. (1992) *Self-organized Learning*, London: Routledge.

6   For an example of personal constructs in educational research see: Derry, S. J. and Potts, M. K. (1998) How tutors model students: a study of personal constructs in adaptive tutoring, *American Educational Research Journal*, 35 (1), 65–99.

20 MULTI-DIMENSIONAL MEASUREMENT

1   For a fuller discussion of clustering methods, see Everitt, B. S. (1974) *Cluster Analysis*, London: Heinemann Educational Books.

2   See also Bennett, S. N. and Jordan, J. (1975) A typology of teaching styles in primary schools, *British Journal of Educational Psychology*, 45, 20–8. Powerful cluster programmes such as SAS, Version 5 Edition, (1985) SAS Institute Inc., Cary, NC, USA, can throw new light on data and reveal dimensions previously obscure. Using SAS in an analysis of the perceptions of some 686 teachers about their working lives, Poppleton and Riseborough (1990) identified four clusters of teachers with distinctively different orientations towards the pursuit of a career. See Poppleton, P. and Riseborough, G. (1990) Teaching in the mid–1980s: the centrality of work in secondary teachers' lives, *British Educational Research Journal*, 16 (2), 105–24.

3   Gray, J. and Satterly, D. (1976) A chapter of errors: teaching styles and pupil progress in retrospect, *Educational Research*, 19, 45–56; Aitken, M., Bennett, S. N. and Hesketh, J. (1981) Teaching styles and pupil progress: a reanalysis, *British Journal of Educational Psychology*, 51 (2), 170–86; Aitken, M., Anderson, D. and Hinde, J. (1981) Statistical modelling of data on teaching styles, *Journal of the Royal Statistical Society*, 144 (4), 419–61; Prais, S. J. (1983) Formal and informal teaching: a further reconsideration of Professor Bennett's statistics, *Journal of the Royal Statistical Society*, 146 (2), 163–9; Chatfield, C. (1985) The initial examination of data, *Journal of the Royal Statistical Society*, 148 (3), 214–53.

4   Self-serving bias refers to our propensity to accept responsibility for our successes, but to deny responsibility for our failures.

5   For examples of research conducted using factor analysis see: Andrews, P. and Hatch, G. (1999) A new look at secondary teachers' conception of mathematics and its teaching, *British Educational Research Journal*, 25 (2), 203–23; McEneaney, J. E. and Sheridan, E. M. (1996) A survey-based component for programme assessment in undergraduate pre-service teacher education, *Research in Education*, 55, 49–61; Prosser, M. and Trigwell, K. (1997) Relations between perceptions of the teaching environment and approaches to teaching, *British Journal of Educational Psychology*, 67, 25–35; Valadines, N. (1999) Formal reasoning performance of higher secondary school students: theoretical and educational implications, *European Journal of Psychology of Education*, 14 (1), 109–17; Vermunt, J. D. (1998) The regulation of constructive learning processes, *British Journal of Educational Psychology*, 68, 149–71. For an example of research using cluster analysis see: Seifert, T. L. (1997) Academic goals and emotions: results of a structural equation model and a cluster analysis, *British Journal of Educational Psychology*, 67, 323–38. For examples of research using correlation co-efficients see: Goossens, L., Marcoen, A., van Hees, S. and van de Woestlijne, O. (1998) Attachment style and loneliness in adolescence, *European Journal of Psychology of Education*, 13 (4), 529–42; Lamb, S., Bibby, P., Wood, D. and Leyden, G. (1997) Communication skills, educational achievement and biographic characteristics of children with moderate learning difficulties, *European Journal of Psychology of Education*, 12 (4), 401–14; Okagaki, L. and Frensch, P. A. (1998) Parenting and school achievement: a multiethnic perspective, *American Educational Research Journal*, 35 (1), 123–44.

6   Examples of multilevel modelling in educational research can be seen in: Bell, J. F. (1996) Question choice in English literature examination, *Oxford Review of Education*, 23 (4), 447–58; Croxford, L. (1997) Participation in science subjects: the effect of the Scottish curriculum framework, *Research Papers in Education*, 12 (1) 69–89; Fitz-Gibbon, C. T. (1991) Multilevel modelling in an indicator system, in S. W. Raudenbush and J. D. Willms (eds) *Schools, Classrooms and Pupils. International Studies of Schooling from a Multilevel Perspective*, San Diego, CA: Academic Press Inc.; Hill, P. W. and Rowe, K. J. (1996) Multilevel modelling in school effectiveness research, *School Effectiveness and School Improvement*, 7 (1), 1–34; Kivulu, J. M. and Rogers, W. T. (1998) A multilevel analysis of cultural experience and gender influences on causal attributions to perceived performance in mathematics, *British Journal of Educational Psychology*, 68, 25–37; McNiece, R. and Jolliffe, F. (1998) An investigation into regional differences in educational performance in the National Child Development Study, *Educational Research*, 40 (1), 13–30; Mooij, T. (1998) Pupil–class determinants of aggressive and victim behaviour in pupils, *British Journal of Educational Psychology*, 68, 373–85; Musch, J. and Bröder, A. (1999) Test anxiety versus academic skills: a comparison of two alternative models for predicting performance in a statistics exam, *British Journal of Educational Psychology*, 69, 105–16; Schagen, I. and Sainsbury, M. (1996) Multilevel analysis of the key stage 1 national curriculum data in 1995, *Oxford Review of Education*, 22 (3), 265–72; Thomas, S., Sammons, P., Mortimore, P. and Smees, R. (1997) Differential secondary school effectiveness:

comparing the performance of different pupil groups, *British Educational Research Journal*, 23 (4), 351–69.

21 ROLE-PLAYING

1   For a recent account of a wide range of role-play applications in psychotherapy, see Holmes, P. and Karp, M. (1991) *Psychodrama: Inspiration and Technique*, London: Routledge.
2   However, this is not what advocates of role-play as an alternative to deception generally mean by role-play. See Hamilton (1976) and Forward, Canter and Kirsch (1976) for a fuller discussion.
3   For further sound advice see also, Bolton, G. and Heathcote, D. (1999) *So You Want To Use Role-Play? A New Approach To Planning*, Stoke: Trentham Books.

22 RECENT DEVELOPMENTS

1   For an example of research using Geographical Information Systems see: Higgs, G., Webster, C. J. and White, S. D. (1997) The use of geographical information systems in assessing spatial and socio-economic impacts of parental choice, *Research Papers in Education*, 12 (1) 27–48; Jones, D. and Vann, P. (1994) *Informing School Decisions: GIS in Education*, Luton: Local Government Management Board.

Bibliography

Acker, S. (1989) *Teachers, Gender and Careers*. Lewes: Falmer Press.

Acker, S. (1990) Teachers' culture in an English primary school: continuity and change. *British Journal of Sociology of Education*, 11 (3), 257–73.

Acton, H. B. (1975) Positivism. In J. O. Urmson (ed.) *The Concise Encyclopedia of Western Philosophy*. London: Hutchinson, 253–6.

Adams-Webber, J. R. (1970) Elicited versus provided constructs in repertory grid technique: a review. *British Journal of Medical Psychology*, 43, 349–54.

Adelman, C., Kemmis, S. and Jenkins, D. (1980) Rethinking case study: notes from the Second Cambridge Conference. In H. Simons (ed.) *Towards a Science of the Singular*. Centre for Applied Research in Education, University of East Anglia, 45–61.

Adeyemi, M. B. (1992) The effects of a social studies course on the philosophical orientations of history and geography graduate students in Botswana. *Educational Studies*, 18 (2), 235–44.

Adler, P. A. and Adler, P. (1994) Observational techniques. In N. K. Denzin and Y. S. Lincoln (eds) *Handbook of Qualitative Research*. London: Sage, 377–92.

Agar, M. (1993) Speaking of ethnography. Cited in D. Silverman, *Interpreting Qualitative Data*. London: Sage Publications.

Aitkin, M., Anderson, D. and Hinde, J. (1981) Statistical modelling of data on teaching styles. *Journal of the Royal Statistical Society*, 144 (4), 419–61.

Aitkin, M., Bennett, S. N. and Hesketh, J. (1981) Teaching styles and pupil progress: a reanalysis. *British Journal of Educational Psychology*, 51 (2), 170–86.

Alban-Metcalf, R. J. (1997) Repertory Grid Technique. In J. P. Keeves (ed.) *Educational Research, Methodology and Measurement: an International Handbook* (second edition). Oxford: Elsevier Science Ltd., 315–18.

Alexander, P. C. and Neimeyer, G. J. (1989) Constructivism and family therapy. *International Journal of Personal Construct Psychology*, 2 (2), 111–21.

Alfassi, M. (1998) Reading for meaning: the efficacy of reciprocal teaching in fostering reading comprehension in high school students in remedial reading classes. *American Educational Research Journal*, 35 (2), 309–22.

Alkin, M. C., Daillak, R. and White, P. (1991) Does evaluation make a difference? In D. S. Anderson and B. J. Biddle (eds) *Knowledge for Policy: Improving Education through Research*. London: Falmer, 268–75.

Allison, P. (1984) Event history analysis: regression for longitudinal event data. *Sage University Papers: Quantitative Applications in the Social Sciences*. No. 46. Beverly Hills: Sage Publications.

Altricher, H. and Gstettner, P. (1993) Action research: a closed chapter in the history of German social science? *Educational Action Research*, 1 (3), 329–60.

American Psychological Association (1973) *Ethical Principles in the Conduct of Research with Human Subjects*. Ad Hoc Committee on Ethical Standards in Psychological Research. Washington, DC.

American Psychological Association (1974) *Standards for Educational and Psychological Testing*. Washington, DC. American Psychological Association.

American Psychological Association (1994) *Publication Manual of the American Psychological Association* (fourth edition). Washington, DC: B. Thompson.

Anderson, D. S. and Biddle, B. J. (eds) (1991) *Knowledge for Policy: Improving Education through Research*. London: Falmer.

Andrews, P. and Hatch, G. (1999) A new look at secondary teachers' conception of mathematics and its teaching. *British Educational Research Journal*, 25 (2), 203–23.

Angoff, W. H. (1971) Scales, norms, and equivalent scores. In R. L. Thorndike (ed.) *Educational Measurement* (second edition). Washington, DC: American Council on Education, 508–600.

Antonsen, E. A. (1988) Treatment of a boy of twelve: help with handwriting, play therapy and discussion of problems. *Journal of Education Therapy*, 2 (1), 2–32.

Apple, M. (1990) *Ideology and Curriculum* (second edition). London: Routledge & Kegan Paul.

Applebee, A. N. (1976) The development of children's responses to repertory grids. *British Journal of Social and Clinical Psychology*, 15, 101–2.

Argyle, M. (1978) Discussion chapter: an appraisal of the new approach to the study of social behaviour. In M. Brenner, P. Marsh and M. Brenner (eds), *The Social Contexts of Method*. London: Croom Helm, 237–55.

Argyris, C. (1975) Dangers in applying results from experimental social psychology. *American Psychologist*, 30, 469–85.

Argyris, C. (1990) *Overcoming Organisational Defenses: Facilitating Organisational Learning*. Boston: Allyn and Bacon.

Arnold, P. and Atkins, J. (1991) The social and emotional adjustment of hearing-impaired children integrated in primary schools. *Educational Researcher*, 33 (3), 223–8.

Aronowitz, S. and Giroux, H. (1986) *Education Under Siege*. London: Routledge & Kegan Paul.

Aronson, E. and Carlsmith, J. M. (1969) Experimentation in social psychology. In G. Lindzey and E. Aronson (eds) *The Handbook of Social Psychology*, Vol. 2. Reading, MA: Addison-Wesley, 1–79.

Aronson, E., Ellsworth, P. C., Carlsmith, J. M. and Gonzalez, M. H. (1990) *Methods of Research in Social Psychology*. New York: McGraw-Hill.

Ary, D., Jacobs, L. C. and Razavieh, A. (1972) *Introduction to Research in Education*. New York: Holt, Rinehart & Winston.

Ashmore, M. (1989) *The Reflexive Thesis: Wrighting Sociology of Scientific Knowledge*. Chicago: University of Chicago Press.

Ashton, E. (1994) Managing change in Further Education: some perspectives of college principals. Unpublished Ph.D. dissertation, Loughborough University of Technology.

Atkinson, R. (1998) *The Life Interview*. London: Sage Publications.

Austin, J. L. (1962) *How We Do Things with Words*. Oxford: Oxford University Press.

Bailey, K. D. (1978) *Methods of Social Research*. Basingstoke: Collier-Macmillan.

Ball, S. J. (1981) *Beachside Comprehensive*. Cambridge: Cambridge University Press.

Ball, S. J. (1985) School politics, teachers' careers and educational change: a case study of becoming a comprehensive school. In L. Barton and S. Walker (eds) *Education and Social Change*. Beckenham: Croom Helm, 29–61.

Ball, S. J. (1990) *Politics and Policy-Making in Education*. London: Routledge.

Ball, S. J. (1994a) *Education Reform: a Critical and Post-structuralist Approach*. Buckingham: Open University Press.

Ball, S. J. (1994b) Political interviews and the politics of interviewing. In G. Walford (ed.) *Researching the Powerful in Education*. London: UCL Press, 96–115.

Bannister, D. (ed.) (1970) *Perspectives in Personal Construct Theory*. London: Academic Press.

Bannister, D. and Mair, J. M. M. (1968) *The Evaluation of Personal Constructs*. London: Academic Press.

Banuazizi, A. and Movahedi, A. (1975) Interpersonal dynamics in a simulated prison: a methodological analysis. *American Psychologist*, 30, 152–60.

Barker, C. D. and Johnson, G. (1998) Interview talk as professional practice. *Language and Education*, 12 (4), 229–42.

Barratt, P. E. H. (1971) *Bases of Psychological Methods*. Australasia Pty. Ltd., Queensland, Australia: Wiley & Sons.

Barr Greenfield, T. (1975) Theory about organisations: a new perspective and its implications for schools. In M. G. Hughes (ed.) *Administering Education: International Challenge*. London: Athlone Press, 71–99.

Bates, I. and Dutson, J. (1995) A Bermuda triangle? A case study of the disappearance of competence-based vocational training policy in the context of practice. *British Journal of Education and Work*, 8 (2), 41–59.

Batteson, C. and Ball, S. J. (1995) Autobiographies and interviews as means of 'access' to elite policy making in education. *British Journal of Educational Studies*, 43 (2), 201–16.

Bauman, R. (1986) *Story, Performance and Event*. Cambridge: Cambridge University Press.

Baumrind, D. (1964) Some thoughts on ethics of research. *American Psychologist*, 19, 421–3.

Beck, R. N. (1979) *Handbook in Social Philosophy*. New York: Macmillan.

Becker, H. (1970) *Sociological Work*. Chicago: Aldane.

Becker, H. and Geer, B. (1960) Participant observation: the analysis of qualitative field data. In R. Adams and J. Preiss (eds) *Human Organization Research: Field Relations and Techniques*. Homewood, IL: Dorsey.

Beer, M., Eisenstadt, R. A. and Spector, B. (1990) Why change programs don't produce change. *Harvard Business Review*, Nov.–Dec. (68), 158–66.

Belbin, R. M. (1981) *Management Teams: Why They Succeed or Fail*. London: Heinemann.

Bell, J. (1991) *Doing Your Research Project*. Milton Keynes: Open University Press.

Bell, J. (1996) Question choice in English literature examination. *Oxford Review of Education*, 23 (4), 447–58.

Belson, W. A. (1975) *Juvenile Theft: Causal Factors*. London: Harper & Row.

Belson, W. A. (1986) *Validity in Survey Research*. Aldershot: Gower.

Bennett, C. A. and Lumsdaine, A. A. (1975) *Evaluation and Experimentation*. New York: Academic Press Inc.

Bennett, S. N. (1976) *Teaching Styles and Pupil Progress*. Shepton Mallet: Open Books.

Bennett, S. N. and Jordan, J. (1975) A typology of teaching styles in primary schools. *British Journal of Educational Psychology*, 45, 20–8.

Bennett, S. N., Desforges, C. and Wilkinson, E. (1984) *The Quality of Pupil Learning Experiences*. London: Lawrence Erlbaum Associates.

Bennett, S. and Bowers, D. (1977) *An Introduction to Multivariate Techniques for Social and Behavioural Sciences*. London: Macmillan.

Ben-Peretz, M. and Kremer-Hayon, L. (1990) The content and context of professional dilemmas encountered by novice and senior teachers. *Educational Review*, 42 (1), 31–40.

Benstead, D. and Constantine, S. (1998) *The Inward Revolution*. London: Little, Brown & Co.

Berger, P. L. and Luckmann, T. (1967) *The Social Construction of Reality*. Harmondsworth: Penguin.

Bernstein, B. (1970) Education cannot compensate for society. *New Society*, February, 387, 344–57.

Bernstein, B. (1971) On the classification and framing of educational knowledge. In M. F. D. Young (ed.) *Knowledge and Control*. Basingstoke: Collier-Macmillan, 47–69.

Bernstein, B. (1974) Sociology and the sociology of education: a brief account. In J. Rex (ed.) *Approaches to Sociology: an Introduction to Major Trends in British Sociology*. London: Routledge & Kegan Paul, 145–59.

Bernstein, R. J. (1976) *The Restructuring of Social and Political Theory*. Oxford: Blackwell.

Bernstein, R. J. (1983) *Beyond Objectivism and Relativism*. Oxford: Blackwell.

Best, J. W. (1970) *Research in Education*. Englewood Cliffs, NJ: Prentice-Hall.

Beynon, J. (1985a) Historical change and career histories in a comprehensive school. In S. J. Ball and I. F. Goodson (eds) *Teachers' Lives and Careers*. Lewes: Falmer Press, 158–79.

Beynon, J. (1985b) *Initial Encounters in the Secondary School*. Lewes: Falmer Press.

Bhadwal, S. C. and Panda, P. K. (1991) The effects of a package of some curricular strategies on the study habits of rural primary school students: a year long study. *Educational Studies*, 17 (3), 261–72.

Biddle, B. J. and Anderson, D. S. (1991) Social research and educational change. In D. S. Anderson and B. J. Biddle (eds) *Knowledge for Policy: Improving Education through Research*. London: Falmer, 1–20.

Bielinski, J. and Davison, M. L. (1998) Gender differences by item difficulty interactions in multiple choice mathematics items. *American Educational Research Journal*, 35 (3), 455–76.

Bijstra, J. O. and Jackson, S. (1998) Social skills training with early adolescents: effects on social skills, well-being, self-esteem and coping. *European Journal of Psychology of Education*, 13 (4), 569–83.

Binet, A. (1905) Methode nouvelle pour le diagnostic de l'intelligence des anormaux. Cited in G. de Landsheere (1997) History of educational research. In J. P. Keeves (ed.) *Educational Research, Methodology, and Measurement: an International Handbook* (second edition). Oxford: Elsevier Science Ltd., 8–16.

Black, D. R. and Scott, W. A. H. (1997) Factors affecting the employment of teachers returning to the United Kingdom after teaching abroad. *Educational Research*, 39 (1), 37–63.

Blalock, H. M. (1979) *Social Statistics* (second edition). Tokyo: McGraw-Hill-Kogakusha.

Blalock, H. M. (1991) Dilemmas of social research.

In D. S. Anderson and B. J. Biddle (eds) *Knowledge for Policy: Improving Education through Research.* London: Falmer, 60–9.

Blatchford, P. (1992) Children's attitudes to work at 11 years. *Educational Studies*, 18 (1), 107–18.

Blease, D. and Cohen, L. (1990) *Coping with Computers: An Ethnographic Study in Primary Classrooms.* London: Paul Chapman Publishing.

Bliss, J., Monk, M. and Ogborn, J. (1983) *Qualitative Data Analysis for Educational Research.* London: Croom Helm.

Bloom, B. (ed.) (1956) *Taxonomy of Educational Objectives: Handbook 1: Cognitive Domain.* London: Longman.

Bloor, M. (1978) On the analysis of observational data: a discussion of the worth and uses of induction techniques and respondent validation. *Sociology*, 12 (3), 545–52.

Blumenfeld-Jones, D. (1995) Fidelity as a criterion for practising and evaluating narrative inquiry. *International Journal of Qualitative Studies in Education*, 8 (1), 25–33.

Blumer, H. (1969) *Symbolic Interactionism.* Englewood Cliffs, NJ: Prentice-Hall.

Boas, F. (1943) Recent anthropology. *Science*, 98, 311–14.

Bogdan, R. G. and Biklen, S. K. (1992) *Qualitative Research for Education* (second edition). Boston, MA: Allyn & Bacon.

Bolton, G. and Heathcote, D. (1999) *So You Want to Use Role-Play? A New Approach to Planning.* Stoke: Trentham Books.

Borg, M. G. (1998) Secondary school teachers' perceptions of pupils' undesirable behaviours. *British Journal of Educational Psychology*, 68, 67–79.

Borg, W. R. (1963) *Educational Research: an Introduction.* London: Longman.

Borg, W. R. (1981) *Applying Educational Research: a Practical Guide for Teachers.* New York: Longman.

Borg, W. R. and Gall, M. D. (1979) *Educational Research: an Introduction* (third edition). London: Longman.

Borg, W. R. and Gall, M. D. (1996) *Educational Research: an Introduction* (sixth edition). New York: Longman.

Boring, E. G. (1953) The role of theory in experimental psychology. *American Journal of Psychology*, 66, 169–84.

Borkowsky, F. T. (1970) The relationship of work quality in undergraduate music curricula to effectiveness in instrumental music teaching in the public schools. *Journal of Experimental Education*, 39, 14–19.

Boruch, R. F. (1997) *Randomized Experiments for Planning and Evaluation.* Applied social research methods series, Vol. 44. Thousand Oaks, CA: Sage Publications.

Boulton, M. J. (1992) Participation in playground activities at middle school. *Education Research*, 34 (3), 167–82.

Boulton, M. J. (1997) Teachers' views on bullying: definitions, attitudes and abilities to cope. *British Journal of Educational Psychology*, 67, 223–33.

Bowe, R., Ball, S. J. and Gold, A. (1992) *Reforming Education and Changing Schools.* London: Routledge.

Bowles, S. and Gintis, H. (1976) *Schooling in Capitalist America.* London: Routledge & Kegan Paul.

Boyd-Barrett, D. and Scanlon, E. (1991) *Computers and Learning.* Wokingham: Addison-Wesley Publishing Co.

Bracht, G. H. and Glass, G. V. (1968) The external validity of experiments. *American Educational Research Journal*, 4 (5), 437–74.

Bradburn, N. M. and Berlew, D. E. (1961) *Economic Development and Cultural Change.* Chicago: University of Chicago Press.

Breakwell, G. (1990) *Interviewing.* London: Routledge/British Psychological Society.

Brenner, M., Brown, J. and Canter, D. (1985) *The Research Interview.* London: Academic Press Inc.

Broad, W. and Wade, N. (1983) *Betrayers of Truth: Fraud and Deceit in the Halls of Science.* New York: Century.

Brock-Utne, B. (1996) Reliability and validity in qualitative research within education in Africa. *International Review of Education*, 42 (6), 605–21.

Bromley, D. B. (1986) *The Case Study Method in Psychology and Related Disciplines.* Chichester: John Wiley.

Brown, J. and Sime, J. D. (1977) Accounts as general methodology. Paper presented to the British Psychological Society Conference. University of Exeter.

Brown, J. and Sime, J. D. (1981) A methodology of accounts. In M. Brenner (ed.) *Social Method and Social Life.* London: Academic Press, 159–88.

Brown, J., Collins, A. and Duguid, P. (1989) Situated cognition and the culture of learning. *Educational Researcher*, 32, 32–42.

Brown, R. and Herrnstein, R. J. (1975) *Psychology.* London: Methuen.

Bruner, J. (1986) *Actual Minds, Possible Worlds.* Cambridge, MA: Harvard University Press.

Bryant, P., Devine, M., Ledward, A. and Nunes, T. (1997) Spelling with apostrophes and understanding possession. *British Journal of Educational Psychology*, 67, 91–110.

Buhler, C. and Allen, M. (1972) *Introduction to Humanistic Psychology.* Monterey, California: Brooks/Cole.

Bulmer, M. (ed.) (1982) *Social Research Ethics.* London and Basingstoke: Macmillan.

Burgess, R. G. (ed.) (1982) *Field Research: A Sourcebook and Field Manual.* London: George Allen & Unwin.

Burgess, R. G. (1983) *Experiencing Comprehensive Education.* London: Methuen.

Burgess, R. G. (1985a) Conversations with a purpose? The ethnographic interview in educational research. Paper presented at the British Educational Research Association Annual Conference, Sheffield.

Burgess, R. G. (1985b) *Issues in Educational Research: Qualitative Methods.* Lewes: Falmer.

Burgess, R. G. (ed.) (1989a) *The Ethics of Educational Research.* Lewes: Falmer Press.

Burgess, R. G. (1989b) Grey areas: ethical dilemmas in educational ethnography. In R. G. Burgess (ed.) *The Ethics of Educational Research.* Lewes: Falmer Press, 60–76.

Burgess, R. G. (1993) Biting the hand that feeds you? Educational research for policy and practice. In R. G. Burgess (ed.) *Educational Research and Evaluation for Policy and Practice.* London: Falmer, 1–18.

Burke, M., Noller, P. and Caird, D. (1992) Transition from probationer to educator: a repertory grid analysis. *International Journal of Personal Construct Psychology*, 5 (2), 159–82.

Burrell, G. and Morgan, G. (1979) *Sociological Paradigms and Organizational Analysis.* London: Heinemann Educational Books.

Busato, V. V., Prins, F. J., Elshant, J. J. and Hamaker, C. (1998) Learning styles: a cross-sectional and longitudinal study in higher education. *British Journal of Educational Psychology*, 68, 427–41.

Butler, N. R. and Golding, J. (1986) *From Birth to Five.* Oxford: Pergamon Press.

Butzkamm, W. (1998) Code-switching in a bilingual history lesson: the mother tongue as a conversational lubricant. *Bilingual Education and Bilingualism*, 1 (2): 81–99.

Calder, J. (1979) Introduction to applied sampling. *Research Methods in Education and the Social Sciences.* Block 3, part 4, DE304. Milton Keynes: Open University Press.

Callawaert, S. (1999) Philosophy of Education, Frankfurt critical theory, and the sociology of Pierre Bourdieu. In T. Popkewitz and L. Fendler (eds) *Critical Theories in Education: Changing Terrains of Knowledge and Politics.* London: Routledge, 117–44.

Campbell, D. T. and Fiske, D. W. (1959) Convergent and discriminant validation by the multitrait–multimethod matrix, *Psychological Bulletin*, 56, 81–105.

Campbell, D. T. and Stanley, J. (1963) Experimental and quasi-experimental designs for research on teaching. In N. Gage (ed.) *Handbook of Research on Teaching.* Chicago: Rand McNally, 171–246.

Campbell, D. T., Sanderson, R. E. and Laverty, S. G. (1964) Characteristics of a conditioned response in human subjects during extinction trials following a single traumatic conditioning trial. *Journal of Abnormal and Social Psychology*, 68, 627–39.

Cannell, C. F. and Kahn, R. L. (1968) Interviewing. In G. Lindzey and A. Aronson (eds) *The Handbook of Social Psychology, Vol. 2: Research Methods.* New York: Addison Wesley, 526–95.

Caplan, N. (1991) The use of social research knowledge at the national level. In D. S. Anderson and B. J. Biddle (eds) *Knowledge for Policy: Improving Education through Research.* London: Falmer, 193–202.

Carr, W, and Kemmis, S. (1986) *Becoming Critical.* Lewes: Falmer.

Carroll, S. and Walford, G. (1997) Parents' responses to the school quasi-market. *Research Papers in Education*, 12 (1), 3–26.

Carspecken, P. F. (1996) *Critical Ethnography in Educational Research.* London: Routledge.

Carspecken, P. F. and Apple, M. (1992) Critical qualitative research: theory, methodology, and practice. In M. LeCompte, W. L. Millroy and J. Preissle (eds) *The Handbook of Qualitative Research in Education.* London: Academic Press Ltd., 507–53.

Cartwright, D. (1991) Basic and applied social psychology. In D. S. Anderson and B. J. Biddle (eds) *Knowledge for Policy: Improving Education through Research.* London: Falmer, 23–31.

Carver, R. P. (1978) The case against significance testing. *Harvard Educational Review*, 48 (3), 378–99.

Cassell, J. (1993) The relationship of observer to observed when studying up. Cited in R. M. Lee, *Doing Research on Sensitive Topics.* London: Sage Publications.

Cavan, S. (1977) Review of J. D. Douglas's (1976) 'Investigative Social Review: Individual and Team Field Research'. *The American Journal of Sociology*, 83 (3), 809–11.

Central Advisory Council for Education (1967) *Children and their Primary Schools*. London: HMSO.

Chalmers, A. F. (1982) *What Is This Thing Called Science?* (second edition). Milton Keynes: Open University Press.

Chapin, F. S. (1947) *Experimental Designs in Sociological Research*. New York: Harper & Row.

Chatfield, C. (1985) The initial examination of data. *Journal of the Royal Statistical Society*, 148 (3), 214–53.

Chelinsky, E. and Mulhauser, F. (1993) Educational evaluations for the US Congress: some reflections on recent experience. In R. G. Burgess (ed.) *Educational Research and Evaluation for Policy and Practice*. London: Falmer, 44–60.

Chetwynd, S. J. (1974) *Outline of the analyses available with G.A.P., the Grid Analysis Package*. London: St George's Hospital.

Child, D. (1970) *The Essentials of Factor Analysis*. New York: Holt, Rinehart & Winston.

Childs, G. (1997) A concurrent validity study of teachers' ratings for nominated 'problem' children. *British Journal of Educational Psychology*, 67, 457–74.

Chomsky, N. (1959) Review of Skinner's *Verbal Behaviour*. In *Language*, 35 (1), 26–58.

Cicognani, C. (1998) Parents' educational styles and adolescent autonomy. *European Journal of Psychology of Education*, 13 (4), 485–502.

Cicourel, A. V. (1964) *Method and Measurement in Sociology*. New York: The Free Press.

Claxton, G. (1981) *Wholly Human*. London: Routledge & Kegan Paul.

Cline, T. and Ertubney, C. (1997) The impact of gender on primary teachers' evaluations of children's difficulties in school. *British Journal of Educational Psychology*, 67, 447–56.

Cline, T., Proto, A., Raval, P. D. and Paolo T. (1998) The effects of brief exposure and of classroom teaching on attitudes children express towards facial disfigurement in peers. *Educational Research*, 40 (1), 55–68.

Cochrane, A. L. (1972) *Effectiveness and Efficiency: Random Reflections on Health Services*. London: Nuffield Provincial Hospitals Trust.

Cogan, J. J. and Derricot, R. (eds) (1998) *Citizenship for the 21st Century*. London: Kogan Page.

Cohen, D. K. and Garet, M. S. (1991) Reforming educational policy with applied social research. In D. S. Anderson and B. J. Biddle (eds) *Knowledge for Policy: Improving Education through Research*. London: Falmer, 123–40.

Cohen, L. (1977) *Educational Research in Classrooms and Schools: a Manual of Materials and Methods*. London: Harper & Row.

Cohen, L. (1993) *Racism Awareness Materials in Initial Teacher Training*. Report to the Leverhulme Trust, 11–19 New Fetter Lane, London, EC4A 1NR.

Cohen, L. and Holliday, M. (1979) *Statistics for Education and Physical Education*. London: Harper & Row.

Cohen, L. and Holliday, M. (1982) *Statistics for Social Scientists*. London: Harper & Row.

Cohen, L. and Holliday, M. (1996) *Practical Statistics for Students*. London: Paul Chapman Publishing Ltd.

Cohen, L. and Manion, L. (1981) *Perspectives on Classrooms and Schools*. Eastbourne: Holt, Rinehart & Winston.

Cohen, L. and Manion, L. (1994) *Research Methods in Education* (fourth edition). London: Routledge.

Cohen, L., Manion, L. and Morrison, K. R. B. (1996) *A Guide to Teaching Practice* (fourth edition). London: Routledge.

Cohen, M. R. and Nagel, E. (1961) *An Introduction to Logic and Scientific Method*. London: Routledge & Kegan Paul.

Cohen, P. A., Kulik, J. A. and Kulik, C. L. (1982) Educational outcomes of tutoring: a meta-analysis of findings. *American Educational Research Journal*, 19 (2), 237–48.

Cole, A. L. (1991) Personal theories of teaching: development in the formative years, *Alberta Journal of Educational Research*, 37 (2), 119–32.

Coleman, J. S. (1991) Social policy research and societal decision-making. In D. S. Anderson and B. J. Biddle (eds) *Knowledge for Policy: Improving Education through Research*. London: Falmer, 113–22.

Collins, J. S. and Duguid, P. (1989) Situated cognition and the culture of learning. *Educational Researcher*, 32, 32–42.

Collins, L. (ed.) (1976) *The Use of Models in the Social Sciences*. London: Tavistock Publications.

Connell, R. W., Ashenden, D. J., Kessler, S. and Doswett, G. W. (1996) Making the difference: schools, families and social division. Cited in B. Limerick, T. Burgess-Limerick, and M. Grace, The politics of interviewing: power relations and accepting the gift. *International Journal of Qualitative Studies in Education*, 9 (4), 449–60.

Connelly, F. M. and Clandinin, D. J. (1999) Narrative inquiry. In J. P. Keeves and G. Lakomski (eds) *Issues in Educational Research* (second edition). Oxford: Elsevier Science Ltd, 132–40.

Cook, T. D. (1991) Postpositivist criticisms, reform associations, and uncertainties about social research. In D. S. Anderson and B. J. Biddle (eds) *Knowledge for Policy: Improving Education through Research*. London: Falmer, 43–59.

Cook, T. D., Cooper, H., Cordray, D. S., Hartmann, H., Hedges, L. V., Light, R. J., Louis, T. A., Mosteller, F. (1992) *Meta-analysis for Explanation*. New York: Russell Sage Foundation.

Cooley, C. H. (1902) *Human Nature and the Social Order*. New York: Charles Scribner.

Cooper, H. M. and Rosenthal, R. (1980) Statistical versus traditional procedures for summarizing research findings. *Psychological Bulletin*, 87, 442–9.

Corey, S. M. (1949) Action research, fundamental research and educational practices. *Teachers College Record*, 50, 509–14.

Corey, S. M. (1953) *Action Research to Improve School Practice*. New York: Teachers College, Columbia University.

Corporal, A. H. (1991) Repertory grid research into cognitions of prospective primary school teachers. *Teaching and Teacher Education*, 36, 315–29.

Coser, L. A. and Rosenberg, B. (1969) *Sociological Theory: a Book of Readings* (third edition). New York: Macmillan.

Cox, E. (1994) *The Fuzzy Systems Handbook: a Practitioner's Guide to Building, Using and Maintaining Fuzzy Systems*. London: Academic Press.

Coyle, A. (1995) Discourse analysis. In G. M. Breakwell, S. Hammond and C. Fife-Shaw (1995) *Research Methods in Psychology*. London: Sage Publications, 243–58.

Cresswell, M. J. and Houston, J. G.(1991) Assessment of the national curriculum – some fundamental considerations. *Educational Review*, 43 (1), 63–78.

Crocker, A. C. and Cheeseman, R. G. (1988) The ability of young children to rank themselves for academic ability. *Educational Studies*, 14 (1), 105–10.

Croll, P. (1985) *Systematic Observation*. Lewes: Falmer Press.

Cronbach, L. J. (1949) *Essentials of Psychological Testing* (first edition). New York: Harper & Row.

Cronbach, L. J. (1970) *Essentials of Psychological Testing* (third edition). New York: Harper & Row.

Crow, G. M. (1992) The principalship as a career: in need of a theory. *Educational Management and Administration*, 21 (2), 80–7.

Croxford, L. (1997) Participation in science subjects: the effect of the Scottish curriculum framework. *Research Papers in Education*, 12 (1) 69–89.

Cuff, E. G. and Payne, G. C. F. (eds) (1979) *Perspectives in Sociology*. London: George Allen & Unwin.

Cullen, K. (1997) Headteacher appraisal: a view from the inside. *Research Papers in Education*, 12 (2), 177–204.

Cunningham, G. K. (1998) *Assessment in the Classroom*. London: Falmer Press.

Cunningham, D., McMahon, H. and O'Neill, B. (1991) *Bubble Dialogue: a New Tool for Instruction and Assessment*. Language Development and Hypermedia Research Group, Faculty of Education, University of Ulster at Coleraine.

Curtis, B. (1978) Introduction to Curtis, B. and Mays, W. (eds) *Phenomenology and Education*. London: Methuen.

Daly, P. (1996) The effects of single-sex and co-educational secondary schooling on girls' achievement. *Research Papers in Education*, 11 (3), 289–306.

Daly, P. and Shuttleworth, I. (1997) Determinants of public examination entry and attainment in mathematics: evidence of gender and gender-type of school from the 1980s and 1990s in Northern Ireland. *Evaluation and Research in Education*, 11 (2), 91–101.

Data Protection Act 1984. London: HMSO.

Davenport, E. C. Jr, Davison, M. L., Kuang, H., Ding, S., Kin, S.-K. and Kwak, N. (1998) High school mathematics course-taking by gender and ethnicity. *American Educational Research Journal*, 35 (3), 497–514.

Davidson, J. (1970) *Outdoor Recreation Surveys: the Design and Use of Questionnaires for Site Surveys*. London: Countryside Commission.

Davie, R. (1972) The longitudinal approach. *Trends in Education*, 28, 8–13.

Davies, B. (1982) *Life in the Classroom and Playground: the Accounts of Primary School Children*. London: Routledge & Kegan Paul.

Davies, J. and Brember, I (1997) Monitoring reading standards in year 6: a 7-year cross-sectional study. *British Educational Research Journal*, 23 (5), 615–22.

Bibliography

Davies, J. and Brember, I. (1998) Standards in reading at key stage 1 – a cross-sectional study. *Educational Research*, 40 (2), 153–60.

Davies, L. (1984) *Pupil Power: Deviance and Gender in School*. Lewes: Falmer Press.

Delamont, S. (1976) *Interaction in the Classroom*. London: Methuen.

Delamont, S. (1981) All too familiar? A decade of classroom research. *Educational Analysis*, 3 (1), 69–83.

Delamont, S. (1992) *Fieldwork in Educational Settings: Methods, Pitfalls and Perspectives*. London: Falmer.

Delamont, S. (1998) Review of 'Understanding Social Research'. *Evaluation and Research in Education*, 12 (3), 176–7.

de Landsheere, G. (1997) History of educational research. In J. P. Keeves (ed.) *Educational Research, Methodology, and Measurement: an International Handbook* (second edition). Oxford: Elsevier Science Ltd., 8–16.

Denscombe, M. (1995) Explorations in group interviews: an evaluation of a reflexive and partisan approach. *British Educational Research Journal*, 21 (2), 131–48.

Denzin, N. K. (1970) *The Research Act in Sociology: a Theoretical Introduction to Sociological Methods*. London: Butterworth.

Denzin, N. K. (1989) *The Research Act* (third edition). Englewood Cliffs, NJ: Prentice-Hall.

Denzin, N. K. (1997) Triangulation in educational research. In J. P. Keeves (ed.) *Educational Research, Methodology and Measurement: an International Handbook* (second edition). Oxford: Elsevier Science Ltd., 318–22.

Denzin, N. K. (1999) Biographical research methods. In J. P. Keeves and G. Lakomski (eds) *Issues in Educational Research*. Oxford: Elsevier Science Ltd., 92–102.

Denzin, N. K. and Lincoln, Y. S. (eds) (1994) *Handbook of Qualitative Research*. Thousand Oaks, California: Sage Publications Inc.

Department of Education and Science (1977) *A Study of School Buildings*. Annex 1. London: HMSO.

Derry, S. J. and Potts, M. K. (1998) How tutors model students: a study of personal constructs in adaptive tutoring. *American Educational Research Journal*, 35 (1), 65–99.

Deyle, D. L., Hess, G. and LeCompte, M. L. (1992) Approaching ethical issues for qualitative researchers in education. In M. LeCompte, W. L. Millroy and J. Preissle (eds) *The Handbook of Qualitative Research in Education*. London: Academic Press Ltd., 597–642.

Diaper, G. (1990) The Hawthorne Effect: a fresh examination. *Educational Studies*, 16 (3), 261–7.

Dicker, R. and Gilbert, J. (1988) The role of the telephone in educational research. *British Educational Research Journal*, 14 (1), 65–72.

Didierjean, A. and Cauzinille-Marmèche, E. (1998) Reasoning by analogy: is it schema-mediated or case-based? *European Journal of Psychology of Education*, 13 (3), 385–98.

Diener, E. and Crandall, R. (1978) *Ethics in Social and Behavioral Research*. Chicago: University of Chicago Press.

Dietz, S. M. (1977) An analysis of programming DRL schedules in educational settings, *Behaviour Research and Therapy*, 15, 103–11.

Dobbert, M. L. and Kurth-Schai, R. (1992) Systematic ethnography: toward an evolutionary science of education and culture. In M. LeCompte, W. L. Millroy and J. Preissle (eds) *The Handbook of Qualitative Research in Education*. London: Academic Press Ltd., 93–160.

Doll, W. E. (1993) *A Post-modern Perspective on Curriculum*. New York: Teachers College Press.

Dollard, J. (1949) *Criteria for the Life History*. New Haven, CT: Yale University Press.

Dosanjh, J. S. and Ghuman, P. A. S. (1997) Asian parents and English education – 20 years on: a study of two generations. *Educational Studies*, 23 (3), 459–72.

Douglas, J. D. (1973) *Understanding Everyday Life*. London: Routledge & Kegan Paul.

Douglas, J. D. (1976) *Investigative Social Research*. Beverly Hills: Sage Publications.

Douglas, J. W. B. (1976) The use and abuse of national cohorts. In M. D. Shipman (ed.) *The Organization and Impact of Social Research*. London: Routledge & Kegan Paul, 3–21.

Dugard, P. and Todman, J. (1995) Analysis of pre-test and post-test control group designs in educational research. *Educational Psychology*, 15 (2), 181–98.

Duncan Mitchell, G. (1968) *A Dictionary of Sociology*. London: Routledge & Kegan Paul.

Dunham, R. B. and Smith, F. J. (1979) *Organizational Surveys: an Internal Assessment of Organizational Health*. Glenview, IL: Scott, Foreman and Co.

Dunn, S. and Morgan, V. (1987) Nursery and infant school play patterns: sex-related differences.

British Educational Research Journal, 13, (3), 271–81.

Dunning, G. (1993) Managing the small primary school: the problem role of the teaching head. *Educational Management and Administration*, 21 (2), 79–89.

Durkheim, E. (1956) *Education and Sociology*. Glencoe: IL.: Free Press.

Eagleton, T. (1991) *Ideology*. London: Verso.

Ebbinghaus, H. (1897) Über eine neue methode zur Prüfung geistiger Fähigkeiten. Cited in G. de Landsheere (1997) History of educational research. In J. P. Keeves (ed.) *Educational Research, Methodology, and Measurement: an International Handbook* (second edition). Oxford: Elsevier Science Ltd., 8–16.

Ebbutt, D. (1985) Educational action research: some general concerns and specific quibbles. In R. G. Burgess (ed.) (1985b) *Issues in Educational Research: Qualitative Methods*. Lewes: Falmer, 152–74.

Ebel, R. L. (1972) *Essentials of Educational Measurement*. Englewood Cliffs, NJ: Prentice-Hall.

Ebel, R. L. (1979) *Essentials of Educational Measurement* (third edition). Englewood Cliffs, NJ: Prentice-Hall.

Edwards, A. (1990) *Practitioner Research*. Study Guide No. 1. Lancaster: St Martin's College.

Edwards, A. D. (1976) *Language in Culture and Class*. London: Heinemann.

Edwards, A. D. (1980) Patterns of power and authority in classroom talk. In P. Woods (ed.) *Teacher Strategies: Explorations in the Sociology of the School*. London: Croom Helm, 237–53.

Edwards, A. D. and Westgate, D. P. G. (1987) *Investigating Classroom Talk*. Lewes: Falmer Press.

Edwards, D. (1991) Discourse and the development of understanding in the classroom. In O. Boyd-Barrett and E. Scanlon (eds) *Computers and Learning*. Wokingham: Addison-Wesley Publishing Co., 186–204.

Edwards, D. (1993) Concepts, memory and the organisation of pedagogic discourse: a case study. *International Journal of Educational Research*, 19 (3), 205–25.

Edwards, D. and Mercer, N. M. (1987) *Common Knowledge: The Development of Understanding in the Classroom*. London: Routledge & Kegan Paul.

Edwards, D. and Mercer, N. M. (1989) Reconstructing context: the conventionalization of classroom knowledge. *Discourse Processes*, 12, 91–104.

Edwards, D. and Potter, J. (1993) Language and causation: a discursive action model of description and attribution. *Psychological Review*, 100 (1), 23–41.

Eisenhart, M. A. and Howe, K. R. (1992) Validity in educational research. In M. D. LeCompte, W. L. Millroy and J. Preissle (eds) *The Handbook of Qualitative Studies in Education*. New York: Academic Press, 643–80.

Eisner, E. (1985) *The Art of Educational Evaluation*. Lewes: Falmer.

Eisner, E. (1991) *The Enlightened Eye: Qualitative Inquiry and the Enhancement of Educational Practice*. New York: Macmillan.

Ekehammar, B. and Magnusson, D. (1973) A method to study stressful situations. *Journal of Personality and Social Psychology*, 27 (2), 176–9.

Elliott, J. (1978) What is Action-Research in Schools? *Journal of Curriculum Studies* 10 (4), 355–7.

Elliott, J. (1991) *Action Research for Educational Change*. Buckingham: Open University Press.

English, H. B. and English, A. C. (1958) *A Comprehensive Dictionary of Psychological and Psychoanalytic Terms*. London: Longman.

Entwistle, N. J. and Ramsden, P. (1983) *Understanding Student Learning*. Beckenham: Croom Helm.

Epting, F. R. (1988) Journeying into the personal constructs of children. *International Journal of Personal Construct Psychology*, 1 (1), 53–61.

Epting, F. R., Suchman, D. I. and Nickeson, K. J. (1971) An evaluation of elicitation procedures for personal constructs. *British Journal of Psychology*, 62, 513–17.

Erickson, F. (1973) What makes school ethnography 'ethnographic'? *Anthropology and Education Quarterly*, 4 (2), 10–19.

Erickson, F. E. (1992) Ethnographic microanalysis of interaction. In M. LeCompte, W. L. Millroy and J. Preissle (eds) *The Handbook of Qualitative Research in Education*. London: Academic Press Ltd., 201–26.

Erikson, K. T. (1967) A comment on disguised observation in sociology. *Social Problems*, 14, 366–73.

Evans, K. M. (1978) *Planning Small Scale Research*. Windsor: NFER Publishing Co.

Everett, M. (1984) The Scottish comprehensive school: its function and the roles of its teachers with special reference to the opinions of pupils and student teachers. Unpublished Ph.D. dissertation, School of Education, University of Durham.

Everitt, B. S. (1974) *Cluster Analysis*. London: Heinemann Educational Books.

Everitt, B. S. (1977) *The Analysis of Contingency Tables*. London: Chapman & Hall.

Evetts, J. (1990) *Women in Primary Teaching*. London: Unwin Hyman.

Evetts, J. (1991) The experience of secondary headship selection: continuity and change. *Educational Studies*, 17 (3), 285–94.

Eysenck, H. (1978) An exercise in mega-silliness. *American Psychologist*, 33, 517.

Fay, B. (1987) *Critical Social Science*. New York: Cornell University Press.

Feixas, G., Marti, J. and Villegas, M. (1989) Personal construct assessment of sports teams. *International Journal of Personal Construct Psychology*, 2 (1), 49–54.

Feldt, L. S. and Brennan, R. L. (1993) Reliability. In R. Linn (ed.) *Educational Measurement*. New York: Macmillan Publishing Co., 105–46.

Fendler, L. (1999) Making trouble: prediction, agency, critical intellectuals. In T. S. Popkewitz and L. Fendler (eds) *Critical Theories in Education: Changing Terrains of Knowledge and Politics*. London: Routledge, 169–88.

Ferris, J. and Gerber, R. (1996) Mature-age students' feelings of enjoying learning in a further education context. *European Journal of Psychology of Education*, 11 (1), 79–96.

Festinger, L. and Katz, D. (1966) *Research Methods in the Behavioral Sciences*. New York: Holt, Rinehart & Winston.

Fiedler, J. (1978) *Field Research: a Manual For Logistics and Management of Scientific Studies in Natural Settings*. London: Jossey-Bass.

Field, P. A. and Morse, J. M. (1989) *Nursing Research: the Application of Qualitative Methods*. London: Chapman and Hall.

Fielding, N. G. and Fielding, J. L. (1986) *Linking Data*. Beverly Hills, CA: Sage Publications.

Finch, J. (1985) Social policy and education: problems and possibilities of using qualitative research. In R. G. Burgess (ed.) *Issues in Educational Research*. Lewes: Falmer Press, 109–28.

Finch, J. (1986) *Research and Policy: the Uses of Qualitative Methods in Social and Educational Research*. Lewes: Falmer Press.

Fine, G. A. and Sandstrom, K. L. (1988) *Knowing Children: Participant Observation with Minors*. Qualitative Research Methods Series 15. Beverly Hills: Sage Publications.

Finn, C. E. (1991) What ails education research? In D. S. Anderson and B. J. Biddle (eds) *Knowledge for Policy: Improving Education through Research*. London: Falmer, 39–42.

Finnegan, R. (1996) Using documents. In R. Sapsford and V. Jupp (1996) (eds) *Data Collection and Analysis*. London: Sage Publications and the Open University Press, 138–51.

Fisher, B., Russell, T. and McSweeney, P. (1991) Using personal constructs for course evaluation. *Journal of Further and Higher Education*, 15 (1), 44–57.

Fitz-Gibbon, C. T. (1984) Meta-analysis: an explanation. *British Educational Research Journal*, 10 (2) 135–44.

Fitz-Gibbon, C. T. (1985) The implications of meta-analysis for educational research, *British Educational Research Journal*, 11 (1), 45–9.

Fitz-Gibbon, C. T. (1991) Multilevel modelling in an indicator system. In S. W. Raudenbush and J. D. Willms (eds) *Schools, Classrooms and Pupils. International Studies of Schooling from a Multilevel Perspective*. San Diego, CA: Academic Press Inc., 67–83.

Fitz-Gibbon, C. T. (1996) *Monitoring Education: Indicators, Quality and Effectiveness*. London: Cassell.

Fitz-Gibbon, C. T. (1997) *The Value Added National Project. Final Report*. London: School Curriculum and Assessment Authority.

Fitz-Gibbon, C. T. (1999) Education: high potential not yet realized. *Public Money and Management*, Jan.–March, 19 (1), 33–9.

Flanagan, J. (1949) Critical requirements: a new approach to employee evaluation. Cited in E. C. Wragg *An Introduction to Classroom Observation*. London: Routledge.

Flanders, N. (1970) *Analyzing Teacher Behaviour*. Reading, MA: Addison-Wesley.

Flaugher, R. (1990) Item pools. In H. Wainer (ed.) *Computerized Adaptive Testing: a Primer*. New Jersey: Lawrence Erlbaum, 41–64.

Floud, R. (1979) *An Introduction to Quantitative Methods for Historians* (second edition). London: Methuen.

Fogelman, K. (ed.) (1983) *Growing Up in Great Britain: Papers from the National Child Development Study*. London: Macmillan.

Forgas, J. P. (1976) The perception of social episodes: categoric and dimensional representations in two different social milieux. *Journal of Personality and Social Psychology*, 34 (2), 199–209.

Forgas, J. P. (1978) Social episodes and social structure in an academic setting: the social environment of an intact group. *Journal of Experimental Social Psychology*, 14, 434–48.

Forgas, J. P. (1981) *Social Episodes: The Study of Interaction Routines*. London: Academic Press.

Forward, J., Canter, R. and Kirsch, N. (1976) Role-enactment and deception methodologies. *American Psychologist*, 35, 595–604.

Foskett, N. H. and Hesketh, A. J. (1997) Constructing choice in continuous and parallel markets: institutional and school leavers' responses to the new post-16 marketplace. *Oxford Review of Education*, 23 (3), 299–319.

Foster, J. R. (1992) Eliciting personal constructs and articulating goals. *Journal of Career Development*, 18 (3), 175–85.

Foster, P. (1989) Change and adjustment in a Further Education College. In R. G. Burgess (ed.) *The Ethics of Educational Research*. Lewes: Falmer Press, 188–204.

Fourali, C. (1997) Using fuzzy logic in educational measurement: the case of portfolio assessment. *Evaluation and Research in Education*, 11 (3), 129–48.

Fox, D. J. (1969) *The Research Process in Education*. New York: Holt, Rinehart & Winston.

Francis, H. (1992) Patterns of reading development in the first school. *British Journal of Educational Psychology*, 62, 225–32.

Frankfort-Nachmias, C. and Nachmias, D. (1992) *Research Methods in the Social Sciences*. London: Edward Arnold.

Fransella, F. (1975) *Need to Change?* London: Methuen.

Fransella, F. and Bannister, D. (1977) *A Manual for Repertory Grid Technique*. London: Academic Press.

Fredericksen, J. R. and Collins, A. (1989) A systems approach to educational testing. *Educational Researcher*, 189, 27–32.

Freire, P. (1970) *The Pedagogy of the Oppressed*. Harmondsworth: Penguin.

Frisbie, D. (1981) The relative difficulty ratio – a test and item index. *Educational and Psychological Measurement*, 41 (2), 333–9.

Fullan, M. (1999) *Change Forces* (second edition). London: Falmer.

Gadamer, H. G. (1975) *Truth and Method*. New York: Polity Press.

Gage, N. L. (1989) The paradigm wars and their aftermath. *Teachers College Record*, 91 (2), 135–50.

Gallagher, T., McEwen, A. and Knip, D. (1997) Science education policy: a survey of the participation of sixth-form pupils in science and the subjects over a 10-year period, 1985–95. *Research Papers in Education*, 12 (2), 121–42.

Galton, M., Simon, B. and Coll, P. (1980) *Inside the Primary Classroom*. London: Routledge & Kegan Paul.

Galton, M., Hargreaves, L, Comber, C., Wall, D. and Pell, T. (1999) Changes in patterns in teacher interaction in primary classrooms, 1976–1996. *British Educational Research Journal*, 25 (1), 23–37.

Gardiner, P. (1961) *The Nature of Historical Explanation*. Oxford: Oxford University Press.

Gardner, G. (1978) *Social Surveys for Social Planners*. Milton Keynes: Open University Press.

Gardner, H. (1993) *Multiple Intelligences: the Theory in Practice*. New York: Basic Books.

Garfinkel, H. (1967) *Studies in Ethnomethodology*. Englewood Cliffs, NJ: Prentice-Hall.

Garner, C. and Raudenbush, S. W. (1991) Neighbourhood effects in educational attainment: a multilevel analysis. *Sociology of Education*, 64 (4), 251–62.

Garrahan, P. and Stewart, P. (1992) *The Nissan Enigma: Flexibility at Work in a Local Economy*. London: Mansell.

Gaukroger, A. and Schwartz, L. (1997) A university and its region: student recruitment to Birmingham, 1945–75. *Oxford Review of Education*, 23 (2), 185–202.

Geertz, C. (1973) Thick description: towards an interpretive theory of culture. In C. Geertz (ed.) *The Interpretation of Cultures*. New York: Basic Books.

Geertz, C. (ed.) (1973) *The Interpretation of Cultures*. New York: Basic Books.

Geertz, C. (1974) From the native's point of view: on the nature of anthropological understanding. *Bulletin of the American Academy of Arts and Sciences*, 28 (1), 26–45.

Gersch, I. (1984) Behaviour modification and systems analysis in a secondary school: combining two approaches. *Behavioural Approaches with Children*, 8, 83–91.

Geuss, R. (1981) *The Idea of a Critical Theory*. London: Cambridge University Press.

Gewirtz, S. and Ozga. J. (1993) Sex, lies and audiotape: interviewing the education policy elite. Paper presented to the Economic and Research Council, 1988 Education Reform Act Research seminar. University of Warwick.

Gewirtz, S. and Ozga, J. (1994) Interviewing the

education policy elite. In G. Walford (ed.) *Researching the Powerful in Education*. London: UCL Press, 186–203.

Gibson, R. (1985) Critical times for action research. *Cambridge Journal of Education*, 15 (1), 59–64.

Giddens, A. (ed.) (1975) *Positivism and Sociology*. London: Heinemann Educational Books.

Giddens, A. (1976) *New Rules of Sociological Method: a Positive Critique of Interpretative Sociologies*. London: Hutchinson.

Giddens, A. (1979) *Central Problems in Social Theory*. London: Macmillan.

Gilbert, G. N. (1983) Accounts and those accounts called actions. In G. N. Gilbert and P. Abell, *Accounts and Action*. Aldershot: Gower, 183–7.

Ginsburg, G. P. (1978) Role playing and role performance in social psychological research. In M. Brenner, P. Marsh and M. Brenner (eds), *The Social Contexts of Method*. London: Croom Helm, 91–121.

Gipps, C. (1994) *Beyond Testing: towards a Theory of Educational Assessment*. London: Falmer.

Giroux, H. (1989) *Schooling for Democracy*. London: Routledge.

Glaser, B. G. (1978) *Theoretical Sensitivity: Advances in the Methodology of Grounded Theory*. Mill Valley, CA: Sociology Press.

Glaser, B. G. and Strauss, A. L. (1967) *The Discovery of Grounded Theory*. Chicago: Aldane.

Glass, G. V. (1976) Primary, secondary and meta-analysis. *Educational Research*, 5, 3–8.

Glass, G. V. (1977) Integrating findings: the meta-analysis of research. *Review of Research in Education*, 5, 351–79.

Glass, G. V. and Hopkins, K. D. (1996) *Statistical Methods in Education and Psychology* (third edition). Boston: Allyn & Bacon.

Glass, G. V. and Smith, M. L. (1978) *Meta-analysis of Research on the Relationship of Class-size and Achievement*. San Francisco: Farwest Laboratory.

Glass, G. V., McGaw, B. and Smith, M. L. (1981) *Meta-analysis in Social Research*. Beverly Hills: Sage Publications.

Glass, G. V., Cahen, L. S., Smith, M. L. and Filby, N. N. (1982) *School Class Size: Research and Policy*. Beverly Hills: Sage Publications.

Gleick, J. (1987) *Chaos*. London: Abacus.

Goffman, E. (1968) *Asylums*. Harmondsworth: Penguin.

Goffman, E. (1969) *The Presentation of Self in Everyday Life*. Harmondsworth: Penguin.

Gold, R. L. (1958) Roles in sociological field observations. *Social Forces*, 36, 217–23.

Goldstein, H. (1987) *Multilevel Modelling in Educational and Social Research*. London: Charles Griffin and Co. Ltd.

Good, C. V. (1963) *Introduction to Educational Research*. New York: Appleton-Century-Crofts.

Goodson, I. (1983) The use of life histories in the study of teaching. In M. Hammersley (ed.) *The Ethnography of Schooling*. Driffield: Nafferton Books, 129–54.

Goodson, I. (1990) *The Making of Curriculum*. Lewes: Falmer Press.

Goodson, I. and Walker, R. (1988) Putting life into educational research. In R. R. Sherman and R. B. Webb (eds) *Qualitative Research in Education: Focus and Methods*. Lewes: Falmer Press, 110–22.

Goossens, L., Marcoen, A., van Hees, S. and van de Woestlijne, O. (1998) Attachment style and loneliness in adolescence. *European Journal of Psychology of Education*, 13 (4), 529–42.

Gottschalk, L. (1951) *Understanding History*. New York: Alfred A. Knopf.

Graue, M. E. and Walsh, D. J. (1998) *Studying Children in Context: Theories, Methods and Ethics*. London: Sage Publications.

Gray, J. and Satterly, D. (1976) A chapter of errors: teaching styles and pupil progress in retrospect. *Educational Research*, 19, 45–56.

Gray, J., Reynolds, D., Fitz-Gibbon, C. T. and Jesson, D. (eds) (1996) *Merging Traditions: The Future of Research on School Effectiveness and School Improvement*. London: Cassell.

Greig, A. D. and Taylor, J. (1998) *Doing Research with Children*. London: Sage Publications.

Gronlund, N. E. (1981) *Measurement and Evaluation in Teaching* (fourth edition). New York: Collier-Macmillan.

Gronlund, N. E. (1985) *Stating Objectives for Classroom Instruction* (third edition). New York: Macmillan.

Gronlund, N. E. and Linn, R. L. (1990) *Measurement and Evaluation in Teaching* (sixth edition). New York: Macmillan.

Grundy, S. (1987) *Curriculum: Product or Praxis*. Lewes: Falmer.

Grundy, S. (1996) Towards empowering leadership: the importance of imagining. In O. Zuber-Skerritt (ed.) *New Directions in Action Research*. London: Falmer, 106–20.

Grundy, S. and Kemmis, S. (1988) Educational action research in Australia: the state of the art (an overview). In S. Kemmis and R. McTaggart (eds) *The Action Research Reader* (second edition). Victoria: Deakin University Press, 83–97.

Guba, E. G. and Lincoln, Y. S. (1989) *Fourth Generation Evaluation*. Beverly Hills: Sage Publications.

Guba, E. G. and Lincoln, Y. S. (1991) What is the constructivist paradigm? In D. S. Anderson and B. J. Biddle (eds) *Knowledge for Policy: Improving Education through Research*. London: Falmer, 158–70.

Guba, E. G. and Lincoln, Y. S. (1994) Competing paradigms in qualitative research. In N. K. Denzin and Y. S. Lincoln (eds) *Handbook of Qualitative Research*. Beverly Hills: Sage Publications, 105–17.

Guilford, J. P. and Fruchter, B. (1973) *Fundamental Statistics in Psychology and Education*. New York: McGraw-Hill.

Habermas, J. (1970) Toward a theory of communicative competence. *Inquiry*, 13, 360–75.

Habermas, J. (1972) *Knowledge and Human Interests* (trans. J. Shapiro). London: Heinemann.

Habermas, J. (1974) *Theory and Practice* (trans. J. Viertel). London: Heinemann.

Habermas, J. (1976) *Legitimation Crisis* (trans. T. McCarthy). London: Heinemann.

Habermas, J. (1979) *Communication and the Evolution of Society*. London: Heinemann.

Habermas, J. (1982) A reply to my critics. In J. Thompson and D. Held (eds) *Habermas: Critical Debates*. London: Macmillan, 219–83.

Habermas, J. (1984) *The Theory of Communicative Action. Vol. 1: Reason and the Rationalization of Society* (trans. T. McCarthy). Boston: Beacon Press.

Habermas, J. (1988) *On the Logic of the Social Sciences* (trans. S. Nicholsen and J. Stark). Oxford: Polity Press in association with Basil Blackwell.

Habermas, J. (1990) *Moral Consciousness and Communicative Action* (trans. C. Lenhardt and S. Nicholsen). Cambridge: Polity Press in association with Basil Blackwell.

Haig, B. D. (1997) Feminist research methodology. In J. P. Keeves (ed.) *Educational Research, Methodology, and Measurement: an International Handbook* (second edition). Oxford: Elsevier Science Ltd. 180–5.

Haig, B. D. (1999) Feminist research methodology. In J. P. Keeves and G. Lakomski (eds) *Issues in Educational Research*. Oxford: Elsevier Science Ltd., 222–31.

Hakim, C. (1987) *Research Design, Contemporary Social Research: 13*. London: Allen & Unwin.

Haladyna, T., Nolen, S. and Haas, N. (1991) Raising standardised achievement test scores and the origins of test score pollution. *Educational Researcher*, 20 (5), 2–7.

Hall, E., Hall, C. and Abaci, R. (1997) The effects of human relations training on reported teacher stress, pupil control ideology and locus of control. *British Journal of Educational Psychology*, 67, 483–96.

Hall, K. and Nuttall, W. (1999) The *relative* importance of class size to infant teachers in England. *British Educational Research Journal*, 25 (2), 245–58.

Hall, S. (1996) Reflexivity in emancipatory action research: illustrating the researcher's constitutiveness. In O. Zuber-Skerritt (ed.) *New Directions in Action Research*. London: Falmer.

Halpin, D., Croll, P. and Redman, K. (1990) Teachers' perceptions of the effects of inservice education. *British Educational Research Journal*, 16 (2), 163–77.

Halsey, A. H. (ed.) (1972) *Educational Priority: Vol. 1: E. P. A. Problems and Policies*. London: HMSO.

Hambleton, R. K. (1993), Principles and selected application of item response theory, in R. Linn (1993) (ed.) *Educational Measurement* (third edition). American Council on Education and the Oryx Press, Phoenix, Arizona, 147–200.

Hamilton, D. (1981) Generalisation in the educational sciences: problems and purposes. In T. S. Popkewitz and R. S. Tabachnick (eds) *The Study of Schooling*. New York: Praeger.

Hamilton, V. L. (1976) Role play and deception: a reexamination of the controversy. *Journal for the Theory of Social Behaviour*, 6, 233–50.

Hammersley, M. (1979) Analysing ethnographic data. Unit 1, Block 6, DE304 *Research Methods in Education and the Social Sciences*. Milton Keynes: Open University Press.

Hammersley, M. (1987) Some notes on the terms 'validity' and 'reliability'. *British Educational Research Journal*, 13 (1), 73–81.

Hammersley, M. (1992) *What's Wrong with Ethnography?* London: Routledge.

Hammersley, M. (ed.) (1993) *Social Research: Philosophy, Politics and Practice*. London: Sage Publications in association with the Open University Press.

Hammersley, M. and Atkinson. P. (1983) *Ethnography: Principles on Practice*. London: Methuen.

Hampden-Turner, C. (1970) *Radical Man*. Cambridge, MA: Schenkman.

Haney, C., Ranks, C. and Zimbardo, P. (1973) Interpersonal dynamics in a simulated prison. *International Journal of Criminology and Penology*, 1, 69–97.

Hanna, G. S. (1993) *Better Teaching through Better Measurement*. Fort Worth: Harcourt Brace Jovanovich Inc.

Hannan, A. and Newby, M. (1992) Student teacher and headteacher views on current provision and proposals for the future of Initial Teacher Education for primary schools (mimeo). Rolle Faculty of Education, University of Plymouth.

Hargreaves, D. H., Hester, S. K. and Mellor, F. J. (1975) *Deviance in Classrooms*. London: Routledge & Kegan Paul.

Harlen, W. (ed.) (1994) *Enhancing Quality in Assessment*. London: Paul Chapman Publishing.

Harré, R. (1974) Some remarks on 'rule' as a scientific concept. In T. Mischel (ed.) *On Understanding Persons*. Oxford: Basil Blackwell, 143–84.

Harré, R. (1976) The constructive role of models. In L. Collins (ed.) *The Use of Models in the Social Sciences*. London: Tavistock Publications, 16–43.

Harré, R. (1977a) The ethogenic approach: theory and practice. In L. Berkowitz (ed.) *Advances in Experimental Social Psychology*, Vol. 10. New York: Academic Press, 284–314.

Harré, R. (1977b) Friendship as an accomplishment. In S. Duck (ed.) *Theory and Practice in Interpersonal Attraction*. London: Academic Press, 339–54.

Harré, R. (1978) Accounts, actions and meanings: the practice of participatory psychology. In M. Brenner, P. Marsh and M. Brenner (eds) *The Social Contexts of Method*. London: Croom Helm, 44–66.

Harré, R. and Rosser, E. (1975) The rules of disorder. *The Times Educational Supplement*, 25 July.

Harré, R. and Secord, P. (1972) *The Explanation of Social Behaviour*. Oxford: Basil Blackwell.

Harris, N., Pearce, P. and Johnstone, S. (1992) *The Legal Context of Teaching*. London: Longman.

Harvey, C. D. H. (1988) Telephone survey techniques. *Canadian Home Economics Journal*, 38 (1), 30–5.

Heath, S. B., (1982) Questioning at home and at school: a comparative study, in G. Spindler (ed.) *Doing the Ethnography of Schooling*. New York: Holt, Rinehart & Winston, 102–31.

Hedges, A. (1985) Group interviewing. In R. Walker (ed.) (1985) *Applied Qualitative Research*. Aldershot: Gower, 71–91.

Hedges, L. (1981) Distribution theory for Glass's estimator of effect size and related estimators. *Journal of Educational Statistics*, 6, 107–28.

Hedges, L. (1990) Directions for future methodology. In. K. W. Wachter and M. L. Straf (eds) *The Future of Meta-analysis*. New York: Russell Sage Foundation, cited in B. McGaw, Meta-analysis. In J. P. Keeves (ed.) *Educational Research, Methodology, and Measurement: an International Handbook* (second edition). Oxford: Elsevier Science Ltd., 371–80.

Hedges, L. and Olkin, I. (1980) Vote-counting methods in research synthesis. *Psychological Bulletin*, 88 (2), 359–69.

Hedges, L. and Olkin, I. (1985) *Statistical Methods for Meta-analysis*. New York: Academic Press.

Held, D. (1980) *Introduction to Critical Theory*. Los Angeles: University of California Press.

Hesse, M. (1982) Science and objectivity. In J. Thompson and D. Held (eds) *Habermas: Critical Debates*. London: Macmillan, 98–115.

Hibbett, A., Fogelman, K. and Manor, O. (1990) Occupational outcomes of truancy. *British Journal of Educational Psychology*, 60, 23–36.

Higgs, G., Webster, C. J. and White, S. D. (1997) The use of geographical information systems in assessing spatial and socio-economic impacts of parental choice. *Research Papers in Education*, 12 (1) 27–48.

Hill, J. E. and Kerber, A. (1967) *Models, Methods and Analytical Procedures in Educational Research*. Detroit: Wayne State University Press.

Hill, P. W. and Rowe, K. J. (1996) Multilevel modelling in school effectiveness research. *School Effectiveness and School Improvement*. 7 (1), 1–34.

Hinkle, D. N. (1965) The change of personal constructs from the viewpoint of a theory of implications. Unpublished Ph.D. thesis. Ohio State University.

Hitchcock, G. and Hughes, D. (1989) *Research and the Teacher*. London: Routledge.

Hitchcock, G. and Hughes, D. (1995) *Research and the Teacher* (second edition). London: Routledge.

Hockett, H. C. (1955) *The Critical Method in Historical Research and Writing*. London: Macmillan.

Hodgkinson, H. L. (1957) Action research – a critique. *Journal of Educational Sociology*. 31 (4), 137–53.

Hoinville, G. and Jowell, R. (1978) *Survey Research Practice*. London: Heinemann.

Holbrook, D. (1977) *Education, Nihilism and Survival*. London: Darton, Longman & Todd.

Holland, J. L. (1985) *Making Vocational Choices: a Theory of Vocational Personalities and Work Environments*. Englewood Cliffs, NJ: Prentice-Hall.

Holly, P. (1984) *Action Research: a Cautionary Note*. Classroom Action Research Network, bulletin No. 6. Cambridge Institute of Education.

Holly, P. and Whitehead, D. (1986) *Action Research in Schools: Getting It into Perspective*. Classroom Action Research Network.

Holmes, P. and Karp, M. (1991) *Psychodrama: Inspiration and Technique*. London: Routledge.

Holmes, R. M. (1998) *Fieldwork with Children*. London: Sage Publications.

Holsti, O. R. (1968) Content analysis. In G. Lindzey and E. Aronson (eds), *The Handbook of Social Psychology. Vol. 2: Research Methods*. Reading, MA: Addison-Wesley, 596–692.

Hopkins, D. (1985) *A Teacher's Guide to Classroom Research*. Milton Keynes: Open University Press.

Hopkins, K. D., Hopkins, B. R. and Glass, G. V. (1996) *Basic Statistics for the Behavioral Sciences* (third edition). Boston: Allyn & Bacon.

Horkheimer, M. (1972) *Critical Theory: Selected Essays* (trans. M. Connell *et al.*). New York: Herder & Herder.

Horowitz, I. L. and Katz, J. E. (1991) Brown vs Board of Education. In D. S. Anderson and B. J. Biddle (eds) *Knowledge for Policy: Improving Education through Research*. London: Falmer, 237–44.

Houghton, D. (1991) Mr Chong: a case study of a dependent learner of English for academic purposes. *System*, 19 (1–2), 75–90.

House, E. R. (1979) Technology versus craft: a tenyear perspective on innovation, *Journal of Curriculum Studies*, 11 (1), 1–15.

Hoyle, E. (1986) *The Politics of School Management*. Sevenoaks: Hodder & Stoughton.

Hudson, P. and Miller, C. (1997) The treasure hunt: strategies for obtaining maximum response to a postal survey. *Evaluation and Research in Education*, 11 (2), 102–12.

Hughes, J. A. (1976) *Sociological Analysis: Methods of Discovery*. Sunbury-on-Thames: Nelson & Sons.

Hull, C. (1985) Between the lines: the analysis of interview data as an exact art. *British Educational Research Journal*, 11 (1), 27–31.

Hult, M. and Lennung, S. (1980) Towards a definition of action-research: a note and bibliography. *Journal of Management Studies*, 17 (2), 241–50.

Humphreys, L. (1975) *Tearoom Trade: Impersonal Sex in Public Places* (enlarged edition). New York: Aldine.

Hunter, J. E., Schmidt, F. L. and Jackson, G. B. (1982) *Meta-analysis: Cumulating Research Findings across Studies*. Beverly Hills: Sage Publications.

Hurn, C. J. (1978) *The Limits and Possibilities of Schooling*. Boston, MA: Allyn & Bacon.

Hutchinson, B. and Whitehouse, P. (1986) Action research, professional competence and school organization. *British Educational Research Journal*, 12 (1) 85–94.

Hycner, R. H. (1985) Some guidelines for the phenomenological analysis of interview data. *Human Studies*, 8, 279–303.

Ions, E. (1977) *Against Behaviouralism: a Critique of Behavioural Science*. Oxford: Basil Blackwell.

Jacklin, A. and Lacey, C. (1997) Gender integration in the infant classroom: a case study. *British Educational Research Journal*, 23 (5), 623–40.

Jackson, D. and Marsden, D. (1962) *Education and the Working Class*. London: Routledge & Kegan Paul.

Jackson, G. B. (1980) Methods for integrative reviews. *Review of Educational Research*. 50 (3), 438–60.

Jacob, E. (1987) Qualitative research traditions: a review. *Review of Educational Research*, 57 (1), 1–50.

James, M. (1993) Evaluation for policy: rationality and political reality: the paradigm case of PRAISE? In R. G. Burgess (ed.) *Educational Research and Evaluation for Policy and Practice*. London: Falmer.

Jayaratne, T. E. (1993) The value of quantitative methodology for feminist research. In M. Hammersley (ed.) *Social Research: philosophy, politics and practice*. London: Sage Publications, in association with the Open University Press, 109–23.

Jones, D. and Vann, P. (1994) *Informing School Decisions: GIS in Education*. Luton: Local Government Management Board.

Jones, J. (1990) The role of the headteacher in staff development. *Educational Management and Administration*, 18 (1), 27–36.

Jones, J. L. (1998) Managing the induction of newly appointed governors. *Educational Research*, 40 (3), 329–51.

Jones, S. (1987) The analysis of depth interviews. In R. Murphy and H. Torrance (eds) *Evaluating*

Education: Issues and Methods. London: Paul Chapman Publishing, 263–77.

Jules, V. and Kutnick, P. (1997) Student perceptions of a good teacher: the gender perspective. *British Journal of Educational Psychology*, 67, 497–511.

Kamin, L. (1991) Some historical facts about IQ testing. In D. S. Anderson and B. J. Biddle (eds) *Knowledge for Policy: Improving Education through Research*. London: Falmer, 259–67.

Kaplan, A. (1973) *The Conduct of Inquiry*. Aylesbury: Intertext Books.

Kauffmann, S. (1995) *At Home in the Universe*. Harmondsworth: Penguin.

Kazdin, A. E. (1982) *Single-case Research Designs*. New York: Oxford University Press.

Keat, R. (1981) *The Politics of Social Theory*. Oxford: Basil Blackwell.

Keeves, J. P. (ed.) (1997) *Educational Research, Methodology and Measurement: an International Handbook* (second edition). Oxford: Elsevier Science Ltd.

Keeves, J. P. and Lakomski, G. (eds) (1999) *Issues in Educational Research*. Oxford: Elsevier Science Ltd.

Keeves, J. P. and Sellin, N. (1997) Multilevel analysis. In J. P. Keeves (ed.) *Educational Research, Methodology and Measurement: An International Handbook*. Oxford: Elsevier Science Ltd, 394–403.

Kelle, U. (ed.) (1995) *Computer-Aided Qualitative Data Analysis*. London: Sage Publications.

Kelle, U. and Laurie, H. (1995) Computer use in qualitative research and issues of validity. In U. Kelle (ed.) (1995) *Computer-Aided Qualitative Data Analysis*. London: Sage Publications, 19–28.

Kelly, A. (1986) The development of children's attitudes to science: a longitudinal study. *European Journal of Science Education*, 8, 399–412.

Kelly, A. (1987) *Science for Girls?* Milton Keynes: Open University Press.

Kelly, A. (1989a) Education or indoctrination? The ethics of school-based action research. In R. G. Burgess (ed.) *The Ethics of Educational Research*. Lewes: Falmer, 100–13.

Kelly, A. (1989b) *Getting the GIST: a qualitative study of the effects of the Girls Into Science and Technology Project*. Manchester Sociology Occasional Papers, no. 22. Manchester: University of Manchester.

Kelly, A. and Smail, B. (1986) Sex stereotypes and attitudes to science among eleven-year-old children. *British Journal of Educational Psychology*. 56, 158–68.

Kelly, G. A. (1955) *The Psychology of Personal Constructs*. New York: Norton.

Kelly, G. A. (1969) *Clinical Psychology and Personality: the Selected Papers of George Kelly*, edited by B.A. Maher. New York: Wiley.

Kelman, H. C. (1967) Human use of human subjects. *Psychological Bulletin*, 67 (1), 1–11.

Kemmis, S. (1982) Seven principles for programme evaluation in curriculum development and innovation. *Journal of Curriculum Studies*, 14 (3), 221–40.

Kemmis, S. (1997) Action Research. In J. P. Keeves (ed.) *Educational Research, Methodology, and Measurement: an International Handbook* (second edition). Oxford: Elsevier Science Ltd., 173–9.

Kemmis, S. (1999) Action Research. In J. P. Keeves and G. Lakomski (eds) *Issues in Educational Research*. Oxford: Elsevier Science Ltd., 150–60.

Kemmis, S. and McTaggart, R. (eds) (1981) *The Action Research Planner* (first edition). Geelong, Victoria: Deakin University Press.

Kemmis. S. and McTaggart, R. (eds) (1988) *The Action Research Planner* (second edition). Geelong, Victoria: Deakin University Press.

Kemmis, S. and McTaggart, R. (eds) (1992) *The Action Research Planner* (third edition) Geelong, Victoria, Australia: Deakin University Press.

Kerlinger, F. N. (1970) *Foundations of Behavioral Research*. New York: Holt, Rinehart & Winston.

Kerlinger, F. N. (1986) *Foundations of Behavioral Research* (third edition). New York: Holt, Rinehart & Winston.

Kerlinger, F. N. (1991) Science and behavioural research. In D. S. Anderson and B. J. Biddle (eds) *Knowledge for Policy: Improving Education through Research*. London: Falmer, 87–102.

Kierkegaard, S. (1974) *Concluding Unscientific Postscript*. Princeton: Princeton University Press.

Kimmel, A. J. (1988) *Ethics and Values in Applied Social Research*. Beverly Hills: Sage Publications.

Kincheloe, J. L. (1991) *Teachers as Researchers: Qualitative Inquiry as a Path to Empowerment*. London: Falmer.

Kincheloe, J. and McLaren, P. (1994) Rethinking critical theory and qualitative research. In N. K. Denzin and Y. S. Lincoln (eds) *Handbook of Qualitative Research*. Beverly Hills: Sage Publications, 105–17.

King, J. A., Morris, L. L. and Fitz-Gibbon, C. T. (1987) *How to Assess Programme Implementation*. Beverly Hills: Sage Publications.

King, R. (1979) *All Things Bright and Beautiful?* Chichester: John Wiley.

Kirk, J. and Miller, M. L. (1986) *Reliability and Validity in Qualitative Research.* Qualitative Research Methods Series No. 1. Beverly Hills: Sage Publications.

Kitwood, T. M. (1977) Values in adolescent life: towards a critical description, Unpublished Ph. D. dissertation, School of Education, University of Bradford.

Kivulu, J. M. and Rogers, W. T. (1998) A multilevel analysis of cultural experience and gender influences on causal attributions to perceived performance in mathematics. *British Journal of Educational Psychology*, 68, 25–37.

Knott, J. and Wildavsky, A. (1991) If dissemination is the solution, what is the problem? In D. S. Anderson and B. J. Biddle (eds) *Knowledge for Policy: Improving Education through Research*. London: Falmer, 214–24.

Kogan, M. and Atkin, J. M. (1991) Special commissions and educational policy in the U.S.A. and U.K. In D. S. Anderson and B. J. Biddle (eds) *Knowledge for Policy: Improving Education through Research*. London: Falmer, 245–58.

Kolakowski, L. (1978) *Main Currents of Marxism, Volume Three: the Breakdown* (trans. P. S. Falla). Oxford: Clarendon Press.

Kosko, B. (1994) *Fuzzy Thinking*. London: Flamingo.

Krejcie, R. V. and Morgan, D. W. (1970) Determining sample size for research activities. *Educational and Psychological Measurement*, 30: 607–10.

Kremer-Hayon, L. (1991) Personal constructs of elementary school principals in relation to teachers. *Research in Education*, 43, 15–21.

Krueger, R. A. (1988) *Focus Groups: a Practical Guide for Applied Research*. Beverly Hills: Sage Publications.

Kshir, M. A. M. (1999) An evaluative survey of the role of INSET in managing innovations in schools in Libya. Unpublished Ph. D. thesis, School of Education: University of Durham.

Kuhn, T. S. (1962) *The Structure of Scientific Revolutions*. Chicago: University of Chicago Press

Kumar, D. D. (1991) A meta-analysis of the relationship between science instruction and student engagement, *Educational Review*, 43 (1), 49–56.

Kvale, S. (1996) *Interviews*. London: Sage Publications.

Labov, W. (1969) The logic of non-standard English. In N. Keddie (ed.) *Tinker, Tailor . . . the Myth of Cultural Deprivation*. Harmondsworth: Penguin, 21–66.

Laing, R. D. (1967) *The Politics of Experience and the Bird of Paradise*. Harmondsworth: Penguin.

Lakatos, I. (1970) Falsification and the methodology of scientific research programmes. In I. Lakatos and A. Musgrave (eds) *Criticism and the Growth of Knowledge*. London: Cambridge University Press, 91–195.

Lakomski, G. (1999) Critical theory. In J. P. Keeves and G. Lakomski (eds) *Issues in Educational Research*. Oxford: Elsevier Science Ltd., 174–83.

Lamb, S., Bibby, P., Wood, D. and Leyden, G. (1997) Communication skills, educational achievement and biographic characteristics of children with moderate learning difficulties. *European Journal of Psychology of Education*, 12 (4), 401–14.

Lansing, J. B., Ginsberg, G. P. and Braaten, K. (1961) *An Investigation of Response Error*. Bureau of Economic and Business Research University of Illinois.

Lather, P. (1986) Research as praxis. *Harvard Educational Review*, 56, 257–77.

Lather, P. (1991) *Getting Smart: Feminist Research and Pedagogy within the Post Modern*. New York: Routledge.

Laudan, L. (1990) *Science and Relativism*. Chicago: University of Chicago Press Ltd.

Lave, J. and Kvale, S. (1995) What is anthropological research? An interview with Jean Lave by Steiner Kvale. *International Journal of Qualitative Studies in Education*, 8 (3), 219–28.

Lawless, L., Smee, P. and O'Shea, T. (1998) Using concept sorting and concept mapping in business and public administration, and education: an overview. *Educational Research*, 40 (2), 219–35.

Layder, D. (1994) *Understanding Social Theory*. London: Sage Publications.

Lazarsfeld, P. P. and Barton, A. (1951) Qualitative measurement in the social sciences: classification, typologies and indices. In D. P. Lerner and H. D. Lasswell (eds) *The Policy Sciences*. Stanford: Stanford University Press, 155–92.

LeCompte, M. and Preissle, J. (1993) *Ethnography and Qualitative Design in Educational Research* (second edition). London: Academic Press Ltd.

LeCompte, M., Millroy, W. L. and Preissle, J. (eds) (1992) *The Handbook of Qualitative Research in Education*. London: Academic Press Ltd.

Lee, R. M. (1993) *Doing Research on Sensitive Topics*. London: Sage Publications.

Lehrer, R. and Franke, M. L. (1992) Applying personal construct psychology to the study of teachers' knowledge of fractions. *Journal for Research in Mathematical Education*, 23 (3), 223–41.

Leistyna, P., Woodrum, A. and Sherblom, S. A. (1996) *Breaking Free*. Cambridge, MA: Harvard Educational Review.

Levin, H. M. (1991) Why isn't educational research more useful? In D. S. Anderson and B. J. Biddle (eds) *Knowledge for Policy: Improving Education through Research*. London: Falmer, 70–8.

Levine, M. (1984) *Canonical Analysis and Factor Comparisons*. Beverly Hills: Sage Publications.

Levine, R. A. (1966) Towards a psychology of populations: the cross-cultural study of personality. *Human Development*, 3, 30–6.

Lewin, K. (1946) Action research and minority problems. *Journal of Social Issues*, 2 (4), 34–46.

Lewin, K. (1948) *Resolving Social Conflicts*. New York: Harper.

Lewin, K. (1952) *Field Theory in Social Science*. London: Tavistock Publications.

Lewin, R. (1993) *Complexity: Life on the Edge of Chaos*. London: Phoenix.

Lewis, A. (1992) Group child interviews as a research tool. *British Educational Research Journal*, 18 (4), 413–21.

Lewis, D. (1974) *Assessment in Education*. London: University of London Press.

Lewis-Beck, M. S. (ed.) (1993) *Experimental Design and Methods*. London: Toppan Co., with the co-operation of Sage Publications, Inc.

Lietz, P. and Keeves, J. P. (1997) Cross-sectional research methods. In J. P. Keeves (ed.) *Educational Research, Methodology and Measurement: an International Handbook* (second edition). Oxford: Elsevier Science Ltd., 138–49.

Light, R. J. and Smith, P. V. (1971) Accumulating evidence: procedures for resolving contradictions among different research studies. *Harvard Educational Review*, 41, 429–71.

Likert, R. (1932) *A Technique for the Measurement of Attitudes*. New York: Columbia University Press.

Limerick, B., Burgess-Limerick, T. and Grace, M. (1996) The politics of interviewing: power relations and accepting the gift. *International Journal of Qualitative Studies in Education*, 9 (4), 449–60.

Lin, N. (1976) *Foundations of Social Research*. New York: McGraw-Hill.

Lincoln, Y. S. and Guba, E. G. (1985) *Naturalistic Inquiry*. Beverly Hills: Sage Publications.

Lincoln, Y. S. and Guba, E. G. (1986) But is it rigorous? Trustworthiness and authenticity in naturalistic inquiry. In D. D. Williams (ed.) *Naturalistic Evaluation*. San Francisco: Jossey-Bass, 73–84.

Linn, R. L. (ed.) (1993) *Educational Measurement* (third edition). Phoenix, Arizona: American Council on Education and the Oryx Press.

Lipsey, M. W. (1992) Juvenile delinquency treatment: a meta-analytic inquiry into the variability of effects. In T. D. Cook, H. Cooper, D. S. Cordray, H. Hartmann, L. V. Hedges, R. J. Light, T. A. Louis and F. Mosteller (eds) *Meta-analysis for Explanation*. New York: Russell Sage Foundation.

Littleton, K., Ashman, H., Light, P., Artis, J., Roberts, T. and Oosterwegel, A. (1999) Gender, task contexts, and children's performance on a computer-based task. *European Journal of Psychology of Education*, 14 (1), 129–39.

Loevinger, J. (1957) Objective tests as instruments of psychological theory. *Psychological Review*, 72, 143–55.

Lofland, J. (1970) Interactionist imagery and analytic interruptus. In T. Shibutani (ed.) *Human Nature and Collective Behaviour: Papers in Honour of Herbert Blumer*. Englewood Cliffs, NJ: Prentice-Hall, 35–45.

Lofland, J. (1971) *Analyzing Social Settings*. Belmont, CA: Wadsworth.

Lonkila, M. (1995) Grounded theory as an emerging paradigm for computer-assisted qualitative data analysis. In U. Kelle (1995) (ed.) *Computer-aided Qualitative Data Analysis*. London: Sage Publications, 41–51.

Lund, B. and McGechan, S. (1981) *CE Programmer's Manual*. Victoria, Australia: Ministry of Education, Continuing Education Division.

McClelland, D. C., Atkinson, J. W., Clark, R. A. and Lowell, E. L. (1953) *The Achievement Motive*. New York: Appleton-Century-Crofts.

McCormick, J. and Solman, R. (1992) Teachers' attributions of responsibility for occupational stress and satisfaction: an organisational perspective. *Educational Studies*, 18 (2), 201–22.

McCormick, R. and James, M. (1988) *Curriculum Evaluation in Schools* (second edition). London: Croom Helm.

MacDonald, B. (1987) *Research and Action in the Context of Policing*. Paper commissioned by the Police Federation. Norwich: Centre for Applied Research in Education, University of East Anglia.

MacDonald, G. (1997) Social work: beyond control?

In A. Maynard and I. Chalmers (eds) *Non-random Reflections on Health Service Research*. London: BMJ Publishing Group, 122–46.

McEneaney, J. E. and Sheridan, E. M. (1996) A survey-based component for programme assessment in undergraduate pre-service teacher education. *Research in Education*, 55, 49–61.

McFee, G. (1993) Reflections on the nature of action research. *Cambridge Journal of Education*, 23 (2), 173–83.

McGaw, B. (1997) Meta-analysis. In J. P. Keeves (ed.) *Educational Research, Methodology and Measurement: an International Handbook* (second edition). Oxford: Elsevier Science Ltd, 371–80.

McIntyre, D. and MacLeod, G. (1978) The characteristics and uses of systematic classroom observation. In R. McAleese and D. Hamilton (eds), *Understanding Classroom Life*. Windsor: NFER, 102–31.

McKernan, J. (1991) *Curriculum Action Research*. London: Kogan Page.

McLaren, P. (1995) *Critical Pedagogy and Predatory Culture*. London: Routledge.

McLaughlin, J. F., Owen, S. L., Fors, S. W. and Levinson, R. M (1992) The schoolchild as health educator: diffusion of hypertension information from sixth-grade children to their parents. *Qualitative Studies in Education*, 5 (2), 147–65.

McNamara, E. (1986) The effectiveness of incentive and sanction systems used in secondary schools: a behavioural analysis. *Durham and Newcastle Research Review*, 10, 285–90.

McNiece, R. and Jolliffe, F. (1998) An investigation into regional differences in educational performance in the National Child Development Study. *Educational Research*, 40 (1), 13–30.

McNiff, J. (1988) *Action Research: Principles and Practice*. Basingstoke: Macmillan.

McNiff, J., Lomax, P. and Whitehead, J. (1996) *You and Your Action Research Project*. London: Routledge, in association with Hyde Publications, Bournemouth.

McQuitty, L. L. (1957) Elementary linkage analysis for isolating orthogonal and oblique types and typal relevancies. *Educational and Psychological Measurement*, 17, 207–29.

McTaggart, R. (1996) Issues for participatory action researchers. In O. Zuber-Skerritt (ed.) *New Directions in Action Research*. London: Falmer, 243–55.

Madge, J. (1963) *The Origin of Scientific Sociology*. London: Tavistock.

Madge, J. (1965) *The Tools of Social Science*. London: Longman.

Mager, R. F. (1962) *Preparing Instructional Objectives*. Belmont, CA: Fearon Publishers.

Magnusson, D. (1971) An analysis of situational dimensions. *Perceptual and Motor Skills*, 32, 851–67.

Malinowski, B. (1922) *Argonauts of the Western Pacific: an Account of Native Enterprise and Adventure in the Archipelagoes of Melanesian New Guinea*. New York: Dutton.

Mannheim, K. (1936) *Ideology and Utopia*. London: Routledge & Kegan Paul.

Marcinkiewicz, H. R. and Clariana, R. B. (1997) The performance effects of headings within multi-choice tests. *British Journal of Educational Psychology*, 67, 111–17.

Marris, P. and Rein, M. (1967) *Dilemmas of Social Reform: Poverty and Community Action in the United States*. London: Routledge & Kegan Paul.

Marsh, H. W. and Yeung, A. S. (1998) Longitudinal structural equation models of academic self-concept and achievement: gender differences in the development of math and English constructs. *American Educational Research Journal*, 35 (4), 705–38.

Marsh, P., Rosser, E. and Harré, R. (1978) *The Rules of Disorder*. London: Routledge & Kegan Paul.

Maslow, A. H. (1954) *Motivation and Personality*. New York: Harper & Row.

Mason, M., Mason, B. and Quayle, T. (1992) Illuminating English: how explicit language teaching improved public examination results in a comprehensive school. *Educational Studies*, 18 (3), 341–54.

Masschelein, J. (1991) The relevance of Habermas's communicative turn. *Studies in Philosophy and Education*, 11 (2), 95–111.

Maxwell, J. A. (1992) Understanding and validity in qualitative research. *Harvard Educational Review*, 62 (3), 279–300.

Maynard, A. and Chalmers, I. (eds) (1997) *Non-random Reflections on Health Service Research*. London: BMJ Publishing Group.

Mead, G. H. (ed. Charles Morris) (1934) *Mind, Self and Society*. Chicago: University of Chicago Press.

Medawar, P. B. (1972) *The Hope of Progress*. London: Methuen.

Medawar, P. B. (1981) *Advice to a Young Scientist*. London: Pan Books.

Medawar, P. B. (1991) Scientific fraud. In D. Pike (ed.)

The Threat and the Glory: Reflections on Science and Scientists. Oxford: Oxford University Press, 64–70.

Megarry, J. (1978) Retrospect and prospect. In R. McAleese (ed.) *Perspectives on Academic Gaming and Simulation 3: Training and Professional Education.* London: Kogan Page, 187–207.

Mehrens, W. and Kaminski, J. (1989) Methods for improving standardised test scores: fruitful, fruitless or fraudulent? *Educational Measurement: Issues and Practice,* Spring, 14–22.

Melrose, M. J. (1996) Got a philosophical match? Does it matter? In O. Zuber-Skerritt (ed.) *New Directions in Action Research.* London: Falmer.

Menzel, H. (1978) Meaning – who needs it? In M. Brenner, P. Marsh and M. Brenner (eds) *The Social Contexts of Method.* London: Croom Helm, 140–71.

Mercer, N., Wegerif, R. and Dawes, L. (1999) Children's talk and the development of reasoning in the classroom. *British Educational Research Journal,* 25 (1) 95–111.

Merrett, F., Wilkins, J., Houghton, S. and Wheldall, K. (1988) Rules, sanctions and rewards in secondary schools. *Educational Studies,* 14 (2), 139–49.

Merriam, S. B. (1988) *Case Study Research in Education.* San Francisco: Jossey Bass.

Merton, R. K. (1949) *Social Theory and Social Structure.* Illinois: Glencoe Press.

Merton, R. K. (1967) *On Theoretical Sociology.* New York: The Free Press.

Merton, R. K. and Kendall, P. L. (1946) The focused interview. *American Journal of Sociology* 51, 541–57.

Merton, R. K., Fiske, M. and Kendall, P. L. (1956) *The Focused Interview.* Glencoe, IL: Free Press.

Messick, S. (1993) Validity. In R. Linn (ed.) *Educational Measurement* (third edition). Phoenix, Arizona: American Council on Education and the Oryx Press, 13–103.

Miedama, S. and Wardekker, W. L. (1999) Emergent identity versus consistent identity: possibilities for a postmodern repoliticization of critical pedagogy. In T. Popkewitz and L. Fendler (eds) *Critical Theories in Education: Changing Terrains of Knowledge and Politics.* London: Routledge, 67–83.

Mies, M. (1993) Towards a methodology for feminist research. In M. Hammersley (ed.) *Social Research: Philosophy, Politics and Practice.* London: Sage Publications, in association with the Open University Press, 64–82.

Miles, M. and Huberman, M. A. (1984) *Qualitative Data Analysis.* Beverly Hills: Sage Publications.

Miles, M. and Huberman, M. A. (1994) *Qualitative Data Analysis* (second edition). Beverly Hills: Sage Publications.

Milgram, S. (1963) Behavioral study of obedience. *Journal of Abnormal and Social Psychology,* 67, 371–8.

Milgram, S. (1974) *Obedience to Authority.* New York: Harper & Row.

Millan, R., Gallagher, M. and Ellis, R. (1993) Surveying adolescent worries: development of the 'Things I Worry About' scale. *Pastoral Care in Education,* 11 (1), 43–57.

Miller, C. (1995) In-depth interviewing by telephone: some practical considerations. *Evaluation and Research in Education,* 9 (1), 29–38.

Miller, P. V. and Cannell, C. F. (1997) Interviewing for social research. In J. P. Keeves (ed.) *Educational Research, Methodology and Measurement: an International Handbook* (second edition). Oxford: Elsevier Science Ltd., 361–70.

Miller, R. L. (1999) *Researching Life Stories and Family Histories.* London: Sage Publications.

Millman, J. and Darling-Hammond, L. (eds) (1991) *The New Handbook of Teacher Evaluation.* Newbury Park, CA: Corwin Press.

Millman, J. and Greene, J. (1993) The specification and development of tests of achievement and ability, in R. Linn (1993) (ed.) *Educational Measurement* (third edition). American Council on Education and the Oryx Press, Phoenix, AZ, 147–200.

Mishler, E. G. (1986) *Research Interviewing: Context and Narrative.* Cambridge, MA: Harvard University Press.

Mishler, E. G. (1990) Validation in inquiry-guided research: the role of exemplars in narrative studies. *Harvard Educational Review,* 60 (4): 415–42.

Mishler, E. G. (1991) Representing discourse: the rhetoric of transcription. *Journal of Narrative and Life History,* 1, 225–80.

Mitchell, M. and Jolley, J. (1988) *Research Design Explained.* New York: Holt, Rinehart & Winston.

Mitchell, R. G. (1993) *Secrecy and Fieldwork.* London: Sage Publications.

Mixon, D. (1972) Instead of deception. *Journal for the Theory of Social Behaviour,* 2, 146–77.

Mixon, D. (1974) If you won't deceive, what can you do? In N. Armistead (ed.) *Reconstructing Social Psychology.* Harmondsworth: Penguin, 72–85.

Mooij, T. (1998) Pupil-class determinants of aggressive and victim behaviour in pupils. *British Journal of Educational Psychology*, 68, 373–85.

Morgan, C. (1999) Personal communication with one of the authors. University of Bath, Department of Education.

Morgan, D. L. (1988) *Focus Groups as Qualitative Research*. Beverly Hills: Sage Publications.

Morris, L. L., Fitz-Gibbon, C. T. and Lindheim, E. (1987) *How to Measure Performance and Use Tests*. Beverly Hills: Sage Publications.

Morrison, K. R. B. (1993) *Planning and Accomplishing School-centred Evaluation*. Norfolk: Peter Francis Publishers.

Morrison, K. R. B. (1995a) Habermas and the school curriculum. Unpublished Ph.D. thesis, School of Education, University of Durham.

Morrison, K. R. B. (1995b) Dewey, Habermas and reflective practice. *Curriculum*, 16 (2), 82–94.

Morrison, K. R. B. (1996a) Developing reflective practice in higher degree students through a learning journal. *Studies in Higher Education*, 21 (3), 317–32.

Morrison, K. R. B. (1996b) Structuralism, post-modernity and the discourses of control. *Curriculum*, 17 (3), 164–77.

Morrison, K. R. B. (1996c) Why present school inspections are unethical. *Forum*, 38 (3), 79–80.

Morrison, K. R. B. (1997) Researching the need for multicultural perspectives in counsellor training: a critique of Bimrose and Bayne. *British Journal of Guidance and Counselling*, 25 (1), 95–102.

Morrison, K. R. B. (1998) *Management Theories for Educational Change*. London: Paul Chapman Publishing.

Mortimore, P., Sammons, P., Stoll, L., Lewis, D. and Ecob, R. (1988) *School Matters: the Junior Years*. London: Open Books.

Moser, C. and Kalton, G. (1977) *Survey Methods in Social Investigation*. London: Heinemann.

Mouly, G. J. (1978) *Educational Research: the Art and Science of Investigation*. Boston: Allyn & Bacon.

Mullen, B. (1993) Meta-analysis. *Thornfield Journal*, 16, 36–41.

Munn, P., Johnstone, M. and Holligan, C. (1990) Pupils' perceptions of effective disciplinarians. *British Educational Research Journal*, 16 (2), 191–8.

Musch, J. and Bröder, A. (1999) Test anxiety versus academic skills: a comparison of two alternative models for predicting performance in a statistics exam. *British Journal of Educational Psychology*, 69, 105–16.

Nash, R. (1976) *Classrooms Observed*. London: Routledge & Kegan Paul.

National Education Association of the United States: Association for Supervision and Curriculum Development (1959) *Learning about Learning from Action Research*. Washington: National Education Association of the United States.

Naylor, P. (1995) Pupils' perceptions of teacher racism. Unpublished Ph.D. dissertation, Loughborough University of Technology.

Neal, S. (1995) Researching powerful people from a feminist and anti-racist perspective: a note on gender, collusion and marginality. *British Educational Research Journal*, 21 (4), 517–31.

Nedelsky, L. (1954) Absolute grading standards for objective tests. *Educational and Psychological Measurement*, 14, 3–19.

Neimeyer, G. J. (1992) Personal constructs in career counselling and development. *Journal of Career Development*, 18 (3), 163–73.

Nesfield-Cookson, B. (1987) *William Blake: Prophet of Universal Brotherhood*. London: Crucible.

Nias, J. (1991) Primary teachers talking: a reflexive account of longitudinal research. In G. Walford (ed.) *Doing Educational Research*. London: Routledge, 147–65.

Nisbet, J. and Watt, J. (1984) Case study. In J. Bell, T. Bush, A. Fox, J. Goodey and S. Goulding (eds) *Conducting Small-scale Investigations in Educational Management*. London: Harper & Row, 79–92.

Nixon, J. (ed.) (1981) *A Teacher's Guide to Action Research*. London: Grant McIntyre.

Noack, P. (1998) School achievement and adolescents' interactions with their fathers, mothers, and friends. *European Journal of Psychology of Education*, 13 (4), 503–13.

Noffke, S. E. and Zeichner, K. M. (1987) Action research and teacher thinking. Paper presented at the annual meeting of the American Educational Research Association, Washington, DC.

Norris, N. (1990) *Understanding Educational Evaluation*. London: Kogan Page.

Nuttall, D. (1987) The validity of assessments. *European Journal of Psychology of Education*, 11 (2), 109–18.

Oakley, A. (1981) Interviewing women: a contradiction in terms. In H. Roberts (ed.) *Doing Feminist Research*. London: Routledge & Kegan Paul, 30–61.

Oja, S. N. and Smulyan, L. (1989) *Collaborative Action Research: a Developmental Approach.* Lewes: Falmer.

Okagaki, L. and Frensch, P. A. (1998) Parenting and school achievement: a multiethnic perspective. *American Educational Research Journal*, 35 (1), 123–44.

Okakura, K. (1991) *The Book of Tea.* Tokyo: Kodansha International.

Oldroyd, D. (1986) *The Arch of Knowledge: an Introductory Study of the History of the Philosophy and Methodology of Science.* New York: Methuen.

O'Neill, B. and McMahon, H. (1990) *Opening New Windows with Bubble Dialogue.* Language Development and Hypermedia Research Group, Faculty of Education, University of Ulster at Coleraine.

Oppenheim, A. N. (1966) *Questionnaire Design and Attitude Measurement.* London: Heinemann.

Oppenheim, A. N. (1992) *Questionnaire Design, Interviewing and Attitude Measurement.* London: Pinter Publishers Ltd.

Osborne, J. I. (1977) College of education students' perceptions of the teaching situation. Unpublished M.Ed. dissertation. University of Liverpool.

Osgood, C. E., Suci, G. S. and Tannenbaum, P. H. (1957) *The Measurement of Meaning.* Urbana: University of Illinois.

Overett, S. and Donald, D. (1998) Paired reading: effects of a parental involvement programme in a disadvantaged community in South Africa. *British Journal of Educational Psychology*, 68, 347–56.

Page, R. N. (1997) Teaching about validity. *International Journal of Qualitative Studies in Education*, 10 (2), 145–55.

Palmer, M. (1976) An experimental study of the use of archive materials in the secondary school history curriculum. Unpublished Ph.D. dissertation. Leicester: University of Leicester.

Palys, T. S. (1978) Simulation methods and social psychology. *Journal for the Theory of Social Behaviour*, 8, 341–68.

Papasolomoutos, C. and Christie, T. (1998) Using national surveys: a review of secondary analyses with special reference to schools. *Educational Research*, 40 (3), 295–310.

Parker, H. J. (1974) *View from the Boys.* Newton Abbot: David & Charles.

Parker, I. (1992) *Discourse Dynamics: Critical Analysis for Social and Individual Psychology.* London: Routledge.

Parlett, M. and Hamilton, D. (1976) Evaluation as illumination. In D. Tawney (ed.) *Curriculum Evaluation Today: Trends and Implications.* London: Macmillan, 84–101.

Parsons, E., Chalkley, B. and Jones, A. (1996) The role of Geographic Information Systems in the study of parental choice and secondary school catchments. *Evaluation and Research in Education*, 10 (1), 23–34.

Parsons, J. M., Graham, N. and Honess, T. (1983) A teacher's implicit model of how children learn. *British Educational Research Journal*, 9 (1), 91–101.

Parsons, M. and Lyons, G. (1979) An alternative approach to inquiry in educational management. *Educational Management and Administration*, 8 (1), 75–84.

Paterson, L. (1991) An introduction to multilevel modelling. In S. W. Raudenbush and J. Willms (eds) *Schools, Classrooms and Pupils: International Studies of Schooling from a Multilevel Perspective.* San Diego: Academic Press, 13–24.

Paterson, L. and Goldstein, H. (1991) New statistical methods for analysing social structures: an introduction of multilevel models. *British Educational Research Journal*, 17 (4), 387–93.

Patrick, J. (1973) *A Glasgow Gang Observed.* London: Eyre Methuen.

Patton, M. Q. (1980) *Qualitative Evaluation Methods.* Beverly Hills: Sage Publications.

Patton, M. Q. (1990) *Qualitative Evaluation and Research Methods* (second edition). London: Sage Publications.

Peak, D. and Frame, M. (1994) *Chaos under Control: the Art and Science of Complexity.* New York: W. H. Freeman.

Peevers, B. H. and Secord, P. F. (1973) Developmental changes in attribution of descriptive concepts to persons. *Journal of Personality and Social Psychology*, 27 (1), 120–8.

Percival, F. (1978) Evaluation procedures for simulating gaming exercises. In R. McAleese (ed.) *Perspectives on Academic Gaming and Simulation 3: Training and Professional Education.* London: Kogan Page, 163–9.

Phillips, R. (1998) Some methodological and ethical dilemmas in élite-based research. *British Educational Research Journal*, 24 (1), 5–20.

Pierce, C. M. B. and Molloy, G. N. (1990) Psychological and biographical differences between secondary school teachers experiencing high and low levels of burnout. *British Journal of Educational Psychology*, 60, 37–51.

Pilliner, A. (1973) *Experiment in Educational Research.* E 341. Milton Keynes: Open University Press.

Pirsig, R. (1976) *Zen and the Art of Motorcycle Maintenance.* London: Corgi.

Pithers, R. T. and Soden, R. (1999) Person–environment fit and teacher stress. *Educational Research,* 41, 51–61.

Pitman, M. A. and Maxwell, J. A. Qualitative approaches to evaluation: models and methods. In M. LeCompte, W. L. Millroy and J. Preissle (eds) *The Handbook of Qualitative Research in Education.* London: Academic Press Ltd., 729–70.

Platt, J. (1981) Evidence and proof in documentary research: some specific problems of documentary research. *Sociological Review,* 29 (1), 31–52.

Plewis, I. (1985) *Analysing Change: Measurement and Explanation Using Longitudinal Data.* Chichester: John Wiley.

Plewis, I. (1991a) Using multilevel models to link educational progress with curriculum coverage. In S. W. Raudenbush and J. Willms (eds) *Schools, Classrooms and Pupils: International Studies of Schooling from a Multilevel Perspective.* San Diego: Academic Press, 53–65.

Plewis, I. (1991b) Pupils' progress in reading and maths during primary school: associations with ethnic group and sex. *Educational Research,* 33, 133–40.

Plewis, I. (1997) *Statistics in Education.* London: Arnold.

Plummer, K. (1983) *Documents of Life: an Introduction to the Problems and Literature of a Humanistic Method.* London: Allen & Unwin.

Pollard, A. (1985) *The Social World of the Primary School.* Eastbourne: Holt, Rinehart & Winston.

Pope, M. L. and Keen, T. R. (1981) *Personal Construct Psychology and Education.* London: Academic Press.

Popper, K. (1968) *The Logic of Scientific Discovery* (second edition). London: Hutchinson.

Poppleton, P. and Riseborough, G. (1990) Teaching in the mid–1980s: the centrality of work in secondary teachers' lives. *British Educational Research Journal,* 16 (2), 105–24.

Postlethwaite, K. and Haggarty, L. (1998) Towards effective and transferable learning in secondary school: the development of an approach based on mastery learning. *British Educational Research Journal,* 24 (3), 333–53.

Potter, J. and Wetherall, M. (1987) *Discourse and Social Psychology: Beyond Attitudes and Behaviour.* London: Sage Publications.

Powney, J. and Watts, M. (1987) *Interviewing in Educational Research.* London: Routledge & Kegan Paul.

Prais, S. J. (1983) Formal and informal teaching: a further reconsideration of Professor Bennett's statistics. *Journal of the Royal Statistical Society,* 146 (2), 163–9.

Prein, G., Kelle, U. and Bird, K. (1995) An overview of software. In U. Kelle (1995) (ed.) *Computer-Aided Qualitative Data Analysis.* London: Sage Publications.

Preisler, G. M. and Ahström, M. (1997) Sign language for hard of hearing children – a hindrance or a benefit for their development? *European Journal of Psychology of Education,* 12 (4), 465–77.

Pring, R. (1984) The problems of confidentiality. In M. Skilbeck (ed.) *Evaluating the Curriculum in the Eighties.* Sevenoaks: Hodder & Stoughton, 38–44.

Prosser, M. and Trigwell, K. (1997) Relations between perceptions of the teaching environment and approaches to teaching. *British Journal of Educational Psychology,* 67, 25–35.

Quantz, R. A. (1992) On critical ethnography (with some postmodern considerations). In M. LeCompte, W. L. Millroy and J. Preissle (eds) *The Handbook of Qualitative Research in Education.* London: Academic Press Ltd., 447–506.

Raffe, D., Bundell, I. and Bibby, J. (1989) Ethics and tactics: issues arising from an educational survey. In R. G. Burgess (ed.) *The Ethics of Educational Research.* Lewes: Falmer, 13–30.

Ramsden, C. and Reason, D. (1997) Conversation – discourse analysis in library and information services. *Education for Information,* 15 (4), 283–95.

Rapoport, R. N. (1970) Three dilemmas in action research. *Human Relations,* 23 (6), 499–513.

Rasmussen, D. M. (1990) *Reading Habermas.* Oxford: Basil Blackwell Ltd.

Ravenette, A. T. (1977) Personal construct theory: an approach to the psychological investigation of children and young people. In D. Bannister (ed.) *New Perspectives in Personal Construct Theory.* London: Academic Press, 251–80.

Reid, S. (1987) *Working with Statistics: an Introduction to Quantitative Methods for Social Scientists.* Cambridge: Polity Press.

Rex, J. (ed.) (1974) *Approaches to Sociology: an Introduction to Major Trends in British Sociology.* London: Routledge & Kegan Paul.

Reynolds, D. (1995) The effective school: an inaugural lecture. *Evaluation and Research in Education,* 9 (2), 57–73.

Reynolds, P. D. (1979) *Ethical Dilemmas and Social Science Research*. San Francisco: Jossey-Bass.

Ribbens, J. and Edwards, R. (1997) *Feminist Dilemmas in Qualitative Research: Public Knowledge and Private Lives*. London: Sage Publications.

Rice, J. M. (1897) The futility of the spelling grind. Cited in G. de Landsheere (1997) History of educational research. In J. P. Keeves (ed.) *Educational Research, Methodology, and Measurement: an International Handbook* (second edition). Oxford: Elsevier Science Ltd., 8–16.

Ridgway, J. (1998) *The Modeling of Systems and Macro-Systemic Change: Lessons for Evaluation from Epidemiology and Ecology*. Research Monograph 8. University of Wisconsin–Madison: National Institute for Science Education.

Riecken, H. W. and Boruch, R. F. (1974) *Social Explanation: a Method for Planning and Evaluating Social Intervention*. New York: Academic Press Inc.

Rigby, K. (1999) Peer victimisation at school and the health of secondary school students. *British Journal of Educational Psychology*, 69, 95–104.

Riley, M. W. (1963). *Sociological Research 1: a Case Approach*. New York: Harcourt, Brace & World Inc.

Riseborough, G. F. (1992) The Cream Team: an ethnography of BTEC National Diploma (Catering and Hotel Management) students in a tertiary college. *British Journal of Sociology and Education*, 13 (2), 215–45.

Roberts, H. (1981) *Doing Feminist Research*. London: Routledge.

Robinson, B. (1982) *Tutoring by Telephone: a Handbook*. Milton Keynes: Open University Press.

Robinson, P. and Smithers, A. (1999) Should the sexes be separated for secondary education – comparisons of single-sex and co-educational schools. *Research Papers in Education*, 14 (1), 23–49.

Robson, J. and Collier, K. (1991) Designing 'Sugar 'n' Spice': An anti-sexist simulation. *Simulation/Games For Learning*, 21 (3), 213–19.

Roderick, R. (1986) *Habermas and the Foundations of Critical Theory*. Basingstoke: Macmillan.

Rogers, C. R. (1942) *Counselling and Psychotherapy*. Boston: Houghton Mifflin.

Rogers, C. R. (1945) The non-directive method as a technique for social research. *American Journal of Sociology*, 50, 279–83.

Rogers, C. R. (1969) *Freedom to Learn*. Columbus, OH: Merrill Pub. Co.

Rogers, C. R. and Stevens, B. (1967) *Person to Person: The Problem of Being Human*. London: Souvenir Press.

Rogers, V. M. and Atwood, R. K. (1974) Can we put ourselves in their place? *Yearbook of the National Council for Social Studies*, 44, 80–111.

Roman, L. G. and Apple, M. (1990) Is naturalism a move away from positivism? Materialist and feminist approaches to subjectivity in ethnographic research. In E. Eisner and A. Peshkin (eds) *Qualitative Inquiry in Education: the continuing debate*. New York: Teachers College Press, 38–73.

Rose, D. and Sullivan, O. (1993) *Introducing Data Analysis for Social Scientists*. Buckingham: Open University Press.

Rosenthal, R. (1991) *Meta-analysis Procedures for Social Research*. Beverly Hills: Sage Publications.

Rosier, M. J. (1997) Survey research methods. In J. P. Keeves (ed.) *Educational Research, Methodology and Measurement: an International Handbook* (second edition). Oxford: Elsevier Science Ltd., 154–62.

Ross, K. N. and Rust, K. (1997) Sampling in survey research. In J. P. Keeves (ed.) *Educational Research, Methodology and Measurement: an International Handbook* (second edition). Oxford: Elsevier Science Ltd., 427–38.

Ross, K. N. and Wilson, M. (1997) Sampling error in survey research. In J. P. Keeves (ed.) *Educational Research, Methodology and Measurement: an International Handbook* (second edition). Oxford: Elsevier Science Ltd., 663–670.

Rossi, P. H. and Freeman, H. E. (1993) *Evaluation: a Systematic Approach*. London: Sage Publications.

Roszak, T. (1970) *The Making of a Counter Culture*. London: Faber & Faber.

Roszak, T. (1972) *Where the Wasteland Ends*. London: Faber & Faber.

Rozeboom, W. W. (1997) Good science is abductive, not hypothetico-deductive. In L. L. Harlow, S. A. Muliak and J. H. Steiger (eds) *What if There Were No Significance Tests?* Mahwah, NJ: Erlbaum, 335–92.

Ruddock, J. (1981) *Evaluation: a Consideration of Principles and Methods*. Manchester Monographs 10: University of Manchester.

Ryle, A. (1975) *Frames and Cages: the Repertory Grid Approach to Human Understanding*. Brighton: Sussex University Press.

Ryle, G. (1949) *The Concept of Mind*. Harmondsworth: Penguin

Sacks, H. (1992) *Lectures on Conversation* (ed. G. Jefferson). Oxford: Basil Blackwell.

Sainsbury, M., Whetton, C., Mason, K. and Schagen, I. (1998) Fallback in attainment on transfer at age 11: evidence from the summer literacy schools evaluation. *Educational Research*, 40 (1), 73–81.

Salmon, P. (1969) Differential conforming of the developmental process. *British Journal of Social and Clinical Psychology*, 8, 22–31.

Sanday, A. (1993) The relationship between educational research and evaluation and the role of the Local Education Authority. In R. G. Burgess (ed.) *Educational Research and Evaluation for Policy and Practice*. London: Falmer, 32–43.

Schagen. I. and Sainsbury, M. (1996) Multilevel analysis of the key stage 1 national curriculum data in 1995. *Oxford Review of Education*, 22 (3), 265–72.

Schatzman, L. and Strauss, A. L. (1973) *Field Research: Strategies for a Natural Sociology*. Englewood Cliffs, NJ: Prentice-Hall.

Scheurich, J. J. (1995) A postmodernist critique of research interviewing. *International Journal of Qualitative Studies in Education*, 8 (3), 239–52.

Scheurich, J. J. (1996) The masks of validity: a deconstructive investigation. *International Journal of Qualitative Studies in Education*, 9 (1), 49–60.

Schofield, J. W. (1993) Increasing the generalizability of qualitative research. In M. Hammersley (ed.) *Social Research: Philosophy, Politics and Practice*. London: Sage Publications in association with the Open University Press, 200–25.

Schofield, W. (1996) Survey sampling. In R. Sapsford and V. Jupp (1996) (eds) *Data Collection and Analysis*. London: Sage Publications and the Open University Press, 25–55.

Schön, D. (1983) *The Reflective Practitioner: How Professionals Think in Action*. London: Temple Smith.

Schön, D. (1987) *Educating the Reflective Practitioner*. San Francisco: Jossey-Bass.

Schonbach, P. (1990) *Account Episodes: the Management or Escalation of Conflict*. Cambridge: Cambridge University Press.

Schutz, A. (1962) *Collected Papers*. The Hague: Nijhoff.

Scriven, M. and Roth, J. (1978) Needs assessment: concept and practice. *New Directions for Program Evaluation*, 1, 1–11.

Searle, J. (1969) *Speech Acts*. London: Cambridge University Press.

Sears, R., Maccoby, E. and Levin, H. (1957) *Patterns of Child Rearing*. New York: Harper & Row.

Secord, P. F. and Peevers, B. H. (1974) The development and attribution of person concepts. In T. Mischel (ed.) *On Understanding Persons*. Oxford: Basil Blackwell.

Seidel, J. and Kelle, U. (1995) Different functions of coding in the analysis of textual data. In U. Kelle (1995) (ed.) *Computer-Aided Qualitative Data Analysis*. London: Sage Publications.

Seifert, T. L. (1997) Academic goals and emotions: results of a structural equation model and a cluster analysis. *British Journal of Educational Psychology*, 67, 323–38.

Selleck, R. W. J. (1991) The Manchester Statistical Society and the foundation of social science research. In D. S. Anderson and B. J. Biddle (eds) *Knowledge for Policy: Improving Education through Research*. London: Falmer, 291–304.

Sellitz, C., Wrightsman, L. S. and Cook, S. W. (1976) *Research Methods in Social Relations*. New York: Holt, Rinehart & Winston.

Semin, G. R. and Manstead, A. S. R. (1983) *The Accountability of Conduct: a Social Psychological Analysis*. London: Academic Press.

Serafini, A. (ed.) (1989) *Ethics and Social Concern*. New York: Paragon House.

Severiens, S. and ten Dam, G. (1998) A multilevel meta-analysis of gender differences in learning orientations. *British Journal of Educational Psychology*, 68, 595–618.

Shapiro, B. L. (1990) A collaborative approach to help novice science teachers reflect on changes in their construction of the role of the science teacher. *Alberta Journal of Educational Research*, 36 (3), 203–22.

Sharp, R. and Green, A. (1975) *Education and Social Control: a Study in Progressive Primary Education*. London: Routledge & Kegan Paul.

Sharpe, P. (1985) Behaviour modification in the secondary school: a survey of students' attitudes to rewards and praise. *Behavioural Approaches with Children*, 9, 109–12.

Shavelson, R. J. and Berliner, D. C. (1991) Erosion of the education research infrastructure: a reply to Finn. In D. S. Anderson and B. J. Biddle (eds) *Knowledge for Policy: Improving Education through Research*. London: Falmer, 79–84.

Shaw, E. L. (1992) The influence of methods instruction on the beliefs of preservice elementary and secondary science teachers: preliminary comparative analyses. *School Science and Mathematics*, 92, 14–22.

Shaw, M. L. G. (ed.) (1981) *Recent Advances in Personal Construct Technology*. London: Academic Press.

Sherrard, P. (1987) *The Eclipse of Man and Nature*. London: Inner Traditions, Lindisfarne Press.

Shipman, M. D. (1972) *The Limitations of Social Research*. London: Longman.

Shipman, M. D. (1974) *Inside a Curriculum Project*. London: Methuen Co.

Sideris, G. (1998) Direct classroom observation. *Research in Education*, 59, 19–28.

Siegel, H. (1987) *Relativism Refuted*. Netherlands: D. Reidel Publishing Ltd.

Siegel, S. (1956) *Nonparametric Statistics for the Behavioral Sciences*. New York: McGraw-Hill.

Sikes, P. and Troyna, B. (1991) True stories: a case study in the use of life histories in teacher education. *Educational Review*, 43 (1), 3–16.

Sikes, P., Measor, L. and Woods, P. (1985) *Teacher Careers*. Lewes: Falmer Press.

Silverman, D. (1985) *Qualitative Methodology and Sociology: Describing the Social World*. Brookfield, VT: Gower.

Silverman, D. (1993) *Interpreting Qualitative Data*. London: Sage Publications.

Simon, H. A. (1996) *The Sciences of the Artificial* (third edition). Cambridge, MA: The MIT Press.

Simon, J. L. (1978) *Basic Research Methods in Social Science*. New York: Random House.

Simons, H. (1982) Conversation piece: the practice of interviewing in case study research. In R. McCormick (ed.) *Calling Education to Account*. London: Heinemann, 239–46.

Simons, H. (1996) The paradox of case study. *Cambridge Journal of Education*, 26 (2), 225–40.

Slater, P. (1977) *The Measurement of Interpersonal Space*, Vol. 2. Chichester: Wiley.

Slavin, R. E. (1984a) Meta-analysis in education: how has it been used? *Educational Researcher*. American Educational Research Association, 13 (8), 6–15.

Slavin, R. E. (1984b) A rejoinder to Carlberg *et al*. *Educational Researcher*. American Educational Research Association, 13 (8), 24–7.

Sluckin, A. (1981) *Growing up in the Playground: The Social Development of Children*. London: Routledge & Kegan Paul.

Smith, H. W. (1991) *Strategies of Social Research* (third edition). Orlando, FL: Holt, Rinehart & Winston.

Smith, L. M. (1987) *Kensington Revisited*. Lewes: Falmer Press.

Smith, M. L. and Glass, G. V. (1977) Meta-analysis of psychotherapy outcome studies. *American Psychologist*, 32, 752–60.

Smith, M. L. and Glass, G. V. (1987) *Research and Evaluation in Education and the Social Sciences*. Englewood Cliffs, NJ: Prentice-Hall.

Smith, R. W. (1975) *Strategies of Social Research: the Methodological Imagination*. London: Prentice-Hall.

Smith, S. and Leach, C. (1972) A hierarchical measure of cognitive complexity. *British Journal of Psychology*, 63 (4), 561–8.

Smithson, M. (1988) Possibility theory, fuzzy logic, and psychological explanation. In B. Zetenyi (ed.) *Fuzzy Sets in Psychology*. North Holland: Elsevier Science Publishers.

Smyth, J. (1989) Developing and sustaining critical reflection in teacher education. *Journal of Teacher Education*, 40 (2), 2–9.

Soble, A. (1978) Deception in social science research: is informed consent possible? *Hastings Center Report*, 8, 40–6.

Social and Community Planning Research (1972) *Questionnaire Design Manual No. 5*. London: 16 Duncan Terrace, NI 8BZ.

Social Science Research Council (1971) *Research in Economic and Social History*. London: Heinemann.

Social Sciences and Humanities Research Council of Canada (1981) *Ethical Guidelines for the Institutional Review Committee for Research with Human Subjects*.

Solomon, R. L. (1949) An extension of control group design. *Psychological Bulletin*, 46, 137–50.

Somekh, B. (1995) The contribution of action research to development in social endeavours: a position paper on action research methodology. *British Educational Research Journal*, 21 (3), 339–55.

Southgate, V., Arnold, H. and Johnson, S. (1981) *Extending Beginning Reading*. London: Heinemann Educational Books for the Schools Council.

Spector, P. E. (1993) Research designs. In M. L. Lewis-Beck (ed.) *Experimental Design and Methods. International Handbook of Quantitative Applications in the Social Sciences*, Vol. 3. London: Sage Publications, 1–74.

Spencer, J. R. and Flin, R. (1990) *The Evidence of Children*. London: Blackstone.

Spindler, G. (ed.) (1982) *Doing the Ethnography of Schooling*. New York: Holt, Rinehart & Winston.

Spindler, G. and Spindler, L. (1992) Cultural process and ethnography: an anthropological perspective. In M. LeCompte, W. L. Millroy and J. Preissle (eds) *The Handbook of Qualitative Research in Education*. London: Academic Press Ltd., 53–92.

Spradley, J. P. (1979) *The Ethnographic Interview*. New York: Holt, Rinehart & Winston.

Spradley, J. P. (1980) *Participant Observation*. New York: Holt, Rinehart & Winston.

Stables, A. (1990) Differences between pupils from mixed and single-sex schools in their enjoyment of school subjects and in their attitude to Science in school. *Educational Review*, 42 (3), 221–30.

Stake, R. E. (1978) The case study method in social inquiry. *Educational Researcher*, 7 (2), 5–8.

Stake, R. E. (1994) Case studies. In N. K. Denzin and Y. S. Lincoln (eds) *Handbook of Qualitative Research*. London: Sage Publications, 236–47.

Steiner, G. (1978) *Heidegger*. Glasgow: Fontana/Collins.

Stenhouse, L. (1975) *An Introduction to Curriculum Research and Development*. London: Heinemann.

Stenhouse, L. (1979) What is action research? (mimeo). Norwich: Classroom Action Research Network.

Stenhouse, L. (1985) Case study methods. In T. Husen and T. N. Postlethwaite (eds) *International Encyclopaedia of Education* (first edition). Oxford: Pergamon, 640–6.

Stewart, I. (1990) *Does God Play Dice?* Harmondsworth: Penguin.

Stillar, G. F. (1998) *Analysing Everyday Texts: Discourses, Rhetoric, and Social Perspectives*. London: Sage Publications.

Strand, S. (1999) Ethnic group, sex and economic disadvantage: associations with pupils' educational progress from Baseline to the end of Key Stage 1. *British Educational Research Journal*, 25 (2), 179–202.

Strauss, A. M. (1987) *Qualitative Analysis for Social Scientists*. Cambridge: Cambridge University Press.

Strike, K. A. (1990) The ethics of educational evaluation. In J. Millman and L. Darling-Hammond (eds) *A New Handbook of Teacher Evaluation*. Beverly Hills: Corwin Press, Sage Publications, 356–73.

Stringfield, S. (1997) Underlying the chaos: factors explaining exemplary US elementary schools and the case for high-reliability organisations. In T. Townsend (ed.) *Restructuring and Quality: Issues for Tomorrow's Schools*. London: Routledge, 143–60.

Stronach, I. and Morris, B. (1994) Polemical notes on educational evaluation in an age of 'policy hysteria'. *Evaluation and Research in Education*, 8 (1 & 2), 5–19.

Stubbs, M. and Delamont, S. (eds) (1976) *Explorations in Classroom Observation*. Chichester: John Wiley.

Stufflebeam, D. L., McCormick, C. H., Brinkerhoff, R. O. and Nelson, C. O. (1985) *Conducting Educational Needs Assessment*. Boston, MA: Kluwer Nijhoff.

Sturman, A. (1997) Case study methods. In J. P. Keeves (ed.) *Educational Research, Methodology and Measurement: an International Handbook* (second edition). Oxford: Elsevier Science Ltd., 61–6.

Sturman, A. (1999) Case study methods. In J. P. Keeves and G. Lakomski (eds) *Issues in Educational Research*. Oxford: Elsevier Science Ltd., 103–12.

Suarez, T. M. (1994) Needs assessment. In T. Husen and T. N. Postlethwaite (eds) *The International Encyclopedia of Education*, Volume 7 (second edition). Oxford: Pergamon, 4,056–60.

Sudman, S. and Bradburn, N. M. (1982) *Asking Questions: a Practical Guide to Questionnaire Design*. San Francisco, CA: Jossey-Bass Inc.

Sutherland, G. (1969) The study of the history of education. *History*, 54 (180).

Sykes, W. and Hoinville, G. (1985) *Telephone Interviewing on a Survey of Social Attitudes*. London: Social and Community Planning Research.

Task Group on Assessment and Testing (1988) *National Curriculum: Testing and Assessment: a Report*. London: HMSO.

Tatar, M. (1998) Teachers as significant others: gender differences in secondary school pupils' perceptions. *British Journal of Educational Psychology*, 68, 217–27.

Taylor, J. L. and Walford, R. (1972) *Simulation in the Classroom*. Harmondsworth: Penguin Books.

Terry, A. A. (1998) Teachers as targets of bullying by their pupils: a study to investigate incidence. *British Journal of Educational Psychology*, 68, 255–68.

Tesch, R. (1990) *Qualitative Research: Analysis Types and Software Tools*. London: Falmer.

Thissen, D. (1990) Reliability and measurement precision. In H. Wainer (ed.) *Computer Adaptive Testing: a Primer*. Hillsdale, NJ: Lawrence Erlbaum Associates, 161–86.

Thody, A. (1997) Lies, damned lies – and storytelling. *Educational Management and Administration*, 25 (3), 325–38.

Thomas, J. B. (1992) Birmingham University and teacher training: day training college to department of education. *History of Education*, 21 (3), 307–21.

Thomas, L. F. (1978) A personal construct approach to learning in education, training and therapy. In F. Fransella (ed.) *Personal Construct Psychology*. London: Academic Press, 45–58.

Thomas, L. F. and Harri-Augstein, E. S. (1992) *Self-organized Learning*. London: Routledge.

Thomas, P. (1991) Research models: insiders, gadflies, limestone. In D. S. Anderson and B. J. Biddle (eds) *Knowledge for Policy: Improving Education through Research*. London: Falmer, 225–33.

Thomas, S., Sammons, P., Mortimore, P. and Smees, R. (1997) Differential secondary school effectiveness: comparing the performance of different pupil groups. *British Educational Research Journal*, 23 (4), 351–69.

Thomas, W. I. (1923) *The Unadjusted Girl*. Boston: Little, Brown

Thomas, W. I. (1928) *The Child in America*. New York: Knopf..

Thomas, W. I. and Znaniecki, F. (1918) *The Polish Peasant in Europe and America*. Chicago: University of Chicago Press.

Thompson, B. (1994) Guidelines for authors. *Educational and Psychological Measurement*, 54, 837–47.

Thompson, B. (1996) AERA editorial policies regarding statistical significance testing: three suggested reforms. *Educational Researcher*, 25 (2), 26–30.

Thompson, B. (1998) In praise of brilliance: where that praise really belongs. *American Psychologist*, 53, 799–800.

Thompson, B. and Snyder, P. A. (1997) Statistical significance testing practices in the *Journal of Experimental Education*. *Journal of Experimental Education*, 66, 75–83.

Thurstone, L. L. and Chave, E. J. (1929) *The Measurement of Attitudes*. Chicago: University of Chicago Press.

Tones, K. (1997) Beyond the randomized controlled trial: a case for 'judicial review'. *Health Education Research*, 12 (2) i–iv.

Torres, C. A. (1992) Participatory action research and popular education in Latin America. *International Journal of Qualitative Studies in Education*, 5 (1), 51–62.

Travers, R. M. W. (1969) *An Introduction to Educational Research*. London: Collier-Macmillan.

Tripp, D. H. (1985) Case study generalisation: an agenda for action. *British Educational Research Journal*, 11(1), 33–43.

Tripp, D. (1994) Teachers' lives, critical incidents and professional practice. *International Journal of Qualitative Studies in Education*, 7 (1) 65–72.

Troyna, B. and Hatcher, R. (1992) *Racism in Children's Lives: a Study in Mainly-White Primary Schools*. London: Routledge.

Tuckman, B. W. (1972) *Conducting Educational Research*. New York: Harcourt Brace Jovanovich.

Tyler, R. (1949) *Basic Principles of Curriculum and Instruction*. Chicago: University of Chicago Press.

Tymms, P. B. (1996) Theories, models and simulations: school effectiveness at an impasse. In J. Gray, D. Reynolds, C. T. Fitz-Gibbon, D. Jesson (eds) *Merging Traditions: the Future of Research on School Effectiveness and School Improvement*. London: Cassell, 121–35.

Tymms, P. B. (1997) *The Security of Inspection of Initial Teacher Training*. http://www.leeds.ac.uk/educol/index.html.

UNESCO (1996) *Learning: the Treasure Within*. Paris: UNESCO.

United States Department of Health, Education and Welfare (1971) *The Institutional Guide to D. H. E. W. Policy on Protecting Human Subjects* DHEW Publication (NIH), December 2, 1971, 72–102.

University of Manchester Regional Computing Centre (UMRCC) (1981) *GAP: Grid Analysis Package*. Manchester: University of Manchester Regional Computing Centre.

Usher, P. (1996) Feminist approaches to research. In D. Scott and R. Usher (eds) *Understanding Educational Research*. London: Routledge, 120–42.

Usher, R. and Scott, D. (1996) Afterword: the politics of educational research. In D. Scott and R. Usher (eds) *Understanding Educational Research*. London: Routledge, 175–80.

Valadines, N. (1999) Formal reasoning performance of higher secondary school students: theoretical and educational implications. *European Journal of Psychology of Education*, 14 (1), 109–17.

Van Etten, S., Pressley, M., Freebern, G. and Echevarria, M. (1998) An interview study of college freshmen's beliefs about their academic motivation. *European Journal of Psychology of Education*, 13 (1), 105–30.

van Ments, M. (1978) Role playing: playing a part or a mirror to meaning? *Sagset Journal*, 8 (3), 83–92.

van Ments, M. (1983) *The Effective Use of Role-Play: a Handbook for Teachers and Trainers*. London: Croom Helm.

Vasta, R. (1979) *Studying Children: an Introduction to Research Methods*. San Francisco: W. H. Freeman.

Verma, G. K. and Beard, R. M. (1981) *What is Educational Research?* Aldershot: Gower.

Verma, G. K. and Mallick, K. (1999) *Researching Education: Perspectives and Techniques*. London: Falmer.

Vermunt, J. D. (1998) The regulation of constructive learning processes. *British Journal of Educational Psychology*, 68, 149–71.

Von Eye, A. (1990) *Statistical Methods in Longitudinal Research*. New York: Academic Press Inc.

Vulliamy, G. (1990) The potential of qualitative educational research in developing countries. In G. Vulliamy, K. Lewin, and D. Stephens (1990) *Doing Educational Research in Developing Countries: Qualitative Strategies*. London: Falmer, 7–25.

Vulliamy, G., Lewin, K. and Stephens, D. (1990) *Doing Educational Research in Developing Countries: Qualitative Strategies*. London: Falmer.

Wainer, H. (1990) (ed.) *Computerized Adaptive Testing: a Primer*. New Jersey: Lawrence Erlbaum Associates.

Wainer, H. and Mislevy, R. J. (1990) Item response theory, item calibration and proficiency estimation. In H. Wainer (ed.) *Computerized Adaptive Testing: a Primer*. New Jersey: Lawrence Erlbaum Associates, 65–102.

Waldrop, M. M. (1992) *Complexity*. Harmondsworth: Penguin.

Walford, G. (ed.) (1994) *Researching the Powerful in Education*. London, UCL Press.

Walker, J. C. and Evers. C. W. (1988) The epistemological unity of educational research. In J. P. Keeves. (ed.) *Educational Research, Methodology and Measurement: an International Handbook*. Oxford: Pergamon Press, 28–36.

Walker, R. (1980) Making sense and losing meaning: problems of selection in doing Case Study. In H. Simons (ed.) *Towards a Science of the Singular*. University of East Anglia: Centre for Applied Research in Education, 222–35.

Walkerdine, V. (1988) *The Mastery of Reason: Cognitive Development and the Production of Rationality*. London: Routledge.

Wardekker, W. L. and Miedama, S. (1997) Critical pedagogy: an evaluation and a direction for reformulation. *Curriculum Inquiry*, 27 (1), 45–61.

Warnock, M. (1970) *Existentialism*. London: Oxford University Press.

Watts, M. and Ebbutt, D. (1987) More than the sum of the parts: research methods in group interviewing. *British Educational Research Journal*, 13 (1), 25–34.

Webb, G. (1996) Becoming critical of action research for development. In O. Zuber-Skerritt (ed.) *New Directions in Action Research*. London: Falmer, 137–61.

Weiskopf, R. and Laske, S. (1996) Emancipatory action research: a critical alternative to personnel development or a new way of patronising people? In O. Zuber-Skerritt (ed.) *New Directions in Action Research*. London: Falmer, 121–36.

Weiss, C. (1991a) The many meanings of research utilization. In D. S. Anderson and B. J. Biddle (eds) *Knowledge for Policy: Improving Education through Research*. London: Falmer, 173–82.

Weiss, C. (1991b) Knowledge creep and decision accretion. In D. S. Anderson and B. J. Biddle (eds) *Knowledge for Policy: Improving Education through Research*. London: Falmer, 183–92.

Wheldall, K. and Panagopoulou-Stamatelatou, A. (1991) The effects of pupil self-recording of on-task behaviour in primary school children. *British Educational Research Journal*, 17 (2), 113–27.

Whitehead, J. (1985) An analysis of an individual's educational development: the basis for personally oriented action research. In M. Shipman (ed.) *Educational Research: Principles, Policies and Practices*. Lewes: Falmer, 97–108.

Whiteley, P. (1983) The analysis of contingency tables. In D. McKay, N. Schofield and P. Whiteley (eds) (1983) *Data Analysis and the Social Sciences*. London: Frances Pinter, 72–119.

Whyte, J. (1986) *Girls into Science and Technology: the Story of a Project*. London: Routledge & Kegan Paul.

Whyte, W. F. (1982) Interviewing in field research. In R. Burgess (ed.) *Field Research: a Sourcebook and Field Manual*. London: Allen & Unwin, 111–22.

Wickens, P. (1987) *The Road to Nissan: Flexibility, Quality, Teamwork*. Basingstoke: Macmillan.

Wilcox, R. R. (1997) Simulation as a research technique. In J. P. Keeves (ed.) *Educational Research, Methodology and Measurement: an International Handbook* (second edition). Oxford: Elsevier Science Ltd., 150–4.

Wild, P., Scivier, J. E. and Richardson, S. J. (1992) Evaluating information technology-supported local management of schools: the user acceptability audit. *Educational Management and Administration*, 20 (1), 40–8.

Wiles, J. and Bondi, J. C. (1984) *Curriculum Development: a Guide to Practice* (second edition). Columbus, OH: Charles E. Merrill Publishing.

Wiliam, D. (1996) Standards in examinations: a matter of trust. *The Curriculum Journal*, 7 (3), 293–306.

Willis, P. E., (1977) *Learning to Labour*. Farnborough: Saxon House.

Willms, J. D. (1992) Pride or prejudice? Opportunity structure and the effects of Catholic schools in Scotland. In A. Yogev (ed.) *International Perspectives on Education and Society: a Research and Policy Annual (Vol. 2)*. Greenwich, CT: JAI Press.

Wilson, M. (1996) Asking questions. In R. Sapsford and V. Jupp (1996) (eds) *Data Collection and Analysis*. London: Sage Publications and the Open University Press, 94–120.

Wilson, N. and McLean, S. (1994) *Questionnaire Design: a Practical Introduction*. Newtown Abbey, Co. Antrim: University of Ulster Press.

Windisch, V. (1990) *Speech and Reasoning in Everyday Life*. Cambridge: Cambridge University Press.

Wineburg, S. S. (1991) The self-fulfilment of the self-fulfilling prophecy. In D. S. Anderson and B. J. Biddle (eds) *Knowledge for Policy: Improving Education through Research*. London: Falmer, 276–90.

Winter, R. (1982) Dilemma analysis: a contribution to methodology for action research. *Cambridge Journal of Education*, 12 (3) 161–74.

Winter, R. (1996) Some principles and procedures for the conduct of action research. In O. Zuber-Skerritt (ed.) *New Directions in Action Research*. London: Falmer.

Witkin, B. R. (1984) *Assessing Needs in Educational and Social Programs*. San Francisco: Jossey-Bass.

Wittgenstein, L. (1974) *Tractatus Logico-Philosophicus* (trans. D. Pears and B. McGuiness). London: Routledge & Kegan Paul.

Wolcott, H. F. (1973) *The Man in the Principal's Office*. New York: Holt, Rinehart & Winston.

Wolcott, H. F. (1992) Posturing in qualitative research. In M. LeCompte, W. L. Millroy and J. Preissle (eds) *The Handbook of Qualitative Research in Education*. London: Academic Press Ltd., 3–52.

Wolf, R. M. (1994) The validity and reliability of outcome measure. In A. C. Tuijnman and T. N. Postlethwaite (eds) *Monitoring the Standards of Education*. Oxford: Pergamon, 121–32.

Wood, P. (1995) Meta-analysis. In G. M. Breakwell, S. Hammond and C. Fife-Shaw (eds) *Research Methods in Psychology*. London: Sage Publications, 396–9.

Woods, P. (1979) *The Divided School*. London: Routledge & Kegan Paul.

Woods, P. (1983) *Sociology and the School*. London: Routledge & Kegan Paul.

Woods, P. (1986) *Inside Schools: Ethnography in Educational Research*. London: Routledge & Kegan Paul.

Woods, P. (1989) *Working for Teacher Development*. Dereham, Norfolk: Peter Francis Publishers.

Woods, P. (1992) Symbolic interactionism: theory and method. In M. LeCompte, W. L. Millroy and J. Preissle (eds) *The Handbook of Qualitative Research in Education*. London: Academic Press Ltd., 337–404.

Woods, P. (1993) Managing marginality: teacher development through grounded life history. *British Educational Research Journal*, 19 (5), 447–88.

Woods, P. and Hammersley, M. (1993) *Gender and Ethnicity in Schools: Ethnographic Accounts*. London: Routledge.

Worrall, L. (ed.) (1990) *Geographic Information Systems: Developments and Applications*. London: Belhaven Press.

Wragg, E. C. (1994) *An Introduction to Classroom Observation*. London: Routledge.

Yin, R. K. (1984) *Case Study Research: Design and Methods*. Beverly Hills: Sage Publications.

Yorke, D. M. (1978) Repertory grids in educational research: some methodological considerations. *British Educational Research Journal*, 4 (2), 63–74.

Yorke, D. M. (1985) Indexes of stability in repertory grids: a small-scale comparison. *British Educational Research Journal*, 11 (3), 221–5.

Young, J. (1971) *The Drugtakers*. London: Paladin.

Youngman, M. B. (1984) Designing questionnaires. In J. Bell, T. Bush, A. Fox, J. Goodey and S. Goulding (eds) *Conducting Small-scale Investigations in Educational Management*. London: Harper & Row, 156–76.

Zechmeister, E. B. and Shaughnessy, J. J. (1992) *A Practical Introduction to Research Methods in Psychology*. New York: McGraw-Hill.

Ziegahn, L. and Hinchman, K. A. (1999) Liberation or reproduction: explaining meaning in college tutors' adult literacy tutoring. *International Jour-*

nal of Qualitative Studies in Education, 12 (1), 85–101.

Zimbardo, P. C. (1984) On the ethics of intervention in human psychological research with specific reference to the 'Stanford Prison Experiment'. In J. Murphy, M. John and H. Brown (eds) *Dialogues and Debates in Social Psychology*. London: Lawrence Erlbaum Associates in association with the Open University Press.

Znaniecki, F. (1934) *The Method of Sociology*. New York: Farrar & Rinehart.

Zuber-Skerritt, O. (1996a) Introduction. In O. Zuber-Skerritt (ed.) *New Directions in Action Research*. London: Falmer, 3–9.

Zuber-Skerritt, O. (1996b) Emancipatory action research for organisational change and management development. In O. Zuber-Skerritt (ed.) *New Directions in Action Research*. London: Falmer, 83–105.

Zuzovsky, R. and Aitkin, M. (1991) Curriculum change and science achievement in Israel elementary schools. In S. W. Raudenbush and J. Willms (eds) *Schools, Classrooms and Pupils: International Studies of Schooling from a Multilevel Perspective*. San Diego: Academic Press, 25–36.

Bibliography

Index